OXFORD ISLAMIC LEGAL STUDIES

Series Editors:
Anver M. Emon, Clark Lombardi, and Lynn Welchman

ISLAMIC LEGAL REVIVAL

OXFORD ISLAMIC LEGAL STUDIES

Series Editors
Anver M. Emon, Clark Lombardi, and Lynn Welchman

Satisfying the growing interest in Islam and Islamic law, the *Oxford Islamic Legal Studies* series speaks to both specialists and those interested in the study of a legal tradition that shapes lives and societies across the globe. Islamic law operates at several levels. It shapes private decision making, binds communities, and it is also imposed by states as domestic positive law. The series features innovative and interdisciplinary studies that explore Islamic law as it operates at each of these levels. The series also sheds new light on the history and jurisprudence of Islamic law and provides for a richer understanding of the state of Islamic law in the contemporary Muslim world, including parts of the world where Muslims are minorities.

Islamic Legal Revival

Reception of European Law and Transformations in Islamic Legal Thought in Egypt, 1875–1952

LEONARD WOOD

OXFORD
UNIVERSITY PRESS

OXFORD
UNIVERSITY PRESS

Great Clarendon Street, Oxford, OX2 6DP,
United Kingdom

Oxford University Press is a department of the University of Oxford.
It furthers the University's objective of excellence in research, scholarship,
and education by publishing worldwide. Oxford is a registered trade mark of
Oxford University Press in the UK and in certain other countries

First published in 2016

Published in the United States of America by Oxford University Press
198 Madison Avenue, New York, NY 10016, United States of America

British Library Cataloguing in Publication Data
Data available

Library of Congress Control Number: 2016936815

ISBN 978–0–19–878601–6

For A. R. Jones

Series Editors' Preface

In this meticulously researched volume, Leonard Wood adds greatly to the scholarship on the intellectual history of Islamic revivalist thinking about Islamic law. *Islamic Legal Revival: Reception of European Law and Transformations in Islamic Legal Thought in Egypt, 1875–1952* strengthens our understanding of the impact of colonial interventions on Islamic legal consciousness during the nineteenth and early twentieth centuries. The work begins by describing the history of the decision to displace Egyptian law with transplanted European codes, and it explores how this decision led to the evolution of a movement to revive Islamic law. This "revivalist" movement was committed to the ideal of developing a "modern" version of Islamic law that could be codified and would replace the newly imposed European codes. The challenge, however, was to develop a methodology for mining from the Islamic legal tradition a set of rules that would be suitable for inclusion in a modern style code, but would maintain their fundamental "Islamic" characteristics. In this work, Wood explores with great subtlety how the approach of Egyptian revivalists was informed by their engagement with cutting-edge trends in European legal scholarship. These trends, many of them controversial within the European academy, were carefully studied and vigorously debated in the recently established modern Egyptian law faculties. Wood convincingly shows how, over time, sophisticated engagement with European scholarship on comparative legal theory and Islamic law helped to inspire influential revivalists and to inform their methods for developing a modern, codifiable version of Islamic law. The story Wood tells has important implications for our understanding of Egyptian history, Islamic legal history, the history of comparative law as a discipline, and, more broadly, of the multi-faceted, deeply contested, and highly transformative interactions between European and Islamic thought during the colonial period.

Anver M. Emon
Clark B. Lombardi
Lynn Welchman

Acknowledgements

The concept for this book was born in Oxford and carried to fruition at Harvard and in Egypt. At Oxford, Eugene Rogan, Ronald Nettler, and James Piscatori inspired interests and questions that remain at the heart of this work. I was also fortunate during those years to have met Lucie Ryzova, who became a friend and interlocutor. Subsequently in Cairo, our conversations about sources and methods, her sharing of rare historical materials, and our trips to markets of books and ephemera all provided fertile ground for the textual research on which this work is based. At Harvard, E. Roger Owen, Charles Donahue Jr., Baber Johansen, and William Granara served as advisers and mentors, discussing ideas, teaching me in their respective fields, commenting on my research, and facilitating scholarships and international connections that were indispensable to the completion of this work. I must emphasize additionally my particular debt to Professor Owen for having been my principal research adviser for many years and for sharing with me on countless occasions his precious insights and characteristic good cheer. I remain ever-mindful of each contribution and kindness that he and my mentors offered.

My gratitude to the Harvard community extends also to Kristen A. Stilt, Chibli Mallat, Susan Kahn, Helga Anetshofer, Hakan Karateke, Himmet Taskomur, Ahmad Atif Ahmad, Havva Guney-Ruebenacker, Sayed Elsisi, Aron Zysow, Sara Roy, Salmaan Mirza, Zehra Hirji, and the late Wolfhart Heinrichs. I also acknowledge with gratitude Janet Halley and Duncan Kennedy, who among other contributions helped me in a later stage of this book to improve it, and vested me with a capacity to envision theoretical and methodological agendas beyond it.

In Egypt, I thank Amr Shalakany for facilitating connections and illuminating Egyptian history in ways that proved critical to the conception and pursuit of this project. I learned from interviews with law professors of Cairo University and Alexandria University, including Borham Atallah, Muhammad Serag, Fu'ad Arini, and Muhammad Kamal al-Din al-Imam. I thank the teachers of the American University of Cairo's Arabic language faculty, especially Zaynab Taha and Nevenka Korica; and Muhammad Salama of Helwan University and Muhammad Habib, then of Al-Azhar University, for honing my skills in the study of Islamic texts. I am indebted to the librarians and archivists of the Cairo University Law Faculty, the Alexandria Law Faculty, La College de la Sainte Famille, Centre d'études et de documentation économiques, juridiques et sociales (CEDEJ), Institut français d'archéologie orientale (IFAO), and the Egyptian National Archives (Dar al-Watha'iq).

In England and France, I drew routinely on the expertise of librarians and archivists at the Bodleian Library, St Antony's College Middle East Centre, and Centre des archives diplomatiques of Nantes. Sir Thomas Legg, KCB, QC and Ruth Hawthorn of London invited me into their homes so that I could access the personal papers of their ancestors Sheldon Amos, Maurice Sheldon Amos, and Colin

Scott-Moncrieff. Hilary Kalmbach shared valuable insights and primary sources that supported my research on Islamic legal education.

For material support, I gratefully acknowledge a Fulbright-Hays fellowship, a research fellowship at the Islamic Legal Studies Program of Harvard Law School, the Harvard Center for Middle Eastern Studies, and Foreign Language and Area Studies grants from the U.S. Department of Education.

Several scholars I have known or met labored before me to reconstruct modern Egyptian and Islamic legal history. Among them are Guy Bechor, Bernard Botiveau, Nathan J. Brown, Kenneth M. Cuno, Baudouin Dupret, Mona El-Ghobashy, Khaled Fahmy, Israel Gershoni, Ellis Goldberg, Baber Johansen, Wael Hallaq, Will Hanley, Enid Hill, Clark Lombardi, Chibli Mallat, Tamir Moustafa, Rudolph Peters, Donald M. Reid, Bruce K. Rutherford, Amr Shalakany, Justice Adel Omar Sherif, Frank E. Vogel, and Farhat J. Ziadeh. Throughout this work I have made arguments and used methods that at times diverge from their respective commitments. I hope that my footnotes sufficiently reflect their prior contributions and influences without connecting them to arguments or methods from which they may have distanced themselves.

For sustained friendship, encouragement, and substantive exchanges, I thank Andrew March, Naz Modirzadeh, Guy Bechor, Jonathan Smolin, Robert Wipfler, and Hasina Sinha. I especially thank Walter Young for the best of times and profitable discussions and collaborations in Cairo and Montreal. The professional trajectory that undergirded this effort was made possible in the first instance by Thomas Naff and Ian S. Lustick of the University of Pennsylvania, mentors who trained me in historical research.

Peri Bearman guided me in the conversion of this work from a manuscript to a book, deploying unique skills and insights with respect to both editing and content development. No individual had a greater impact than she in making this a publishable work. Tim Laurio and Hassan Shiban provided assistance in editing, research, and translations. Clark Lombardi and Anver Emon, the series editors for Oxford University Press, made useful comments; while Elinor Shields and Alex Flach of Oxford University Press shepherded the work through its production process.

My wife, Kristin, has provided love, support, joie de vivre, and forbearance that were essential to allowing this work to finally see the light of day.

My stepfather, W. C. Jones, has been a source of inspiration and counsel. An expert in humanities, writing, languages, and law, he encouraged my interests in these same fields. The first ideas for this book unfolded during our memorable lunch in Saint-Germain-des-Prés in 2001.

I dedicate this work to my mother, A. R. Jones, with love, gratitude, and the highest respect. She has been the core inspiration to every worthy cause I have ever pursued. Insofar as this project was the outgrowth of personal industry and care for important matters, its foundations were established well before I knew anything about this or any other topic.

Permissions

I would like to thank the following publishers and author for permission to reproduce certain materials included in this book.

An earlier version of Chapter 3 has appeared in the form of an article: Leonard Wood, "Sharīʿah Revivalist Thought in the First Years of the *Sharīʿah Lawyers' Bar Association Journal*, 1929–31," *The Maghreb Review*, 32,2–3 (2007): 196–217 (copyright, The Maghreb Review 2007). This material has been reproduced with permission from The Maghreb Review.

Table 1.1 entitled "Jurisdiction ranges for British, French, and Egyptian subjects" previously appeared in Will Hanley, "Foreignness and Localness in Alexandria, 1880–1940" (Ph.D. diss., Princeton University, 2007), 170. A revised version of the table is scheduled to be published in Will Hanley, *Identifying with Nationality: Europeans, Ottomans, and Egyptians in Alexandria* (New York: Columbia University Press, 2017). This material has been reproduced with permission from Will Hanley.

Figure 9.1 entitled "Title page and first dedication page of Muḥammad ʿAbd al-Jawād's *L'Exécution testamentaire en droit musulman* (1926)" presents the title and dedication pages from Mohamed Abdel Gawad, *L'Exécution testamentaire en droit musulman* (Paris: Librairie Orientaliste Paul Geuthner, 1926). This material has been reproduced with permission from Librairie Orientaliste Paul Geuthner.

Figure 11.1 entitled "Chafik Chehata and Louis Milliot, Paris, 1951" presents an image that originally appeared in Louis Milliot and Université de Paris, *Travaux de la semaine internationale de droit musulman, Paris, 2–7 juillet 1951* (Paris: Recueil Sirey, 1953). This material has been reproduced under the designation "D.R." (droits réservés) in coordination with Dalloz.

Table of Contents

List of Abbreviations and Translation and Transliteration

F.O.	British Foreign Office (records housed at the British National Archives in Kew, England)
F.O. Conf.	Foreign Office Confidential Print
Nantes	Centre des archives diplomatiques de Nantes (Diplomatic Archives Center, Nantes, France)
P.P.	Parliamentary Papers

Arabic and French sources quoted herein are translated by the author except where noted otherwise.

Arabic words are most commonly rendered in full transliteration based on the system of the *International Journal of Middle Eastern Studies*. The transliteration herein differs in three respects. The *ṭā marbūṭah* in the non-construct state is *-ah*. The *alif maqṣūrah* is *á*. If an Arabic word appears in the Oxford University Press online dictionary of U.S. English, the Oxford spelling is generally used.

List of Tables and Figures

About the Author

Leonard Wood lectured at Harvard University on Middle Eastern political and intellectual history and is a former research fellow of the Islamic Legal Studies Program of Harvard Law School. He holds a J.D. from Harvard Law School, a Ph.D. in History and Middle Eastern Studies from Harvard University, and an M.Phil. in Modern Middle Eastern Studies from Oxford University. He is a practicing attorney in the United States specializing in corporate governance, mergers and acquisitions, and capital markets.

Your laws are marvelous;
therefore my soul has kept them.
The unfolding of your words gives light;
it gives understanding to the simple.
I opened my mouth and panted,
because I longed for your commands.
Turn to me and have mercy on me,
as you always do to those who love your name.
Direct my steps according to your word;
let no iniquity rule over me.
Deliver me from the oppression of man,
so I will obey your precepts.
Make your face to shine on your servant
and teach me your statutes.
Streams of tears run down from my eyes,
for they do not keep your law.

Psalms 119:129–136.

Introduction

The history of modern Arab and Islamic law centers on Egypt.[1] The legal past of this regionally powerful and influential country presents a treasure trove of insights into contemporary applications of Islamic law and into the future of modern Middle Eastern law as a phenomenon related to, but distinct from, Islamic law.[2] From 1875 to 1952, Egypt was a European colony and a developing country, with sophisticated political and legal systems, robust scholarly and literary cultures, and law faculties abounding with publishing scholars. Its law libraries were filled with the best scholarly books from around the world. As part of the sphere of continental European law,[3] Egypt had adopted a civil code twenty-five years before Germany, and its legal profession operated in a complex and multicultural legal system that served as a market for competing ideas and agendas touching on every aspect of life.

An appreciation of the history of legal thought in Egypt is integral to evaluating the evolution and facets of present-day movements in the Middle East and the wider Islamic world to revive Islamic law. Leaders of such movements and authoritative writers in Islamic law have adopted attitudes and methods regarding Islamic law that were developed in Egypt between 1875 and 1952. Prevailing notions and methods of present-day Islamist jurists and politicians—proponents of the revival of Islamic law—have emerged and thrived in the face of competing ideas, including secular-oriented worldviews, because of the vision and tenacity of nineteenth- and twentieth-century jurists who toiled to modernize, reform, and revive Islamic law.

[1] Modern Arab law does not necessarily begin with Egypt. See, for example, Michael Brett, "Legislating for Inequality in Algeria: The Senatus-Consulte of 14 July 1865," *Bulletin of the School of Oriental and African Studies* 51,3 (1988): 440–61; Alan Christelow, *Muslim Law Courts and the French Colonial State in Algeria* (Princeton: Princeton University Press, 1985).

[2] See Chibli Mallat, *Introduction to Middle Eastern Law* (Oxford: Oxford University Press, 2007).

[3] The term "European law" in this book most often refers to continental European law and more specifically to the law and legal thought of France. To a lesser extent, the term encompasses the law and legal thought of other continental European countries such as Germany, Italy, and Belgium. "European law" as used here does not imply pan-European law, which is the present-day sense of the same term. For all of its faults and potentially misleading qualities, the term "European law" is appropriate since it distinguishes "civil law" countries on the European continent from those of the Anglo-American tradition on the one hand, and the Ottoman, Egyptian, and Islamic legal systems and traditions on the other hand. This was the way jurists in Egypt conceptualized the families of law, legal systems, and legal thought.

Islamic Legal Revival: Reception of European Law and Transformations in Islamic Legal Thought in Egypt, 1875–1952. First Edition. Leonard Wood.

A journey into the origins of modern movements to revive Islamic law also opens the door to shedding new analytical light on writings on Islamic law published from the mid-twentieth century to the present that seamlessly meld classical and modern Islamic notions and methods. These works habitually present distinctly modern notions and approaches to law—sometimes French, German, or American notions—as if they were deeply historical and autochthonous features of Islamic legal thought and practice. Such conflations of entirely modern concepts with concepts from the earliest centuries of Islam emerge on every topic in Islamic law, from claims about the laws of war and statecraft to claims about the intricacies of more routine fields such as contract law and civil procedure.

This book examines the reception of continental European law in Egypt, the consequent evolution of Islamic legal revivalism, and the foundations of transformations in modern Arab-Islamic legal thought between 1875 and 1952. The period under investigation incorporates two political eras in Egyptian history: from 1875 until 1922, an era of European colonial control and British occupation, and from 1922 until 1952, an era of nominal Egyptian independence and sustained British imperial control. Three developments were paramount during these two eras. First, transformations were occurring in all areas of Egyptian legal thought, Islamic and non-Islamic; second, the reception of European law sparked changes in Egypt's culture, legal-educational institutions, and the alignment patterns of its law scholars; and third, European influence gave rise to Islamic legal activism and both inspired and shaped changes in legal thought at levels of theory, method, and substance.[4]

These developments will be examined in nine chapters, divided among three sections as outlined here; the book's tenth and final chapter—making up the fourth section "New Forms of Islamic Legal Thought"—elaborates on substantive changes in Islamic legal doctrine by examining a transformational treatise in the field of Islamic contract law. Through this final chapter it will be seen that a portion of post-1936 Islamic legal thought looked European, and was European in its immediate origins, even though it was presented as authentically Islamic.

THE ORIGINS OF ISLAMIC LEGAL REVIVALISM

The first section of this book is concerned with explaining the origins of the abiding enthusiasm among contemporary Egyptians for a revival of Islamic law. The story begins between 1875 and 1884, a period when European powers and Egyptian elites engineered a thorough adoption of European laws in Egypt. The Egyptian government, operated by Egyptians but controlled by Europeans, lost little time in promulgating new codes based on the Napoleonic codes of France. A new system of centralized courts, modeled on French courts, was established to

[4] For Wael Hallaq, European imperialism was the central driving force behind changes in Islamic law and legal thought during the nineteenth and twentieth centuries. See Wael B. Hallaq, *Sharīʿa: Theory, Practice, Transformations* (Cambridge: Cambridge University Press, 2009), 396–499.

apply the new Egyptian codes. Applied Egyptian law experienced transitions in the eight decades following 1875, particularly where Islamic law was concerned. With the appearance of European-style law, legal thought, and legal education, the period witnessed both supplanting and transformation of traditional laws and institutions—Islamic, Egyptian, and Ottoman—that had once been applied in the country's legal sphere. To this day, the Egyptian legal system retains many of its essentially European legal characteristics, attitudes, and presumptions.

The changes in Egyptian law and legal thought brought about by the penetration of European law inspired a popular ideological sentiment and a movement that advocated the revival, reform, and reapplication of Islamic law. This sentiment and this multilayered movement together constitute what this book has termed Islamic legal revivalism.[5]

The desire to revive Islamic law in the face of European legal reception has long been and continues to be a popular ideological sentiment among Egyptians.[6] It is common in present-day Egypt for intellectuals, political and religious leaders, and members of the public to criticize the presence of Western law and to esteem the ambition of reviving Islamic law. In the years before the Arab Spring of 2011, this view was a frequent rallying point in popular slogans and academic writing. For decades prior to the adoption of a new constitution in 2012 that contained a heavy measure of Islamic revivalist norms, voices were heard at political rallies, particularly those of the Muslim Brotherhood, proclaiming: "The Quran is our constitution." But the Quran was not, and still is not, the constitution of Egypt. The many twentieth-century Egyptian constitutions, prior to and including the 2012 Constitution, were modeled in most respects on American and European constitutions. A 2006 Gallup poll from Egypt reported that 66 percent of Egyptians thought that Islamic law should be the only source of legislation, while 24 percent stated it should be one among other sources.[7] Such sentiments have persisted even though public pressure led President Anwar Sadat to amend the

[5] The term and its variations do not have a precise Arabic equivalent, but a treasury of common Arabic expressions and aphorisms amount to the same meaning.

[6] The failure of the Muslim Brotherhood in 2013 notwithstanding, abundant academic and journalistic writing in the last thirty years has addressed the desire among portions of Egyptians for a revival of Sharia. For a few examples from Arab academic scholarship, see ʿAlī ʿAlī Manṣūr, *Niẓām al-tajrīm wa-l-ʿiqāb fī l-islām: Muqāranan bi-l-qawānīn al-waḍʿiyyah* (Medina: Muʾassasat al-Zahrāʾ li-l-Īmān wa-l-Khayr, 1976); Fatḥī Marṣafāwī, *Dirāsat taṭbīq al-sharīʿah al-islāmiyyah fī Miṣr* ([Cairo]: Dār al-Fikr al-ʿArabī, 1981); ʿAbd al-ʿAzīz Hindī, *al-Azhar wa-taqnīn al-sharīʿah al-islāmiyyah* (Cairo: Majmaʿ al-Buḥūth al-Islāmiyyah, 1982); Jamāl al-Bannā, *al-Ḥukm bi-l-qurʾān wa-qaḍīyat taṭbīq al-sharīʿah* (Cairo: Dār al-Fikr al-Islāmī, 1986); Ṣalāḥ Ṣāwī, *Qaḍīyat taṭbīq al-sharīʿah* (Shubrah al-Khaymah, Egypt: Bayt al-Ḥikmah, 1990); M. K. Qaṭṭān, *Muʿawwiqāt taṭbīq al-sharīʿah al-islāmiyyah* (Cairo: Maktabat Wahbah, 1991); Muḥammad Quṭb, *Ḥawla taṭbīq al-sharīʿah* (Cairo: Maktabat al-Sunnah, 1991); ʿAbd al-Nāṣir Tawfīq ʿAṭṭār, *Taṭbīq al-sharīʿah al-islāmiyyah fī l-ʿālam al-islāmī* (Cairo: Dār al-Faḍīlah, 1993); Muḥammad Saʿīd al-ʿAshmāwī, *al-Sharīʿah al-islāmiyyah wa-l-qānūn al-miṣrī* (Cairo: Maktabat Madbūlī al-Ṣaghīr, 1996); Ṭāriq al-Bishrī, *al-Waḍʿ al-qānūnī al-muʿāṣir bayna l-sharīʿah al-islāmiyyah wa-l-qānūn al-waḍʿī* (Cairo: Dār al-Shurūq, 1996). Media coverage has been extensive in all languages for at least twenty years and even more since the Arab Spring. See, for example, Anthony Shadid, "Egypt's Islamists Show Their Might and Numbers, Demanding Religious Law," *New York Times*, July 30, 2011, 1.

[7] Commensurate figures were reported in Pakistan, Jordan, Bangladesh, Morocco, and Iran. Dalia Mogahed, "Islam and Democracy," Special Report: Muslim World. The Gallup Organization, Princeton, NJ (2006).

constitution in 1980 to provide that "principles of Islamic Sharia are the principal source for legislation." In the eyes of Islamic legal revivalists, the courts and the government did not go far enough. During the revolutionary upheaval in Egypt of 2011 and 2012, a Muslim Brotherhood leader Mohamed Morsi was elected as president of Egypt based in part on a platform of further advancing the application of Islamic law. The Muslim Brotherhood is still Egypt's leading proponent of this agenda, even though the movement fell from power in 2012 at the hands of the national army.

For many proponents of Islamic legal revival, their enthusiasm has long reduced to a simple desire for greater political and economic justice in society. This adaptation of Islamic legal revivalism is frequently highlighted by Western academics of the present day who wish to cast Islamic political movements, like the Egyptian Muslim Brotherhood, in a light that is benevolent and palatable to skeptical Western audiences. Yet there have always been other dimensions to the Islamic legal cause, in Egypt as in most other countries, that are more particularistic, less concerned with Western-defined concepts of political and economic justice, and more concerned in the first instance with rigorously implementing the word and will of God, whatever the political and social byproducts of this action might be. In the particularistic dimensions of Islamic legal revivalist thought, the focus is on elaborating and reviving an enormous range of specific rules derived from sacred sources and thought to be intrinsically and entirely Islamic in origin.

Apart from pure ideology and political activism, the desire to revive Islamic law in Egypt has also long been the raison d'être for a field of technical legal scholarship that is the domain of professional jurists who toil in analyzing, reforming, and positing Islamic law and legal methods. The presence of European law inspired the creation of a prolific genre of academic writing about modern Islamic law, which developed concertedly in the mid-1920s and 1930s and continues to thrive in today's academic publishing market. And since the 1870s at least, there has been a thriving field of academic and legal-professional discourse in Egypt wherein jurists, lawyers, professors, politicians, judges, ideologues, and other members of the public have debated the content of applied and hypothetical Islamic law. Discussions have ranged from questions of the highest magnitude in legal theory to the minutiae of substantive law. Positions taken in these debates have also appeared in courts through judgments. One inspiration to pursue a revival of Islamic law was that Egypt had adopted European laws. Proponents of Islamic legal revival interpreted Egypt's European law as an affront to Egypt's religious, cultural, national, and transnational Muslim identity. They championed the revival of Islamic law as a priority in restoring Egypt's independence and authentic character.

The story of the growth of Islamic legal revivalism pertains in part to how the very conception of "Sharia" changed during the decades in question.[8] The existence

[8] See Baber Johansen, *Contingency in a Sacred Law: Legal and Ethical Norms in the Muslim* Fiqh (Leiden: Brill, 1999), 40–72; Hallaq, *Sharīʿa*; Murteza Bedir, "*Fıkıh* to Law: Secularization through Curriculum," *Islamic Law and Society* 11,3 (2004): 378–401.

of the Western-language term "Islamic law" (*droit musulman, diritto musulmano, islamisches Recht*, etc.) as an ostensible synonym for Sharia is a manifestation of how its conception changed during the nineteenth and twentieth centuries, not only in Egypt but around the world. The coinage "Islamic law" reflects the particular impact of European ideas and institutions on a pre-modern, Arabic-Islamic concept that was arguably broader than common Western European notions of "law," in particular of law as a tool of control employed and managed, above all, by states.

For much of the nineteenth century, Sharia was understood as a flexible source of law and one that could live side by side with state-made law. After the 1880s, and particularly after the 1920s, Sharia was increasingly identified and advertised as a singularly complete and valid source for the development of a comprehensive system of positive laws that was created, managed, and enforced by the state. Proponents of this view saw Sharia as a body of law that trumped all other law and could not exist comfortably parallel, let alone in a state of subjugation, to "man-made" laws that were considered morally inferior. Simultaneously, Egyptian jurists advanced a theory that, to be legitimate, all law needed to be the product of specific methodological procedures beginning with consultation of the Quran. The jurists and law professionals encountered in this book were proponents of these prevalent points of view, and in some regards they were pioneers of these views insofar as they intended to make such perspectives the cornerstone of law in the modern nation.

EUROPE'S INTERVENTIONS IN ISLAMIC LAW

At the same time as Egyptians were aspiring to revive an authentic Islamic law, and to thereby supplant the invasive European law, their approaches to law generally and their conception of Islamic law specifically were being influenced by their long experience with Europeans. It became common for Egyptians to meld their ideas about Islamic law with their experiences in European law, and through contacts with European law professors, who were experts in comparative law, European law, Egypt's particular version of European law, and Islamic law, they encountered European plans for the reform of Islamic law. European scholars and colonial authorities had studied Islamic law for more than a century before the European assumption of authority in Egypt in 1875, and they had already generated an extensive range of treatises, articles, and field manuals about Islamic law. By the 1920s and 1930s, this literature was large and informed. For better or for worse, these works positioned Europeans to influence Islamic legal thought and practice in colonial settings.

European scholars who became interested in Islamic law in the nineteenth and early twentieth centuries did not merely describe Islamic law and legal thought as they found it; they wrote about and sought practical ways to reform Islamic law and legal thought. Some lived in the Muslim world where they taught in schools and trained generations of indigenous lawyers and judges. Some worked in government offices in their home countries and in colonized countries around the world. Their approaches to Islamic law and their ideas about Islamic legal reform, however, were often not value-free, politically neutral, or purely inductive. Their intellectual industry created tools for European and Egyptian jurists who wanted to reform Islamic law according to European ideas, practices, trends, values, and policies.

The effects of these European efforts are still felt in Islamic legal thought in Egypt, even among those who claim to want to revive an authentic and autochthonous Islamic legal practice. As part of an examination of European law's influence on Egyptian legal thought, a chapter in this book is devoted to a study of Édouard Lambert's ideas about Islamic law. A leading French comparativist who had formed well-defined views about Islamic law and the future of Islamic legal reform, Lambert worked for decades with Egyptians on legal reform projects.

EGYPTIAN LAW SCHOOLS AND THE RECEPTION OF EUROPEAN DOCTRINES

Egyptians were masters as well as objects in Egypt's "reception" of European law. They engaged European ideas rigorously in their own pedagogy and scholarship. In particular, Egyptian law professors played central roles in pursuing the reception of European legal thought in native Egyptian legal thought.

The world of legal education in Egypt in the period under study in this book was complex, mirroring the complexity of a legal system that played host to several separate but interworking legal spaces that took their laws, lawyers, and judges from multiple countries—Egypt, France, England, and Italy to name a few. There were several schools of higher education for training legal professionals and scholars, each school differing in its ideological, political, religious, and cultural outlook. Three law schools concentrated on teaching the new Franco-Egyptian legal system, while three high Islamic institutions produced judges, lawyers, and clerks for the Sharia courts and produced professors versed in Sharia. Yet, as this book will show, the graduates of these schools interacted with one another, and this collaboration pushed Egypt's legal thought and practice—as well as that of the Middle East and the Islamic world—in new directions.

The years between the mid-1920s and the mid-1950s were an especially creative era in the history of legal thought and activism in Egypt. The period was characterized by diverse approaches and ideas, cross-cultural and multilingual engagements, methodological and philosophical rigor, theoretical awareness on a world-class level, piously construed innovations in Islamic legal thought, and controlled experiments with the modernization of classical Islamic laws and methods. In these years, scholars offered competing visions for the path to revival, reform, and reapplication of Islamic law.

Offering insights into transformations in law, the final chapter of this book will display all of the factors discussed in previous sections coalescing to produce new approaches, concepts, and rules in Islamic legal thought. The chapter explains how European legal ideas inspired the formation of the "general theory" legal genre in Egypt, and it explains how the innovation of general theory in European legal writing played a role in encouraging Egyptian jurists to articulate a new "theory of obligation," "theory of contract," and theory of "freedom of contract" for Egyptian-Islamic legal doctrine.

In the process of this analysis, the final chapter offers observations on the politics of the reception of European law and legal ideas within Egyptian legal-intellectual culture between the 1920s and 1950s. The chapter explains differences that arose between professors of law who came from the European-oriented side of Egypt's legal academy and those who were trained in the country's preeminent Islamic institutions.

SCHOLARSHIP ON EGYPTIAN LEGAL HISTORY

Since this book responds to and engages with pre-existing historical writing, comments are in order about where this book fits into existing knowledge about the history of Islamic law in Egypt and the wider Islamic law world.

Scholarship on Egyptian legal history of the nineteenth and twentieth centuries is divided by the transitional years 1875–1884.[9] The earlier period witnessed the Ottoman-Egyptian ruling elite enact criminal laws, land laws, constitutional laws, and elements of criminal and investigative procedure that had European origins, and establish secular-oriented Nizami courts (Ar. adj. < *niẓām* "order"). Light was originally brought to this era of Egyptian legal history by Gabriel Baer, Daniel Crecelius, and D. G. Nadolski;[10] recently, Khaled Fahmy, Rudolph Peters, Avi Rubin, Liat Kozma, Imad Hilal, and Omar Cheta have upended generalizations about pre-1875 Egyptian law.[11] The older works emphasized that innovations in the practice

[9] In recent years, scholars working on both sides of the divide have met to exchange ideas, including at a June 2009 conference at the American University of Cairo entitled "New Approaches to Egyptian Legal History."

[10] See Gabriel Baer, "Tanzimat in Egypt: The Penal Code," *Bulletin of the School of Oriental and African Studies* 26 (1963): 29–49; Baer, "The Development of Private Ownership of Land," in Baer, *Studies in the Social History of Modern Egypt* (Chicago: University of Chicago Press, 1969), 62–78; Daniel Crecelius, "Nonideological Responses of the Egyptian Ulama to Modernization," in *Scholars, Saints, and Sufis: Muslim Religious Institutions in the Middle East since 1500*, ed. Nikki R. Keddie (Berkeley and Los Angeles: University of California Press, 1972), 167–209; Keddie, "The Emergence of the Shaykh of al-Azhar as the Preeminent Religious Leader in Egypt," in *Colloque international sur l'histoire du Caire, 27 mars–5 avril 1969*, ed. Ministry of Culture of the Arab Republic of Egypt ([Cairo]: General Egyptian Book Organization, 1972), 109–203; Dora Glidewell Nadolski, "Ottoman and Secular Civil Law," *International Journal of Middle East Studies* 8,4 (1977): 517–43.

[11] See, for example, Khaled Fahmy, "The Police and the People in Nineteenth-Century Egypt," *Die Welt des Islams* 39,3 (1999): 340–77; Fahmy, "The Sound of Silence: Criminal Law, Forensic Medicine and Subaltern Agency in Khedival Egypt" (unpubl. art., 2005); Fahmy, "Justice, Law and Pain in Khedival Egypt," in *Standing Trial: Law and the Person in the Modern Middle East*, ed. Baudouin Dupret (London: I. B. Tauris, 2004), 85–116; Rudolph Peters, "Islamic and Secular Criminal Law in Nineteenth Century Egypt," *Islamic Law and Society* 4,1 (1997): 70–90; Peters, "State, Law and Society in Nineteenth Century Egypt," *Die Welt des Islams* 39 (1999): 267–72; Avi Rubin, *Ottoman Nizamiyye Courts: Law and Modernity* (New York: Palgrave Macmillan, 2011); Omar Youssef Cheta, "Rule of Merchants: The Practice of Commerce and Law in Late Ottoman Egypt, 1841–1876" (Ph.D. diss., New York University, 2014). See also Wael B. Hallaq, "A Prelude to Ottoman Reform: Ibn ʿĀbidīn on Custom and Legal Change," in *Histories of the Modern Middle East: New Directions*, ed. Israel Gershoni et al. (Boulder: Rienner, 2002), 37–61.

of Egyptian courts flowed from European influences; new works have shown that much innovation was attributable to autochthonous Egyptian and Ottoman design.[12]

Scholars investigating the second period, when the Ottoman and Islamic institutions made way for a regime based more thoroughly on French law, are fewer and have produced less in the way of work that reshapes fundamental understandings. Mid-twentieth-century writings by Joseph Schacht, Malcom Kerr, Herbert Liebesny, Farhat Ziadeh, Yvon Linant de Bellefonds, and Chafik Chehata took a broad look at changes in law in Egypt during the colonial era,[13] while more recent histories of Islamic law describe Islamic law's interaction with modernity in Egypt.[14] Although these works serve as essential starting points—and in some respects also provide new analytical arguments for experts—they do not explain how the Egyptian legal system was experienced, developed, and practiced by Egyptian jurists with strong religious conviction or Islamic-ideological inclinations other than Muḥammad ʿAbduh and ʿAlī ʿAbd al-Rāziq.

Nathan Brown, Byron Cannon, Will Hanley, Enid Hill, Latifah Salim, Donald Reid, and Herbert Liebesny have most developed the macro history of legal institutions and legal education in colonial Egypt between 1875 and the 1950s,[15] while Anne Clément and Samera Esmeir are perhaps the only historians to have written in recent times rigorous social histories of the administration of law under British rule.[16] Through an analysis of court records and ordinary life in the

[12] See Peters, "State, Law and Society," 268.

[13] Joseph Schacht is considered a leading figure of Islamic legal studies in the West, but he has also been the subject of harsh theoretical critique and empirical revisionism for over thirty years. See generally Amr A. Shalakany, "Islamic Legal Histories," *Berkeley Journal of Middle Eastern and Islamic Law* 1 (2010): 1–82. See also Joseph Schacht, "L'Évolution moderne du droit musulman en Égypte," *Melanges Maspero* 3 (1940): 323–34; Schacht, "Islamic Law in Contemporary States," *American Journal of Comparative Law* 8,2 (1959): 133–47; Malcolm H. Kerr, *Islamic Reform: The Political and Legal Theories of Muḥammad ʿAbduh and Rashīd Riḍā* (Berkeley and Los Angeles: University of California Press, 1966); Herbert J. Liebesny, *The Law of the Near and Middle East: Readings, Cases, and Materials* (Albany: State University of New York Press, 1975); Farhat Ziadeh, *Lawyers, the Rule of Law and Liberalism in Modern Egypt* (Stanford: Hoover Institution, 1968); Yvon Linant de Bellefonds, *Traité de droit musulman comparé* (Paris: Mouton, 1965); Shafīq Shiḥātah (Chafik Chehata), *Tārīkh ḥarakat al-tajdīd fī l-nuẓum al-qānūniyyah fī Miṣr mundh ʿahd Muḥammad ʿAlī* (Cairo: al-Jamʿiyyah al-Miṣriyyah li-l-Dirāsāt al-Tārīkhiyyah, 1961).

[14] See Wael B. Hallaq, *An Introduction to Islamic Law* (Cambridge: Cambridge University Press, 2009), 396–442; Sami Zubaida, *Law and Power in the Islamic World* (London: I. B. Tauris, 2003), 158–81; Talal Asad, *Formations of the Secular: Christianity, Islam, Modernity* (Stanford: Stanford University Press, 2003), 203–56. See also n. 11.

[15] Nathan J. Brown, "The Precarious Life and Slow Death of the Mixed Courts of Egypt," *International Journal of the Middle East* 25,1 (1993): 33–52; Brown, "Law and Imperialism: Egypt in Comparative Perspective," *Law and Society Review* 29,1 (1995): 103–26; Brown, *The Rule of Law in the Arab World: Courts in Egypt and the Gulf* (Cambridge: Cambridge University Press, 1997); Byron Cannon, *Politics of Law and the Courts in Nineteenth-Century Egypt* (Salt Lake City: University of Utah Press, 1988); Will Hanley, "Foreignness and Localness in Alexandria, 1880–1940" (Ph.D. diss., Princeton University, 2007); Liebesny, *The Law of the Near and Middle East*; Donald M. Reid, "The National Bar Association and Egyptian Politics, 1912–1954," *International Journal of African Historical Studies* 7,4 (1974): 608–46; Reid, *Lawyers and Politics in the Arab World, 1880–1960* (Minneapolis: Bibliotheca Islamica, 1981); Laṭīfah Muḥammad Sālim, *al-Niẓām al-qaḍāʾī al-miṣrī al-ḥadīth 1875–1914*, 2 vols. (Cairo: al-Hayʾah al-Miṣriyyah al-ʿĀmmah li-l-Kitāb, 2000).

[16] Anne Marie Clément, "*Fallāḥīn* on Trial in Colonial Egypt: Apprehending the Peasantry through Orality, Writing, and Performance (1884–1914)" (Ph.D. diss., University of Toronto, 2012); Samera Esmeir, *Juridical Humanity: A Colonial History* (Stanford: Stanford University Press, 2012). I cite this work where there is overlap in topical material, although Esmeir's approach to Egyptian legal history not only differs from, but is even antithetical to the approach used in this book.

courts, Clément has brought a law-in-action and ethnographic perspective to colonial Egypt's legal history. Esmeir, on the other hand, investigates aspects of Egyptian legal history through an analytically ambitious fusion of studies in juridical texts, legal institutions, legal practice, and social theory. Another study, by Noah Feldman, is a discussion of the stamina of Islamic legal revivalism that puts less weight on empirical research but is heavy on insights, grounded in historical perspective, and considers its subject matter from a unique range of empirical and theoretical angles.[17] Although these scholars provide essential, original research as well as analytical points of departure for scholars interested in the field, still too little is known about how the Egyptian courts—Mixed Courts, Native Courts, consular courts, Sharia Courts, and guardian courts—advanced Islamic law and legal thought.[18] There is equally an inadequate understanding of legal education and the inclinations of academic jurists.[19]

Having probed little into the substance of Egyptian academic legal thought,[20] legal historians have often taken for granted, mistakenly, that European law mostly replaced Islamic law in the work and consciousness of the mainstream Egyptian lawyers and that this transformation occurred without significant protest.[21] In an academically fashionable endeavour to afford as much credit as possible to efforts that took place on Egyptian soil and to the work of Egyptians, influences in Egypt—beyond codes—from Europe, European colonies, and European personnel within Egypt have been overlooked. Ideological and theoretical topics, such as secularism,[22] and political themes in colonial history, such as whether Europeans or Egyptians should be credited for constructing the modern Egyptian legal system, have been the subject of much study in the prevailing scholarly literature.[23]

[17] Noah Feldman, *The Fall and Rise of the Islamic State* (Princeton: Princeton University Press, 2008). See also Zubaida, *Law and Power*; Asad, *Formations of the Secular*.

[18] But see Ron Shaham, *Family and the Courts in Modern Egypt: A Study Based on Decisions by the Sharīʿa Courts, 1900–1955* (Leiden: Brill, 1997). See also the historical introduction in Chapter 2. For Mixed Courts, see Jasper Yeates Brinton, *The Mixed Courts of Egypt*, rev. ed. (New Haven: Yale University Press, 1930); Mark S. W. Hoyle, "The Structure and Laws of the Mixed Courts of Egypt," *Arab Law Quarterly* 1,3 (1986): 327–45; Hoyle, *Mixed Courts of Egypt* (London: Graham and Trotman, 1991); Brown, "Precarious Life"; B. A. Roberson, "The Emergence of the Modern Judiciary in the Middle East," in *Islam and Public Law: Classical and Contemporary Studies*, ed. C. Mallat (London: Graham and Trotman, 1993), 107–39. For legal practice, see Clément, "*Fallāḥīn* on Trial," 7 n. 15, 118, 148, 232, 252, 294–6, 309; Hanan Kholoussy, *For Better or Worse: The Marriage Crisis That Made Modern Egypt* (Stanford: Stanford University Press, 2010).

[19] More knowledge about Egypt's six law schools would yield insights into how Islamic legal thought changed after 1875, at the root of which inquiry lies the aspiration to understand how institutional factors shaped new trends. See Hilary Kalmbach, "From Turban to Tarboush: Dār al-ʿUlūm and Social, Linguistic, and Religious Change in Interwar Egypt" (D.Phil. diss., University of Oxford, 2011).

[20] For exceptions, see Guy Bechor, *God in the Courtroom: The Transformation of Courtroom Oath and Perjury between Islamic and Franco-Egyptian Law* (Leiden: Brill, 2011); Oussama Arabi, *Studies in Modern Islamic Law and Jurisprudence* (The Hague: Kluwer Law International, 2001); Esmeir, *Juridical Humanity*.

[21] This prevailing tendency in historical literature was observed and critiqued in Lama Abu-Odeh, "Politics of (Mis)Recognition: Islamic Law Pedagogy in American Academia," *American Journal of Comparative Law* 52 (2004): 789–824.

[22] Asad, *Formations of the Secular*, 205–56.

[23] Brown, "Precarious Life"; Brown, "Law and Imperialism."

Although Bernard Botiveau's *Loi islamique et droit dans les sociétés arabes* (1993) has provided a singularly exemplary model for what a more comprehensive study on general developments in Islamic legal thought for the period 1875 to the 1950s can look like,[24] there is no study that programmatically explains, through in-depth and broad research in primary sources, the main characteristics, issues, changes, challenges, and developments that shaped and defined modern Islamic legal thought as understood and practiced by leading lawyers and law professors of these decades.

Several factors impede the writing of such a comprehensive study. The time range and geographical spans are wide. Morocco, Algeria, Egypt, and Syria, to mention only a few countries, had different experiences in the arena of modern Islamic legal thought and revivalism. Moreover, the scope of primary source material is vast and probably over 98 percent of it remains unread. The legal historian is faced with hundreds of books and articles—primary sources—that have not been subjected to historical scrutiny. Even the most important works by well-known figures such as Muḥammad ʿAbduh[25] and ʿAbd al-Razzāq al-Sanhūrī, the Arab world's most prolific civil jurist and self-styled modernizer of applied Islamic law, remain largely untreated.[26] This is to say nothing of the works of influential, but much less celebrated, writers such as Muḥammad Zayd al-Abyānī, Aḥmad Ibrāhīm, Muḥammad Abū Zahrah, ʿAlī al-Khafīf, ʿAbd al-Wahhāb Khallāf, and Muḥammad Yūsuf Mūsá. Even the authors of recent, short biographies on some of those figures have heavily generalized on the content of their juridical treatises.[27]

[24] Botiveau mentions, if often only in passing, the emergence of new genres and approaches in legal thought and writing. He views social, economic, and political history as integral to legal history and looks at change in the substance of legal thought at the highest levels of conceptualization down to the medium-level rules. He notes a number of historical figures who were influential in their own time but who have not been adequately recognized by historical literature, and shows that an understanding of reformist Islamic legal thought in Egypt should be formed in concert with an understanding of what was happening in the non-Islamic spheres of Egyptian law. Bernard Botiveau, *Loi islamique et droit dans les sociétés arabes: Mutations des systèmes juridiques du Moyen-Orient* (Paris: Karthala, 1993). See also Zubaida, *Law and Power*.

[25] The bulk of Muḥammad ʿAbduh's work specifically in private law and legal theory remains unknown in spite of the great deal of attention he has received from historians. On ʿAbduh, see ʿAbd Allāh Mabrūk al-Najjār, *Fatāwá l-imām Muḥammad ʿAbduh: Dirāsah fiqhiyyah taʾṣīliyyah* (Cairo: Dār al-Nahḍah al-ʿArabiyyah, 1995); ʿAbd Allāh Maḥmūd Shiḥātah, *Manhaj al-imām Muḥammad ʿAbduh fī tafsīr al-qurʾān al-karīm* ([Cairo]: al-Majlis al-Aʿlá li-Riʿāyat al-Funūn wa-l-Ādāb wa-l-ʿUlūm al-Ijtimāʿiyyah, 1963); Arabi, *Modern Islamic Law*, "Muhammad Abduh and the Modern Demands on Islamic Law," 19–38; Fāʾiz Muḥammad Ḥusayn Muḥammad, *al-Manhaj al-fiqhī li-l-imām Muḥammad ʿAbduh* (Cairo: Dār al-Nahḍah al-Miṣriyyah, 2000); Yasir S. Ibrahim, "The Spirit of Islamic Law and Modern Religious Reform: Maqasid al-Shariʿa in Muhammad ʿAbduh and Rashid Rida's Legal Thought" (Ph.D. diss., Princeton University, 2004); Kerr, *Islamic Reform*; Muḥammad Rashīd Riḍā, *Tārīkh al-ustādh al-imām al-shaykh Muḥammad ʿAbduh: Wa-fih tafṣīl sīratih wa-khulāṣat sīrat mūqiẓ al-sharq al-ḥakīm wa-l-islām Jamāl al-Dīn al-Afghānī*, 3 vols. (Miṣr: Maṭbaʿat al-Manār, 1906–31).

[26] No critical studies exist on al-Sanhūrī's six-volume *Maṣādir al-ḥaqq fī l-fiqh al-islāmī* (Sources of Rights in Islamic *Fiqh*), on his ten-volume commentary on the Egyptian Civil Code of 1948, or on the Iraqi Civil Code of 1953 that he authored. See Enid Hill, "Al-Sanhuri and Islamic Law: The Place and Significance of Islamic Law in the Life and Work of ʿAbd Al-Razzaq Ahmad al-Sanhuri, Egyptian Jurist and Scholar, 1895–1971," *Arab Law Quarterly* 3,1–2 (1988): 33–64, 182–218.

[27] Muḥammad al-Sayyid Dasūqī, *Muḥammad Yūsuf Mūsá, 1317–1383h/1899–1963m: al-Faqīh al-faylasūf wa-l-muṣliḥ al-mujaddid* (Damascus: Dār al-Qalam, 2003); Muḥammad ʿUthmān Shubayr, *al-Shaykh ʿAlī al-Khafīf 1309–1398h/1891–1978m: al-Faqīh al-mujaddid* (Damascus: Dār al-Qalam, 2002); Shubayr,

To appreciate the significance of the legal writings and legislative projects of this period, one must be prepared to read thousands of pages on the specifics of contract, property, procedural, administrative, and constitutional law in several national, religious, and cultural traditions. Because the Egyptian jurists were products of a wealth of intellectual traditions, the reader should ideally also be versed in, at least, Arabic, French, English, pre-modern Sunni jurisprudence, late nineteenth-century Ottoman jurisprudence, Roman law, French law, German law, early twentieth-century British common law, post-1875 Franco-Egyptian law, post-1948 Egyptian civil law, continental European legal history post-Gaius, European socialism, labor studies, schools of legal theory that were being studied in France, Germany, Italy, England, and the United States between 1804 and 1952, and, finally, Egyptian and Islamic intellectual and political history since the chronicler ʿAbd al-Raḥmān al-Jabartī (d. 1825). The legal thought that was produced intentionally aimed to handle, balance, or even merge all of these various traditions—sidelining none—and the jurists often assumed an awareness of these traditions and their ongoing relevance with their readers.

Despite accomplishments to date, knowing more about the variety of impetuses for change, the processes of change, and the effects of change are still needed. We also need to know more about how the substance of Islamic legal thinking changed, especially in the bulk of legal matters in private and public law.[28] For the bulk of law—contracts, property, procedure, administration, commercial and business law, constitutional law, and the rest—few studies have made progress in explaining how, why, in what way, and to what effects legal thinking on these matters shifted. Efforts have also been too limited to identify the best-known jurists working at the time, to account for what they wrote, and to discuss how they related to each other and responded to their own intellectual, political, and cultural contexts. Prevailing arguments in modern Egyptian-Islamic legal history also need to be reconsidered. One idea in need of revision is that Islamic legal thought did not change much as a result of Western incursions, but was sidelined over time and left to develop, if at all, on its own terms.[29] Another is the familiar habit of placing Muḥammad ʿAbduh at the absolute center of Egyptian reformism. This book aims to fill the gaps and revise the paradigm, and to provide new pathways and ideas to facilitate sophisticated historical and legal analyses.

Muḥammad Abū Zahrah: Imām al-fuqahāʾ al-muʿāṣirīn wa-l-mudāfiʿ al-jarīʾ ʿan ḥaqāʾiq al-dīn (Damascus: Dār al-Qalam, 2006); Shubayr, *ʿAbd al-Wahhāb Khallāf: al-Faqīh al-uṣūlī al-mujaddid* (Dimashq: Dār al-Qalam, 2010); Muḥammad ʿImārah, *al-Duktūr ʿAbd al-Razzāq al-Sanhūrī: Islāmiyyat al-dawlah wa-l-madaniyyah wa-l-qānūn* (Cairo: Dār al-Rashād, 1999).

28 This book employs the term "public law" to refer to law controlling the chief branches of government, akin to "constitutional law" in the American legal system. Due to the connection with the French legal system, "public law" (Ar. *al-qānūn al-ʿāmm*) was used in tandem with "constitutional law" (Ar. *al-qānūn al-dustūrī*) in the period 1875–1952.

29 See Aharon Layish's comment that Muḥammad ʿAbduh and Rashīd Riḍā "did not succeed in shaping a new legal doctrine amalgamating Islamic ideas with liberal elements of Western civilization.... Their attempt to ... reopen the gates of *ijtihād* by refashioning traditional mechanisms was ... unenduring. Their efforts were not continued, at any rate, not by the authorized exponents of the sharīʿah." Aharon Layish, "The Contribution of the Modernists to the Secularization of Islamic Law," *Middle Eastern Studies* 14,3 (1978): 263–77, 267.

METHODOLOGY

This is a book of intellectual history and legal-institutional history; it is not a work devoted to traditional, critical, anthropological, or social legal analysis of laws or legal practice.[30] A degree of overlap exists between the methods of intellectual and legal-institutional history, but there is enough of a difference to warrant making this distinction. On the side of intellectual history, my ambition was to trace the origins and development of one main idea—that of problematizing Western law and championing Islamic law as an alternative legal system—and its associated ideas. In Egyptian, British, and French archives, I read newspapers, journals, memoirs, law treatises, scholarly articles, dissertations, law codes, committee transcripts, and official government reports that shed light on developments in Egypt's law, courts, and law schools. I examined ideas articulated by law students, judges, jurists, legislators, and political and administrative leaders in order to demonstrate how the precepts of Islamic legal revivalism emerged, developed, and intensified over a period of approximately eighty years.

This book mentions, with varying degrees of depth, over forty Egyptian and European jurists whose contributions to modern Islamic legal thought in Egypt have not been sufficiently appreciated. Since is not possible to write in detail about all of these jurists, the analysis of jurists and their generations is largely, and at best, prosopographical. I analyze the institutional, political, ideological, and socio-economic contexts in which they operated, and examine how they made changes to the curricula and structures of the multiple law schools in order to serve their ideological and nationalist agendas. Where possible, I account for links that were established between jurists and leading nationalists and Islamists.

If there were two prevailing methodological curves in Middle Eastern historical studies in American universities during the years when this book was being written, one was the study of social and economic history and the other was the study of court records. Academics in the field commonly rejected the notion that ideology, including Islamism, could be a revolutionary force in Middle Eastern political life as great as or greater than economics and malaise over the economy. Furthermore, it was widely held that economic, social, ethnographic, and "bottom-up" history are not only useful keys to unlocking history, but superior to all others. The study of printed texts and of institutions where comparatively influential persons worked—in essence, intellectual history—was therefore out of fashion, perhaps even a target for hostility. Nevertheless, this kind of history has a rightful place among other methodological inclinations, and its revival would seem to be all the more justified in light of the fact that the recent Arab Spring was shaped to such a great extent by ideological aspirations.

[30] On the methods of traditional and critical legal analysis, see generally Stephen E. Gottlieb, *Jurisprudence: Cases and Materials. An Introduction to the Philosophy of Law and Its Applications*, 2nd ed. (Newark, NJ: LexisNexis, 2006), 410–63; Robert L. Hayman Jr. et al., *Jurisprudence: Classical and Contemporary*, 2nd ed. (St. Paul: West Group, 2002); Gary Minda, *Postmodern Legal Movements: Law and Jurisprudence at Century's End* (New York: New York University Press, 1995), 67–88, 106–48; Mario Jori, "Formalisme," in *Dictionnaire encyclopédique de théorie et de sociologie du droit*, eds. A. J. Arnaud and J. G. Belley (Paris: Libraire générale de droit et de jurisprudence, 1993); Roberto Unger, "The CLS Movement," *Harvard Law Review* 96 (1983): 561–73, 665–75.

The research methods and preoccupations of this project were also informed by the field of Western legal history, as taught and practiced in European and U.S. universities. There, the examination of how the "reception" of a foreign legal system can impact an already existing legal system is a topic of ongoing interest. This gave me the idea to examine how the reception of French law influenced local, customary, and religious law in Egypt, a recipient thereby also of European customary law, Roman law, and canon law. I was influenced by Alan Watson's conception of a "block effect" of Roman law, or the proposition that Roman law has most influenced non-Roman legal systems by encouraging jurists to repackage substantive law into Roman categories.[31] The influence of Watson's theory of legal influence is seen in Section IV's analysis of the work of Chafik Chehata.

Another common theme of research in legal history concerns the origins, conduct, and impact of the nineteenth-century movement to codify law in Western Europe.[32] The fact that European law came to Egypt in codified form was one of the reasons that it both survived in Egypt and subsequently influenced developments in Islamic legal thought. Advancing our understanding of how the introduction of European codes into Egypt affected Egyptian and Islamic legal doctrine would be a useful contribution to the field of comparative legal history.

Western legal historians have also developed a range of approaches to answering three recurring questions in their field. Specifically, how did legal thought change in a given country and in a given period of time, who changed the legal thought, and why did the legal thought change? Those who have focused on developments in the intellectual sphere and in the profession of juridical science more precisely have concerned themselves, to varying degrees, with the influence of external political, social, economic, and ideological factors on jurists,[33] having in mind a premise that these are the central factors driving changes in legal thought.[34] Others have placed the most focus on the development of institutions, having in mind a theoretical premise that institutions play a driving role in the development of law and legal thought.[35] Change in legal thought has been analyzed as the result of changes in intellectual culture, or as the result of new problems and modes of adjudicating that arise in courts. In the final analysis, selecting only one of these approaches unnecessarily limits one's research and findings.

[31] Alan Watson, *The Making of the Civil Law* (Cambridge, MA: Harvard University Press, 1981). See also Charles Donahue's review, "Roman Law Influence on the Civil Law," *Michigan Law Review* 81,4 (1983): 972–6.

[32] Watson, *Making of the Civil Law*, chaps. 2, 8, 9, 11; James Q. Whitman, *The Legacy of Roman Law in the German Romantic Era: Historical Vision and Legal Change* (Princeton: Princeton University Press, 1990); S. Bayitch, "Codification in Modern Times," in *Civil Law in the Modern World*, ed. A. N. Yiannopoulus (Baton Rouge: Louisiana State University Press, 1965), 161–91.

[33] See, for example, Franz Wieacker, *A History of Private Law in Europe* (Oxford: Oxford University Press, 1995); Watson, *Making of the Civil Law*; Paul Ourliac and J. de Malafosse, *Histoire du droit privé*, 3 vols. (Paris: Presses Universitaires de France, 1961–68).

[34] See, for example, Whitman, *Legacy of Roman Law*; Oussama Arabi, "Intention and Method in Sanhūrī's Fiqh: Cause as Ulterior Motive," *Islamic Law and Society* 4,2 (1997): 200–23.

[35] See, for example, Jacques Ellul, *Histoire des institutions*, 2nd ed. (Paris: Presses Universitaires de France, 1958); Richard L. Kagan, *Lawsuits and Litigants in Castile, 1500–1700* (Chapel Hill: University of North Carolina Press, 1981).

My approach is to focus on academic jurists—professors and authors, but not judges writing from the bench—and their roles in developing Franco-Egyptian and Islamic legal thought, while considering the influence of political, ideological, and economic events external to the strict practice and study of law, such as the popular waves of nationalism, Islamism, and various left-leaning inclinations of the period of Egyptian history between 1922 and 1952. However, a working premise and theme of the book is that these influences had their limits and Egyptian jurists were themselves the major engines of change in Egyptian juridical science and the law itself during the period 1875–1952. Egyptian jurists could be influenced by prevailing trends in political and legal thought in one moment, yet unmoved by changes in these same areas in another moment. One example touched upon by this book is that many Islamic legal revivalists embraced a measure of nineteenth-century Europe's legal formalism, yet did not avail themselves of the anti-formalism that soon after (and to an extent concomitantly) prevailed in much of European and Franco-Egyptian legal thought. Egyptian jurists retained and used their powers to control the direction of legal academia as they deemed most fit, even when their intellectual inclinations clashed with other political, economic, religious, ideological, and legal-theoretical trends in Egyptian society.

A central part of this book's effort is the attempt to reconstruct the outlooks and institutional culture of sophisticated Egyptian law students and jurists of the periods under study. Although a historian can never fully appreciate the psychology or mentality of a historical person, it is possible to reconstruct the education, knowledge, and intellectual orientation of Egyptian law scholars. We can know, as they did, the French, German, and Egyptian civil codes and the theoretical works of European and Arab scholars that were circulating in the 1930s, and we can imagine having their confidence in European notions of legal universalism and internationalism, in global legal unification, and in the merits of European social science, codes, and European-style comparative law studies.

This book is more interested in juridical thought and less interested in juridical practice[36] for the simple reason that during the period under study, the practice of Islamic law became nominally limited to matters of personal status, inheritances, and trusts. It was this marginalization of Sharia that prompted Muslim jurists to try to modernize and expand Islamic law by writing academic tracts. Egyptians were looking for ways to make Islamic laws and courts newly competent and relevant. Their doctrinal thought laid the groundwork for substantive developments, practical and theoretical, in Islamic legal revivalism after 1952. Although one cannot dispute that the juridical practice in Sharia Courts influenced what scholars wrote, one is hard pressed to find Islamic legal theorists of the 1950s and beyond referring to court records. They refer instead to doctrinal premises, methods, aphorisms, and notions that were popularized between 1875 and 1952 within doctrinal literature.

[36] See generally Dror Ze'evi, "The Use of Ottoman Sharīʿa Court Records as a Source for Middle Eastern Social History," *Islamic Law and Society* 5,1 (1998): 35–56.

CONTENTS

Section I. Origins of Islamic Legal Revivalism

Chapters 1, 2, and 3 discuss the period 1875–1884, when European powers and Egyptian elites engineered a thorough adoption of European laws in Egypt, albeit an adoption that had certain, substantial precursors in the nineteenth century. While people in that historical era spoke of "Egyptian law" (*qānūn miṣrī*), this work refers to Egypt's new laws and to things associated with those laws—courts, professors, university departments—as "Franco-Egyptian." However neologistic, the term is useful because it allows one to distinguish between the portion of Egyptian law with distinctly French origins (civil, criminal, commercial, civil procedure, maritime, constitutional, and administrative law) and the Egyptian Sharia laws that regulated family, inheritance, and trusts, and which prevailed in the separate system of Sharia Courts. Both types of law were "Egyptian" and both were called "law" (*droit, qānūn*). The term "Franco-Egyptian" allows the analyst to single out portions of "Egyptian" law with a European genealogy.

The first chapter sets the historical background for the penetration of European law and the changes it wrought; Chapters 2 and 3 treat what the reception of European law inspired: a popular ideological sentiment and a multilayered movement that advocated the revival, reform, and reapplication of Islamic law.

Section II. European Law and Imperialist Campaigns for Islamic Legal Reform

Chapters 4, 5, and 6 treat European law and its specific influence on Islamic legal reform. It is a mistake to presume that the solely predominant innovation European law brought to the Egyptian legal system was the "code" in its nineteenth-century form.[37] New law codes were tools that changed law and legal ideas in Europe and Egypt, but there was much more to the world of European law and legal thought than the code. There was legal theory, doctrinal literature, comparative law, and case law, all pertaining to European law and all transportable to the Arab world. There was also reformist scholarship written in Europe, by Europeans, about Islamic law itself; the ideas and agendas of this literature were also transportable to the Arab world.

Chapter 4 begins by telling the story of European legal thought of the late nineteenth and early twentieth centuries as it concerned Islamic law, before European laws and law professors exerted power and influence in Egypt's law schools. Chapter 5 discusses comparative law's influence on Egyptian legal thought, and

[37] See the approaches of Aharon Layish, "The Transformation of the Shariʿa from Jurists' Law to Statutory Law in the Contemporary Muslim World," *Die Welt des Islams* 44,1 (2004): 85–112; Bedir, "*Fıkıh* to Law"; Rudolph Peters, "The Codification of Criminal Law in Nineteenth Century Egypt: Tradition or Modernization?" in *Law, Society, and National Identity in Africa*, ed. J. M. Abun-Nasr et al. (Hamburg: H. Buske, 1990), 211–25; Peters, "From Jurists' Law to Statute Law or What Happens When the Sharia Is Codified," in *Shaping the Current Islamic Reformation*, ed. B. A. Roberson (London: Frank Cass, 2003), 82–95.

Chapter 6 analyzes the well-defined perspectives of Édouard Lambert—the most famous European comparative law scholar to have become engaged with Egypt—concerning Islamic law and the future of Islamic legal reform. Lambert's initiatives influenced a number of jurists—among them the most famous Egyptian jurist, ʿAbd al-Razzāq al-Sanhūrī—who identified with the "Franco-Egyptian" part of the Egyptian legal academy and inclined toward embracing European influences.

Section III. Transformations in Education and Scholarship

Chapters 7, 8, and 9 examine the history of Egypt's law faculties in the interest of tracing the "reception" of European law, legal thought, and legal education.[38] Particular attention is given to the history of the Cairo University Law Faculty (*Kulliyyat al-Ḥuqūq*) and its professors and students.

Egyptian law professors played central roles in facilitating the reception of European legal thought into native Egyptian legal academia and culture. Prior studies have tended to reduce Islamic legal thought of the pre-1952 era to debates on the caliphate, jihad, the most controversial questions about the rights of women, secularism, and general ideas about the necessity of reviving independent religious thought (*ijtihād*). Islamic legal academia in Egypt, however, was also concerned with elaborating other areas of law that are fundamental building blocks for sophisticated and populous states and economies in the modern world: contracts, property, penal law, procedure, administrative law, tax, commercial law, conflict of laws principles, and rights jurisprudence. Sharia jurists were concerned with demonstrating that Islam could produce laws on a par with Franco-Egyptian laws with respect to prestige, sophistication, reasonableness, practicality, and ideological moderation. The scholars encountered in this book did not spend their careers in extensive introspection worrying about the meaning of secularism or features of a theoretical neo-caliphate nearly so much as they labored to build an Islamic corpus of modern contract, commercial, and administrative law that could supplant the Franco-Egyptian system. They took for granted the necessity of energizing *ijtihād*, i.e., independent juridical reasoning; many lived for *ijtihād* and pursued it tirelessly, since they were concerned with the rigorous creation of rules and regulations on which to build a flourishing country that could compete in the globalizing economy. Although this kind of Islamic legal

[38] The reception, or imposition, of European legal ideas was an intellectual and professional phenomenon that had a life of its own and was not wholly determined by the framework of European-Egyptian power relations. Nevertheless, politics, war, imperialism, coercion, and the deployment of European capital created important, if not the most important, institutional mechanisms that brought Egyptians into extensive contact with European law. On the political and military aspects of European occupation and the imposition of European law, see Nathan J. Brown, "Brigands and State Building: The Invention of Banditry in Modern Egypt," *Comparative Studies in Society and History* 32,2 (1990): 258–81; Brown, "Precarious Life"; Brown, "Law and Imperialism"; Brown, *Rule of Law*; Esmeir, *Juridical Humanity*, 14–15. Egypt has received some attention in the field of historical scholarship that theorizes on imperialism and, in doing so, examines the legal dimensions of imperialism. See, for example, Asad, *Formations of the Secular*, but see how Nathan Brown adds nuance by stressing in his writings that much legal development was homegrown and not the product of imperial control (e.g., *Rule of Law*, 44–8, and the articles cited earlier).

thought does not capture the world's attention today, it still fills the shelves of bookstores throughout the Middle East.

Section IV. New Forms of Islamic Legal Thought

Finally, as mentioned, Chapter 10 offers insights into transformations in substantive legal doctrine. The text of principal interest is Chafik Chehata's 1936 treatise on the general theory of obligation in Islamic law. The emergence of the "general theory" genre in Egypt was significant because the genre became a device that reformist jurists used to reshape premises and substantive rules of Egyptian-Islamic legal doctrine, and to bridge or otherwise confirm differences between European and Islamic law. The genre also bore practical effects on legislative reform initiatives.

Chapter 10 proposes an analytical model for explaining how European legal ideas influenced modern Muslim jurists working in other areas of Islamic legal thought, such as criminal, procedural, family, and constitutional law. This chapter suggests that one can identify nexuses of influence where European ideas influenced Islamic legal thought: expository, conceptual-and-categorical, substantive, methodological, social scientific, religious-and-philosophical, and policy-and-theoretical. The same kind of innovation and maneuvering that jurists displayed in the contract field can be seen at work in other areas of modern Islamic legal thought across the twentieth century.

Section I

Origins of Islamic Legal Revivalism

1

The Reception of European Law in Political and Social Context

Although occupied briefly by France from 1798 to 1801, until 1875—when it came under the political authority of Britain—Egypt lived under the nominal sovereignty of the Ottoman sultans in Istanbul and the actual sovereignty of a dynasty of local rulers founded by the rogue Ottoman governor and autocrat, Muḥammad ʿAlī Pasha (Mehmet Ali, r. 1804–1848). The rulers of this dynasty were known as the khedives of Egypt until 1914.[1]

The significant loss of local sovereignty in 1875 occurred when the Egyptian government defaulted on foreign debt owed to European creditors.[2] The British and French governments responded by placing their ministers into the khedive's cabinet. They did not have colonial governors or military forces on the ground initially, but the period between 1875 and 1882 became known as the Dual Control. Following domestic upheavals partly directed at European interests, the British then unilaterally occupied Egypt, exerting control over domestic politics and administration from 1882 until 1952 and maintaining army bases there until 1956. Egypt remained a province of the Ottoman Empire until 1914 as a formal matter, but the British controlled the province in all important respects the entire time.

As the British and French governments began to manage Egypt's finances, economy, and infrastructure in the 1870s, an array of European nations assumed a correspondingly greater interest in reforming Egypt's legal and judicial systems. In the early 1870s, European powers pressed for a reformed system of local justice that would be better understood by the Europeans living in Egypt (whose population, 80,000 in 1875 and 90,000 in 1882, was considerable[3]), would serve their interests, and would ensure more predictable adjudication in disputes among foreign parties of different nationalities or national origins.[4] The justice

[1] See generally P. J. Vatikiotis, *The History of Egypt*, 2nd ed. (Baltimore: Johns Hopkins University Press, 1980), 124–66; M. W. Daly, ed., *The Cambridge History of Egypt*, vol. 2: *Modern Egypt from 1517 to the End of the Twentieth Century* (Cambridge: Cambridge University Press, 1998), 113–38, 180–97.

[2] See Donald Malcolm Reid, "The ʿUrabi Revolution and the British Conquest, 1879–1882," in *Cambridge History of Egypt*, ed. Daly, 2: 217–38.

[3] Brinton, *Mixed Courts*, 18; Hanley, "Foreignness and Localness," 273. Europeans were called by the collective term "foreigners."

[4] This observation is based on extensive research in the archives of the foreign offices of Great Britain and France. Although the documents consulted are too extensive to list here, relevant collections are listed in References.

Islamic Legal Revival: Reception of European Law and Transformations in Islamic Legal Thought in Egypt, 1875–1952. First Edition. Leonard Wood.

system available to Egyptians was also perceived to be in need of reform, and it was thought among European political agents in Egypt that reforming the justice system available to foreigners would open a door to improvement for Egyptians.[5]

The term "Egyptians" was ambiguous during the nineteenth century and had different meanings for different purposes. It always included native-born, Arabic-speaking people who constituted the majority of inhabitants and could also generally be called Arab. Egypt was also home to people of Turkish, southeastern European, Anatolian, and Caucasian descent who had come to Egypt from the non-Arab parts of the Ottoman Empire and spoke languages such as Ottoman Turkish, various dialects of Turkish, Albanian, Georgian, and Armenian. Although the number of so-called "Turco-Egyptians" (or "Turco-Circassians") never exceeded 20,000, they dominated Egypt's political, military, and commercial elite throughout the nineteenth century, albeit with diminishing prominence in the final two decades of the century.[6] The ruling dynasty of khedives, for example, traced their lineage to the Albanian parents of Muḥammad ʿAlī who resided in the area of present-day Greek Macedonia. Finally, a relatively small number of people of Greek and Italian descent lived as permanent inhabitants.

All of these people were rooted in Egypt by virtue of domicile and history, but one should bear in mind that in the 1870s and 1880s Egypt was not yet a "nation state," as the category had recently been refined in Europe—rather, Egypt was a subject territory of the Ottoman Empire, and although its name (*Miṣr*) had existed in Arabic parlance since before the formation of Islam, it is anachronistic to speak of "Egyptians" during this period under the assumption that the term denoted citizenship in a nation state or a sovereign country. In sum, whether one was called "Egyptian" depended on the purpose of creating the distinction, and delineations were commonly made according to the relevant ethnic and language groups.

Although reception of European law in Egypt had also occurred in earlier decades, the 1870s and 1880s stand out as a distinct era of concerted and forceful reception and one that brought different consequences for the legal system.[7] A series of European-style reforms between 1875 and 1884 established a new regime of laws and courts based on French models. These developments ended the dominance of Ottoman and Islamic legal institutions in Egypt, despite the fact that Egypt remained a nominal subject of the Ottoman Empire until the outbreak of the First World War.

An appreciation of the political context between 1882 and 1952 is helpful for following the legal history. From 1882 to 1914, Britain ruled Egypt through successive British officials who managed an Egyptian government composed mainly of Egyptians but also including a large number of British public servants, of which the greater number was employed by the Egyptian, not British, government.

[5] See n. 4. Whether or not this perception was warranted is another matter.

[6] Gabriel Baer, "Social Change in Egypt: 1800–1914," in *Political and Social Change in Modern Egypt: Historical Studies from the Ottoman Conquest to the United Arab Republic*, ed. P. M. Holt (London: Oxford University Press, 1968), 135–61, at 147–50.

[7] For the pre-1875 years, see, for example, Fahmy, "Sound of Silence"; Peters, "Islamic and Secular Criminal Law"; Peters, "State, Law and Society"; Rubin, *Ottoman Nizamiyye Courts*. Wael Hallaq's writings contribute to this interest also, for example, "Prelude to Ottoman Reform."

Regardless of their official employer, the British employees were often unofficially and ultimately serving the British government. An example is the Judicial Adviser, which position was typically held by a British figure, employed by the Egyptian government and serving the Egyptian Minister of Justice, yet also reporting to the British political officers on the ground and ensuring that British directives were carried out by the given Egyptian Minister of Justice. The longest-serving British authority was Lord Cromer, born Evelyn Baring, who was resident in Egypt periodically before 1883 and then permanently from 1883 until 1907. First as Controller-General (1883–1892) and then as Consul-General (1901–1907), Cromer and his charges managed Egyptian affairs by directing the policies of the hereditary rulers—for example, the khedives Muḥammad Tawfīq (r. 1879–1892) and ʿAbbās Ḥilmī (r. 1892–1914)—their cabinet ministers, and the ministries and public departments. This was not always an easy process from the standpoint of the British as the khedives and their administrations often resisted British directives. The British nevertheless maintained leverage in shaping policies while Egypt formally remained a province of the Ottoman Empire.

Although Egypt was a British colony for most practical purposes, it was never declared as such. It was referred to in Britain as a "veiled protectorate" prior to 1914. Egyptians predominated throughout the state bureaucracy, but they worked side by side with large numbers of European locals—in 1887, more than 1,600 Europeans were employed in the Egyptian public service[8]—who often earned considerably higher salaries than their Egyptian counterparts. They also often doubled as informal supervisors serving the British residency or their own country's vigilant embassies, and were placed strategically into important positions throughout the government and public service.

Between 1914 and 1918, the era of the First World War, Britain severed Egypt from the Ottoman Empire and declared it a protectorate. The khedive was forcibly replaced by his uncle who was given the new title of sultan, a more illustrious and independent designation and one that signified that the Egyptian ruling house was no longer under even nominal Ottoman sovereignty. Yet the new title did not conceal that the sultan was a subject of British power. Moreover, while the question of the Ottoman Empire's sovereignty over Egypt had loomed for many years over the pre-1914 "veiled protectorate," the prospect of any revival of Ottoman power in Egypt ended decisively with the abolition of the Ottoman caliphate in 1924 at the hands of the newly formed Grand National Assembly of Turkey. The loss of the Islamic world's premier figurehead was a source of consternation for many Muslims and led to successive conferences focused on reconstituting the caliphate, which took place in Mecca, Cairo, and Jerusalem in the 1920s and 1930s.

As a consequence of Britain's denying Egypt a seat at the Paris Peace Conference, the years 1919 to 1923 were marked by a series of national upheavals led by

[8] The greatest numbers were Italians (511), English, (427), and French (319). Greeks, Austrians, and Germans were also well represented. Britain and Lord Cromer, *P.P., Despatches from Sir E. Baring Respecting the Employment of Europeans in the Egyptian Public Service, Egypt. No. 6 (1887), C. 4997 XCII 1888* (London, 1887).

civilian politicians. The new terms of an ostensible independence were ironed out during these years. In 1922, the British formally acquiesced to Egyptian independence and issued a "Declaration to Egypt" that Great Britain would thereafter "recognise Egypt as an independent sovereign State."[9] Until 1953 the country was known as the Egyptian Kingdom. Yet, although the post-1922 era is referred to as one of Egyptian independence, the reality was more complicated.[10] In 1923, a new constitution was established, transforming the sultan into a king and establishing a constitutional monarchy with the power of the king balanced by a parliament.[11] The constitution afforded the British no role in domestic governance, but until 1952, the British managed Egyptian politics behind the scenes, manipulating the parliamentary process and the policies of the monarchy. At times, and in cycles, the troubled parliamentary life of Egypt gave way to less-than-democratic styles of rule backed by leading Egyptians and the British authorities alike.[12] Thus, between 1923 and 1952, the British exercised their authority over domestic politics when it came to managing affairs most crucial to their interests. The more mundane affairs of governance and administration were generally left to the Egyptians, in particular to the Egyptian elite. This policy is especially relevant to the history of Egypt's legal system and its legal education. The post-1923 era saw greater Egyptian independence in the management of both of these spheres.

LEGAL AND JUDICIAL REFORMS OF 1875–1876 AND 1883–1884

While not all questions of Egypt's legal history should be approached by accepting the years 1875–1876 and 1883–1884 as turning points, these dates facilitate an outlining of institutional history. In 1875, a concert of European diplomatic missions, jurists, and lawyers reformed part of Egypt's legal and judicial systems by establishing new codes and courts to adjudicate legal matters involving foreigners, while in 1883, following the British occupation of 1882, the Egyptian government established new codes and courts to adjudicate legal matters involving Egyptians.[13]

[9] Albert P. Blaustein et al., *Independence Documents of the World* (Dobbs Ferry, NY: Oceana Publications, 1977), 1: 204–5.

[10] See Selma Botman, "The Liberal Age, 1923–1952," in *Cambridge History of Egypt*, ed. Daly, 2: 285–308.

[11] Elie Kedourie, "The Genesis of the Egyptian Constitution of 1923," in *Political and Social Change in Modern Egypt*, ed. Holt, 347–61.

[12] Ibid.

[13] Ideas for the project were discussed in the British and French embassies before the occupation. In 1878, John Scott submitted a report on the topic. F.O. 78/2855/256ff/fol.365 (July 19, 1878), "Avis de Monsieur le Conseiller Scott" (also printed in "No. 201: Mr. Vivian to the Marquis of Salisbury" [Jul. 20, 1878], F.O. Conf., "Further Correspondence Respecting Judicial Reforms in Egypt," No. 3869, pp. 188–211, at 202–4 [1876–1878] [Foreign Office: Mar. 1879]). See also F.O. Conf., "Judicial Reforms Part 5," Mallet to Granville, Paper No. 4720 (Sep. 29, 1881). Nathan Brown (*Rule of Law*, 44), emphasizes that European legal reforms preceded the advent of the Mixed and Native Courts, based on his view that "key periods in legal reform hardly coincide with the height of imperial penetration."

Mixed, Native, and Consular Courts

The new courts designed to apply the new Egyptian laws were, respectively, the Mixed Courts (*al-maḥākim al-mukhtalṭah, tribunaux mixtes*) in 1875–1876 and the Native Courts (*al-maḥākim al-ahliyyah, tribunaux indigènes*) in 1883–1884. The Mixed Courts adjudicated civil and commercial cases between foreigners of different nationalities and between foreigners and Egyptians. They also adjudicated the bulk of real property litigation, much of which concerned pious endowments (sg. *waqf*).[14] The Native Courts were, in simple terms, the courts for Egyptians. They adjudicated all criminal cases involving Egyptians and foreigners and all civil and commercial cases between Egyptians in which no foreigners were involved or foreign-owned property was at stake.[15] The Native Courts did not handle cases that pertained primarily to family law and inheritance. Those cases were reserved for the Islamic court system and the separate courts belonging to each religious minority group (e.g., Coptic and Jewish).

Although the Mixed Courts are remembered as institutions imposed on Egypt by foreigners, local Egyptian leaders took much initiative in establishing them.[16] The genesis and early development of the Native Courts involved a high degree of direct European responsibility as they were envisioned by European officials in the 1870s and created in 1883–1884 under the conditions of direct occupation. Records of the British Foreign Office indicate that the British exercised a systematic, protracted, and dominant role in establishing and managing the Native Courts.[17] On the other hand, Nathan Brown has argued that these same records

[14] Pious endowment is one English translation for *waqf* (pl. *awqāf*), a category of property in Islamic law that is similar to the charitable trust or the common law trust.

[15] This wording follows that of Hanley, "Foreignness and Localness," 5.

[16] Nubar Pasha traveled in Europe gathering signatures for his own plan to build the new courts. See Brown, *Rule of Law*, 27–37; Hoyle, *Mixed Courts of Egypt*, 9–10; Cannon, *Politics of Law*, 124, 190, 210.

[17] The solution to the question of who contributed how much to the evolution and function of the Native Courts is most likely to be found in Arabic sources in Egyptian archives. But within the records of the British Foreign Office, see, for example, "No. 201: Mr. Vivian to the Marquis of Salisbury" (Jul. 20, 1878) (cited at n. 13); "No. 62: Mr. Mallet to Earl Granville, Memorandum Respecting the Establishment of Courts of Law for the Administration of Justice to Natives" (Sep. 29, 1881), in F.O. Conf., "Part V: Further Correspondence Respecting Judicial Reforms in Egypt (in continuation of Confidential Paper 4489) (1881) (Foreign Office: January 1883), 76–8; "Edward Mallet to Granville, Report on the Decree Organizing the New Native Tribunals," (Draft), F.O. 141/144/348 (Nov. 28, 1881); "Mallet to Granville" (Sep. 13, 1882), in *P.P., Correspondence Respecting Reorganization in Egypt*, No. 1 (1883), C. 3462 (London: 1883); "No. 7: Granville to Mallet" (Oct. 2, 1882), in ibid.; "Earl of Dufferin to Earl Granville, Report on the Delta" (Mar. 12, 1883), in *P.P., Reports by Mr. Villiers Stuart M.P., Respecting Reorganization in Egypt*, No. 7 (1883), C. 3554 (London: 1883); F.O. Conf., "Part VIII: Further Correspondence Respecting Judicial Reforms in Egypt," No. 5084 (1884) (Foreign Office: Mar. 1885); "No. 26: E. Baring to Salisbury" (Jan. 10, 1889), F.O. Conf., "Judicial Reforms," No. 5807 (1889); "No. 92: E. Baring to Salisbury" (Feb. 4, 1889), in ibid.; "Nos 6, 10, 11: Mr. Clarke to the Marquis of Salisbury" (Jul. 18, 1889, Aug. 30, 1889), F.O. Conf., "Further Correspondence Respecting Judicial Reforms in Egypt," No. 5880 (1889) (Foreign Office: Feb. 1890); "Nos. 2, 3, 5, 9, 16, 25: Sir E. Baring to the Marquis of Salisbury" (Jan. 17, Feb. 11, Feb. 8, Feb. 25, Jun. 27, Nov. 6, 1890, respectively), F.O. Conf., "Further Correspondence Respecting Judicial Reforms in Egypt" (Foreign Office: Feb. 1891). In 1892, Lord Cromer averred in an assessment of the Egyptian ministries that the policy of English officials was to do all the work "but to appear to do it as little as possible; to efface themselves, and to put the Khedive to the front. . . . [T]he fact that they alone really pulled the strings was rarely brought in any striking manner before the public." F.O. Conf., "State of Affairs (Cromer)," No. 6248 (1892).

collectively highlight the limits of British power and the centrality of contributions by Egyptians.[18]

Both the Mixed and Native Courts were modeled on the courts of France with multiple judges on each bench and a hierarchical organization for appeals (small claims, first instance, and appeal). The Mixed Courts remained in place until 1949 when their jurisdiction was folded into the Native Courts; they were known thereafter as the National Courts (*al-maḥākim al-waṭaniyyah*), which in Egypt today have jurisdiction in all matters of private law, including family law, inheritance, and succession.

The Mixed and Native systems managed a substantial caseload from their inception due to litigious residents. In 1910, for example, Native Courts issued 208,500 judgments in civil and commercial cases and 154,450 judgments in criminal cases. The Mixed Courts issued 45,900 judgments in civil and commercial cases.[19]

The Mixed benches and Bar Association were initially dominated by Europeans and North Americans, but Egyptians increasingly appeared as lawyers and judges. The Mixed Courts—where the official languages were French and English, with French being the principal language—were the prestige forum of legal practice for European and Egyptian law professionals. Some foreigners worked in the courts as transient personnel, but most employees worked in the courts as a career.

In the Native Court system, the benches and Native Bar Association were dominated by Egyptians, many of whom had worked in Egypt's previously known "courts of reform" (*niẓāmī*), the secular-oriented courts established on an Ottoman model in the 1860s. Their language of operation was Arabic. Europeans were included in the Native Courts and Bar Association. During the 1880s and 1890s, European judges on benches were strategically distributed to double as quality-control supervisors on behalf of the British personnel charged with overseeing the judicial reforms, and at least one European judge served on a given appellate court. This policy furthered European influence over the decisions of Egyptian courts, particularly for significant questions of law. Most of these Europeans worked as lawyers and judges for their livelihoods.

Finally, a category of courts belonging to consulates of foreign nations adjudicated civil and commercial cases arising among foreign parties of the same nationality. They handled cases of foreign civil status[20] and criminal cases with a foreign defendant.[21] By comparison, the Mixed Courts had only very limited competence in penal matters. Like the Mixed and Native Courts, consular courts also had a hierarchical organization for appeals. British consular courts within the Ottoman Empire, for example, were considered part of the same system. Thus for Egypt there were three tiers of British consular courts: the provincial consular

[18] Brown, "Law and Imperialism," 109–13.

[19] These figures are rounded and do not include cases handled but not settled within that year. They also do not include penal judgments of the Mixed Courts. Egyptian Ministry of Justice, *Rapport pour l'année 1910 presenté par le Conseiller Judiciaire* (Cairo: Imprimerie Nationale, 1911).

[20] Consular courts did not have jurisdiction over all matters of civil status. Since personal status and civil status overlapped, religious courts undertook a portion of civil status work. This was particularly true for foreign Muslims and Jews. See Hanley, "Foreignness and Localness."

[21] This language is from ibid., 170.

Table 1.1. Jurisdiction ranges for British, French, and Egyptian subjects.

Case type and defendant		Plaintiff or Petitioner: British subject	French subject	Local subject
Civil or Commercial	British	British consular	Mixed	Mixed
	French	Mixed	French consular	Mixed
	Local	Mixed	Mixed	Native
Criminal	British	British consular	British consular	British consular
	French	French consular	French consular	French consular
	Local	Native	Native	Native
Personal Status		British consular or religious courts	French consular or religious courts	Religious courts

Source: Will Hanley, "Foreignness and Localness in Alexandria, 1880–1940" (Ph.D. diss., Princeton University, 2007), 170.

court, the Chief Consular Court in Alexandria, and the Supreme Consular Court, which sat in Istanbul and Cairo, depending on the year.

The jurisdiction of these three judicial arenas among the British, French, and Egyptians is illustrated by Table 1.1, borrowed from the historian Will Hanley. Although the table does not include other European nationalities, jurisdiction was managed in a similar manner for Italians, Greeks, Belgians, and so on. The patterns of jurisdictional logic are apparent. In civil law and commercial law, the jurisdictional arrangement aimed to afford the maximum possible neutrality of the judicial forum. In criminal law, the arrangement aimed to afford the defendant a home-field advantage.

Conflicts of jurisdiction arose routinely given that there were four primary court jurisdictions: Mixed, Native, religious, and consular. Frederick Walton, a dean of the Khedivial Law School, observed: "The question is not whether a foreign law is to be applied or which foreign law, but which of the legal systems in force in Egyptian territory is to govern the question."[22] Judges, lawyers, and law professionals were accustomed to inter-jurisdictional tussles. Titles like "Conflict of Jurisdiction" appeared regularly as columns in the law journals and case reporters of the different courts. The questions were not wholly resolved in the first thirty years of the new Egyptian legal order. In 1912, Pierre Arminjon, a prolific French lawyer in Egypt, creatively addressed this problem by proposing the foundation for a field of law to be called "domestic international private law."[23]

The new law codes adopted by Egypt for the Mixed and Native Courts were codes of civil law, civil procedure, criminal law, criminal procedure, commercial law, and maritime commercial law. The Mixed Courts enforced one complete set of these six codes known as the Mixed Codes; the Native Courts enforced their

[22] Frederick Parker Walton, "Egyptian Law, Sources and Judicial Organisation," in *Pars Orientalis (Aegyptus—Palaestina—Sina—Japonia)*, ed. Elemér Balogh (Berlin: Sack et Montanus, 1929), 11–38, at 33.
[23] P. Arminjon, "Le Droit international privé interne," *Journal Clunet* (1912, 1913): 79–172.

own complete set of six known as the Native Codes. There were thus twelve new codes in all. The Mixed Codes and the Native Codes were similar in form and substance, and they were all based on the Napoleonic codes of 1804–1806. Perhaps most significantly, and symbolically, the new Egyptian civil codes were modeled to a large extent on the form and substance of the French *Code civil* (1804), the most famous European legislation of the nineteenth century. Some important differences existed between the Egyptian codes and the Napoleonic codes, but that does not alter the fact that the codes were modeled on French codes. Egypt also became further acquainted in the 1870s and beyond with European approaches to public law that established rules and protocols for the exercise of governmental and administrative authority.

Rupture versus Continuity in Legal Traditions, 1875–1884

The years 1875 to 1884 were not the first in Egyptian history to witness an appearance of European-style laws. In the middle of the nineteenth century, the Ottoman-Egyptian ruling elite enacted criminal laws, land laws, constitutional laws, and elements of criminal and investigative procedure that had European—primarily Swiss and French—origins. The political authority also established the body of secular- and reform-oriented Nizami courts that preceded the Mixed and Native Courts.[24]

Certain elements of law, procedure, legal thought, and legal culture from the pre-1875 era also carried into the later legal order, which is to be expected. If judges from an older system are appointed, features of the old system and the old legal culture are likely to persist in a new set of courts. These features may even shape in some fundamental ways the ostensibly "new" order. In fact, chronological boundaries are blurred. British judicial advisers complained routinely in the 1880s and 1890s about older Egyptian judges and lawyers who persisted in their ways and refused to conduct their courtrooms according to the European expectations. British public servants worked throughout the 1880s and 1890s to jettison older people and older habits from the new courts.

Yet there is also much about the period 1875–1884 that suggests facets of rupture in legal thought and practice.[25] These years witnessed the most thoroughgoing imposition of European-style laws to date, and by far. It was an imposition of a new judicial order, backed by the power of Britain. Not only were elderly judges and all other remnants of the past pushed out, colonial personnel systematically trained new generations of Egyptians and judges. Since the laws on book were in fact different from previous laws, they became the only secure basis for new trajectories in court-produced law and legal scholarship. Egyptian law textbooks

[24] Taking a position against the concept of rupture, Nathan Brown (*Rule of Law*, 44) states, "There was certainly no sudden break from a system based largely on Islamic jurisprudence to the Code Napoléon; rather there was a gradual emergence of a centralized and hierarchical state-sponsored system."

[25] Esmeir, *Juridical Humanity*, 39–42.

published after 1890 had minimal interest in laws and practice of the previous legal order. By 1900, the history of that old order was lost on new generations of Egyptian practitioners of the civil, criminal, and commercial law.

Egyptian chroniclers of the legal system operative around 1900, renowned and prestigious authorities of their time, wrote of living in a revolutionized legal order. They depicted 1875–1876 and 1883–1884 as breaking points.[26] This does not mean, of course, that Egypt really was living in a completely new legal order in 1900. These chroniclers overlooked continuities, overstated the effects of reforms, and perhaps too eagerly valorized the reforms. But, imagined rupture itself proved a relevant and powerful form of rupture. Egyptian law professionals believed they were living in an age of new laws and legal culture. They believed they were living in an age in which the old legal order no longer mattered—and they conducted their work accordingly. The most notable exceptions to this trend are found among personnel who worked in the Islamic courts and experts in Islamic law. Yet, even these figures had little apparent, overt interest in the laws and practices of the Ottoman courts of reform. There is a need in the field of Egyptian legal history to understand better how, and to what degree, if any, aspects of Ottoman law and practice continued to influence Egyptian law after 1882.

FRENCH LAW UNDER BRITISH RULE

In light of local and global circumstances surrounding the British occupation, it was not surprising to contemporary observers that the British allowed the perpetuation of French law in Egypt. Following the sudden occupation of 1882, the British scrambled to stabilize their position and design workable reform policies. The French urged for an immediate withdrawal of British forces, and the vigor of their urgings cannot be understated. Although Britain assured European powers of a quick withdrawal, the British were not certain initially as to how long the occupation would continue. All they appear to have been certain of is that they would use the occupation as an opportunity to launch as many reforms, for as many domestic institutions, as possible.[27] British personnel were of the view that reforms of local institutions—political, judicial, economic, infrastructural, and military—would offset the possibility of further domestic upheavals threatening European interests.

British officials endorsed the continuity of the French system as a matter of practicality. English common law was, at least for the first twenty years of occupation,

[26] Aḥmad Fatḥī Zaghlūl, *al-Muḥāmāh* (Miṣr: Maṭbaʿat al-Maʿārif, 1900); Maḥmūd ibn Muḥammad Ibn ʿArnūs, *Kitāb Tārīkh al-qaḍāʾ fī l-islām* (Cairo: al-Maṭbaʿah al-Miṣriyyah al-Ahliyyah al-Ḥadīthah, 1934); ʿAzīz Khankī, "al-Tashrīʿ wa-l-qaḍāʾ qabla inshāʾ al-maḥākim al-ahliyyah," in *al-Kitāb al-dhahabī li-l-maḥākim al-ahliyyah 1883–1933*, 2 vols. (Bulaq: al-Maṭbaʿah al-Amīriyyah, 1937), 1: 62–96.

[27] A well-known report by the Earl of Dufferin identified legal reform as a paramount reform issue. F.O. Conf., Earl of Dufferin, "General Report by the Earl of Dufferin Respecting Reorganization in Egypt," No. 4770 (1883).

a comparatively unknown and irrelevant quantity in Egypt, and the Mixed legal system, with its strong roots in French and continental European law ("civil law"), was already well in place by 1882. The Mixed Courts were supported and managed by the various European states as well as by the foreign communities in Egypt—especially the French, Italian, and Greek communities, which were among the communities that Britain claimed to be protecting by its occupation. The British also chose to entrench the new Native Courts, envisioned in the mid- to late 1870s by John Scott, a British lawyer who had worked in the colonial service in India but who was knowledgeable in French law, and contributed to by the English scholar of French and Roman law, Sheldon Amos.[28] It was practical to have two similar sets of laws applied in both court systems and the British had to acknowledge, if grudgingly, the worldwide prestige of French law—as it was the global prestige law of the mid- and late-nineteenth century. In these years, a reference to the prestige of "French" law was often a reference more broadly to the law codes of continental Europe, all of which were based to some extent on the Napoleonic models. Napoleonic law in the 1870s and 1880s was the subject of extensive, groundbreaking critique by jurists throughout Europe, particularly in Germany and Italy, while Egyptian jurists had known about Napoleonic law as early as its creation through mid-nineteenth-century Arabic translations and the original French.

The sustaining of French legal traditions in Egypt was a convenient compromise that the British government could offer the French, a palliative to acute French resentment over Britain's unilateral occupation of a territory that both powers had been managing jointly. And at least initially, the British left the mundane affairs of legal practice and legal education in the hands of the French and other continental European experts while assuming control of most high-level aspects of Egyptian administration.

After 1890, British representatives in Egypt increasingly took steps to put the law and legal education more in British hands. This work had some success, if measured solely by the extension of control by British personnel. Egypt's law, however, would continue to remain French-inspired in its essential aspects. Despite English-style changes to aspects of Egyptian law (for example, in criminal procedure), British law and legal culture never replaced the French law and legal culture in Egypt in terms of prestige or as the parent source of Egyptian civil and criminal laws.

British personnel often spoke French as part of the business of government in Egypt. Lord Cromer's office conducted certain government and diplomatic business in French. Those who worked as lawyers, judges, and law professors needed to know French law. Some personnel were more competent than others in this regard, but all who lasted in their offices managed. British personnel in the legal system took foreign language acquisition seriously. Judges serving in the Native Courts passed difficult examinations in written and colloquial Arabic.

[28] John Scott became a powerful judicial adviser in the 1880s. Sheldon Amos served as a judge in India and was the father of Maurice Sheldon Amos who became a scholar of European continental law and eventually dean of the Khedivial Law School in Cairo.

Three factors in particular helped to guarantee the continuation and prestige of French law. First, a result of the British occupation was that Egyptians often favored French culture and all things French more than British culture and all things British. Even ardent Egyptian nationalists were more disposed toward French elements in society, which sentiment French personnel in Egypt encouraged. Second, the prestigious legal forum of the Mixed Courts continued to operate in French, enforcing the prestige of French law. Third, leading Egyptian law jurists of civil, criminal, and constitutional law were trained in France and by Francophone jurists in Egypt. Although Egyptian students of law eventually learned English and read Bentham and Austin, and although they might have been apprenticed by British lawyers or judges, the influence of British professors and jurists on generations of Egyptian jurists was comparatively less weighty than the influence enjoyed by their French and Francophone counterparts.

Another perspective to be considered when accounting for the perpetuation of French law is that of Nathan Brown, that Egyptian leaders and lawyers, as nationalists above all, regarded French law and the Mixed Courts as tools for resisting British dominance.[29] Insofar as these two institutions afforded Egyptians autonomy from day-to-day British control, the survival of French law through the maintenance of the Mixed Courts and by other means could be interpreted as less the result of British imperialism and designs imposed on Egyptians and rather as an upshot of the efforts and designs of both Egyptians and French to counter British imperialism. Brown goes a great distance in substantiating this view through his study of the Mixed Courts from their inception to their termination.

NARROWED JURISDICTION OF ISLAMIC COURTS AND LAW

As noted, religious courts inhabited the universe of legal systems in Egypt because the Native Courts did not hear Egyptians' cases on family law, inheritance, succession, some questions pertaining to *waqf*, and related matters; they only handled family and inheritance questions when they were ancillary questions of a case. This was a fundamental difference between French and Egyptian conceptions of "civil law." French civil law included family and inheritance laws; the Egyptian civil law did not.

The reforms of 1884 gave a different name to the body of law handling family and inheritance law, which became known as "personal status" (*al-aḥwāl al-shakhṣiyyah*). When the term was used by itself without any further qualifications, it was usually understood to connote Muslim personal status law. When speaking of law for non-Muslims, lawyers spoke of "personal status for non-Muslims" (*al-aḥwāl al-shakhṣiyyah li-ghayr al-muslimīn*). The personal status disputes of Egyptian Christians and Jews were adjudicated before their own religious

[29] Brown, "Precarious Life"; Brown, *Rule of Law*, 48; Brown, "Law and Imperialism."

courts (*majālis milliyyah*), which were institutional holdovers from the Ottoman tradition.

Muslim personal status law was the competence of Egypt's surviving Islamic courts (*al-maḥākim al-sharʿiyyah*) known in the European parlance of the times as "Moslem Courts," "Mehkemes," and *tribunaux musulmanes*. The Islamic courts handled a sizeable caseload—13,000 in 1910.[30] The substantive and procedural laws of these courts remained uncodified, if the standards for codification were those of the Mixed and Native Courts. Piecemeal codifications of procedures were issued as early as 1880,[31] and sets of statutes were passed throughout the 1940s, but officially, there was no "code" of the substantive law of personal status law for Muslims. However, Muḥammad Qadrī Pasha's 1875 draft code of Hanafi personal status law was known to enjoy authority in the courts.[32] How much authority is still an open question.

Studies typically claim that the Native Courts usurped the jurisdiction of Egypt's Islamic courts. This notion requires a more precise formulation. Islamic courts had been competent to handle the full scope of civil cases as well as many types of tort and crime. The foundation of the Native Courts permanently relegated the jurisdiction of Islamic law primarily to family law and inheritance (certain other elements were incorporated into new Franco-Egyptian civil law), while the Mixed Courts assumed much of the litigation on *waqf*. The Native Courts and the Mixed Courts were therefore together responsible for cementing the narrowed jurisdiction of Islamic courts. As of the 1880s and beyond, anyone in Egypt who wanted to claim a broader jurisdiction for Egypt's Islamic courts was essentially proposing to reclaim some aspect of jurisdiction enjoyed by the Native and Mixed Courts.

The Native Courts did not initiate the process of usurping jurisdiction from traditional Islamic courts; much of the Islamic legal jurisdiction had already been usurped by Ottoman-style reform courts established by the Egyptian khedives throughout the nineteenth century before 1883.[33] The Native Courts advanced the process, entrenched it, and stamped it with the imprints of British power and French law.[34]

[30] Egyptian Ministry of Justice, *Rapport pour l'année 1910*, 100.

[31] See, for example, from July 11, 1897, "Règlement général judiciaire des Mehkémés," *Recueil des documents officiels du gouvernement égyptien* (Cairo: Imprimerie Nationale, 1897), 382–97; J. A. Wathelet et al., *Codes égyptiens et lois usuelles en vigueur en Égypte*, 5th ed. (Cairo: Imprimerie Noury, 1939).

[32] Walton, "Egyptian Law," 36. The code was commented upon in Arabic, and portions were translated into French and English. [Muḥammad Qadrī], *Droit musulman: Du statut personnel et des successions d'après le rite hanafite* (Alexandria: Imprimerie Française A. Mourès, 1875); Eng. trans., Nasib Abcarius and Wasey Sterry, *Code of Mohammedan Personal Law According to the Hanafite School* (London: Spottiswoode and Co., 1914); Muḥammad Zayd al-Abyānī, *Sharḥ al-Aḥkām al-sharʿiyyah fī l-aḥwāl al-shakhṣiyyah* (Miṣr: Maṭbaʿat ʿAlī Sukkar Aḥmad, 1903); Muḥammad Qadrī, *al-Aḥkām al-sharʿiyyah fī l-aḥwāl al-shakhṣiyyah (wa-sharḥ li-Muḥammad Zayd al-Abyānī)*, ed. Muḥammad Aḥmad Sirāj and ʿAlī Jumʿah Muḥammad, 4 vols. (Cairo: Dār al-Salām, 2006).

[33] See Peters, "Codification of Criminal Law"; Botiveau, *Loi islamique*, 54, 143; Knut S. Vikør, *Between God and the Sultan* (Oxford: Oxford University Press, 2005), 236–7.

[34] The Native Courts did not acquire jurisdiction over the entire country until 1889. The more remote parts of Egypt maintained their original courts until this time.

The Native Courts were not the only set of "civil" courts that compromised the jurisdiction of Islamic laws and courts. A system of Guardian Courts, known as the Majlis Hasby (pl. *majālis ḥisbiyyah*), managed the financial interests of persons who lacked full legal capacity, such as minors and the mentally disabled.[35] The Guardian Courts were originally considered part of the civil system, but their jurisdiction encroached on that of the Islamic courts. They were therefore a source of debate among practitioners and scholars. Lawyers in the Islamic court system took an interest in these courts and recorded many of their cases in the Islamic court reporters. There are arguments as to how much the European colonial influence can be credited or blamed for the separate existence of the Guardian Courts. The Egyptian government enhanced the jurisdiction of these courts in 1896 and 1925 at the expense of the Islamic courts.[36] On the other hand, Khedive Ismail established these courts in 1873, prior to the onset of the Dual Control in 1875.

EGYPTIAN RECEPTION OF EUROPEAN LAW

The 1870s and 1880s in Egypt witnessed a wide range of European-inspired developments, including the introduction of new technologies, infrastructure, educational institutions, and cultural developments. In the eyes of European colonial authorities, and of many among the Egyptian elite, the innovations in the Egyptian justice system were consistent with the other Westernization and modernization efforts already underway in the country, and were originally welcomed.[37] Egyptian leaders and intellectuals referred to their own era as an era of "reform." The new courts were correspondingly referred to in French, English, and Arabic as "the courts of reform" (*maḥākim al-iṣlāḥ, maḥākim iṣlāḥiyyah*).

Not all Egyptians, however, were enthusiastic about the changes in Egyptian laws. Jurists in particular viewed the legal transformations in Egypt as having robbed the country of its rightful legal heritage, one they believed was rooted in Islamic laws, courts, and customs. At the same time as the new French-style laws and courts in Egypt became monuments of modern reform, they also became enduring symbols of Egypt's subjugation to foreign powers. For many, the new laws and courts became symbols of a European assault on Islam, Islamic institutions, and traditional law and values.

Yet others passively accepted the new courts as a *fait accompli* in what they viewed as their "ever-changing" society, one that faced both inevitable European control and the implacable dawn of the new, "modern" era. The word "modern" (*muʿāṣir, ḥadīth, jadīd*) was commonly used in the colonial period to refer to all of the new aspects of life in Egypt—new technologies, dress, institutions, manners, and so forth. Thus, to many Egyptian writers and legal practitioners of the period,

[35] Shaham, *Family and the Courts*, 12.

[36] The Guardian Courts were merged into the National Courts in 1947 as the Maḥākim Ḥisbiyyah. Brinton, *Mixed Courts*, 59.

[37] Ṭāriq al-Bishrī, *al-Ḥiwār al-islāmī al-ʿalmānī* (Cairo: Dār al-Shurūq, 1996), 9; Asad, *Formations of the Secular*, 212.

the imposition of French law seemed as much an inevitable consequence of "modernization" as the expansion of railroads and electric grids.

Egypt's political circumstances of the 1870s and 1880s help explain the scarcity of evidence of explicit Egyptian opposition to the new Franco-Egyptian law. Today, certain Egyptians blame Egyptians of that past era for not having done more to curtail the rise of Franco-Egyptian law. A leading proponent of this critique has been the historian and former judge Tariq al-Bishri.[38] However, such critique ignores past political circumstances, past intellectual culture, and the particular ways in which Egyptians of a past era understood Sharia and maintained expectations of the Egyptian legal order. This strain of present-day criticism assumes that Egyptians knew more than they did about the behind-the-scenes plans to establish the Native Courts, that they had more agency than they had during a time of foreign occupation and domestic elite-driven politics, and that they viewed Sharia and the Egyptian legal order with the same premises and expectations that prevail in the present day.

When the Mixed jurisdiction appeared, it was commonly understood in Egypt as the continuation of extraterritorial jurisdiction by a new name and new institutions. The Mixed system was the latest manifestation of "capitulations laws" (*imtiyāzāt*) affecting foreigners in the Ottoman Empire. But such laws had existed for hundreds of years as a fundamental feature of legal life in Egypt.[39] If the Mixed system presented an offense to Egyptian sensibilities in the 1870s—as it did for some—this was because the Mixed system was perceived principally as an affront to both Egyptian and Ottoman sovereignty.[40]

The Native system emerged somewhat precipitously, surprisingly, and violently out of the Mixed system. True, the Native system was negotiated and prepared for in the late 1870s, but these negotiations took place in the highest levels of the Justice Ministry. It was only the sudden and mostly unexpected British occupation in 1882 that catalyzed preparations and brought its planning to rapid fruition. The drafters of the Native Codes rushed to complete their work; the Justice Ministry operating under the new British occupation scrambled to assign judges to new posts.

[38] Ṭāriq al-Bishrī, *al-Muslimūn wa-l-aqbāṭ fī iṭār al-jamāʿah al-waṭaniyyah* (Cairo: al-Hayʾah al-Miṣriyyah al-ʿĀmmah li-l-Kitāb, 1980); al-Bishrī, *al-Waḍʿ al-qānūnī al-muʿāṣir*. See also Jumaʿah ʿAbd al-Ḥamīd ʿAlī Saʿūdī, "al-Qānūn fī Miṣr bayna l-sharīʿah al-islāmiyyah wa-l-tashrīʿāt al-waḍʿiyyah" (doct. diss., Cairo University Faculty of Law, 1995).

[39] Alexandre de Miltitz, *Manuel des consuls* (London and Berlin: A. Asher, 1837), xxxvi ff., 516–31; Domenico Gatteschi et al., *Manuale di diritto pubblico e privato ottomano* (Alexandria: V. Minasi, 1865); Stanislas Genton, *De la juridiction française dans les échelles du levant* (Lyon: Imprimerie du Salut Public, 1873); Gregorius Aristarches, *Législation ottomane, ou recueil des lois, réglements, ordonnances, traités, capitulations et autres documents officiels de l'empire ottoman* (Constantinople: Freres Nicolaïdes, 1873–88); J. C. Aristide Gavillot, *Essai sur les droits des européens en Turquie et en Égypte* (Paris: E. Dentu, 1875); G. Timmermans, *La Réforme judiciaire en Égypte et les capitulations* (Ghent: Librairie Générale de Ad. Hoste, 1875); G. Pélissié du Rausas, *Le Régime des capitulations dans l'empire ottoman* (Paris: A. Rousseau, 1902); ʿAbd al-Ḥamīd Badawī, "Athar al-imtiyāzāt fī l-qaḍāʾ wa-l-tashrīʿ fī Miṣr," in *al-Kitāb al-dhahabī*, 1: 1–61; Muḥammad ʿAbd al-Bārī and ʿAbd al-Razzāq Aḥmad al-Sanhūrī, *al-Imtiyāzāt al-ajnabiyyah* (Miṣr: Lajnat al-Taʾlīf wa-l-Tarjamah wa-l-Nashr, 1930); Brinton, *Mixed Courts*.

[40] Brown, "Precarious Life"; Brown, "Law and Imperialism"; Brown, *Rule of Law*, 28–9, 34, 41.

During the months when the British occupying power commanded the establishment of the Native system, outright opponents of British rule enjoyed no sustained power in directing affairs of state. Moreover, many of the Egyptians in the government after 1882 were the same Egyptians who had constructed the Mixed system and conceived of the Native system. One of the architects of the Mixed Courts was Nubar Pasha, an Armenian Christian who served as Prime Minister three times between 1878 and 1895. He showed little interest in preserving or recovering Islamic jurisdictions, let alone in expanding them once they had been constricted.

Like Nubar Pasha, substantial numbers of Egypt's political and economic elite in the late nineteenth century were Christian, including Copts, Armenians, Greek Orthodox, and Anglican Protestants. The Coptic community experienced a cultural and economic revival during the first decades of British occupation. One estimate holds that at the beginning of the twentieth century, Coptic Christians, accounting for less than a tenth of the native population, controlled one-fifth of the natively held wealth in Egypt.[41] In addition to Nubar Pasha, important Christian political and legal figures operative between 1875 and 1914 included Buṭrūs Ghālī (Prime Minister, 1908–1910), Yaqub Artin, Akhnūkh Fanūs, Makram ʿUbayd, and Yūsuf Wahbah. Between 1919 and 1944, Copts held the presidency of the National Bar Association half of the time.[42] Between 1887 and 1910, 21 percent of the graduates of the Khedivial Law School were Copts.[43] One of the first law journals established in Egypt, *al-Ḥuqūq*, was edited by the Syrian Christian journalist Antun Shumayyil. The journal took an interest in European styles of legal philosophy and was committed to the improvement of the Egyptian legal system, but paid little attention to Islamic legal revival as a principle of legal development. In essence, the story of non-Muslims and their role in the construction of Egypt's new legal order is worthy of further inquiry. Such a story would also need to account for figures such as Riyāḍ Pasha, three times Prime Minister between 1879 and 1894, who was Circassian and likely of Jewish ancestry.[44]

When the Native Courts were proposed in the 1870s, European and Egyptian political figures considered them a continuation of a reform process that began in the 1860s with the Ottoman-styled Nizami courts.[45] These courts had already annexed portions of the jurisdiction of the traditional Sharia Courts, and this process had taken place under the leadership of independent Egyptian and Ottoman officials. The Native Courts were sometimes called, colloquially, Nizami courts.[46] Egyptian leaders were well aware of the fact that these courts helped to keep Egypt within the Ottoman imperial ambit; but Egypt was a semi-autonomous part of the Ottoman Empire.[47] Egyptian leaders did not necessarily imagine that the Europeans would control these courts after 1882 and use them as tools for

[41] Samir Seikaly, "Coptic Communal Reform: 1860–1914," *Middle Eastern Studies* 6,3 (1970): 247–75, at 268.

[42] Reid, "National Bar Association," 621. [43] Ibid. [44] Ibid., 621–2.

[45] On the Nizami courts, see Avi Rubin, *Ottoman Nizamiye Courts*.

[46] See discussions of capitulations during the 1870s in *Majallat al-qaḍāʾ al-sharʿī* 4 (1926–7).

[47] See Brown, "Law and Imperialism."

European imperial domination; they could not reliably predict a full-scale British occupation. Egyptian political figures also favored the idea of Native Courts, having been persuaded that the Native Courts would eventually subsume the Mixed Courts, and thus ultimately bring all civil and criminal cases in Egypt under the jurisdiction of Egyptian judges. From this perspective, Egyptian politicians were inclined to view the Native Courts as desirable (if not also inevitable) because they would be a tool for both phasing out extraterritorial jurisdiction and justifying Egyptian calls for independence from European political control.

The British occupation and ascent to power was rapid, brutal, and forceful. In 1882 the British Navy set fire to Alexandria and the Marines put Cairo under martial law. Elite Egyptians who opposed British directives were ejected from their offices; intellectuals, journalists, and teachers who made too much noise were silenced on threat of jailing or losing their jobs; the poor who engaged in brigandage and insurrection were jailed and tortured.

The history of 1882–1884 furnishes countless stories of minor Egyptian heroics and political standstills caused by Egyptian resistance in the face of British control. The archives and personal papers of European agents in Egypt, including those involved with legal reform, are filled with accounts of daily struggles in coercing the cooperation of an Egyptian political elite whose members were often less than cooperative. But the larger picture is that British agents in Cairo advanced their major reform objectives outlined in the Dufferin Report of 1883. They pursued their purposes through the exercise of power in many forms. They did so with the help of an Egyptian political elite that was just sufficiently compliant, an Egyptian army commanded by British officers, and an Egyptian bureaucracy commanded by European managers. When historians or present-day Egyptians aggrieved by Franco-Egyptian law's existence look back on the 1880s, they should be no more surprised that the British established the Native system than that the British interfered in Egypt's bureaucracy, its army, taxation, the budget, education, foreign policy, trade policy, agricultural policy, water policy, public works, and every other significant portfolio of concern to the management of the state.

Although the construction of the Native Courts was an operation with far-reaching consequences for law, justice, order, economy, and culture in Egypt, and although it might have been objectionable to some elite proponents of Egyptian sovereignty, Egyptian elites had few cards at their disposal for opposing the courts and little incentive for doing so. The courts' creation looked to most observers, even those in the Egyptian government itself, like a straightforward, predictable, rapid, and inexorable process managed by untouchable elites—many of whom were Egyptians.

One of the keys to the successful transition to the Native Court system was that it happened rapidly. It took twenty years for the Egyptian government to make the Native Courts work as the British judicial advisers wanted them to work, but it only took two years for the Egyptian government to put the Native Courts in operation in most of the country. The work involved giving jobs to a relatively small number of judges and clerks, almost all of whom were white-collar workers in need of jobs; they were not heroes, martyrs, public intellectuals, or revolutionaries. The Native Courts were established within the facilities of previously existing courts. Former judges and clerks accepted work in the same buildings that they had labored in before the occupation. Even jobless graduates of the mosque-university al-Azhar found judgeships in the courts during the 1880s, two decades before they were shut out from such positions.

A historian should not expect to find in historical sources significant and sustained opposition to the Native Court system in 1882–1884. An important aspect of the history of the early British occupation is that the British were for several years insecure in Egypt and not confident that they would stay. The French and the Ottomans campaigned and intrigued relentlessly against the occupation, inside and outside of Egypt, while Egyptians put up notable resistance as well. Nevertheless, the British were forceful, and they remained. When the British wanted to build extensive networks of dams, canals, ports, and roads at great cost in money and manpower, they built dams, canals, ports, and roads; when they wanted to create a new system of prisons, they built the prisons and filled them with prisoners. When they wanted to quash small-scale rebellions and demonstrations, they did so. Similarly, when they wanted to create new courts and to manage the white-collar workers and bureaucrats in them, they did, with comparatively less money and bloodshed than they put into their other reform initiatives. The post-1882 administration restored stability and the better part of the political pre-occupation status quo. With each reform, the British provided jobs to assuage unemployment among white-collar workers. They fired those whom they disliked and hired those whom they liked, as reflected in meticulous government records spanning several decades. This is not to put a benevolent face on British policy, but to underline that occupation and post-occupation policy lulled lower-middle, middle, and upper-class Egyptian society, overall, into compliance with the occupation's state of order. It is possible that the British implemented reforms more slowly than they might otherwise have done due to a lack of confidence in the projected timeline of their occupation. All the same, they operated purposefully from the moment their forces touched down in 1882.[48]

THE MODERN LEGAL PROFESSION IN ECONOMIC, SOCIAL, AND CULTURAL CONTEXT

Institutional and intellectual history only go so far in explaining the relationship of Egyptians to their legal system and courts, given that this relationship was also conditioned by economic, social, and cultural factors of the times. This angle on the history begins by illuminating how Egyptian law professionals could be nationalists or Islamists on the one hand and common workers on the other, intent on obtaining and maintaining a particular social status and lifestyle.

[48] British government records from the first years of the occupation generally bear out this assertion. See, for example, Bodleian Library, Papers of Lord Milner, Papers relating to Egypt, Mss. Milner dep., 443, fols. 1–3, Egypt No. 2 1882, letters of Nov. 3, 1882 and Jan. 3, 1883.

From the mid-nineteenth century through the era of European control, law professionals enjoyed newfound prestige and enhanced opportunities for social mobility within the context of an expanding economy, new state institutions, and changing patterns in social life and culture.[49] This was true most of all for lawyers, but judges, law professors, and administrators partook as well.[50]

Although not advocates in the modern sense, legal representatives were not unknown in the pre-modern Islamic legal system;[51] a semi-professional trade of private advocates practiced in the Ottoman cities of the sixteenth century.[52] Whereas the pre-modern advocate was not commonly viewed as having received extensive training and was not necessarily a prestigious figure in society, let alone a political figure, the opposite was true for Egyptian lawyers throughout the British occupation, even if individual lawyers could be accused of incompetence or corruption and lawyers as a group were periodically marked out for scorn and ridicule, which resulted from public malaise over political and economic problems.[53]

Historians still have before them the task of exploring and explaining, in precise terms, what made late nineteenth- and early twentieth-century lawyers and

[49] On economic and social history, see generally Ehud R. Toledano, "Social and Economic Change in the 'Long Nineteenth Century'," in *Cambridge History of Egypt*, ed. Daly, 2: 252–84; Joel Beinin, "Egypt: Society and Economy, 1923–1952," in *Cambridge History of* Egypt, ed. Daly, 2: 309–33; Roger Owen, *The Middle East in the World Economy, 1800–1914*, rev. ed. (London: I. B. Tauris, 1993), 216–43; Jacques Berque, *Egypt: Imperialism and Revolution*, trans. J. Stewart (London: Faber and Faber, 1972); Gabriel Baer, "Social Change in Egypt: 1800–1914"; Charles P. Issawi, ed., *The Economic History of the Middle East, 1800–1914: A Book of Readings* (Chicago: University of Chicago Press, 1966), 357–452; Issawi, "Egypt since 1800: A Study in Lopsided Development," *Journal of Economic History* 21,1 (1961): 1–25; John S. Badeau, "Book review of Daniel Lerner with Lucille W. Pevsner, *The Passing of Traditional Society: Modernizing the Middle East*, and Sir Reader Bullard, *The Middle East: A Political and Economic Survey*," *American Political Science Review* 53,4 (1959): 1133–5.

[50] On the prestige of lawyers, see ʿAzīz Khānkī and Jamīl Khānkī, *al-Muḥāmāh qadīman wa-ḥadīthan* (Cairo: s.n., 1940), 29–31; Zaghlūl, *al-Muḥāmāh*, introduction. On the professional trajectories of law professionals in social and cultural context, see generally all works by Nathan Brown listed in References; ʿAmr Shalaqānī (Amr Shalakany), *Izdihār wa-inhiyār al-nukhbah al-qānūniyyah al-Miṣriyyah, 1805–2005* (Cairo: Dār al-Shurūq, 2013); idem, "'I Heard it All Before': Egyptian Tales of Law and Development," *Third World Quarterly* 5,27 (2006): 833–53; Reid, *Lawyers and Politics*; Reid, "National Bar Association"; Ziadeh, *Lawyers, the Rule of Law and Liberalism*; Khānkī and Khānkī, *al-Muḥāmāh qadīman wa-ḥadīthan*; Zaghlūl, *al-Muḥāmāh*. For an exceptional bibliography of Arabic works and documents concerning the lives of lawyers, see ʿAbd al-Ḥalīm Jindī, *Nujūm al-muḥāmāh fī Miṣr wa-Ūrubbā: al-Hilbāwī, al-Sanhūrī, Muṣṭafá Marʿī, Marshāl Hawl, Ḥanrī Rawbayr* (Cairo: Dār al-Maʿārif, 1991). For representative autobiographies and memoirs of lawyers and judges, see Muḥammad Muḥammad Jawādī, *Fī riḥāb al-ʿadālah: Mudhakkirāt ʿAbd al-Fattāḥ Ḥasan, Fatḥī Raḍwān, Yūsuf Naḥḥās, Maḥmūd Kāmil* (Cairo: al-Hayʾah al-Miṣriyyah al-ʿĀmmah li-l-Kitāb, 2007); ʿAbd al-Razzāq al-Sanhūrī, *al-Sanhūrī min khilāl awrāqihi l-shakhṣiyyah*, ed. N. al-Sanhūrī and T. al-Shāwī (Cairo: Dār al-Shurūq, 2005); Ibrāhīm Hilbāwī, *Mudhakkirāt Ibrāhīm al-Hilbāwī: Tārīkh ḥayāt Ibrāhīm al-Hilbāwī Bik, 1858–1940*, ed. ʿI. Ḍiyāʾ al-Dīn Sayyid (Cairo: al-Hayʾah al-Miṣriyyah al-ʿĀmmah li-l-Kitāb, 1995); Maḥmūd Kāmil, *Yawmiyyāt muḥāmin miṣrī: al-Jānib al-insānī min ḥayāt al-maḥākim fī ʿishrīn ʿāman* (Cairo: al-Dār al-Qawmiyyah li-l-Ṭibāʿah wa-l-Nashr, 1963), Eng. trans., *Diary of an Egyptian Lawyer: The Human Side of a Court of Law* ([Cairo]: General Egyptian Book Organization, 1980); Ṣalāḥ Shāhīd, *Dhikrayātī fī ʿahdayn* (Miṣr: Dār al-Maʿārif, 1976); Tādrus Mikhāʾīl Tādrus, *Dhikrayāt min ʿālam al-muḥāmāh wa-l-qaḍāʾ* (Cairo: al-Dār al-Qawmiyyah li-l-Ṭibāʿah wa-l-Nashr, 1966); Fatḥ Allāh Ṣaqqāl, *Min dhikrayātī fī l-muḥāmāh fī Miṣr wa-Sūriyā* (Aleppo: Maṭbaʿat al-Ḍād, 1958); ʿAzīz Khānkī, *Majmūʿat Mudhakkirāt* (Miṣr: Maṭbaʿat al-Akhbār, 1912) (ʿAzīz Khānkī's personal papers are maintained at the library of CEDEJ, Cairo).

[51] These representatives were known by various titles, among which *wakīl bi-l-khuṣūmah* (lit. agent for the dispute). See Ahmad Atif Ahmad, "Lawyers: Islamic Law," *Oxford Encyclopedia of Legal History* (Oxford: Oxford University Press, 2009), 4: 47–8.

[52] Ibid., 47. The professional in Ottoman Turkish was called *daʿwá wekīli*.

[53] See Chapter 2, n. 46.

legal practice different from historical precursors. Nevertheless, aspects of lawyers' distinctive social and economic trajectories of the nineteenth and twentieth centuries are clear. The evolving status of "lawyers" resulted in part from trends in professionalization that prevailed across many areas of work in Egypt; like engineers, Egyptian lawyers gradually became a recognized professional group and one whose ranks were relatively selective.[54] In 1845, Muḥammad ʿAlī established "merchants' councils" (*majālis al-tujjār*), the regulations of which specified that parties were entitled to hire legal representatives. In the 1870s, Egyptian lawyers pleaded before the reputedly sophisticated[55] Mixed Courts as "advocates"—on a European model—alongside European attorneys and judges of an international class. Egyptian lawyers increasingly pressed the government to adopt the terms "lawyer," *avocat*, *avvocato*, and *muḥāmī* for regulatory and legislative purposes.[56] Clearer regulations regarding age and training came in the mid- and late 1880s, as entry to a law career became tied to the acquisition of a law degree and less to apprenticing, and by 1893 it was almost a necessity for an advocate in the Native Courts to hold a degree from the Khedivial Law School or a similar institution in Egypt or Europe.[57] The lawyers of the Mixed Courts organized in a professional society as early as 1876—although the official law promulgating a Mixed Bar Association was not until 1887, with bar associations for the National and Sharia Courts following in 1912 and 1916 respectively.

In light of the developing economy and attendant state of affairs—urbanization, social problems induced by shocks to traditional society, and crime—lawyers and judges flourished and became more highly valued, and their law professions evolved.[58] Entrepreneurship, investment, finance, industry, commerce, agriculture, and trade involved contracts, taxes, tariffs, new investment schemes and corporate forms, and disputes. These were precisely the kinds of hurdles that lawyers were uniquely trained to navigate for the benefit of individuals, companies, and the government.[59] The expanding Egyptian bureaucracy also needed lawyers, prosecutors, judges, investigators, regulators, supervisors, clerks, researchers, statisticians, and penal administrators.

University faculties, law schools among them, were founded to meet the new economic needs and social consequences of the changing economics and demographics; new programs of every kind in tertiary education, with relatively demanding standards for admission and graduation, elevated aspiring youth into

[54] For Donald Reid (*Lawyers and Politics*, 42), advocacy became a full-fledged profession though five factors among others: the establishment of a law school, the founding of law journals, the introduction of official regulation of advocacy, the growth of numbers of qualified lawyers, and the founding of a national bar association. See also Reid, "The Rise of Professions and Professional Organizations in Modern Egypt," *Comparative Studies in Society and History* 16,1 (1974): 24–57, at 41.

[55] See Brinton, *Mixed Courts*, 144–56; Jasper Y. Brinton, "The Closing of the Mixed Courts of Egypt," *American Journal of International Law* 44,2 (1950): 303–12.

[56] See n. 54.

[57] J. Scott, "Rapport sur les Tribunaux indigènes 1890–1894," *Recueil des documents officiels du gouvernement égyptien* (1894), 81–100, at 84; Brinton, *Mixed Courts*, 144–46; Byron Cannon, "Social Tensions and the Teaching of European Law in Egypt before 1900," *History of Education Quarterly* 15,3 (1975): 299–315, at 304–5. See also Chapter 7.

[58] Reid, *Lawyers and Politics*, 12–13, 40, 92, 118, 395.

[59] The many case reporters and legal encyclopedias of Egypt testify to the rich opportunities that lawyers encountered in these areas.

new professional, social, and income-based ranks. Government policies intentionally capped enrollments, however, so that many Egyptian secondary school graduates could not obtain admission.

Despite the classism of Egyptian society of the nineteenth and early twentieth centuries, the new professional schools provided non-aristocratic graduates with paths to upward economic and social mobility.[60] Lawyers in particular were increasingly and especially numerous among the professional classes.[61] The most successful lawyers moved fluidly between practicing law and working in government,[62] and prosperous lawyers, whose success was obtained through merit rather than birth and family connections, found colleagues among Egypt's aristocratic, landed elite.[63] Being educated in law schools founded and controlled by Europeans, in both Egypt and Europe, was central to their improving status. Graduation from one of these schools meant being fluent in a European language, acquiring elevated mannerisms, rubbing elbows with richer students, and being introduced at least to the rudiments of economics and finance. A degree from Cairo's École Française de Droit gave the graduate equal right to practice in France; a degree from Cairo's Khedivial Law School facilitated admission to the courts of France.

Such facts had prestige value. A practitioner before the Mixed or Native Courts could boast a respectable salary, knowledge of French or English, and a collection of suits. It suffices to mention for now that these practitioners wore modern dress (as distinct from traditional Egyptian attire) and this was a meaningful signifier of status—real or desired—in Egyptian society.

Economic expansion and a growth in national wealth naturally shaped the expanding fortunes of legal professionals. Since Egypt was a litigious society, as well as one filled with business, social, and criminal problems, there were jobs to be had in law, even if job insecurity was a feeling shared by many educated Egyptians.[64] Lawyers, judges, and law professors also enjoyed notable successes outside of law as newspaper editors, writers, and teachers in fields such as history, sociology, psychology, poetry, literature, theater, medicine, and oratory.[65]

Some have viewed the Mixed Courts as the starting point and foundation of the prestige and the relatively good incomes of modern Egyptian legal professionals.[66]

[60] On the economic and social bases of the ascending Egyptian legal profession, see n. 50. See also Reid, *Lawyers and Politics*, 10–13. There was some limited mobility for women, although this topic is in need of further research. Khānkī and Khānkī, *Muḥāmāh*, 63.

[61] In 1907, there were 2,237 registered lawyers and lawyers' clerks. Gabriel Baer, "Social Change in Egypt: 1800–1914," 156.

[62] See Chapter 2, n. 46.

[63] Reid, *Lawyers and Politics*, 13, 41, 396.

[64] On job insecurity, see Roger Allen, *A Study of Hadīth ʿĪsā ibn Hishām: Muhammad al-Muwaylihī's View of Egyptian Society during the British Occupation* (Albany: State University of New York Press, 1974), 92–3. For differing wage incentives for the various kinds of jobs in law, see Reid, *Lawyers and Politics*, 42.

[65] For a list of accomplishments and a bibliography, see Khānkī and Khānkī, *Muḥāmāh*, 63.

[66] Shalakany, "'I Heard it All Before'," 841–2; Reid, "National Bar Association," 610–12; Mark S. W. Hoyle, "The Mixed Courts of Egypt: An Anniversary Assessment," *Arab Law Quarterly* 1, 1 (1985): 60–8, at 60. For a primary-source illustration of the prestige of professionals in the Mixed Courts, see *Les juridictions mixtes d'Égypte 1876–1926: Livre d'or édité sous le patronage du Conseil de l'ordre des avocats à l'occasion du cinquantenaire des tribunaux de la réforme* (Alexandria: Journal des tribunaux mixtes, 1926).

The presence of Europeans within these courts—as professionals and parties—along with the sophistication of pleadings assured the Mixed Courts the top spot in Egypt's legal hierarchy, and thus in its professional-social hierarchy. Next in the line of prestige—if one discounts the consular courts—were practitioners admitted to the Native Courts, where lawyers aspired to be like the lawyers who were admitted to the Mixed Courts. The Native Courts had within themselves a social hierarchy. Judges aspired to reach the appellate benches; litigators competed for lucrative business; and prosecutors competed for high-profile prosecutions.

A law degree was thus a source of social and cultural capital insofar as Egyptians embraced an energized ideal of the era that contemporary public law was the chief foundation for legitimizing political power and a key to participating in it. A high proportion of the country's prime ministers, politicians, ministers, diplomats, high political advisers, governors, and local mayors was comprised of lawyers.[67] The Native Court Bar Association was continuously involved in national politics.[68] The stature of lawyers increased as some became prominent in the independence campaign after the First World War;[69] while in a society and profession whose interests were newly piqued in concepts such as separation of powers, judicial independence, appellate review, and constitutional jurisprudence, judges could envision themselves as striving to make a tangible, positive impact in politics, economy, and social affairs.[70] Law professors also saw similar promise in contemporary society. Scholars of law had existed in Egypt since antiquity, and they had obtained varying degrees of practical influence at different times, but in the Franco-Egyptian legal system, rooted in French tradition, they were definitively regarded as active creators of law.

These economic and social developments, favorable as they were from the material perspective, are one reason Egyptian law professionals could be fervent nationalists or Islamists while remaining attracted to, rooted in, or invested in European-oriented legal traditions, languages, and customs. In the courts and bar associations there was plenty of malaise and critique of the courts that stemmed from secular-oriented nationalism and antagonism to the British occupation, but radical criticisms of the legal system's European-law foundations were more muted than they might have been, particularly before the 1930s. It was not just that a practitioner's knowledge and identity, forged in a law school, were hard to discount, supplant, or forego entirely: many profited from the status

[67] Reid, *Lawyers and Politics*, 56; J. N. D. Anderson, "Law Reform in Egypt: 1850–1950," in *Political and Social Change in Modern Egypt*, ed. Holt, 209–30, at 216; Amānī al-Ṭawīl, *al-Muḥāmūn bayna l-nahḍah wa-l-siyāsah* (Cairo: Dār al-Shurūq, 2007); ʿAbd al-Ḥalīm Jindī, *Ibrāhīm al-Hilbāwī: al-Muḥāmūn wa-siyādat al-qānūn* (Egypt: Majallat al-Muḥāmāh Niqābat al-Muḥāmīn, 1982); Khānkī and Khānkī, *Muḥāmāh*, 33–4, 53–7.

[68] Ninette S. Fahmy, *The Politics of Egypt: State-Society Relationship* (London: RoutledgeCurzon, 2002), 110; Brown, *Rule of Law*, 74–95; Reid, "National Bar Association."

[69] The first independence-era prime minister was the outspoken lawyer and nationalist, Saʿd Zaghlūl. Another of Egypt's leading nationalists in this period was the lawyer Muḥammad Kāmil Ḥusayn. On his leadership of the Cairo Tramway Worker's Union during the 1919 nationalist uprising, see Beinin, "Egypt: Society and Economy, 1923–1952," 317. See also Shalakany, " 'I Heard it All Before'," 844; Reid, *Lawyers and Politics*, 59, 395–6.

[70] Shalakany, " 'I Heard it All Before'," 841; Ibn ʿArnūs, *Kitāb Tārīkh al-qaḍaʾ*, 196.

that the legal system afforded them, however much they may have resented the system for its foreign roots.

In the Islamic courts, practitioners, who were typically graduates of the homegrown Islamic institutions, and professors in all areas of law—Franco-Egyptian and Islamic—felt more comfortable critiquing the Franco-Egyptian legal system. Their comparative distance from day-to-day accountability was a rare kind of freedom. For the critics in the Franco-Egyptian courts (the Mixed and Native Courts), however, who by their practice were more able to see certain problems, but less able to assail them publicly, concerns for religious values and political ideology apparently gave way to concerns about sustaining livelihood and status as well as to inevitable realizations about the practical limitations of effecting radical change. Their livelihood and ambitions were dependent upon a professional system that was far larger and more historically entrenched than any individual and one that was too sizeable to be changed by individual action. The ideas and practices of this system were valuable and valued even by its critics. Above all, it was a system that, for all its warts, was exponentially more intelligent, capable, and resilient than any single person or group.

THE "ISLAMIC REVIVAL" AND THE PIVOTAL 1930S

Returning to the general overview of malaise over the origins of the Egyptian legal system, the reason present-day critics expect or hope to find Egyptian opposition to the Native Courts in the 1880s is that this system is now associated with the imposition of European imperialism, and their point of departure is that Egypt's legal order should ideally be based on the Sharia. But the more one examines the situation in Egypt in the 1870s and in the decades beforehand, the more anachronistic the present-day expectations of past actors appear. Egyptian Muslims in the 1870s and 1880s esteemed Islamic law, and they esteemed Islam. The Sharia Courts had been losing ground to secular courts for decades, however, at the hands of Egyptian leaders. The creation of the Native Courts in 1883–1884 was alarming to some, but it could not have been very surprising. The British occupation quashed the ulema (Ar. *ʿulamāʾ* "Islamic religious scholars") as an effective political force, at least during the 1880s. The occupation in general was overwhelming in its forcefulness. The key principle for empowered Egyptian leaders—some of whom were not Muslim—was protecting Egyptian political sovereignty as far as possible under the circumstances of occupation. And, radical reform of the courts was the least of most leaders' concerns, particularly since the trajectories of reform predated the occupation itself. Every indication is that the major aspiration for law professionals—judges and clerks, principally—was to work. Moreover, it was commonly said in Egypt that the British would stay only for a short time. This meant that the British would leave the courts in Egyptian hands and then Egyptians could do with them what they liked. These were the circumstances of the early and mid-1880s.

The 1930s, by contrast, were pivotal for the broader movement of Islamic revivalism in Egypt generally, not limited to Islamic *legal* revivalism alone. While ideology in Egypt during the 1920s had been marked by secular-oriented nationalism, Egyptian culture witnessed an "Islamic turn" during the 1930s as intellectuals, academics, and artists become more interested in Islamic and pan-Arab themes.[71] Although a movement of general "Islamic revival" had roots tracing back to the 1870s at least,[72] the 1930s marked a new phase. In this decade, proponents of Egyptian independence became particularly inclined to cast the "national" cause as an "Islamic" cause. At the same time, Egyptians became more prone to situating their national struggle and identity within a wider Arab context, as opposed to a predominantly European-national context. In explaining the transformation of popular cultural symbols and ambitions, Israel Gershoni and James Jankowski speak of a transcendence of "territorial" nationalism and the evolution of "supra-national" nationalism in Egypt.[73]

Older Egyptian intellectuals who had previously been more focused on territorial Egyptian nationalism began to engage with Islamic and Arab themes. Among those who made this paradigmatic shift were Aḥmad Amīn, Abbās Maḥmūd al-ʿAqqād, and Muḥammad Ḥusayn Haykal.[74] This Islamic turn was also shaped by younger intellectuals, journalists, and activists who came from the (lower-) middle classes. They included Ḥasan al-Bannā, Ṣāliḥ Muṣṭafá ʿAshmāwī, Aḥmad Ḥusayn, Fatḥī Raḍwān, and Sayyid Quṭb in his pre-fundamentalist phase as a literary critic.[75] They challenged the notion that Egypt should accept Westernization as the mode for modernizing and coping with demands of a rapidly changing modern world.[76]

The 1930s and 1940s witnessed economic hard times, political instability, and widespread dissatisfaction with the status quo.[77] While Egypt's national income doubled between the 1920s and the 1950s, the wealth was not distributed evenly. Many Egyptians became poorer in real terms.[78] In cities during the 1930s, Egypt experienced patterns in urbanization and industrialization similar to those that Europe had experienced in the later nineteenth century, and familiar issues appeared relating to poor urban living conditions, low wages, and dissatisfied urban classes. By 1947, a third of the total population was living in towns and cities.[79] These urban populations were dissatisfied with turbulent and disappointing politics.

Academic analyses of social and political life in the 1930s have made much of the emergence of a new, urban, lower-middle class comprised mostly of white-

[71] See generally I. Gershoni and James P. Jankowski, *Redefining the Egyptian Nation, 1930–1945* (New York: Cambridge University Press, 1995); Charles D. Smith, *Islam and the Search for Social Order in Modern Egypt* (Albany: State University of New York Press, 1983).

[72] See generally Ali Rahnema, ed., *Pioneers of Islamic Revival* (Atlantic Highlands, NJ: Zed Books, 1994), 1–63; Albert Hourani, *Arabic Thought in the Liberal Age, 1798–1939* (London: Oxford University Press, 1962), 161–82, 222–44.

[73] See generally Gershoni and Jankowski, *Redefining the Egyptian Nation.*

[74] Ibid., 37. [75] Ibid. [76] Ibid.

[77] See Smith, *Islam and the Search for Social Order*; Roger Owen and Sevket Pamuk, *History of Middle East Economies in the Twentieth Century* (London: I. B. Tauris, 1998), 30–40; Berque, *Egypt*, 280–300.

[78] Berque, *Egypt*, 280–300. [79] Ibid.

collar workers (*effendiyyah*).[80] The effendiyyah were products of new urbanization, expansion of the public sector, and the broadening of public education. As urbanization intensified and more Egyptians were educated in state schooling, a greater number of young Egyptians who worked in the capacity of lower-level white-collar workers appeared in society. While the native elite structure of Egyptian society remained more or less intact and closed to outsiders, the numbers of these lower-middle class types swelled.

If one is looking into history for people disappointed with political, social, and economic life, the effendiyyah class is one place to look. They were more vulnerable than higher-ranking people to the economic, political, and social vicissitudes of the age. They were based in urban settings like Cairo, Alexandria, and Ismailiyya. They were susceptible to shifting trends in popular culture, such as the Islamic turn. Notably, they were prevalent in the Sharia Court system and in the middle and lower echelons of the Native and Mixed systems.

Although the effendiyyah were likely to be well disposed to Western-oriented aspects of Egyptian modernity, the individual effendi was likely to have fewer real connections to Western culture and the Western aspects of his society than the *basha*s and the *bey*s of the elites.[81] The effendi wore a suit and tie, he might have smoked fashionable cigarettes and frequented fashionable clubs, and he may have learned a European language. However, for many effendis, their education was mostly in Arabic.

In the 1930s and 1940s, new Islamic political and cultural sentiments spread among the effendiyyah.[82] Grassroots movements emerged from within the effendi class. Non-effendi, higher-ranked members of the intellectual and political elite also reached down into the effendiyyah for followers. The two most famous Islamic movements of the 1930s and 1940s—al-Fatḥ (Conquest) and the Muslim Brotherhood—found their base among the effendiyyah. Ḥasan al-Bannā and Sayyid Quṭb were both effendis.

The effendiyyah and the various ranks of persons in society appear throughout this work. Most of the law students encountered below were effendis. This term was applied to students in law school and many students at the Sharia College aspired to have it applied to them. All of the professors of Franco-Egyptian law had earned doctorates (their title was *duktūr*); and several of them were *bey*s. The professional jurists and professors of Sharia, however, did not take any of these honorifics—they assumed the more traditional titles of *shaykh* or *ustādh* (teacher). They dressed differently, wearing the turban and cloak (*ridā'*).

[80] As all historical notions about class and classes, a conception of the effendiyyah must be broad and allow for variances; one can speak of the effendiyyah as a "class" as long as one has an appreciation for the limitations of generalizing about class identity and behavior. See Lucie Ryzova, *The Age of the Efendiyya: Passages to Modernity in National-Colonial Egypt* (Oxford University Press, 2014); Ryzova, "Egyptianizing Modernity through the New Effendiya," in *Re-Envisioning Egypt, 1919–1952*, ed. Arthur Goldschmidt et al. (Cairo: American University in Cairo Press, 2005), 124–63; Yoav Di-Capua, "The Professional Worldview of the *Effendi* Historian," *History Compass* 7,1 (2009): 306–28.

[81] Now an honorific, used in the sense of "Mr.," *bey* (< T. *beg* "lord") was a title carried by Turkish landowners in Ottoman Egypt; by the beginning of the twentieth century, the title *bey*—along with *pasha*—was commonly handed out by the Egyptian monarchy to the upper or upper-middle classes as a token of favor.

[82] Di-Capua, "Professional Worldview."

The notion of a "rising middle class" and its unsettling effects on a political status quo is now so common a historical concept that historians are cautious to invoke it. Nonetheless, invocation of a frustrated lower-middle class is useful for explaining changes in ideology and culture in Egypt. Identifying a frustrated lower-middle class goes a long way in explaining the flourishing of Islamic rhetoric and agendas. The proliferation of effendis and Islamic sentiment occurred during a period of effervescence in printed media. There was a burgeoning landscape of writers. Ordinary people were finding new outlets and freedoms for sharing their ideas. The legal journals dedicated to Islamic legal revivalism, discussed in the following chapters, were thus part of a larger movement of Islamic-oriented publications that appeared in the 1930s.

POLITICS AND INSTITUTIONS AFTER 1922

This book will refer sparingly to aspects of political history after 1922—in an effort to remain focused on the legal topics most at hand—but it must be borne in mind throughout the forthcoming discussions that jurists and law professionals of the post-1922 period were acting in light of, and in direct response to, the major political and institutional events of their times.[83] The summary above of Islamic legal activism in social and economic context has already referred to the links between Islamic activism and the contentious politics of the 1930s, but the major political and institutional events of this period captured the attention of all law professionals in Egypt, irrespective of their particular ideological inclinations. Law professionals generally shared in common sentiments of nationalism (or supra-nationalism) as directed against the occupiers, and almost all harbored an ongoing concern for improving the quality of Egypt's fledging democratic process.

Great Britain's 1922 Declaration of Egyptian Independence, for example, was an abiding source of discontent among lawyers and politicians because of Great Britain's failure to yield full control to Egyptians. This failure sparked the engagement of legal professionals and scholars with the topic of shoring up Egyptian sovereignty from the top down (e.g., on the level of treaties and parliamentary integrity) and from the bottom up (e.g., in the day-to-day operation and independence of the courts). The 1923 Constitution became the touchstone for a lively field of legal literature and activism with respect to the parliamentary process, the obligations of the state, and the political rights of citizens. In the 1920s and 1930s, the British and Egyptian governments engaged in successive negotiations to reform and end the capitulations regime which buttressed the Mixed Courts system and prevented the unification of the court system under native Egyptian control. The 1936 Anglo-Egyptian Treaty, which secured to the British certain military-related prerogatives, aroused the nationalism of Egyptian law

[83] See generally, Brown, *Rule of Law*, 23–74.

professionals and politicians and strengthened their desire for institutional reform. The Montreux Conventions of 1937 between Egypt and Great Britan set in motion a twelve-year process designed to phase out the capitulations regime in Egypt.[84] Egypt's law professionals and jurists, particularly those who rotated in and out of government office, contributed to the formation, critique, and implementation of this process.

The "post-independence" period naturally also witnessed the evolution of important institutions, in addition to the parliament and Mixed and Native Courts, which shaped the discourse and work of law professionals. The National Bar Association and the Sharia Lawyers Bar Association became mechanisms through which law professionals could define their priorities and channel their activism. In 1946, Egypt established an administrative judiciary known as Majlis al-Dawlah ("State Council") that, based on its French precursor in the *Conseil d'État*, was tasked with reviewing draft legislation and hearing disputes concerning actions of administrative bodies.[85] In 1948, Majlis al-Dawlah, under the leadership of ʿAbd al-Razzaq al-Sanhūrī, announced that it possessed the authority to review the constitutionality of legislation. This decision gave rise to a series of ambitious and controversial decisions that aimed to check the power of the executive branch. The development was a source of pride for Egypt's law professionals but also a source of conflict between them and the state. Finally, the year 1948 can hardly be mentioned in Egyptian historical context without reference to the Arab-Israeli War of that year. Egypt's failures in the war deepened the commitment of Egyptian lawyers to furthering the cause of Egyptian independence. For some, these failures deepened their commitment to Islamic-oriented solutions.

Topics and events of this magnitude, when they sparked debate at a national level, involved considerations of Islamic law only relatively infrequently. Yet as this book will demonstrate, the Islamic legal discourse was transpiring in every year beneath the most evident surface of the national stage. One notable exception might be the rise of the Muslim Brotherhood in the 1930s and 1940s; but the movement at this time was more commonly considered a marginal political movement, and it is only in recent decades that historians have focused on the Islamic legal revivalist thought that was ancillary to its political objectives. Such possible exceptions aside, there is a broader point at stake. If proponents of Islamic legal revival were intent on discussing ideas about how to integrate Islamic law into the legal fabric of the state during the interwar period, they were not alone among Egyptians in focusing on fundamental political and legal questions about the country's future. They were engaging with national topics and interests, but approaching these topics from an angle which received less attention on the national and international levels of discourse. The most vocal proponents of Islamic legal revivalism were generally not as powerful as the more secular-oriented politicians and lawyers who dominated the national political stage during the interwar period and into 1952.

[84] Ibid., 43–4, 64–9. [85] Ibid., 71–2.

2

Early Islamic Legal Revivalism and National Complacency

When European law began taking firmer root in Egyptian legislation, as early as the 1870s, law schools and the courts, select jurists, law professionals, and political figures in Egypt looked skeptically upon the Europeanization of their law. Their skepticism prompted an aspiration for the revival of Islamic law. But it was only in the 1920s, 1930s, and 1940s that Egypt saw more outward, explicit, and common opposition to European law and a confluence of a general revival of Islamic sentiment with revivalist trajectories in Islamic legal thought. The gradual ambition to revive Islamic law in the face of European incursion became more explicit and widespread as a result of many factors. Politics and culture during the 1870s through the 1920s differed from that during the 1920s through the 1950s; still other factors pertain to changing understandings of Sharia, changing expectations of the modern legal order, and changing interpretations of Egypt's pre-colonial legal past.

From 1882 into the 1920s, Egyptians lived under foreign occupation and a government that monitored the publishing market and classroom education in tertiary institutions. Journals dealing with Islamic legal practice before the 1920s betrayed cautious self-censorship among their authors. The media showed an aversion or at best ambivalence toward printing oppositional views on European law, most often legitimizing the Franco-Egyptian legal order.

Egyptian law professionals and jurists who were already operative and established during the 1870s were accustomed to a decades-old process of European legal incursion into Egyptian laws and to the presence of government-created legislation in the legal order.[1] Laws had been passed by the Muḥammad ʿAlī dynasty in Cairo, the Ottoman government in Istanbul, and other local leaders. A web of capitulations laws had long existed granting foreigners extra-territorial jurisdiction within Egypt. As such, the expectation that Egypt's laws could and should be based on Sharia alone was somewhat new and it took time to develop and become more widespread under the auspices of Islamic legal revivalist ideology.

[1] See generally articles by Rudolph Peters in References, as well as his "Egypt in the Age of the Triumphant Prison: Legal Punishment in Nineteenth Century Egypt," *Annales Islamologiques* 36 (2002): 253–85 and *Crime and Punishment in Islamic Law: Theory and Practice from the Sixteenth to the Twenty-First Century* (Cambridge: Cambridge University Press, 2005). See also Shiḥātah, *Tārīkh ḥarakat al-tajdīd*; Ibn ʿArnūs, *Tārīkh al-qaḍāʾ*; Zaghlūl, *al-Muḥāmāh*.

Islamic Legal Revival: Reception of European Law and Transformations in Islamic Legal Thought in Egypt, 1875–1952. First Edition. Leonard Wood.

The Egyptian political elite was empowered to direct policy and make law, and from 1875 into the 1930s most of them maintained an outwardly ambivalent posture in the face of the marginalization of Islamic law. Focused on nationalist politics and urgent political problems, they took for granted Islamic law's reduced jurisdiction as a consequence of colonization and an upshot of modernization. These same elites were also the ones who stood to lose the most from resisting European pressures on the Egyptian legal system. The Europeans held sufficient power to impose their will on the Egyptian political class. For an Egyptian, opposing this will meant risking disempowering oneself. A famous proponent of Islamic law, Muḥammad Qadrī Pasha (d. 1886), may have lost his position as Minister of Justice in 1883 for this very reason. For the native political elite, practicality, power politics, and capitulation to superior European power became orders of the day. Aversion to disempowerment was likely a particular concern for certain Christians, who from 1882 into the 1940s enjoyed political overrepresentation relative to their population numbers. They held positions in government ministries, led nationalist parties, and wielded power in the National Bar Association. There is scant evidence that empowered Copts in this period, prominent among the elite, took an interest in the revival of Islamic law. The outspoken proponents of Islamic legal revival were Muslim jurists, lawyers, and judges affiliated with the Sharia Courts or the high Islamic educational institutions.

One of the bastions of skepticism toward European law in the late nineteenth century was al-Azhar, the preeminent center of Sunni religious teaching. The faculty of this institution found themselves removed from political power during the years of British occupation. The institutions of Islamic higher education were autonomous enough to expand the discourse of Islamic legal revivalism within intellectual corners, but their power did not extend much beyond this academic capability.

Those with the power to spread ideas—prominent intellectuals—did not consider the marginalization of Sharia among the most pressing problems facing Egypt during the first forty years of colonization. They were alarmed by colonization. They had neither zeroed in on the decline of Sharia as a principal—let alone *the* principal—manifestation of Islamic society's weakness, nor had they yet identified the revival of Islamic law as a tool for restoring Islamic society's greatness and independence. The crystallization of these notions emerged in the 1920s and 1930s in concert with other trends in Egyptian culture that were similarly, and somewhat newly, concerned with Islamic themes and rhetoric.

It took some decades before a significant number of Egyptians could forget the actual history of nineteenth-century Sharia theory and practice and then be convinced by a new conception of nineteenth- and pre-nineteenth-century Egyptian and Muslim legal history, one that held that Egypt had once been a country ruled almost exclusively by laws of Sharia. Yet Egyptians writing in the first decades of the twentieth century also depicted Islamic law as having been stagnant and inflexible in the nineteenth century and in need of substantial revival.[2] They emphasized that the pre-1883 courts of Egypt had been lacking in quality and were in

[2] Cf. Esmeir, *Juridical Humanity*, 30–2.

need of comprehensive reform. Although there was much in Islamic legal theory and practice in the pre-modern centuries that would suggest a flexible and adaptable system in the fields of doctrine and practice, many Egyptians became convinced that Islamic legal thought and practice had long been in stasis, thus making state-made law and legal reform a practical necessity and even something desirable from the standpoint of Islam. Before the 1940s, Egyptians, even the Islamic legal revivalists among them, were not adept at overturning this prevailing conception of a historically immobile legal system. But they were adept at taking the position that the history of legal practice in Muslim societies mattered less than the potential of Islamic law in the present day. They found whatever they could in historical practice of the pre-tenth century and doctrine of the post-seventh century that would open up Islamic law to modernization so that it could address the needs of the present as they understood those needs.

CHAMPIONING THE THEORETICAL IDEAL OF THE ISLAMIC LEGAL ORDER

The story of Islamic legal revivalism concerns, in part, how popular conceptions and moreover expectations of Sharia, *fiqh*, and legal order changed or were adapted to respond to contemporary controversies. During the late nineteenth and early twentieth centuries, Muslim jurists and proponents of Islamic revival spoke constantly and purposefully of Sharia and *fiqh* as a body of "laws" (*ḥukm/aḥkām, sharʿ/sharāʾiʿ, qāʿidah/qawāʿid, qānūn/qawānīn, ḥaqq/ḥuqūq, nāmūs/nawāmīs, tashrīʿ/tashrīʿāt*) that was "complete" (*kāmil*), "comprehensive" (*shāmil*), and "eternally and ubiquitously applicable" (*ṣāliḥ li-kull zamān wa-makān*). They did not use any specific term meaning "superior," but rather they expressed in manifold ways the concept of Sharia's superiority over other laws. Islamic legal revivalists also maintained that a modern legal order should be based exclusively on Sharia.

There are good reasons for being cautious about assuming that "law" (or *droit*), in the sense of positive law, is a reliable translation and equivalent for Sharia.[3] However interesting and important questions are about the differences in legal theory and historical practice between and among the terms Sharia, *ḥuqūq, fiqh, tashrīʿ, sharāʾiʿ, aḥkām*, law, *droit, jurisprudence* (French, i.e., judge-made law), and jurisprudence (English), the fact of the matter is that the Egyptian and European jurists discussed later were either content with viewing Sharia and *fiqh* as a system of positive laws or they were intent on turning Sharia and *fiqh*

[3] On the meaning of "Sharia" and "law," and on problems of translation in general, see Baber Johansen, *Contingency in a Sacred Law: Legal and Ethical Norms in the Muslim* Fiqh (Leiden: Brill, 1999); Hallaq, *Sharīʿa*. For a critique of translating "Sharia" as "Islamic law," see Shalakany, "Islamic Legal Histories," 10. This critique of modern scholars, particulary Western scholars, is essential to a fuller understanding of particular distortions that contemporary scholars make in their accounts of Islamic law. At the same time, the critique could be equally levied against the Arab and Muslim scholars encountered in this book, who themselves made "Sharia" and "Islamic law" their topics of study, while partaking in the same distortions.

into a system of positive laws. This process of transforming Sharia and *fiqh* into positive law, created and managed by the state as opposed to a class of jurists, was part of the championing of a theoretical ideal and the reimagining of the history of Muslim legal practice at this period in time.

The actual legal systems of pre-modern Muslim societies were rarely based exclusively on the primary sources of the Sharia or even the jurisprudence of jurists formally deduced from those sources.[4] However, the actual history of Islamic legal doctrine and legal practice matters less than what Egypt's Islamic legal revivalists viewed it to be. Islamic legal revivalists intervened in what they took to be "tradition" in various ways that will be seen throughout the coming chapters, but two examples follow.

First, Islamic legal revivalists asserted the ideal of a comprehensively Sharia-based legal system as a practical ambition in modern legal reform. In other words, they advocated for all law to be changed until the law was solely and fully based on the primary sources of Sharia or otherwise derived through traditionally recognized modes of legal reasoning as elaborated in Islamic legal theory (*uṣūl al-fiqh*). Their understanding of Muslim history engendered some degree of confidence that a comprehensive revival and application of Islamic law was desirable, necessary, feasible, and with historical precedent.

Second, they imagined that the history of legal practice in Muslim countries had featured a practice centered around Sharia, where Sharia was held up as the first and best source of all law, and where the legal system was commonly identified as a Sharia-enforcing legal system. Some jurists took for granted that this situation obtained in Muslim countries until the advent of modern European colonialism, with a few prominent exceptions such as the Mongol invasions and the Crusades. Other jurists took for granted that pre-colonial centuries had witnessed a persistent intermingling of Sharia and secular law. Those jurists focused their historical imagination on the lifetime of the Prophet Muhammad and the behavior of the earliest Muslim leaders after his death, claiming that those early communities had established binding principles for all time by having based all of their laws on the Sharia. For these jurists, the contemporary period presented an opportunity to break a centuries-long cycle of non-Sharia law interfering in the legal practice of Muslim communities.

Islamic legal revivalism harbored the objective of making Sharia more flexible and thus more adaptable to modern circumstances, while relying on a historical theory that revered the practices of the first Muslim communities, those from during and immediately after the lifetime of the Prophet Muhammad. Certain proponents of Islamic revival imagined that they were doing a service to the project of reviving and modernizing Islamic law by focusing on the examples of those earliest Muslim communities. However, technically minded jurists of the twentieth century who labored to reconstruct the technicalities of Islamic law in its various fields realized that a narrow focus on the earliest Muslim societies was too limiting as a legal method. They ultimately revived a number of juridical theories and

[4] See generally Shalakany, "Islamic Legal Histories."

methods that had been elaborated in the centuries following Muhammad's death, from both before and after the consolidation of the *madhhabs* in the tenth century. Thus, while eschewing what they saw as the dogmatism and conformism (*taqlīd*) of most post-tenth-century jurists, influential revivalist jurists ultimately revived many of the views of the classical jurists, putting Islamic legal theory not so far from where it had been in thirteenth-century Andalusia (in the mind of al-Shāṭibī, at least), thirteenth-century Syria (in the mind of Ibn Taymiyyah, at least), or the high Ottoman Empire of the eighteenth century.

SKEPTICAL RESPONSES

Evidence from the early 1880s of Egyptian elites trying to work Islamic legal rules into the Native Codes is scarce, but it exists. I introduce below two manuscripts from the end of the 1870s that indicate Egyptian caution regarding the adoption of European law for Egyptian courts. Otherwise, official reports from 1882–1884 do not appear to have taken an interest in Islamic law when dealing with matters beyond the confines of the Sharia Courts. The Justice Minister who presided over the opening of the Native Courts in 1884, Ḥusayn Fakhrī, wrote that the question of putting more Islamic law into the Native Codes was entertained briefly, but that Islamic law was not considered ready for application in modern society.[5] Extensive records of the Committee for Legislative Counsel pay relatively minimal regard to Islamic law in hundreds of pages of official minutes.[6] Islamic law was not a central part of mainstream discourse as it appeared in print.

Two of the most famous proponents of Islamic revival operative in Egypt during the 1870s were Jamāl al-Dīn al-Afghānī (d. 1897) and Muḥammad ʿAbduh (d. 1905). Both of these figures were connected to al-Azhar and the anti-European movement. They were exiled from Egypt as the result of anti-government activity: Afghānī in 1879 and ʿAbduh in 1882. In Paris following the British occupation, they founded together a small journal that ran between 1884 and 1886 and was entitled *al-ʿUrwah al-wuthqá* (The Strongest Link). Less a journal than a series of monthly pamphlets, *al-ʿUrwah al-wuthqá* published short, pointed articles assailing European encroachment on Muslim countries.

Al-ʿUrwah al-wuthqá displays an Egyptian brand of Islamic political activism in its early phases. The authors worked to formulate a repertoire of terms and concepts to frame anti-European sentiment in an Islamic discourse. They seem not to have taken many cues from the Algerians who had been developing this repertoire since the 1830s. The main concern was the loss of sovereignty of Muslim nations to European, non-Muslim nations. Contributors argued for a revival of Islamic consciousness as a means to support the independence of Muslim people,

[5] "Mudhakkirāt Ḥusayn Fakhrī bāshā nāẓir al-ḥaqqāniyyah li-majlis al-nuẓẓār," in *al-Kitāb al-dhahabī*, 1: 107–16, at 113.

[6] Majlis al-shūrá li-qawānīn, *Majmūʿat maḥādir jalsāt sanat 1884, 1885, 1886 (24 nūvambir sanat 1883–22 dīsambir sanat 1886* (Miṣr: 1895).

and they made copious references to the Quran to support their arguments and principles.

A modern-day reader who turns to *al-ʿUrwah al-wuthqá* looking for explicit condemnations of European legal incursion into Egyptian and Islamic law is disappointed. Although one finds a generalist Islamic revivalist discourse in the making, the term Sharia was deployed to mean something akin to "the Islamic way of life," not as a synonym for a specific system of law and legislation. The authors' main concerns were power politics, the Islamic faith generally, and the integrity of Islamic society.

Al-ʿUrwah al-wuthqá's silence on the matter of Sharia as a system of specific laws is significant if we are tracing the historical evolution of Islamic legal revivalism. Muḥammad ʿAbduh would be known in later years for having regarded Franco-Egyptian law skeptically.[7] By the 1930s, it was impossible to imagine Islamic political activism without Sharia occupying a central position as a rallying point and a cause. Yet, in these critical years of Egyptian legal transformation during the 1880s, lamentation over the decline of Sharia and the call for its revival and application as a corpus of specific positive laws were not core concepts in writings by Afghānī and ʿAbduh, chief pioneers of anti-European Islamic revivalism.

The lack of specificity displayed by Afghānī and ʿAbduh on the future of Sharia does not mean that the matter was not important for others. There are indications that public figures associated with Islam were skeptical of European incursions against the jurisdiction of Sharia laws and courts. Rashīd Riḍā related the story of a moment in the late 1870s when Khedive Ismail found himself under pressure to apply French law to Egyptians. According to Riḍā, the khedive understood instinctively that such a decision might be unpopular among Egyptians, and so he implored the shaykhs of al-Azhar to write codes of Islamic civil and criminal law, similar to the Ottoman *Mecelle*. According to Riḍā, the shaykhs refused this opportunity for fear of arousing public scorn.[8]

The Ottoman *Mecelle*—a code of Islamic positive law in sixteen books on contracts, delicts, and civil procedure—was the most prominent manifestation of skeptical attitudes to European law present among political elites of the Ottoman and Arab worlds in the 1870s. Composed in Istanbul at the direction of the Ottoman Ministry of Justice, the *Mecelle* was the first official attempt by a state in the Ottoman and Arab world to codify Islamic contract rules comprehensively and apply them in a hierarchical system of courts. It is unimaginable that the khedive was unaware of the pro-Islamic and pro-Ottoman sentiments that led to its drafting in the first place. Not only did the *Mecelle* represent the views of Ottoman political elites whom he knew personally, but it represented the views of the Ottoman Turkish and Arab ulema. Several of the clerics who contributed to the drafting of the *Mecelle* were well-known Syrian Arabs, including the son of the most renowned nineteenth-century Syrian jurist, Ibn ʿĀbidīn (d. 1836).

The question arises as to why the khedive did not adopt the *Mecelle* in Egypt if he was keen to avoid applying French law to Egyptians in the form of the Native Codes.

[7] See Chapter 3. [8] *Al-Manār* 2 (1899): 120.

Here the answer is multipronged but straightforward given the logics of Egyptian, Ottoman, and European imperial politics in the 1870s. Although the khedive was, legally speaking, a governor of a province of the Ottoman Empire, his family had long been in the business of expanding Egyptian autonomy against Ottoman authority wherever and whenever possible. This khedive also displayed during his reign only a limited interest in Islamic tradition. He was formally the caretaker of al-Azhar, the chief trustee of pious endowments, and the delegate of the Ottoman caliphate in Egypt. However, as a ruler who made policies that impacted the cultural landscape of Egypt, he was known above all else for his efforts to Europeanize the society and its institutions.[9] British and French agents in Cairo who controlled the khedive's policies between 1875 and 1882 in the most important affairs of state had little interest in seeing Egypt move more firmly into the domain of Ottoman law. Finally, a problem with the *Mecelle* from an Egyptian standpoint was that its structure and rules did not correspond to the Mixed civil, commercial, and civil procedural codes. By 1878, the Mixed Courts were already the most prestigious courts in Egypt, and Egyptian leaders envisioned that the Native system would eventually subsume the Mixed system. There needed to be as much correspondence between Mixed and Native laws as possible so as to facilitate legal uniformity and an eventual fusion of systems. The *Mecelle* was too different from the Mixed Code both in substance and organizational form to support this agenda.

It is conceivable that Khedive Ismail was not as eager to reject European law codes or to create modern Islamic law codes as he was to find a way to legitimately claim that French law and Islamic law were approximately the same—with the exception of a handful of sticking points that could be left for negotiation. As a ruler who had ruled since 1863, as one who knew the pre-1875 Egyptian legal system, and as one who was cognizant of broad Ottoman conceptions about the rule of law, it is likely that the khedive was tolerant of the notion that French law and imperial law could be imported and adopted and then be declared, retroactively, Islamic or at least as conforming to Islam.

Finding no one in al-Azhar who would or could help him draft a code of Islamic positive laws as he wanted to see it, Ismail commissioned Shaykh Makhlūf al-Minyāwī (d. 1878), a Sharia Court judge in Minya, to write a book comparing the French *Code civil* to Islamic law.[10] The resulting work, *al-Muqāranāt al-tashrīʿiyyah* (Legislative Comparisons), which compared the civil code to Maliki law, was Egypt's first known academic study of the *Code civil* and its first scholarly comparison of the *Code civil* to Islamic law. The book's purpose was either to create the basis for writing a code of Islamic civil law or to justify the adoption of French civil laws on the argument that the two systems were approximately the same.

One of the better known law books to appear in Egypt was Muḥammad Qadrī Pasha's *Murshid al-ḥayrān* (Guide for the Perplexed), composed in the late 1870s and early 1880s, and finally published in 1890. The book was an early attempt—and

[9] Panayiotis Vatikiotis (*History of Egypt*, 124–66) described him as "the impatient Europeanizer."

[10] Makhlūf ibn Muḥammad al-Badawī al-Minyāwī, *al-Muqāranāt al-tashrīʿiyyah: Taṭbīq al-qānūn al-madanī wa-l-jināʾī ʿalá madhhab al-imām Mālik*, ed. Muḥammad Aḥmad Sirāj and ʿAlī Jumʿah Muḥammad, 2 vols. (Cairo: Dār al-Salām, 1999), 1: 1–13.

a purely Egyptian attempt—to codify Hanafi rules of contract and property. It was one of three unofficial codes that Qadrī Pasha wrote, as he also wrote a book of *waqf* law and one on personal status law. Since he left behind no comments about the process of writing *Murshid al-ḥayrān*, historians can only speculate on its purpose. Since Qadrī sat on the drafting committees for both the Mixed and Native Codes, it seems likely that he wrote the book with the idea that its rules would become part of the new Native Code.[11]

Muḥammad Qadrī was forced out of his position as Minister of Justice in 1883. He had been the Minister of Justice twice: first, during the writing of the Native Codes, and second, in 1883, when the government promulgated the organic law of the Native Courts. Archival reports suggest that his leaving the office in 1883 was connected to his disappointment with the content of the Native Codes and the occupation.[12] The government did not publish *Murshid al-ḥayrān* until 1890, eight years after the promulgation of the Native Codes. The reasons for this delay will perhaps never be known. What is certain, however, is that the Egyptian government did not rush to publish this work, even though it was the most coherent expression of Islamic legal revivalism composed in the 1880s.

INCIPIENT REVIVALISM IN THE PRESS AND LAW SCHOOLS

Islamic legal revivalism became more pronounced after 1882 as Egypt settled into the British occupation. The first years of this occupation saw tumult and opposition, but war receded and occupation became a fact of life. Journals and newspapers appeared in greater numbers, institutions functioned more regularly, and the Egyptian government adopted regular patterns of operation. Egyptians understood that the British would not leave voluntarily in the immediate future. Nationalists became famous, including Muṣṭafá Kāmil, Shaykh ʿAlī Yūsuf, and Shaykh ʿAbd al-ʿAzīz Jāwīsh. By the 1890s, social dividing lines among Egyptians became clearer than they had been during the uprisings and oppression of the early 1880s. Egyptians knew who represented the collaborating elites, the partially collaborating elites, and ardent opponents of the colonial order.

[11] Insofar as *Murshid al-ḥayrān* was a "code" of contract law, it was similar to the Ottoman *Mecelle* in the single sense that it contained tersely stated, codified rules from the Hanafi tradition. Beyond this, it differed from the *Mecelle* in important respects; its chapters and articles, for example, were modeled on the format of the Egyptian Mixed codes.

[12] "The nature of the mission must not, however, be judged by the character of the chief plenipotentiaries, nor by the official instructions of which they are the bearers....The soul of it, I have reason to believe, is Kadri Bey, an imperial chamberlain and an Arab by birth, who has played a considerable part in all the Pan-Islamitic intrigues which [Sultan] Abdul Hamid's genius so clearly loves to weave. He indeed only accompanies the special mission in the humbler part of interpreter, but there is little doubt that to the Palace confidant is committed the delicate task of vindicating at Cairo the supreme authority of the Khalifate." Letter from Constantinople, Oct. 7, *Pall Mall Gazette*, October 12, 1881, as cited in Karl von Malortie, *Egypt: Native Rulers and Foreign Interference*, 2nd ed. (London: W. Ridgway, 1883), 190. See also Byron Cannon, "Social Tensions," 303; Cannon, *Politics of Law and the Courts*, 129–30, 303 n. 38; At the British National Archives, see F.O. 605, 236–7 (1875), F.O. 328 (1880), F.O. 238 (1880), F.O. 240 (1882), and F.O. 245–6 (1889).

The years between 1882 and the 1890s afforded Egyptians time to process the long-term consequences of reform policies set in motion in the early 1880s. They had now witnessed the deepening impact of Europeanization in Egyptian culture. Few explicit statements were printed before 1898 to the effect that Islamic law should supplant Egypt's Franco-Egyptian laws. However, it was common for Egyptians to lament publicly that Islamic traditions and institutions were under attack by the British. In 1889, public debate fixated on the future of Islamic law in the curriculum of the Khedivial Law School. The Khedivial Law School was established in the 1860s to train lawyers for the Ottoman-based Nizami courts and then, after 1875, the Mixed Courts. The school was not an Islamic institution, but a tertiary educational institution established on European models and intending to serve the secular-oriented courts. When the Native Courts were established in 1883–1884, it took five years for the Khedivial Law School to adjust its curriculum to prepare students for work in those courts as advocates, judges, and clerks. The faculty and administration of the law school were dominated by European teachers, the curricular focus was on the Franco-Egyptian codes, and all classes were taught in French except those dealing with the laws of the Sharia Courts. Courses in Sharia law were taught in Arabic by faculty from al-Azhar and the higher educational institution Dār al-ʿUlūm, founded in 1871.

In 1889, the founder and dean of the Khedivial Law School, Victor Vidal, died. A controversy erupted over who would succeed Vidal as dean. Egyptians nominated an Egyptian candidate. Lord Cromer, the British Controller-General, backed a Frenchman, Charles Testoud. Cromer's decision precipitated an outcry in Egyptian newspapers over European domination in Egypt's most prestigious faculty. The newspaper *al-Adab* criticized the fact that secular-oriented law (*sharīʿah qānūniyyah*) was becoming dominant in the country. It criticized the fact that an education in Franco-Egyptian law was the primary road leading to work in the law profession. The paper charged that the legal system was being overtaken by French language and law, and that Egyptian lawyers were losing contact with their own legal heritage. The paper observed that Egyptians were increasingly less competent to practice in the Sharia Courts, and lamented that Egyptians now thought about Islamic law as relevant only to personal status matters. The article argued that Islamic law could be introduced into Egypt's civil law.[13] The authors then exhorted the Khedivial Law School to enhance its program in Islamic law.

In 1891, a discussion again appeared in the newspapers about the notions of "Egyptianizing" the Khedivial Law School and increasing education in Islamic law. Prime Minister Muṣṭafá Fahmī had adopted the concept of "Egyptianization" as a pillar of his cabinet's policy.[14] A supporter of this campaign, the outspoken Islamic-oriented nationalist, Shaykh ʿAlī Yūsuf, complained in the newspaper *al-Muʾayyad* about the lack of Islamic law at the law school, writing, "The law

[13] *Al-Adab*, March 30, 1889, as cited in Cannon, "Social Tensions," 314 n. 27.

[14] Cannon, "Social Tensions," 309.

school needs a . . . program of Islamic law in each of its sections. No one can deny the connections between civil law and the mores of the country . . . which are based on Quranic law."[15]

The pressure successfully prompted changes at the Khedivial Law School, which reformed its curriculum in 1892 to afford the Sharia courses the most number of classroom hours in comparison to other courses at the school. Muḥammad Qadrī Pasha's codification of Hanafi contract law, which ʿAlī Mubārak, the Egyptian education minister, had arranged to have published in 1890, became a textbook.[16] The Sharia courses were the only courses at the school in which students studied laws that were not applied, but which might possibly be applied as alternatives to Franco-Egyptian civil law at some time in the future.

Three reform efforts of the Justice Ministry during the 1890s aroused consternation among Sharia law professionals. The British Judicial Adviser, John Scott, spent much of the decade trying to reform the organization and procedure of Sharia Courts along the lines of Native Courts and Franco-Egyptian procedures. His first measure was to propose new rules of civil procedure based on the French rules. Despite opposition from Sharia professionals, this reform was passed in 1897 as the procedural law of the Sharia Courts. The second measure was to allow graduates of the Khedivial Law School to work as lawyers in the Sharia Courts. Until this time, only graduates of al-Azhar and Dār al-ʿUlūm became Sharia law professionals. Despite opposition from al-Azhar, this reform passed in 1898.[17] Finally, in the most famous of these conflicts, John Scott attempted to place two Native Court judges on the High Sharia Appeals Court.[18] In response to this, pro-Islamic intellectuals and al-Azhar faculty organized a press campaign and hostile protests.[19] As Grand Mufti of Egypt, Muḥammad ʿAbduh issued a fatwa

[15] Ibid., 309.

[16] Muḥammad Qadrī, *Kitāb Murshid al-ḥayrān ilá maʿrifat aḥwāl al-insān fī l-muʿāmalāt al-sharʿiyyah ʿalá madhhab al-imām al-aʿẓam Abī Ḥanīfah al-Nuʿmān mulāʾimān li-ʿurf al-diyār al-miṣriyyah wa-sāʾir al-aqṭār al-islāmiyyah* (Bulaq: al-Maṭbaʿah al-Kubrá al-Amīriyyah, 1890).

[17] *Recueil des documents officiels du gouvernement égyptien* (Cairo: Imprimerie Nationale, 1899), 167–70.

[18] This measure would have constituted an advancement on a controversial policy of 1891 that appointed two judges of the Native Court of Appeals to be inspectors in the Sharia Courts.

[19] See Maḥmūd [Ibn] ʿArnūs, "Tārīkh al-qaḍāʾ wa-l-quḍāh fī l-islām: Ṣaḥīfah maṭwiyyah min tārīkh al-qaḍāʾ bi-Miṣr (Part 3)," *al-Muḥāmāh al-sharʿiyyah* 1,10 (1930): 869–71; ʿAbd Allāh Ḥusayn, "Taghyīr lāʾiḥat al-maḥākim al-sharʿiyyah sanat 1899," *al-Muḥāmāh al-sharʿiyyah* 2,4 (1931): 306–9. Riḍā reports that Muḥammad ʿAbduh told him: "The person who wrote that was not a Muslim. . . . [His] aim is to make the Muslims increasingly accustomed to rule by those who wear the tarboush, even in Sharia law matters, until it comes to a point where there is nothing left in the Egyptian government of religious characteristics." Muḥammad Rashīd Riḍā, "Musāwāt al-marʾah bi-l-rajul: al-Ḥukm fī l-bilād al-islāmiyyah, ʿalāqat al-maḥākim al-sharʿiyyah wa-l-ahliyyah bi-l-sharīʿah al-islāmiyyah," *al-Muḥāmāh al-sharʿiyyah* 1,7 (1929): 574–8, at 575. Evidence suggests that ʿAbduh's understanding of the situation was accurate. In 1896, Cromer expressed to Lord Salisbury his view that the Sharia Courts should eventually be folded into the Native Courts: "There is only one effective remedy for this state of things. It is to abolish the Mehkeme Sheraieh as a separate institution altogether, and to transfer their jurisdiction to the ordinary Civil Courts. This is what was done many years ago in India, and I do not altogether despair of seeing a similar change eventually made in Egypt." Cromer to Salisbury, Nov. 8, 1896, F.O. 371/14620 no. 30, as cited in Nathan J. Brown, "Shariʿa and State in the Modern Muslim Middle East," *International Journal of Middle East Studies* 29,3 (1997): 367–8.

declaring the reform contrary to Islam.[20] Subsequent to the fatwa, the Committee for Legislative Counsel rejected the proposal. The input of the Counsel created an impasse and the Justice Ministry retreated.

Challenging though it may be to locate written evidence of Islamic legal revivalist sentiment from the late 1880s and early 1890s, it appears that Lord Cromer was aware of this sentiment. In 1892 he commented in a report to the Foreign Office (in characteristically pejorative terms) that, "A system under which the Mahommedan clings to the primitive simplicity of the law and customs of Islam has, somehow or other, to find a modus vivendi side by side with the Napoleonic Code, with the privileges conferred on Europeans by the Capitulations, with a legislative system... and with a financial administration which must look at one time to the requirements of the Stock Exchange and to sound fiscal principle, and at another to the wants of a backward agricultural population."[21]

From the 1890s into the 1920s, there were at least three basic approaches to evaluating the Egyptian legal system with regard to the state of Islamic law. The first approach involved supporting the legal system as it was, developing it, and ignoring Sharia as a topic except where the applied Sharia laws of the Sharia Courts were concerned. If one collects the bulk of material printed on Egyptian law and reads through the archives and personal papers of those who worked full-time on the legal system, one is left with the impression that the marginalization of Sharia was a non-issue for almost everyone involved at a high level in the Mixed and Native systems. Both the second and third approaches involved viewing the legal system skeptically for sidelining the Sharia. The second approach made remarks in cautious, limited, implicit, or otherwise veiled terms, while the third approach opposed the legal system explicitly, publicly, and forcefully. Rashīd Riḍā is an exemplar of the third approach.

RASHĪD RIḌĀʾS CONTRIBUTION TO ISLAMIC LEGAL REVIVALISM AS IDEOLOGY

Among the first outspoken proponents of Islamic legal revivalism in Egypt was Rashīd Riḍā, a Syrian cleric who spent his professional life in Cairo and played a prominent role in general Islamic intellectual culture in Egypt. A salafist, a forerunner of the Muslim Brotherhood, and an eventual champion of the Wahhabi movement in Arabia, he advocated early in his career the revival of Muslim society through the revival of Islamic institutions and piety. Although a member of the clerical class and associated with graduates of al-Azhar, he used his writings to distance himself from Egypt's ulema and to accuse them of blind conformism.

[20] His rationale was that only the Ottoman sultan held the power to appoint judges to the Sharia Courts, and this through his delegate, the khedive of Egypt; moreover, the mufti claimed that any judge appointed to the Sharia bench needed to be sufficiently schooled in Hanafi law and Sharia procedure. Rashīd Riḍā, "al-Taʿlīm al-qaḍāʾī," *al-Manār* 2 (1899): 117–21. Following the 1898 controversy, Lord Cromer removed the uncooperative mufti and replaced him with ʿAbduh, considering ʿAbduh to be more amenable to British legal policy.

[21] F.O. Conf., "State of Affiars (Cromer)," No. 6248 (1892), 13–16.

Before Riḍā launched his influential journal, *al-Manār* (The Beacon), public pronouncements in support of Islamic law mostly appeared as ad hoc responses to controversial government policies that impinged on the autonomy of the Sharia Courts, the power of al-Azhar, or the place of Egyptians and Arabic within school curriculums. The concept of Islamic legal revival as a means to supplant Franco-Egyptian law had not reached the level, before 1899, of a well-defined theory or concept.

Riḍā was among the first writers in Egypt to expound consistently on the non-desirability of European law and the necessity of reforming, reviving, and reapplying Islamic law in Egypt. Whereas some students of Muḥammad ʿAbduh honored his legacy by tending toward more liberal, modernist, and secular-leaning approaches to Islam, Riḍā honored his legacy by developing ʿAbduh's salafist tendencies, his emphasis on the Quran and Sunnah as the bases for modern religious and political revival, his moral conservatism, and his belief in the unity of religion and state in Islam.

Riḍā's *al-Manār* helped Islamic legal revivalism to crystallize into a theory, an agenda, and a repertoire of attitudes, concepts, and ambitions. He founded the journal in 1898 for the purpose of spreading religious knowledge, news, and consciousness. Published until 1935, it became a mouthpiece of Islamic political sentiment, which Riḍā generated and compiled extensively. Each annual volume ran to at least three hundred pages and was sold around the world. It was autonomous from al-Azhar and evidently managed to avoid government control.

In the first volume of *al-Manār*, it was clear that Riḍā had little liking for Franco-Egyptian law. One article entitled "The Caliphate and Caliphs" criticized modern positive law. He lamented to readers that their rulers had "substituted your divine law for positive laws."[22] He was not opposed to positive law as such (that is, *qānūn*), but he insisted that it be compliant with and guided by Sharia. In another article, he criticized colonizers for having put themselves "above both Sharia and *qānūn*."[23] Overall, his attitudes corresponded with traditional Ottoman attitudes about the place of non-Islamic law in the legal order of a Muslim society.

In the second volume, Riḍā escalated his commitment to the revival, reform, and theoretical supremacy of Sharia. Rather than focusing his discussions on the necessity of protecting Islam in general, he focused on the protection and advancement of Sharia as one of the principal means for protecting Islam, the integrity of the faith, and the independence of Muslim societies. In an article entitled "Religious Reform," he insisted that Sharia be the guide to religious and political reformers alike.[24] He assailed the ulema for traditionalism in *fiqh*, identifying this traditionalism as one of their greatest foibles. He argued that traditional loyalty to a single *madhhab* had constrained the scope of law, and criticized the *Mecelle* for having drawn only from the *fiqh* of the Hanafi *madhhab*.

22 Riḍā, "Rabbanā innā aṭaʾnā sādatanā wa-kubarāʾanā fa-aḍallūnā al-sabīlā," *al-Manār* 1 (1898): 606.

23 Rashīd Riḍā, "Iqtirāḥ al-qayṣar," *al-Manār* 1 (1898): 484–95.

24 Rashīd Riḍā, "al-Iṣlāḥ al-dīnī: al-Muqtaraḥ ʿalá maqām al-khilāfah al-islāmiyyah," *al-Manār* 1 (1898): 764–71.

Riḍā may have been the first writer in Egypt to write a negative historical account of the post-occupation legal transformation. He portrayed the adoption of Franco-Egyptian codes as a retrogressive, impious, and unnatural change. Previously, Egyptian historical accounts had treated the new codes and courts as monuments of modernization and progress. Aḥmad Fatḥī Zaghlūl wrote one such account in a 1900 treatise on Egyptian and Arab legal history.[25] But, building on ʿAbduh's description, in 1881, of Egypt's legal past as a disorganized system that haphazardly applied laws from different sources,[26] Riḍā argued that Egyptians and Turks had adopted European laws only because their ulema were ignorant of the requirements of the times and unwilling to develop *fiqh* accordingly. He lamented the decline of Sharia in the Ottoman Empire. A supporter of the Islamic caliphate, Riḍā claimed that the Ottoman Empire's core point of unity—since it was comprised of many linguistic and ethnic groups—was its basis in the Sharia.[27] Moreover, Sharia was the central tool for promoting unity in the Islamic community (*ummah*). Through Sharia, he claimed, Islam gives mankind a "single Islamic (positive) law" (*qānūn sharʿī wāḥid*).[28]

Riḍā's championing of the Sharia was based on no particular hierarchy of principles or concepts; all arguments were equal units in a constellation of interlocking ideas that collectively supported a conception of Sharia's supremacy, relevance, vitality, and applicability. Riḍā rejected the notion of a separation between religion and state in Muslim societies, calling this concept a Christian innovation.[29] In another article, he claimed that Christians were spreading the notion that Islam distinguishes between religion and state as part of a conspiracy to weaken Islam and the Egyptian people.[30] On another topic, he argued that it was right to apply Sharia to Christians and other non-Muslim minorities, since this had been done successfully for centuries. He took direct, polemic aim at the Mixed Courts, insisting that Muslims should be the ones to adjudicate cases involving foreigners in their midst, and that Muslims ought to do so according to Sharia. He argued that although Islam forbids compulsion in religion and allows for "freedom of religion," Muslims must still judge foreigners by Sharia.[31] He condemned Muslim nations that did not follow Sharia, noting, "The Muslim only follows man-made law with repudiation and under pressure of force."[32] Still elsewhere, he claimed that "a fundamental rule of life in the *ummah*" is that no one should obey any law that contravenes the Sharia.[33] Among *al-Manār*'s main

[25] Zaghlūl, *al-Muḥāmāh*, 1.

[26] Muḥammad ʿAbduh, "Ikhtilāf al-qawānīn bi-ikhtilāf al-umam," *al-Waqāʾiʿ al-miṣriyyah* (June 19, 1881). Reprinted in Muḥammad ʿAbduh, *Aʿmāl al-kāmilah li-l-imām Muḥammad ʿAbduh*, ed. Muḥammad ʿImārah (Cairo: Dār al-Shurūq, 2001), 1: 337–42.

[27] Rashīd Riḍā, "Muwāfaqah wa-intiqād," *al-Manār* 1 (1899): 841–3.

[28] Riḍā, "al-Iṣlāḥ al-dīnī," 764–71.

[29] Riḍā, "al-Dīn wa-l-dawlah aw al-khilāfah wa-l-salṭānah," *al-Manār* 2 (1899): 353–60.

[30] Riḍā, "Taḥrīf al-kalim ʿan mawāḍiʿih," *al-Manār* 2 (1899): 385–91.

[31] Riḍā, "Muwāfaqah wa-intiqād."

[32] Riḍā, "al-Iṣlāḥ al-dīnī," 764–71. See also Rashīd Riḍā, "Khiṭāb waʿẓī li-l-insān," *al-Manār* 2 (1899): 1–2.

[33] Rafīq Bey al-ʿAẓm, "al-Iṣlāḥ al-islāmī bi-ʿadl al-qiwām aw al-takāful al-ʿāmm," *al-Manār* 2 (1899): 71–8.

interests, he wrote, was to discuss the problems that flow from having states that are not based on Islamic law but on other laws.[34]

The second volume of *al-Manār* thus took important steps to develop Islamic legal revivalist ideology. This conception sprang from Riḍā's tendency to imagine the history of legal practice in Muslim societies as having been centered on Sharia. The conception also sprang from his enthusiasm for Sharia and a notion that the application of Sharia was paramount in defining the identity of Muslim society and in distinguishing it from Western society.

To support his arguments, Riḍā cited the passages in the Quran that most clearly, and overtly, suggest the necessity of applying Sharia in Muslim lands. The clearest of these passages, and those Riḍā cited most frequently, are found in *al-Mā'idah*, verses 44–49,[35] which warn that "If any fail to judge by what God has revealed, they are unbelievers." Riḍā cited these passages in various articles and elaborated on them in *Tafsīr al-manār*, the multi-volume Quranic commentary he wrote in collaboration with ʿAbduh.[36]

Riḍā used the pages of *al-Manār* to compensate for ʿAbduh's outwardly moderate position on the existence of foreign law in Egypt[37] as, for example, in an article by ʿAbduh that Riḍā published entitled "Power and Law," in which ʿAbduh wrote that "law" exists to serve justice for the people, promote equality, and combat authoritarianism.[38] He used the words Sharia and *qānūn* interchangeably to mean "law," and he insisted that Muslims should respect *qānūn* and Sharia equally.[39] At the end, Riḍā averred that ʿAbduh had been too general: he was not clear when he was speaking of man-made positive law (*sharīʿah waḍʿiyyah*) and when he was speaking of divine law (*sharīʿah samāwiyyah*); ʿAbduh had conflated man-made legal philosophy with the religious law that Muslims follow. Riḍā ultimately claimed that ʿAbduh's mistakes should not lead readers to misunderstand ʿAbduh's true position on man-made law, which was, in essence, that ʿAbduh did not support man-made law. "As for the existence of rule by man-made positive law," Riḍā concluded, and speaking on behalf of ʿAbduh, "it is not pleasing to God."[40]

The distinction made by Riḍā between "God-made law" and "man-made law" proved to be one of the most important distinctions in twentieth-century Egyptian

[34] Riḍā, "Taḥrīf al-kalim ʿan mawāḍiʿih," 385–91.

[35] Elsewhere Riḍā references other Quranic verses to support his positions. For example, *al-Aḥzāb* (33):67: "They would say: ʿOur Lord! We obeyed our chiefs and our great ones, and they misled us as to the (right) Path'." *Al-Tawbah* (9):32: "Fain would they extinguish God's light with their mouths, but God will not allow but that His light should be perfected, even though the Unbelievers may detest (it)." *Al-Ṭāhā* (20):48–50: [48] "Verily it has been revealed to us that the Penalty (awaits) those who reject and turn away. [49] (When this message was delivered), (Pharaoh) said: ʿWho, then, O Moses, is the Lord of you two?' [50] He said: ʿOur Lord is He Who gave to each (created) thing its form and nature, and further, gave (it) guidance'." *Yūnūs* (10):101: "Say: ʿBehold all that is in the heavens and on earth'; but neither Signs nor Warners profit those who believe not." Translation based on Yusuf Ali.

[36] Although his commentary on the verses above did not assail the current Egyptian legal order in the most direct fashion imaginable, it strongly implied that there was something amiss about the Egyptian legal order. Rashīd Riḍā, *Tafsīr al-manār* (Cairo: Dār al-Manār, 1948–56), 6: 399–416; 7: 577.

[37] After ʿAbduh's death, Riḍā worked to define ʿAbduh's legacy by writing his biography (*Tārīkh al-ustādh*), which appeared first as numbers in *al-Manār*. In this text, Riḍā selectively emphasized those ideas of ʿAbduh that corresponded most closely to his own.

[38] Muḥammad ʿAbduh, "al-Quwwah wa-l-qānūn," *al-Manār* 1 (1899): 917–23.

[39] Riḍā had suggested as much himself in the first volume.

[40] ʿAbduh, "al-Quwwah wa-l-qānūn," 923.

legal discourse. There was nothing new about this distinction in view of Islamic legal doctrine across the pre-modern centuries. What was relatively new, as of 1899, is that this distinction was being articulated publicly and forcefully, and being used to critique the state of the contemporary Egyptian legal order.

Riḍā's comments on the necessity of reviving, reforming, and reapplying Islamic law were not merely theoretical. He addressed real-world events. In an article titled "Sharia in the Sudan," he explained that Sudanese leaders asked Lord Cromer to ensure that the Sharia would be the law of the land under British occupation. Cromer promised to make it so, but then appointed English judges in their courts. Riḍā commented by asking sarcastically, "Since when do they know the Sharia? When did Kitchener become the caliph?"[41]

Riḍā also examined the issue of judicial education for Sharia judges, a popular topic in 1899.[42] He discussed competing methods for training Sharia judges and drew a distinction between "education through practice" and "education through book learning." He stressed the importance of Sharia Court judges knowing the texts of classical writers. From this unsurprising argument, he arrived at a more interesting question: why would judges need to study laws and texts that are no longer applied in Egypt's courts—not even in the Sharia Courts?

> You might ask: what is the use of studying laws that we don't actually use, now that the leaders of the Muslims have wiped them out with positive laws? The answer is that the absence of book education caused the divine and wide-ranging Sharia to become too narrow, until it could not serve the needs of our time. The princes and the rulers found themselves forced to go along with the exigencies of the times....
>
> We could improve our education and have in this *ummah* ulema who understand the nature of the present age. They could extrapolate rules from the general principles of Sharia (*qawāʿid al-sharīʿah al-ʿāmmah*) for which the Sharia is famously known. The Sharia is known for being applicable to situations in all times and places, according to the welfare (*maṣlaḥah*) of people in their own time. If we had done this already, there is no doubt that the Muslim princes and rulers would have been able to apply laws built on their own religion....this, had their command not been usurped by foreign powers.
>
> By saying this, I do not exculpate the princes from the responsibility of straying from the Sharia (*inḥirāf al-sharīʿah*[43]), or the ulema from the consequences of limiting its relevance. No! And twice over, no![44]

[41] Rashīd Riḍā, "al-Ḥukm bi-l-sharīʿah fī l-Sūdān," *al-Manār* 1 (1899): 759–60. On the issue of application of Sharia in Sudan, Muḥammad Harūn was an Egyptian judge who went to Sudan and asserted the supremacy of Islamic law. He wanted to apply and teach only Islamic law. Cromer rebuffed the attempt and sent a new chief judge to replace him. Horatio Herbert Kitchener, 1st Earl Kitchener (1850–1916), was a senior British army officer who became Governor-General of the Sudan in 1898. See Gabriel Warburg, *The Sudan under Wingate: Administration in the Anglo-Egyptian Sudan, 1899–1916* (London: Cass, 1971), 131; Warburg, *Islam, Sectarianism, and Politics in Sudan since the Mahdiyya* (London: Hurst and Co., 2003), 66.

[42] See Chapter 8 on the origins of the Sharia College and the judicial section at Dār al-ʿUlūm.

[43] *Inḥirāf* was a common term in *al-Manār* to refer to "straying" from the Sharia and the right path (*al-ṭarīq al-mustaqīm*).

[44] Riḍā, "al-Taʿlīm al-qaḍāʾī," 120.

Riḍā completed the article by addressing the importance of improving education in Sharia law and practice at al-Azhar, and by insisting that law students continue to study aspects of Islamic law that were not in fact applied in Egypt but which could hypothetically be applied at some future date. The article was published during a year when al-Azhar was trying, and failing, to prevent graduates of the Khedivial Law School from entering the Sharia law profession.

THE CAUTIOUS APPROACH

As noted, the majority in Egypt were unconcerned with principles of the emergent Islamic legal revivalism. The personal papers and archival records of dozens of European personnel involved in the Egyptian legal system show that they seem to have had no regard for or awareness of a movement or need for Islamic legal revival. Most of the literature addressed issues and problems in the legal system as it was. Egyptians were litigious and used their courts intensively,[45] and even if journalists and writers lampooned the courts for their inefficiency and foreignness,[46] Egyptian lawyers worked to improve the courts far more than they assailed the courts' legitimacy. Nevertheless, the suggestion that the lack of Sharia was a problem did appear in some publications. For those who critiqued the declining place of Sharia in the legal system, the second approach—the cautious and implicit approach—predominated in the 1890s and the first two decades of the 1900s.

In 1902, the Ministry of Justice founded a monthly journal entitled *al-Aḥkām al-sharʿiyyah* (Sharia Decisions). A semi-official case reporter with commentary on noteworthy cases, the journal critically discussed law but did not criticize the legal order as a whole. For example, a series of articles commented on the new Sharia Court procedures that were implemented in the 1890s. The journal regularly discussed conflict of jurisdiction questions between the Sharia Courts and the Mixed and Native Courts. In these cases, the journal sometimes advocated for the right of Sharia Courts to adjudicate the cases in question, or the journal criticized the manner in which the Mixed or Native Court had handled a case. These criticisms, however, were not elevated to a higher level that involved openly criticizing the legal system and the restricted function of Sharia therein.

A variety of European and Egyptian lawyers commented on the state of Sharia in Egypt. In 1897, the Egyptian law professor ʿUmar Bey Luṭfī authored a book on Islamic criminal law that discussed the interest of Egyptians in Islamic legal revival in that field.[47] The book sought to find a way to marginalize traditional

[45] See text accompanying Chapter 1, n. 19; Brown, *Rule of Law*, 46–7.

[46] See, for example, Roger Allen, *A Period of Time*, part 1: *A Study of Muhammad al-Muwaylihi's Hadith ʿIsa Ibn Hisham* (Oxford: Ithica Press, 1992). And later in time, in the 1930s, Tawfīq al-Ḥakīm, *The Maze of Justice: Diary of a Country Prosecutor* (London: Saqi Books, 1989).

[47] Omar Bey Loutfy (ʿUmar Luṭfī), *De l'Action pénale en droit musulman: Rite hanefite* (Paris: Marchal et Billard, 1897).

features of Islamic criminal law, to adopt European approaches, and to find ways of declaring these approaches as comporting with the spirit of Sharia. In 1898, the Ottoman minister Savvas Pacha discussed the common esteem among Muslims for the project of reviving Sharia law in the Ottoman Empire.[48] In 1902, Muḥammad Ḥāfiẓ Ṣabrī produced the first published comparative study in Egypt of Islamic and European law.[49] In 1914, a comparative work was written by Muḥammad Ḥilmī ʿĪsá, an advocate in the Native Courts. Under the title *Sharḥ al-bayʿ fī l-qawānīn al-miṣriyyah wa-l-faransiyyah wa-fī l-sharīʿah al-islāmiyyah* (Commentary on Sales in Egyptian, French, and Islamic Law),[50] it compared laws between the *Code civil*, the Franco-Egyptian civil codes, and the two Hanafi Islamic codes, the *Mecelle* and *Murshid al-ḥayrān*. One of the author's purposes was to show that the Franco-Egyptian civil codes were similar to Hanafi law in many respects. Another purpose was to point out the many places in sales law where the Franco-Egyptian law had departed from the rules of Sharia. In 1914, the lawyer ʿAbd al-Ḥamīd Badawī penned an article for *L'Égypte contemporaine* criticizing the approach of the Egyptian legal system to Sharia and discussing how the mixture of Islamic rules with French rules had created problems in the Sharia Courts and the legal system generally.[51]

In 1911, ʿAbd al-ʿAziz Jāwīsh, editor of *al-Liwāʾ* newspaper, spoke at a public conference about the necessity of Islamic legal revival. He was a leading anti-British activist, a well-known antagonist of the khedive, and he was considered by many a proponent of violence.[52] His paper advocated a reformist style of Islamic legal method that emphasized the flexibility of the Sharia, the equitable doctrine of "welfare" (*maṣlaḥah*), and the Sharia's adaptability to modern exigencies and values.[53] Although Jāwīsh did not state as explicitly as he might have that Egypt's laws should be replaced by Islamic laws, he evidently intended for the article to have this implication. He made a separate speech at the conference implicitly criticizing the overrepresentation of Christians in the Egyptian legal field.

In the 1920s, debate ensued among Egyptian writers over the relationship between Roman and Islamic law, specifically the notion that much of classical Islamic jurisprudence had its origins in Roman law. A handful of scholars in Europe had proposed this idea, especially Ignaz Goldziher, Alfred von Kremer,

[48] Savvas Pacha, *Étude sur la théorie du droit musulman, 2ème partie*, 2 vols. (Paris: Marchal et Billard, 1898). See also comments by Savvas in *Journal des Économistes* (1892): 286–7; George Young, *Corps de droit ottoman* (Oxford: Clarendon, 1906), 6: viii n. 3.

[49] Muḥammad Ḥāfiẓ Ṣabrī, *al-Muqāranāt wa-l-muqābalāt bayna aḥkām al-murāfaʿāt wa-l-muʿāmalāt wa-l-ḥudūd fī sharʿ al-yahūd wa-naẓāʾirihā min al-sharīʿah al-islāmiyyah al-gharāʾ wa-min al-qānūn al-miṣrī wa-l-qawānīn al-waḍʿiyyah al-ukhrá* (Miṣr: Maṭbaʿah Hindiyyah, 1902).

[50] Muḥammad Ḥilmī ʿĪsá, *Sharḥ al-bayʿ fī l-qawānīn al-miṣriyyah wa-l-faransiyyah wa-fī l-sharīʿah al-islāmiyyah* ([Cairo]: Maṭbaʿat al-Maʿārif, 1916).

[51] Abd El-Hamid Bey Badawi (ʿAbd al-Ḥamīd Badawī), "Du Principe qu'en droit musulman: La Succession n'est ouverte qu'après aquittement des dettes," *L'Égypte contemporaine* 5 (1914): 14–51.

[52] Amira El Azhary Sonbol, *The Last Khedive of Egypt: Memoirs of Abbas Hilmi II* (Cairo: American University in Cairo Press, 2006), 13, 41, 36–7, 101. Jāwīsh was implicated in the murder of Prime Minister Buṭrūs Ghālī.

[53] Abd el Aziz Chaouiche (ʿAbd al-ʿAzīz Jāwīsh), "Nécessité d'avoir égard aux circonstances de temps et de lieu dans l'application des préceptes de la chériat," in *Recueil des travaux du premier congrès égyptien réuni à Héliopolis du samedi 30 rabi-ul-sani 1329 (29 avril 1911) au mercredi 5 gamadi-ul-awl 1329*, ed. Congrès égyptien (Alexandrie: Imprimerie d'Alexandrie, 1911).

and Theodore Ion. It was then adopted by European law professors who had direct connections with Egyptian law students, such as Édouard Lambert.[54] Sheldon Amos, a British judge in Egypt and co-author of the first Native Civil Code, also articulated the view in his *History and Principles of the Civil Law of Rome* (1883). In the Egyptian political-legal context, the claim of Roman origins of Islamic law bore a serious implication: to Europeans in Egypt who ascribed to the view, it meant that Egyptians had nothing to fear from adopting European law, because it was the fount of Islamic law.

Egyptian and other Arab writers rejected the Roman origins theory out of hand, and they recognized the consequences of accepting it. Makhlūf Muḥammad (al-Minyāwī) dismissed the theory in his circa 1875 comparison of French and Maliki law and claimed that the converse was true: Islamic law was the fount of European law. In 1924, the young Syrian Fāʾiz Khūrī rejected the Roman origins theory, supporting the Islamic-influence-on-Roman-law thesis and championing the traditional concept of Islamic law's originality and genealogical autonomy.[55] This topic would be picked up again by other Sharia jurists in Egypt during the 1930s.[56]

In the first decades of the 1900s, law professors at the Khedivial Law School used textbooks to champion Islamic law in the face of an increasingly dominant Franco-Egyptian law. In 1908, Shaykhs Muḥammad Zayd al-Abyānī and Muḥammad Salāmah Sanjalfī, professors at the Khedivial Law School, published a commentary on Muḥammad Qadrī's *Murshid al-ḥayrān*.[57] In 1911, Shaykh Muḥammad Khuḍarī called for reformed methods in modern Islamic legal thought.[58] In 1913, Shaykh Aḥmad Abū al-Fatḥ's treatise on Islamic contract and property laws called for reviving interest in Sharia, which had flagged after 1883.[59] He praised Islamic law for its divineness and contrasted this characteristic with man-made law.[60] In 1923, Aḥmad Qamḥah and ʿAbd al-Fattāḥ al-Sayyid introduced their long treatise on Sharia Court procedures with an encomium to the virtues of procedural law in Sharia.[61]

Europeans also recognized that some Egyptians desired a revival and reapplication of Islamic law. In 1882, a Dutch judge in the Mixed Courts contemplated the idea of writing codes of Islamic law to create an Islamic legal system in Egypt

[54] See Chapter 6.

[55] Fāʾiz Khūrī, *Muqābalah bayna l-ḥuqūq al-rūmāniyyah wa-l-ḥuqūq al-islāmiyyah wa-l-faransiyyah wa-l-inkiliziyyah* (Damascus: al-Maṭbaʿah al-Ḥadīthah, 1924).

[56] Aḥmad Amīn, "al-Qānūn al-rūmānī wa-l-fiqh al-islāmī (Part 1)," *al-Muḥāmāh al-sharʿiyyah* 1,1 (1929): 20; ʿĀrif Bey al-Nakadī, "al-Qānūn al-rūmānī wa-l-fiqh al-islāmī (Part 2)," ibid., 1,2 (1929): 72–3; Murād al-Ghāzī, "al-Qānūn al-rūmānī wa-l-fiqh al-islāmī (Part 3)," ibid., 1,3 (1929): 167–70.

[57] Muḥammad Zayd al-Abyānī and Muḥammad Salāmah al-Sanjalfī, *Sharḥ Murshid al-ḥayrān ilá maʿrifat aḥwāl al-insān fī l-muʿāmalāt al-sharʿiyyah ʿalá madhhab al-imām al-aʿẓam Abī Ḥanīfah al-Nuʿmān mulāʾiman li-ʿurf al-diyār al-miṣriyyah wa-sāʾir al-aqṭār al-islāmiyyah* (Miṣr: Maṭbaʿat al-Wāʿiẓ, 1908).

[58] Muḥammad Khuḍarī, *Kitāb Uṣūl al-fiqh* (Miṣr: Maṭbaʿat al-Jamāliyyah Muḥammad Amīn al-Khānjī, 1911), introduction.

[59] Aḥmad Abū al-Fatḥ, *Kitāb al-Muʿāmalāt fī l-sharīʿah al-islāmiyyah wa-l-qawānīn al-miṣriyyah*, 2 vols. (Miṣr: Maṭbaʿat al-Busfūr, 1913).

[60] Ibid., 1: 1–9.

[61] Aḥmad Qamḥah and ʿAbd al-Fattāḥ al-Sayyid, *Sharḥ lāʾiḥat al-ijrāʾāt al-sharʿiyyah wa-l-qawānīn wa-lawāʾiḥ al-murtabiṭah bihā* (Miṣr: Maṭbaʿat al-Nahḍah, 1923), 1–40.

as an alternative to the Franco-Egyptian system;[62] in 1896, the Dutch orientalist Christiaan Snouck Hurgronje showed a similar awareness of such an interest among Muslim clerics in Egypt, the Ottoman Empire, and elsewhere;[63] and in 1900, a British judicial adviser in Egypt, Raymond West, examined the concept of Islamization.[64]

OPEN SKEPTICISM IN THE SHARIA COLLEGE JOURNAL

Sharia revivalist rhetoric escalated in the 1920s with respect to openness, forcefulness, coherence, and regularity. Such elevation partly resulted from political events: Egypt obtained nominal independence in 1923, Saʿd Zaghlūl became Prime Minister in 1924, the Wafd party enjoyed popular support, and many Egyptians believed the closure of the Mixed Courts to be imminent. The disintegration of the Ottoman caliphate opened the door to discussions about new pathways for Islamic public law.

A locus for heightened expression of Islamic legal revivalism was the Sharia College, an institution that existed between 1907 and 1929 and prepared students for professional life in the Sharia Courts. The Sharia College was established at the instigation of Muḥammad ʿAbduh and Saʿd Zaghlūl to promote reform by producing more modern-minded Sharia professionals than those trained at al-Azhar. The college trained students in traditional Islamic subjects and offered light training in more "modern" fields such as history and geography. Students learned classical Islamic sources and theories, with some input from modernist approaches to Islamic jurisprudence.

In the wake of Egypt's quasi-independence, the Sharia College's students and faculty expressed views in their journal, *Majallat al-qaḍāʾ al-sharʿī* (Sharia Law Journal),[65] which ran between 1922 and 1929 and published court decisions, academic articles on both law and the natural and social sciences,[66] and Arabic poetry. The articles tended to advance ideas rather than rigorous research. Contributors were avowed proponents of Egyptian and Islamic revival, or, in the parlance of the times, simply "revival" (*al-nahḍah*). Egyptian intellectuals of the

62 See Pieter van Bemmelen, *L'Égypte et l'Europe* (Leiden: E. J. Brill, 1882).

63 C. Snouck Hurgronje, "Le Droit musulman (Review of Savvas Pacha, *Le Droit musulman expliqué: Réponse à un article de M. Ignace Goldziher* (1893)," *Revue de l'histoire des religions* 37 (1896): 1–22, 174–203, at 190–5. See also C. Snouck Hurgronje, *Verspreide geschriften* (Bonn and Leipzig: K. Schroeder, 1924), 4,2: 259.

64 Raymond West, "Modern Developments of Mohammedan Law: Its Origin and Growth," *Journal of the Society of Comparative Legislation* 2,2 (1900): 271–5.

65 *Majallat al-qaḍāʾ al-sharʿī: Sharʿiyyah, ʿilmiyyah, adabiyyah*, ed. Muḥammad Ibrāhīm Jazīrī (Cairo, 1922–31).

66 Aḥmad Amīn writes in his memoirs that the rector of al-Azhar once tried to prevent him from lecturing to the student body on Darwin, natural selection, and genetics. This did not prevent him from eventually publishing a series of articles about Darwin and genetics in the college's student journal. Ahmad Amin, *My Life: The Autobiography of an Egyptian Scholar, Writer and Cultural Leader*, trans. I. J. Boullata (Leiden: E. J. Brill, 1978), 117.

1920s tended to support secular-oriented aspects of the Egyptian revival, and the journal displayed some deference to that trend. However, this deference had its limits.[67]

Collectively, the Sharia Law Journal comprised the largest concentration of revivalist technical works dedicated to Islamic substantive law that had appeared to date in Egyptian journals. The articles went further than any other collection since Rashīd Riḍa's first volumes of *al-Manār* in fleshing out conceptions and aims of Islamic legal revivalism. Although these were not the most rigorous legal articles conceivable, they advanced the technical discourse of Islamic legal revivalism.

The journal pushed the Islamic conception of the Egyptian *nahḍah* in ways that other journals at the time, especially law journals, did not. Articles on Islamic and Egyptian history emphasized aspects of the Islamic legal past that could be beneficial to the modern Islamic legal reformer. One author wrote about the *ijtihād* (independent reasoning) of the caliph ʿUmar with an eye toward suggesting how such *ijithād* could be performed in the present-day legal order. ʿAbd al-Wahhāb ʿAẓẓām criticized European involvement in "Eastern affairs" and suggested that Egypt adopt laws matching its particular needs and temperament.[68] Aḥmad Amīn wrote about the importance of innovating piously in laws and ethics and not unquestioningly following either Islamic tradition or the ways of the West.[69] The journal also published moderately technical articles about substantive Islamic law.[70] These articles had the intention of serving, or at least contemplating, an Islamic legal revival.

The journal showed interest in dimensions of Islamic law that were not applied in Egypt but which might hypothetically be applied in the modern era. In 1922, ʿAbd al-Wahhāb Khallāf wrote a series of articles on penal law in Sharia.[71] This was an early piece of comparative Islamic-European legal inquiry that assailed Franco-Egyptian law for having sidelined the Quranic penalties (*ḥudūd*, sg. *ḥadd*) and for having usurped from the family of murder victims the right to retribution and bloodwit.[72] Another article examined a sophisticated concept in Islamic public

[67] The journal displayed its enthusiasm for certain secular-oriented dimensions of Egyptian revival by publishing articles on natural and social sciences; for instance, Aḥmad Amīn wrote about Darwin, and others about Socrates, Arabic-language pedagogy, literary criticism, and rhetoric. Much of the literary prose and poetry was non-political. Many articles on Islam were of a traditional nature, praising the literary quality of the Quran, the importance of the Prophet Muhammad's message, or the relative quality of different hadith. The journal showed its commitment to current trends in Egyptian nationalism, for example, by praising Saʿd Zaghlūl at the opening of every volume. This praise could have served a double function. On the one hand, Zaghlūl was the leader of Egypt's most powerful independence party and leaned toward secular-oriented policies and rhetoric. On the other hand, he was a graduate of al-Azhar and the founder of the Sharia College. His possession of Islamic credentials made it easier for the College to revere him as its hero.

[68] ʿAbd al-Wahhāb ʿAẓẓām, "al-Nahḍah," *Majallat al-qaḍāʾ al-sharʿī* 1,2 (1922): 81–6.

[69] Aḥmad Amīn, "Khaṭarāt," *Majallat al-qaḍāʾ al-sharʿī* 1,3 (1922): 139–41.

[70] The journal published many articles on family law, inheritances, and trusts. See, for example, Muḥammad Makhlūf, "al-Zawāj fī l-islām," *Majallat al-qaḍāʾ al-sharʿī*, 1,4 (1922): 149–58.

[71] ʿAbd al-Wahhāb Khallāf, "al-ʿUqūbāt al-sharʿiyyah: Li-man ḥaqq al-ʿiqāb?" *Majallat al-qaḍāʾ al-sharʿī* 1,1 (1922): 12–17; 1,2 (1922): 59–61.

[72] ʿAbd al-Wahhāb Khallāf's reform proposal suggested that in case of murder, the kin of the victim should have the option to demand punishment; in especially serious crimes, such as premeditated murder, the state would be entitled to seek punishment if the victim's kin declined to do so.

law, the state's rights to control property in the caliphate.[73] Still another article on Sharia and international public law touted the Islamic laws of warfare regulating combat and the treatment of captured combatants.[74] The article concluded that European war law fell short because it lacked an underpinning in divine commands.[75]

In the area of legal theory and methodology, the fourth volume presented a series of articles on *siyāsah sharʿiyyah*. This topic—governance and state-sponsored lawmaking in accordance with Sharia—would be of increasing interest to reformist jurists in the 1930s and 1940s. Still other articles lamented the jurisdictional boundaries on the Sharia Courts.[76]

The journal offered rudimentary forays into the field of comparative Islamic-European legal research. The science of Islamic-European comparative law developed mostly in the 1930s and 1940s, when it became a more defined science that involved multilingual research and methodological rigor. The articles in this journal showed relatively weak efforts in comparative law. The authors knew Islamic law. However, they did not demonstrate knowledge of European languages; they did not posit a theory or defined target for their comparative inquiries; and they did not produce much in the way of original comparative research. Their comparative remarks were limited mainly to highlighting salient commonalities and differences between Islamic and European laws. On the other hand, these articles showed an awareness of developments in Islamic legislation in other Arab countries.[77]

The journal offered a few explicit attacks on the Franco-Egyptian legal order. The first volume published a series of articles relating a sermon delivered by Shaykh Muḥammad Sulaymān at Ramadan.[78] The shaykh berated Egyptians for not applying God's law.[79] He quoted the same Quranic verses that Rashīd Riḍā had used to critique the legal order.[80] He attacked Franco-Egyptian criminal law for depriving the relatives of murder victims of the right of retribution (*qiṣāṣ*) and for having placed this power solely in the hands of the public prosecutor. The shaykh discussed each Quranic punishment in classical Islamic penal law and assailed the positive law (*qānūn*) for neglecting these punishments. He criticized Franco-Egyptian law's permissive rules on fornication. He claimed that Sharia penal law was more flexible in its doctrine of discretionary punishments for

73 *Majallat al-qaḍāʾ al-sharʿī* 1.3 (1922).

74 "Al-Sharīʿah al-islāmiyyah wa-l-qānūn al-dawlī," *Majallat al-qaḍāʾ al-sharʿī*, 1,3 (1922): 105–10.

75 In the eyes of the author of this article, the problem posed by European war law is that the combatant is free to do as he pleases where law is silent. By contrast, the author argued, the Muslim combatant faces a comprehensive set of controls because he must consider the consequences of unethical actions in the afterlife.

76 For example, "al-Nafaqāt fī l-maḥākim al-ahliyyah," *Majallat al-qaḍāʾ al-sharʿī* 1,10 (1923): 544.

77 For example, "al-Qānūn nimrat 25 li-sanat 1920" (1,7 [1922]: 356–9), which discussed new Islamic legislation in North Africa, citing the Code Morand, the Code Santillana, and Arthur Giraud's *Principes de colonisation et de législation coloniale*, 4th ed. (Paris: L. Tenin, 1921–3).

78 Muḥammad Sulaymān, "Ḥaqq al-ruʾyah (Part 2)," *Majallat al-qaḍāʾ al-sharʿī* 1,3 (1922): 144.

79 The editors took special care to underline polemic text. See ibid., 9–24, at 21(in the copy consulted, these pages appear out of sequence at the end of vol. 1,3 (1922) in an appendix (*mulḥaq*) after p. 144).

80 For example, *al-Māʾidah* (5):56: "Those in the party of God are they who will be triumphant"; *al-Māʾidah* (5):44: "If any do fail to judge by what God has revealed, they are unbelievers."

those crimes that fall outside the categories of *ḥadd* and *qiṣāṣ*. He criticized weak regulations on loan interest. He called foreigners in Egypt representatives of the "party of Satan." He called European laws wicked and exhorted Egyptians to avoid being a nation of "unbelievers" (*kāfirūn*). Finally, the shaykh contrasted European laws and values with Sharia and its values—while European law represented wickedness, Islamic law represented freedom of religion, freedom of the individual, freedom of opinion, rights jurisprudence, and the values of love, justice, social welfare, and international order. He lamented:

> Is it not a national shame that a court judgment can be issued by an Egyptian, concerning an Egyptian, for an Egyptian, and in an Egyptian court, all in the name of a court that sits in Egypt, and meanwhile the judgment is from a law that is not Egyptian? Let's say nothing of the fact that the law is not even from the continent of Africa. Our Sharia is appropriate for all places and times. It is richer than all laws combined. Our jurists are the best.

This article was among a handful of other articles in the journal that criticized the legal order to the same degree. The first volume reprinted a portion of a book by Shaykh ʿAfīfī ʿImār on the caliphate and political power, which insisted that spiritual and temporal authority must be fused in a Muslim country. Elsewhere, the editors published an announcement asking readers to submit opinions on three questions: "Can the Islamic Sharia be effective as applied law in this country? How so? What are the means for facilitating this process and for accomplishing it by studying and writing about Sharia?"[81]

The single aspect of Islamic revivalist discourse of the 1920s that has been recognized and analyzed by historical literature is the controversy that erupted after the publication of ʿAlī ʿAbd al-Rāziq's *al-Islām wa-uṣūl al-ḥukm* (Islam and the Theory of Government, 1925), an infamous book by an Azharite who argued that Islam demands a separation between religion and state. The shaykh argued that there was no sure basis in Sharia for the existence of a caliph, and so, by extension, he was effectively a proponent of the notion that Islam supports a separation between religion and state. The controversy resulted in the author's being stripped of his Azhar degree.

ʿAlī ʿAbd al-Rāziq's book occupies an important place in the history of Egypt, Islamic revivalism, and Islamic legal revivalism. The question of the caliphate and the debate over Islam and secularism were important in the 1920s. The forceful response of Azharite leaders to the book is evidence of aspirations shared in conservative Muslim quarters for the role of Islam and Islamic law in the state.

There was a discursive relationship between the authors of the articles in the journal of the Sharia College and the writings of Alī ʿAbd al-Rāziq. Discussions about Islamic law during the 1920s were concerned with more than the fundamentals of constitutional law in Muslim societies. Jurists were debating the nature of the Egyptian legal system where many other fields of law were concerned—not just in family law, inheritances, and trusts, and not just in constitutional law,

[81] Editorial comment, *Majallat al-qaḍāʾ al-sharʿī* 1,8 (1923): 366.

but in civil, criminal, procedural, and international law as well. They were also discussing legal theory and method, as displayed in the articles focusing on the doctrine of *siyāsah sharʿiyyah*.

In sum, the sentiments underlying articles of the Sharia Law Journal had been present in clerical quarters since at least the 1890s. There is evidence of similar sentiments in the 1870s. But, before this journal's appearance, public articulations of such sentiments in print were rare. In the Islamic-oriented newspapers such as *al-Liwāʾ* and *al-Risālah*, a few articles discussed the legal order skeptically while pointing out the limited jurisdiction of the Sharia Courts. The Sharia Law Journal was the first law journal to articulate these sentiments pointedly. Yet still, although the journal contained a few articles that expressed explicit hostility to the Egyptian legal system, the majority of revivalist articles opposed the system only implicitly, displaying more guarded skepticism rather than outright opposition. Or, articles criticized specific aspects of Franco-Egyptian law without broadening the critique to issue blanket condemnations of the legal order. It is only in the 1930s that more consistent and outright opposition appeared in law journals.

The comparative Islamic-European articles in the Sharia Law Journal were rudimentary in academic quality. They focused on the most controversial differences between Islamic and European law, and they did not engage deeply with European law and legal theory or go far in fleshing out the details of modern Islamic legal order in the civil, criminal, procedural, and constitutional fields. This kind of work would be left to writers in the 1930s and 1940s. When the Sharia Law Journal ceased operations in 1929, its purposes were adopted and advanced by a new journal of the Sharia Bar Association.

3

The Sharia Bar Association Journal and the Islamic Turn

The secular-oriented nationalism of the 1920s gave way to Islamic and pan-Arab themes; for many, the national cause became an Islamic cause, the national struggle part of a wider Arab struggle.[1] The 1930s witnessed a flourishing of writings by Egyptian lawyers, judges, and academic jurists who advocated the revival of Islamic law and promoted Islamic law as an alternative to Franco-Egyptian law. These ideas now appeared not only in Islamic publications and institutions, or through the writings of clerics and Sharia lawyers, but in publications and institutions that were not identified as Islamic, and through the writings of professionals who had been trained outside of the Sharia's traditional institutions. In 1932, ʿAbd al-Razzāq al-Sanhūrī, professor of civil law at the Cairo Faculty, began outlining plans to revise the Egyptian Civil Code taking inspiration from Sharia.[2]

The most popular Egyptian social science journal, *L'Égypte contemporaine*, which had avoided the topic of Islamic law, published in 1935 an oration by Shaykh Muḥammad Sulaymān advocating a comprehensive revival of Islamic law.[3] With his emphasis on the inherent superiority of Islamic law, his enthusiasm for the Islamic equitable doctrine of welfare (*maṣlaḥah*) and for *siyāsah sharʿiyyah* (state lawmaking within the parameters of the religious law),[4] and his belief that a modern legal system could take inspiration, at the very least, from the general principles of Sharia, the speech echoed ideas of Rashīd Riḍā.

In the world of Islamic institutions during the 1930s, the foremost forum for publicly critiquing the Franco-Egyptian law and advocating the revival of Islamic law was the journal *al-Muḥāmāh al-sharʿiyyah* (The Sharia Lawyers). The Egyptian Sharia Bar Association published the journal's first issue in 1929 and followed it with consecutive volumes, comprising ten issues per year, until 1955.

[1] See generally Gershoni and Jankowski, *Redefining the Egyptian Nation*.

[2] ʿAbdel Razzak al-Sanhoury (ʿAbd al-Razzāq al-Sanhūrī), "Le Droit musulman comme élément de refonte du code civil égyptien," in *Introduction à l'étude du droit comparé: Recueil d'études en l'honneur d'Édouard Lambert* (Paris: LGDJ, 1935), 621–42; ʿAbd al-Razzāq Aḥmad al-Sanhūrī, "Wujūb tanqīḥ al-qānūn al-madanī al-miṣrī," *Majallat al-qānūn wa-l-iqtiṣād* 6,1 (1936): 3–144; al-Sanhūrī, "ʿAlá ayy asās yakūn tanqīḥ al-qānūn al-madanī al-miṣrī," in *al-Kitāb al-dhahabī*, 2: 76–94.

[3] Muḥammad Sulaymān, "Bi-ayy sharʿ nuḥkam?," *L'Égypte contemporaine* 26 (1935): 289–365; Mohamed Soliman (Muḥammad Sulaymān), "Mise en harmonie de la nouvelle législation égyptienne avec le concept de la loi musulmane," *L'Égypte contemporaine* 26 (1935): 367–84.

[4] See text accompanying n. 12.

Islamic Legal Revival: Reception of European Law and Transformations in Islamic Legal Thought in Egypt, 1875–1952. First Edition. Leonard Wood.

Most of the contributors to this journal were professionals in the Sharia Courts or academics affiliated with al-Azhar, Dār al-ʿUlūm, and the formerly extant Sharia College.

The Sharia Lawyers Journal displayed a shift in content and rhetoric from the patterns of the 1920s and the decades before. The editors and contributors made an ideological commitment to Islamic revival generally and to the revival and improvement of Islamic jurisprudence more specifically. The journal openly expressed skepticism toward European law and enthusiasm for the revival of Islamic law in all fields. The editors and contributors promoted expanding the jurisdiction of Islamic law beyond family law and returning the jurisdiction of Sharia to the civil, criminal, and constitutional spheres of Egyptian law. They explored the principles, intellectual methods, and political strategies of hypothetical Islamic legal reform. Importantly, the contributors did not merely advocate the revival, modernization, and expansion of Islamic law at a notional level, but they used published academic research that argued, in substantive and empirical terms, that it was necessary from a religious standpoint, and feasible from a practical standpoint, for Islamic law to supplant Egypt's European-inspired laws.

The contributors in the early years endeavored to use "comparative law" as a tool for creating revived and modern Islamic positive law. They experimented with rudimentary comparative studies. However, they did not make thorough efforts in this regard by the emergent standards of the era. They did not have the same understanding of "comparative law" as their contemporaries affiliated with the Franco-Egyptian spheres of legal education. They were not equipped with the methods, premises, and language tools that would have made their studies rigorous in the view of their contemporaries at the Cairo University Law Faculty. They had not, by the mid-1930s, solved several of the most pressing questions about Islamic legal methodology and substance that concerned them. An examination of the technical content of this journal's academic articles reveals a style of academic writing on Sharia that would be challenged by a more powerful strain of legal thought that came from the Cairo University Law Faculty, and which represented the Franco-Egyptian side of legal education.

REFORM, RESEARCH, AND ENTHUSIASM

The editors stated in their introduction to the first volume that the journal would advocate the revival of Islamic law and serve the everyday needs of Sharia law professionals by publishing decisions, critiques, and academic articles.[5] Each month, the journal published Sharia Court decisions from every level of the system. It commented on decisions in the Native and Mixed Courts where Sharia law had been implicated. It assessed conflict of jurisdiction questions that arose between the Sharia Courts and the Native and Mixed Courts. It published news relevant to the Sharia bar, announced job openings and competitions, distributed

[5] "Iftitāḥiyyat al-majallah wa-bayān khiṭaṭihā," *al-Muḥāmāh al-sharʿiyyah* 1,1 (1929): 3–4.

petitions, and solicited reader input. Contributors discussed issues in legal education, such as al-Azhar's bid to close the Sharia College. The editors were also interested in raising the level of professionalism among lawyers and judges. They printed editorials, poems, and anecdotes that addressed the importance of honesty, fairness, integrity, and independence among law professionals. They related anecdotes about caliphs who had demonstrated qualities of fairness and reason as judges.

Although this journal did not have the same interest in literature and poetry as its predecessor, the Sharia Law Journal, readers sent in poems. Poems often praised the Sharia law profession for its leadership and its resilience against the ever-expanding power and jurisdiction of the Native and Mixed Courts. The following poem sent by Ḥusayn Zahrān, a lawyer in Ismailiyya, reflects the spirit of optimism and measured defiance that characterized the journal in its first years:

For the Journal

So much you endeavored in crafting, of wit and understanding,
    a "journal," that it blotted out shining bands of pearls
It appeared to fellows of the trade with a brimming visage,
    twinkling with hope, and aspirations pure
It shone with a gleaming smile, like the burst of dawn's breaking light
    or like pearls upon the necks of beautiful girls
No effort spared in the full elaboration of meaning and elucidation,
    all radiant, like rows of blossoms in the garden
Fruits hanging down, all the easier for plucking
    for the gatherer seeking new learning and understanding
How excellent a drinking place!
    as if its pages contained the barmaid's spirits,
It struts in mantles of erudition, and with what eloquence!
    So it scoffs at pendants of gemstones and pearls.

For the Profession

Yours is a profession hidden from sight, pushed aside,
    its gleaming face shuttered by curtains of the age
and days' trials, it had pulled down its tent on all sides
    for fear of its debasement.
It was nearly trampled underfoot, beneath the feet of time,
    and was nearly struck down by a hail of arrows and spears
O had it not been for you! For you rescued it from the abyss
    and boldly raised it up, higher than Saturn.

For the Lawyers

You fought for those who saw that there is life
    for a new nation.
As noontime waned, they came forth with banners raised,
    and they appeared like the sun in the heavens,

They achieved the minimum required,
then ascended further to the highest of ranks
They are a people who came in aid of the downtrodden
and spoke truth in the face of treacherous falsehood
How many a one in need, crying out, went to them,
telling of suffering, their tears burning?
So he was put at ease, cured of his weeping
eager to express his gratitude in a thousand different ways
Of their praise you have a pleasant, sweet-scented breeze
and of my praise, bands of pearls.[6]

The editors and contributors engaged with the ideas and vocabulary of general Islamic revivalism, which had intensified since the mid-1920s with the emergence of more pointed Islamic political sentiment and more powerful nationalist organizations. Key ideas typically associated with Islamic revivalist writings from the interwar period included "revival" (*nahḍah*), "reform" (*iṣlāḥ*), and "renewal" (*tajdīd*).[7] The general Islamic revivalists focused their criticisms on what they considered to be excessive traditionalism (*taqlīd*) and stasis (*jumūd*) in Islamic thought. Revivalist thinkers were keenly interested in modernity and developing an Islamic way of life and governing system. They frequently discussed the concept of modernity, deploying various terms for "modern" such as *ḥadīth* and *muʿāṣir*.[8] All of these terms and concepts were topics of frequent and protracted discussion in the early years of the Sharia Lawyers Journal. The terms of general Islamic revival were harnessed and put in the service of an increasingly coherent ideology of Islamic legal revival.

In the journal's first issue of September 1929, the editors boldly asserted their revivalist agenda. The frontispiece featured a dedication to King Fuʾād that praised him as the "the defender of Islam" and "the protector of the Islamic nation."[9] It was followed by a pointedly revivalist introduction: "In the name of God, the merciful and compassionate, and peace and blessings upon the greatest of all reformers (*khayr al-muṣliḥīn*), the master of the revivalists (*sayyid al-mujaddidīn*), the messenger of God, Muḥammad." Such a style was absent from journals published by members of the Native and Mixed bar associations. Even in the Sharia College's journal of the 1920s, this kind of language, when it did appear, was not put to the fore in such a manner.[10]

6 "Qaṣīdah," *al-Muḥāmāh al-sharʿiyyah* 1,6 (1929): 486–7.

7 These three ideas, which were also powerful rhetorical terms, were not unique to the Islamic discourse in Egypt of the 1930s and 1940s. The terms had been common in pan-Arab and other Islamic-oriented writings dating to the beginning of the twentieth century. In the 1920s, Egyptian nationalists employed these terms in a brand of nationalist rhetoric that was largely independent of Islamic sentiment. Proponents of Islamic revival also adopted these terms and infused them with Islamic import. See Charles C. Adams, *Islam and Modernism in Egypt: A Study of the Modern Reform Movement Inaugurated by Muhammad Abduh* (London: Oxford University Press, 1933); Hourani, *Arabic Thought.*

8 Both words might be translated as "modern" or "contemporary."

9 "Iftitāḥiyyat al-majallah," 2.

10 See, for example, the first volumes of *Majallat al-qaḍāʾ al-sharʿī* (1922–9) and *Majallat al-aḥkām al-sharʿiyyah* (1902–10).

The editors set forth in their introductory statement an ambitious program for advancing new scholarship in Islamic law. They promised to publish "research and articles on comparative jurisprudence (*al-fiqh al-muqāran*)," "comparisons between the Islamic systems (*al-nuẓum al-islāmiyyah*) and other modern systems," and "research in *al-siyāsah al-sharʿiyyah*." The editors envisioned this research agenda as serving the revival, reform, and reapplication of Islamic law.

The Sharia Lawyers Journal inducted the dawn of the movement toward a sophisticated field of comparative Islamic-European law studies. This is true even if the journal was more successful in proposing and starting that agenda than it was in accomplishing it. The 1930s were experimental years for Islamic-European comparative law in Egypt, and the articles of this journal show the field's rudimentary beginnings. The Arabic term for comparative law, *al-fiqh al-muqāran*, was a relatively new coinage in the country. It appeared infrequently before the late 1920s. Comparative law was commonly known before the 1930s by its French term, *droit comparé*.[11]

Although comparative studies in Arabic had appeared in Egypt since the 1870s, it was not recognized as a field unto itself or regularly practiced as a discipline until the late 1920s at the earliest. It was only at the end of the 1930s, and more so in the 1940s, that Egyptians in significant numbers began to publish rigorous studies in this field, in Arabic. In the latter part of the 1930s, and for all of the 1940s, the academic field of comparative law would become a scholarly laboratory for research on the hypothetical future of Islamic private and public law.

The editors were ambitious in stating that contributors to the journal would compare "Islamic systems and other modern systems." In the 1930s, one could have argued that no comprehensive Islamic legal or political system existed in the Arab world. Nor did the editors espouse any notion that Egypt could return to the specific system of a previous century. The purpose of comparing theoretical Islamic systems to the actual European legal systems was to use comparative analysis as a tool to build substantive ideas about which specific laws, principles, and institutions might constitute the legal framework of a viable Islamic system of private and public law in the modern world. Their intention was to go far beyond discussions in family law, inheritance, successions, and trusts. The Sharia jurists writing in the journal saw themselves as specially qualified to develop comprehensively the building blocks for a modern Islamic legal and political system.

The journal also took an interest in studying *siyāsah sharʿiyyah*, the classical theory of jurisprudence that sought to accommodate tensions between government-made policy and law with the Islamic jurisprudence of scholars and judges. In essence, the purpose of the classical theory was to render state-made law compliant with or equivalent to Islamic law.[12] Some authors in the journal understood

[11] See the following chapters on the evolution of the comparative law discipline in Egypt's law schools. Before the 1920s, legal "comparison" was commonly termed *taṭbīq* in Arabic. The term *muqāran* appeared occasionally.

[12] See ʿAbd Allāh Ṣiyām, "al-Siyāsah al-sharʿiyyah wa-qawāʿid al-ʿadl wa-l-inṣāf," *al-Muḥāmāh al-sharʿiyyah* 1,7 (1929): 579–81; ʿAbd al-Wahhāb Khallāf, "al-Siyāsah al-sharʿiyyah aw niẓām al-dawlah al-islāmiyyah," *al-Muḥāmāh al-sharʿiyyah* 2,3 (1930): 196–206.

siyāsah sharʿiyyah as a synonym for *ijtihād*, or legal reasoning that is undertaken when the answer to a legal question is not readily and incontrovertibly found in the four primary sources of Islamic law. The journal's interest in *siyāsah sharʿiyyah* related to its interests in expanding the range of modern Islamic law in the private and public dimensions.

CRYSTALLIZATION OF CORE TENETS

In the Sharia Lawyers Journal, the ideological tenets of Islamic legal revivalism developed as follows. First, there was lamentation over a lethargy that had ostensibly infected Islamic juridical science. Second, there was admiration for European advancements in juridical science. This entailed a reverence for European accomplishments in codifying European customary and Roman law, and for publishing authoritative commentaries and reference works on the European codes. Third, there was an effort to advance the view that the Franco-Egyptian laws were "foreign" and not suitable for the Egyptian people. Fourth, there was an effort to advance the view that Sharia was relevant in all places and all eras, including the present era, and that Sharia was totally comprehensive. The implication of this view was that the jurisdiction of Islamic law should not be limited to family law, but should include all legal matters, civil, commercial, criminal, procedural, constitutional, and beyond. Fifth, there was an effort to advance the view that Islamic jurisprudence, as an academic science, needed to be reformed and revived so that it could better power a practical movement of Islamic legislation that was envisioned to be forthcoming. Sixth, the authors advocated the view that Islamic positive laws should replace Egypt's Franco-Egyptian laws, in parts or in whole. In essence, this was an argument that Sharia law of the civil, commercial, criminal, procedural, and constitutional fields needed to be revived (and in many cases created), reorganized, codified, and adopted. Finally, seventh, the writers believed that the work of Islamizing the legal system was the special work of jurists, as jurists were especially competent to compare European and Islamic laws, and to write modern laws and set up courts. These ideas set the stage for the technical developments in Islamic legal doctrine and pedagogy.

The first article published by the journal came from Muḥibb al-Dīn al-Khaṭīb (1886–1969), a popular journalist and proponent of Arab nationalism and Salafi thought. His article "al-Fiqh al-islāmī wa-l-tashrīʿ" (Islamic Jurisprudence and Legislation) reflected the spirit, ambition, ideological orientation, and rhetorical mode of the journal:

> Scholars have long known that Islamic legal thought (*fiqh*) is a vast ocean, that it is the scale of justice, and that it includes everything that mankind needs for legislating.... I reflect on the words of the orientalist, Vambery, who said to the Turkish litterateur Haşım Vali Effendi, "Your Islamic legal doctrine (*fiqh*) has such great breadth, I am amazed to learn that you have never derived from it institutions or rules that would be of use to your people in the present era."

It is true that the Sharia is expansive. It comprises institutions and laws that are relevant for all places and times. This is so much the case that even those who spend their lives studying Sharia, although they are not Muslims... believe with all confidence that in this jurisprudence there is everything for the needs of man regarding their contracts, commerce, issues, and disputes.... But our corpus of Islamic legal doctrine (*fiqh*) has a deficiency I cannot deny. It is that we have become indolent and ascetic in dealing with our inheritance, and we are ignorant of its value. We have not worked to improve our jurisprudence. We have not been dutiful toward it....

If the precious treasure of Islamic jurisprudence had come upon the modern Europeans, and had they counted it as part of what they had inherited from their Roman and Greek ancestors, then by now it would have been published in reference encyclopedias, in every language of the world, and organized to the utmost degree. In the European system there is no such thing as a law that cannot be easily found by referring to an encyclopedia of reference. All of their various law schools agreed on a single law for each problem. Their laws contain sophisticated ideas, rules, and opinions. After a long period of comprehensive research, the Europeans masterfully distilled thirteen centuries of jurisprudence to its essences.

As for us, we have not thought about doing anything like that.... Our researchers are forced to read sixty volumes just to attain a result that could be accomplished in fifteen minutes if they were able to work in a single reference book, or had we thought to write a reference encyclopedia of *fiqh* along the models of Carpentier, Dalloz, and Benedict.[13]

In addition to the Islamic nation having perpetrated disgraces in the technical organization of Islamic legal thought, our Islamic governments have adopted foreign laws like the French and Swiss civil codes....[14] But what does that law have to do with the Sharia, with which the Muslims are well acquainted, and which has embodied their spirit for fourteen centuries?....

As for the men of the Sharia, who know the encyclopedias of Western law in foreign languages, and who are amazed by the precision of their formation... who will earn for himself a page of eternal glory and present himself for such work in the field of Sharia, appointing alongside of him bands of brothers and colleagues? For if we had a uniform reference encyclopedia of Islamic jurisprudence that brought together all the schools (*madhāhib*) and rules, and that pointed to the rules reliably and precisely, that would open the path for extending our academic knowledge of Islamic doctrine (*fiqh*) to the legislative sphere when the opportunity arises. We could then move beyond our shameful position before God and mankind.[15]

Muḥibb al-Dīn's article did not detail how these goals would be accomplished. However, in plain and pointed language, it assailed the ostensible backwardness of Islamic legal thought, hailed the accomplishments of European jurists, criticized the predominance of European law in Egypt, and suggested reform of Islamic juridical science as a prerequisite task for replacing European laws.

[13] Adrien Carpentier authored encyclopedic works on French, Algerian, and international law. The brothers Désiré and Armand Dalloz were the founders of France's leading legal publishing house and published reference works. The reference to Benedict is unclear. Muḥammad Ḥilmī ʿĪsá (*Sharḥ al-bayʿ*, 8) reports having relied on a source by "Banadikt Fransīz."

[14] The Turkish Republic adopted the Swiss Civil Code in 1926.

[15] Muḥibb al-Dīn al-Khaṭīb, "al-Fiqh al-islāmī wa-l-tashrīʿ," *al-Muḥāmāh al-sharʿiyyah* 1,1 (1929): 5–7.

The suggestion that Muslim jurists should compile a uniform reference work to unite the Sunni law schools (*madhāhib*) was of lasting significance. This idea had been occupying the minds of other jurists since the early twentieth century—but they had done little with it.[16] By 1930, Egyptian proponents of Sharia were aware of the story that Azharites had refused to compile Islamic law codes in the 1870s for fear of writing uniform codes that would eclectically choose rulings from different *madhāhib*. For any who had forgotten this story, Rashīd Riḍā related it again, in this journal, in 1929. He even made the rendition more elaborate than the version he rendered in 1899 in *al-Manār*. According to this story, the Azharites originally thought that codification would erode the authority and autonomy of the four juridical schools, whose cooperative coexistence had been enshrined in classical Islamic legal theory under the doctrine of *ikhtilāf* (difference).

Muḥibb al-Dīn encouraged the creation of codes and authoritative reference works that would "bring together" the *madhāhib*. This was an important premise to have advanced in the field of modern Islamic legal theory and one that was adopted by legal reformers throughout the 1930s, 1940s, and 1950s. Once applied in the later 1930s and throughout the 1940s, the premise affected how Sharia jurists envisioned Islamic legal revival taking place: through the writing of uniform Islamic legal codes and academic doctrine in civil, commercial, criminal, procedural, constitutional, and other areas of law.

ALLEGATION OF LETHARGY IN ISLAMIC JURIDICAL SCIENCE

Several leading Egyptian jurists in the early twentieth century believed that the field of Islamic jurisprudence lacked the virtues of French law in regard to organization, accessibility, clarity, decisiveness, uniformity, and above all, relevance to the modern world. The modern world, as these jurists saw it, had brought forth new political, economic, commercial, and social issues. Judges and lawyers needed to be able to access laws about these issues efficiently. Moreover, in the view of many jurists, it was important for judges in a single country to apply the same laws to the same situations. The heightened interest in that point resulted from the influence of imported, Western legal instruments, texts, and institutions.

In the view of these critical jurists, the European codes were prepared to handle new issues of the contemporary world, but Islamic legal doctrine, for its part, had fallen behind in its ability to respond quickly, decisively, and uniformly to modern situations. In this vein, one of the central ideas to surface in the journal's critique of contemporary Islamic jurisprudence was, relatedly, the insufficient organization in books of Islamic *fiqh*, which hindered the modern jurist's effort to expand Islamic jurisprudence, codify parts of Sharia, and rule on novel disputes

[16] See, however, ʿAbd al-Raḥmān al-Jazīrī, *Kitāb al-Fiqh ʿalá al-madhāhib al-arbaʿah* (Cairo: Dār al-Kitāb al-ʿArabī, 1938). See also Aḥmad Ibrāhīm's contribution to the first volume of the students' journal of the Cairo University Law Faculty, "Wujūb waḍʿ qānūn sharʿī ghayr muqayyad bi-madhhab muʿayyin," *Majallat Kulliyyat al-Ḥuqūq li-l-mabāḥith al-qānūniyyah wa-l-iqtiṣādiyyah* 1,1 (1927): 2–5.

efficiently. The contributors were troubled by this ostensible deficiency in the *fiqh* books because, in their view, Sharia was superior to European law substantively and spiritually. In an editorial, the journal summarized Egypt's predicament:

> When the French code law was translated into Arabic for the Native Courts, the best of our Muslim scholars took that law and . . . laid it side by side with the great Islamic Sharia. They found that this code law did not approach the preciseness of the Sharia and was not better than the Sharia. . . . The Sharia's rulings are the best rulings, and its system is the best system. . . . If only we could organize those rules into a convenient treatise along the lines of Dalloz, it would be the greatest source of guidance to our codifiers (*muqannīn*).[17]

In the sixth issue of the first volume, a Sharia judge named ʿAbd al-Raʾūf Ibrāhīm ʿAlī criticized the state of publishing in *fiqh*:

> The first problem with *fiqh* books is that they jumble the topics. . . . When you open a *fiqh* book, you find chapters and sub-headings and sub-sub-headings haphazardly piled on top of each other. You do not know what connects to what, or under what heading you should be searching for what. I am not saying that *fiqh* books lack organization totally. But what there is in the way of organization does not fulfill people's needs or conform to the spirit of our age, and does not encourage the student in his research to invent (*ibtikār*) new ideas in a variety of areas of law.[18]

The judge continued in his discussion of the predicament of *fiqh* books, describing the evolution of *fiqh* genres.

> There is a peculiar style that many writers follow in *fiqh*. If one of them finds an older and famous book, he cuts out from it what he wants, he drops what he doesn't want, and then he publishes it as a new book under his own name. Then another person comes along and looks at that book and says it needs commentary (*taʿlīq*), so he writes a commentary. Someone comes to that commentary and writes a new commentary on it. He calls that the marginal commentary (*ḥāshiyah*). Somebody reads this marginal commentary and writes a summary on it (*taqrīr*). Then someone looks at these books with their marginal commentaries and summaries, and writes a commentary. That commentary then needs a commentary. And that commentary then needs a marginal commentary. And that marginal commentary then needs a summary. This is what I call circular and repetitive writing.[19]

ʿAbd al-Raʾūf claimed that Egyptian *fiqh* books were unbalanced in their focus on substantive legal questions. There is a "lack of distribution of practical efforts in writing about the varying points of jurisprudence in proportion to their value and the extent of people's needs. . . . The jurists have expounded in matters where they should have economized, namely, the *ʿibādāt*, and they should have expounded in the matters where they economized, namely the *muʿāmalāt*."[20] He claimed that

[17] Editorial comment preceding Makhlūf Muḥammad, "Bāb al-muwāzanāt wa-l-muqāranāt bayna l-sharīʿah al-islāmiyyah al-gharrāʾ wa-bayna l-qawānīn al-waḍʿiyyah," *al-Muḥāmāh al-sharʿiyyah* 2,2 (1930): 135–7, at 135. On Dalloz, see n. 13.

[18] ʿAbd al-Raʾūf Ibrāhīm ʿAlī, "Kutub al-fiqh al-islāmī," *al-Muḥāmāh al-sharʿiyyah* 1,6 (1929): 482–4, at 484.

[19] Ibid. [20] Ibid.

jurists had dedicated the lion's share of space in *fiqh* books to minutiae (*ṣaghā'ir*) associated with the laws of ritual (*ʿibādāt*), whereas there was a dearth of research and commentary on the Islamic laws of transactions (*muʿāmalāt*).[21] ʿAbd al-Raʾūf was referring here to Islamic laws on contracts, commerce, torts, crimes, procedure, and constitution—those areas of law within the Franco-Egyptian jurisdiction.

ʿAbd al-Raʾūf expressed a view that the shortcomings of Islamic legal literature, as a genre, were responsible for the fact that Egyptians needed to live under foreign laws. "These and other faults," he averred, "and still others I do not even know about, have led the Islamic nations away from the application of the Islamic Sharia. Because of these problems, people think that the Sharia has no relevance to the present age."[22] It was this popular conception of the Sharia—that it had no relevance—that he and other contributors to the journal hoped to change.

UNSUITABILITY OF EUROPEAN LAW

Rashīd Riḍā wrote one article for the Sharia Lawyers Journal which criticized the adoption of foreign law in Egypt.[23] Riḍā told a story about Khedive Ismail, in the 1870s, asking the clerics of al-Azhar to draft Islamic law codes so that he could avoid adopting French law as Egyptian law. According to the story, the shaykhs of al-Azhar refused this request because they did not want to consolidate the varying rules of the four Sunni law schools into uniform codes:

> Khedive Ismail one day called in Shakyh ʿAlī Rifāʿah for an audience. The khedive said, "Shaykh Rifāʿah, you are an Azharite who has studied and was raised in al-Azhar. You are the most learned of the Azharites. I would like to appoint you to convince the Azharites of something, because you are the most capable for the task. A number of contracts and rights have fallen to the European foreigners in our lands and thus many judicial proceedings have arisen both among them and between their people and our people. The foreigners complain that they do not know which laws are for them or against them in these claims.... They say they do not know which laws to pay attention to and which laws to use to defend themselves, because the books of *fiqh* by our jurists are numerous, complicated, and at variance with one another. So they have asked if the learned men of al-Azhar would write a book of positive Islamic civil law (*aḥkām madaniyyah sharʿiyyah*) that will be like the books of positive laws (*qawānīn*): detailed, organized by topic, and without internal contradictions as to specific rules. If we do not do this, then I will be forced to adopt the laws of the Napoleonic Code, or something similar."
>
> Rifāʿah Pasha responded, "Your Highness, I have traveled to Europe and I have studied there. I have served the government and translated many books from French to English. I have done my share of work. I have reached an old age, and no one has ever separated me from my religion. If I suggested this idea to the ulema of al-Azhar by the

[21] M. Bernand, "Muʿāmalāt," *Encyclopaedia of Islam*, 2nd ed. (Leiden: Brill, 1960–2004).
[22] ʿAlī, "Kutub al-fiqh al-islāmī." [23] Riḍā, "Musāwāt al-marʾah bi-l-rajul."

command of your Highness, I fear they would say that Shaykh Rifāʿah apostatized from Islam in his old age, wanting to transform the books of Sharia into positive laws (*qawānīn waḍʿiyyah*). I beg you to excuse me from this risk before my death, so that it will not be said that I died an unbeliever (*kāfir*)."[24]

The intended effect of this anecdote is of greater interest than the question of its authenticity. Riḍā's story makes at least three points about how Egypt came to adopt foreign legal codes. First, it depicts the khedive as having had misgivings about the adoption of the foreign codes. (It also suggests that the shaykhs of al-Azhar, the traditional purveyors of Islamic law, may have had even deeper misgivings about codified law than the khedive.) Second, it indicates that the khedive was forced to accept the codes because he was in a position of political weakness. And, third, it shows that the shaykhs of al-Azhar had dangerously committed themselves to traditionalism. The overall effect was to underline that European laws had been imposed on Egypt by outside forces. Present-day observers of the Egyptian legal system commonly take this polemical perspective for granted. For many Egyptians in 1929, including lawyers and jurists, the existence of French law in Egypt was still not viewed as deeply problematic or even contrary to Islam.

Riḍā's article proceeded to criticize the Egyptian lawyers and politicians who favored the Franco-Egyptian law and who, he claims, were endeavoring to expand the reach of this foreign law even further, at the expense of Sharia laws and courts.

> A time came when the Muslims fell into a weak state and foreigners assumed power over their governments and the political and moral authority of those governments.... There are still opponents of Islamic law and those who despise the Islamic character of these nations and who cast a great black cloud over Islam while renewing the present campaigns and internal schemes to suppress all that is Islamic in them.[25]

Riḍā viewed Egypt's legal sphere as divided between proponents of Islamic law and proponents of Franco-Egyptian law. He used the article, along with his commentary on it, to lay conceptual and historical groundwork for the call to Egyptian jurists to write new codes of Islamic civil and criminal law. In his conclusion, he showed his interest in practical, immediate reform:

> The Egyptian government recently became constitutional and representative. As a result, a number of scholars from al-Azhar and other religious institutions have reasserted themselves, with a new independence of thought and greater awareness of the modern situation. The country has come close to freeing itself of foreign control, which was the primary cause for our having left behind the Sharia in civil and criminal matters. These changes in government have paved the way for a return to things as they were before, and to make apparent the highest form of justice. Thus, there is only one thing for the reforming scholars (*al-ʿulamāʾ al-mujaddidīn*) to do, and it is that which I have recommended repeatedly. They are to undertake an organization of Sharia law books of civil and penal rules (*aḥkām madaniyyah wa-taʾdībiyyah*) that cor-

[24] Ibid., 577. (The same story appeared in *al-Manār* 2 [1899]: 120.)
[25] Riḍā, "Musāwāt al-marʾah bi-l-rajul," 585.

respond to the general needs of this age. These books will guarantee justice and equality among the people. And the Egyptian parliament will then have the opportunity to act on them.[26]

DICHOTOMOUS LEGAL VOCABULARY AS AN IDEOLOGICAL TOOL

The Sharia Lawyers Journal employed a dichotomous technical vocabulary that reinforced the conception of European law as foreign and un-Islamic. This lexicon served to emphasize that there indeed existed important differences between Islamic law and European law, both substantive and spiritual.

The terms used were not new, but they were deployed with newfound enthusiasm and intent. Islamic law was called *al-sharīʿah, al-aḥkām al-sharʿiyyah* (Sharia rules), and *al-qawānīn al-sharʿiyyah* (Sharia positive laws).[27] Sharia was called "the glorious Sharia" (*al-sharīʿah al-gharrāʾ*) and "the magnanimous Sharia" (*al-sharīʿah al-samḥāʾ*). These terms were juxtaposed to terms for Franco-Egyptian law. When used by itself, *qānūn* connoted the secular-oriented, Franco-Egyptian code law. The Sharia professors of Cairo University innovated the term *qānūn Allāh*, "the positive law of God," as a way of appropriating the term *qānūn* from purely secular ownership. In comparative studies, *qānūn* was most often juxtaposed to *aḥkām sharʿiyyah*. A second term was *al-qānūn al-miṣrī*, or the secular-oriented code law of Egyptian Native and Mixed Courts. A third term was *al-qānūn al-waḍʿī* (pl. *al-qawānīn al-waḍʿiyyah*), or the positive law. Finally, there was the term *al-qānūn al-ūrūbī* (European law), used to describe both the laws of European nations and the Franco-Egyptian law.

Most of these expressions were in place before the 1930s. Importantly, however, the contributors were now discussing law in these terms, at this specific time in history, with a heightened emphasis and purpose. The terms of the discourse were stabilized and concentrated, and consistently deployed to support the dual agenda of opposing European law and championing the revival of Islamic law.

The deployment of this vocabulary shows how the authors in the journal perceived the legal playing field. They envisioned two legal systems in place simultaneously, the Islamic law and the Franco-Egyptian law. The Sharia law professionals were working for the Sharia law; the other law professionals were working for

[26] Ibid., 578.

[27] It is significant to see the terms *qawānīn* (sg. *qānūn*) and *sharʿiyyah* bound in the same phrase. *Aḥkām sharʿiyyah* was a historical term for rules of Islamic jurisprudence that had deep roots in classical Islamic legal literature. *Qawānīn*, as noted earlier, historically referred to positive laws that did not have their origin in Islamic sources, but rather from government order. By the 1930s and 1940s, Arab jurists had become accustomed to thinking of positive laws of any origin as *qānūn*, so that it came to pass that even Islamic laws of personal status would be called *qānūn*. This was the case with Syrian and Iraqi codes of personal status from 1953 and 1959. The Egyptian personal status law was eventually known as *qānūn sharʿī* ("Sharia-compliant *qānūn*") or *qānūn al-aḥwāl al-shakhṣiyyah* ("the *qānūn* of personal status law"). Thus, the journal's authors would occasionally describe Islamic laws as *al-qawānīn al-sharʿiyyah* (sg. *qānūn sharʿī*). See Y. Linant de Bellefonds et al., "Ḳānūn," *Encyclopaedia of Islam*, 2nd ed.

the Franco-Egyptian law. This reinforced commitment to recognizing a dichotomy in Egyptian law influenced the way Egyptian law was studied and written about in the coming decades, particularly in studies of comparative law.

"SHARIA IS PRACTICABLE IN ALL TIMES AND PLACES"

The twentieth century was not the first era in which certain outspoken Muslim jurists lamented the failure of their countries to apply Islamic law. In the thirteenth century, Ibn Taymiyyah assailed the application of foreign laws by Mongol invaders. In the fourteenth century, Abū Isḥāq al-Shāṭibī argued that Muslim jurists were too narrow-minded and tradition-bound in their interpretations of Quran and prophetic tradition. More traditionally minded scholars at al-Azhar contributed to the movement of Islamic legal reform in the 1920s and 1930s by printing new editions of works by Ibn Taymiyyah, al-Shāṭibī, and other classical writers whose ideas could be applied to modern Islamic legal thought. However, for the more ambitious writers who contributed to the Sharia Lawyers Journal, it did not suffice to exhume the classical writers and make them proxies for complaining about the state of contemporary law.

The Egyptian legal system of the 1930s and its move away from traditional patterns in legal order—that is, what was widely thought to have been legal tradition—required the comment of contemporary reform-minded jurists. The shift toward European and secular-leaning modes of law, judiciary, and juridical thought appeared newly and uniquely inexorable in the early twentieth century. Many Egyptians now appreciated these new laws and institutions. Leading Egyptian law professionals, professors, and legislators had become comfortable with the European-style codes. They liked uniform codes, codified procedural rules, and formal protocols for appeals, and deemed the new codes and the new system practical and relevant for the present age. They did not presume that the Franco-Egyptian codes were comprehensive or perfect, but many took for granted that it was easier to amend the extant codes than to write new codes of Islamic law.

The acquiescence of so many Egyptians to the legal status quo made it necessary for the journal's contributors to hammer at the notion that Islamic law was comprehensive and practicable for all times and places, and could therefore be applied in a modern setting, even if that meant putting the Islamic law into codes. Contributors asserted over and again that Sharia was "comprehensive" (*shāmil*) and complete (*kāmil*). The phrase Sharia "is practicable in all times and in all places" (*ṣāliḥah li-kull zamān wa-makān*) became a slogan in the journal, repeated in tens of articles.

In most regards, this claim was not new to the 1930s. It was a common expression in Islamic discourse,[28] and can be traced back to classical literature. The concept

[28] It appeared in the revivalist texts discussed in the previous chapter, such as in Chaouiche (Jāwīsh), "Nécessité d'avoir égard aux circonstances de temps et de lieu" (1911).

was expressed frequently during the nineteenth century in Arabic and Turkish. The preamble to the *Mecelle* articulated the principle, and Rashīd Riḍā invoked it in *al-Manār*. If the Sharia Lawyers Journal made any new contribution to this conception of a timelessly relevant and geographically boundless Sharia, it was by making it a mantra and a foundational precept for the claim that Islamic law should be thoroughly applied in the present day, and that the revival of Sharia was an essential component of Egyptian nationalism and pan-Islamist transnationalism.

The journal established a running column entitled "Sharia is Practicable in All Times and in Places." Different authors wrote for the column over the years. The first author was Muḥammad al-Khiḍr Ḥusayn, a future rector of al-Azhar.[29] In a typical expression of the concept, he explained:

> All Muslims agree that the Islamic Sharia came down to provide rules for human affairs. All Muslims agree that there is no issue in life that does not have a ruling based on the Quran, or on one of the sources of law derived the from the Quran.... The Sharia is tolerant and wise, and it governs every issue that one could possibly imagine from all of the issues that citizens and humankind have faced across the generations.[30]

Rashīd Riḍā also weighed in, arguing, "Rule in Islamic countries used to be entirely based on the glorious Sharia because it is comprehensive and encompasses all of the beneficial things for humankind on the basis of justice and equality between the people."[31]

IJTIHĀD AS "RESEARCH"

If Sharia was indeed comprehensive and could be applied to modern circumstances, then the jurists needed to set upon the task of making this application possible through new legislation. New legislation, however, needed to be preceded by new thinking—*ijtihād*—in the realm of academic doctrine.[32] One of the most concerted appeals for a new wave of *ijtihād* was the first article written for the second year of the journal. The author, ʿAbd al-Raʾūf Ibrāhīm, wrote:

> The Sharia cannot be time-bound, nor can it be right when people who speak of it mention stasis and lack of flexibility. It is incredible that one could believe it has no pertinence to the present age or that it does not address the needs of the people.... It is surprising and strange that the prevailing opinion and belief is that *ijtihād* should be prevented in the branches of Sharia, regardless of whether it be undertaken by the

[29] Muḥammad al-Khiḍr Ḥusayn (1876–1958) was born in Tunisia but spent his career in Egypt as a scholar and teacher. He served as the rector of al-Azhar between 1950 and 1952, and was the only non-Egyptian to have held the position.

[30] Muḥammad al-Khiḍr Ḥusayn, "al-Sharīʿah al-islāmiyyah ṣāliḥah li-kull zamān wa-makān," *al-Muḥāmāh al-sharʿiyyah* 2,2 (1930): 119.

[31] Riḍā, "Musāwāt al-marʾah bi-l-rajul," 584.

[32] *Ijtihād* (from the same Arabic root as jihad) connotes the effort (exertion) to derive law—or here, newly articulated rules—from the revelatory sources through interpretation where God's commands are not categorically clear (*qaṭʿī*); for an explanation why this was a struggle or effort, see Bernard G. Weiss, *The Spirit of Islamic Law* (Athens, GA: University of Georgia Press, 1998), esp. 88–92.

> scholar, who has a religious obligation to perform *ijtihād* in the sources of Sharia, or whether it be undertaken by the layman....
>
> The living truth is that the existence of a *mujtahid*[33] among our scholars today is rare. Nay, I might even say that the *mujtahid* is completely absent. That is attributable to extreme lassitude, weakness in resolution, and a spreading of some false belief that people have asked us to believe. It is a belief that keeps everyone from trying to open the wide door and to see what is behind it in the way of grace. If one could only have the opportunity to go beyond this door, it would awaken him to the Islamic Sharia. Then there would be no need to take refuge in foreign laws that the Islamic nations apply on their people.
>
> If only the supporters of traditionalism (*taqlīd*) knew that they, in fact, were committing a crime against the Sharia and promoting doubt as to its validity and adequacy for our times. Sharia lacks nothing except the *mujathids* who understand it, as it was understood by our pious ancestors who discerned its rules on the scales of reason and judgment.[34]

One fact known about Islamic reformism since at least the mid-nineteenth century is that Muslim reformists supported the "opening of the door" of *ijtihād*.[35] The Sharia Lawyers Journal added new elements to this long-running interest in *ijtihād*.

The journal took the call for a revival of *ijtihād*, which had long circulated in rarefied clerical circles, and brought it to mainstream professionals and academics involved with the courts. Moreover, the call for a revival of *ijithād* was being outfitted with more clearly defined practical goals. The aim was to apply Islamic law in the state, as far as possible, and to supplant European law, as far as possible. Specific suggestions were made about what kind of *ijtihād* should be undertaken, and how Islamic legal doctrine would be written in the future. Certain methodological ideas that had been discussed in the previous thirty years received attention. For example, jurists discussed theories of *maṣlaḥah* and *siyāsah sharʿiyyah*; they discussed Sharia "principles" (*mabādiʾ*) and aims (*maqāṣid*). The purpose of exploring such interests was to serve the ambition to expand the substantive range of Islamic jurisprudence and to codify its rules.

The contributors tried to determine how new *ijtihād* could address the needs of Egypt's modern legal system, a system now thoroughly accustomed to uniform codes, the particular categories of Franco-Egyptian law, and new, contemporary outlooks on values, social relations, and legal priorities of the state. To address these concerns, the editors and contributors held that *ijtihād* needed to transcend the current practices of traditionally-minded scholars and of the judges operating in Egypt's courts. New *ijithād* needed to take the form of "research": *baḥth, buḥūth, mabāḥith*.

Egyptian law scholars became interested during the 1920s and early 1930s in the concept of legal research and how the concept had developed in recent decades

[33] I.e., one who practices *ijtihād*.

[34] ʿAbd al-Raʾūf Ibrāhīm ʿAlī, "al-Ijtihād wa-l-taqlīd," *al-Muḥāmāh al-sharʿiyyah* 2,1 (1930): 16–18. See also ʿAbd al-Qādir al-Maghribī, "Najtahid fī ījād al-mujtahid," *al-Muḥāmāh al-sharʿiyyah* 1,10 (1930): 873–8.

[35] See Chapter 6.

in Egypt and Europe.[36] When the Sharia College was opened in 1907, its purpose was to advance modern legal thought and practice among Sharia professionals, and particularly judges. The school pursued this goal to an extent through a somewhat pioneering curriculum. However, before the 1920s, the college did not produce much of what would have been called "research" by evolving standards in Europe and the new, secular-oriented law schools of Egypt. The transforming factor in promoting a new conception of research in Sharia was the flourishing of the Cairo University Law Faculty in the 1920s. During this decade, Egyptian scholars returned from France with doctorates in law and began new programs in academic research. They were mostly experts in European and Franco-Egyptian law, but they were interested in Islamic law. They wrote in Arabic, French, and English, and they defined for their Egyptian students the meaning of modern legal research. They expounded on the imperative to produce "original" and innovative ideas; they sparked discussions about intellectual property in scholarship; they demanded certain conventions for academic writing that they had encountered in France; they demanded rigor and theoretical awareness in academic writing; and they expected researchers in comparative legal studies to be fluent in more than one language.[37] Their journals, chief vehicles for publishing their best research, included the official faculty law journal, *Majallat al-qānūn wa-l-iqtiṣād* (The Law and Economy Review), which began in 1932, and the student journal *Majallat Kulliyyat al-Ḥuqūq li-l-mabāḥith al-qānūniyyah wa-l-iqtiṣādiyyah* (The Law Faculty Review of Legal and Economic Research), which began in 1927.

The Sharia Lawyers Journal was not at that level. In the first volume, Shaykh Muḥammad Aḥmad Jād al-Mawlá Bey contributed an article entitled "al-Qurʾān al-karīm" (The Glorious Quran). The shaykh was not an academic but an inspector in the Ministry of Education.[38] He had been educated in the Islamic institutions. The possibility that he knew any European languages or was familiar with newly emergent practices in "research" at Cairo University is slight. The editors prefaced the article by praising it as a specimen of research:

> The divine source for the judicial procedure and all legislation—social, political, criminal, civil, military, or otherwise—is the Glorious Quran. We have not seen a piece of research this year that has been better than this piece. It analyzes the Quran, clarifies its contents, discusses its linguistic attributes, and explains its injunctions in matters pertaining to legislation, social life, creation, science, and reformism (*iṣlāḥiyyah*). It discusses how the Quran raises the level of the people.[39]

The author's purpose was to take all of the major concerns and categories of Franco-Egyptian law and argue that these concerns and categories had equivalents, and superior manifestations, in the Quran. He began by discussing the supremacy of the Quran as a source of human law. Then, he enumerated the areas of law covered by the Quran that provide for a just and effective legal system.

[36] See pp. 212–15. [37] See Chapter 9.
[38] Muḥammad Aḥmad Jād al-Mawlá Bey, "al-Qurʾān al-karīm," *al-Muḥāmāh al-sharʿiyyah* 1,10 (1930): 838–50.
[39] Ibid., 838.

He argued that the Quran provides "social, political, criminal, and civil" legislation (*tashrīʿ*). He claimed that all guidance necessary for civil, criminal, and public law was found in the Quran ("It has all that man needs in his life"). Additionally, he discussed Quranic rules of ritual and ethics, the Quran's place in Arabic grammar, its scientific precepts, and its role in confirming that Muḥammad was the "greatest reformer who ever lived."

In fleshing out the Quran's rules in these categories of law, the author did not go very far. But, he tried, and he made a fair point that the rules of the Quran could, as a theoretical exercise, be organized into manifestly European and Franco-Egyptian categories—social, political, criminal, and civil. His method was to state a legal category and then cite a few verses from the Quran that showed the Quran's contribution to the category. On social law, for instance, he mentioned the Quran's requirement that people pay alms.[40] On political legislation, he cited verses that discuss the obedience of people to their leaders.[41] For criminal legislation, he cited one verse on punishment, remedies, and the requirement of just judging.[42] On civil legislation, he cited two verses on the prohibition of usury[43] and two verses on inheritance.[44]

This was the extent of what the editors considered to be the best piece of research produced in the judicial year 1929–1930.[45] It is impossible to say that there is anything bad about the article, but the article could not have lived up to the emergent expectations of legal research at the Cairo Faculty. It showed no interest in taking the substantive law further than the articulation of very basic principles and a handful of salient rules. It said nothing extensive about reformist methodology and did not problematize the European categories that it adopted. For example, the author did not inquire as to whether the Quran or Islamic law naturally recognized a category like "civil" law. It showed no knowledge of Franco-Egyptian and European legal thought and sources or interest in the emergent social science fields and their possible relevance to legal research. In sum, the article was heavy on ideology and agenda, but light on rigor and technical content by emerging standards of the times. This was the kind and level of research in Sharia that other Egyptian jurists tried to transcend during the later 1930s and throughout the 1940s.

SIGNIFICANCE OF THE JURISTS' IDEAS

On their face, the notions about the shortcomings of European law and the virtues and possibilities of Islamic law were no more than ideas, similar to the very

[40] See *al-Tawbah* (9):60; *al-Baqarah* (2):215. [41] *Al-Nisāʾ* (4):59. [42] *Al-Māʾidah* (5):45.

[43] *Al-Rūm* (30):39; *al-Baqarah* (2):276. [44] *Al-Baqarah* (2):11, 12.

[45] ʿAbd al-Wahhāb Khallāf wrote a similar kind of article in a series on *siyāsah sharʿiyyah*, which became a book. He similarly discussed how Islamic law fits into new categories, such as "constitutional law," and spoke of how Islamic law addresses personal freedom, individual freedom, freedom of property, freedom of belief, freedom of opinion, freedom of education, and equality. Khallāf, "al-Siyāsah al-sharʿiyyah," *al-Muḥāmāh al-sharʿiyyah* 2,2 (1930): 100–6; 2,3 (1930): 196–206.

general ideas about modern Egyptian law posited by Islamic thinkers such as Ḥasan al-Bannā, founder of the Muslim Brotherhood. However, when professional jurists expanded upon these ideas in a professional and technical forum, the ideas took on important practical implications. By articulating and positing these ideas as religiously based facts, the jurists established theoretical premises on which the revival of Islamic law could be based. By de-legitimizing the Franco-Egyptian system and by championing the potential for Islamic law to be applied in modern times, the contributors gave their colleagues intellectual justification and spiritual incentive to seek Islamic reform of Egyptian laws and courts.

It was important that these revivalist articles came from the minds and pens of practicing, professional Sharia jurists. Compared to non-jurists, jurists were capable of giving an added measure of credibility and substance to the notion of Sharia revivalism. They could take an otherwise vague ambition for the legal system and flesh out its foundational concepts and programmatic points in specific legal terms. Many of the writers were already highly respected thinkers in Egypt and in the wider Islamic world. Others who were unknown added the popular voice to the journal. Jurists were thus capable of attracting the interest and confidence of other jurists, the people who would be responsible for reforming and reviving Islamic jurisprudence. How exactly this confidence and interest in the jurists' articles was manifested in subsequent years, in the wider field of Egyptian jurisprudence, is seen in the forthcoming chapters.

The editors and contributors believed that reform and revival in the academic area of *fiqh* were prerequisites for a legislative movement. The contributors wrote articles on comparative European-Islamic law and hypothetical Islamic legislation with an eye toward influencing lawyers, judges, scholars, and legislators. These articles were exploratory studies in how Islamic law could be revived and reapplied. In reading them, it is difficult to escape the observation that writers were following the lead of European laws and legal categories, picking out various articles and theories from Franco-Egyptian codes and then looking for their parallels in books of classical Islamic *fiqh*. Nevertheless, one finds in the journal some of earliest attempts by twentieth-century jurists to use comparative law with the aim of creating modern Islamic legislation. One also finds examples of Muslim jurists looking within classical Islamic tradition for ideas that could assist in or drive the reform process.

The contributors who wrote comparative articles examined theories and philosophies that were current in Islamic and European thought. From the Islamic side, the contributors worked with Islamic theoretical principles like *maṣlaḥah* and *maqāṣid al-sharīʿah*. They also dealt with theories of "justice" (*ʿadl*) and "equality" (*musāwāh*). In the case of these latter two principles, it is not always clear whether the jurists were drawing primarily on ideas from traditional Islamic thought, or whether they were initially drawing on European ideas and then projecting those ideas into their research in the Quran and prophetic tradition. From the European side, the jurists engaged with a range of European theories and philosophies. In this period, European jurists were writing extensively on theories about independence of the judiciary, civil and political rights, and the legal status of women. The progressive French jurists were interested in injecting socialism, social reform agendas, and welfare principles into French law. Some of these French jurists taught law in Cairo and trained Egyptian students in France. In the journal, one finds authors writing about similar theories in Islamic law. The journal's early volumes contain articles about social rights, workers' rights, socialism, and independence of the judiciary "in Islamic law" (*fī l-fiqh al-islāmī*). This was the beginning of a genre of legal writing in the Arab world, which continues to this day, wherein writers search out the existence or origins of a concept, encountered in explorations in Western law, "in Islamic law." It is also remarkable to see studies about "equality of men and women" in the journal, which became a running column. It is plausible that a primary impetus for such research was Egyptian contact with European scholarship.

It is particularly important to read the articles that treated the topic of creating Islamic civil, commercial, criminal, procedural, constitutional, and international law codes. Here we are looking not at the comparison or creation of legal theories and philosophies, but at the comparison and creation of positive legislation (in the sense of *qawānīn*). An analysis of comparative law writings is the topic of the next chapters. It will suffice to stress here that the articles on comparative law were for the most part short, exploratory, and often rudimentary. By the 1940s, Egyptian jurists in greater numbers would be publishing sophisticated studies in comparative Islamic-European law although not in this journal. The comparative law articles found in the early volumes of the Sharia Lawyers Journal underline that a period of greater sophistication in Egyptian comparative law was still to come as of the early 1930s.

The early history of the journal is not entirely about accomplishment and success. Perhaps the greatest failing of the journal in its first years was that the contributors did not make a concerted effort to reach or even broach consensus on a number of thorny juridical questions that were certain to encumber a revival of Islamic jurisprudence.

One such question on which the jurists did not come to an agreement was how to work with *ikhtilāf* (literally, "difference"), the principle that a single legal question can have multiple but equally valid rulings both among and within the four Sunni schools of law.[46] Such a theory was at odds with one of the core objectives of European-style code writing and civil law, which was that for every known legal question the law should provide one authoritative resolution. Another question on which the contributors did not arrive at a uniform conclusion was the extent to which traditional Islamic crimes and punishments should be applied in a modern Islamic system of law. A third difficult issue was how modern Islamic law should treat women and non-Muslims. Additionally, it was difficult for jurists in the journal to make breakthroughs or to establish fundamental points of consensus about the hypothetical future of Islamic constitutional law. In the first year of the journal, ʿAbd al-Razzāq al-Sanhūrī and Rashīd Riḍā argued that Sharia

[46] See J. Schacht, "Ikhtilāf," *Encyclopaedia of Islam*, 2nd ed., 3: 1088.

necessitated unity between religion and state.[47] However, when ʿAlī ʿAbd al-Rāziq assumed editorship of the journal in 1935, he was already famous for having taken the position that Sharia necessitates a division between religion and state. Discussions about the relationship between religion and constitutional law thereafter dropped from the journal's pages.

Like all academic and professional journals, the Sharia Lawyers Journal was challenged to maintain its popularity, its flow of writers and readers, and its standards of quality. From approximately 1940 onward, the journal published increasingly fewer research articles, and by the mid-1940s it had mainly become a monthly case reporter. The waning of research articles may have been tied to the demise of the Sharia College and the fact that Dār al-ʿUlūm and al-Azhar published their own journals. And it may have resulted from the ascendance of comparative law studies at the Cairo Faculty and competition from that Faculty's journals. The Cairo Faculty's Law and Economy Review was a larger academic journal that enjoyed the backing of Egypt's most prestigious law professionals and professors. When it began to take an interest in Sharia in the later 1930s, its articles made those in the Sharia Lawyers Journal appear brief and amateurish. Leading scholars of Islamic jurisprudence began publishing their articles in the Law and Economy Review instead.

[47] ʿAbd al-Razzāq Aḥmad al-Sanhūrī, "al-Dīn wa-l-dawlah fī l-islām," *al-Muḥāmāh al-sharʿiyyah* 1,1 (1929): 8–14; Riḍā, "Musāwāt al-marʾah bi-l-rajul."

Section II

European Law and Imperialist Campaigns for Islamic Legal Reform

4

Foreign Interventions in Islamic Law

Islamic legal revivalism was influenced by the reception of both European law and European ideas about Islamic law, and more generally it was influenced by distinctly non-Islamic, non-Egyptian, and non-Arab factors. Europeans intervened in Islamic legal thought and practice by way of the intellectual as well as the political and institutional mechanisms of imperialism. As a result, to appreciate the full spectrum of Egypt's modern legal heritage there is no greater mistake than limiting the range of inquiry to events and history that occurred in Egypt. At some point, one must shift the focus to Europe and to other European colonies.

It offends nationalist and certain Islamist sensibilities to grapple with the proposition that much of Egyptian law and legal thought, including aspects of modern Islamic legal thought, comes from outside of Egypt. This proposition also tests the patience of postcolonial sensibilities. But many of Egypt's legal instruments, institutions, and doctrinal inclinations were developed in other countries. Leading Europeans on the Egyptian legal scene hailed from Europe and European colonies. Leading Egyptians in Franco-Egyptian law held European degrees, studied in Europe, spoke European languages, and took pride in their European pedigree in spite of their own nationalism. The consequent impacts to Egyptian law were felt in both the Franco-Egyptian and the Islamic legal spheres.

In colonial Egypt, as in other colonies, Europeans wanted to change Islamic law. They did not arrive in Egypt merely proposing that the commercial and penal laws of the state—the areas that had previously seen some incursion of European influence at the invitation of Egyptian leaders themselves—should become more like European law. But Europeans also had their reformist sights set on the heart of Islamic legal doctrine, in its theory as well as its practice. European scholars and agents of colonial authority had studied Islamic law for more than a century before the British occupation of Egypt, and had pre-formed ideas about Islamic law that in turn shaped reform initiatives within Egypt. As of 1900, they had created a field of learning built on scores of treatises, articles, and field manuals. To understand the effects that European law, legal thought, legal education, and the European academic field of "comparative law" had on Egyptian and Islamic legal thought, it is necessary to know about origins and accomplishments of legal orientalism. In this investigative context, simply dismissing European orientalism as a malicious reductionism, or wishing it away, is unhelpful to the recovering of history.

Islamic Legal Revival: Reception of European Law and Transformations in Islamic Legal Thought in Egypt, 1875–1952. First Edition. Leonard Wood.

The European intellectual engagement with Islamic law and legal thought produced several effects insofar as Egyptian-Islamic legal thought was concerned. First, as Europeans became knowledgeable about Islamic law, they presumed themselves to have the requisite capacity and right to critique it and intervene in its future. Second, the European conception of "Islamic law" was different from classical conceptions of Sharia. Consequently, Europeans contributed to a gradual transformation in what Sharia meant to Muslim jurists themselves. Third, Europeans tried to change Islamic law in practice and in theory—often with the intention of making Islamic legal thought more European in form, substance, method, and premises. Finally, the European engagement with Islamic law informed the field of European comparative law, a school of thought that took new form at the beginning of the twentieth century.

The example *par excellence* of foreign influence on the Franco-Egyptian and Islamic legal spheres is that of Édouard Lambert, the most influential European law scholar and legal comparativist to have become directly and personally involved with Egypt. He advised in the drafting of the Egyptian Civil Code of 1948, which is still in force and known for its objective of melding Islamic law with civil law. He acquired his prestige and power in part by convincing Egyptian law scholars of his own affinity for Islamic law and his academic understanding of it, despite knowing no Arabic.

When Lambert and other European comparativist scholars seized upon the Islamic legal tradition around the turn of the twentieth century and contemplated integrating Islamic law into a rising field of global, comparative law studies—as a way of using academic studies to actually change Islamic law—they relied on European scholarship from a variety of disciplines and intellectual milieus that had already been written on Islamic religion, history, civilization, and law in contemporary Arab, Ottoman, and other Muslim societies. Comparativists like Lambert were themselves not schooled in Arabic, Persian, and Middle Eastern and Islamic history. The research of their European colleagues who specialized in oriental studies made it possible for them to engage with the Islamic legal tradition.

This chapter and the next are concerned with how European scholarly perspectives on Islam informed European comparative law scholars and pioneered paths for changing Islamic law and legal doctrine.

Before the British occupation of 1882, European scholars of Islamic law, as imperialist agents, had already pursued a rudimentary and distorting type of Islamic legal revivalism. Acting on the premise that if Islamic law could not be eradicated, it could at least be changed, they tried their hands at codifying Islamic legal rules. Before 1882, they had reorganized Islamic legal rules according to the categorical arrangements of particular European codes and doctrinal treatises; they had critiqued the field of Islamic legal theory and method (*uṣūl al-fiqh*); and they had discussed ways in which this field facilitated and obstructed modern Islamic legal reform. They had developed mechanisms for efficiently comparing European and Islamic law, such as with the innovation of concordances and cross-referencing footnotes, and had attacked substantive rules of Islamic *fiqh* that they considered inconvenient, lacking, backward, or morally abhorrent. They had formed and acted upon the premise that a European scholar, armed with knowledge of Islamic law, had the right to intervene in the scholarship and practice of Islamic law, and they had developed the confident belief that it was the right of the informed European scholar to instruct Muslims in matters relating to the law of their faith.

The term "European scholarship" must be used with caution. Many ideas, arguments, books, and articles were produced by European armchair academics who researched in libraries and spent some time visiting Muslim countries for research. However, as Europe became increasingly present and powerful in Muslim countries, the European intellectual engagement in the study of Sharia often flowed from and directly served Europe's imperial agendas. European scholars collaborated with their governments to learn more about local laws and legal traditions sometimes for the mere pursuit of knowledge, but often they did it to facilitate the processes of manipulating, controlling, and changing the colonized people and their indigenous law and legal traditions.

ACADEMIC STUDY OF SHARIA IN EUROPE

The tradition of European scholars studying Near Eastern languages, the Arabs, the Ottomans, and Islamic civilizations may be traced to at least the eleventh century.[1] In Leiden, Oriental studies are thought to have begun in the 1590s.[2] Oxford appointed the first Laudian professor of Arabic, Edward Pococke, in 1636. Pococke's counterparts and near-contemporaries in Europe included François Pétis de la Croix (1653–1713) of France and Thomas Erpenius (1584–1624) of Holland.

Scholars working in this field of research acquired the designation of "orientalists" in French and English during the last quarter of the eighteenth century.[3] They gathered and published through professional societies such as the Royal Asiatic Society and the Société Asiatique. With their editions and annotations of manuscripts, "the growing accessibility of the relevant literary and historical sources" facilitated the emergence of "Islamic studies proper" at the end of the nineteenth century and the beginning of the twentieth.[4] The most celebrated pioneers included Ignác Goldziher (1850–1921), Hellmut Ritter (1892–1971), and

[1] See J. D. J. Waardenburg, "Mustashriḳūn," in *Encyclopaedia of Islam*, 2nd ed. For a famously critical analysis of this body of scholarship, see Edward W. Said, *Orientalism*, 2nd ed. (New York: Vintage Books, 1994). See also Bernard Lewis, "The Question of Orientalism," *New York Review of Books* 29,11 (1982): 49–56; Azim Nanji, ed., *Mapping Islamic Studies: Genealogy, Continuity, and Change* (Berlin: Mouton de Gruyter, 1997); and for a comprehensive stocktaking of the effect of Said's *Orientalism*, Daniel M. Varisco, *Reading Orientalism: Said and the Unsaid* (Seattle: University of Washington Press, 2007).

[2] W. Otterspeer, ed., *Leiden Oriental Connections, 1850–1940* (Leiden: E. J. Brill, 1989).

[3] The designation of "orientalists" is polysemous with the same term, "orientalists," that has been applied to nineteenth- and twentieth-century painters of Arab and Muslim life. On this artistic genre, see, for example, Christine Peltre, *Orientalism* (Paris: Terrail, 2004).

[4] Waardenburg, "Mustashrikūn," 743a. See generally J. D. J. Waardenburg, *L'Islam dans le miroir de l'occident* (Paris: Mouton, 1963).

Louis Massignon (1883–1962). Additionally there was Joseph Schacht (1902–1969) who wrote on Islamic law, Hamilton Alexander Rosskeen Gibb (1895–1971), who wrote on the history of institutions in the Islamic world, Gustave Edmund von Grunebaum (1909–1972), who specialized in the general history of Islamic civilization, and Arendt Jan Wensinck (1882–1939), who examined Islam from the standpoint of religious studies.[5]

A more concerted interest in Sharia, or more specifically in the history, theory, and practice of Islamic law, was shown by some in the later nineteenth century—approximately between 1880 and 1900.[6] Although Goldziher and Schacht were leaders in the early twentieth century (highly regarded European contemporaries were Louis Milliot, Georges-Henri Bousquet, and Octave Pesle), an even earlier generation of scholars made their work possible. Among those historians were T. W. J. Juynboll (1802–1861), Aloys Sprenger (1813–1893), Reinhart Dozy (1820–1883), Alfred Freiherr Kremer (1828–1899), Michael Jan de Goeje (1836–1909), David Margoliouth (1858–1940), Christiaan Snouck Hurgronje (1857–1936), and Eduard Sachau (1845–1930). Some of Schacht's career-defining arguments found their origins in the hypotheses and arguments of these scholars.[7]

These historians produced new interpretations of Islamic history and of the formation of Islamic law that challenged conventional interpretations prevailing within the Islamic world. We will encounter these arguments in the next chapter in seeing how they were reproduced in the writings of Édouard Lambert. Lambert put their ideas about Islamic legal history to practical use by training his Egyptian students with them. One may thereby see how the ideas and methods of European orientalists eventually came to influence the rising generation of Egyptian comparativists.

ORIENTALISTS AND COLONIAL SCHOLARS

The increasing attention that European researchers devoted to Islamic law in the mid- and late-nineteenth century was motivated by two factors. The first can be attributed to their academic interests. Orientalists who worked on Islamic law and legal history were driven to ask and answer as many questions as possible, to construct new understandings of the past, to undermine older understandings,

[5] Waardenburg, "Mustashriḳūn," 743a. Ignác Goldziher was a Hungarian orientalist and one of the founders of modern Islamic studies in Europe. Having studied at the European universities of Budapest, Berlin, Leipzig, and Leiden, he also attended lectures at al-Azhar. He became the first Jewish professor at Budapest University in 1905 and published widely in Hungarian and English. Representative publications translated into English include Ignác Goldziher, *Muslim Studies: On the Development of Hadith* (Chicago: Aldine Pub. Co., 1968); Ignác Goldziher, *Introduction to Islamic Theology and Law* (Princeton: Princeton University Press, 1981).

[6] There were orientalists who in earlier times explored topics in Islamic law. See M. B. Vincent, *Études sur la loi musulmane: Législation criminelle* (Paris: Joubert, 1842). See also Botiveau, *Loi islamique*, 74–102 ("Les Études orientales et le droit musulman").

[7] See Aharon Layish, "Notes on Joseph Schacht's Contribution to the Study of Islamic Law," *BRISMES Bulletin* 9,2 (1985): 132–3.

to create theoretical superstructures, and above all, to create as true a picture of the past as possible. At least, this is how they characterized their own work. They held that history was—speaking in French—a *science*. The word implied to them the pursuit of rigorous, logical, dispassionate, non-ideological study of the past according to the close study of primary sources. Whether they were faithful to such objectives or accomplished them is not relevant for the moment. More important is that they thought this way and made pronouncements to this effect. They spoke often of historical method as "scientific method." This was in keeping with the general upswing of enthusiasm for and confidence in the social sciences and scientific method in nineteenth-century European academia.[8]

The second driving factor was the fact that European countries were engaged in colonial projects in the Muslim world. By the mid-nineteenth century, Britain had long been present in Muslim regions of India, Malaya, and sub-Saharan Africa. France was active in almost all the Ottoman and Arab provinces, the Dutch were in the Indies, Russia had entered Muslim parts of the Caucasus and Central Asia, and a nascent Germany was working to build its young empire. Even the lesser colonial powers of the nineteenth century—for example, Italy and America—were taking an interest in the legal doctrines of the Ottoman, Arab, and Muslim worlds.[9]

The interest of European governments in Muslim regions afforded the study of Muslim and other local customary laws strategic value. European nationals developed an expertise in local laws. Sometimes they went to the colonial regions as established scholars, or sometimes they would go to the colonial regions as government officials and develop expertise, even ostensibly "scholarly" expertise, through their practical activities in service to a colonial administration. A number of treatises produced by Europeans in the colonies were funded by their home governments or by the colonial administrations in place.

Scholarship on Islamic, Arab, and Ottoman law was therefore not the unique pursuit of purely armchair academics. Further complicating the picture, a number of European writers on Islamic law from the nineteenth century had a background in academia but pursued research and published from the colonies, doubling as ostensible scholars and agents of colonial power. Later sections will

[8] The conception of history as a "science" has a long tradition in European and Islamic scholarship. For leading exponents of the conception of history as a science, see the writings of Immanuel Kant, Althusser, Arnold Toynbee, Marc Bloch, Wilhem Windelband, Heinrich Rickert, Wilhem Dilthey, Carl Gustav Hempel, Benedetto Croce, William Dampier, and Thomas Kuhn. European historians of Islam often found justification in pursuing the scientific study of history by citing the work of Ibn Khaldūn, whose conception of "scientific history" corresponded to the modern conception. Had the orientalists known better the work of early modern Ottoman historians, they might also have found correspondence in the theory of history propounded by Mustafa Naima (1655–1716).

[9] Italians constituted one of the largest European minorities in Egypt, second for a long time only to the Greeks. Their jurists were instrumental in reforming Egyptian courts from the 1850s and in the 1870s with the creation of the Mixed Courts. Moriondo, a drafter of the Egyptian codes, was an Italian (I have not been able to confirm Moriondo's first name despite efforts). Americans were involved in the Mixed Courts as judges and lawyers. The most famous American to have been involved in the Mixed Courts was probably Jasper Yates Brinton, author of *The Mixed Courts of Egypt*.

encounter examples in Snouck Hurgronje[10] and L. W. C. (Lodewijk Willem Christiaan) van den Berg, a Dutch jurist without orientalist training who published manuals on Islamic law.[11]

FOUNDATIONS OF A FIELD: BRITISH, RUSSIAN, AND DUTCH WRITINGS

Already in the late eighteenth century, agents of British authority began producing technical works to inform British personnel of the laws and customs of Indian Muslims. This genre of work became increasingly prevalent as the nineteenth century progressed. Some major translation works from British India were the 1791 translation of al-Marghīnānī's *al-Hidāyah* (Guidance) (with successive editions in 1869 and beyond), the 1792 translation of al-Sajāwandī's *Sirājiyyah*, a book on successions, and 1850 translations of the *Fatāwá l-ʿĀlamgīriyyah* (The Fatwas of Alamgir, a.k.a. the Indian Fatwas) concerning contracts.[12] A multitude of technical treatises also appeared, comprised of compendia and syntheses of rules, technical dictionaries, and manuals for legal practitioners and judges.[13] All of these works became reference works, and because they addressed Hanafi law—the Islamic legal school followed in India—British writers in Egypt used the "Indian Fatwas" as a source for understanding aspects of Islamic law as known or practiced in Egypt.

Russian manuals on Islamic law appeared as the Russian Empire became increasingly involved in the Caucasus and Central Asia during the nineteenth

[10] Christiaan Snouck Hurgronje was a Dutch scholar of Oriental cultures and an adviser to the colonial government in the Dutch East Indies. An expert in Malay and Islamic civilization, he lived in Indonesia from 1889 until 1906 and was a professor at the University of Leiden thereafter until his death in 1936. See J. Brugman, "Snouck Hurgronje's Study of Islamic Law," in *Leiden Oriental Connections*, ed. Otterspeer, 82–93; Harry J. Benda, "Christiaan Snouck Hurgronje and the Foundations of Dutch Islamic Policy in Indonesia," *The Journal of Modern History* 30,4 (1958): 338–47.

[11] L. W. C. van den Berg (1845–1927) obtained a doctorate from Leiden in 1868, writing a thesis on Islamic law. See Brugman, "Snouck Hurgronje's Study of Islamic Law," 84.

[12] Charles Hamilton, trans., *The Hedaya, or Guide: A Commentary on the Mussulman Laws* (London: T. Bensley, 1791). Hamilton's English translation of the *Hidāyah* was from a Persian translation of the Arabic original. Muḥammad Awrangzeb ʿĀlamgīr and al-Ḥasan ibn Manṣūr al-Ūzjandī al-Farghānī Qāḍīkhān, *al-Fatāwá al-hindiyyah wa-tuʿarraf bi-l-fatāwá al-ʿālamgīriyyah fī madhhab al-imām Abī Ḥanīfah al-Nuʿmān*, repr. of Bulaq ed. 1310/1891, 6 vols. (Beirut: Dār al-Maʿrifah li-l-Ṭibāʿah wa-l-Nashr, 1973). William Jones, trans., *Al Sirájiyyah, or, the Mohammedan Law of Inheritance, with a Commentary* (Calcutta: Printed by Joseph Cooper, 1792).

[13] Some examples are S. Rousseau, *A Dictionary of Mohammedan Law, Bengal Revenue Terms, Shanscrit, Hindoo, and Other Words, Used in the East Indies* (London: Printed for J. Sewell, 1802); William Macnaghten, *Principles and Precedents of Moohummudan Law* (Calcutta: Church Mission Press, 1825); Roland Knyvet Wilson, *Tables Shewing the Differences between English and Indian Law, under the Several Heads of I. Substantive Criminal Law. II. Law of Evidence. III. Contract Law* (Cambridge: University Press, 1890); Wilson, *An Introduction to the Study of Anglo-Muhammadan Law* (London: W. Thacker, 1894); Wilson, *A Digest of Anglo-Muhammadan Law, Setting Forth in the Form of a Code, with Full References to Modern and Ancient Authorities, the Special Rules Now Applicable to Muhammadans as Such by the Civil Courts of British India* (London: W. Thacker, 1895).

Indian authors and experts published on Islamic law in English. This became more common after 1900. The most prominent examples from before 1900 are the works of Syed Ameer ʿAli (1849–1928).

century.[14] Russian contributions enhanced European literature on Shafiʿi and Shiʿi law, but since most of this writing was in Russian and Shafiʿism was only a marginal *madhhab* to most Arab regions, the Russian works were infrequently cited. However, a relatively prominent Russian known to European scholars was Nikolay Egorovich Tournau (1812–1882).[15] A political post in Azerbaijan facilitated his writing of the *Explication of the Sources of Muslim Law* (1850), which was translated into French.[16] Other Russian works known to Europeans were those of Nauphal on family law.[17]

Holland's colonial interest in the East Indies prompted Dutch scholars to produce new studies on Islamic law. Before 1900, Dutch colonial scholarship was matched in quantity and quality only by French writers in Algeria. A number of important Shafiʿi works were translated.[18] Although Eduard Sachau was German, his 1897 German translation of Abū Shujāʿ al-Iṣfahānī's *Mukhtaṣar fī l-Risālah* should be added here, since it built on the previous work of Juynboll and Van den

[14] On intersections between Russian imperialism, Russian orientalism, and Islamic law, see Austin Jersild, *Orientalism and Empire: North Caucasus Mountain Peoples and the Georgian Frontier, 1845–1917* (Montreal: McGill-Queen's University Press, 2002); Daniel R. Brower and Edward J. Lazzerini, eds., *Russia's Orient: Imperial Borderlands and Peoples, 1700–1917* (Bloomington: Indiana University Press, 1997); Nathaniel Knight, "Grigor'ev in Orenburg, 1851–1862: Russian Orientalism in the Service of Empire?," *Slavic Review* 59,1 (2000): 74–100.

For a discussion of Islamic law under Russian rule, see Alex Marshall, *The Russian General Staff and Asia, 1800–1917* (London: Routledge, 2006); Robert D. Crews, *For Prophet and Tsar* (Cambridge, MA: Harvard University Press, 2006).

See also reviews of present-day, Russian-language scholarship on this topic: Willard Sunderland, "The Caucasian Tangle," *Kritika: Explorations in Russian and Eurasian History* 7,1 (2006): 111–22; Serge A. Zenkovsky, "Kulturkampf in Pre-Revolutionary Central Asia," *American Slavic and East European Review* 14,1 (1955): 15–41. According to Sunderland, a strong Russian-language discussion of Russian treatment of Islamic law in the Caucusus is in Vladimir O. Bobrovnikov, *Musul'mane severnogo Kavkaza: Obychai, pravo, nasilie* (Moscow: Vostochnaia Literatura, 2002).

[15] Alternative spellings are Nikolay, N. N. (as opposed to N. E.), Tounau, and Tournaw. He became active in the Russian imperial administration in the Caucasus, Central Asia, and Persia. He was vice governor for five years in Shemahi, Azerbaijan, or the center of the region historically known as Shirvan. There was another Tornau—Fedor Fedorovich (F. F.) Tornau (1810–1890)—who wrote memoirs of service in the Caucasus during the 1830s.

[16] The English title given is my translation. Baron Nikoli Egorovich Tornau, *Izlozhenīe nachal musul'manskago zakonoviedienīia* (St. Petersburg: 1850), Fr. trans. N. N. Tornau, *Le Droit musulman, exposé d'après les sources*, trans. Louis Prosper Auguste Eschbach (Paris: Cotillon, 1860).

[17] I. de Nauphal, *Cours de droit musulman présenté à l'Institut des langues orientales du Ministère des Affaires Étrangères en l'année 1884/85*, fasc. 1: *La Propriété* (St. Petersburg: Trenké et Fusnot, 1886); idem, *Système législatif musulman: Mariage* (St. Petersburg: Trenké et Fusnot, 1890); idem, *Législation musulmane: Filiation et divorce* (St. Petersburg: Trenké et Fusnot, 1893).

[18] Salomon Keijzer, *Handboek voor het mohammedaansch regt* [trans. of *al-Tanbīh* of Fīrūzābādī] (The Hague: Belinfante, 1853); Keijzer, trans., *Précis de jurisprudence musulmane selon le rite châfeite* [annot. trans. of al-Iṣfahānī's *Mukhtaṣar fī l-fiqh ʿalá madhhab al-Shāfiʿī*] (Leiden: E. J. Brill, 1859); A. W. T Juynboll, trans., *Jus Shafiiticum: At-Tanbîh* [of al-Shīrāzī] (Leiden: E. J. Brill, 1879); L. W. C. van den Berg, trans., *Minhâdj aṭ-ṭâlibīn: Le Guide des zélés croyants. Manuel de jurisprudence musulmane selon le rite de Châfiʿī* [trans. of al-Nawawī's *Minhāj al-ṭālibīn*] (Batavia: Imprimerie du Gouvernement, 1882). In terms of popularity and influence in the colonial period, the *Minhāj* could be compared to the *Hidāyah* of al-Marghīnānī in the Hanafi regions and the *Mukhtaṣar* of Sīdī Khalīl in the Maliki regions. Van den Berg's work is singular in that it presents the translation and original text on the same page. However, the French translation was not made directly from the Arabic, but is a translation of the Dutch manuscript that was Van den Berg's original translation of the Arabic. Later scholars who examined the work found that the Dutch version was more precise and that the French translation of the Dutch was lacking. See unfavorable reviews by Snouck Hurgronje, "Droit musulman." See also citations in Benda, "Christiaan Snouck Hurgronje," 84, 92.

Berg. Sachau's translation added to the translations and editions of Abū Shujāʿ, this important Shafiʿi authority in the East Indies.[19]

Beyond translations and editions of Arabic manuscripts, Dutch writers produced technical treatises synthesizing and summarizing Islamic law and legal history. Th. W. Juynboll (1866–1948) produced two Dutch-language textbooks on Shafiʿi law.[20] His 1903 textbook was, according to many European scholars, the only real textbook of Islamic law, in the sense of a "secondary" work, of its time. The book drew heavily from the disparate articles and book reviews written by Snouck Hurgronje. Another example was L. W. C. van den Berg's Dutch-language, secondary treatise on Islamic law according to the Hanafi and Shafiʿi schools. Its reception among Francophone and English scholars was due principally to a French translation published in Algiers in 1896.[21]

The works of Th. W. Juynboll and Van den Berg are of special concern, for their work reflected the incipient consolidation of Islamic law studies as a distinctive field of European scholarship. The work of Dutch scholars reveals that the building blocks of a "field" in Islamic law studies were coalescing with increasing cogency at the end of the nineteenth century. The field's literature now included edited primary sources in the original Arabic, translated Arabic primary sources, technical manuals explaining the law, legal histories, and secondary treatises explaining and commenting on both Islamic law and legal history. A body of knowledge, conventions, and popular arguments and conceptual taboos—in other words, a professional, disciplinary discourse—was coming into existence. The production of their two textbooks is especially important because a textbook synthesizes the state of the art in a field's findings.

Even though Van den Berg's textbook was scathingly reviewed, the book constituted one of the few concise handbooks of Islamic law available to specialists, and more importantly, to non-specialists, in the 1870s and 1880s.[22] Even the later French translation of Van den Berg's textbook is an example of the cumulative developments of the field, since it includes references to a number of works that had been recently published by French scholars in Algeria.[23]

[19] Eduard Sachau, *Muhammedanisches Recht nach schafiitischer Lehre* (Stuttgart: W. Spemann, 1897).

[20] For biographical comments, see Otterspeer, ed., *Leiden Oriental Connections*, 28–32, 43–7. For his texts, see Th. W. Juynboll, *De hoofdregelen der Sjafi'itische leer van het pandrecht, met een onderzoek naar haar ontstaan en naar haren invloed in Ned.-Indië* (Leiden: E. J. Brill, 1893); Juynboll, *Handleiding tot de kennis van de mohammedaansche wet volgens de leer der Sjâfi'itische school* (Leiden: E. J. Brill, 1903).

[21] L. W. C. van den Berg, *De beginselen van het mohammedaansche recht volgens de imâm's Aboe Hanîfat en Sjâfe'î* (Batavia: Bruining, 1874), Russ. trans. V. F. Girgas (St. Petersburg, 1882), Fr. trans. R. de France de Tersant (Algiers: A. Jourdan, 1896). Van den Berg also worked in India and wrote about Islamic law in India, as well as on legislative reforms in the Ottoman Empire. He wrote many other smaller but more focused case studies, for example, on Muslim clerics and religious learning on Java and Madura in the East Indies. For a fuller bibliography of his production up to 1906, see *Winkler Prins' geïllustreerde encyclopaedie*, 3rd ed., 3: 276–7.

[22] Benda, "Christiaan Snouck Hurgronje," 84, 92.

[23] Van den Berg claims that he wrote the book with the intention of using only "Arabic" sources (i.e., especially those in translation) without reference to the European secondary sources. He considered translated works to fall within the category of Arabic sources. The book reflects the organization and content of the Arabic *fiqh* books from which he derived it, principally the *Mukhtaṣar* of Sīdī Khalīl and his own translation of *Minhāj al-ṭālibīn*. For Hanafis he followed al-Qudūrī's *Mukhtaṣar*, Hamilton's translation of the *Hidāyah*, and the *Fatāwá ʿĀlamgīriyyah*, which also had translations. He appears to

Certain points that Snouck Hurgronje criticized about Van den Berg's treatise were arguably advantages that advanced the field of European studies on Islamic law. Van den Berg's book did not go deeply into historical problems that occupied the full-time historians of Islamic law. It did not delve into the complex mass of Arabic primary sources, did not address in detail the authenticity of hadith literature (a major interest of Goldziher), did not discuss the ostensibly non-Islamic origins of Islamic law (an increasingly popular idea among orientalists), did not talk about the complex aspects of and inter-*madhhab* variances in Islamic legal theory, and did not give the reader a full sense of the diversity of rules that occur in Islamic law. Van den Berg's book also did not handle issues such as the difference between theory and practice in Islamic law and the relationship between law and custom. The problem for Snouck Hurgronje was that, in his view, all of these topics needed to be familiar to the European reader who wanted to understand Islamic law and realize how difficult it would be to apply in modern circumstances. This is not to say that Van den Berg was necessarily ignorant of the details he left out. His aim was, in several respects, only to provide a summary. Such an effort can produce positive results for building a field. A field is only a field if it possesses a well-known book that scholars can accept or critique as they like.

Snouck Hurgronje, one of the most famous and influential of all Dutch orientalists, represents a classic example of the combined orientalist-cum-colonial agent. Yet his significance here is not in the area of his translations and technical treatises; it is that he was a historian of Islam and Islamic law who advanced many theses that challenged conventional interpretations of Islamic law and legal history that prevailed in the Muslim world during his lifetime. His influence on European scholars of comparative law will become central to the subsequent discussion concerning intellectual influences on Édouard Lambert.

OTTOMAN LAW AND EUROPEAN-ISLAMIC COMPARATIVISM

At the beginning of the nineteenth century, the cities of the North African coastline in Algeria, Tunisia, and Libya were only nominally under Ottoman control. The case was similar in Egypt and parts of the Levant, Ottoman portions of the Caucasus and Crimea, much of Muslim Eastern Europe, and parts of modern-day Greece. Moreover, Ottoman Istanbul and Anatolia were never colonized in the nineteenth century like the regions mentioned earlier. This makes it problematic to refer to colonial scholarship of "law of the Ottoman Empire." Nevertheless, the Ottoman Empire was an empire for all of its complexity, and writers did speak of

have been aware of the literature from India, Malay, and Istanbul, and the French-Algerian writings of the 1880s. For a discussion of his sources, see Van den Berg, *Principes du droit musulman*, 1–19. One of the peculiar aspects of the long bibliography at the end of his first chapter in this French edition is that it includes all of the Algerian sources from the 1880s and 1890s that post-dated his original Dutch edition of 1874. It is not clear whether he or the translator added these.

"a law of the Ottoman empire" even when they were describing legal systems and places that were not exclusively or precisely Ottoman.

European writers with interests in the Ottoman Empire and whose geographical focus was on Istanbul were active early in the nineteenth century. They also presented Europeans with scholarship on Hanafi law of Ottoman Eastern Europe, Anatolia, Syria, and Egypt. One of these was Ignatius Mouradgea, or Baron D'Ohsson (1740–1807), who does not fit neatly within a mold of nineteenth-century European writers.[24] Although he possessed French lineage and a title of Swedish nobility, he was an Ottoman of Armenian origins. Nevertheless, he was fluent in European languages and culture. Between 1787 and 1820, he produced (in part posthumously, via his son) a French treatise entitled *Tableau général de l'empire othoman*. For all of its imperfections, the book became a widely read statement on Ottoman and Hanafi laws and customs.[25] For its portion on private law, the work depended heavily on the sixteenth-century treatise *Multaqá al-abḥur* (Confluence of the Seas) by Ibrāhīm al-Ḥalabī (d. 1549), which in its original Arabic was a popular primary textbook of Islamic law in Istanbul during the eighteenth century.[26]

D'Ohsson's translation was more like a paraphrase: it condensed the contents of Ibrāhīm al-Ḥalabī's *Multaqá* into terse statements of positive law. For European agents and scholars operating in the Ottoman Empire, D'Ohsson's translation became a reference tool of first resort.[27] The author may also have found popularity among European scholars due to his professed respect for the "rapid progress of Christian Europe in all aspects of science."[28] The book was referenced by later European scholars and certain of its ideas about the nature of Islamic jurisprudence, specifically the state of Islamic legal reasoning (*ijtihād*), influenced the powerful French jurist in Egypt, Lambert.

D'Ohsson's paraphrase of the *Multaqá* did more for European writers than allow them to cite a primary Arabic source on questions of Hanafi law. Because

[24] Ignatius Mouradgea, born outside of Istanbul to a family of French and Armenian background, was ennobled as Baron D'Ohsson in 1775 (or 1786) by King Gustav III with whom he had formed ties. He was a Swedish-Ottoman translator for the Swedish legation in Istanbul, and from 1795 to 1799 he was the equivalent of the Swedish ambassador to the sultan. See Sture Theolin, *The Torch of the Empire* (Istanbul: Yapi Kredi Kültür, 2002), 38–40; Fatma Müge Göçek, *Rise of the Bourgeoisie, Demise of Empire: Ottoman Westernization and Social Change* (New York: Oxford University Press, 1996), 94–5.

[25] The seven-volume *Tableau général de l'empire othoman* (1787–1820) was D'Ohsson's most notable work. He produced it, in part, to counter prevailing views in Europe that the Ottoman Empire was devoid of a justice system and a conception of justice. These views were given famous articulation in the work of Baron de Montesquieu in his *De l'Esprit des lois* (1748). The volumes printed before the French Revolution cover Ottoman and Islamic law, including an examination of Islamic *fiqh*, state law (*ḳānūn*), custom (*ʿādet*), and the sultan's power of decree (*örf*).

[26] It does not appear that D'Ohsson could read Arabic. It is possible that he translated the *Multaqá* from an Ottoman translation and commentary composed by a certain Mevkufat in the seventeenth century (alternatively: Mawkufat). The Mevkufat edition was reprinted several times in the nineteenth century.

[27] See de Miltitz, *Manuel des consuls*, xxxvii ff., 516–31. This extensive handbook was prepared for Prussian diplomats to provide knowledge about politics, diplomacy, law, and history for major areas of the world. In addition to providing a summary of Ottoman legal institutions, it includes a detailed appendix on the history of Islam and Islamic legal history. The work is heavily concerned with commercial law and capitulations, for which it draws on an extensive body of European writings. For all matters of law outside of commerce, it relies heavily on D'Ohsson.

[28] D'Ohsson, *Tableau général de l'empire ottoman, divisé en deux parties, dont l'une comprend la législation mahométane, l'autre, l'histoire de l'empire ottoman*, 7 vols. in 5 (Istanbul: Isis, 2001), 1: 7.

the rules of the *Multaqá* were presented in concise form, not unlike the articles in the *Code civil*, the translation helped European writers to learn Islamic legal rules, to manipulate them, and to compare them with rules of continental European codes.[29]

One early European who used recent translations to directly compare Islamic and European private law was Domenico Gatteschi, author of *Manuale di diritto pubblico e privato ottomano* (1865).[30] He was an Italian lawyer, trained in Pisa, and resident in Alexandria. His book was an encyclopedia of Ottoman laws and those pertaining to Egypt, with a particular focus on commercial law, capitulations, and the legal status of foreigners in the Empire. The work was written in the same spirit as the works of French lawyers in Algeria: it was intended as a technical treatise to help Europeans resident in Egypt to understand the multiple legal systems in Egypt.[31] The book dedicated over one hundred pages to a concordance of Islamic private law with continental European law. This kind of concordance would become important for later attempts to rewrite and re-theorize on the fundamentals of Islamic contract law.[32]

Gatteschi's *Manuale* reorganized statements of Islamic positive law according to the *Code civil*'s structural hierarchy of Books, Titles, Chapters, and Articles, with Book I pertaining to the law of Persons, Book II pertaining to the law of Property, and Book III on the law of Obligations. Gatteschi then enumerated the individual rules: literally, he gave them numbers.[33] This mode of organization marked a departure from the manner in which Islamic law had traditionally been conceptualized and organized in the manuals of classical Muslim jurists, and later we will see that structural reorganizations of this sort had implications for the substantive content of the Islamic positive law, at least as it was articulated by academic jurists. Gatteschi's *Manuale* represents the first instance of European comparativism and concordance writing that would influence later Egyptian jurists to reassess the organizational and conceptual paradigms, as well as substance, of classical Islamic law.

Another significance of the *Manuale* as a forerunner to Islamic-European legal comparativism is that the book cross-references many of the articles of Islamic positive law to corresponding articles from Roman law in Justinian's *Institutes* and *Digest*. Gatteschi's cross-referencing is the work of an Italian lawyer attuned to trends in contemporary Italian scholarship of the precise period in which he published the book. His citation format is that of the continental scholars of

[29] D'Ohsson's style of translation was taken up soon after in European paraphrases of Khalīl by Perron and Abū Shujāʿ by Keijzer.

[30] Gatteschi et al., *Manuale di diritto*. The book on property was translated by Edward A. Van Dyck as *Real Property, Mortgage and Wakf According to Ottoman Law* (London: Wyman and Sons, 1884). On his biography, see L. A. Balboni, *Gl'italiani nella civiltà egiziana del secolo XIX°: Storia, biografie, monografie* (Alexandria: V. Penasson, 1906), 2: 109–10.

[31] See his prefatory writings in *Giornale di legislazione e di giurisprudenza* 7 (1859): 649, 721. See also Amédée Roux's review, "Manuel de droit public et privé ottoman, par le docteur Domenico Gatteschi," *Revue historique de droit français et étranger* 11 (1865), 646–50.

[32] See Chapter 10.

[33] The Ottoman *Mecelle*, which also enumerated articles of Islamic law in a code, had not yet been produced.

Roman law (e.g., "L. 7. § 13 D. *De acquir. rer.* <<Ratio non permittit...>>"). He had received his legal training in Pisa in the 1850s, a decade when Italian jurists were studying classical Roman law as an ancillary project to building the Italian *Codice civile* of 1865.

It is not clear why Gatteschi did not cross-reference the Islamic rules he enumerated to the French *Code civil*. One might surmise that his book was the product of an era of Italian nationalism, Italian enthusiasm for Italy's emergent *Codice civile*, and a premonition among Italian jurists that the French *Code civil* was a flawed work and declining in international influence. Moreover, in the 1860s, Italians—the largest European minority in Egypt—perhaps considered themselves equal or superior to the French in the area of influence and prominence in Egyptian law.

Unfortunately for the Islamic law specialist, Gatteschi did not provide an equally competent footnoting apparatus for the 526 articles of Islamic law. It is therefore not certain where each article in his codification of the Islamic law actually found its primary source. Gatteschi did, however, include a bibliography at the top of each "Title." Taken together, the bibliography reflects almost the entirety of European translations and textbooks written up to 1865. The work on which he most closely relied was that of D'Ohsson.

As a foundational work in Islamic-European comparative law studies, Gatteschi's book was a start. It demonstrated that Islamic law could be comprehended by the European lawyer who was not an expert in Islamic law (although one might equally argue that the format and approach led the inexperienced European reader to a colossal miscomprehension). The book also demonstrated that Islamic law could be organized and codified according to a conceptual and organizational framework that resonated with continental European lawyers. Furthermore, it purported to show that Islamic substantive law was in many aspects similar to continental European law. The book was a forerunner to a number of concordances of Egyptian, Islamic, and French law that aided in the production of new comparative Islamic-European law research in the 1900s.[34]

SAVVAS PACHA, SNOUCK HURGRONJE, AND LAMBERT ON ISLAMIC LAW

In the 1890s, the Ottoman Savvas Pacha participated in the development of the European field of Islamic law studies. He was similar to Baron D'Ohsson in that he was not a native of a European state; on the other hand, as a prominent Ottoman diplomat who served as the Ottoman governor of Crete in 1880 and as foreign minister in the government of Saʿīd Pāshā in 1886, he was internationally known, and was taken seriously enough by Europeans that his work became part of the canon of European scholarly literature on Islamic law.

[34] Two of importance are Joseph Aziz, *Concordance des codes égyptiens mixtes et indigènes avec le code Napoléon, suivie d'un appendice relatant la jurisprudence de la Cour d'Appel Mixte d'Alexandrie* (Alexandria, 1886), an early concordance of the Egyptian and French civil codes; and the earlier-referenced al-Minyāwī, *al-Muqāranāt al-tashrīʿiyyah*, a concordance of the *Code civil* and Maliki law.

Savvas was of Greek origin and a Christian, although in his works he professed absolute faith in Islamic revelation, the supremacy of Islamic law, and the truth and reliability of the Quran and prophetic tradition. In his retirement, he wrote three books on the theories and methods of Islamic law (*uṣūl al-fiqh*): *Étude sur la théorie du droit musulman* (1892), *Le droit musulman expliqué* (1896), and *Étude sur la théorie du droit musulman, deuxième partie* (1898). The first two works were assailed in reviews by Goldziher and Snouck Hurgronje.[35] Savvas's 1896 book was specifically dedicated to refuting Goldziher's review, and his 1898 work was pitched to address both scholars.

The heated exchanges in journals and books between the European orientalists and Savvas are essential background to understanding Édouard Lambert's interventions in Egyptian and Islamic law. The importance does not lie in who was right and wrong, or who wrote the better books. The importance lies in the fact that we see in these exchanges the crystallizing of state-of-the-art, European-language, textbook explanations of Islamic law in history and practice. Their contrary views pertained not only to Islamic legal history, but to how Islamic law should be understood, approached, and reformed by contemporary jurists.

It would be impractical to detail all of the points on which the three scholars disagreed; the important point concerns the kinds of disagreements that arose. One dispute pertained to the role of scientific inquiry and empirically verifiable learning in the conception and production of historical writing. These were topics in Ottoman and Egyptian literature in the 1880s, and an increasing body of historical scholarship is now tracing the evolution of debates on social science methods in the Ottoman and Arab world.[36] Savvas believed in Muslim revelation, although he stated it could not be factually proven. But Snouck Hurgronje and Goldziher considered this professed belief in Islamic revelation to be a "scientific" deficiency on Savvas's part, and they argued that this premise would necessarily prevent him from making scientific and logical explanations in the effort to conceptualize a viable legal system for modern Islamic law.

Savvas claimed that Islamic law was a fluid and adaptive law, open to constant changes and pious innovations. He rejected the notion that a gate of *ijtihād* had closed in a previous century. Snouck Hurgronje and Goldziher, by contrast, viewed Islamic law as trapped in methodological and ideological impasses. They traced these impasses to an ostensible closure of the gate of *ijtihād*, which they claimed was an empirically proven phenomenon. Savvas believed that Islamic law could be the basis of a modern, legal system for the Muslim world, and one that would keep Muslims up to date with the changing circumstances of life. (However, he also urged fusions of European and Islamic law.) Snouck Hurgronje considered this aspiration to be a fantasy. He had little faith in the capacity for classical *fiqh* to become the basis of a modern, applied law.

Finally, Savvas thought that *uṣūl al-fiqh*—its study and its revival—was the essential tool for producing a modern Islamic law; Snouck Hurgronje thought

[35] Goldziher, in *Byzantinische Zeitschrift* 2,2 (1893); Snouck Hurgronje, in *Revue de l'histoire des religions* 37 (1896).

[36] See recent work by Marwa El-Shakry, Omnia El-Shakry, and Hakan Karateke.

that *uṣūl al-fiqh* was not legal methodology but a fractious and dated theoretical literature that could not be relied upon to make modern law.

In the short term, the two Europeans won the day among their European colleagues. The ideas of Goldziher and Snouck Hurgronje, having formed against those of Savvas, evidently influenced Édouard Lambert and his conceptions about Islamic law and legal reform. In turn, such ideas and practices as formulated in Berlin, Paris, Amsterdam, Istanbul, Algiers, and Batavia would eventually find their way to Egypt, and once there, into the content of Islamic legal revivalist thought.

5

The Long Arms of Legal Thought from Algeria, France, and Germany

Comparative law emerged as a powerful school of thought in Europe at the end of the nineteenth century. As important to Egypt as the codification movement, it helped to transform Egyptian legal thought and law.[1] A timeless field of study reified by European scholars, the new comparative law compared laws for more than the mere sake of it: comparative law promoted legal change in European and non-European countries. As a discipline purposively developed by European law scholars who knew each other and shared objectives, it comprised premises, theories, and ambitions that had express implications for reform agendas in Islamic legal thought and practice. Within and around the ambit of comparative law, scholars also reified a discipline they called "legal history," which they equipped with ideas, premises, and agendas that served projects of reforming domestic laws and legal traditions in the colonies. Related to their zeal for both comparative law and legal history, European jurists at the turn of the twentieth century also took an increasing interest in utilizing new social sciences to facilitate legal progress. This enthusiasm also found its way into Egyptian legal thought.

This chapter explores the key trends in European legal writing beyond orientalism that impacted legal education and thought in Egypt. The first part discusses developments in French Algeria, where late nineteenth-century scholars developed a basic comparative method to compare European and Islamic law and, from there, to reform the latter on the model of the former. The second part will discuss developments on the European continent in comparative law, legal history, and other social science interventions in the law, highlighting ideas that were to become prominent and transformative in the writings and work of French and Egyptian jurists.

THE DRIVE TO CODIFY, COMPARE, AND MANIPULATE LEGAL TRADITION IN ALGERIA

An indicator of the need to investigate connections between the legal scholarship of French Algeria and Egypt is the work of the Egyptian Muḥammad Qadrī Pasha.

[1] If contemporary lawyers were to think of the field of Law and Economics and its transformative powers in interpreting case law and legal history, it would be an approximate comparison for appreciating the power comparative law was intended to deliver for continental European law.

Islamic Legal Revival: Reception of European Law and Transformations in Islamic Legal Thought in Egypt, 1875–1952. First Edition. Leonard Wood.

His 1875 codification of Islamic personal status rules bears unmistakable similarities to a book with the same title by Édouard Sautayra and Eugène Cherbonneau, published in Algiers in 1873. Qadrī's code of Islamic contract laws, often hailed for its originality, was structurally modeled on the Franco-Egyptian civil codes.

Reorganizing Islamic substantive rules to match the structural paradigms of French codes was not invented in Egypt but was a well-established practice in French Algeria before 1875. Since the 1830s, Islamic law had been an integral part of the colonial Algerian legal sphere. As a result, more groundbreaking, transformational ideas and approaches appeared in Algeria. Writers produced translations, critical editions of classical texts, historical studies, analytical studies, field manuals, and new codifications, both official and unofficial.

Connections formed between Algerian and Egyptian legal scholars and scholarship. British Egypt was closer to French Algeria than British India, the Dutch Indies, or the Russian Caucasus. Whereas in British India Anglo-Muhammadan law consisted of substantive Hanafi family law subjected to British procedural law, in Egypt Muslim family law was increasingly influenced by Franco-Egyptian civil procedures and Francophone professors of civil law. Also, French professors and writers routinely moved between Algiers and Cairo. Eugène Clavel taught at the Algiers Law Faculty and founded a law journal in Cairo.[2] L. W. C. van den Berg, the colonial scholar, Henri Lamba, a professor at the Khedivial Law School, and Gérard Pélissié du Rausas, first dean of the École Française de Droit du Caire all moved to Cairo from Algiers. When the Cairo University Law Faculty excluded French professors between 1907 and 1923, they continued to teach and shape the course of Egypt's legal thought at the École Française de Droit.

French-Algerian models for performing comparative studies between French and Islamic law were not neutral but pro-French. They assumed the aggressive disposition of the *mission civilatrice* and as such French jurists made no apologies about their intention to reform the theory and practice of *fiqh*. Their writings adopted the premise that an informed European had every right to intervene in and to change Islamic doctrine and practice.

When Édouard Lambert wrote about Islamic law mindful of an Egyptian audience, he displayed more sensitivity to Muslim sensibilities than his Francophone peers in Algeria. His more cooperative disposition resulted from his left-of-center politics and the requirements of French policy in Egypt, which focused on disparaging the British rather than the Egyptians. Nevertheless, Lambert held that Europeans had a right to intervene in Islamic law by virtue of their grasp on rational and social sciences and because of the civilizational advancement of Europe. For Lambert, as for the French jurists in Algeria, comparing law was a process whereby two systems of law were laid side by side, the superior laws (generally European) were identified, and European laws updated Islamic law.

[2] *Revue internationale de législation et de jurisprudence musulmane* (Cairo, 1895–96).

CODIFIERS AND COMPARATIVISTS BEFORE THE FOUNDATION OF THE ALGIERS LAW SCHOOL

Before Algerian-Islamic norms could be laid alongside French law, they needed to be made accessible to French jurists. Moreover, demand in Algeria for education, scholarship, and field manuals on Islamic law resulted from the fact that French lawyers and judges handled Islamic law across the spectrum of private law. Therefore French texts on the history, theory, and substance of Islamic law appeared, of which several were additionally concerned with transforming Islamic *fiqh* in theory and practice. Before the foundation of the École de Droit d'Alger in 1880, such books were produced by scholars and colonial agents variously working for universities in France and the French government. The beginning was a nineteenth-century translation wave paralleling that of the Dutch Indies. The first and most influential work was Nicolas Perron's *Précis* (1848), a six-volume translation and commentary of the *Mukhtaṣar* by Sīdī Khalīl (ibn Isḥāq al-Jundī), published with support by the French Ministry of War.[3] In 1882, O. Houdas and F. Martel translated the *Tuḥfah* of Ibn ʿĀṣim (1359–1426), another Maliki authority.[4] In 1898, Perron translated *al-Mizān al-ṣughrá* (The Great Scales) of Aḥmad al-Shaʿrānī (d. ca. 1565).

An early French textbook on Islamic and Algerian law, in part comparative, was Charles Gillotte's *Traité de droit musulman* (1854). Gillotte was among the civilian lawyers in the colonial administration who advocated suppressing the Muslim courts and subsuming all jurisdictions under French law. This objective did not stop him from recognizing that French judges still handled issues under the jurisdiction of Islamic law.[5] Insofar as French courts were appeals courts to *qāḍī* courts, he envisioned that French law could exert a downward pressure to modernize Algerian-Islamic law—that is, to make it more French.

Gillotte summarized Islamic laws based on the translations of D'Ohsson and Perron and related what he considered the most important "*principes*" across the

[3] Its full title was *Précis de jurisprudence musulmane ou principes de législation musulmane civile et religieuse selon le droit malékite* (Paris: Imprimerie Nationale, 1848–54). The first edition was printed in Paris in 1855, although it was dated as 1848. There were additional printings until 1883. G. Delphin made an edition in 1900. In 1889, E. Fagnan published in Algiers the *Concordances du manuel de Sidi Khalîl* in reference to the edition of 1883. An Italian translation was made in 1919 by I. Guidi and D. Santillana. Other partial translations appeared, among them those of E. Sautayra and E. Cherbonneau on personal status and on succession (Paris, 1873–74), of N. Seignette (Constantine, 1878; Paris, 1911), of E. Fagnan on jihad (Algiers, 1908), then marriage and divorce (Algiers, 1909), and of L. Bercher on apostasy (1923). The most recent was G. H. Bousquet, *Abrégé de la loi musulmane selon la rite de l'imâm Mâlek*, 4 vols. (Algiers-Paris, 1956–62), 62. See M. Bencheneb, "Khalīl b. Isḥāḳ," *Encyclopaedia of Islam*, 2nd ed.; C. Brockelmann, *Geschichte der arabischen Litteratur* (Leiden: E. J. Brill, 1937–49), 2: 83; S 2: 96–99. Arabic sources are rich with biographies of Khalīl and indices of the commentaries on the *Mukhtaṣar*. A recent summary is found in ʿAlī Jumʿah Muḥammad, *al-Madkhal ilá dirāsat al-madhāhib al-fiqhiyyah* (Cairo: Dār al-Salām, 2004).

For an English translation of Perron's *Précis de jurisprudence musulmane*, see F. H. Ruxton, trans., *Mâliki Law: Being a Summary from French Translations of the Mukhtasar of Sîdî Khalîl* (London: Luzac and Co., 1916).

[4] Muḥammad b. Muḥammad (Ibn ʿĀṣim), *Traité de droit musulman: La Tohfat d'Ebn Acem*, trans. O. Houdas and F. Martel (Algiers: Gavault Saint-Lager, 1882).

[5] Ch. Gillotte et al., *Traité de droit musulman précédé du décret du 31 décembre, 1859*, 2nd ed. (Constantine: Alessi and Arnolet, 1860), xi.

private law spectrum. The focus on principles—pithy articulations of middle-level generalities—was intended to help French judges who needed handbooks of easy reference. Gillotte organized the rules from Sīdī Khalīl's *Mukhtaṣar* into three books of persons, property, and contracts, on the categorical model of the *Code civil*. He cross-referenced Islamic rules to corollaries in the *Code civil*. For example, on property, the first rules Gillotte posits are cross-referenced to *Code civil* articles 516, 528, and 529, the first articles on property. This was a transformative act: the Islamic rules were approximated to civil law, and where possible, Gillotte claimed the Islamic rules were the same as in civil law. In these ways, the book prepared the way for further Islamic-European concordances.

Gillotte looked down on Islamic law and hoped to change it, even by way of a book that was supposed to translate it.[6] He wrote:

> All of our efforts must serve the fusion [of French and Muslim law], to make a special and perfect mix of all interests. The justice that we exercise is the product of civilization and the best expression of our victories in the preceding centuries.
>
> Justice must be a common force creating an obstacle against injustice. Like order, it begins with force. Since we are the strongest, we do not need to hesitate to impose the benefits of our institutions on those we have vanquished and on those whom we must protect from themselves.
>
> One must not believe that the ideas of our law are difficult to make popular among the Muslims. Roman law represents a common source from which people take their inspirations. Muslim law and French law have retained its ineffaceable imprint. And, apart from questions related to personal status and some rare exceptions, the same rules are observed.
>
> Reassured by the wisdom of those who preside over the destinies of Algeria, we await with confidence that moment when, on the basis of justice, the Government will do away forever more with any barrier that separates Arab society from ours.[7]

Nineteenth-century orientalist historians commonly asserted that Islamic law's origins lay in Roman law. This notion became a basis upon which comparativists championed their project of comparing and combining European and Islamic law. Lambert argued, for example, that Islamic and French law could be reunited as one law because they both had Roman law as a common parent.[8]

In 1873, Édouard Sautayra, a colonial official, and Eugène Cherbonneau, an orientalist, advanced the works of Gillotte and Perron.[9] Their source text was Perron's translation of Khalīl's *Mukhtaṣar*. They took the material further by rearranging the *Précis* according to the order of the *Code civil*. Going further still, their commentary pointed to differing rules in the Hanafi and Shafiʿi schools.

[6] For a similar attitude, see E. Sautayra and E. Cherbonneau, *Droit musulman du statut personnel et des successions* (Paris: Maisonneuve et cie., 1873–74), i–viii.

[7] Gillotte et al., *Traité de droit musulman*, xix–xx.

[8] See pp. 63–4, 103–4, 137, 140, 145, 149–50.

[9] See Sautayra and Cherbonneau, *Droit musulman*. See also Justin Brun-Durand, "Edouard Sautayra," *Dictionnaire biographique et biblio-iconographique de la Drôme* (Grenoble: Librairie Dauphinoise, 1901), 2: 334–5; David S. Powers, "Orientalism, Colonialism, and Legal History: The Attack on Muslim Family Endowments in Algeria and India," *Comparative Studies in Society and History* 31,3 (1989): 535–71, at 544.

Table 5.1. Tables of content of Sautayra and Cherbonneau's *Droit musulman* (1873) and Qadrī Pasha's *Droit musulman* (1875) compared.[10]

Édouard Sautayra and Eugene Cherbonneau, *Droit musulman. Du statut personnel et des successions.* Vol. I. (1873)	Qadri Pasha, *Droit musulman. Du statut personnel et des successions* (1875)
1: Demand in Marriage	1.1.1: Demand in Marriage
2: Conditions to Validity	1.1.2: Conditions to Validity
3: Dowry	1.1.7: Dowry
4: Impediments to Marriage	1.1.3: Impediments to Marriage
5: Formalities in Marriage	
6: Vitiating Factors: Absolute and Relative	1.1.9: Vitiating Factors: Absolute and Relative
7: Evidence of Marriage	
8: Marriage between Infidels and between Muslims and Infidels	1.1.8: Union of Muslims with Christians and Jewish Women; Marriage of Non-Muslims
9: Rights and Duties of Spouses	1.2: Rights and Obligations of Spouses
Obligations of the Husband	1.2.1: Obligations of the Husband
[Obligations of the Wife]	1.2.3.4.1: Obligations of the Wife
[Rights of the Wife]	1.2.3.4.2: Rights of the Wife
10: Obligations Triggered by Marriage; Alimony	1.2.2: Obligations of the Husband for Wives' Maintenance
11: Idda and Istibra (Waiting Periods for Women after Divorce)	1.3.5: Idda
12: Divorce	1.3: Dissolution of Marriage by Repudiation and Divorce
12.1. Mutual Consent	1.3.1.2: Mutual Consent
12.2. By Law	
12.2: Impotence	1.3.3: Impotence
12.2: Blasphemy	1.3.4: Apostasy
13: Repudiation	1.3.1: Repudiation
14: Vow of Continence, Assertion of Prohibited Degree, Accusation of Unchastity (Ila, Zihar, Liʿan)	
15: Paternity, Filiation, Verification of Kinship and Milk Kinship	1.4: Children
1. Paternity and Filiation	1.4.1: Paternity and Filiation
2. Adoption	1.4.5: Found Children
3. Verification of Paternity	1.4.1.4: Verification of Birth, Paternity, and Kinship
4. Milk Kinship	
16: Paternal Authority	1.4.5: Paternal Authority
17: Maternal Guardianship (Hadana)	1.4.2.3 Maternal Guardianship (Hadana)
	1.5: Guardianship, Interdiction, Donations Inter Vivos, and Bequests
18: Guardianship	1.5.1: Guardianship
19: Majority	1.5.2.2: Age of Reason, Adolescence, Majority
20: Incapacity	1.5.2.1: Incapacity
21: Dowry	1.1.7: Dowry
22: Succession	2: Succession

Cross-references were made to the European-language translations of al-Ḥalabī's *Multaqá*, Abū Shujāʿ's *Mukhtaṣar*, and al-Marghīnānī's *Hidāyah*.

As already mentioned, Muḥammad Qadrī Pasha may have loosely patterned the structure and approach of his unofficial codification of personal status law on Sautayra and Cherbonneau. There is no sure proof, but occasional resemblances in wording, ordering, and appearances are suggestive (see Table 5.1 and Fig. 5.1).

[10] This summary of the tables of contents of each work is abridged to highlight similiarities.

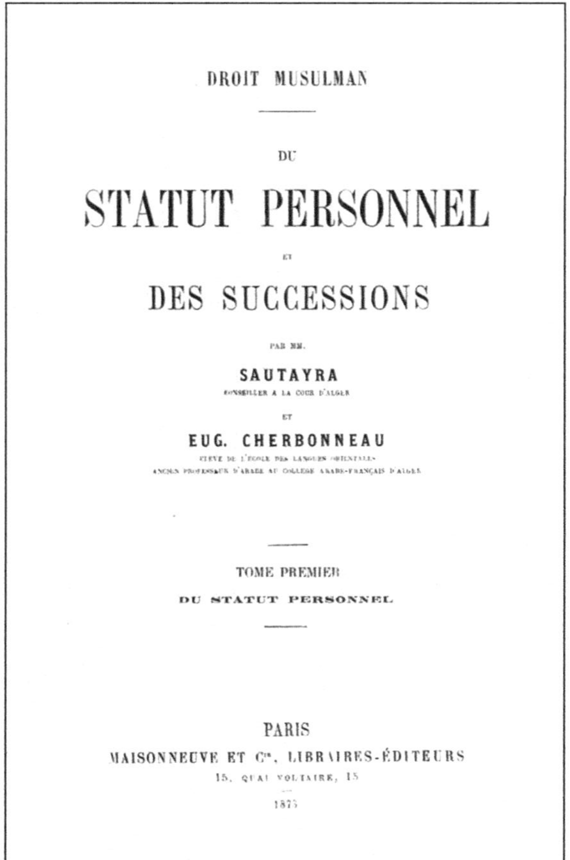

DROIT MUSULMAN

DU

STATUT PERSONNEL

ET

DES SUCCESSIONS

PAR MM.

SAUTAYRA

CONSEILLER A LA COUR D'ALGER

ET

EUG. CHERBONNEAU

ÉLÈVE DE L'ÉCOLE DES LANGUES ORIENTALES

ANCIEN PROFESSEUR D'ARABE AU COLLÈGE ARABE-FRANÇAIS D'ALGER

TOME PREMIER

DU STATUT PERSONNEL

PARIS

MAISONNEUVE ET Cie, LIBRAIRES-ÉDITEURS

15, QUAI VOLTAIRE, 15

1873

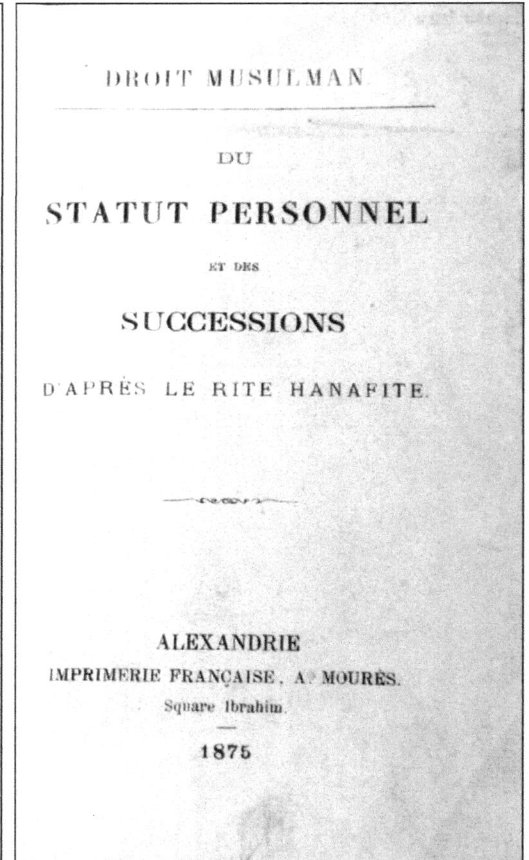

DROIT MUSULMAN

DU

STATUT PERSONNEL

ET DES

SUCCESSIONS

D'APRÈS LE RITE HANAFITE.

ALEXANDRIE

IMPRIMERIE FRANÇAISE, A. MOURÈS.

Square Ibrahim.

1875

Fig. 5.1. Title pages of Sautayra and Cherbonneau's *Droit musulman* (1873) and Qadrī Pasha's *Droit musulman* (1875) compared.

ENHANCED TREATISES AT THE ALGIERS LAW SCHOOL

Improved publications on Islamic law appeared after the establishment of the École de Droit d'Alger in 1879.[11] As part of his bid to make the "school" a proper "faculty" of law, the Director, Robert Estoublon, developed chairs in colonial and comparative law and encouraged scholarly publication. In addition to hiring professors to teach French civil, criminal, administrative, and commercial law, Estoublon created a chair in Algerian and Tunisian Law and another in Muslim Law and Customs.

For young professors, the Algiers Faculty was a stepping stone to more prestigious positions in the metropole. This created an incentive for them to publish, and in turn scholars moved from Europe to Algiers, and back to Europe. The Law Faculty at Aix-en-Provence hired from Algiers Eugène Audinet and Paul Lacoste, Rennes hired Robert Piédlèvre, and Paris hired René Maunier, who eventually distinguished himself in Egypt.[12] Leading figures elsewhere in French academia also spent time at the Algiers School: Marcel Morand, Émile Larcher, Georges-Henri Bousquet, Louis Milliot, and Estoublon himself.[13] The teachers of Muslim law before 1910 were principally Estoublon, Sautayra, Ernest Zeys, and Marcel Morand, all prominent names in Francophone Islamic law studies.[14]

In 1885, Estoublon founded the *Revue algérienne, tunisienne et marocaine de législation et de jurisprudence*.[15] The school's faculty members were the editors and contributors. It was a recorder of cases, a repository for commentaries on cases, and a forum for academic articles. Over the years, prominent comparativists based in France joined the editorial board, among them François Gény, Emmanuel Lévy, and Henri Capitant.[16] This journal was the model for a journal established by Eugène Clavel in Cairo which ran for one year, *Revue internationale de législation et de jurisprudence musulmanes* (1895–96). Had the journal continued, it might have led to an aberration from the norm of European legal-academic publishing in Cairo, which tended to shy away from academic studies on Islamic law before the 1920s.

Ernest Zeys's *Essai d'un traité méthodique de droit musulman* reflects the state of learning among French jurists in Algeria in 1884.[17] Zeys had been the President of the Algiers Court of Appeal and had recently taken up the first chair in Muslim law studies at the Algiers Faculty. The book advanced on Gillotte and Sautayra by

[11] On the school's history, see Laure Blevis, "Une Université française en terre coloniale: Naissance et reconversion de la Faculté de Droit d'Alger (1879–1962)," *Politix* 4,76 (2006): 53–73; G. H. Bousquet, "L'École de Droit (1880–1909)," available at http://alger-roi.fr/Alger/documents_algeriens/culturel/pages/30_droit.htm (last accessed April 21, 2015).

[12] Blevis, "Une Université française en terre coloniale," 62.

[13] Estoublon was director until his death in 1895. He was succeeded by Cyprien Dujarier (1895–1906), Marcel Morand (1906–1932), and Louis Milliot (1933–1934).

[14] See Louis Milliot, "Le Mouvement des études juridiques musulmanes en France," *Revue algerienne, tunisienne et marocaine de legislation et de jurisprudence* (1922–23): 103–10.

[15] Blevis, "Une Université française en terre coloniale," 64–5.

[16] Ibid., 62.

[17] Ernest Zeys, *Essai d'un traité méthodique de droit musulman (école malékite)* (Algiers: A. Jourdan, 1884).

pushing Muslim law further in the direction of a fuller code form, positing Maliki rules following the order of the *Code civil* and organized into three books of persons, property, and contracts. On each page, the text enumerates the rules, literally giving each rule a number. After each rule, Zeys lists his supporting primary sources, which is to say previous translations.

In Zeys's *Traité élémentaire de droit musulman algérien* (1885), a longer work in two volumes,[18] one sees the beginnings of a comparative approach in Algeria. This was comparative law before its reification at the turn of the twentieth century. Intended as a textbook for students at the Algiers Faculty, the book focused on contracts. Zeys was one of the first to put the French and Muslim contract laws, other than marriage, side by side. He was one of the first who thought about advancing and transforming the Islamic laws of contracts, and about how French law and local Muslim law could be "conciliated," that is, compared and unified.[19]

This approach was a forerunner to V. Meysonasse's *Code civil musulman suivant la cadre du Code civil française: rite malekite* (1898), a work that went further than Zeys in reordering and changing the textbook rendition of the Islamic law of Algeria. While relating ostensible Islamic rules of contracts in his Book III.3, Meysonasse drew guidance from the text of articles in the *Code civil*.[20]

Finally, Nicolas Perron's translation of *al-Mīzān al-kubrá* (The Supreme Scale) by al-Shaʿrānī intended to address the interest among French and Muslim jurists in unifying the various Islamic law schools into a single school of law.[21] The chief idea was that by taking the best rules from the four Sunni law schools, Islamic law could be modernized on the basis of its own terms, traditions, theories, and rules. The idea was not wholly French in its origins. Al-Shaʿrānī wrote his book in the sixteenth century with a similar interest in a classical genre known as *ikhtilāf* ("difference"). For Perron, the *Mīzān*, taken together with his translation of Khalīl's *Précis*, provided French judges in Algeria with the "complete Islamic Digest" and precious insights into how Islamic law could be reformed on its own terms:

> Having this knowledge in Muslim law (*la loi et le droit musulmans*), our judges will know the modifications and improvements that must be made. They will know the tolerant and intolerant aspects of Muslim law, and the tools of legal reasoning that, from a Muslim point of view, can augment or help to develop the flexibility of the law. Having some background in philosophy and social science, our judges will find the proper means and tools to facilitate their project of *reformation*. They will see with greater clarity that which they should reject outright, gradually modify, or tolerate temporarily. They will know what to include in our codes and what needs to be clarified

[18] Ernest Zeys, *Traité élémentaire de droit musulman algérien (école malékite)*, 2 vols. in 1 (Algiers: A. Jourdan, 1885).

[19] Ibid., ix.

[20] V. Meysonasse, *Code civil musulman suivant le cadre du code civil français: Rite malekite* (Paris: A. Chevalier-Marescq et cie., 1898), 3–4. The introduction reports: "We may recall the spiritual words of Seignette in his introduction to this translation of Sidi Khalil that Islam (*islamisme*) has turned its back on the future and faces the past."

[21] ʿAbd al-Wahhāb ibn Aḥmad al-Shaʿrānī, *Balance de la loi musulmane, ou, esprit de la législation islamique et divergences de ses quatre rites jurisprudentiels*, trans. Nicolas Perron and J. D. Luciani (Algiers: Imprimerie orientale, P. Fontana, 1898).

and made more precise. In a word, they will know what they have to instill in the legal regime of the Muslims.[22]

Although Perron was teaching law in Paris by the time the book was printed, he still had in mind the objective of using the book to modernize the "civil law" of Algeria. His choice of the term "civil law" was not just an act of designation, translation, and description, but also another act of transformation:

> The reformation of [Islamic] civil law is a project of profound benefit for the Muslims in general, and, above all, for the Muslims of Algeria in particular. This law, which is no longer sufficient for life of our times, this law, having transformed itself into dogma, has, in fact, blocked the horizon of progress to all people whom it governs. This horizon must be made to give way. It must open. It must enlarge itself. It must not close itself again. Otherwise, the Muslims cannot live in a progressive manner.
>
> Today, a new manner of living is required. It is necessary to throw out the old, worn out, and worm-eaten baggage. The Muslim people are a people who made their law but have not been able to improve it for a long time. From now on, it is necessary for this law to be improved and corrected by these people who are being enlightened, called to reason, and brought to a justice more just, to fairness (*équité*) more fair, and to the sincere conviction that all law, whether between individuals or nationalities, must be tempered by fairness.
>
> It is not enough to know what a body of *législation* has decreed, defended, or tolerated for many centuries. It also matters what the law may still offer. From the moment that the law becomes incapable of keeping its people at the level comparable to that known in the past or regenerating that level—when it originally brought them to that level and promised to maintain them at that level—this is an indication and a proof, for the social order, for life, and for the development and wellbeing of the masses, that it is necessary to improve the law and the moral, intellectual, and physical order of these masses. In that way, they can and do advance to a level evidently higher than where the older (*primordial*) law left them and still leaves them. So, laws and customs must change. All legal traditions have faced this. A law that has become closed and a dead end is an unreasonable thing, a monstrosity, and even a blasphemy.[23]

As much as Perron wished to see a rapid reformation of Islamic law, he allowed that change could be pursued and justified according to concepts and methods that would appeal to the Muslims themselves, taking into account both the general taste of the masses and the methodological sensibilities of the Muslim law scholars. In Perron's view, it was important for modern Islamic legal thought to have some grounding in the methods of the *madhhabs*. He showed a measure of deference to *uṣūl al-fiqh* as a relevant field of knowledge, acknowledging that *uṣūl al-fiqh* was a field of scholarship with which the modern, reforming European jurist would need to contend. By invoking "blasphemy," he contributed to a European strategy that encouraged Muslims to change their own views on Islamic law through the proposition that their current views were not consonant with Islam.

[22] Ibid., viii–ix. [23] Ibid., xii–xiii.

In sum, the French lawyer-colonists in Algeria had their eyes set on reforming Islamic law before and after the British occupation of 1882. Only willful ignorance permits, ultimately, a notion that they did not find ways to make their influence felt in Egypt.

ON THE EUROPEAN CONTINENT: UNDERSTANDING THE INTELLECTUAL EQUIPMENT OF THE CIVIL LAW JURISTS IN EGYPT

Eight years before Édouard Lambert arrived in Egypt in 1906 to serve as dean of the Khedivial Law School, and almost twenty years before his input on the Egyptian Civil Code of 1948 began, Europe knew him as a reviver, innovator, and mastermind of comparative law.[24] He obtained his doctorate in law at the University of Paris in 1893 where he had worked under Raymond Saleilles.[25] When Saleilles assumed a new chair in comparative civil law in Paris in 1898, he positioned Lambert to become a foremost builder of the field. Lambert delivered the keynote address at the International Congress of Comparative Law in Paris in 1900. He edited the Congress's papers and contributed the lead chapter.[26] In 1903, he published a one-thousand-page treatise on the aims and methods of comparative law and on what he considered to be its empirical foundations.

Lambert's treatise, *La Fonction du droit civil comparé*, also elaborated in over eighty pages his revisionist account of Islamic legal history, Islamic *fiqh*, and Islamic legal theory, and he proposed the outlines of a reform program.[27] A portion of interwar Egyptian legal thought and portions of the Egyptian Civil Code of 1948 are explained by returning to *Fonction*. However, understanding Lambert's explanation of Islamic law is complicated because the explanation is infused with underlying premises, concepts, and agendas that can only be discerned by a reader equally familiar with European orientalism, European comparative law, contemporary legal theory, and Lambert's personal and intellectual ambitions, to which we now turn.

[24] René David, *Le Droit comparé* (Paris: Economica, 1982), 10–20; Amr Shalakany, "Sanhuri and the Historical Origins of Comparative Law in the Arab World (or How Sometimes Losing Your Asalah Can Be Good for You)," in *Rethinking the Masters of Comparative Law,* ed. Annelise Riles (Oxford: Hart, 2001), 152–88; Bénédicte Fauvarque-Cosson, "Development of Comparative Law in France," in *The Oxford Handbook of Comparative Law*, ed. Reinhard Zimmermann and Mathias Reimann (Oxford: Oxford University Press, 2006), 35–67.

[25] On Saleilles, see E. Gaudemet, "Raymond Saleilles (1855–1912)," *Revue bourguignonne de l'université de Dijon*, 22,4 (1912): 161–263; Alfons Aragoneses, *Recht im* Fin de Siècle*: Briefe von Raymond Saleilles an Eugen Huber (1895–1911)* (Frankfurt am Main: V. Klostermann, 2007), 11–20.

[26] Société de législation comparée, *Congrès international de droit comparé tenu á Paris du 31 juillet au 4 août 1900* (Paris: Librairie générale de droit et de jurisprudence, 1905), 26–61; Édouard Lambert, "Une Réforme nécessaire des études de droit civil," *Revue international d'enseignement* 40 (1900): 216–43.

[27] Édouard Lambert, *Études de droit commun législatif ou de droit civil comparé. Première série. Le régime successoral. Introduction: La fonction du droit civil comparé. Tome I.* (Paris: V. Giard et E. Brière, 1903); henceforth referenced as *Fonction.*

THE REIFICATION OF COMPARATIVE LAW

The reification of comparativism resulted partly from attacks of the 1890s on the School of Exegesis, a mode of juridical analysis that had been embraced by French jurists in the early nineteenth century.[28] The school believed in natural and universal law and in turn held that the *Code civil* had presented private law perfectly and completely. In its most conservative manifestation, it eschewed the study of private law beyond the *Code civil*. For tools to interpret the *Code civil* in such a way that it met all new problems that could ever arise in private law, the exegetes resorted to philological analysis, hermeneutics, and deductive logic to extend the code's articles.[29] The exegetes did not consider the *Code civil* gapless, but they considered its articles and their interpretive methods entirely sufficent for filling the gaps. The school formed part of a broader constellation of nineteenth-century sensibilities that Duncan Kennedy has termed "classical legal thought," a set of formalistic trends, methods, and premises in juridical thought that were eclipsed in Europe, and later in the United States, from the 1890s through 1920s.[30]

Lambert and his colleagues assailed the exegetes from angles that became premises of comparative law and which are maximally important to the history of Egyptian legal thought.[31] First, they lambasted the notion that any single code could be, on its own, a complete and comprehensive source of law for any given area of law. Second, they insisted that jurists in France examine laws of other societies to enhance the French legal order. Third, they insisted that jurists' work should transcend the mere interpretation of existing codes through formalistic methods in philology, hermeneutics, and deductive logic. Fourth, developing what they called the "social" angle of critique, they insisted that jurists enhance the legal order by shaping law to address society's urgent, present-day needs. Fifth, they insisted that the legal systems of Europe had a common legal heritage and that this justified comparative analysis of national legal systems. Sixth, they believed that because of Europe's common legal heritage, Europe should therefore pursue a common legal future and tear down the artificial boundaries that currently separated national, religious, and cultural legal systems. And, seventh, they held great confidence in the ability of newly emergent social science disciplines to unlock truths of Europe's legal past and to shed light on how contemporary law could best serve the needs of contemporary society. In addition to the leading

[28] Mid-nineteenth-century legal thought was not fully dominated by exegetes and it is problematic to overstate or overgeneralize their formalism. Europeans before Lambert argued that the *Code civil* was incomplete and imperfect. M. Bellomo, *The Common Legal Past of Europe, 1000–1800* (Washington, DC: Catholic University of America Press, 1995), 41; W. Hug, "The History of Comparative Law," *Harvard Law Review* 45,6 (1932), 1027–70, at 1060. Nevertheless, some French scholars still characterized the nineteenth century as having been dominated by exegetes. Christophe Jamin, "Le Vieux rêve de Saleilles et Lambert revisité: À Propos du centenaire du congrès international de droit comparé de Paris," *Revue internationale de droit comparé* 52,4 (2000): 733–51, at 736.

[29] See Julien Bonnecase, *L'École de l'exégèse en droit civil* (Paris, 1919).

[30] Duncan Kennedy, *The Rise and Fall of Classical Legal Thought* (Washington, DC: Beard Books, 2006); see also n. 30.

[31] Marie-Claude Belleau, "The 'Juristes Inquiets': Legal Classicism and Criticism in Early Twentieth-Century France," *Utah Law Review* 2 (1997): 379–424.

French critics Saleilles, François Gény, and Lambert,[32] professors from all over Europe participated in this comparative law movement, particularly from Germany,[33] Italy, and Great Britain.[34]

Saleilles followed in the footsteps of German critics of the *Code civil* as well as other European legal theorists.[35] Railing against the exegetes for adopting myopic fixations on grammar and logic, Saleilles championed a "historical method,"[36] but unlike earlier proponents of the German "historical school,"[37] he was not opposed to modern codification efforts.[38] Instead, he advocated that Europe's codes be interpreted more flexibly to meet the needs of the era.[39] He thought that French

[32] The origins of their critical drive against the exegetical school are not certain. Saleilles traced the movement to Jean Charles Demolombe (1804–1887) while others traced it to Émile Labbé and Claude Bufnoir (1832–1898). See nn. 33, 35.

[33] Much of the critical drive originated in Germany with scholars such as Rudolph von Jhering. See Jamin, "Vieux rêve"; Philippe Jestaz and Christophe Jamin, *La Doctrine* (Paris: Dalloz, 2004); Philippe Jestaz, *Doctrine et jurisprudence: Une Liaison de 25 siècles* (Montreal: Thémis, 2001).

[34] Elisabetta Grande, "Development of Comparative Law in Italy," in *Oxford Handbook of Comparative Law*, ed. Zimmermann and Reimann, 107–30; John W. Cairns, "Development of Comparative Law in Great Britain," in ibid., 131–74.

[35] Precedents for anti-exegesis, social jurisprudence, interdisciplinary studies, and comparativism can be found in earlier nineteenth-century European legal thought. Ideas of social and sociological jurists had precedents in European classical legal thought. New comparativists and sociological jurists, often one and the same, took from Savigny's historical school what they liked and left out what they did not. They liked the idea that historical study could inform the study and creation of present-day law, but they rejected the idea that historical law should be the only or the necessarily primary model for its reform and creation. They also rejected Savigny's opposition to codification.

Universalist theory had precedents in classical legal thought as well. Concepts of universalism had been present in natural law, as for example in the "philosophical school." Hegel posited a universalistic conception of law and history. Universalism was also manifested in at least one writing of an early nineteenth-century German jurist, Eduard Gans (*Das Erbrecht in Weltgeschichtlicher Entwicklung* [Berlin: Maurer, 1824]), and two Bavarian codes from the early 1800s: Bavarian Civil Code (1808) and Bavarian Penal Code (1813). See Wieacker, *History of Private Law*, 327; Cairns, "Development of Comparative Law in Great Britain," 73. Savigny's historical school had universalistic implications, however partially ironic given the central place the historical school afforded to the concept of the *Volksgeist*.

Ideas correlating to "the social" were not without mid-nineteenth-century precedents. Marx is one example. More within the mainstream of politics and law was the social dimension of classical liberalism. The German Civil Code placed constraints on contractual freedom, usury, and punishment for contract breaches. See Wieacker, *History of Private Law in Europe*, 380–1. The social dimension of classical liberalism manifested in social-legislative reforms of the Third Republic. Lisa DiCaprio, *The Origins of the Welfare State* (Urbana: University of Illinois Press, 2007), 199–203. See generally Jean Bron, *Histoire du movement ouvrier français* (Paris: Editions Ouvrières, 1968); Edouard Dolleans and Gerard Dehove, *Histoire du travail en France* (Paris: Domat-Montchrestien, 1953); Émile Levasseur, *Questions ouvrières et industrielles en France sous la troisième république* (Paris: A. Rousseau, 1907), 434. The final decades of the nineteenth century saw the evolution of labor laws, protection of child workers, and a reexamination of contractual freedom and competition laws. Eltjo Schrage and Viola Heutger, "Legal History and Comparative Law," in *Elgar Encyclopedia of Comparative Law*, edited by J. Smits (Cheltenham: Edward Elgar, 2006), 393–406, at 400.

Optimism for the truth-yielding power of social science had roots in the classical era. The seventeenth and eighteenth European centuries produced mathematicians and natural scientists who dominated intellectual milieus. Mathematicians advanced for the intellectual world the science of abstract deductions, while natural scientists advanced empiricism. Some of these thinkers also engaged with juridical thought, such as Leibnitz and Christian Wolff.

[36] Jamin, "Vieux rêve," 734.

[37] See pp. 122–3. [38] Jamin, "Vieux rêve," 737.

[39] Raymond Saleilles, "Quelques mots sur le rôle de la méthode historique dans l'enseignement du droit," *Revue internationale de l'enseignement* 19 (1890): 482–505; Saleilles, "École historique et droit naturel," *Revue trimestrielle de droit civil* 1 (1902): 80–112; Saleilles, "Préface," in Francois Gény, *Méthode d'interprétation et sources en droit privé positif* (Paris: A. Chevalier-Marescq et cie., 1899); Saleilles, "Droit civil et droit comparé," *Revue international de l'enseignement* 61 (1911): 5–32.

private law could be reformed without abrogating the *Code civil* and thereby became known for the expression: "Beyond the *Code civil*, but by the *Code civil*."[40]

François Gény influenced the movement through arguments that post-exegetic jurists should avail themselves of the power of modern disciplines such as sociology, psychology, and economics. He advanced the concept of "free scientific research," the idea that open-ended, disciplined research would lead to a more perfect understanding of society and its needs with regard to rule formation.[41]

Lambert was concerned about the capacity of social sciences to yield truths about the social world that could then be reliably acted upon to pursue legal reform, and he critiqued Gény for placing too much faith in the truth-yielding capacity of social sciences.[42] At the same time, this position ultimately meant for Lambert that any attempt to pursue social science research to support modern legal development needed to be thorough. As such, he wrote the one-thousand-page *Fonction* to be a comparative history of European and world laws, all as prefatory work to the more important work of creating new laws for Europe and the colonies. The objective was to find common historical bases of law in Europe and the world as a preface to unifying European and eventually world law. He called the project of *Fonction* "descriptive legal history" and "comparative legal history." In his terms, these studies would furnish the necessary, empirical basis for the next stage of effort: "comparative lawmaking" (*legislation comparative*).[43]

Related to the rise of the social jurisprudence already described was the evolution of new strands of interdisciplinary legal studies.[44] In the view of Duncan Kennedy, the eclipse of European classical legal thought resulted in part from the advent of new trends in "social legal thought."[45] Ambitions for social reform through legal reform were popularized, globalized, and integrated into the comparative law movement by such Francophone scholars as Saleilles, Gény, and

[40] This account closely follows Jamin, "Vieux rêve," 737–8.

[41] Saleilles, "Préface," 457.

[42] Lambert, "Réforme nécessaire."

[43] There were other dimensions of the critique of Gény. For example, Lambert argued that Gény did not go far enough in attacking the formalism of the school of exegesis.

[44] If we see the "historical school" of Savigny as a precursor to this rise of interdisciplinary legal studies, we could trace this approach to the mid-nineteenth century when the historical school was popularized in Germany. There was an interdisciplinary flavor to this school of legal thought insofar as it brought historical studies into the domain of contemporary legal studies and projects of legal reform. However, the historical school might not be included in the flowering of the social and interdisciplinary legal studies because of its predominant interest in the law of past societies as opposed to contemporary law and contemporary social realities; and if not, then we find more certain precedents in academic trends from the later nineteenth century. One example comes from pre-1900 efforts in legal comparativism. In 1878, German jurists founded the *Zeitschrift für vergleichende Rechtswissenschaft*, which aspired to an "enlargement of the boundaries of legal science." See Franz Bernhöft, "Über Zweck und Mittel der vergleichenden Rechtswissenschaft," *Zeitschrift für vergleichende Rechtswissenschaft* 1,1 (1878), as cited in Cairns, "Development of Comparative Law in Great Britain," 73. The work in that journal has been associated with early, ethnological legal studies. It has also been associated with a new wave of historical legal studies wherein law was studied within evolutionary paradigms.

[45] See Duncan Kennedy, "Three Globalizations of Law and Legal Thought: 1850–2000," in *The New Law and Economic Development: A Critical Appraisal*, ed. David Trubek and Alvaro Santos (Cambridge: Cambridge University Press, 2006), 19–73, at 37–46.

Lambert.[46] Another proponent was Léon Duguit, a founder of reformed syndicalism and the dean of Cairo Faculty in 1926–27.[47]

LEGAL UNIFICATION, UNIVERSALISM, SCIENTISM, AND IMPERIALISM AT THE CONGRESS OF 1900

The newly formed *Société de législation comparée* convened in Paris in 1900 for the first International Congress of Comparative Law (*Congrès international de droit comparé*). This was "the first major world congress on the discipline" and it became "famous because it symbolizes... the birth of comparative law."[48] The Congress "developed the modern conception of comparative law as a legal science, closely linked to philosophy, legal history, ethnology, and sociology."[49] Most participants represented non-common law countries and shared in an enthusiasm for code law. The British participants were more cautious about the promises of comparative law and markedly less enthusiastic about the codification movement.

Saleilles's presentation in 1900 posited four aims for the Congress: to define the methods of the field, to clarify how comparative law is used in teaching, to clarify how comparative law could benefit the world of lawmaking and justice, and to determine paths of future research.[50] He argued that comparative law was not only a tool for academic study, but moreover a tool for producing practical benefits for civilization. By comparing the laws of different legal systems, legal systems would help one another to improve the lives of individuals and societies. Jurists would need to derive "theories, systems, and principles" in this interest, availing themselves of other disciplines. His interest in political economy reflected the Congress's "social" inclinations.[51]

At the Congress, Lambert and others claimed that comparative law's ultimate goal was to form a "common law of humanity" (*droit commun de l'humanité*) through its "unifying capability" (*action unificatrice*).[52] Henri Lévy-Ullmann envisioned a "world law of the 20th century."[53] At the core of this proposition was a desire to replace Natural Law as a prevalent theory and to make comparative law, as history, the basis on which individual nations would improve their laws and then unify them, through "comparative legislation." "Comparative law," Reinhard

[46] This narrative follows closely on ibid., 37.

[47] J. E. S. Hayward, "Solidarist Syndicalism: Durkheim and Duguit," *Sociological Review* 8 (1960): 17–36. And see pp. 203–4.

[48] Fauvarque-Cosson, "Development of Comparative Law in France," 36. [49] Ibid., 43.

[50] Société de législation comparée, *Congrès international de droit comparé*, 9–17.

[51] See Pavel Kalenský, *Trends of Private International Law* (Prague: Academia, 1971), 205–32.

[52] Société de législation comparée, *Congrès international de droit comparé*, 38.

[53] Henri Lévy-Ullmann, "Vers le droit mondial du XXème siècle," in P. Lepaulle, *De la Condition des sociétés étrangères aux États Unis d'Amérique* (Paris: Rousseau et cie., 1923), preface. See also M. Ancel, "La Tendance universaliste dans la doctrine comparative française au début du XXème siecle," in *Festschrift für Ernst Rabel*, ed. H. Dölle et al. (Tübingen: J. C. B. Mohr, 1954), 1: 17–38; R. Hyland, "Comparative Law," in *A Companion to Philosophy of Law and Legal Theory*, ed. D. Patterson (Cambridge, MA: Blackwell, 1996), 184–99, at 186.

Zimmerman observes, intended "to resolve the accidental differences which divide the laws of the various modern nation states."[54] As formulated by Saleilles, comparative law would "discover the common foundation of institutions and conceptions beneath the apparent statutory diversity, to collect maxims common to these legal systems, and thereby constantly to encroach on the domain of particularism."[55]

Underlying most presentations at the Congress was universalist theory, the notion that all law derives from similar origins, has fundamental similarities, and can and should be fused into a coherent system. This universalism bore similarities to natural law theory, but now the goal was to replace the ineluctable mysteries of natural law theory with the practical, rational, truth-yielding capabilities of legal history and other social sciences.[56]

The comparativists have been critiqued for having harbored overly optimistic expectations of the "scientific" comparison of laws,[57] but their papers reveal that the leaders were ambitious but not naïve. Similar to the comparativists of the present day, they were pursuing the ambition of perfection as a lesser evil to comparing nothing. They sought conciliations and synergies; they did not expect to necessarily reach perfection.[58] Lambert stressed that comparativism needed to be gradual. He advocated a first stage of arduous research into the commonalities and differences among legal systems. He urged that comparativists begin this work by focusing on a smaller group of nations "linked by traditions of common upbringing, history, and economy."[59] Rather than focusing first on principles of law that stretched across all of humanity, he wished to first compare rules adopted by countries already "standing on the same level of civilization."[60]

THE PERVASIVE GERMAN INFLUENCE IN COMPARATIVE LAW AND LEGAL THEORY

It is essential to turn to German history to locate several elements of nineteenth-century legal thought that were to have an afterlife in Egyptian legal scholarship.

[54] Reinhard Zimmermann, "Comparative Law and the Europeanization of Private Law," in *Oxford Handbook of Comparative Law*, ed. Zimmermann and Reimann, 539–78.

[55] He continued: "The unifying force attributed to comparative law... results in the progressive effacement of the accidental diversity that prevails among legal systems located in countries of similar development and economic condition and the reduction of statutory differences that are not justified by political, moral, or social reasons and which, therefore, are due to historical accident or to transitory and superficial causes." Translation by Hyland, "Comparative Law," 186.

[56] Kalenský, *Trends of Private International Law*, 210.

[57] Lawrence Rosen, "Beyond Compare," in *Comparative Legal Studies: Traditions and Transitions*, ed. Pierre Legrand and R. J. C. Munday (Cambridge: Cambridge University Press, 2003), 439–510, at 493.

[58] See, for example, Reinhard Zimmermann, "Roman Law and European Legal Unity," in A. S. Hartkamp and Christian von Bar, *Towards a European Civil Code*, 2nd ed. (Nijmegen: Ars Aequi Libri, 1998), 21–43, at 44; Andrew Huxley, *Religion, Law and Tradition: Comparative Studies in Religious Law* (London: Routledge Curzon, 2002), 7.

[59] Kalenský, *Trends of Private International Law*, 211.

[60] Ibid.

Many pre-Lambertian roots of comparative law are to be found in Germany, but these can be put aside for our purposes. The key aspects of German legal thought and history to bear in mind when approaching early twentieth-century Egypt are the historical school, conceptual jurisprudence, pandectism, and Rudolph von Jhering's proto legal realism.

The Historical School

Two schools of thought that dominated nineteenth-century German legal thought were the "historical school" and "conceptual jurisprudence." This occurred in contrast to prevailing trends during the eighteenth century, when German legal thought was preoccupied by the school of "natural law" (alternatively, the "law of reason"), a philosophy developed from Aquinas through Grotius, Pufendorf, Spinoza, and Christian Wolff. Kant received much of the credit for dismantling the authority of the natural law school in Germany, yet he did not pioneer a clear and reliable method that could replace natural law theory for the purposes of discerning new positive law. Facing a vacuum in the way of philosophy and methods that could guide the creation of positive law for their own era, nineteenth-century German jurists worked to create new philosophies and methods. They coined the term "legal science" (*Rechtswissenschaft*) and worked to define the premises, preoccupations, and methods of this science.

The historical school emerged as a replacement for natural law. The jurists Paul Feuerbach (d. 1833) and Anton Thibaut (d. 1840) held that the process of creating law needed to involve both "historical" and "philosophical" research. This is to say that a jurist produced law by studying the history of law among a people, and that a jurist also created law by making philosophical speculations. The interest in philosophy was a holdover from the centuries of jurisprudence in the law of reason.

The historical school was redefined and reborn at the hands of Friedrich Karl von Savigny (d. 1861), who departed from Thibault during a famous debate over the question of whether to codify German civil law. The latter proposed the writing of a German civil code, and Savigny insisted that more research into Roman and German legal history needed to be undertaken before this could be accomplished. Savigny developed the science of legal history as it became known, and was elaborated on, for the rest of the century.

Under Savigny, the historical school's approach to studying and creating law was defined by three principles.

One, Savigny advocated the study of Roman legal history as the chief method for discerning and producing modern law for Germans.[61] He dropped philosophical speculation and natural law theory from legal science, championing the notion that law emanated not from philosophy but from the experience and "spirit of a

[61] The discussion on pp. 122–3 draws heavily on Reimann; see n. 64. See also Friedrich Karl von Savigny, *Vom Beruf unserer Zeit für Gesetzgebung und Rechtswissenschaft* (Heidelberg: Mohr und Zimmer, 1814); von Savigny, *Geschichte des römischen Rechts im Mittelalter*, 6 vols. (Heidelberg: Mohr und Zimmer, 1815), Fr. trans. Charles Guenoux, *Histoire du droit romain au moyen age*, 4 vols. (Paris: Alexandre Mesnier, 1830). See also Wieacker, *A History of Private Law*, 307.

people." In this view, the task of the jurist was to study the history of a people to extract from it the rules and principles proper to their disposition and society. His notion of a "spirit of the people" was an established concept in German philosophy, and the term he used for it, *Volksgeist*, was a coinage of his contemporary, Georg Puchta. Whereas legal history had formerly been known as *Rechtsgeschichte* (legal history), Savigny coined the term *geschichtliche Rechtswissenschaft* to mean "scientific legal history."

Two, Savigny held that the task of the jurist was to erect a *comprehensive system* of laws. Much in contrast to the worldview of a common law jurist, he believed that empirical research in legal history would lead jurists to create immense treatises of doctrines and rules to govern, ex ante, all conceivable conflicts in private law.

Three, whereas Feuerbach and Thibaut envisioned a methodology for building positive law that was both *historical* and *philosophical*, Savigny envisaged a methodology that was *historical* and *systematic*. The system of modern law was to have total "internal coherence."

Two of these ideas would flourish in Egypt. The first was Savigny's argument that laws in all places and regions shared a common historical trajectory: law begins as custom, progresses into systematic state law, and is managed by jurists.[62] This theory of global legal history profoundly shaped Lambert's theory of Islamic legal history, and he in turn taught the theory to Egyptian students. In essence, the power of the idea in Egypt was the suggestion that even sacred law was not as sacred as it seemed, and that jurists in turn were empowered to change the law. The second idea to take hold was Savigny's immense faith in the truth-yielding power of revisionist history. The Egyptians adopted his confidence in the power of "scientific legal history" to tell truths about a people and their past—they appreciated the concept that this kind of history could be the basis for thoroughgoing legal reform.

Conceptual Jurisprudence

Savigny's students transformed the historical approach into a corollary school of thought known as "conceptual jurisprudence," which is important for Egypt because its twentieth-century jurists labored to create grand, comprehensive, hierarchical structures of legal principles and lower-order rules in private law. The most notable jurists in this field, Georg Friedrich Puchta and Rudolph von Jhering, maintained that "legal order" was formed, organized, and even itself *produced* by a hierarchy of legal concepts.[63] In other words, the mass of casuistry constituting the legal tradition of a people could be placed side by side and compared in order to derive general rules of life that were paramount and should

[62] Eventually this theory was refined by Jhering, who argued that the current state of law in a legally advanced society is always the function of a push-and-pull dynamic between the ever-changing needs of society, the conservatism of institutionalized law, and the power of the jurist who recognizes the advancing needs of society and reforms the law accordingly.

[63] Heikki E. S. Mattila, *Comparative Legal Linguistics* (Aldershot: Ashgate, 2006), 171.

guide the lower-order laws beneath them. Each concept was to find its right place in the system, thus enabling an overview of legal effects. As put by Reimann, Puchta worked to construct "a comprehensive order of the concepts of positive law that organized them according to their internal relationship and the hierarchy of their generality. From the most general concepts, he deduced increasingly particular ones and in this manner created a pyramid of concepts in which all parts were logically interconnected."[64]

According to Reimann, and critically to the future of Egyptian-Islamic legal thought, "A perhaps even more important step beyond Savigny was the assumption that the system itself was capable of generating new law."[65]

> [The system's] logic was not only organizational but also productive. The basis for this claim was Puchta's refinement of Savigny's "Volksgeist" theory. Puchta agreed that the law emanated from the spirit of the people, and the jurists were its keepers in advanced times. But he distinguished three kinds of law stemming from different sources: customary law emanating directly from the people (*Volksrecht*), legislative law coming from the lawgiver (*Gesetzesrecht*), and the law of the jurists created by legal science (*Juristenrecht*). Puchta went beyond Savigny when he claimed that legislation and legal science were not only advanced expressions of originally customary law, but sources of law in their own right. "Thus science is not only a receptive activity . . . but also a productive one. It is itself a source of law, besides customary law and legislative law there is scientific law." At advanced stages of development customary law became less important, while legislation and, most of all, legal science became more important.[66]

The idea of a hierarchical system of principles found its way into Egyptian legal literature during the interwar years as a result of Egyptian jurists' exposure to conceptual jurisprudence. The exposure occurred not though Egyptians' direct encounters with German texts, for they rarely read German, but through works of French-language *doctrine*[67] literature that had internalized German approaches. A symbol of such internationalization was Marcel Planiol's *Traité élémentaire de droit civil* (1899), which was widely studied in Egypt. On that basis, Egyptian scholars in the 1910s, 1920s, and 1930s formulated new Arabic-language *doctrine* works. These were Arabic-language treatises on Roman Law and Franco-Egyptian civil law, produced by none other than Lambert's Egyptian doctoral students and other Egyptians returning to Cairo holding French doctorates obtained under the supervision of other scholars.

Jhering began his career as a conceptual jurist. He proposed moving beyond Roman law, was attracted to the natural sciences, and spoke of a new "natural-historical" method. In the 1860s, he definitively turned away from the strict belief that the study of Roman law was the key to designing Germany's modern law (by this time, that school of thought was known as pandectism, as discussed next)

[64] Mathias Reimann, "Nineteenth Century German Legal Science," *Boston College Law Review* 31 (1990): 837–900, at 860.
[65] Ibid. [66] Ibid., 860–1.
[67] That is, the legal thought and rules posited by academic jurists.

and thereafter became a proponent of the new social approach to legal thought. His aim was to give jurists greater freedom to extrapolate new laws as a means to address pressing changes and turbulence in German political, social, and economic life. Jhering's engagement with social questions in German law foreshadowed the emergence of sociological jurisprudence, and for that matter, the later, twentieth-century emergence of legal realism.

The gradual rise of sociological jurisprudence in Germany before 1900 was accompanied by the rise of the Free Law Movement (*Freirechtslehre*), a school of thought that countered Romanist and conceptual jurisprudence. The view was that jurists and judges could not study and understand law only in the abstract, but needed to take account of present day social, economic, and psychological needs, as well as consider the fundamental role played by law in preserving and advancing political order. They came to view conceptual jurisprudence as a modern form of overly introspective and circular scholasticism. There was a linkage between this German school of thought and the anti-exegetical movement of the French *juristes inquiètes*.

Pandectism and the German Civil Code

Despite Jhering's antagonistic attitudes during the 1860s to the historical school, his favorable attitude to the nascent sociological jurisprudence, and the spreading of the Free Law Movement, the second half of the nineteenth century in Germany was nevertheless dominated by pandectism (*Pandektenwissenschaft*). The pandectists were the Romanists of this time period working in the intellectual heritage of Savigny. They continued to work to build a systematic and ideally gapless, modern positive law on the basis of their knowledge of principles and rules from classical Roman law. They articulated the crucial concepts of person, property, obligation, contract, delict, and succession. The leading figure in this movement was Bernard Windscheid (d. 1892), who strove to demonstrate how conceptual jurisprudence could create a comprehensive, internally coherent, and hierarchical system of rules. The otherwise chaotic mass of laws would thus be tamed and organized into such a system.

German jurists working in private law spent the final third of the nineteenth century drafting a new civil code for Germany which was to look, superficially, like the *Code civil*, but was intended to improve on the latter code's failings and its alleged lack of conceptual hierarchy, internal coherence, and precision. The *Bürgerliches Gesetzbuch* (BGB) was completed in 1896 and promulgated on January 1, 1900. Alongside the German jurists were Swiss jurists who worked toward the foundation of the Swiss Civil Code (*Zivilgesetzbuch*), promulgated in 1912.

The BGB was the outgrowth of the historical school, conceptual jurisprudence, and pandectism.[68] Conceptual jurisprudence and ideas of the historical school also contributed to the creation of the first book of the German Civil Code, the

[68] While the civil code was organized following a Roman model, much of its substance was taken from German custom as worked out in the *Usus modernus Pandectarum*.

Allgemeiner Teil, a novel text that set out controlling principles of the German private law which were to be referred to when interpreting articles of the code.

Promulgated in 1900, the BGB represented the previous century of juridical thought as opposed to the new school of social juridical thought that would come to dominate German legal thought in the coming decades. Put another way, the BGB was the product of classical legal thought, despite the fact that modes of classical legal thought would soon be eclipsed in the law faculties.[69]

IMPACT OF GERMAN IDEAS ON FRENCH DOCTRINE

In Reimann's account, nineteenth-century German legal thought was characterized by positivism, idealism, and formalism. "[N]ineteenth-century German legal science," he explains, "was positivist in its focus on historical sources and in its renunciation of the search for normative standards. It was idealist in its belief that the historically contingent rules contained timeless principles and in its assumption that in reality there is reason. And it was formalist in its definition of law that excluded substantive considerations and in its adherence to deductive logic."[70]

Putting aside the rising school of sociological jurisprudence, it is now possible to summarize the concepts that most influenced doctrine in France and Egypt.

First, there was the conception of law as a science, and the notion that a perfect science could be designed for discerning and elaborating the law. Second, there was the concept of legal history as a tool for elaborating law of the present day. Third, there was the concept that law could be organized in a hierarchy of interlocking principles. Fourth was the conception that the superstructure of interlocking concepts and principles could be productive of new law. Fifth was the premise that law should be produced and enforced by a central authority, which was to say the state. Finally, important for Muslim jurists accustomed to legal pluralism within the *fiqh* itself, the sixth was a concept that there should be one answer to any legal question. For German jurists, this was the concept of "unity" in the law.[71] The drive to unify the law and to create a hierarchical superstructure of principles collectively formed the impetus for the construction of general theories of contracts and obligations that prevailed in French doctrinal works of the later nineteenth and early twentieth centuries.

As German jurists began using conceptual jurisprudence to elaborate on overarching principles for property and contracts, they developed a literature on "sources of the law." This field strove to explain, according to hierarchical concepts, the perfect system for deriving and elaborating upon the law by reference to its underlying premises, objectives, and sources. As put by James Herget,

> The importance of the university of the Legal Order [was] illustrated in the area of legal education. Courses in General Legal Theory (Allgemeine Rechtslehre) are taught

[69] Kennedy, *Rise and Fall*; Reimann, "Nineteenth Century German Legal Science," 838 n. 2.

[70] Reimann, "Nineteenth Century German Legal Science," 894–5.

[71] James E. Herget, *Contemporary German Legal Philosophy* (Philadelphia: University of Pennsylvania Press, 1996), 116–18.

> at some German universities, and books are written on this subject. Texts of this type will have as their content such things as the concept of law, the basis of legal scientific theory, classification of legal norms, the distinction between subjective and objective law, sources of law, legal method, and the relationship between law and justice. Such an exposition is premised on the unity and rationality of the Legal Order. Also, the term "legal dogmatics" is often used to describe the contents of traditional law courses. The implication of this term is that each area of the law (e.g., civil law, administrative law, commercial law) is constituted by a highly structured system of norms and concepts based in legislation and that this doctrine constitutes the sole subject matter to be studied. Textbooks present this doctrine in dogmatic form.[72]

The influence of German scholarship on French theoretical literature went still further. At the beginning of the nineteenth century, when French commentary literature on the *Code civil* was still in the exegetic mode, the typical method for commenting on the code was to follow its order. A change to this method came with the work of Charles Aubry and Charles Rau, entitled *Cours de droit civil français d'après l'ouvrage allemande de K.S. Zacharia* (3rd ed., 1856). Their book was a translation of a manual by the German Karl Salomo Zachariae (d. 1843) who had organized his study of French civil law according to categorical hierarchies of conceptual jurisprudence, rather than according to the categorical hierarchies of the *Code civil*. Zachariae had been influenced by the methods of the pandectists. This pattern was then taken up by later *doctrine* writers. It is therefore with Aubry and Rau that one sees a system, in French *doctrine*, come into place that is extrapolated from the *Code civil*. This approach became the basis for the formation of general theories of civil law as something more advanced than mere exegetical commentary on the *Code civil*.

The method of Aubry and Rau did not catch on among the French *doctrine* writers until the end of the nineteenth century. This may be because it was a new method, and it may be because Aubry and Rau were more closely identified with legal practice than legal academia. The delay may have resulted from the hostile attitude of the French legal academy in the mid-nineteenth century to ideas brought from Germany. Nevertheless, the approach of Aubry and Rau eventually prevailed in France.

French *doctrine* in its twentieth-century form was consolidated between roughly 1880 and 1920.[73] Marcel Planiol's 1899 *Traité* solidified the "general theory" approach to explaining French private law. He was the inheritor of the method advanced by Aubry and Rau. It was then Planiol, more than Aubry and Rau, who set the standard for how theories and large concepts would dominate the style of explaining the law for the next century. Planiol's style was also found in the work of his immediate contemporaries such as Saleilles and Gény, and it was followed by jurists who came after him, most notably Henri Capitant, Louis Josserand, and Georges Ripert. Planiol's approach informed writers in Egypt who

[72] Ibid., 118. [73] Jestaz and Jamin, *La Doctrine*, 120.

wrote new books on Franco-Egyptian and Islamic contract doctrine. His book was first known at the Khedivial Law School to British authors of early, English-language commentaries on the Franco-Egyptian civil codes. They used his structure loosely in the first decade of the twentieth century to structure their own commentaries. Planiol's book and its offspring then received even greater attention from Egyptians themselves after 1923; this happened when the Khedivial Law School, under new Egyptian leadership, pursued a renaissance in the study of French law, French language, and legal education on a French model.

6

The Comparativist Program for Islamic Legal Reform

In addition to being the most famous comparativist of the first half of the twentieth century, Édouard Lambert counts among the European scholars who most influenced legal scholarship in Egypt.[1] Lambert spent one year in Egypt as dean of the Khedivial Law School in 1906–7. Following disputes with British personnel, he returned to the University of Lyon in 1907 where he mentored Egyptian students and established a club for his Arab students called the *Séminaire oriental d'études juridiques et sociales.* The *Séminaire* occupied much of his time and energy. The only works he published between 1910 and 1919 were a mission statement for the *Séminaire* and introductions to the theses of his Arab students.[2] In turn, the *Séminaire* was the institutional forerunner to his Institut de Droit Comparé in Lyon. In the 1930s he worked with ʿAbd al-Razzāq al-Sanhūrī to revise the Egyptian Civil Code. In 1936, he accepted the Cairo University Law Faculty's first honorary doctorate. (See Fig. 6.1.)

The most commonly acknowledged aspect of Lambert's influence on Egyptian and Islamic legal thought is his relationship to al-Sanhūrī, Egypt's most famous native comparativist, civil lawyer, and codifier.[3] Lambert served as al-Sanhūrī's doctoral adviser in Lyon between 1921 and 1926. Al-Sanhūrī received two doctoral degrees, one in *sciences juridiques* and another in *sciences politiques et économiques.* Lambert advised both dissertations: one on English contract law and the other on Islamic public law. Lambert trained al-Sanhūrī in European law, comparative law, and the methods and sensibilities of related social science fields from the French and European traditions. He inspired al-Sanhūrī to study Islamic

[1] Shalakany, "Sanhuri," 86; Maurice Flory and Jean-Robert Henry, *L'Enseignement du droit musulman* (Paris: Editions du CNRS, 1989); David, *Droit comparé*, 10–20; Suzanne Basdevant-Bastid, "L'Institut de Droit Comparé de Lyon," in *Introduction à l'étude du droit comparé*, 11–15, at 12.

[2] Mahmoud Fathy, *La Doctrine musulmane de l'abus des droits (étude d'histoire juridique et de droit comparé)* (Lyon: H. Georg, 1913); Édouard Lambert, *L'Institut oriental d'études juridiques et sociales de Lyon: Séminaire libre ouvert aux étudiants de l'orient musulman* (Lyon: Imprimerie du Moniteur Judiciaire, 1910); Lambert, "Muḥāḍarāt al-ustādh Lāmbīr bi-Kulliyyat al-Ḥuqūq," *Majallat al-qānūn wa-l-iqtiṣād* 7,3 (1937): 439–54.

[3] Shalakany, "Sanhuri"; Botiveau, *Loi islamique*, 18, 83–95; Hill, "Al-Sanhuri and Islamic Law," 44; Enid Hill, "Islamic Law as a Source for the Development of a Comparative Jurisprudence: Theory and Practice in the Life and Work of Sanhuri," in *Islamic Law: Social and Historical Contexts*, ed. Aziz Al-Azmeh (London: Routledge, 1988), 146–97; Ziadeh, *Lawyers, the Rule of Law and Liberalism*, 141; ʿImārah, *al-Duktūr ʿAbd al-Razzāq al-Sanhūrī.*

Islamic Legal Revival: Reception of European Law and Transformations in Islamic Legal Thought in Egypt, 1875–1952. First Edition. Leonard Wood.

Fig. 6.1. Édouard Lambert. Taken from *al-Kitāb al-dhahabī li-l-maḥākim al-ahliyyah 1883–1933* (Egypt, 1937) celebrating the fiftieth anniversary of the Native Courts.

law within the context of comparative law, and nurtured al-Sanhūrī's ambition to revive and reform Egyptian law. He also inspired al-Sanhūrī's social consciousness with regard to law and legal reform. When al-Sanhūrī returned to Cairo in 1926, he worked to improve education at the Cairo Faculty along the lines of what he had encountered in Lyon and aspired to write books that Lambert would have found methodologically and empirically satisfying. Lambert made al-Sanhūrī a principal Arab representative to the Hague Conference on comparative law in 1932. When Lambert received his honorary doctorate at the Cairo Faculty, in the academic year 1936–37, al-Sanhūrī was dean of the Faculty.

Al-Sanhūrī was not the oldest or the first of Lambert's students, but he was one among many students and devotees of Lambert who impacted the course of Egyptian legal thought and education. Other leading professors at the Cairo Faculty among Lambert's students were ʿAbd al-Salām Dhuhnī and Muḥammad Ṣādiq Fahmī. Still other professors who were enthusiasts of Lambert, but not his students, were ʿAbd al-Ḥamīd Abū Hayf, Muḥammad Kāmil Mursī, Sulaymān Murqus, and Chafik Chehata. Since enthusiasm for comparative law was part of the spirit of the age among professors of the Cairo Faculty in the 1920s and 1930s, faculty members lived in the shadow of his ideas, however removed they may have been from him personally.

Lambert introduced Egyptians to new horizons of methods and scholarly literature. Through him and his writings they encountered the great theorists and doctrinalists of European legal thought. This encounter is reflected in Arabic textbooks composed in the 1910s, 1920s, and 1930s. Lambert encouraged Egyptian students to think ambitiously: to regain control of their own legal heritage and institutions and to think critically and rigorously about the reform and revival of their legal heritage. In spite of his own misgivings about Islamic *fiqh* in its current state, he reinforced preconceptions they had about Islamic and Arab law as a distinct legal heritage worthy of preservation and, moreover, advancement. He afforded his Egyptian doctoral students latitude in their research—some of his students wrote monographs with findings that surprised him and with which he disagreed.

Although Lambert has long been recognized as an innovator in European legal thought, and although he has more recently been studied as one who inspired those who innovated in Egyptian legal thought, he has not been credited as an innovator in Islamic legal thought. But Lambert was an originator and innovator of reformed premises, methods, ambitions, and substantive content in Islamic *fiqh*. He imparted to his students specific ideas about Islamic law and legal history that found a way into their reformist legal writings and intellectual approaches during the 1930s and 1940s.

In his treatise of 1903, before he became involved with Egypt, Lambert had already formulated ideas about how Islamic law should be integrated into comparative law studies, and his plan came pre-equipped with well-defined ambitions. Specifically, he had formulated revisionist views concerning Islamic legal history and a series of critiques regarding the current state of Islamic legal thought and methods. He had also formulated plans for the reform and revival of Islamic law. These ideas took shape at least four years before he traveled to Cairo to assume the deanship at the Cairo Faculty and at least eighteen years before he met al-Sanhūrī in 1921. To grasp these ideas is to grasp an essential key to appreciating the meaning and origins of important writings on Islamic law that appeared at Cairo University Law Faculty in the interwar period.

COMPARATIVISM AND ISLAMIC REFORM IN THE LAMBERTIAN WORLDVIEW

Why did a young professor at a high point in his career in France move to the Cairo Faculty in 1906? This is a thought-provoking question posed and explored by Amr Shalakany.[4] Egypt was not a prime posting for a person of Lambert's sta-

[4] Shalakany, "Sanhuri," 167.

tus in Europe. Professors usually tried to move in the opposite direction, from the colony to the metropole. Lambert already held a post in Lyon and was an established expert of French law. Unlike the young professors who went to Algeria, he did not need expertise in a foreign field as a strategic means to acquire a prestigious post at home. Secure in his post at Lyon, Lambert knew that he could leave and return. He was young but not junior. It is also possible that he was seeking to escape the pressures of living in a hostile academic environment—his contrary positions vis-à-vis the legal profession had made him unpopular in some quarters.

Lambert was attracted to the multicultural legal culture of Egypt, complete with the Native law, Sharia, the consular law, and Mixed law, which was internally diverse in its sources.[5] He mentioned after 1907 that he saw Egypt as a premier site of "comparative law experimentalism." As put by Shalakany, "Egypt posed the world's first juristic laboratory, a space where comparative law might be observed in action.... Lambert expected the study of both Islamic law and the case law of the Mixed Courts to furnish him with invaluable comparativist energy to rejuvenate the ossified body of French private law."[6]

His interests in Islamic law ran deeper than a desire to learn from Egyptians about Egyptian law, for Lambert also wanted to instruct and direct Egyptians. The first indication of this inclination was the portion of his seminal treatise, *La Fonction du droit civil comparé*, analyzing Islamic *fiqh* and its history, rules, problems, and avenues for reform and revival.

To understand Lambert's objectives in his section on Islamic law in *Fonction*, one must understand how the book as a whole—above and beyond its section on Islam—was designed to advance the ambitions Lambert had for the study of world comparative law generally. Although the explanation of Islamic law stood on its own in certain respects, it served in other respects to support Lambert's broader claims about human law and the future of global legal reform.

AMBITIONS, METHODS, AND PREMISES OF COMPARATIVE LAW IN GENERAL

Fonction explained the methodological, theoretical, empirical, and historical premises of Europe's new comparative law. It advanced theories about global legal history, European legal history, and other families of law. Lambert made two types of claims about law generally and the study of comparative law generally. One pertained to the ambitions and methods of comparative law; the other had to do with empirical propositions about the past, present, and future of laws. Lambert asked the scholar of comparative law to share in his own ambitions and to accept his empirical findings as premises that would precede further comparative inquiries and the project of comparative legislation.

The first section of *Fonction* defined comparative law and outlined its core

[5] Ibid. [6] Ibid. See also Lambert, "Muḥāḍarāt al-ustādh Lāmbīr."

ambitions and methods. It clarified what set the new field apart from previous incarnations—above all, the purpose of the new comparative law was to improve current legal systems in European countries. Lambert was already famous for his attacks on the nineteenth-century legal formalism. He argued that France and other countries could improve their law by studying the laws of their neighbors.

Lambert proposed that comparative law comprised three distinct sub-fields: "comparative history of law," "descriptive comparative law,"[7] and "comparative legislation."[8] *Fonction* was a project of the first and second fields, although more of the book was dedicated to "descriptive comparative law" than to "comparative history of law." That is, Lambert used most of the book to describe the history of individual legal traditions. The repeated formula of information was: tradition *x* uses method *y* and applies rule *z*. That is the "descriptive" part. At various points throughout the text, he compared traditions. Here, the recurrent formulas were: system *x* uses method *y*, and system *w* also uses method *y*, or, system *x* arrives at result *z*, and system *y* also arrives at result *z*. That was the "comparative" part.

The book's length resulted from its description of multiple legal traditions in Europe and around the world. It focused primarily on the European continental and English legal traditions, with much attention to Roman law. Other space was allocated to Jewish, Greek, Indian, ancient Egyptian, and Islamic law.

THE THEORY OF GLOBAL LEGAL HISTORY

Fonction narrated and compared the history of different legal traditions to prove Lambert's thesis that the world's various systems possessed common historical origins, premises, methods, and substance. In the typical mode of a comparativist, Lambert synthesized secondary historical scholarship on law (for he could not undertake extensive primary-source research on every legal system he discussed), but he also offered sufficient insights to make the work original. Only a careful reading of the text and its notes ensures that one knows where he is following the work of others, revising the work of others, or injecting his own insights. He delved into the most important historical and legal debates of the day and infused his analysis with the formidable power of his critique. He foregrounded the social critique of law, universalism, and an antipathy to scholastic modes of legal reasoning.

[7] Further explaining the "comparative history of law" and "descriptive comparative law," Lambert distinguished between "the study of foreign law" and "comparative law" (American law faculties conflate the two under the term "comparative law"). Cf. Charles Donahue, "Comparative Legal History in America: A Report," *Tijdschrift voor rechtsgeschiedenis* 65, 1–2 (1997): 1–17. In Lambert's view, "the study of foreign law" involved studying the legal tradition of another country, while "comparative law" involved comparing legal traditions in an effort to improve a given country's legal system and to advance the cause of nations in unifying their laws. Lambert viewed the study of legal history as integral to the "study of foreign law" and the study of "comparative law." Legal history was assumed to be necessary for the critical study of laws in force. Société de législation comparée, *Congrès international de droit comparé*, 32; Lambert, *Institut*, 7, 10, 17.

[8] See also E. Lambert, "Comparative Law," in *Encyclopaedia of the Social Sciences*, ed. Edwin R. A. Seligman (New York: Macmillan Company, 1931), 127.

The root of Lambert's theory of global legal history begins with notions that were common among his colleagues. The first notion is that all legal traditions followed similar historical patterns, from their origins through to their consolidation and systematization.[9] Law originated from local custom. Over time, local customs of different groups were fused into a broader and ever-expanding, more general system of customary law. Subsequently and concomitantly, the administration of this broader law was taken over by political organizations that sought to stabilize and cement the legal tradition either by legislating or solidifying the authority of juridical institutions and precedent. When this happens, the new politically controlled law begins to become distinct from customary law. Political law and customary law then exist in a state of both cooperative reciprocity and tension. Sometimes the politically administrated law yields to ever-changing customs and incorporates them; sometimes the politically administrated law fights custom. In the end, however, law in large political entities is eventually taken from the power of ordinary people and their customary preferences and put into the hands of political figures, professional jurists, or both.

This view of legal history amounted to a notion that legal systems move from customary, small, regional, and particularistic frameworks to larger systems governing towns, cities, provinces, states, and empires. If law could be expanded in this way to cover more and more people, then law could be expanded, by way of unification, to apply across the whole world. Eventually, ostensibly "different" legal traditions would coalesce, just as ostensibly "different" customary traditions had once coalesced in some ancient time.

Lambert augments and revises this theory by adding a consideration of the importance of *jurisprudence* (in the French sense, viz., judge-applied law) and *doctrine* (in the French sense, viz., the legal thought and rules posited by academic jurists). The traditional theory just elaborated, which Lambert otherwise accepted in great part, treats *doctrine* as the academic analysis of customary and state-made law. It is a tool to explain the law, but it is not a source of law. Lambert altered the theory by emphasizing what he considered to be the role of *doctrine* in the historical formation of law. For him, academic commentary on the law had always been a source of law; it had historically provided the important work of updating old laws to meet the changing needs of societies. This view was much in concert with institutional practices of civil law countries, where academic jurists are accorded a kind of lawmaking power, as distinct from common law countries where academic jurists are supposed to be merely producers of academic commentary.

In this aspect of the theory, not only has *doctrine* been ever-present in the history of legal development, but it has served a necessary social function by helping to adopt law to the social needs of the times. Thus, although *doctrine* is an informal source of law, it is a powerful and necessary source of influence for transforming applied law.[10] Notably, it followed from this premise that if *doctrine* was

[9] Jamin, "Vieux rêve."
[10] Raoul de la Grasserie, "Analyses: E. Lambert, *Études de droit commun législatif ou de droit civil comparé*," *Revue de l'histoire des religions* 49 (1904): 195–200.

powerful and necessary to legal development, then the academic jurist was also powerful and necessary to legal development. In essence, Lambert's theory assigned power and relevance to the academic jurist in tailoring the law to address the "social" needs of the times. What was true for history, it follows, should be true for the present. Put another way, a practice that was adopted in civil law countries—according academic jurists (like him) lawmaking power—was a practice grounded in world history and should be continued in the present day.

Lambert's focus on custom as the fount of human law did not prevent him from accommodating religion and religious law into his historical model. He took "revelation" to be the manifestation of customary laws or whatever laws were known at the time of the ostensible revelation. For many societies, Lambert claimed, religion was a source of customary law and politically created law. People start with the notion of religious law as complete and infallible. They eventually realize, through their own *jurisprudence* and critical evaluation, that they need to continually develop the law and fill its infinite gaps. According to Lambert, a curious aspect of human nature over time is that humans forget that much of law they consider to be infallible was in fact, originally, a human creation, fallible and incomplete. In this way, he saw religious law as comparable to customary law for the purposes of comparative analysis.

A few powerful, analytical implications followed from this approach to religious law. One implication is that few rules in the mass of private law casuistry in any society are sacred. Lambert never explicitly cast doubt on the truth of revelation in Islam,[11] but everything he wrote indicated that he did not believe in revelation as a historical fact. An implication of this doubt in the truth of revelation is that there is no reason to presume that Islam has the best or the right answers to every legal question. Recognizing that religious jurists would never accept that proposition, Lambert presented other arguments that he thought they would find more palatable. First, dead jurists were not sources of revelation, and therefore could not and should not exercise posthumous monopoly on legal authority. Second, since most rules in private law originally sprang from custom, it is conceivable that all human laws could coalesce into a single, united system of law on earth through the formation of modern custom.[12] The ultimate implication was that there are no insurmountable barriers to the final unification of all human laws among the different traditions in the "civilized" world.

THE PRE-PACKAGED METHODOLOGICAL FRAMEWORK OF COMPARATIVISM

Lambert believed there was an intimate, symbiotic relationship between the correct understanding of legal history and the wise plotting out of the future of law.

[11] In one exception, he casts aspersions on the authenticity of revelation of Quran *al-Aḥzāb* (33):5 and 37. See n. 21.

[12] He asserted that Jewish law was customary law in its essence. Lambert, *Fonction,* 278.

The scholar's understanding of the legal past was to inform his work in reforming law in the present day. He had confidence in his understanding of history and that of other historians on whom he relied. He wrote as though he expected his readers to have the same confidence in him as a legal historian. He made hundreds of arguments about legal history which he presented as pure facts. This approach was common among historical writers of the period, just as it is common today. The difference is that Lambert's historical writing was about more than discussing history. Lambert was proposing a program of practical reforms, to Islamic law for example, that were based on historical arguments that he treated as facts.

His interest and faith in legal history reflected the faith of European scholars in the capabilities of social sciences. These views were also an upshot of the influence of the German "historical school." Lambert took from Savigny the latter's confidence in the value of historical research for modern legal reform, even though he discarded other of Savigny's ideas, such as the opposition to codification and his narrow focus on history as the chief repository for present-day legal guidance. On these latter topics, Lambert was closer to the school of Jhering.

One now begins to understand the comparative law framework in which Lambert situated Islamic law studies. It was not an open-ended field of inquiry, set up purely for exploratory, empirical fact-finding. It was a field pre-packed with historical premises, research methods, and theoretical predispositions. Moreover, this is only the beginning of the ways in which Lambert's comparative law prejudiced free and open inquiries into Islamic law and legal history. When he turned his attention to Islamic law, he molded the historical narrative to support his larger claims about the history of global law; he also posited a set of historical arguments that flew in the face of accepted wisdom in the Muslim world.

It is strange to the social scientist of the present day that Lambert would have introduced a discipline (such as comparative law) or a field (such as Islamic law studies) by predetermining their core empirical findings, methods, and theoretical inclinations. The explanation is perhaps not that Lambert was overzealous or naively credulous in social science and the work of other scholars. It may be that Lambert carried the burden of creating a discipline and its sub-fields and convincing others of their significance and analytical power. Perhaps he could not have constructed his new projects with such success on the basis of qualified arguments. He was not the first scholar in history to overstate his claims as a means to solidify his standing in the academy on the basis of his firm conclusions in historical territory that most other scholars admitted was murky and slippery. In elite academia, then as now, overstating claims was one path to power.

COMPARATIVISM'S ENCOUNTER WITH ORIENTALISM AND FRENCH ALGERIA

For a scholar who had not learned Arabic, traveled to the Muslim world, or formally studied Islam, Lambert spoke authoritatively in *Fonction* about Islamic history, law, and legal history. His treatment began with pre-Islamic Arabia and continued beyond the foundations of the *madhhabs*. He discussed topics such as Quranic hermeneutics, hadith interpretation, analogical reasoning, and custom in legal practice. He critiqued contemporary Islamic legal thought. His confidence in his own knowledge of this foreign material is striking. On what was his confidence based?

Lambert's confidence in his understanding of Islamic history and law was based on his trust in the orientalist and technical-colonial sources discussed in Chapters 4 and 5. Almost all of the discussion on Islam in *Fonction* is a synthesis of such works. Lambert cites approximately forty European works: historical treatises, translations of classical legal texts, and unofficial codifications of Algerian and Indian law. The most commonly cited authors were Goldziher, Snouck Hurgronje, Sachau, Kremer, Kohler, Van den Berg, Savvas Pacha, and Ibn Khaldūn.[13]

The narrative combined the standard interpretations of Arab-Muslim scholars, as related by orientalists, with revisionist arguments put forth by the same orientalists. The chief sources of the revisionist claims were Goldziher and Snouck Hurgronje. As a result, many of the claims Lambert made about Islamic law, legal history, and legal theory contradicted traditional conceptions held by Muslim scholars of the Arab and Ottoman worlds. Only a reader schooled in both conventional Arab-Islamic history, as rendered by Arabs, Persians, Ottomans, and orientalist historiography would know where the conventional or revisionist ideas are being marshaled in the text. Without such expertise, the narrative in *Fonction* appears to the reader as a series of equally valid and accepted truth claims.

Into this mix of traditional Arab interpretations and revisionist arguments about Islam, Lambert wove his own unique commentary as a comparativist, social jurist, anti-exegete, legal historian, Romanist, and devotee of Jhering. He moved fluidly between reciting the arguments of specialists, revising the arguments of specialists, and inserting his own opinions about the quality of other scholars' works.[14] He often drew from his theories of global legal development to suggest how Islamic legal history bore out his claims about the similarities of legal development across cultures. He was approving, for example, of arguments of Kremer and Goldziher on the Roman, Jewish, and Arabian customary (i.e., non-revelationary) origins of Islamic law.

European orientalists such as Goldziher, Snouck Hurgronje, and Kremer have never been seen as having played an instrumental or direct role in the revival of Islamic law studies or Islamic law through the emergence of comparativism. Yet their influence moved through Lambert who followed their most well-evidenced arguments as well as their greatest conjectures.

Goldziher and Snouck Hurgronje were easy choices for Lambert. More than preeminent orientalists, they were students of Savigny's historical school and proponents of the "science" of history.[15] They claimed to write history on the

[13] See Chapter 5.

[14] On the French Algerian literature of Zeys, Sautayra, Cherbonneau, and others, see Lambert, *Fonction*, 438–9 n. 5.

[15] Snouck Hurgronje made his methodological sensibilities explicit. In his destructive review of Savvas Pacha's *Le Droit musulman expliqué* (1896), he attacked Savvas's credence in received wisdom

basis of scrutiny in primary sources and to be averse to received wisdom. However religious they may or may not have been,[16] they claimed that dogma had no place in the construction of historical narrative. They posited a rigid distinction between scientific historical truth and historical fictions created by religion and folk heritage. They believed that the other social sciences could be marshaled in the service of history. Lambert shared with Savigny the optimism that the study of legal history could bring present-day benefits. Snouck Hurgronje was somewhat different on this score. He used the historical sensibility to more skeptical ends; he tended to see Islamic legal history as proof that Islamic law could never be modernized on its own terms.

Lambert was far more politic and optimistic in his treatment of Muslims' credence in the historical tenets of their faith. Lambert usually contented himself with delicately suggesting alternative ways of understanding Islam, avoiding the most charged conflicts with his rationalist sensibilities, for example, the belief of Muslims that God revealed the Quran to the Prophet Muhammad. Snouck Hurgronje openly cast doubt on that claim, but Lambert was more circumspect. Lambert perhaps realized that this question was not necessarily fundamental, let alone helpful, to a European historical study of the evolution of Islamic juridical thought. Much like Perron in his translation of al-Sharʿānī, Lambert believed that much of Islamic legal reform could, should, and would have to take place on Islam's own terms.

Lambert shared Snouck Hurgronje's faith in European social sciences. He wrote, "Of all the religious codes that conserve for us juridical conceptions of semi-civilized societies, the *Qorân* is certainly among those that have most escaped the investigations of science."[17] The Muslim "sciences" of investigating the Quran were insufficient to Lambert. Out the door went classical Arab genres of Muslim history (*tāʾrikh*), Quranic commentary (*tafsīr*), prophetic biography (*sīrah*), speculative theology (*kalām*), and other fields that Muslims had developed for centuries in their pursuit of understanding the Quran. In came Snouck Hurgronje and Savigny.

THE APPLICATION OF LEGAL HISTORY AND COMPARATIVIST PRINCIPLES TO ISLAM

Lambert deployed revisionist historical arguments as a springboard for proposing pathways to the reform of contemporary Islamic law. This was a strategic approach to attacking orthodox precepts and method in Islamic legal thought,

about Islamic history. He refers to this wisdom as a "marvelous ontological system... no longer accepted by any historian." He praised the alternative knowledge system offered by European historical research methods and "European science." Snouck Hurgronje, "Droit musulman," 203; Otterspeer, ed., *Leiden Oriental Connections*, 86–9.

[16] Some comparativists, legal historians, and theorists of the age were religious. Gény is an example of a European comparativist who was influenced by and considered himself to be serving Catholic ideals.

[17] Lambert, *Fonction*, 304.

since much of orthodox Islamic legal methodology is based on historical understandings among Muslim scholars as to how law was understood and practiced by the Prophet Muhammad and the first generations of Muslim leaders and scholars.

Table 6.1 illustrates how the historical method operated when applied to Islamic law and the question of its reform. The method was to identify a "misunderstanding" of conventional Islamic legal history, to assert the correct revisionist understanding, and to propose a reform plan that would honor the correct understanding.

Lambert made six core claims, empirical and theoretical, about Islamic legal history that were to be bases for contemporary reform. It is striking how similar some of these ideas were to the ideas of his Muslim contemporaries, Muḥammad ʿAbduh and Rashīd Riḍā,[18] despite Lambert's showing no awareness of contemporary Egyptian clerics.

Authenticism. Lambert believed that Islamic law had an authentic core, that some of this core had been lost, and that this core could be and needed

Table 6.1. Examples of Lambert's historical method.

Traditional Claims of Sunni Legal History	Lambert's Historical Revisionist Claims	Reform Proposals
The current *fiqh* as known and practiced by the scholars is the authentic *fiqh* and the pious *fiqh*.	Muslims are wrong to think that their current *fiqh* is the authentic *fiqh*.	Muslims should reconstitute *fiqh* so that it is consistent with the authentic *fiqh*.
The four *madhhabs* are integral to the practice of *fiqh*; their evolution was a pious event; their authority and autonomy should be respected.	Muslims are wrong to think that the consolidation of the four *madhhabs* was a good event.	Muslims should see the consolidation of *madhhabs* as a bad event and challenge the authority and autonomy of the *madhhabs*.
Islamic law is different in essence and fundamental origins from other legal systems of the world. Islamic law is a superior law among other systems known on earth.	Muslims are wrong to think that Islamic law is different in essence and fundamental origins from other legal systems of the world; and they are wrong to think that Islamic law is a superior law among other systems known on earth.	Muslims should see that Islamic law has an intrinsic connection to the common law of humanity, and plays an *equal* (not a superior) part in the common legal future of humanity.
"Consensus" (*ijmāʿ*) as a source and tool of Islamic legal reasoning is currently correctly understood and properly applied by Muslim scholars and judges.	Muslims do not understand correctly the function of consensus (*ijmāʿ*) in Islamic legal method. Their understanding of this tool is inauthentic and contravenes the way that the earliest Muslim jurists meant for it to be used.	Muslims can still reacquire a proper understanding of the function of consensus (*ijmāʿ*) in modern law, and in turn they can use consensus in the present day to make new rules and amend or abolish old ones.

[18] Aziz Al-Azmeh claims that Savigny and Herder influenced ʿAbduh's thinking regarding law. Aziz Al-Azmeh, *Islams and Modernities* (London: Verso, 1993), 28, 44–5, 52–3.

to be restored. This notion was analytically powerful because it meant that modern "reforms" could be advertised as the resuscitation of authentic faith and practice. According to this logic, by "reforming" Islamic law, one was not engaging in an impious innovation, but rather one was returning the law and belief to its authentic state.

Universalism. Lambert believed that Islamic law was a subsidiary set of values to more overarching principles shared by humanity.[19] While Islam was a source of legal and ethical guidance in the world, it was not the first, last, or best source. He rejected the notion that all law, even law for Muslims, flowed from Islam.

Common Origins. Related to universalism but important enough to merit its own mention was Lambert's premise that Islamic law had come originally in large part from Roman and Jewish law and that its methods had come from Greek logic. Therefore, Lambert reasoned, there was no need for Muslim jurists to fear the influence of contemporary European laws which have only served to advance ancient and shared traditions of legal method and substance.

*Flexibility and Anti-Formalism (*or, *Ijtihād as Flexibility)*. Lambert argued that Islamic law historically had been flexible, and was meant to be flexible, but in recent centuries had become static, fixed, and overly formalistic. He referred to this as the closure of independent legal reasoning (*ijtihād*) and argued that the necessity of reopening *ijtihād* came from the core of authentic Islamic religion. This was essentially a critique of conservative traditionalism (*taqlīd*)—offered by ʿAbduh and other Muslim reformists—without the use of the term *taqlīd* and without reference to contemporary Muslim authorities.

Social Imperatives. Lambert argued that Islam needed to address society's contemporary needs as it had, in his view, in the age before the closure of *ijtihād*. For Lambert, *ijtihād* in the earliest days of Islam had been a kind of legal reasoning that addressed "social" reform imperatives. The authentic *ijtihād* was *ijtihād* that engaged with social needs.

Methods and Sources. Lambert had specific ideas about how Islamic legal methodology (*uṣūl al-fiqh*) would be reformed. These reforms, he claimed, would not be impious innovations but rather would facilitate a return to authentic faith and practice, which consisted of new ideas concerning consensus (*ijmāʿ*), custom (*ʿurf*), hadith skepticism, and anti-madhhabism (specifically, cross-madhhabism and trans-madhhabism as features of juridical method).

Lambert made the historical claim (uncontested by the traditional Sunni view) that the consensus of jurists had once been a key tool for jurists to determine law,

[19] For an alternative, richly theoretical take on the universal concept and its role in Egyptian legal history, see Esmeir, *Juridical Humanity*, 1–3.

and that the consensus of Muslim jurists of later centuries had no value as a primary source of law. That development, Lambert argued in a revisionist manner, was a piously construed impiety, an accident of history that Muslims had unfortunately and wrongly memorialized as a pious and divinely sanctioned occurrence. Thus, according to Lambert, consensus needed to be revived as an operative source of law and returned to the methodological toolkit of contemporary Muslim jurists. He thought that the present-day consensus of jurists should be a primary source of law, and argued that authentic faith and practice would have looked favorably on that view.

Lambert believed strongly in the importance of custom as a source of law for all societies. He saw customary practice as the reflection of society's attempt to regulate itself, bottom up, in the face of ever-changing circumstances and needs. In his view, custom was a key source of Islamic law and a key guarantor of its flexibility. He found a doctrine of custom present in Islamic legal history and theory, but also found that it had been downgraded as a source of law and was no longer considered a principal source of *fiqh*. He argued that custom should be taken more seriously as a source of law in Muslim societies.[20]

In Lambert's revisionist view, the greater part of prophetic tradition (hadith) was fabricated, and in any case was created in the first place to justify Arab customary practice. Such fabrication, Lambert argued revisionistically, was another piously construed impiety, or an accident of history. The corresponding reform, he implied, was for jurists to now free themselves from the constraints of canonical hadith literature.

According to Lambert's revisionism, the consolidation of the four Sunni law schools (sg. *madhhab*) and their hegemony over jurists was an accident of history that, albeit piously intended, corrupted authentic Islamic practice and belief. The remedy, Lambert suggested, was to devolve the boundaries around the individual *madhhab*s. This would be a critical step in supporting the reform points mentioned above. This does not mean that the modern jurist should have no regard for wisdom of the *madhhab*s. It means only that, at a minimum, a modern jurist need not be constrained by the classical jurists, and certainly not by the rulings of one single *madhhab*.

Lambert made six additional claims about how to apply comparative law to reform Islamic law.

> *Comparative Study of Codes and Doctrine.* Lambert held that Islamic *fiqh* manuals could be organized in such a manner that it would be possible to compare them side by side with European law manuals. This would be done to serve comparative law study and then comparative legislation.
>
> *Universalism*, or *Global Legal Unification*. Lambert held that Islamic law could eventually be subsumed into a broader global law. Islamic law would

[20] Historical knowledge today suggests that the scope of custom's relevance in historical practice vastly exceeded its scope in theory. Its place in the world of theory was also not entirely negligible. See Hallaq, "Prelude to Ottoman Reform"; G. Libson and F. H. Stewart, "ʿUrf," *Encyclopaedia of Islam*, 2nd ed.; Gideon Libson, "On the Development of Custom as a Source of Law," *Islamic Law and Society* 4,2 (1997): 131–55.

not necessarily hold the first position as a source of normative guidance in this global law, but it would, at best, share first position with other traditions. Islamic law could also inform European law in places where the former held advantages over the latter.

Scientific Legal History. Lambert held that the "scientific" study of legal history could uncover lost truths about the history of Islam and Islamic law that would show why and how modern Islamic legal thought could be improved. Although he did not profess belief in ultimate truths of history, he wrote and acted as if he did. The idea was that a legal historian could say something about legal history, then accept it as given, and then act upon it as a premise for contemporary reform. The idea was also that jurists should be skeptical of received historical wisdom.

Social Science. Lambert believed that utilization of social science was essential to studying and advancing law. He was not as explicit as he might have been on this point in *Fonction* (it was a view he expressed more forcefully in other writings), but one sees in *Fonction* hints of his desire to incorporate interdisciplinary legal studies into Islamic law studies as a means to serve all of the social goals already discussed.

Social Consciousness. Lambert believed that Islamic law, in its most authentic form during the first three Islamic centuries, was socially conscious in a manner akin to the new social jurists of Europe. The role of jurists was now to develop the Islamic law in such a way that it would address contemporary problems. To restore the authentic Islamic legal order, Muslim jurists needed to eschew their "scholastic" methods of legal reasoning and begin deriving rules that would better serve modern-day, "social" needs.

Islamization, or *Islamization of Law*. Lambert is one of the first European figures who used this new term. The more complicated question is what he meant by it. This topic will be explained further in what follows.

Flexibility and Anti-Formalism in *Ijtihād*

Whereas the typical Muslim jurist in the orientalist view tended to be cautious toward innovations in the substance of Islamic positive law, Lambert wanted to make the argument that most rules in Islamic law should be open for revision. He looked for cases where the Prophet, caliphs, or classical jurists made law or performed *ijtihād*, and he portrays these examples as instances of expedient and socially beneficial reasoning. In a rare instance when he explicitly challenges sacred historical dogma, Lambert narrated the revelation of the thirty-third chapter of the Quran, *al-Aḥzāb* (The Coalition), and he cast the Prophet Muhammad as having bent the law of the Quran itself to suit "considerations of political order."[21] This is the text's most daring moment of casting doubt on sacred

[21] Lambert tells the story of Prophet Muhammad becoming enamored of Zaynab, a wife of his adopted son, Zayd. Zayd divorced his wife to gain the Prophet's favor. The Prophet subsequently married

history to encourage flexible reasoning. Lambert tended to avoid the history of the Prophet, whom Muslims consider to have made no errors in expounding the law and to have delivered revelations directly to the public, unmediated. Instead, he typically focused on the fallibility of early jurists.

Closer to the mainstream of Islamic legal thought, one of his arguments pertained to the question of the closure of the gates of independent legal reasoning (*ijtihād*) in Islamic legal history. Staying true to his model of the common historical development of human laws, Lambert argued that Islamic law historically had been a flexible system: Islam was always meant to be flexible, but in recent centuries it had become immobile. The cause of this immobility, he said, was consolidation of the Sunni *madhhabs*, which occurred concomitantly with, and prompted, the closure of the gates of *ijtihād* in the third Islamic century.

His claim was that closure of the gates of *ijtihād* was not supposed to have happened. This was a historical claim only (it is not even clear if such a closure ever happened), but he argued that reopening *ijtihād* was a necessity mandated by the authentic Islamic religion. He averred that practitioners of *taqlīd* in Islam were more extreme than the French exegetes in conformism, anti-rationalism, and scholasticism.[22]

Lambert adopted his narrative of the closure of *ijtihād* from Goldziher and Snouck Hurgronje. Specifically, he adopted the position they had taken in their recent debate with Savvas Pacha. The crux of the debate was not whether a closure of *ijtihād* had occurred—on that they all agreed—but rather what the characteristics and scope of the closure were. Goldziher and Snouck Hurgronje argued that there had been absolute closure on all significant pursuits of independent reasoning and lawmaking; they claimed the gate had been sealed and was never opened again, either for the creation of new legal methods or for the creation of new laws to handle modern circumstances. By contrast, Savvas argued that the closure was more nuanced. Savvas said that with the consolidation of the four Sunni schools between the ninth and tenth centuries, the era of creating fundamental methods and principles in legal reasoning had mostly closed; however, he argued, the practice of jurists using independent reasoning to create new rules had never ceased. Today, Savvas's interpretation is the dominant view among most scholars of Islamic law.[23]

Zaynab. This much of the story is standard. Then Lambert diverges from traditional accounts—according to him, Muhammad recognized that his decision to marry Zaynab might shock public sentiment and custom. He thus "made use of his power to reveal law," "issuing" the Quranic verses *al-Aḥzāb* (33):5 and 37 to legitimize that category of marital union. By Muslim standards, this account would have been considered blasphemy, but to Lambert it was scientific history. He attributed his interpretation to Sprenger and Dozy. Lambert, *Fonction*, 300. See also Aloys Sprenger, *Das Leben und die Lehre des Mohammad* (Berlin: Nicolai'sche Verlagsbuchandlung, 1861), 300; Reinhart Dozy, *Essai sur l'histoire de l'islamisme*, trans. V. Chauvin (Leiden: E. J. Brill, 1879), 78.

[22] Lambert, *Fonction*, 376.

[23] Many studies now argue that *ijtihād* was continued well into the nineteenth century. See, for example, Haim Gerber, *State, Society, and Law in Islam: Ottoman Law in Comparative Perspective* (New York: SUNY Press, 1994); Gerber, "Rigidity Versus Openness in Late Classical Islamic Law: The Case of the Seventeenth-Century Palestinian Muftī Khayr al-Dīn al-Ramlī," *Islamic Law and Society* 5,2 (1998): 165–95; Rudolph Peters, "Ijtihad and Taqlid in 18th and 19th Century Islam," *Die Welt des Islams* 20,3–4 (1980): 131–45; Wael B. Hallaq, "Was the Gate of Ijtihad Closed?," *International Journal of*

Lambert took sides with orientalists who found in the historical record a total closing of *ijtihād* and one that ended all abilities of Muslim jurists to respond to new problems of modern society. He did so while inserting his own unique gloss on the revisionist narrative.

> During the thirteenth and fourteenth centuries, and to speak in the parlance of Muslims, the door of *ijtihād*... was definitively closed.[24] This progressive decadence of Islamic juridical science, which ultimately caused an abdication of the highest of its functions, and the renunciation of the exercise of *ijtihād*, and of the reasoning power of the jurist, was the consequence of upholding indefinitely the line between the religion and law.... It is known by universal accord of the Sunni community that, after the third Islamic century, there was no longer a single general *mujtahid* in Islam.... The authority of the most ancient jurists imposed itself on the most recent ones. The jurist has today definitively abdicated from all use of free examination....
>
> The classical Muslim scholars succeeded in cutting all ties that connected *fiqh* to the *social environment, in blocking any reconsiderations on the basis of economic life, and in shielding it from contemporary influences*. The idea that an "Islamization" is possible for modern law is advanced only by two or three Europeanized Easterners, who are detached from the traditional beliefs of their race.[25] Those writers who know best the present-day spirit of Islam, consider this not only a grave heresy and an indubitable anachronism, but moreover the most unrealizable of all dreams. The *jurisprudence* of Islam has existed for a long time in a state of complete and definitive repose, which, as one person has put it,[26] "brings to mind the tranquility of a cemetery."[27]

Lambert adopted ideas of orientalists, adapted them, and added his perspectives as a comparativist and social jurist. He turned the story of the closure of *ijtihād* into an argument for why *ijtihād* must be revived. What Goldziher and Snouck Hurgronje described as Islamic jurists' habitual inability to modernize their law, Lambert cast as an inability to engage with the "social environment."

Lambert cast the closure of *ijtihād* as a mistake of history, or of the Muslims having turned their back on their own religious-historical traditions. During the first three centuries of Islam, he says, the Islamic legal tradition and its jurists were anti-formalist. From Muhammad to the first caliphs to the eponyms of three Sunni schools, the hallmark of Islamic jurists was that they adapted their rules to meet contemporary needs. The aberration point in this story was then the fourth imam and madhhabic eponym, Aḥmad Ibn Ḥanbal (d. 855), who tightened the reigns on *ijtihād*, enforced faith in hadith, and dealt a blow to rationalists of the tenth century. Ibn Ḥanbal's triumph, Lambert averred, was a mistake and an

Middle East Studies 16,1 (1984): 3–41; Baber Johansen, "Legal Literature and the Problem of Change: The Case of Land Rent," in Johansen, *Contingency*, 446–64; Johansen, "Casuistry: Between Legal Concept and Social Praxis," *Islamic Law and Society* 2,2 (1995): 135–56.

[24] Here he cites *Les Prolégomènes* (*al-Muqaddimah*) of Ibn Khaldūn, pp. 18–19. It has not been possible to confirm the edition. It may have been that by M. de Slane (1862/1863). But although it is commonly reported that Ibn Khaldūn propagated the notion of a closure of *ijtihād*, he does not do so on pp. 18–19 of this edition.

[25] One of these is Savvas Pacha. The other may be Mirza Ghulam Ahmad.

[26] See Snouck Hurgronje, "Droit musulman," 13.

[27] Lambert, *Fonction*, 373–7 (emphasis added).

irony that ran counter to all previous legal practice of the early and pious Muslims, including the Prophet himself. In Lambert's exhortation, contemporary *ijtihād* should be a full-scale *ijtihād* of the kind known to the first century of Islam: it should be used for establishing and refining legal methods, and for changing substantive law to meet new needs.

The most interesting comparative moment occurs when Lambert indirectly associates Ibn Ḥanbal with scholasticism and the French school of exegesis, accusing him of anti-scientism and narrow-minded textualism.[28] "The scrupulous conservative guardians of the teachings of the Prophet," he wrote, "viewed the effort of scientific investigation as an act of non-belief, or a veritable sacrilege."[29]

Lambert contrasted Ibn Ḥanbal's position with that of Abū Ḥanīfah and Mālik ibn Anas, whom he compared to France's liberal and progressive jurists. He lauded Mālik for acceptance of early Medinese custom as a source of law. He portrayed Abū Ḥanīfah as anti-formalist, inclined to reason, less bound to literalism, and averse to scholastic thought.[30] He claimed further that Abū Ḥanīfah and al-Shāfiʿī were more liberal in their reasoning methods than the French school of exegesis.[31] He compared Abū Ḥanīfah's "school of opinion" (*raʾy*) to Gény's conception of "free scientific research."[32] Lambert found a measure of "positivism" in the legal thought of Abū Ḥanīfah and compared him in this regard to Gény.

Common Origins in Roman and Jewish Law

In the late nineteenth century, some orientalists conjectured that the law of the Quran, the Sunnah, and methods of early jurists were derived partly from Roman and Jewish law.[33] Lambert turned this conjecture into a historical claim and one that could guide contemporary reformist thought. In his adaptation of this notion, he discussed how Muslims in the first three centuries of Islam had been receptive to and would even incorporate the customary and formal legal practices of non-Muslim communities. Influences included the laws and customs of pre-Islamic Arabia, Romans, Persians, Byzantines, and Jews.[34] Roman law's influence was particularly pronounced.[35] For Lambert, the implication of this historical "fact" was that Muslims of today should not fear comparing their laws to European law. Since Muslim and Western laws sprang from a common well, there would be nothing to fear in borrowing rules from Europe.

Consensus and Custom

Since Lambert's theory of global legal history held that custom is the fount of law, he embraced the orientalists' arguments about Islamic law's customary origins.

[28] Ibid., 363–4, 368–74. [29] Ibid., 360. [30] Ibid., 352–60.
[31] Ibid., 364. [32] Ibid., 361. [33] Ibid., 279–90.
[34] Ibid. On the origins of the positions of Goldziher and Savvas, see Patricia Crone, *Roman, Provincial, and Islamic Law: The Origins of the Islamic Patronate* (Cambridge: Cambridge University Press, 1987), 102.
[35] Lambert, *Fonction*, 283.

He presented their evidence and conjectures alike as a basis for claiming that custom should be revived as a source of law in present-day Muslim legal doctrine.

Lambert argued for reformed conceptions of consensus and custom that would allow both to become tools of common recourse for making law in the contemporary period. "Consensus" was considered by Muslim jurists the third primary source (*aṣl* pl. *uṣūl*) after Quran and Sunnah. Problematically for the reformer of modern-day law, classical Sunni legal theory held that it was the prerogative of scholars of the first generations and could no longer be applied contemporarily. As for custom, this had long been recognized as a source of law by Muslims, but it was not considered among the primary sources. It had a second-class status as a source of law, and it certainly did not have the power, legally speaking, to override a norm established by the Quran, hadith, or consensus, or a ruling based on a firm and undisputed analogy to a rule in Quran, hadith, or consensus.

Following the leads of Snouck Hurgronje, Goldziher, Sachau, and Van den Berg, Lambert sought to revive the practice of consensus by reinterpreting history. He began by arguing that consensus is a feature of custom, and that it is a tool to legitimize the incorporation of custom into the formal law. He also pointed out a similarity between consensus and a European (thus, in his mind, universal) concept:

> It is possible to recognize, in a brief review of the origins of diverse juridical systems that have veritably made their mark in the general history of humanity, scientific proof of the accuracy of the Romano-canonical conception of custom (*coutume*). It is in that conception that we may hope to find [the equivalent of consensus, *ijmāʿ*]. We see, in effect, the reappearance here of the dogma on which the entire doctrine of the pandectists rests: the idea that the juridical norm finds its origins in a mysterious harmony of wills that is accomplished non-violently within a social community, according to the spontaneous and instinctive practice of all interested parties. The designation of this phenomenon as the third primary source of canonical Muslim *fiqh* seems highly significant. The "*ijmāʿ* of the ummah," which is the agreement of the community, is the *tacitus consensus populi* of canonists and glossators; and it is the *gemeinsame Rechtsüberzeugung* of the historical school.[36]

The argument was that contemporary Muslims misunderstood *ijmāʿ* because they misunderstood its history. *Ijmāʿ* was originally a manifestation of custom and was an early practice of Muslims that gave legal force to custom. However, with the passage of time, Muslims came to believe that early *ijmāʿ* was of a higher and inimitable status because it reflected lost hadiths, the benefit of living close to the time of the Prophet, and perfect correspondence with his instructions and norms. Muslim tradition over time mistakenly turned the first generation's *ijmāʿ* into a sacred restatement and elaboration of the Quran and prophetic example. Consensus, he argued, was not and is never worked out as a result of perfect consensus of wills, but is always the result of conflict between jurists and the ability of one group to triumph over others. He likened *ijmāʿ* to English and French case law:

[36] Ibid., 325–6.

> The spectator, mistaking effect for cause, forgets or ignores the preceding conflicts and unrest that prepared the phenomena of appeasement and harmony.... I don't understand why the jurist or historian allows himself to be duped by such grand illusions. It does not take an extremely penetrating analysis to realize the fiction that has been accorded to *ijmāʿ*—the façade of being a *Volksrecht*, or a people's law, when it is in fact a *Juristenrecht*, or a law elaborated by the jurists.[37]

The argument casts *ijmāʿ* in such a way that it could be used to justify a new, modern lawmaking project. The first consensus, he claims, was the work of jurists, not God. He casts doubt on their monopoly of authority. By this, he meant to empower contemporary jurists with the power of forming consensus. He says that Muslim societies had had to create extra-Sharia law (*qānūn*) because they turned their back on *ijmāʿ*, custom, and science.[38] A return to *ijmāʿ* and custom would allow Muslims to once again live under the true Islamic law, thus having no need for *qānūn*, which they could call *ijmāʿ*.

Islamization as Authenticity, Universality, Flexibility, Sensitivity to Social Needs, and Openness to Comparative Legislation

Lambert supported "Islamization" of law. The question is what this meant to him. For Lambert, to "Islamize" law meant to acknowledge Islam's authentic nature; this meant, in turn, to understand that Islam mandates flexibility and spontaneous, practical-minded innovation in legal reasoning, requires jurists to take stock of social needs to develop the law to address those needs, and requires jurists and Muslim society to be open to all beneficial legal reforms, even those that were unprecedented or forbidden in historical memory. He stopped short of suggesting that there is nothing inherently Islamic about an Islamic law.

Around 1903, there was little public and published discourse in French and English about "Islamization" of law. The word appeared rarely in scholarly discourse before the mid-1920s. When used, it referred to the ancient Islamic conquests or to spiritual conversion. English- and French-language writers did not use the term to mean converting European legal systems of the colonies into Islamic legal systems. Those ideas were present in some quarters of the world, but that coinage was not common.

Among the exceptions were Savvas Pacha, Goldziher, and Lambert. In 1896, Savvas wrote in *Le Droit musulman expliqué* (1886) about "*islamisation du droit*":

> Ethnological studies in recent years have placed beyond doubt the existence of more than two hundred million Muslims on three continents, which form the ancient hemisphere. It is the duty of civilized peoples and above all the most cosmopolitan nation

[37] Ibid., 334–8.

[38] On *qānūn*, see Leonard Wood, "Legislation as an Instrument of Islamic Law," *The Oxford Handbook of Islamic Law*, Oxford Handbooks Online, ed. Anver Emon and Rumee Ahmed (Oxford: May 2016), available online at http://www.oxfordhandbooks.com.

> of Europe, France, to seek out the proper means for improving the wellbeing of such a considerable portion of humanity.
>
> It has seemed to me that adapting our laws to principles that guide Muslim society—that is, the Islamization of modern law—would achieve this goal. It would allow two hundred million men, our fellow man, worthy in every respect, to benefit from our more advanced institutions. Their religious beliefs are so strong that they merit our most serious attention....
>
> I have shown by reference to facts, we can make not only acceptable, but mandatory, for the conscience of the Muslims, all progress, all truth, and every legal attitude that to this point has not been accepted by Muslim society and that has not yet been enshrined in its law.
>
> This is the most important aspect of the present situation that I have come to know, which I witnessed from my particular point of view. It is also the reason to assure the two hundred million Muslims who live today... a prosperous future and an advantageous position in modern society.
>
> The path that will lead to the progress of Islam is undoubtedly the Islamization of modern law. Provided we know deeply the sources of Islamic law and the legislative methods particular to them, we can broaden the scope of Islamic law (*code*) and make it accomplish, *without impiety*, all of the improvements for which civilized peoples are justly proud.[39]

These excerpts come from a complex text that debates with Ignaz Goldziher on dozens of historical questions. Only the most pivotal of these debates needs be addressed. When Savvas referred to "adapting our laws," he meant "by ensuring that all laws in the Ottoman Empire are compliant with Islam." He did not mean supplanting the Ottoman Empire's *qānūn* or European-inspired laws with laws extracted from canonical works of *fiqh*.[40] For Savvas, Islamization meant keeping most contemporary Ottoman laws in place, including *qānūn* and laws of European extraction, by calling such laws "Islamic" on the basis they were sufficiently compliant with Islam. The means to this end, for Savvas, was to claim that most contemporary laws of the Ottoman Empire were in the service of progress and modernization. One would argue that the existing laws have a foundation in the principles and spirit of Islam and the primary sources of Islamic revelation. As the means to pursue and accomplish this objective, he urged revision and reformation of traditional methods and theories of Islamic legal reasoning (*uṣūl al-fiqh*).

Goldziher ridiculed Savvas's concept of Islamization because he held the idea infeasible from a methodological standpoint. He thought *uṣūl al-fiqh* was too doctrinally rigid to meet modern demands and to achieve the ends envisioned by Savvas. Moreover, he said that Savvas had made a proposition that Muslims would find totally objectionable. Goldziher was like other orientalists who held that Islamic law could only "modernize" if it were to change its laws and methods so drastically that it was fundamentally altered from its essences.

[39] Savvas Pacha, *Le Droit musulman expliqué: Réponse à un article de M. Ignace Goldziher paru dans le Byzantinische Zeitschrift, II, 2, p. 317–325, 1893* (Paris: Marchal et Billard, 1896), 1, 152. Note that the ellipsis in this excerpt excludes 150 intervening pages. Savvas articulated these ideas earlier at a conference in 1892. See "Société d'économie politique: Réunion du 5 février 1892," *Journal des économistes* 5e sér., 9 (1892): 284–300, at 286–8.

[40] See Wood, "Legislation as an Instrument of Islamic Law."

Lambert considered Savvas's vision of Islamization to be the wrong way for approaching reform, because the view proposed that a project of complex reform in technical aspects of Islamic legal theory was needed for modern legal systems to become "Islamic." Lambert did not want to wade in and tinker with the technicalities, complexities, and doctrinal strictures and rigidities of Islamic legal theory as it had been elaborated during and after the third century of Islam; instead, Lambert wanted to sidestep many of the technicalities and doctrinal rigidities of that literature altogether, by revisiting and revising the history of the first three Islamic centuries. He wanted to change understandings of the earliest moments of Islamic history as a means to reset the field of Islamic legal theory that had gone astray, and to return Islam to what he took to be its original practices and outlooks.

Lambert's argument about Islamization was that if Islamic law and society's earliest, authentic characteristics were merely and correctly recognized, all would see that Islamic law and European law were already fundamentally very close, and moreover flexible and adaptable. If Muslims could grasp the authentic Islamic faith and practice, with all of its intrinsic flexibility, then there would be no major, or at least no intractable, gaps between the systems. Lambert saw the concept of Islamization as the result of the conceptualization of a false problem: there was no need to bridge two systems that were already the same.

> I do not use the word *islamisation* here in the sense that it has been given recently by Muslim writers, who endeavor to demonstrate that sensible efforts in juridical thought (*doctrine*), if they are well enough directed, will arrive at this result: to render acceptable for the Muslims all the achievements of modern civilization and to make such achievements conform with all of the principles of Muslim canonical law; that is (in the words of those writers) to "Islamize" all of the juridical ideas that today form the base of our Christian legislations. This theory of a possible Islamization of modern law has been developed by Savvas Pacha [and] a professor from Cairo, Omar Bey Loutfi.[41] It was also restated by Raymond West.[42] The purely utopian character of these plans of reform have been pitilessly denounced by Snouck Hurgronje.[43]
>
> But the principal causes that explain the powerlessness of contemporary Islamic law to bend itself to the necessities of progress, and the quasi-immobility into which it has fallen, did not yet exist in the time when the corpus of canonical law was elaborated in Mecca [i.e., in the first Islamic century] and transported to Iraq [i.e., in the second and third Islamic centuries] and in the ancient Roman provinces [e.g., Syria and Egypt]. The juridical institutions of these areas were Islamized (*islamisées*) in great number. Most often these institutions were not deformed by being squeezed into the restrictive framework of primitive traditions; instead, Muslim tradition was enlarged and transformed to take the place of those institutions. *Islamisation* was therefore not developed systematically by the schools of *fiqh*; it was rather developed spontaneously in the face of compelling urgencies and the everyday needs of practice. This was achieved in large part by means of falsified or fabricated hadith.[44]

41 Presumably the reference is to Loutfy, *De l'Action pénale.*
42 See West, "Modern Developments."
43 Snouck Hurgronje, "Droit Musulman," 190.
44 Lambert, *Fonction*, 322–3 (internal citations omitted).

Lambert was convinced that Islamic law in its original manifestation in the first three centuries of Islam was flexible and adaptable in matters of law. He believed this not only because that was the manner of Islamic jurists as he understood it, but because, in his understanding of history, Muslims had learned these methods through exposure to the laws and legal systems of the Romans (Western and Eastern) who had previously occupied Syria and Mesopotamia or otherwise made their legal influence felt in North Africa and Egypt. The idea was that if Muslims would finally accept this historical narrative as fact, they would accept returning to the previous methods from before the consolidation of the Sunni *madhhabs* and would be more open to collaborative efforts with European law.

FROM LAMBERT TO EGYPT

A study of Lambert's earliest ideas about Islamic law yields insights into the contribution of comparative law to the development of reformist approaches in Egyptian legal thought. It partly explains the origins and characteristics of comparative law in early twentieth-century Egypt. The most important of Lambert's ideas for Egypt may have been universalism. Universalist theory made comparativist agendas palatable to Egyptian jurists who might otherwise have been wary of comparativism's ambitious, interventionist, transformative, and sometimes hostile animus with respect to well-established doctrines and conceptions of history long held by Muslims in Islamic societies. Who these Egyptian scholars were and what they consequently accomplished in their own country's legal thought are treated in the following section.

Section III

Transformations in Education and Scholarship

7

Education and Scholarship in Franco-Egyptian and French Law before 1923

Beginning in 1923 and for three decades afterward, scholars at the Cairo University Law Faculty pursued groundbreaking pedagogy and scholarship in Franco-Egyptian and Islamic law. Developments characterizing that golden era included the transition of Franco-Egyptian legal academia from European languages into Arabic, the creation of new genres of legal-academic literature, the advancement of new methods and the reconfiguration of old methods, the popularization of advanced legal theory, innovation in substantive and procedural law, the embrace of European-styled social sciences, and the ascendance of comparative law as a discipline to inspire new research, thinking, teaching, and substantive law.

If the jurists of Franco-Egyptian law at this Cairo Faculty[1] were original, prolific, and powerful after 1923, and if their scholarship and pedagogy became newly sophisticated, an explanation is required for how this flourishing came about and why it occurred in earnest only after four decades of British occupation. For this, one turns to the history of the Cairo Faculty between 1867 and 1923. The school has been known for having produced Egypt's most famous lawyers, judges, and professional and political elites, but the history of its curriculum and the intellectual production by its scholars are largely unknown.[2] Related developments at the French School of Law of Cairo, a separate and private institution, also played a role in developing scholarship.

British hegemony was a leading factor in impeding the expansion of new scholarship at the Cairo Faculty. Before the 1920s the Cairo Faculty trained students to

[1] The Cairo University Law Faculty (*Kulliyyat al Ḥuqūq, Faculté de Droit*) is referred to as the "Cairo Faculty" because the institution changed names several times. It began in 1868 as the Oriental School of Languages and Administration. In 1875, the legal division of the Oriental School became known as "The Law School," the Khedivial Law School, and the Royal Law School. In 1914–1923, the school was known as the Sultanic Law School. In 1925, it became the Law Faculty of the Egyptian University, which became King Fu'ād I University, and in 1952 became Cairo University. Shalakany, "Sanhuri," 164 n. 28.

[2] There is no comprehensive history of the school and no study evaluating the intellectual history of the school and its faculty. See *al-ʿĪd al-miʾawī li-Kulliyyat al-Ḥuqūq* (Cairo: Jāmiʿat al-Qāhirah, 1980), 1–9, 21–7. This book contains historical data pertinent to the law school but only a short narrative that mostly repeats what was originally published in the school's annual prospectuses of the 1930s. See also "Kulliyyat al-Ḥuqūq," in *al-Kitāb al-dhahabī*, 2: 409–32; al-Jāmiʿah al-Miṣriyyah, *Taqwīm Kulliyyat al-Ḥuqūq* (Cairo: al-Maṭbaʿah al-Amīriyyah, 1929–40); Botiveau, *Loi islamique*, 170–4; Ziadeh, *Lawyers, the Rule of Law and Liberalism*, 19–21; Cannon, *Politics of Law*, 225, 270, 278; Donald M. Reid, *Cairo University and the Making of Modern Egypt* (Cambridge: Cambridge University Press, 1990), 21.

Islamic Legal Revival: Reception of European Law and Transformations in Islamic Legal Thought in Egypt, 1875–1952. First Edition. Leonard Wood.

practice law and operate the judiciary, but the administrators did not promote advanced legal research and thought among students or professors. Although French personnel founded the school, the British wrested control at the turn of the twentieth century. Afterward, the school taught only in English and squeezed out French personnel. Leaders blocked initiatives that would have advanced training in legal thought and scholarship beyond that which was immediately required to serve the practical needs of an expanding and complex legal system. The school remained especially uninterested in promoting sophisticated legal scholarship in Arabic. The French- and English-language textbooks written during those years by professors of Franco-Egyptian law sought to explain the law for the use of practitioners. They showed little in the way of exploratory research or engagement with elevated modes of legal theory and critique that were current and popular in contemporary European scholarship.

The period of British hegemony at the Cairo Faculty from 1907 to 1923 was, on the other hand, a period of reception and entrenchment of Franco-Egyptian law as a fact of life, in spite of British administrators making certain English-style reforms to the laws and courts. Students learned continental European and Franco-Egyptian law and became lawyers, judges, ministers, and administrators in the colonial state, and in this way they became invested in the system itself. However, the Cairo Faculty remained insulated from the lively world of continental European legal theory that would have been useful to students and scholars of Franco-Egyptian law, which was still a product of the continental European heritage. Given the lack of opportunities and encouragement for advanced and graduate-level research, students and faculty were not incentivized to critically investigate the Franco-Egyptian law. The British system of control deprived them of opportunities to rigorously contemplate a revival of Islamic law and its mechanics.

THE CAIRO FACULTY BEFORE THE FOUNDATION OF THE NATIVE COURTS

The Cairo Faculty started out as the Oriental School of Languages and Administration, founded in 1868; it began its work by training Egyptian students in European law. Its creators included Europeans, Egyptians, and Turco-Circassian elites.[3] In 1865, Khedive Ismail asked Victor Vidal, a French engineer and lawyer, to draft a criminal code and submit a memorandum on the establishment of the Ottoman-style Nizami courts in Egypt.[4] Vidal opened the Oriental School to train Egyptians

[3] Contributions came from Nubar Pasha, Yaqub Artin, and ʿAlī Mubārak. Botiveau, *Loi islamique*, 169–76, citing the description of a memorandum from Victor Vidal to M. de Régny Bey on legal education in Egypt, in "Séance du 20 février 1874," *Bulletin de l'Institut Égyptien, année 1874–1875*, no. 13: 7–10; also citing A. Gavillot, "Notice sur Vidal Pacha," ibid., *année 1891*, 3rd ser., no. 2: 122–34. See following note.

[4] Cannon, "Social Tensions," 300–1; Vidal reported that his memorandum on this topic, for the Institut Égyptien, was entitled "État actuel de l'enseignement du droit en Égypte." V. Vidal Bey, "Notice sur les travaux de l'Institut Égyptien depuis sa fondation," in *Verhandlungen des VII. internationalen Orientalisten-Congresses, gehalten in Wien im Jahre 1886*, 4 vols. (Wien: Alfred Holder, 1886–89),

Table 7.1. Cairo Faculty enrollment, 1873–1882.

Year	Total enrollment	Graduating Students
1873	30[5]	
1874	35	7
1875	35	5
1876	31	5
1877	35	
1878	48	3
1879		9
1880	37	10
1881	48	7
1882		4

Compiled from *Recueil des documents officiels du gouvernement égyptien* (Port Said: Imprimerie Française J. Serrière, 1881), 207. Blank spaces indicate a lack of reliable numbers.

for work in the Nizami courts, and he modified the curriculum in 1875 to train students for the Mixed Courts. He was the first director and remained in the position until his death in 1890.

The school was small and its curriculum experimental. The first year of a four-year program taught foreign languages, translation, and bookkeeping. The remaining three years taught contracts, property, criminal law, and procedures for practice in the Mixed and Sharia Courts. Students received occasional instruction in European personal status law to prepare for practice in the consular courts. By 1881, the number of graduating students had never exceeded ten. (See Table 7.1.) The school had two full-time law professors and four full-time language instructors. Other courses were taught by practitioners, graduates, and the director.

Although a *licence* from this school would eventually become the best ticket to a prestigious career in the Mixed and Native Courts, apprenticeship and patronage were still the keys to employment before the mid-1880s.[6] In the Mixed Courts, lawyers and judges held degrees from European and North American law schools. When the Native Courts were established, the lawyers and judges were recruited from the Nizami courts. At the Sharia Courts, al-Azhar was the feeder—a daunting competitor for Vidal, having a large enrollment, robust training in Islamic law, and prestige. Its graduates could assume positions in the Native and Mixed Courts and did so into the early 1900s. Vidal therefore focused on producing practitioners before scholars. He taught academic questions in the law insofar as such topics would prepare them for practice. He fostered internships with judges, prosecutors, and investigators.

The school's approach to languages—it taught Turkish, French, Italian, Latin, and Arabic—reflects its limited capacity for supporting research. Language studies were

1: 89–108, at 103. See also *Bulletin de l'Institut Égyptien, année 1874–1875*, no. 13: 7–10, 30, 243; ibid., *année 1880*, 2nd ser., no. 1: 77–80, 150, 153–5.

[5] Botiveau (*Loi islamique*, 171 n. 11) reports 44.

[6] Cannon, "Social Tensions," 304–5.

important at the Cairo Faculty because of Egypt's multi-jurisdictional landscape. This is the primary reason law was originally taught in a language school. But legal translation posed challenges that the school itself could not resolve in Vidal's time.

Vidal reduced instruction in Turkish and increased instruction in Arabic in 1881.[7] The interest in Arabic reflected an awareness that a new legal system was evolving but that the Arabic used to express terms and ideas from French law was new even to native Arabic speakers. European jurists had been analyzing for decades problems with the *Code civil* that stemmed from overlapping and inconsistent use of technical terms in French. These problems were replicated in the French versions of the Mixed and Native Codes and compounded in the Arabic translations. Bilingual Egyptians saw that there was no definitive Arabic lexicon for translating French legal terms.[8]

The presence of French laws in Egypt required late nineteenth-century Egyptians to develop a technical Arabic vocabulary to express French legal concepts, for which there were approximate—but not perfect—parallels in Arabic. To meet translation needs, Egyptians assigned new or revised meanings to technical legal terms from the lexicon of classical Islamic *fiqh*, but this tended to create new problems while fixing others. This translation phenomenon was not a regulated and standardized process in which one single group of skilled jurists, working in one place, and within a discrete period of time, finalized and agreed on Arabic translations for French words.

The process of stabilizing Arabic-French translations was a project that Vidal envisioned but not one that he could accomplish. The handful of scholarly works on law from before the 1910s reveals that this was a limited operation. Few Arabic-language studies were published by scholars on the Franco-Egyptian law before the 1910s. Most were published in French or English. The majority of teachers were Europeans and most instruction occurred in French and English, despite the fact that Egyptian graduates of the school would ultimately practice Native law in Arabic. The hardest work in Arabic-French translation was left for later generations of Egyptian scholars who would be more numerous, more capable of solving translation problems, and surrounded by an incentive structure that rewarded their efforts.

THE CAIRO FACULTY AFTER THE FOUNDATION OF THE NATIVE COURTS

From 1882 to 1886, the institution adjusted to the new political framework of occupation and to the needs of the Native Courts. Lord Dufferin's 1883 *Report* on priorities of the British residency urged that the school be enlarged,[9] but authorities

[7] In 1913, Ottoman students comprised 68 out of 410 students, the largest minority among Greeks, Italians, French, and other groups. *Revue internationale de l'enseignement* 69 (1915): 310.

[8] See Aḥmad Fatḥī Zaghlūl, *Sharḥ al-qānūn al-madanī* (Cairo: al-Maṭbaʿah al-Amīriyyah bi-Miṣr, 1913), introduction.

[9] F.O. Conf., Earl of Dufferin, "General Report" (1883).

only took decisive action in the 1890s after more pressing problems were solved in the Native and Mixed Courts. In 1882, when the Oriental School of Languages and Administration divided into the School of Languages and the School of Administration, the latter taught the law classes. In 1886, the Ministry of Justice renamed it the School of Law.[10] Given the instability of the 1880s, there was little significant expansion of faculty, enrollment, or progress in education and scholarship.

In 1886 the British Judicial Adviser Raymond West called on the school to create its first curriculum in Native law, to hire European judges to lecture, and to expand enrollment.[11] Admission to the bars and benches of the Native and Mixed Courts, he observed, was obtained through clientelism. He argued that admissions should be determined by an applicant's education in the new laws. Although British, West never expressed objection to French control at the school. His sole caveat was that if the law was to remain French, Egyptians should be trained in French law.

West's recommendations ushered in the desired reforms. The Council of Ministers established a five-year curriculum comprising two years of preparatory work and three years of legal education.[12] The preparatory section, for students who would work in middle-level government positions, taught Arabic, French, translation, history, calligraphy, bookkeeping, and judicial procedures.[13] The three-year superior level, for training lawyers, judges, notaries, and high-level government officials, taught Franco-Egyptian law, European law, Sharia, and translation.

BRITISH AND FRENCH COMPETITION FOR PREDOMINANCE

Differences soon arose as to who should control the law school and which cultures and languages would predominate. Turkish and Italian were cut from the curriculum by 1889, even though Italians remained on the faculty teaching in French.[14] The British residency preferred Francophone teachers from civil law countries who were not French: Italians, Belgians, Dutch, Quebecois, Scots, and so on. The struggle for control fell between British administrators associated with the British residency and the Egyptian Ministry of Justice and French professors backed by the French government. Egyptians in government and public life made their case for the role of Egyptians on the faculty and Arabic in the curriculum. (See Table 7.2.)

[10] For the institution's many name changes, see n. 1.

[11] Raymond West, "Note on the Administration of Justice and the Organization of the Courts in Egypt (Incl. in No. 48)," in *P.P.* C. 4679, LXXIV, 397; *Further Correspondence Respecting the Affairs of Egypt*, "Egypt, No. 5, 1886" (London: Harrison and Sons, 1886), 36; Cannon, "Social Tensions," 305.

[12] "Arrêté du Ministre de l'Instruction publique fixant le règlement organique de l'École de Droit," in *Bulletin des lois et décrets et de documents officiels du gouvernement égyptien* (1886), 636–44, at 636.

[13] Ibid., 636–7.

[14] Members of the Italian government and Italian academics worked through diplomatic channels to maintain positions for Italians on the law school's faculty. See, for example, "No. 9: The Marquis of Salisbury to Sir E. Baring (Nov. 5, 1889)," in F.O. Conf., "Further Correspondence Respecting the Affairs of Egypt," No. 5912 (Oct. to Dec. 1889), 10; "No. 10: M. Catalani to the Marquis of Salisbury (Nov. 5, 1889)," in ibid.

Table 7.2. Cairo Faculty, new curriculum, 1886–87.[15]

Elementary section, year 1	Hours	Elementary section, year 2	Hours
Arabic	6	Arabic	6
French	6	French	6
Translation	3	Translation	6
French writing	6	French writing	3
Arabic writing	6	Arabic writing	6
Geography and History	3	Geography and History	3
Judicial organization	3	Bookkeeping	3
Bookkeeping	3	Practical procedure	3
Superior section, year 3	**Hours**	**Superior section, year 4**	**Hours**
Sharia	6	Sharia	3
Civil	3	Civil	3
Penal Law	3	Procedure	3
Roman Law	3	Roman Law	3
French	6	French	6
Italian	6	Italian	6
Translation	6	Translation	6
History and geography	3	History and geography	3
		Redactions in Arabic of juridical works	3
Superior section, year 5	**Hours**		
Sharia	3		
Procedure	3		
Commercial	6		
Roman Law	3		
French	6		
Italian	6		
Translation	6		
Redactions in Arabic of juridical works	3		

Source: "Arrêté du Ministre de l'Instruction publique fixant le règlement organique de l'École de Droit," in *Bulletin des lois et décrets et de documents officiels du gouvernement égyptien, année 1886* (Cairo: Imprimerie Internationale, 1886), 636–44.

When Vidal died in 1890, controversy erupted over the appointment of his successor. The Minister of Education, ʿAlī Mubārak, attempted to appoint Ibrāhīm Najīb, an Egyptian judge from the Cairo Court of Appeals. When British and French officials blocked this proposal through back channels of the ministries, ʿAlī Mubārak attempted to appoint another Egyptian. Ibrāhīm Najīb assumed vice-chairmanship of the law school but could not secure the appointment to director. ʿAlī Mubārak pushed for this promotion until he was replaced by a new Minister of Education, Yaqub Artin, who yielded to the Europeans' designs on the post.[16] (See Table 7.3.)

The controversy over Vidal's successor was one of many flashpoints showcasing the seriousness with which French personnel regarded maintaining their influence in law and legal education. The prosecutor general, a certain Le Grelle

[15] Classes were three or six hours per week.

[16] Cannon, "Social Tensions," 308, citing *The Egyptian Gazette* (Oct. 16, 1889).

Table 7.3. Directors and deans of the Cairo Faculty, 1868–1958.

	Directors and deans	Tenure	*Licence* degree	Doctoral degree
	French period (Directors)			
1	Victor Vidal	Oct 1868–Aug 1891		
2	Charles Testoud	Dec 1891–Mar 1902		
3	M. Grandmoulin	Sep 1903–Sep 1906		
4	Édouard Lambert	Oct 1906–Sep 1907		
	British period (Directors)			
5	W. Hill	Sep 1907–Dec 1912		
6	Maurice Sheldon Amos	Jan 1913–Jul 1915		
7	Hebert Walton	Sep 1915–Jan 1923		
	Interim period (Deans)			
8	ʿAlī Māhir	Apr 1923–Nov 1924	1902	
9	ʿAbd al-Ḥamīd Abū Hayf	Dec 1924–Mar 1925	1909	Cairo
10	Léon Duguit	Nov 1925–Mar 1926		Bordeaux
	Egyptian period (Deans)			
11	Aḥmad Amīn	Apr 1926–Jul 1927	1908	
12	Muḥammad Kāmil Mursī	Oct 1928–May 1936	1910	Paris
13	ʿAbd al-Razzāq Aḥmad al-Sanhūrī	Oct 1936–Oct 1937	1917	Lyon
14	Muḥammad Ṣāliḥ	Oct 1938–Oct 1940	1912	Lyon
15	ʿAlī Muḥammad Badawī	Oct 1940–Nov 1942	1917	Cairo
16	Muḥammad Ṣāliḥ	Nov 1942–Nov 1945	1912	Lyon
17	Muḥammad Muṣṭafá al-Qulalī	Nov 1945–Oct 1949	1922	Cairo
18	Muḥammad Ḥāmid Fahmī	Nov 1949–Jul 1952	1922	Cairo
19	Saʿīd Muṣṭafá al-Saʿīd	Oct 1952–Jul 1953	1927	Cairo
20	Muḥammad ʿAbd al-Munʿim Badr	Jul 1953–Jan 1958	1926	Cairo

Compiled from Jāmiʿat al-Qāhirah, *al-ʿĪd al-miʾawī*, 29–30.

(or Legrelle), pressed his desire for a French dean before the government, arguing it was the only way for the school to successfully pursue its reforms.[17] The French Consul nominated two French candidates, one of whom was Charles Testoud of the Grenoble Law Faculty.[18] Lord Cromer, British Controller-General of Egypt, ultimately pushed the nomination of Testoud through the Ministry of Education.

Cromer opted to accept the French position in the Egyptian legal field for the time being. The law was French. There were French, Belgian, and Italian personnel on hand to teach. Law and legal education were areas of control the British could afford to yield temporarily as a palliative for having seized power without French acquiescence in 1882. The French were already protesting British Judicial

[17] Le Grelle was Belgian. F.O. Conf., "Judicial Reforms," No. 6175 (1891), 26.

[18] On Testoud's career in Egypt, see Pierre Arminjon, "Charles Testoud: Ses années d'Égypte," *Annales (Université de Grenoble)* (1907): 19–25; Charles Tartari, *Charles Testoud, professeur à la Faculté de Droit de Grenoble* (Grenoble: Imprimerie Allier Frères, 1903); Cannon, "Social Tensions," 308. The other nominee, Octave Borelli Bey, was French and an outspoken opponent of British rule. On his career, see Edward Vizetelly, *From Cyprus to Zanzibar* (London: C. A. Pearson Ltd., 1901), 256–60; Alexander M. Broadley, *How We Defended Arabi and His Friends* (London: Chapman and Hall Ltd., 1884), 43–50.

Adviser John Scott's extensive reforms to the Native Court system.[19] The Judicial Adviser was an official charged with issuing British directives to the Egyptian Ministry of Justice.

When Cromer approved the appointment of Testoud, Scott followed suit by announcing that Testoud would be devoted to "continuity in the French tradition."[20] Scott, who took his orders from Cromer, was fluent in French, held a *licence* in French law, and practiced Mixed Law in French; he accepted French personnel in the spheres of Native law and legal education.[21]

INCULCATION OF FRENCH LAW UNDER TESTOUD AND SCOTT

When the Native Courts became secure, Scott, Testoud, and the Justice Ministry turned to improving the Cairo Faculty. Testoud was interested in improving education, and Scott hoped that the school would produce new generations of judges and lawyers to replace older generations in Native and Mixed Courts.[22] French lawyers hoped that rising generations of French-trained Egyptian lawyers would eventually drive out the British rulers; the British hoped that rising generations of French-trained Egyptian lawyers would eventually drive out the French lawyers.

British tolerance for French influence at the Law School lasted long enough for French legal culture and learning to survive and become entrenched in the society. Testoud wrote about teaching students to think for themselves as practically minded practitioners. He followed nineteenth-century priorities in French legal pedagogy. One concept held that a lawyer needed to be well trained to extrapolate rules and principles from the codes so as to apply them properly to situations not covered by the codes. A second concept was that lawyers should analyze the

[19] He served as Judicial Adviser to the Egyptian government from 1890 to 1898.

[20] Cannon, "Social Tensions," 308; "Extract from M. Le Grelle's Report on the School of Law of July 11, 1891 (Inclosure 2 in 26), in F.O. Conf., "Further Correspondence Respecting Judicial Reforms in Egpyt 1891 (in continuation of Confidential Paper No. 6049)," Paper No. 6175 (Mar. 1892), 26–7. Le Grelle reported that the law school had been without a director for more than two years. This information contradicts official histories of the law school, which report that Vidal was director until August 1891. Vidal died, however, in 1890. See *al-ʿĪd al-miʾawī*, 29. John Scott reported ("Rapport sur les Tribuneaux indigènes 1890–1894," *Recueil des documents officiels du gouvernement égyptien* (1894), 81–100, at 82–3): "A European principal, fully capable, will for the moment be necessary, and we had the good fortune of finding the man who turned out to be M. Testoud, who has sacrificed his professional career in France for taking direction of the School of Law."

[21] "Avis de Monsieur le Conseiller Scott." This assertion is based on research in private letter collections of his correspondents. See Bodleian Library, (1) Papers of Lord Kimberley: Letters from 1884, 1894; Mss. Eng. c. 4253, fols. 113–14; Mss. Eng. c. 4409, fols. 20–2. (2) Letters to Lord Bryce: Mss. Bryce 132, fols. 4–51; Mss. Bryce 195, fols. 85–6; Mss. Bryce 228, fols. 227–8. (3) Letters to Lord Milner: Mss. Milner dep. 27, fols. 195–6, 254–7, 285–6; Mss. Milner dep. 28, fols. 194–5; Mss. Milner dep. 30, fols. 134–5; Mss. Milner dep. 206, fol. 74. (4) Copies of Letters from [Milner]: Ms. Milner, dep. 36, fols. 175–6. See also holdings at Rhodes House Oxford and British Library.

[22] Lord Cromer credited John Scott with having realized the connection between improving legal education and the improvement of judges. Evelyn Baring Cromer, *Modern Egypt* (London: Macmillan, 1908), 2: 519. Scott ("Rapport sur les Tribunaux indigènes," 81) considered the school the "breeding-ground for future public officials" and spoke of the importance of its "regeneration."

codes critically, challenging conventional wisdom about the meaning of the codes' articles.

Reforms of 1892 remained more or less in place until political upheavals between 1919 and 1923. The school abolished the elementary section and offered admission only to those holding a secondary school diploma. It reduced "non-juridical" classes and increased "juridical classes." The degree now conferred was a *licence en droit égyptien*.[23] (See Table 7.4.)

Leaders at the Cairo Faculty were committed to instilling students with knowledge and appreciation of Franco-Egyptian law. Teachers took their work seriously as the school was a stepping stone to a higher position in Britain, Europe, and Asia.[24] Private and official papers of figures such as John Scott, Malcom McIlwraith, a judicial adviser, and Maurice Sheldon Amos, a later dean, displayed concern for the quality of education.[25]

Table 7.4. Cairo Faculty, new curriculum, 1891–92.

Year One *Juridical*	Hours	Year Two *Juridical*	Hours
Sharia	3	Sharia	3
Judicial and Administrative Organization	3	Roman	6
General Introduction: Law and Political Economy	6	Criminal	3
Recitation	3	Recitation	6
Non-juridical		*Non-juridical*	
Arabic	6	Arabic	6
French	6	French	6
Translation	6	Translation	6
Bookkeeping	3		
Year Three *Juridical*	Hours	Year Four *Juridical*	Hours
Sharia	3	Sharia	3
Civil	3	Civil	3
Civil Procedure	3	Procedure	3
Criminal	3	Commerical	3
Recitation	6	Administrative	3
Non-juridical		International Private	3
Arabic	6	Recitation	18
French	6		
Translation	6		

Source: *Recueil des documents officiels du gouvernement égyptien 1892* (Cairo: Imprimerie Nationale, 1891), 550–1.

[23] For further details on reforms, see al-Jāmiʿah al-Miṣriyyah, *Taqwīm, 1929–1930*.

[24] They were rewarded for their efforts. Scott became an honorary fellow at Pembroke College Oxford in 1898; Amos obtained the Quain Professorship in Comparative Law at University College London in 1932; and William Brunyate became Vice-Chancellor of Hong Kong University in 1921.

[25] See this chapter's nn. 21, 28.

Testoud and Scott used exams to raise standards and monitor the learning of concepts.[26] They instructed graders to evaluate independent reasoning and to fail inadequate performances.[27] Scott's annual reports on the examinations contained criticism and appreciation. In 1899, he observed that "the majority of students were better prepared and more solidly grounded in legal principles than is the case with the general run of candidates in a European university."[28] He insisted that packing the grading juries with Europeans was essential to maintaining high standards—the same view he applied to staffing judicial benches in the Native Courts. At the same time, insisting on the participation of Egyptians, he found graders in figures no less than Muḥammad ʿAbduh and Qāsim Amīn.[29]

Exemplifying the school's interest in standards was the fate of evening classes, created in 1886 for working students. Testoud and the next British Judicial Adviser, Malcom McIlwraith, annually lamented the performance of the evening students on exams, observing that they struggled because they lacked adequate time for studying.[30] They feared that examiners were too reluctant to fail students with borderline results and were sending underqualified graduates to the profession at a time when good personnel were paramount to improving it. In 1899, they tired of the results and closed the section.[31]

The disappointment of Testoud, British judicial advisers, and grading juries with the evening section sheds further light on pedagogical priorities. The focus was still on training practitioners and not on cultivating higher modes of analysis, theorization, and critique. A source of ongoing criticism from examiners pertained

[26] Official reports on examinations are extensive. Students were required to take an admissions test in Arabic, French, history, and geography. Matriculated students sat final exams each spring to qualify for the next year of study. See, for example, "Arrêté: Règlement organique de l'École de Droit," in *Bulletin des lois et décrets, année 1892* (1891), 537–49, at 542–3.

[27] See nn. 28–30.

[28] "Rapport de Sir J. Scott sur les derniers examens de droit," *Recueil des documents officiels du gouvernement égyptien* (1895), 665–72, at 667. The French lawyer, legal writer, and native court counselor E. De Hults, remarked (ibid.): "[P]laced before a European faculty, all the students I examined would have passed, some with commendation." In 1896, the French lawyer Carton de Wiart wrote of the exams he graded: "I am very satisfied with these students, the top three responded brilliantly. [T]hey were much less given to [repetition of lectures] than the previous group and showed much more facility for finding examples and applications." See also "Rapport adressé à S.E. le Ministre de l'instruction publique par Sir John Scott sur les derniers examens de fin d'année, à l'École Khédiviale de Droit, au Caire," *Recueil des documents officiels du gouvernement égyptien* (1896), 339–44. The sense of overall progress in the estimation of graders continued with the reports of Malcom McIlwraith. See "Rapport de M. le Conseiller Judiciaire sur l'année 1898," *Recueil des documents officiels du gouvernement égyptien* (1899), 152–82.

[29] In 1895, Qāsim Amīn graded exams for the second-year students. He also failed four of seven enrolled in the evening section, observing that the three he passed were barely satisfactory. Muḥammad ʿAbduh examined the students in Arabic and Islamic law during the same year. "Rapport de Sir J. Scott sur les derniers examens de droit," *Recueil des documents officiels du gouvernement égyptien* (1895), 666, 668.

[30] The juries criticized the quality of exams of evening students almost every year the program was in existence. Whereas 75 percent of day students passed exams each year, the pass rate for evening students hovered around 50 percent. In 1895, failure rates in the first through third year were, respectively: six of twelve, two of seven, and four of fourteen. Of the students who passed in the evening section, their total number of points failed to match the combined average of points of those who passed in the day section. "Rapport de M. le Conseiller Judiciaire sur l'année 1898," *Recueil des documents officiels du gouvernement égyptien* (1899), 162; see also n. 28.

[31] Ibid.

to students' ability to reason independently when faced with practical reasoning challenges. The expectation was that students could take a principle of law and apply it to a problem not encountered previously. This was not about critiquing the law but rather about the work of practicing law effectively in a world of codes.

Records of the school's administrators reveal no interest in promoting advanced research. The administration took pride in its pedagogical agenda for the *licence* level and believed it was initiating Egypt into a more scientific approach to legal studies that distinguished education at the Cairo Faculty from al-Azhar. Much of this confidence was tied to the prestige the professors accorded to the codes, instruments of law for which al-Azhar and the Sharia Courts had no equivalent. They were inculcating in Egyptian students the critical faculties of a European lawyer. The question that inevitably surfaced was whether these critical faculties should be French or British.

BRITISH DOMINANCE AND SUPPRESSION OF FRENCH EDUCATION

When the law school opened a section in 1898–99 for students to study law in English, it set in motion a fifteen-year process of phasing out French professors and French-language studies.[32] Before this, education in all branches of European law had been in French; only classes in Sharia and elements of civil procedure were taught in Arabic. Thus, for the most part, only students graduating from Egypt's French secondary schools gained admission to the Cairo Faculty. Under the new regime, students followed either French or English courses exclusively, except those courses given in Arabic to both sections.[33] In 1910, the school stopped admitting students to the first year of the French section, and in 1914, the French section closed. (See Fig. 7.1.)

The rise of the English section and the decline of the French section halted progress toward sophisticated research and education that might have taken root, as Egyptian students were severed from the parent legal culture of Franco-Egyptian law and enmeshed in British institutional hegemony.[34] The triumph came at the expense of initiatives in comparative law or expanded studies in Islamic law. British faculty members hurriedly obtained *licence* degrees in civil law in order to assume teaching responsibilities, while their colleagues in the Ministry of Justice made sporadic efforts to Anglicize parts of the law, especially in criminal law.[35]

[32] "Règlement organique de l'École Khediviale de Droit," *Receuil des documents officiels du gouvenment égyptien* (1899), 527–41, at 528.

[33] Those were Sharia and select courses on criminal law and procedure, and select courses on the organization of public, administrative, and judicial institutions.

[34] See pp. 170–3, on the successful efforts of British colonial agents to foil Édouard Lambert's plans for more advanced legal education at the law school.

[35] See Brown, *Rule of Law*, 38–9; Ebeid Saroufim, "England and the Criminal Legislation of Egypt from 1882" (D.Phil. diss., University of Oxford, 1950); Frederic Maurice Goadby, *Commentary on Egyptian Criminal Law* (Cairo: Government Press, 1914); Clément, "*Fallāḥīn* on Trial."

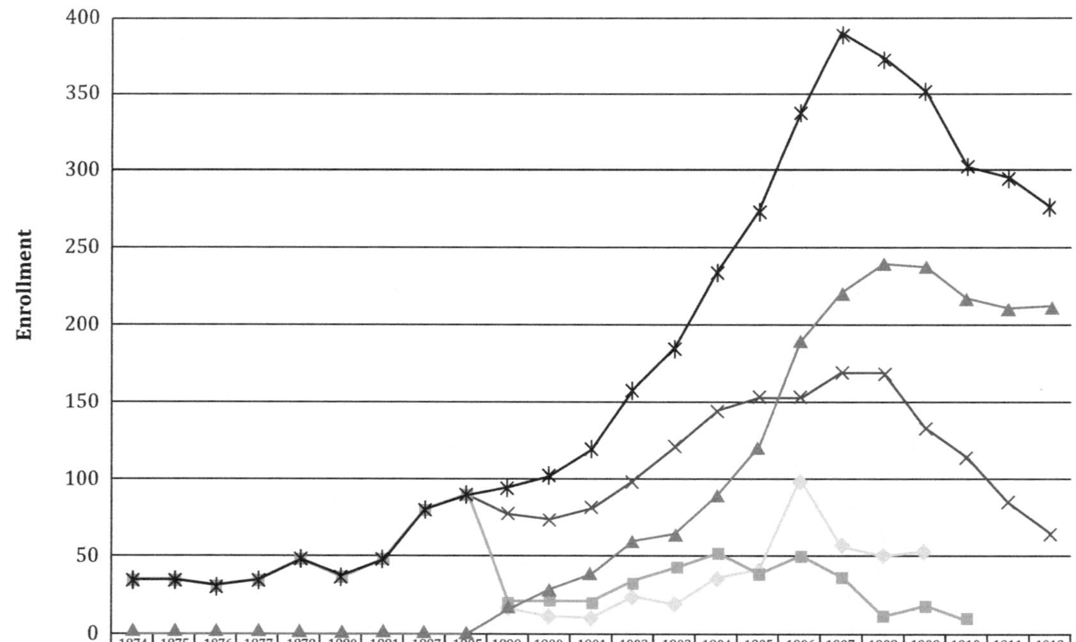

	1874	1875	1876	1877	1878	1880	1881	1887	1895	1899	1900	1901	1902	1903	1904	1905	1906	1907	1908	1909	1910	1911	1912
English Section Admissions	0	0	0	0	0	0	0	0	0	17	11	10	24	19	35	41	99	55	50	53			
French Section Admissions	35	35	31	35	48	37	48	80	90	20	22	20	33	43	52	38	50	37	11	18	10		
English Section Enrollment	0	0	0	0	0	0	0	0	0	17	28	38	59	64	89	120	189	221	240	238	217	211	212
French Section Enrollment	35	35	31	35	48	37	48	80	90	17	74	81	99	121	145	153	153	159	159	133	114	55	55
English and French Enrollment	35	35	31	35	48	37	48	80	90	94	102	119	155	155	234	273	338	390	373	352	302	295	277

Fig. 7.1. Admissions and enrollment at the Cairo Faculty, 1874–1912. Blank spaces indicate a lack of reliable numbers.[36]

[36] Figure 7.1 is compiled from *Recueil des documents officiels du gouvernement égyptien* (1881), 207; *Bulletin des lois et décrets* (1886), 521; *Recueil des documents officiels du gouvernement égyptien* (1890), 795, (1896), 342–4, (1899) 482–3; Jāmiʿat Fuʾād al-Awwal, *Taqwīm Kulliyyat al-Ḥuqūq ʿan al-sanah al-dirāsiyyah 1938–1939* (Cairo, 1939), 181–95; Université Égyptienne, *Annuaire de la Faculté de Droit, année 1936–1937* (Cairo, ca. 1936), 189–96; al-Jāmiʿah al-Miṣriyyah and Kulliyyat al-Ḥuqūq, *Asmāʾ man ḥaṣalū ʿalá līsans fī l-ḥuqūq min sanat 1874 li-sanat 1931 wa ʿalá diblūmāt al-dirāsah al-ʿulyā min sanat 1928–1931* (Cairo: al-Maṭbaʿah al-Amīriyyah, 1933); Botiveau, *Loi islamique*, 171.

The personal papers of Maurice Sheldon Amos, dean of the Cairo Faculty from 1913 to 1915, reveal that plans for an English section were hatched in quiet during the 1890s.[37] In those years, Amos interned as a translator and teacher at this school where his father, the more famous jurist Sheldon Amos,[38] had once taught. He obtained his *licence* in French law in 1897. His letters from that year record discussions with Malcom McIlwraith and Herbert Halton, who wanted to create English books for the Egyptian students, about preparatory work for the English section they intended to establish. Their collaborations with Amos, who was trilingual in French, English, and Arabic, led to publications after 1903 that included English-language commentaries on the Egyptian codes, introductions to law study, and the first English translations of the Egyptian codes.[39] McIlwraith also wanted to translate important French books into English, such as the French version of Savigny's *Geschichte des römischen Rechts*.[40] Those translations never materialized.

French personnel attacked the plan to institute an English section as soon as it was made public.[41] Between 1899 and 1912, French professors from the Cairo Faculty and the École Française de Droit du Caire barraged French diplomats in Cairo and the Ministry of Instruction in Paris with letters of protest.[42] They expressed fear for the decline of French influence and expressed concern for the quality of legal education. They believed they were better equipped than British personnel to teach Egyptian law.

The French also became irritated by the fact that their professors were being replaced by British professors who held only the *licence* in French law and not doctorates and *agrégations*, as was the tradition in France. The last French director, Édouard Lambert, was replaced by the Englishman W. Hill, who obtained a *licence* only after having been promoted to director, and this on his second attempt at the exam. Lambert lampooned this fact in a letter to *Le Temps* published in 1907.[43]

[37] Amos-Bunting-Moncrieff-Legg-Hawthorn Family Papers, MSA, M4, 1897–1901. "MSA to Bonte during Law Degree in Paris and First Years in Egypt" (a letter of June 23, 1898, regarding interview with Malcom McIlwraith). See also Cromer, "Report," *P.P. 1899*.

[38] Sheldon Amos (1835–1886) was a scholar of jurisprudence and Roman law. He sat on the drafting committee for the Native Codes and was a judge on the Native Appeals Court. His personal papers are part of the Amos-Bunting-Moncrieff-Legg-Hawthorn Family Papers.

[39] *Egyptian Native Civil Code* (Oxford: Hart, 1901); *The Code of the Civil and Commerical Procedure of the Egyptian Native Tribunals, Translation* (Oxford: Horace Hart, 1903).

[40] Savigny, *Histoire du droit romain*.

[41] The French archives in Nantes contain letters lamenting the rise of the English section and suggesting ways to counter it. One file comes from a professor at the Cairo Faculty, Albert Chéron, who in letters to the *chargé d'affaires* in Cairo, urged the necessity of bolstering French education at the school as a means of protecting French interests. He predicted that if French was no longer taught at the Cairo Faculty, all instruction would one day be in Arabic and would spell the end of "independent" law instruction in Egypt. See Nantes/Cairo 160 and 171 and further references in nn. 42, 43.

[42] See, for example, letters to the Ministry of Instruction in Paris, complaining that Charles Testoud had underestimated the danger of creating an English section. Nantes/Cairo 171 "Anon. to M. Delané Ministre des affaires étrangères à Paris," Feb. 24, 1899.

[43] See Nantes/Cairo 171, Letter from M. Stéphen Pichon, No. 655, Re: "Remplacement du directeur de l'École de Droit du Caire; L'enseignement français en Égypte," July 28, 1907. Nantes/Cairo 171, No. 2, "Requête de M.H. Lamba," Jan. 4, 1908. Nantes/Cairo 171, Ditto copied letter, in red ink: "École Khediviale" and beginning second paragraph, "Notre École, à peine installée dans un vaste local," signed by Henri Lamba, Nov. 22, 1904.

The British—unpopular colonizers—faced challenges as common law lawyers directing education in civil law in a colony where French was the prestige language, the law was largely French, and French dominated in the Mixed Courts. Having been taught French law in English by British lawyers, Egyptian graduates would then practice in Arabic and French.[44] Yet the British were undaunted by the task of building the English section and they were always able to find personnel to support their projects. John Scott and Maurice Sheldon Amos held the *licence* in civil law. Frederick Walton, a future dean, was a Scottish lawyer who had taught civil law in Montreal.

Defending the British policy, Judicial Adviser McIlwraith claimed that the existing French-language commentaries on French law, as the law of France, were no longer adequate for teaching Franco-Egyptian law. Sixteen years had elapsed since the completion of the Native Codes and Franco-Egyptian law was now different from French law.[45] The French-language texts used at the school, McIlwraith wrote, focused on French law without accounting for differences in Franco-Egyptian codes and twenty years of Egyptian court decisions.

Although McIlwraith's claim about the changing face of Franco-Egyptian law was true to an extent, the textbooks that English professors wrote about Franco-Egyptian law made no attempt to mask the reality that the law was French in content and origin. When the English authors of these commentaries on Franco-Egyptian law needed further insights into the codes, they drew from French law commentaries such as Marcel Planiol's *Traité élémentaire*. Rather than trying to put a British common law spin on Franco-Egyptian law, the British authors styled themselves as authorities on civil law.

Yet for the most part, during a period when French jurists in France were revolutionizing approaches to interpreting the *Code civil*, the new English textbooks for Egyptian students showed awareness of, but minimal interest in, the latest movements in continental European legal theory. English authors availed themselves of some insights by contemporary doctrinalists, but they largely avoided ideas that were changing the face of civil law theory on the European continent.

The opening of the English section corresponded to famous and broader reforms being pursued by Lord Cromer and Douglas Dunlop in Egyptian education. The thrust of their policy was to centralize control of education, increasing the use of English as a language of instruction and reducing the use of Arabic and French.[46]

[44] "Rapport presenté par M. le Conseiller judiciaire sur l'année 1899," *Recueil des documents officiels du gouvernement égyptien* (1900), 151–202, at 171–4; "Reports by His Majesty's Agent and Consul General on the Finances, and Condition of Egypt and the Soudan in 1902," *P.P.* Cd. 1529, LXXXVII, 953, Egypt No. 1 (1903), 58–9.

[45] McIlwraith observed: "The result is that French commentaries and French decisions are often more misleading than helpful to the student of Egyptian law, which is gradually acquiring a distinct and separate individuality of its own." "Rapport presenté par M. le Conseiller judiciaire sur l'année 1899," *Recueil des documents officiels du gouvernement égyptien* (1900), 173. See Eugène Clavel, "Mémoire" in Nantes/Cairo 160, École Française de Droit du Caire, ca. 1900.

[46] In 1899, Cromer appointed Douglas Dunlop and gave him this mission. Dunlop became an inspector for the Ministry of Education. He canceled French as a language of instruction in government secondary schools. See Mona Russell, "Competing, Overlapping, and Contradictory Agendas: Egyptian Education under British Occupation, 1882–1922," *Comparative Studies of South Asia, Africa and the Middle East* 21,1–2 (2001): 50–60.

The objectives were to increase control by British high officials and to hinder a burgeoning of indigenous professional classes. Dunlop pursued these policies from 1890 until his retirement in 1919. Egyptian and French criticism of him were found in the Arabic press and in writings of nationalists such as Khedive ʿAbbās Ḥilmī (r. 1892–1914), Muṣṭafá Kāmil, Muḥammad Farīd, and Saʿd Zaghlūl.

While Cromer and Dunlop pursued educational changes for the purpose of expanding British power, British lawyers argued that English methods of legal education surpassed French methods. They never alluded to British imperial interests. Their critique of the French system was that it was too academic and impractical, and that it produced students who had memorized rules and principles but were unable to work well as independent-minded legal thinkers, ready and able to brief any issue skillfully.[47] The critique was much in the spirit of usual sterotypes held by common law lawyers regarding civil law lawyers. In 1900, McIlwraith criticized the exams of the fourth-year students on this basis:

> The standard of proficiency remains about the same for the majority of students.... [Their] lack of individuality is...no fault of the professors of the school. The French and kindred systems of training do not, in general, make for individuality, as was well pointed out...in the *Journal of the Society of Comparative Legislation*[48] [which] demonstrated the superiority, in this respect, of the English system....This characteristic of the French system becomes intensified when in contact with Oriental constitutions and habits of thought.[49]

Although Vidal and Testoud stressed the importance of practical thinking, and were perhaps even encouraged to think along such lines because of their knowledge of Jhering-style interventions in French pedagogy, the British had no hesitation in seeking to outdo the French in stressing practicality and independent thinking in legal pedagogy. They championed their own preference for practice, practicality, and mastery of case law over the French system's inclination to study what they called "ambiguous principles." Writing from a common law lawyer's perspective, McIlwraith wrote a report in 1904 championing English methods of instruction and the Langdellian pedagogy (known now as the case law method) of Harvard Law School:

[47] McIlwraith claimed Egyptian students in the English section fared better on final exams because "the young Egyptian finds less difficulty in attaining to a certain proficiency in English than in reaching a corresponding plane in French, with its very difficult grammar and syntax." *Report for the Year 1903 Presented by the Judicial Adviser* (Cairo: National Printing Department, 1904), 45.

[48] The cited article claimed that "an English lawyer, with his wretched practical education, his almost total ignorance of principles, his incapacity to deal with a thought in law, is on an average a sounder and more sensible lawyer than the Frenchman." Thomas Barclay, "The Teaching of Law in France," *Journal of the Society of Comparative Legislation* 2,1 (1900): 131–6.

[49] "Reports by His Majesty's Agent and Consul General on the Finances, and Condition of Egypt and the Soudan in 1900," *P.P.* Cd. 441, XCI, 1057, Egypt No. 1 (1901), 53. Elsewhere McIlwraith cited rote memorization as a problem: "In this, as in other Egyptian schools and colleges, the main difficulty against which the professors have to contend is the tendency of the pupils to learn their lessons by heart, and to develop their memories instead of their powers of reasoning. It is satisfactory to learn, on the authority of M. Bernardi, who conducted the examinations last June, that some improvement in this respect is noticeable." "Reports by His Majesty's Agent and Consul General on the Finances, and Condition of Egypt and the Soudan in 1903," *P.P.* Cd. 1951, CXI, 203, Egypt No. 1 (1904), 62.

> Practice, it is superfluous to observe, cannot be taught and must be gradually acquired, but a great deal more could be done, I think, than is usually done at present, in the direction of making the teaching of law less abstract and theoretical and in reducing legal principles to a concrete form in which they may be readily grasped by the novice. Notably students should be made to study collections of judicial decisions (such as the Mixed and Native Bulletins of jurisprudence—and other collections of law problems, specially suitable to students, should be prepared) to analyze the cases reported and to show that they understand the application made to the facts of specific articles of the Code with which—in their abstract terms—they are familiar. As they become more advanced they might even be given [practice cases] to analyse and report upon. Such exercises would be of far greater use to them, as a mental training and a means of developing the juridical instinct than the prolonged study of a certain number of venerable controversies which are often of a highly theoretical nature and such as the student is little likely ever to have to deal with in practice.... Mr. [Maurice] Sheldon Amos, in particular, who has recently visited Harvard Law School... points out to me that there "the distinctive feature of the teaching is the basing of all instruction upon carefully prepared collections of reported cases... and in the almost total banishment of text-books. The method of teaching in class is essentially Socratic. By perpetual question and answer the student is taught to think out the law for himself, the primary object being that he should be as much as possible active, rather than passive, in his studies...."[50]

An irony of this debate of clashing caricatures is that although British lawyers had a strong basis on which to champion legal education through the study of cases and practicalities, contemporary French jurists in France, inspired by Jhering, were championing similar concepts even harder than the British, in spite of their ongoing commitments to codes. Thus it is instructive to observe that the first textbook written for Egyptian students, following the exhortations of McIlwraith, was co-written by the Englishman Maurice Sheldon Amos and the Frenchman Pierre Arminjon, on the inspiration of the German lawyer and civil law theorist, Jhering. They composed a workbook in 1904 that required students to arrive at answers through independent reasoning.[51] It became part of the curriculum under the French director, Grandmoulin. McIlwraith took the credit in his report to Cromer.[52]

The ascendance of the English section and of English personnel persisted through 1914. Administrators enlarged the school.[53] By 1907, it had at least nine British professors. Monteith Smith, Malcom McIlwraith, and a Mr. Sanderson were trained in Scotland. Maurice Sheldon Amos and Herbert Welch Halton held

[50] *Report for the Year 1903 Presented by the Judicial Adviser*, 37–8.

[51] Maurice Sheldon Amos and Pierre Arminjon, *Collection of Problems and Exercises in the Civil and Commercial Law of Egypt* (Cairo, 1904). See also "Book Review: *A Collection of Problems and Exercises in the Civil and Commercial Law of Egypt*," *Harvard Law Review* 18,4 (1905): 324; Fernand Daguin, "Review: *Espèces, problèmes juridiques et questions pratiques de droit civil, de droit commercial et de droit international privé*," *Bulletin de la société de législation comparée* 34 (1905): 110–11.

[52] McIlwraith wrote, "Amos and M. Arminjon have, in response to my suggestions, produced, in collaboration, a very useful collection of practical legal problems.... on the lines of the well known *Civilrechtsfälle* and *Pandectenübunden* of Professor von Jhering." *Report for the Year 1903 Presented by the Judicial Adviser*, 46.

[53] *Recueil des documents officiels du gouvernement égyptien* (1901), 181–236.

licence degrees from Paris. Samuel G. Archibald came from Quebec.[54] Alexander McBarnett came from the English bar and was untrained in French law.[55] Serving briefly were the more famous figures F. M. Goadby and Norman Bentwich. The French section had four French professors and two Belgians. The ratios increasingly favored British over non-British professors and English-section students over French-section students (see Fig. 7.2).[56]

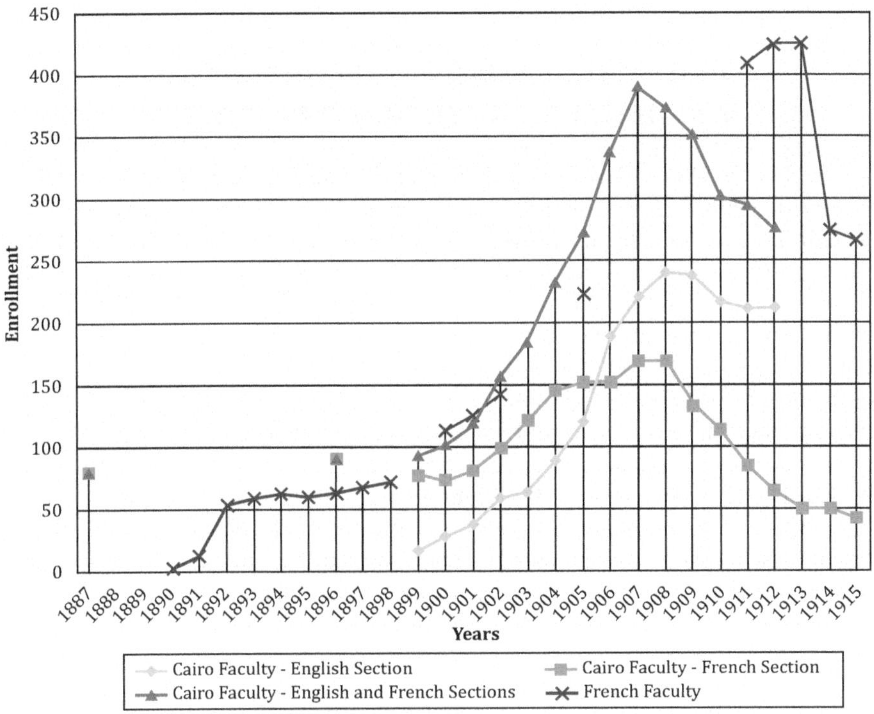

Fig. 7.2. Enrollments compared, the Cairo Faculty and the École Français de Droit du Caire, 1889–1915. Blank spaces indicate a lack of reliable numbers.[57]

[54] Archibald was the son of a chief justice of Quebec, a professor of civil law, and a vice principal of the school.

[55] Alexander Cockburn McBarnett assumed a lectureship at the Cairo Faculty in 1904 and became a judge in the Native Court of First Instance of Assyut. *The Law Journal* (1965): 102.

[56] "Reports by His Majesty's Agent and Consul-General on the Finances, and Condition of Egypt and the Soudan in 1908," *P.P.* Cd. 4580, CV, 333, Egypt No. 1 (1909), 44; Nantes/Cairo 171, "Anon" [probably Henri Lamba], "Note sur l'École Khediviale de Droit," Oct. 1907.

[57] For statistical sources on Cairo Faculty's enrollment, see Figure 7.1. For statistical sources on the French Faculty's enrollment, see as follows. Year 1893: Nantes/Cairo 160, handwritten letter of M. Pélissié du Rausas, "Liste des étudiants." Years 1891–1894: Louis Malosse, *Impressions d'Égypte*, 254. Years 1891–1902: Nantes/Cairo 160, see handwritten files, unsigned but in handwriting of M. Pélissié du Rausas, "Première Année." See also other miscellaneous and untitled documents, in the same folder, that provide numbers until 1902. Years 1902–1913: *Revue internationale de l'enseignement* 69 (1915). Years 1913–1919: see other files in Nantes/Cairo 160, including a letter of Apr. 10, 1916 from the M. Defrance of the École Français de Droit du Caire to M. le Ministre.

The decline in enrollment in the French section was attributable to various factors beyond the mere British desire for such a result. British teachers were allotted more space in their classrooms, while French teachers were given increasingly less space. The school slashed scholarships and maintained high tuition fees, while enrollment at the École Française de Droit du Caire was free.[58] Finally, French was becoming less popular as a language of instruction in Egyptian schools.[59] These were further results of the policies of Cromer and Dunlop.

FROM THE LAMBERT AFFAIR TO THE ENTRENCHMENT OF BRITISH POLICY

Little is known about what Édouard Lambert accomplished as dean of the Cairo Faculty in 1906–7. Given his left-leaning politics, theoretical dispositions, and pride in Francophone legal culture, he could scarcely have arrived in Egypt at a less opportune time to pursue his objectives. Had he been afforded the opportunity, Lambert may have reformed the curriculum and promoted the advanced study of law in critical, comparative, and "social" directions. When Lambert arrived in Cairo, he was already well known in Europe as the doyen of comparative law and social legal reform. He had in mind the goal of building an institute for the study of comparative law in France, and had by this time published his thoughts on the modernization of Islamic law and Arab customary law and his views on the place of these legal traditions within the framework of comparative law studies.

In writings after his departure, Lambert reflected on the plans he had to reform legal education. He recalled having pursued comparative inquiries in Islamic and Western legal history with Azharites, in particular Muṣṭafá ʿAbd al-Rāziq.[60] He recalled efforts to introduce new approaches to social science and political econ-

[58] In the 1880s, the Cairo Faculty afforded a modicum of social mobility to some Egyptians. In 1886, thirty students of approximately seventy were on some form of scholarship. Official enrollment records for scholarship students (*boursiers*) listed the professions or jobs of students' parents, and not all students had white-collar parents. Parental employments included teacher, farmer, Islamic law instructor, soldier, and postman. Between 1886 and 1891, the number of scholarships was reduced. Initially the school instituted a maximum of ten scholarships to be awarded across all five years. Later, a new rule provided that full tuition coverage could not exceed ten percent of the total enrollment. Since total enrollment at the law school did not surpass 100 until 1900, between 1890 and 1899 the school never had more than ten students on full tuition coverage. In 1899, the school abolished scholarships. Compare "Arrêté du Ministre de l'Instruction publique fixant le réglement organique de l'École de Droit (1886)," 639 at Art. 12 (providing a process for obtaining financial aid to attend the school), with "Règlement organique de l'école Khediviale de Droit (1899)," 530, at Art. 12 (affirming the absence of a financial aid program). See also "École de Droit: Élèves boursiers," *Bulletin des lois et décrets* (1887), 996–7; "Arrêté du Ministre de l'Instruction publique déterminant les modifications à apporter au règlement organique de l'École de Droit," *Recueil des documents officiels du gouvernement égyptien* (1891), 731–3.

[59] Primary and secondary education in English overtook French education in the early twentieth century. See Frédéric Abécassis, "De la Protection par l'école: La Sédimentation des traditions d'enseignement du français en Égypte au XIXe siècle," in *France-Levant: De la fin du XVIIe siècle à la première guerre mondiale*, ed. Bernard Delpal et al. (Paris: Geuthner, 2005), 117–44.

[60] Mohamed Abdullah El-Araby, *La Conscription des neutres dans les luttes de la concurrence économique: Les Coalitions du journalisme et la liberté de la presse: Sorrell v. Smith* (Paris: Marcel Giard, 1924), ix.

omy in particular. During a lecture delivered at the Cairo Faculty in 1937, he said he would have undertaken significant curricular changes had he been permitted.[61] He was informed in 1906 of the kinds of advanced institutions and opportunities that could be developed in a colony. He knew about the École de Droit d'Alger, with its programs and research in French, French-Algerian, Islamic, and customary law. He knew that French students at the Algiers Faculty could apply for doctorates in France and that the deans in Algiers were planning to build a doctoral program in Algiers itself. In Cairo, the École Française de Droit du Caire, the local competitor school, had instituted a doctoral program, with its students writing theses on French law and defending them before faculties in France.

Lambert's resignation from the school in 1907 stemmed from political differences with the British, his sympathies for Egyptian nationalism, and his opposition to British attempts to Anglicize the school. These factors appear to have ignited his confrontation with Dunlop more than any plans he may have had for curricular reform.[62] In 1906, Egyptian nationalism was crystallizing to a new level under the leadership of Muṣṭafá Kāmil and Shaykh ʿAlī Yūsuf. The first was a prominent political figure and lawyer, the second a prominent Azharite. The notorious Dinshiway affair, in which a British military officer was killed, took place in June 1906, the summer preceding what would have been Lambert's second academic year.[63] British advisers were uncomfortable with the prospect of student strikes at the law school, which occured. This made the prospect of having a sympathetic British dean more appealing to British agents supervising the law school.

It did not help Lambert's relations with the British advisers that he sympathized with the Egyptians' desire for independence. He was known to hear their complaints about the British control of the curriculum. Egyptians embraced French culture as a manifestation of opposition to British rule.[64] Lambert was also agitating against British favoritism toward the English section. He was director of the law school during a year in which admission of English section outnumbered admission to the French section 99 to 50.[65]

Lambert's letter to *Le Temps* following his resignation revealed his frustration with British interference. He wrote that Dunlop had "fought blindly against the perpetuation of French culture in a school whose teaching of law, is and will

[61] No known records reveal specific changes Lambert intended to make. Because Lambert was at the school only for one year, it is not surprising to find that the final exams of spring 1907 do not reflect substantial curriculum changes from the final exams of spring 1906. Aḥmad ʿUmar and ʿAlī ʿAbd al-ʿAzīz, *Majmūʿat al-imtiḥānāt al-nihāʾiyyah li-madrasat al-ḥuqūq al-malakiyyah min sanat 1906 li-ghāyat imtiḥān māris sanat 1925*, 3rd ed. (Miṣr: Maṭbaʿat al-Iʿtimād, 1925).

[62] René David has argued that the reasons for Lambert's departure remain an open question. However, David favors the interpretation that the departure was tied to problems of politics and nationalism. David, *Droit comparé*, 13–14.

[63] On the Dinshiway incident, see Vatikiotis, *History of Egypt*, 205–6; Roger Owen, *Lord Cromer: Victorial Imperialist, Edwardian Proconsul* (Oxford: Oxford University Press, 2004), 339–40.

[64] Shalakany, "Sanhuri," 168–9.

[65] This had happened for the first time during the admissions round in 1905, but not by such great numbers.

remain, based on French law."[66] He claimed that Dunlop had replaced French teachers with English teachers who were "as ignorant of the principles of the jurisprudence practiced in the country as the students whom they were supposed to teach." He attacked the new English teachers and books ("Several of these English teachers have not at the present time mastered our language to be able to translate without misunderstanding the manuals that supply their course notes") and commented that British policies at the law school encouraged Egyptian nationalism.[67] He indicated that Dunlop's refusal to allow Lambert to hire French or Egyptian teachers provided the final confrontation.

Lambert would not give in, so he quit. Members of the French government assailed him for relinquishing the position without a greater fight or consulting the French government. The decision, they thought, compromised the French position in the law school, the law, and the country.[68] They were right about the law school, but in the longer term erred regarding the consequences for the stamina of French prestige in Egyptian law and legal education.

When the British assumed full control of the school after Lambert's departure, they quashed the possibility of advanced programs in comparative or Islamic law. Inimical to both nationalist and pro-Islamic interests, the prospects for Islamic law studies grew dim. The barring of French-language instruction blocked the pursuit of comparative law, since students without proficiency in French could not engage with the rich, challenging, and dramatically expanding world of continental European law and legal thought. The British remained focused on training for legal practice and instilling British concepts where possible. The few comparative works that did appear between 1900 and 1910 studied relationships between British and Egyptian law, but there were very few of these compared to the numbers of comparative French-Algerian works that had appeared in Algeria and France since 1860.

British paternalism became pronounced in the following decade. In 1918, the Judicial Adviser William Brunyate presented an inaugural lecture at the law school entitled "The Private Reading of a Law Student." This was a year of nationalist ferment when Egyptian university students were still bristling from four years of martial law and forced participation in the First World War. Brunyate, a legal architect of the protectorate, opened by stating, "I myself have never made any system-

[66] Édouard Lambert, "La Lettre de M. Lambert: Dunlop et sa politique anti-française et anti-égytpienne. Comment on étouffe une nation," *Le Temps*, 1907. Precise date unknown. Copy of original in Nantes/Cairo 171, folder: "École Khédiviale de Droit, M. Lambert." Translations provided here are from Sonbol, *Last Khedive*, 183–7.

[67] Sonbol, *Last Khedive*, 183–7.

[68] In a parliamentary session of December 1907, Benazet exhorted: "It is in effect of extreme importance... that a French person direct the Khedivial School of Law.... Instructed by our French teachers and according to the principles of our jurisprudence—given that the Egyptian codes are nothing less than a redaction of our *Code civil*—these functionaries preserve, by their services, the spirit of our teaching, and with this spirit, the respect for our legal traditions.... The judges judge in our language, the lawyers plead in it before the mixed tribunals, to such an extent that for the Egyptians, speaking French is synonymous with speaking justice and reason.... It is natural that we have always sought to conserve the direction of the Khedivial School of Law while the English have made the greatest effort to derail this." Nantes/Cairo 171, folder "École Khédiviale de Droit, M. Lambert."

atic study of Roman law, and, indeed, have never attended any systematic courses of lecture of legal subjects such as those which constitute the program of this school."[69] Yet he proceeded to recommend readings in English law in a speech that must have lasted over an hour. Perhaps most telling was his ringing endorsement of Lord Cromer, of whom he remarked: "He created not only an Egypt, but also an Egyptian people."[70] Cromer was, however, a villain in Egyptian nationalist lore.

The British residency ruled out graduate education for lawyers. Maurice Sheldon Amos, a broad-minded English scholar with strong connections to France and a French license in civil law, reflected on this in memoirs while recounting his years as dean in 1913–15:

> My most ambitious project was the institution of a course of post-graduate studies—a project which came to a picturesque end. I spent the greater part of the early winter of 1913–1914 elaborating, in consultation with the professors, a scheme for the institution of an Egyptian doctorate of laws. It involved a lot of detailed work, but finally we produced a detailed plan which appeared to be workable. This I sent to the Ministry of Justice for approval and promulgation. A few days later McIlwraith sent for me and told me that Lord Kitchner did not approve, and had vetoed my project. I asked for an interview with the great man; and when I saw him he said, "I can't allow a doctorate of laws to be created here; some day we might want to hang one of these fellows, and you don't want to hang a doctor."[71]

By delaying the creation of a graduate program or similar paths to advanced study, the Law School declined to create opportunities for students to embark on sophisticated research. Egyptians wanting post-*licence* training had to travel to Europe and follow a doctoral program lasting several years. The Faculty chose not to implement an incentive structure for those Egyptians who sought foreign doctorates in the hopes of obtaining an academic post back in Egypt. The Cairo Faculty would not necessarily hire them. There were exceptions, as with ʿUmar Luṭfī, but such cases were rare.

THE FRENCH FACULTY AND THE PERSISTENCE OF FRENCH INFLUENCE

When British personnel jettisoned most things French from the Cairo Faculty (excepting the law itself), French law and language professors remained in Egypt. French language continued to dominate in the Mixed Courts. French law continued

[69] William Brunyate, "The Private Reading of a Law Student," *L'Égypte contemporaine* 8 (1918): 195–214, at 197.

[70] Ibid.

[71] He continued, "I have often thought that if I had been a man of independent fortune, I ought to have resigned. It was, of course, absurd to take a man like myself from the bench to be the head of a college and then to shy like a filly at a proposal which anybody might have known *a priori* that I was certain to make." Maurice Sheldon Amos, "Autobiography," in Amos-Bunting-Moncrieff-Legg-Hawthorn Family Papers (ca. 1940).

to be the parent law of the Franco-Egyptian laws. Egyptians traveled to France to obtain *licences* and doctorates. Only a fractional number chose England for this purpose. And French professors who lost their positions transferred to the École Française de Droit du Caire, the "French Faculty," where they held the fort for French influence into the 1920s.

A central feature of the landscape of higher education between 1891 and 1952, the French Faculty produced as many graduates as the Cairo Faculty. Its lawyers dominated the Mixed Bar Association after the 1910s; its faculty traveled back and forth to sister institutions in Algiers, Beirut, and Damascus. Yet, the French Faculty has received almost no attention in histories of Egypt, and its history is difficult to relate because its archives are lost.[72] The mansion that once housed it, now adjoining the French cultural center, still stands on the Rue d'École Française de Droit du Caire. Next door is the venerable Institut Français d'Archéologie Orientale (IFAO), which occupies a splendid palace. Neither institution has records of the pulsing academy that lived on the same street for sixty years.

The French Faculty is of interest from this point forward. Similar to the Cairo Faculty in these years, it seems to have declined to cultivate an atmosphere supportive of advanced research in Franco-Egyptian and Egyptian-Islamic law. It was, after all, a French school for teaching the French law of France and not the Franco-Egyptian law of Egypt. Also, as indicated already, the Faculty helped to maintain the prestige of French law and legal culture in Egypt in spite of the British campaign for domestic predominance. In this way, the Faculty was a preeminent factor in the ongoing reception of French law in Egypt, even at a time when the British controlled the Cairo Faculty and the Native Courts. The school is of further interest because French law and law professors made a comeback in Egyptian legal education after 1923. If one wonders why French scholars were so ready to re-enter the Cairo Faculty's scene in the 1920s, and if one wonders why Egyptian students at the Cairo Faculty were just as admiring of French professors in 1923 as they had been in 1907, the French Faculty's distinguished history provides one answer.

The French Faculty was created to defend the position and prestige of French law and legal culture in Egypt. As noted earlier, a controversy erupted when British personnel attempted to appoint a British dean to succeed Victor Vidal at the Cairo Faculty in 1890. Although the French jurist Charles Testoud was eventually appointed, that outcome had not been certain, and in those months of uncertainty French personnel hedged their bets by planning this separate French school.

The Faculty also emerged in response to the British policy that reduced scholarships for Egyptians wishing to study at the Cairo Faculty. The French Faculty

[72] The librarians at CEDEJ, Cairo, believe that its collection of dissertations is located at the Faculty of Law of Alexandria University. From my own cursory inspection in Alexandria, it appears that almost all of those are dissertations in law written by French students enrolled in French law faculties in France. It was the practice in that period for law students in France to publish their dissertations. Each year's stock of law dissertations would be sold in bulk to university libraries in France and beyond. The Cairo University Law Faculty holds a complete set of these dissertations, as do some American law schools. Whether any of those dissertations were the work of students from the French Faculty remains to be examined.

was free (thus receiving the nickname *l'École libre*). Its existence encouraged Egyptian families to continue sending their children to French *lycées*. As long as the Faculty existed, Egyptian students could graduate from the *lycées* and still obtain a prestigious university degree. In addition, admissions applicants rejected by the Cairo Faculty were applying, in increasing numbers, to law schools in England, Italy, and Russia.[73] The founders envisioned that a free French law school in Egypt would keep Egyptians in Egypt, speaking French, engaging with French culture, and, of course, learning French law.

The founding of the Faculty has been dated to both 1890 and 1892. The school was established by the society of Frères de la doctrine chrétienne in 1890. This arrangement allowed the school to remain private and independent from the Egyptian Ministries of Justice and Education. At the end of 1890, there were three students; a year later, there were thirteen. The French Consul General in Cairo appointed Gérard Pélissié du Rausas as president. All thirteen students passed exams in France in 1892.[74] For this reason, the school considered 1892 its first fully operational year.[75] Thereafter, the French government assumed the responsibility of appointing the school's teachers. Enrollment grew steadily until figures exceeded those of the Cairo Faculty in 1900, and spiked after Lambert's departure in 1907 and then again when the French section at the Cairo Faculty closed.

The French diplomatic archives drip with the complaints and pride of French professors at the Cairo Faculty and the French Faculty who viewed the latter as a bastion for maintaining cultural influence and as an alternate pole of influence to the Cairo Faculty.[76] Henri Lamba, who moved from the Cairo Faculty to the French Faculty, referred to the latter as the "citadel of our influence."[77] Lambert insisted, following his departure from Egypt in 1907, that the only way for France to maintain its legal influence was through the French Faculty.[78]

After the closure of the French section at the Cairo Faculty, the focus of French personnel on the role of the French law school intensified. A French committee charged with reviewing educational institutions commented on its visit to Cairo that Egyptians partial to France "help to spread throughout Egypt not only our language, but our spirit and, in particular, our legal ideas." It continued:

> This is seen, more than anywhere else, in the judicial sphere, especially before the mixed tribunals. Among other languages—English, Arabic and Italian—French holds the title of the original judicial language. In fact, it is the only language used in the Mixed Courts. Egyptian, Italian and Greek lawyers, numerous in Cairo and Alexandria,

[73] Nantes/Cairo 171, Eugène Clavel, "Mémoire."

[74] Students continued to take their final exams in France until 1909. After that year, professors from France traveled to Egypt to administer the exams.

[75] Louis Malosse, *Impressions d'Égypte* (Paris: Librairie Armond Colin, 1896), 253–4.

[76] Société de l'Enseignement Supérieur, "Étudiants et examens," in *Revue internationale de l'enseignement* 30 (1895): 163. See Nantes/Cairo 160 and 171 for letters, memos, and memoirs by Albert Chéron, Eugène Clavel, and Henri Lamba.

[77] Nantes/Cairo 171, No. 2, "Requête de M.H. Lamba," Jan. 4, 1908. Nantes/Cairo 171, Ditto copied letter, in red ink: "École Khediviale" and beginning second paragraph, "Notre École, à peine installée dans un vaste local," signed by Henri Lamba, Nov. 22, 1904.

[78] Sonbol, *Last Khedive*, 183–7.

> can use our language. Why is this so? They have almost all studied at the French School of Law authority of our school. One can be convinced, therefore, of the exceptional power and authority of our school.
>
> It is thanks to the law school that despite the gradual shrinking of the French section of the [Cairo Faculty] in the last ten years, our students in Egypt have not been affected, and our influence and the diffusion of our language has not decreased. Today we can look back on the disappearance of this section without too much fear. The situation of the French School has made us immune to the fear that in time our influence will diminish....
>
> Given the political domination of England, we must preserve our School of Law and if necessary extend its value. England is too enlightened to refuse. She knows as well as we that the French School of Law may serve on the banks of the Nile, at this time, with equal effectiveness, both the major political interests of the British Empire and the major moral interests of France.[79]

The French Faculty held professors and French culture in reserve until the 1920s, when French influence would be welcomed back to the Cairo Faculty.

In sum, from the 1870s to the mid-1920s, the professors of Egypt's various law schools pursued little scholarship in comparative law and Islamic law compared to standards of research, publication, and pedagogy that would prevail after 1923. The principal obstacle at the Cairo Faculty was that the school was controlled by European authorities who displayed little interest in promoting this kind of work. The bulk of responsibility for the sluggishness of the Cairo Faculty in producing new legal research falls on the shoulders of the British personnel. However, French personnel also played their part before they lost all control of the school in 1907. As for the French Faculty, it was concerned with granting a *licence* in French law. There was some movement at the school in the early 1900s to promote academic studies in Islamic law, as will be discussed in the next chapter, but noteworthy developments in scholarship only appeared in substantial quantity in the 1920s and beyond.

[79] Fernand Faure, "L'École Française de Droit du Caire en 1914 (1)," in *Revue internationale de l'enseignement* 69 (1915): 311.

8

Education and Scholarship in Islamic Law, 1868–1923

Law schools in Egypt planted seeds for advanced and comparative studies that transformed technical and ideological aspects of Islamic legal thought during the twentieth century. These schools were the laboratories for increasing the rigor of Islamic legal revivalism. The most significant of such developments emerged in and after the 1920s. Questions therefore arise as to what seeds of change were planted, how these changes served Islamic legal revivalism, and why comparative and modernizing thought in Islamic law flourished in the 1920s rather than in the decades before.

Before 1923, proponents of Islamic law in British Egypt contemplated three futures for Islamic law. In the first vision, Islamic law would recede as a normative or social force. In the march to progress, Sharia would survive in family law and ritual matters, and whatever remained in the legal system would be rendered compatible with European law and left as Islamic in name only. This was the direction French jurists had envisioned for Algeria, and it was the vision held by no less than Ṭāhā Ḥusayn, Cairo University's rector and a doyen of Arabic humanities.[1]

In the second vision, Islamic law would revive and regain lost jurisdictions by updating itself on its own terms, remaining authentic, and competing with, besting, and supplanting Franco-Egyptian law in relevance, prestige, and power. This second view was the ken of Islamic legal revivalism before and after 1923.

The third vision, which had the least traction, was that Islamic law had no need, or at most very little need, to retool to meet demands of the changed world. The answers to modern problems were thought to be in classical books and traditions of reasoning, aggregating, and expounding rules. To the extent that adherents of this inclination envisioned that Islamic law needed some reform to meet modern challenges, they held that the means and methods of such reform could not, should not, and would not come from European inspiration.

Forms of Islamic legal thought and education persisted between 1875 and 1923 amid the clash of these agendas—the British and Egyptian elites advancing the first vision, the most conservative Azharites pressing for the third, and Islamic legal revivalists, from both secular-oriented and Islamic-oriented backgrounds,

[1] See Taha Husayn, *The Future of Culture in Egypt* (Washington, DC: American Council of Learned Societies, 1954).

Islamic Legal Revival: Reception of European Law and Transformations in Islamic Legal Thought in Egypt, 1875–1952. First Edition. Leonard Wood.

aspiring to the second. As a result, little of the pre-1923 story of Islamic legal revivalism involves high politics and legislation. Projects for Islamic legal reform and revival had little traction within the Egyptian government.

Before 1923, the laboratories for deepening the rigor of Islamic legal revivalist ideas were the law schools, where Muslim jurists of various intellectual and religious persuasions studied and taught. The three high Islamic institutions experimented with reforming traditional approaches to Sharia education and scholarship, but struggled to come to terms with the new legal frameworks and intellectual demands that had evolved outside of their walls. Al-Azhar, the bastion of Sunni orthodoxy in Egypt, was the most averse of these to reforming traditional approaches in pedagogy and scholarship. At Dār al-ʿUlūm, a department focused on training Sharia practitioners existed only between 1887 and 1895 and left but a small record of accomplishment. The professors of the Sharia College, on the other hand, had a special mandate to modernize Sharia education and to defend the jurisdiction and prestige of the Sharia Courts. Its faculty was committed to preserving the integrity of Islamic traditions but was open to learning about European law. This atmosphere of openness made it possible for some of its graduates to become Sharia scholars who would critically engage with Franco-Egyptian law and European thought. A handful of its graduates migrated to the Cairo Faculty after 1923 and pursued transformations in Sharia pedagogy and scholarship.

The Cairo and French Faculties offered courses on Sharia and some professors wrote books, but neither came close in the pre-1923 era to producing the volume of work that was appearing in French Algeria. British dominance made the Cairo Faculty uncongenial to pursuing advanced and comparative studies, while the French Faculty's focus on teaching French law, as opposed to Egyptian law, appears to have kept its efforts focused on examinations for the French *licence*. Yet, courses in Sharia lived on at both schools, and revivalist professors joined the faculties. Enthusiasm for pursuing advanced Sharia studies among professors and students thereby survived the period of British hegemony at the Cairo Faculty and ultimately fed a resurgence of Islamic legal studies during a period of both Egyptian nationalist and French revival in the 1920s and 1930s.

REFORM AND THE AZHARITE CURRICULUM

In the same way that Europeans concerned with the quality of the Native Courts took an interest in the quality of legal education at the Cairo Faculty, those concerned with the Sharia Courts took an interest in al-Azhar. European and Egyptian elites pressured for changes in its pedagogy and curriculum. In 1903, a German orientalist and diplomat depicted al-Azhar as harmfully wed to outdated and insular practices that obstructed creative thought and research. Observing that reforms of recent decades had failed, he explained:

> Modern principles look delightful on paper, but, unfortunately, they are not written in the minds of those whose conduct they are designed to direct. The feeling of the majority, whether teachers or scholars, is still predominantly mediaeval, and it can be unquestionably asserted that no more is learned today from printed books in the light of incandescent lamps than half a millennium back out of manuscripts by the flickering glimmer of [oil lamps].... Of lecture-rooms, where the professor can be isolated with his class, theirs are not. A single enormous hall... traversed by eight rows of columns, unites under its roof both professors and pupils. Chaotic confusion, deafening chatter of tongues, ceaseless coming and going, not a moment of quietness... Amid this whirl, the professors, leaning against their columns, or squatting on low stools in the middle of a circle of twenty to thirty students, deliver their lectures....
>
> The professor... is expected to be versed in all the official branches of study. It is clear how much the thoroughness of his accomplishment must thereby suffer. So the professor, apart from laudable exceptions, seldom attempts to introduce the pupil rationally into his subject; he does not trouble himself to give a methodically arranged picture of the present position of the study, freed from all antiquated and superfluous matter. Nor does he ever aim at teaching his pupils to think. He is content with the thankless repetition of the doctrines and principles of past centuries, as they stand in the books hallowed by tradition, and handles them without the slightest criticism as never-changing truths. Doubt, the source of all scientific progress, is most severely prescribed [sic]. *Jura in verba magistri* is the first academical duty, and the disrespectful pupil who puts the too advanced question is smartly called to order with an energetic: "*ʿItakid wa lā tagaddil*" ("Believe, and question not")....
>
> [Reforms] have till now achieved little in face of the stubborn opposition of the professors, who continue unerring in the old paths, less from ill-will, I suppose, than from ignorance of better methods. For not understanding, as is mostly the case, any European language, they cannot inform themselves of Western systems.... [2]

In 1907, Pierre Arminjon, a French professor at the Cairo Faculty, depicted al-Azhar as unscientific, uncritical, and impractical for equipping graduates to operate in the Sharia judiciary and the modern world. In his words, "theoretical, bookish and passive" were "the traits most apparent in the teaching of mosques, and colleges and schools where no room is made for the mode of argumentation that has been applied in Western universities since the Middle Ages."[3] Wrong or right, these were the views of Europeans, Egyptian political elites, and reformist ulema.[4] This is the curriculum, pedagogy, and education culture they imagined they should reform.

Among Egyptians at al-Azhar, power struggles emerged between traditionalists and a clique of reformists who advocated new subjects, disciplines, and

[2] Adolf Heidborn, "A Muslim University," *Imperial and Asiatic Quarterly Review* 16,31–32 (1903): 310–13.

[3] Pierre Arminjon, *L'Enseignement, la doctrine et la vie dans les universités musulmanes d'Égypte* (Paris: Felix Alcan, 1907), 254–73.

[4] See also W. Basil Worsfold, *The Redemption of Egypt* (London: G. Allen, 1899), 101–2; Martin Hartmann, *The Arabic Press of Egypt* (London: Luzac and Co., 1899), 14.

methods of learning from Europe.[5] The majority of clerics opposed changes. Famous conservatives included the Shaykhs al-Azhar Muḥammad al-Inbābī, Salīm al-Bishrī, and ʿAbd al-Raḥmān al-Shirbīnī. The reformists included Muḥammad ʿAbduh, Muḥammad ibn Ibrāhīm al-Ẓawāhirī, Ḥassūna al-Nawawī, and ʿAlī al-Bablāwī.

By the 1860s state primary and secondary schools had begun teaching new subjects such as math, natural sciences, and European philosophy and political thought, and new tertiary educational institutions taught technology and natural sciences. Al-Azhar's earliest reforms skirted substantial change, however. Although a reform of 1872 redesigned its curriculum, courses in philosophy, higher math, natural science, foreign languages, and other subjects considered European were still not offered. The reform's main achievement was that the government now supervised the administration. Between 1895 and 1897, the government incorporated courses in math, chemistry, physics, and astronomy "to increase the capacity of the Muslim community to compete with the contemporary nations."[6] Most of these were optional subjects toward the *ʿālimiyyah* degree.

Reformists considered these curricular changes of the 1890s inadequate.[7] Muḥammad ʿAbduh, the most prominent example, worked to reform the institution until his death in 1905.[8] He lobbied conservative colleagues, collaborated with the government, and published on reform principles. His seminal treatise on Islamic theology attempted to reform Azharite dogma.[9] He circulated a memorandum charging the Shaykh al-Azhar Salīm al-Bishrī (1900–1904) for failing to execute the new laws governing the curriculum.[10] Heated exchanges between him and al-Shirbīnī (Shaykh al-Azhar 1905–1909) appeared in newspapers during 1904 as ʿAbduh pressed al-Azhar to create a "judicial section" to prepare

[5] See Adams, *Islam and Modernism in Egypt*, 70; Lajnat Iṣlāḥ al-Azhar, *Mashrūʿ iṣlāḥ al-azhar* (Cairo, 1919); Muḥammad ʿImārah, *al-Shaykh al-Marāghī wa-l-iṣlāḥ al-dīnī fī l-qarn al-ʿishrīn* (Cairo: Majallat al-Azhar, 1428/2007); Muhammad ʿAbd Allāh ʿInān, *Tārīkh al-jāmiʿ al-Azhar*, 2nd ed. (Cairo: Muʾassasat al-Khānjī, 1958); A. Lutfi al-Sayyid Marsot, "The Ulama of Cairo in the Eighteenth and Nineteenth Centuries," in *Scholars, Saints, and Sufis*, ed. Keddie, 163–5; Mansoor Moaddel and Kamran Talattof, *Contemporary Debates in Islam* (Basingstoke: Macmillan, 2000), 45–52; Saniyyah Qurrāʿah, *Tārīkh al-Azhar fī alf ʿām* (Cairo: Maktabat al-Ṣaḥāfah al-Dawliyyah, 1968); Fazlur Rahman, *Islam and Modernity* (Chicago: University of Chicago Press, 1982), 63–9; Muḥammad Rashīd Riḍā, *al-Manār wa-l-Azhar* (Miṣr: Maṭbaʿat al-Manār, 1353/1934); Riḍā, "Madrasat al-Qaḍāʾ bayna l-Azhar wa-l-Maʿārif," *al-Manār* 10 (1907): 77–8. Riḍā also provides rich documentation elsewhere in *al-Manār*. See Yasushi Kosugi, *Fihris majallat al-Manār, 1898–1935* (Beirut: Turāth, 1998), 19–21. See also ʿAbd al-Mutaʿāl al-Ṣaʿīdī, *Tārīkh al-iṣlāḥ fī l-Azhar wa-ṣafaḥāt min al-jihād fī l-iṣlāḥ* (Miṣr: Maṭbaʿat al-Iʿtimād, 1943); Smith, *Islam and the Search for Social Order*, 18.

[6] See Heidborn, "Muslim University"; Rahman, *Islam and Modernity*, 67; and see ordinances and council decisions of Jan. 3, 1895, Jul. 1, 1896, Mar. 24, 1885, Jan. 24, 1897, Feb. 1, 1897, Feb. 4, 1897, and Mar. 10, 1897, reprinted in Arminjon, *Enseignement*, 293–4.

[7] See, for example, Muḥammad ibn Ibrāhīm al-Aḥmadī al-Ẓawāhirī, *al-ʿIlm wa-l-ʿulamāʾ wa-niẓām al-taʿlīm* (Tanta: al-Maṭbaʿah al-ʿUmūmiyyah, 1904).

[8] See Riḍā, "Madrasat al-Qaḍāʾ bayna l-Azhar wa-l-Maʿārif"; Muḥammad ʿAbduh, "Iṣlāḥ al-Azhar," in *al-Aʿmāl al-kāmilah li-l-imām Muḥammad ʿAbduh*, ed. Muḥammad ʿImārah, 5 vols. (Cairo: Dār al-Shurūq, 2001), 3: 191–215. For an introduction to Muḥammad ʿAbduh, see Chapter 2.

[9] Muḥammad ʿAbduh, *Risālat al-tawḥīd* (Bulaq: al-Maṭbaʿah al-Kubrá al-Amīriyyah, 1898).

[10] Muḥammad ʿAbduh, "Shaykh al-Azhar yukhālif qānūnah," in ʿImārah, ed., *al-Aʿmāl al-kāmilah*, 3: 197–201.

students for work in the Sharia judiciary. ʿAbduh charged al-Azhar publicly with overemphasizing classical texts and insufficiently teaching applied law of the Sharia Courts. He envisioned a new program that would incorporate natural sciences, math, philosophy, and possibly foreign languages. Al-Shirbīnī attacked the initiative in a letter to the nationalist paper *al-Muʾayyad*, asserting, "The aim of our ancestors was to establish a house of God.... [and] worldly affairs and modern learning have nothing to do with al-Azhar."[11] He accused ʿAbduh of wanting "to destroy the clear paths of religious instruction and to convert this great mosque into a school of philosophy and literature."[12] His parting shot was that students at al-Azhar would never read Herbert Spencer.

In a rebuttal, ʿAbduh denied any intention to pursue reform to that extent, and accused al-Shirbīnī of hypocrisy and a mistaken view of al-Azhar. It was error, he wrote, to posit that al-Azhar had historically taught exclusively the Quran, hadith, and theology—al-Shirbīnī displayed through his own letter an education in the same fields that he now sought to inhibit: logic and philosophical reasoning. ʿAbduh cast the shaykh's attitudes as retrogade and harmful to modern thought, reason, and Islam.[13]

REFORM AND THE DĀR AL-ʿULŪM CURRICULUM

Dār al-ʿUlūm was established by Khedive Ismail in 1871 to produce teachers for new state primary and secondary schools, which taught lessons in subjects and sciences that were not part of the Azharite course of study. Until 1887 its curriculum comprised Quranic commentary (*tafsīr*), history, geography, arithmetic, engineering, chemistry, nature, and calligraphy.[14] Although the school was founded to address al-Azhar's limitations, it also became influenced and connected to al-Azhar. Professors wore the cloak and turban, a meaningful symbol, and most had been educated in Islamic primary and secondary schools.

In 1887, the Education Minister ʿAlī Mubārak established a judicial section at Dār al-ʿUlūm in order to train students as Sharia judges and lawyers.[15] For the first four years, students followed the normal Dār al-ʿUlūm curriculum, revised only to incorporate studies in Sharia.[16] They followed a fifth year devoted to Sharia practice. For the brief period between 1887 and 1895 when this fifth year existed, the Justice and Education Ministries considered Dār al-ʿUlūm the "Sharia

[11] Rahman, *Islam and Modernity*, 66; Muḥammad ʿAbduh, "al-Azhar al-sharīf wa-l-gharaḍ min iṣlāḥ ṭuruq al-taʿlīm fīh," in ʿImārah, ed., *al-Aʿmāl al-kāmilah*, 3: 203–9.

[12] Rahman, *Islam and Modernity*, 66.

[13] ʿAbduh, "al-Azhar al-sharīf," 204.

[14] Muḥammad ʿAbd al-Jawād, *Taqwīm Dār al-ʿUlūm: al-ʿAdad al-māsī yuṣdar li-murūr 75 ʿāman ʿalá al-madrasah 1872–1947* (Miṣr: Dār al-Maʿārif, 1952), 19.

[15] Ibid.

[16] For the first four years, the course in *fiqh* was increased from two to five hours per week, and *tafsīr* lessons were reduced from eight to four hours. This loss was compensated by four hours of *uṣūl al-fiqh*. ʿAbd al-Jawād, *Taqwīm*, 25.

law school."[17] There is as yet no evidence that anything particularly new happened in the fifth-year Sharia section or in the *fiqh* courses offered during the four-year curriculum.[18] It is possible that students spent their fifth year learning the outlines of applied law in the Sharia courts and the procedures governing those courts (see Table 8.1).

The program closed in 1895 when ulema of al-Azhar complained that Dār al-ʿUlūm was taking jobs from their graduates.[19] Al-Azhar closed the section and subsequently declined to create a replacement within al-Azhar itself.

Whether curricular reforms at the turn of the century at al-Azhar and Dār al-ʿUlūm made any substantial impact on the way Sharia was studied for the purposes of Islamic legal revivalism is a question in need of further investigation. Clear, however, is that the reforms disappointed the Ministries of Education and Justice, the leaders of the Cairo Faculty, Azharite reformists, and Islamic legal

Table 8.1. Dār al-ʿUlūm curriculum, 1890 (hours per week).

Subject	First Year	Second Year	Third Year	Fourth Year	Fifth Year[20]
Fiqh	5	5	5	5	
Math	4	4	4	4	
Style (*inshāʾ*)	3	3	4	4	
Calligraphy	4	4	2	2	
Geography	2	2	2	2	
General History	1	1	1	1	
Natural History	2	2			
Morphology	3	2			
Rhetoric	2	2			
Drawing	1	1			
Practical Knowledge	1				
Hadith, Theology, Logic		2	1		
Arabic Literature			3	3	
Quranic Commentary			2	2	
Nature and Chemistry			2	2	
Uṣūl al-fiqh			2	2	
Cosmography			1	1	
Pedagogy				1	
Total Hours/Week	28	28	29	29	

Source: Muḥammad ʿAbd al-Jawād, *Taqwīm Dār al-ʿUlūm* (Miṣr: Dār al-Maʿārif, 1952), 25.

[17] In 1898, three years after the judicial section closed, Lord Cromer referred to Dār al-ʿUlūm as the "Mussulman Law School." Lord Cromer, *(P.P.) Reports on the Finances, Administration, and Condition of Egypt, and the Progress of Reforms. May 1898. Egypt. No. 1 (1898)* (London, 1898), 31.

[18] Little is known about the curriculum of the fifth year. Students were required to read Ibn ʿĀbidīn's *Radd al-Mukhtār* on Hanafi *fiqh* before applying for admission.

[19] When this debate occurred between Dār al-ʿUlūm and al-Azhar, an inquiry was made into employment opportunities and the specific number of positions held in the Sharia judiciary and the department of *iftāʾ*. The numbers were 147 in total: 24 judges in the high courts, 25 members in the *majālis al-nuwwāb* of the judges, 19 muftis, and 79 judges in the courts of first instance. This was according to the budget of 1895. ʿAbd al-Jawād, *Taqwīm*, 19–25.

[20] Data for this column are unknown.

revivalists.[21] Al-Azhar was still teaching the same texts, using approximately the same teaching methods, and importantly, it was accused of not teaching the applied laws and procedures of even the Sharia courts.

Rashīd Riḍā remarked that ʿAbduh died in 1905 disappointed to see that little had come of his efforts. "Al-Azhar," Rida related, "resisted the reformists and rejected reformation.... The printing presses had yet to distribute both long-withheld books and the intellectual products of other nations. Thus, the ulema did not acknowledge the existence of any other science but their own knowledge, or any education but their own education. They believed that whoever touched them intended to inflict misdeeds and deformation."[22]

THE SHARIA COLLEGE CURRICULUM

The closure of Dār al-ʿUlūm's judicial department and al-Azhar's refusal to create a replacement caused reformists to envision a school independent from al-Azhar that would teach Sharia in theoretical and applied dimensions as well as math, science, philosophy, and foreign languages.[23] The Sharia College—to which students who had completed three years at al-Azhar could compete for admission by an entrance exam—was established in 1907 to produce worldly judges, muftis, lawyers, and clerks for the Sharia Courts. (See Tables 8.2 and 8.3.) Riḍā considered the founders to have been Muḥammad ʿAbduh, Shaykh Ḥassūnah al-Nawawī (Shaykh al-Azhar 1909), John Scott, and Saʿd Zaghlūl.[24] We last encountered this school through an examination of its student journal, the Sharia Law Journal, a beacon for Islamic legal revivalist sentiment and experimental scholarship of the 1920s.[25]

The Minister of Education Saʿd Zaghlūl (1906–1910), devoted to realizing ʿAbduh's aspirations to establish the college, finessed the project through parliament and negotiated tough compromises with the Azharites. Al-Azhar's opposition launched a press campaign declaring the project a sacrilege (*kufr*) and depicting al-Azhar as an enlightened institution in the process of its own revival (*nahḍah*), poised to incorporate modern learning. It lamented that its own graduates already had competition from Dār al-ʿUlūm graduates for scarce positions in the Sharia Courts.

The collaboration between the government and ʿAbduh had always been a matter of expedience as opposed to ideological alignment. In the 1890s the

[21] Riḍā wrote: "The reforms in Dār al-ʿUlūm and [the Sharia College] were so limited in their effectiveness that they failed to change their outer appearances and to affect the core of these institutions. Up to the present day, the reformation of Dār al-ʿUlūm, the [Sharia College], and other religious institutes has been limited to the introduction of some new sciences and the rewriting of some textbooks. Despite this, the sciences remain the same." Moaddel and Talattof, *Contemporary Debates*, 46.

[22] *Al-Manār* 10,28 (1906). See also Moaddel and Talattof, *Contemporary Debates*, 46.

[23] The school found its original model in a training college for *qāḍīs* established by the Austro-Hungarian Empire in Sarajevo. Cromer recorded having been in contact with the Governor-General of Bosnia on this matter. Cromer, *(P.P.) Reports by His Majesty's Agent and Consul-General on the Finances, Administration, and Condition of Egypt and the Soudan, in 1905. Egypt. No. 1 (1906)*, 81.

[24] Riḍā, "Madrasat al-Qaḍāʾ bayna l-Azhar wa-l-Maʿārif."

[25] See Chapter 2.

Table 8.2. Sharia College enrollment for selected years.

Year	Total Enrollment
1915	432
1919	261

Compiled from Jumayʿī, *Madrasat al-Qaḍāʾ al-Sharʿī.*

Table 8.3. Sharia College admissions for selected years.

Year	Applications	Admissions
1908	1000	191
1909	321	110
1910	405	375

Source: Jumayʿī, *Madrasat al-Qaḍāʾ al-Sharʿī*, 40.

British Judicial Adviser John Scott had understood that Islamic law could not be eliminated as a force in Egypt but could still be managed and reformed by an enlightened vanguard of reformist clerics. Zaghlūl did not share the British lack of enthusiasm for Islam—he had studied under ʿAbduh at al-Azhar—but he shared their aspirations for reforming Islamic education and the worldviews of clerics. The reformist ulema, for their part, needed government support to create the Sharia College against the will of al-Azhar.

The year 1907 presented an opportunity to pass the organic law and bylaws: the Justice Ministry was shifting its focus from Sharia Courts and looked to make a final reform; the Committee for Legislative Counsel supported Zaghlūl; Ḥassūnah al-Nawawī backed the plan; and Lord Cromer agreed to allocate state funds.[26]

The organic law included delicate and fateful compromises with al-Azhar. On a five-member governing board, four were the Minister of Justice, two appointees of the Ministry of Education, and the state mufti—all persons whom the government could in some measure influence. The fifth member was the rector of al-Azhar (Shaykh al-Azhar). Throughout the Sharia College's approximately seventeen-year existence, al-Azhar and the Ministry of Education vied for control.

In the long run, the College never separated from al-Azhar enough to be wholly independent. Its intricate power-sharing arrangement prompted conflicts. The school began as a division of the Ministry of Education and the dean was appointed by the Minister. But the Shaykh al-Azhar supervised the curriculum, even if he exercised little influence in the first years. The College's Arabic name (*Madrasat al-Qaḍāʾ al-Sharʿī*) symbolized independence from al-Azhar, if not also an aspirational peer relationship to the Cairo Faculty (*Madrasat al-Ḥuqūq*). Yet students graduated with an Azharite Certificate of Licensure (*shahādat al-ahliyyah al-azhariyyah*).[27] The College retained practical independence from al-Azhar

[26] The first-year budget was projected at LE 8,074. The budget ultimately exceeded LE 20,000.

[27] ʿAbd al-Munʿim Ibrāhīm al-Dusūqī Jumayʿī, *Madrasat al-Qaḍāʾ al-Sharʿī: Dirāsah tārīkhiyyah li-muʾassasah taʿlīmiyyah, 1907–1930* (Cairo: Maktabat al-Khānjī bi-Miṣr, 1986).

Table 8.4. Reforms in the governance of the Sharia College.

Year	Law/Ordinance	Power Hierarchy	Governance Characteristics
1907	Law 25 of Feb. 25, 1907[28]	(1) Ministry of Education (2) al-Azhar	A five-person administrative council is weighted in the Government's favor.
1911	Law 10, 1911[29]	(1) al-Azhar (2) Ministry of Education	Al-Azhar increases control as the College becomes a department of al-Azhar.
1916		Ministry of Justice	Ministry of Justice resumes control.
1925		al-Azhar	Al-Azhar resumes control. The College's students migrate to al-Azhar or Dār al-ʿUlūm for their classes. To some observers, the College is "closed" for all intents and purposes.[30]
1927		(1) Ministry of Education (2) al-Azhar	The Sharia College and Dār al-ʿUlūm are separated from al-Azhar. The administrative apparatus reverts to the 1907 arrangement.[31]
1928–1930	Law 15 of Nov. 1930	al-Azhar	Al-Azhar integrates the Sharia College into al-Azhar's new Faculty of Sharia.

Compiled from ʿAbd al-Munʿim Jumayʿī, *Madrasat al-Qaḍāʾ al-Sharʿī* (Cairo: Maktabat al-Khānjī bi-Miṣr, 1986).

until 1911,[32] but in the long term, the control structure changed repeatedly, with power shifting away from al-Azhar and then back again (see Table 8.4).

INNOVATIONS AND LIMITATIONS OF THE SHARIA COLLEGE

Students and teachers of the Sharia College considered themselves leaders in the revival of Islamic studies and *ijtihād*. They praised a spirit of free inquiry, new pedagogy, and academic rigor at the school. New expressions popularized in the

[28] Law No. 2 of Feb. 25, 1907. Pierre Arminjon, "Égypte: Notice sur les lois promulguées pendant l'année 1907," in *Annuaire de législation étrangère* (Paris: Libraire Générale de Droit et de Jurisprudence, 1908), 924–6, at 926.

[29] Law No. 10 of 1911, *Journal officiel du gouvernement égyptien* 70 (Jun. 24, 1911).

[30] According to Farhat Ziadeh (*Lawyers, the Rule of Law and Liberalism*, 57), "The Sharia College was abolished in 1923, reactivated in 1927, and finally dissolved in 1929. It was first under the jurisdiction of the Ministry of Education, then the high Azhar council, then the Ministry of Justice, then finally again the Ministry of Education." He bases these claims on an interview with Muḥammad Abū Zahrah. The claim seems to oversimplify the events.

[31] Jumayʿī, *Madrasat al-Qaḍāʾ al-Sharʿī*, 40.

[32] Madrasat al-Qaḍāʾ al-Sharʿī and Wizārat al-Maʿārif al-ʿUmūmiyyah, *Manhaj al-dirāsah al-muʾaqqat* (Cairo: al-Maṭbaʿah al-Amīriyyah, 1929).

discourse of the college included scientific freedom (*ḥurriyyah ʿilmiyyah*), scientific criticism (*naqd ʿilmī*), and "intellectual slavery" (*riqq ʿaqlī*).

One of Egypt's leading intellectuals, Aḥmad Amīn, touted the quality of students and colleagues in his memoirs and recorded that students were given the freedom to critique current ideas about knowledge and learning.[33] He savored the memory of talking with students into the night about philosophy and European books. He recalled that the students studied day and night, faced constant assignments and tests, and that they were prohibited from participating in politics or demonstrations, ostensibly to concentrate their attention on work.[34] Final exams were central to the program and students were dismissed for substandard performance.[35]

The Sharia College program was equally taxing for the faculty, Amīn wrote, who hailed from diverse intellectual backgrounds. Some wore European-style suits and the tarboush and had graduated from European-style faculties; others were from Dār al-ʿUlūm—known as Dar ʿĀmīs—and wore the cloak and turban, such as the Shaykhs Muḥammad Khuḍarī, Muḥammad al-Mahdī, Muḥammad Zayd al-Abyānī, Aḥmad Ibrāhīm, and Ḥasan Manṣūr.[36] Its founding dean, ʿĀṭif Barakāt Bey, a nephew of Saʿd Zaghlūl, was a Dār ʿĀmī.[37] Still others came from al-Azhar, or were lawyers, hired for their experience in the Native Courts.

Students wishing to enter the Sharia judiciary would spend three years at al-Azhar and nine years at the Sharia College. Those aspiring to administrative positions in the courts would graduate after completing the five-year lower division; those aspiring to be lawyers and judges continued to the four-year upper division. This two-tiered system replicated the Cairo Faculty's scheme (see Table 8.5).[38]

The curriculum was long and on the surface innovative. Courses on applied law of the Sharia Courts were integrated into a curriculum of traditional Islamic subjects. In courses on Arabic language, grammar, and literature, students read texts relevant to the study of Quranic commentary, classical *fiqh*, hadith, and theology (see Table 8.6).[39] Learning rules from teachers who expounded on them in printed hornbooks called *mudhakkirāt*, or memoranda, they spent less time than Azharite students studying classical jurists, but they also learned math, natural science, and letters, suggesting that the curriculum pressed them on topics that would make them more aware of the world beyond Islamic sciences and the Sharia Courts. At some point in the 1920s, students began writing a final-year thesis.[40]

[33] See generally Amin, *My Life*, 63–71.

[34] Demonstrations paralyzed the Cairo Faculty in 1906. Ibid., 28–9. The chief chronicler of Dār al-ʿUlūm, writing in 1952, regarded the Sharia College as having imposed strict regimentation in the belief that this produced better students on the model of the Cairo Faculty. ʿAbd al-Jawād, *Taqwīm*, 269.

[35] Jumayʿī, *Madrasat al-Qaḍāʾ al-Sharʿī*, 30.

[36] This follows the articulation in ibid., 23.

[37] Muḥammad ʿĀṭif Barakāt Bāshā (1872–1924) was a younger nephew of Saʿd Zaghlūl. ʿAbd al-Jawād, *Taqwīm*, 276.

[38] See the 1907 Organic Law, Jumayʿī, *Madrasat al-Qaḍāʾ al-Sharʿī*, 32; Madrasat al-Qadāʾ al-Sharʿī, (1) *al-Amr al-ʿālī al-ṣādir 12 muḥarram sanat 1325 (25 fabrāyir 1907) bi-inshāʾ al-madrasah*, (2) *al-Lāʾiḥah al-dākhiliyyah li-l-madrasah*, (3) *Brugrām mawādd al-dirāsah* (Miṣr: al-Maṭbaʿah al-Amīriyyah, 1907).

[39] Ṭāhā Ḥusayn charged that the focus on Sharia was excessive. Jumayʿī, *Madrasat al-Qaḍāʾ al-Sharʿī*, 34.

[40] The college journal, *Majallat al-Qaḍāʾ al-Sharʿī*, refers to these theses, but it is unknown whether copies survive in any Egyptian archive or library.

Table 8.5. Sharia College, lower and upper division curricula, 1907–8 (hours per week). The lower section offered five one-hour classes per day; the upper section offered four lessons per day, each lesson an hour and a quarter.

	Lower Division					Upper Division			
Course	Year One	Year Two	Year Three	Year Four	Year Five	Year One	Year Two	Year Three	Year Four
Tafsīr and Hadith			2	2	2	3	3	3	3
Fiqh and Wisdom of Law	7	7	7	6	6	5	5	5	5
Sharʿī Documents, Formularies, and Notary (*tawthīqāt sharʿiyyah*)				1	1			1	1
Principles of Theology	1			1	1		1		
Logic				1	1	1			
Religious Lit. and Ethics				1	1	1	1		
System of Sharia Courts, *Waqf*, Judiciary, and Administration				1	1	1	1		
Arabic Sciences	9	9	9	7	7	4	4	5	5
Mathematics	5	5	5	3	3	2	2	2	2
Geography and History	3	4	3	3	3	2	2	1	1
Calligraphy	3	3	2	2	2				
Research Literature						2			
Theory of Islamic Law (*uṣūl al-fiqh*)							2	2	2
Sources of Law (*uṣūl al-qawānīn*)								1	1
General Lectures on Sharia Legal Topics								1	1
Medical Topics						2	2	2	2
Total hours per week	28	28	28	28	28	23	23	23	23

Source: Madrasat al-Qaḍāʾ al-Sharʿī, (1) *al-Amr al-ʿālī al-ṣādir 12 muḥarram sanah 1325 (25 fabrāyir 1907) bi-inshāʾ al-madrasah*, (2) *al-Lāʾiḥah al-dākhliyyah li-l-madrasah*, (3) *Brugrām mawādd al-dirāsah* (Miṣr: al-Maṭbaʿah al-Amīriyyah, 1907), 30.

Although an enthusiasm for the revival of *ijtihād* prevailed, the exact content and methods of this spirit are challenging to unearth.[41] Comparative considerations are said to have been part of life at the Sharia College, but they do not seem to have been pursued at the level of rigor envisioned by Lambert.[42] Professors used their unpublished memoranda to share new ideas, which allowed them to express thoughts on a less public stage than the publishing market.[43] Shaykh Aḥmad Ibrāhīm's memorandum on Islamic contract law, from 1909, proposed innovative conceptual reformations of Islamic contract theory, for instance.[44] To

[41] The world of legal practice is another story. See, for example, Shaham, *Family and the Courts*.
[42] See Amin, *My Life*, 88–94.
[43] Jumayʿī claims that this practice started at Dār al-ʿUlūm.
[44] See Madrasat al-Qaḍāʾ al-Sharʿī, *Mudhakkirāt ʿan al-muʿāmalāt fī fiqh al-imām Abī Ḥanīfah raḥimahu Allāh* (Cairo: Maṭbaʿat al-Wāʿiẓ, 1327/1909).

Table 8.6. Sharia College, upper division curriculum, 1929.

(hours per week, across four years)

Upper Division Courses	Year One	Year Two	Year Three	Year Four
Fiqh	6	6	7	7
Quranic Commentary and Hadith	6	6	6	6
Arabic Language and Grammar	5	5	5	5
Research Literature and *uṣūl al-fiqh*	3	3	4	4
Medical Lectures	1	1	1	1
Theology and Logic	2	2		
History of the Judiciary	2	2		
Sharʿī Documents, Formularies, and Notary	1	1		
Ethics	1	1		
Sources of Law (*uṣul al-qawānīn*)	2			
System of Government		2		
History of Islamic Law (*tashrīʿ*)			2	2
Legal Questions and Exercises			2	2
System and Regulations of Sharia Courts and Related Institutions			2	1
International Private Law				1
Total hours per week	29	29	29	29

Source: Madrasat al-Qaḍāʾ al-Sharʿī and Wizārat al-Maʿārif al-ʿUmūmiyyah, *Manhaj al-dirāsah al-muʾaqqat* (Cairo: al-Maṭbaʿah al-Amīriyyah, 1929).

some contemporary observers, however, these were tentative innovations, remodeling old textbooks but not unsettling age-old orthodoxies.[45]

A course entitled "Sources of (Positive) Laws," patterned after one at the Cairo Faculty, taught the history of Roman law, European law, natural law, and proto-positivist philosophies underlying European laws. One reference work it relied on, Muḥammad Raʾfat's *Uṣūl al-qawānīn* (Sources of Law), lamented the decline of Islamic theories of law and the rise of European theories underlying secular and positive law.[46] It was the first book in an Arabic genre of legal literature to which Egyptian jurists of Franco-Egyptian law later contributed.[47] When the organic law was being drafted, Azharites declared the proposal for this course blasphemy (*kufr*). Saʿd Zaghlūl countered, saying the goal was not to inculcate in students an alien and agnostic theory of law but rather to "define" Egypt's applied laws, and to "explain how they are passed, how to use them, when to apply them, and the general principles of the positive law that Sharia judges need to know about."[48]

[45] See, for example, Riḍā, in *al-Manār* 10,28 (1906).

[46] Muḥammad Raʾfat, *Kitāb Uṣūl al-qawānīn* (Cairo, 1898). The genre of which this book was a part may be more properly called, "Sources of Law." Baudouin Bouckaert, "Sources du droit," in *Dictionnaire encyclopédique de théorie et de sociologie du droit*, ed. Arnaud and Belley, 45–53.

[47] See Muḥammad Kāmil Mursī and Sayyid Muṣṭafá, *Uṣūl al-qawānīn* (Miṣr: al-Maṭbaʿah al-Raḥmāniyyah, 1923); Aḥmad Ṣafwat, *Muqaddimat al-qānūn* (Cairo: Maṭbaʿat al-Qāhirah, 1924); ʿAbd al-Razzāq al-Sanhūrī and Aḥmad Ḥishmat Abū Sitīt, *Uṣūl al-qānūn* (Cairo: Maṭbaʿat Lajnat al-Taʾlīf wa-l-Tarjamah wa-l-Nashr, 1941).

[48] Jumayʿī, *Madrasat al-Qaḍāʾ al-Sharʿī*, 34. "al-Akhbār wa-l-ārāʾ: Madrasat al-qaḍāʾ bayna l-Azhar wa-l-maʿārif," *al-Manār* 10,1 (1907): 77–8.

Exposure to the theory of positive law ideally helped students to sharpen their rhetoric and technical arguments against the European philosophies and in favor of the Islamic doctrine. Taken in isolation from the context in which it was read, Raʾfat's book would suggest that the Egyptians who taught and studied these ideas were being converted to a Western way of thinking about law and its bases. Raʾfat writes as if resigned to the inevitable oblivion of traditional Islamic theology and ethics. But for every hour that a student at the Sharia College spent in the class entitled Theories of Positive Law, he spent more than ten times as many hours in traditional classes. The writings of graduates such as Muḥammad Khuḍarī, Aḥmad Abū al-Fatḥ, Muḥammad Zayd, Muḥammad Salāmah, Aḥmad Ibrāhīm, ʿAlī al-Khafīf, and Muḥammad Abū Zahrah show that its most prestigious alumni clung to traditional beliefs, however committed they may have been to reform. They engaged in a prolonged effort to champion traditional Islamic doctrines in the face of secular European philosophies of law into the 1930s and 1940s.

The Sharia College made good on its promise to teach the applied law of the Sharia Courts; and courses on Quran and hadith were organized around passages that were relevant to private, criminal, and constitutional law.[49] In that context, students studied family law, inheritances, and also homicide, bloodwit, theft, illicit gain (*ribā*), advance sales, loans, leases, bankruptcy, and warfare (*jihād*). The first year of the four-year curriculum in *fiqh* taught property, contracts, delicts, usurpation (*ghaṣb*), and illicit gain.[50] Students were aware of the limited jurisdiction of the Sharia Courts and the opportunities for regaining jurisdiction lost to the Native Courts. This is apparent from their curriculum and their student journal. The faculty also gained a technical grasp on what the laws of the Sharia Courts would look like if jurisdiction were recovered, and in the 1930s and 1940s, professors formerly associated with the Sharia College began writing about all of these aspects of Sharia law that might be reapplied in a revival of Islamic law—they eventually wrote books on property, contracts, delicts, procedure, administration, and criminal punishment, all as topics in Islamic law.

However, since the curriculum focused on training students to practice law and not to publish academic work—there were few if any courses offering advanced skills in legal research and writing[51]—such developments crystallized only much later. The culture of Arabic legal-academic publishing—that is, the routine publishing of monographs and articles as a norm for professional law teachers—

[49] The 1929 *Prospectus* lists the Quranic verses and hadith that students were expected to master. All of them were organized under legal rubrics, such as courtroom procedure (*qaḍāʾ*), mutual divorce (*khulʿ*), arbitration (*ṣulḥ*), alimony (*nafaqāt*), divorce via oath-based allegation of adultery (*liʿān*), proven adultery (*zinā*), false allegation of adultery (*qadhf*), dower (*mahr*), and polygamy (*taʿaddud al-zawjāt*).

[50] The four-year curriculum in *fiqh* was weighted in favor of the applied laws and was almost identical to that at the Cairo Faculty. The second-year class taught *sharʿī* procedures (both classical and the contemporary procedures). The third year taught family law, succession, and inheritance. The fourth year taught *waqf*.

[51] The final-year thesis writing requirement imposed in the 1920s might be taken as an exception.

gained ground in Egypt in the 1920s and 1930s at the instigation of professors of Franco-Egyptian law at the Cairo Faculty, and by the time it influenced Sharia scholars to publish new and more searching works in Sharia, the Sharia College had closed and its leading scholars had moved to the Cairo Faculty, al-Azhar, and other schools.

Although Sharia College students learned about the Franco-Egyptian laws, the curriculum did not provide them with the intellectual tools that would have allowed them to engage with these laws as critically, comparatively, constructively, and originally as they might have. The most important impediment in this regard was that they did not learn the foreign languages necessary to deal with the majority of texts on Native and Mixed law, let alone with European legal scholarship. Most of the professors were fluent in Arabic only. Students at the Sharia College wanting to learn French or English needed to go elsewhere for classes, and this was something for which they had little time. Much of their exposure to European ideas came through classroom discussions and books in Arabic translations; they and their teachers may also have read Arabic journals such *al-Muqtaṭaf* or *al-Ḥuqūq*, which published articles explaining ideas from European natural science, social science, and philosophy. When the Cairo Faculty began reintegrating French instruction into its curriculum in the mid-1920s, the Sharia College continued its exclusive use of Arabic. The absence of foreign language courses came with consequences for the intellectual and academic culture of the college. While the Cairo Faculty's renewed engagement with French opened new horizons for its study of law, the Sharia College's curriculum and horizons remained more or less as they had been.

Perhaps most important to longer-term developments in Sharia scholarship was the simple enthusiasm for comparative considerations. This aspect of the Sharia College's environment helps to explain why faculty members who migrated from this college to the Cairo Faculty—although they did not bring with them the tools for pursuing comparativism or much of a publishing record in comparative research or otherwise—worked collegially with their colleagues in Franco-Egyptian law departments, stepped up their comparative studies immensely, and began producing new works on Sharia that showed an imprint of European and Franco-Egyptian legal thought. Their newfound expertise in comparative studies and methodology became a defining feature of their work in the 1930s and 1940s.

The Sharia College's enthusiasm for comparative discussions also helps explain why the Cairo Faculty hired professors from the Sharia College—they were judged to be sufficiently open minded and modern to deserve a position. This did not mean that professors coming from the Sharia College would give up their faith in Islam or prefer Franco-Egyptian law to Sharia; rather, it meant that those Sharia professors were willing to participate cooperatively with professors of Franco-Egyptian departments, and were willing to contribute to the intellectual mission of the Cairo Faculty, as well as meet its standards for producing new scholarship.

THE CAIRO FACULTY CURRICULUM

As we have seen, for a time the government hoped that Dār al-ʿUlūm or al-Azhar would develop improved sections for teaching Sharia and that these schools would be sufficiently reformed to prepare new generations for work in the reformed Sharia Courts. But in the absence of such reforms before 1907, European personnel in the ministries and the Cairo Faculty were keen to ensure that a good program of Sharia instruction was in place.

In the years 1889–1891, the future of the Sharia courses at the Cairo Faculty was at the center of public debate. The context was the fall of Nubar Pasha's cabinet in June 1888 and the rise of Riyāḍ Pasha's government (Jun. 1888–May 1891). Nascent Egyptian and Islamic-oriented nationalist movements were taking firmer shape. As recounted earlier, in 1890 Victor Vidal died and debate ensued over who would succeed him as director of the school. Amid this ferment, the conservative newspaper *al-Adab* published articles criticizing the fact that secular-oriented law (*sharīʿah qānūniyyah*) was becoming dominant in the country. The articles criticized the fact that an education in Franco-Egyptian law was now the key to finding work in the law. The paper charged that the legal system had been overtaken by French language and law, that Egyptian lawyers were losing contact with their own legal heritage, and that Egyptians were increasingly less competent to practice in the Sharia Courts, and it called on the Cairo Faculty to enhance its program in Islamic law. One article lamented that Egyptians had begun to view Islamic law as having relevance only in matters of personal status—Islamic law, it argued, could be relevant also to Egypt's laws on contracts and commerce.[52]

In 1891, there was further public debate about "Egyptianizing" the law school and increasing education in Islamic law. "Egyptianization" became a stated goal of the cabinet under the new Prime Minister Muṣṭafá Fahmī (May 1891–Jan. 1893).[53] One of the contributing figures in this campaign was the outspoken Islamic-oriented nationalist Shaykh ʿAlī Yūsuf, who lodged a complaint in the newspaper *al-Muʾayyad* about the lack of Islamic law at the law school. "The law school," he wrote, "needs a . . . program of Islamic law in each of its sections. No one can deny the connections between civil law and the *mores* of the country . . . which are based on Quranic law."[54]

From 1892 onward, Sharia was a central part of the curriculum. It became more important after 1898 when the government passed a law allowing graduates of the Cairo Faculty to practice before the Sharia Courts.[55] Sharia was one of the few courses that a student encountered in every year of his *licence* program. It was also the class that received either the first or second highest number of classroom hours per year, on average (see Table 8.7). Compared to the curriculum of the three Islamic institutions discussed earlier, where students did not study a

[52] *Al-Adab* (March 30, 1889), as cited in Cannon, "Social Tensions," 307, 314 n. 27.
[53] Cannon, "Social Tensions," 307.
[54] Ibid., 309.
[55] "Rapport de M. le Conseiller Judiciaire sur l'année 1898," 170.

Table 8.7. Cairo Faculty, average hours per week (per class, over the duration of the *licence* program).[56]

	1892	1899	1904	1907	1929	1933	1937
Sharia	12	15	11	14	6	10	10
Civil Law	6	11	10	16	10	14	11
Criminal Law and Procedure	6	5	6	8	7	8	7
Civil and Commercial Procedure	6	5	6	7	5	6	5
Political Economy	3	3	5	5	4	6	6
Roman Law	6	6	5	5	2	3	2
Commercial and Maritime Law	3	3	4	5	3	4	3
International Private Law	3	2			2	3	3
International Private and Public Law				3	3		
International Public Law					2	2	
Administrative Law	3	3				3	2
Administrative and Financial Law			3	3	3		
Financial Law						2	2
Organization of Public Powers	3	3	2	2			
Constitutional Law					2	3	2
General Introduction to the Study of Law	3	4	2	2		3	3
Legal History					2	2	2
Legal Writing			8	8			

Sources: *Recueil des documents officiels du gouvernement égyptien* (1892), 550–51; *Recueil des documents officiels du gouvernement égyptien* (1899), 535; Madrasat al-Ḥuqūq al-Khidīwiyyah, *al-Qawānīn wa-l-brūgrām*, 19–20; al-Jāmiʿah al-Miṣriyyah, *Taqwīm* (1929); *Journal officiel du gouvernement Égyptien*, no. 66, 20 jul. 1933 (1933); Université Égyptienne, *Annuaire, 1936–1937*, 44–6.

subject called Sharia but instead its component parts—Quran, Hadith, Quranic commentary, Islamic legal thought (*fiqh*), legal theory, theology, logic, and so forth—the course at the Cairo Faculty was a simplified program. Students also received rapid training in legal theory (*uṣūl al-fiqh*).

The view of *uṣūl al-fiqh* that students at the Cairo Faculty encountered was traditional, not reformist. Aḥmad Abū al-Fatḥ, a Sharia professor at the Cairo Faculty in the early 1900s, wrote his own *uṣūl al-fiqh* textbook.[57] It was novel in that it was written in the twentieth century and simplified classical material; otherwise, it was traditional in its outlook. It cast normative orthodoxy, or respect for classical precedent (*taqlīd*), in a positive light. It adhered to the Hanafi distinction of three degrees in *ijtihād* and claimed that the door of *ijtihād* had been closed for fundamental questions in doctrine.[58] It declined to expand on theories such as *maqāṣid* (ends of the law) and *maṣlaḥah* (general welfare), theories that Sharia revivalists of the age regarded as tools for producing modern Islamic laws.

Looking broadly from 1899 to 1923, Sharia was usually offered for all four years.[59] Putting Year 1 to the side momentarily, Year 2 was dedicated to personal

[56] In 1892 and 1929, the curriculum was three years. In 1899, 1904, 1907, and 1937, the curriculum was four years. The names of courses varied from year to year. Additional hours per week for language instruction have been omitted.

[57] Aḥmad Abū al-Fatḥ, *Kitāb al-Mukhtārāt al-fatḥiyyah fī tārīkh al-tashrīʿ wa-uṣūl al-fiqh*, 4th ed. (Miṣr: Maṭbaʿat al-Nahḍah, 1924).

[58] On *taqlīd* and *ijtihād*, see Chapter 6.

[59] See Ministère de l'Instruction Publique, *Projet de règlement organique de l'École Khédiviale de Droit* (Cairo: Imprimerie Nationale, 1904), (a copy is in Nantes/Cairo 171). See also statistics and reports on

status, marriage, marital rights, divorce, capacity, alimentary provision, dower, and gifts. Year 3 was devoted to *waqf*.[60] Year 4 was devoted mostly to Sharia court procedure.

As for Year 1, its focus was those parts of the civil law wherein the Franco-Egyptian civil codes were informed by Islamic legal tradition. Of concern were the Native Code's law on options (*khiyārāt*), transfer of obligation (*ḥawālah*), suretyship (*kafālah*), pledge (*rahn*), agency (*tawkīl*), vitiating factors in contract such as coercion and trickery (*ikrāh* and *ghubn fāḥish*), usufruct (*intifāʾ*), capacity (*ahliyyah*), and hiring (*ijārah*). A certain change in the Year 1 class came in the 1910s when Sharia professors began teaching more aspects of Islamic contract law that were not in application in the Egyptian legal system. The textbook for this learning was Muḥammad Qadrī Pasha's codification of Hanafi contract law, *Murshid al-ḥayrān*.

As to whether comparative considerations of law entered the classrooms, such discussions arose as part of lessons on the conflict of jurisdictions within Egypt. Whereas graduates of the Sharia College were likely to work only in Sharia Courts, graduates of the Cairo Faculty might spend their careers moving in and out of multiple jurisdictions—the Native, Mixed, and Sharia, and possibly the consular as well. Comparative legal considerations only appeared in exam questions when they pertained to conflicts of subject-matter jurisdiction between Egyptian courts.[61]

CAIRO FACULTY'S INCORPORATION OF REVIVALISTS

The Cairo Faculty hired professors for its Sharia Department from the high Islamic institutions, preferring the Sharia College and Dār al-ʿUlūm. There were two generations of Sharia professors at the Cairo Faculty before the 1950s. The first generation, appearing in the 1890s and early 1900s, included Shaykhs Muḥammad Salāmah al-Sanjalfī, Aḥmad Abū al-Fatḥ, Muḥammad Zayd al-Abyānī, and Muḥammad Khuḍarī, who were associated with Dār al-ʿUlūm.[62] There were others, from al-Azhar or Dār al-ʿUlūm, but all were "first rate," according to John Scott.[63] The second generation, appearing in the mid-1930s, began with Aḥmad Ibrāhīm, a graduate of Dār al-ʿUlūm and a former teacher at the Sharia College. In the mid-1930s,

1899, 1904, 1907, 1910, and 1916 in, respectively, *Recueil des documents officiels du gouvernement égyptien* (1899), 535; *Recueil des documents officiels du gouvernement égyptien* (1907), 176; Madrasat al-Ḥuqūq al-Khidīwiyyah, *al-Qāwānīn wa-l-brūgrām* (Cairo: al-Maṭbaʿah al-Amīriyyah bi-Miṣr, 1910), 19; *Recueil des documents officiels du gouvernement égyptien* (1917), 24–5. See also ʿUmar and ʿAbd al-ʿAzīz, *Majmūʿat al-imtiḥānāt al-nihāʾiyyah*.

[60] In 1900 a slight change was made. A course was added for courses in Arabic by a Muslim professor on the organization and procedure of the various tribunals dealing with personal status (Sharia courts, patriarchates, etc.). There is commentary on the decrees of June 17, 1880, November 19, 1896, and May 27, 1897, in "Rapport de M. le Conseillier judiciaire sur l'exercice 1900," in *Recueil des documents officiels du gouvernement égyptien* (1901), 181–236.

[61] ʿUmar and ʿAbd al-ʿAzīz, *Majmūʿat al-imtiḥānāt al-nihāʾiyyah*.

[62] Another figure was Aḥmad Qamḥah.

[63] *Recueil des documents officiels du gouvernement égyptien* (1897), 177–8.

Aḥmad Ibrāhīm hired his star students from the Sharia College, ʿAlī al-Khafīf, ʿAbd al-Wahhāb Khallāf, and Muḥammad Abū Zahrah.[64]

In the first two decades of the twentieth century, professors of Franco-Egyptian law at the Cairo Faculty created the modern Egyptian legal-academic publishing arena. Azharites had been publishing legal texts, but their publications focused on editions of classical texts and books that commented on or otherwise recapitulated classical laws and doctrines. By contrast, professors at the Cairo Faculty began a new field of published scholarship on Franco-Egyptian and European law, most of which was in French and English. These books adopted the outward appearance as well as the expository styles and intellectual approaches of Western European law books.

The scholars of Franco-Egyptian law at the Cairo Faculty were prolific, and they increasingly favored colleagues who published new work. The Cairo Faculty Sharia professors thus began publishing new kinds of books for students and practitioners, which sought to keep pace with the constantly changing rules and substantive laws of the Sharia Courts. Most, but not all, of the books were concerned with the laws of the courts in force. For the most part, if these books reflected new ideas about Sharia, they were reflecting the new laws and practices of the Sharia Courts that had been brought into existence as the result of reforms made by legislators.

Commentaries explaining the draft Islamic codes of Qadrī Pasha were published—in 1903, Muḥammad Zayd al-Abyānī's commentary on Muḥammad Qadrī's *al-Aḥkām al-sharʿiyyah fī l-aḥwāl al-shakhṣiyyah* (Rules of Sharia in Personal Status); in 1908, al-Abyānī's partial commentary on Qadrī's *Murshid al-hayrān*, with Muḥammad Salāmah. The commentaries were critical, explaining variations in opinions and ways in which the code changed traditional understandings of the *fiqh*. The commentary on Qadrī's *Murshid al-ḥayrān* reads as a morose review of a body of classical *fiqh* no longer in force. It is interesting to note that they were teaching Qadrī's book, given that it presented many laws that were not part of the national law. Students at the Cairo Faculty were studying not only applied Sharia but also Islamic contract law that could, hypothetically, be applied in a future revival of Sharia.

Aḥmad Ibrāhīm credited members of the first generation of Sharia professors at the Cairo Faculty with having changed traditional methods of writing and teaching *fiqh*. He also suggested that these changes were meant to serve a future revival of Islamic law and legislation in the applied sphere. He wrote of Muḥammad Zayd al-Abyānī's career at the Cairo Faculty:

> When Muḥammad Zayd began teaching, the books of Islamic Sharia taught to the students of Islamic *fiqh* were the books that circulated around al-Azhar and were written in the Azharite style. Except that there was established at that time an intellectual movement aimed at making it easier to learn the rules of Islamic Sharia, and to write the law clearly as articles of positive law. Perhaps that *sharʿī* law would one day become the applied law in Egypt.

[64] Another figure in that mix was Muḥammad Aḥmad Faraj al-Sanhūrī.

> Muḥammad Qadrī Pasha, God Almighty have mercy on him, thought to write three books according to the style of *qānūn* books. He executed this idea and wrote a book on personal status, a second on *waqf*... and a third on the rules of property transactions.
>
> Thus, Qadrī Pasha was the first new pious pioneer in Islamic *fiqh* writings in Egypt, and he removed the heavy burden from students of Sharia laws, such as the *Durr* [*al-mukhtār* of al-Ḥaskafī] and the *Radd al-mukhtār* [*ʿalá durr al-mukhtār* of Ibn ʿĀbidīn].
>
> Our teacher Muḥammad Zayd started teaching from Qadrī Pasha's treatise on personal status law for his students of law while writing his commentaries on it, until he completed the work, penning a complete and satisfying commentary for the book in three volumes .... The people received it with great hope and a strong love, for they found that it fully satisfied their long-cherished wish. I was told that this commentary was translated into French and that for this he was awarded the *Légion d'honneur* by France.[65]
>
> Muḥammad Zayd was considered the second pioneer for that new blessed era of Islamic law. He facilitated its learning and he eased the path with good organization and classification on the basis of the requisite research, and with soundness in its expression and logical flow.[66]

The work of Aḥmad Abū al-Fatḥ is of particular interest.[67] As mentioned earlier, his *uṣūl al-fiqh* book championed traditional *uṣūl al-fiqh* in the face of countervailing theories of positive law.[68] In 1913, he wrote *Kitāb al-Muʿāmalāt fī l-sharīʿah al-islāmiyyah wa-l-qawānīn al-miṣriyyah* (Transactions in Islamic Sharia and Egyptian Law), a two-volume treatise offering a conceptual restructuring of Islamic private law, following a French approach, and its limited reflection in applied Egyptian private law. It outlined a general law of contract and pushed in the direction of articulating a general theory of obligations, reorganizing substantive rules of Islamic contract law according to categorical hierarchies of French law.[69]

The professors of the Cairo Faculty wrote books about the applied law of the Sharia Courts because this law was the subject of ongoing reform. Between the 1880s and 1940s, the government pursued four different kinds of reform for the Sharia Courts and their laws: it altered the distribution of labor among the court systems in the business of property registrations; it restructured the jurisdictional range and internal organization of the Sharia Courts; it changed procedural laws; and it reorganized, changed, and codified the substantive law of the courts.

[65] See Qadrī Pasha, *Droit musulman*.

[66] ʿAbd al-Jawād, *Taqwīm*, 56, 237. See also al-Abyānī and al-Sanjalfī, *Sharḥ Murshid al-ḥayrān*.

[67] Aḥmad Abū al-Fatḥ (1866–1946) entered Dār al-ʿUlūm in 1888 and graduated in 1891. He taught in *madrasahs* between 1891 and 1908, at which time he was appointed as a teacher at the Cairo Faculty. He retired in 1926 and taught as an emeritus professor until retirement in 1931. ʿAbd al-Jawād, *Taqwīm*, 56, 237.

[68] Abū al-Fatḥ, *Kitāb al-Mukhtārāt al-fatḥiyyah*.

[69] The book and its summary version had multiple printings, both in its entirety (Cairo: Maṭbaʿat al-Nahḍah, 1923) and shortened (*Mukhtaṣar Kitāb al-Muʿāmalāt fī l-sharīʿah al-islāmiyyah*, 4th ed. (Miṣr: Maṭbaʿat al-Nahḍah, 1923)).

Among other effects, new laws forced European law and practices into the applied law of the Sharia Court system.[70]

The new books appearing on substantive and procedural laws as well as those on the various organic laws of the Sharia Courts adopted outward attributes of Franco-Egyptian and European law books. Their title pages, contents pages, and indices were formatted on the model of Franco-Egyptian books. Topical rubrics were established on a European model.

There were three types of models for the new Arabic publications on Sharia law written by teachers at the Cairo Faculty: (1) the pamphlets and manuals published by the government in Arabic that contained official compilations of laws. By 1900, the format of these publications was unmistakably French-inspired;[71] (2) the voluminous law manuals published in Arabic by professors of Franco-Egyptian law intended for Egyptian lawyers and judges. These manuals could include sections on applied Sharia law and organizational reforms relevant to the Sharia Courts;[72] and (3) an existing academic literature in French, English, and Arabic—produced by those associated with the Cairo and French Faculties—on Mixed and Native procedural law.[73]

By the 1920s, the visual aspect of the manuals on applied Sharia was wholly Europeanized. Examples are Muḥammad Zayd al-Abyānī's *Kitāb Mabāḥith al-murāfaʿāt* (Topics in Procedural Law) (1924) and two books co-authored by Aḥmad Qamḥah and ʿAbd al-Fattāḥ al-Sayyid: *Niẓām al-qaḍāʾ wa-l-idārah* (The Judicial and Administrative Systems) (1923) and *Sharḥ lāʾiḥat al-ijrāʾāt al-sharʿiyyah* (Commentary on *Sharʿī* Procedural Law) (1923).[74]

For the most part, these were explanatory manuals. Innovations in the Sharia laws printed in these books reflected legislative reforms passed by the government rather than innovative thought on the part of the authors. At the same time, the authors were not silent in these texts; their expertise, and their opinions, on these reforms are apparent. Muḥammad Zayd al-Abyānī, for example, wrote as if lamenting the replacement of an ancient and tried system of Sharia procedures by a more simplistic and less thoughtful system from Europe.

[70] For details on the various legal changes, see Shaham, *Family and the Courts*, 11–15, 240; Leonard Wood, "Reception of European Law, Origins of Islamic Legal Revivalism, and Foundations of Transformations in Islamic Legal Thought in Egypt, 1875–1960" (Ph.D. diss., Harvard University, 2011), 399–400; Ibn ʿArnūs, *Kitāb Tārīkh al-qaḍaʾ*, 195–235; Qamḥah and al-Sayyid, *Sharḥ lāʾiḥat al-ijrāʾāt.*

[71] Appendix provides plates of Arabic law books produced in the 1920s by professors at the Cairo Law Faculty. Although books on Sharia law are not included, the books on contract law and Roman law included depict a "French-inspired" format.

[72] See Octave Borelli, *La Législation égyptienne annotée* (Brussels: P. Weissenbruch, 1892); Homère Sayour, *Répertoire de la jurisprudence des appels sommaires des tribunaux mixtes d'Égypte* (Alexandria: Société des Publications Égyptiennes, 1916); ʿAbd al-Fattāḥ al-Sayyid and Muḥammad Kāmil Mursī, *Majmūʿat qawānīn al-maḥākim al-ahliyyah wa-l-sharʿiyyah* (Miṣr: Maṭbaʿat al-Raghāʾib, 1921); ʿAbd al-ʿAzīz Naṣr, ed., *Marjiʿ al-qaḍāʾ*, 4 vols. (Miṣr: Maṭbaʿat al-Iʿtimād, 1923).

[73] Ugo Lusena Bey, *Eléments de procédure civile et commerciale d'après le code indigène comparé au code mixte*, 3rd ed., 2 vols. (Cairo: Imprimerie Nationale, 1903, 1906); Adib Makad, *Notions générales sur les jurisdictions mixtes d'Égypte* (Alexandria: Imprimerie de l'École Professionelle des Frères, 1922); ʿAbd al-Ḥamīd Abū Hayf, *al-Murāfaʿāt al-madaniyyah wa-l-tijāriyyah wa-l-niẓām al-qaḍāʾī fī Miṣr* (Cairo: Maṭbaʿat al-Maʿārif, 1915).

[74] Muḥammad Zayd al-Abyānī, *Kitāb Mabāḥith al-murāfaʿāt wa-ṣuwar al-tawthīqāt wa-l-daʿāwá l-sharʿiyyah* (Miṣr: ʿAbd Allāh Wahbah al-Katbī, 1924); Aḥmad Qamḥah and ʿAbd al-Fattāḥ al-Sayyid, *Niẓām al-qaḍāʾ wa-l-idārah* (Cairo: Maṭbaʿat al-Nahḍah, 1923); Qamḥah and al-Sayyid, *Sharḥ lāʾiḥat al-ijrāʾāt.*

THE FRENCH FACULTY AND THE CONTINUITY OF FRENCH TRADITION

In the 1890s and early 1900s, a coterie of French legal academics assumed various kinds of teaching positions at both the French Faculty and the Cairo Faculty. Some of the professors were only transient in Cairo but still made their mark in various ways. Among them were Eugène Clavel, Marcel Morand, Henri Lamba, Albert Chéron, and Pierre Arminjon. Lamba and Clavel taught at the French Faculty but moved in and out of the Cairo Faculty. Chéron and Arminjon taught at the Cairo Faculty but kept close relations with their colleagues at the French Faculty. The Dutchman Van den Berg was also part of the Francophone clique.

When the French Faculty opened in the 1890s, its Islamic law offerings were more limited than those of the Cairo Faculty.[75] French Faculty students were studying for the *licence* in the French law of France, and the curriculum afforded them little opportunity to study any subject that did not pertain to the relevant exams. Still, Azharite instructors came to teach some Sharia courses. These courses existed, first and foremost, because graduates of the French Faculty wishing to practice in Egypt needed to take an equivalency exam for admission to the Native and Mixed Bars. This exam was written and administered by the Cairo Faculty. Since students at the Cairo Faculty sat exams in Sharia law to obtain the *licence en droit égyptien*, the equivalency exam included a section on applied Sharia.[76]

The professors at the French Faculty, several of whom had come directly from the Faculté de Droit d'Alger where Islamic law was a central part of the curriculum, sought to control the study of Islamic law and to reform Islamic legal thought.[77] Their interest in expanding Islamic law study was for reasons beyond the mere desire to attract Egyptian students and to prepare them for the equivalency exam in Egyptian law. Eugène Clavel was one such professor. In Cairo, he published in French on Islamic law and founded a journal in 1897 that supported Islamic political sentiment.[78] Clavel's enthusiasm for Islamic law stemmed from his experience at the Algiers Faculty and from the fact that he was part of a broader movement of European orientalist scholarship and legal comparativism that focused on the history and modern practice of Sharia.

In 1896, a letter by Clavel to the French Ministry of Instruction criticized Islamic legal education at the French Faculty. He complained that the Cairo Faculty was doing a better job of teaching both Egyptian and Islamic law. This was a regrettable situation, in his view, since the Cairo Faculty itself had minimal interest in

[75] See folios of the French Consulate of Cairo in Nantes/Cairo 171. Other sources are given later in this chapter and in Chapter 5.

[76] For decades of letters documenting an ongoing debate between the Cairo Faculty and the French Faculty as to whether the equivalency exam should include a section on Sharia, see Nantes/Cairo 171. See also Ministère de la Justice, *Rapport pour l'année 1913 présenté par le Conseiller Judiciaire* (Cairo: Imprimerie Nationale, 1914), 26.

[77] See Chapter 6.

[78] The journal was called *al-Ittiḥād al-islāmī/L'Union islamique*. See also the law journal he edited for one year, *Revue internationale de législation et de jurisprudence musulmanes* (Cairo: Imprimerie Centrale J. Barbier, 1895–96).

Islamic law.[79] He urged the French Faculty to "take better care to teach the Egyptians their own laws, including the personal status law of Muslims." Egyptians, he said, should study their own Muslim law and "have the same opportunities to do this that the Algerians have." The comment was offered without any apparent intent of irony.

The first line of reasoning was that, in the future, Egypt's law would be more thoroughly "Egyptian." This was the typical sentiment of the French professors in Egypt in the 1890s, who, fearing that France was losing control of Egypt's legal system, preferred to see the system become "Egyptian" as opposed to British. Based on his conviction that "Egyptianization" of Egypt's law was almost inevitable, Clavel was convinced it did not make sense to teach only the French and Franco-Egyptian codes at the French Faculty.[80]

Clavel argued that the French Faculty should follow the model in Algiers and establish chairs for the teaching of local law. In particular, he recommended a chair for "*concordance*." The professor holding this chair would be responsible for teaching the differences between French law and local law in practice. Possibly, an implication of establishing such a chair was that the professor would be concerned with reshaping local law to make it look more like French law. Although he did not say as much himself, this is what the French professors of Islamic law in Algeria were in the business of doing.[81] Clavel wrote in his letter, "The day when that has been adopted, our school will be a breeding ground not only for French jurists but for Egyptian jurists. And that, I believe, is not something to be looked down upon." Clavel displays the same interest as Édouard Lambert and French-Algerian writers in experimental and comparativist Islamic law studies, arguing that it was necessary for French teachers to help Egyptians improve their methods for thinking about Islamic law and the role it should play in the contemporary world.

He also went a step further by suggesting that Egyptians should be taught Islamic law by Europeans. This was a quintessentially French and French-Algerian way of thinking about Islamic legal education. Such an important field of study, Clavel reasoned, would be placed ideally in the hands of Europeans who could manage it responsibly and bring their analytical powers to bear upon it. If the Sharia courses at the French Faculty could not be taught by Europeans, Clavel conceded, then at the very least the course could be taught by an Egyptian teacher who was "progressive" and aware of the "most scientific methods" for dealing with law.[82]

[79] Eugène Clavel, "Mémoire," in Nantes/Cairo 160, "École Française de Droit du Caire."

[80] Clavel, "Mémoire."

[81] See Chapter 6.

[82] He wrote: "We have entrusted [in Algeria] these chairs [of Islamic law] not to the ulemas, the great enemies of modern science, but to the French professors, to retired judges, and to people like Mr. Zeys who is today the President Premier of the court of Algiers, or Mr. Estoublon. . . . It is fair to say that all those who opt for our teaching are the progressive youth, friends of serious and detailed study and not fanatics. In fact, today, there are more of them than the fanatics of al-Azhar; and quite a few Europeans." Clavel, "Mémoire."

Clavel supported his position by documenting a conversation with Maḥmūd ʿImād, a president of a Native Court and a "Muslim judge." Clavel asked the judge how he would feel if he found a European teaching Islamic law. The judge responded:

> Why not? . . . Unfortunately, we have today a wave of retrograde and exclusivist scholasticism wherein a deplorable atavism has rendered the teaching of Muslim law if not impossible then at least very difficult. . . . Was it not the Prophet himself who established the principle of free learning? He said: "Seek knowledge, even as far as China."
>
> In the Constantinople Law School . . . the procedure is to translate the works of Muslim law and harmonize them with the laws of Europe. This is taught by non-Muslim professors. . . . If the caliph's government approves these publications, could it be impermissible to allow the same authors to teach? To be certain, if today we had foreigners teaching in the schools of law of Beirut, Cairo, and in the great cities of Europe, it would all be to the advantage of Islam.[83]

These are purportedly the words of an Egyptian judge, but the agenda put forth was also Clavel's own.

It is obvious that Clavel was an exponent of French paternalism in the Egyptian legal sphere. More important, however, and to date unrecognized in Egyptian legal history, is that French scholars like Clavel consistently knocked on the doors of Islamic legal scholarship in Egypt, trying to find any point of entry. They wrote and thought about Islamic law at the French Faculty between 1900 and 1923 when they were marginalized at the Cairo Faculty. In these same years, the French brought Egyptians to France on scholarships, to train them at the *licence* and doctoral levels. In 1923, when the Egyptians assumed control of the Cairo Faculty, Egyptians themselves opened the doors to French professors from the French Faculty and France.

The French professors who were invited back to the Cairo Faculty were knowledgeable about Islamic law and had been thinking about it in scholarly ways for more than twenty years. Their minds regarding Islamic law were already somewhat made up, their agendas for its reform were already in place, and the Egyptian professors who controlled the Egyptian faculty after 1923 and would shape the future of its curriculum had been trained by them in France. French ideas about the reform of Egyptian and Islamic law would thereafter be pursued by their Egyptian students who taught in the departments of Franco-Egyptian law.

[83] Ibid.

9

The Flourishing of Advanced Studies after 1923

The years between the mid-1920s and the mid-1950s marked a distinctive and creative era in the history of legal thought in Egypt. As Egyptians established the upper hand in controlling the administration of the law schools and the future of legal scholarship, their moment in the sun was characterized by diverse approaches and ideas, cross-cultural and multilingual engagements, methodological and philosophical rigor, theoretical awareness on a world-class order, piously construed innovations in Islamic legal thought, and careful experiments with the modernization of classical Islamic laws and methods. Egyptian jurists who were already publishing on Islamic legal topics in the 1920s displayed unmistakable shifts during the 1930s and 1940s.

In this period known as the "interwar," scholars collaborated and debated in offering competing visions for the path of revival, reform, and reapplication of Islamic law. It was a time when Egyptian jurists were valued at international conferences on comparative law, when they were able and willing to appear at such conferences, and when they were eager to participate. It was a time of unprecedented originality in Islamic legal publishing. Authors also recognized original scholarship as intellectual property, incentivizing creativity.

The Cairo Faculty facilitated this flourishing of advanced research and new pedagogy in all areas of law after 1923. As the Cairo Faculty gained greater independence from foreign control, younger Egyptians who had recently received doctorates in France assumed deanships and teaching posts in civil, criminal, commercial, public, and administrative law, political economy, and in at least one case, Sharia.[1] At the same time as they worked to Egyptianize the faculty ranks and Arabize the *licence* curriculum, they revived French intellectual and legal influence that had been marginalized since the departure of Édouard Lambert in 1907. In turn, these Egyptian professors spearheaded a new enthusiasm for comparative law, European legal theory, and international legal history.

The technical dimension of Islamic legal revivalism experienced a high point within the context of the Cairo Faculty's flourishing when reform-minded Egyptian scholars from the Sharia College and Dār al-ʿUlūm joined the Cairo Faculty as professors in the Sharia department. The Sharia professors collaborated and

[1] See Dasūqī, *Muḥammad Yūsuf Mūsá*, for the career of one such Egyptian.

Islamic Legal Revival: Reception of European Law and Transformations in Islamic Legal Thought in Egypt, 1875–1952. First Edition. Leonard Wood.

competed with their colleagues in the Franco-Egyptian departments, and they lent their energies to new efforts in advanced and comparative research.

Broader ideological trends provided context and impetus for new scholarship in the 1930s. Egyptian nationalism coalesced with a wave of Islamic political sentiment, making students and teachers more interested in reform of Islamic law and its advanced study. Professors of Franco-Egyptian law especially shared in enthusiasm for universalism and international progress in comparative legal study and legislation.

Between 1923 and 1952, professors in the Sharia department served the ambition of Islamic legal revival by producing reformist treatises on Islamic doctrine in various fields: contract law, criminal law, procedural law, administrative law, constitutional law, and legal theory.[2] Portions of this scholarship resulted from their interactions with colleagues in the Franco-Egyptian departments. The social and professional interactions between professors of Franco-Egyptian law and Sharia were collegial, but their publications reveal competition for control of the terms, frameworks, and content of comparative law and modern Islamic legal thought.

The Cairo Faculty after 1923 became a lively center for advanced research and comparative law not only because of its motivated Egyptian faculty, but also because it was the home of a newly created graduate program offering diplomas and doctorates. The courses in these programs were more advanced and experimental than those offered at the *licence* level. Professors required students to study issues in the legal system in depth, and students were exposed to the most sophisticated theories and critical considerations from European legal scholarship.[3] Courses introduced students to French-style comparative law and pioneered new directions in comparative Islamic-European legal research. The fruits of these labors appeared in the published dissertations of doctoral students, in the books of the professors, and in the Faculty's law journal, *Majallat al-qānūn wa-l-iqtiṣād/Revue de droit et économie politique*, which became the most prestigious law journal in the Arab world. As a result of these advancements, the Cairo Faculty sent its graduates to teach in law faculties throughout the Arab world, including Lebanon, Syria, Iraq, and Saudi Arabia.

EGYPTIANIZATION, ARABIZATION, AND REVIVAL OF FRENCH AND LAMBERTIAN INFLUENCE

Political changes between 1919 and 1923 opened the way to changes at the Cairo Faculty. Nationalist uprisings ensued in March 1919 when Britain rebuffed Egypt's independence bid at the Paris Peace Conference. After three years of failing to reach an agreement with nationalists, Britain declared Egyptian independence

[2] Lambert also cited 1923 as a turning point in El-Araby, *Conscription des neutres*, ix.

[3] On "international general jurisprudence," see Diego Eduardo López Medina, "Comparative Jurisprudence" (S. J. D. diss., Harvard Law School, 2001), 7.

in 1922. Although Sultan Fu'ād I became King Fu'ād I and a new constitution divided power between his ruling house and a parliament, Egypt's independence was only ever partial.[4] Britain officially retained control over only Egyptian foreign policy, the Suez Canal, and Sudan, but it manipulated the monarchy and the parliamentary process to sustain its occupation until the Egyptian Revolution of 1952.

As mentioned earlier, the Cairo Faculty changed names several times between 1914 and 1952. The Egyptian University was founded in 1923, and in 1925, the Law Faculty was made one of four tertiary schools undergirding the foundation of the new university.[5] Throughout the 1920s and 1930s Egyptian officials at the Egyptian University's central administration tried to remove Europeans from deanships and chairs in the different faculties.[6] It was a difficult project. They faced resistance from high-level British personnel, famously from High Commissioner Lord George Lloyd. Moreover, when chairs opened for new appointments, applicants from different nations continued to appear as they had for similar posts before 1923. The competition for appointments fell between Egyptian, British, French, Italian, and other international candidates, with embassies lobbying on behalf of their respective candidates.

At the Law Faculty, Egyptian deans—after 1923, the deans were all Egyptian but one[7]—and professors assumed new levels of control. They acquired the power to change the curriculum and teaching procedures, but lacked total control over faculty appointments and the hiring and firing of other personnel. It is difficult to generalize beyond this about the power Egyptian deans and professors exercised. Different offices, persons, and committees were vested with different powers at different times. The priorities of the Egyptian deans and professors were Egyptianization of teaching personnel, Arabization of the curriculum and legal scholarship, and the reintroduction of French academic influence.

Egyptians exercised in any event more power after 1923 than they had beforehand. Within the Law Faculty, there were deans, vice-deans, department chairs, and a faculty board. They were all professors of Franco-Egyptian law, except that the vice-dean was most often a professor from the Sharia department. Beyond the faculty were university presidents, university deans, the university administration, the university faculty board, and the Ministry of Education.

After 1923, the Law Faculty expanded the number of Egyptian teaching personnel at the expense of European personnel. For the academic year 1929–30, there were twenty-three Egyptian and nine European instructors at all levels. If the count includes only full and assistant professors, there were nine Egyptians and nine Europeans. In 1938–39, the count of full and assistant professors was seventeen Egyptians to nine Europeans. In the same year, however, Europeans still held the department chairs in public, international, and criminal law, and political economy, and they held on to department chairs and their positions on the governing

[4] See pp. 23–4 and 45–6.

[5] See Chapter 7, n. 1, on the multiple names of the Cairo Faculty. In 1952, the King Fu'ād I University in Cairo became Cairo University, and the Law Faculty became known as the Cairo University Law Faculty. See Reid, *Cairo University*.

[6] Ibid., 100–56.

[7] See Table 7.3.

board into the 1940s. These European professors were by such time all continental Europeans, not British.

The French used every political and diplomatic lever available to safeguard positions within the faculty ranks. Whenever a position opened at the school, French professors and diplomats vigorously petitioned officials in Cairo and Paris to support the French candidate. Arguments for mobilization were still made in terms of the need to "defend and develop French culture."[8] The Ministries of Education and Foreign Affairs considered professors partners in sustaining this objective, as always. Moreover, despite the nationalism of the Egyptian leaders of the Cairo Faculty and the resurgence of Arabic in the curriculum, they pursued a purposeful revival of French cultural, linguistic, and legal influence. After 1923, at which date the Cairo Faculty stopped teaching law in English and converted *licence* classes to Arabic, the Faculty also decided to offer some law courses for the *licence* in French. Revised admissions standards required proficiency in Arabic and stated a preference for proficiency in French.

EGYPTIAN DEANS AND PROFESSORS

The lawyer-politician ʿAlī Māhir became the first Egyptian dean and served in 1923–24.[9] The second post-independence dean was the jurist ʿAbd al-Ḥamid Abū Hayf, who served in 1924–25. The fourth post-independence dean, Aḥmad Amīn, served in 1926–27. The third post-independence dean, the Frenchman Léon Duguit, served in 1925–26 and was an exceptional case. The school's official historical narrative ignores his appointment, but it was a meaningful event.[10] No Frenchman had been appointed to the position since Lambert in 1907. No European would be appointed to the position after Duguit. If the Egyptians had already succeeded in appointing two Egyptian deans in a high period of nationalism, why did they appoint a Frenchman to the prestigious post?

That Léon Duguit's one-year deanship has been ignored in books on Egyptian legal history reflects how that literature has under-appreciated the sophistication of Egyptian legal academia during the interwar period. The Cairo Faculty's official historical narrative claims that Duguit was hired to "to assist in the organization of the school as a university faculty."[11] This explanation sadly misses the point. Duguit was internationally famous and a distinguished scholar of administrative and public law. A globally recognized proponent of syndicalism, he was affiliated with the cause of "social" jurists and interested in sociology and sociological

[8] Nantes/Cairo 171, Untitled document beginning "Une liason étroite . . ." 1935. See also Reid, *Cairo University*, 90–93; Amin, *My Life*, 185.

[9] He was Prime Minister in 1936, 1939–40, and 1952. See Arthur Goldschmidt, *Biographical Dictionary of Modern Egypt* (Boulder, CO: Lynne Rienner, 2000), 117.

[10] Jāmiʿat al-Qāhirah, *al-ʿĪd al-miʾawī li-Kulliyyat al-Ḥuqūq* (Cairo: Jāmiʿat al-Qāhirah, Kulliyyat al-Ḥuqūq, 1980), 25.

[11] *Al-ʿĪd al-miʾawī*, 25. See also Nazih N. M. Ayubi, *Over-Stating the Arab State* (London: I. B. Tauris, 1995), 8, 20, 36, 398.

jurisprudence.[12] He was a colleague of Émile Durkheim at the University of Bordeaux, where they held chairs, and a supporter of comparative law and an intellectual ally of Lambert.[13] He regarded his lectures on public law in Cairo seriously enough to publish them.[14]

In Duguit, the Cairo Faculty thus hired a famous intellectual, a proponent of higher legal and political theory, a proponent of social science and scientific thought, a supporter of comparative law, a social jurist, and a Frenchman. Whatever Duguit may or may not have accomplished during his short tenure as dean, and whichever individuals opposed or supported his appointment, his presence symbolized change. The British deans were out, the Egyptians were in; and French, Francophone, and continental European influence had returned.

With Francophone personnel reinstated, the theories and preoccupations of higher-level French legal scholarship could now be issues of concern at the Cairo Faculty. Duguit's placement represents the integration into the curriculum of the continental European methods and sensibilities described in Chapter 7. The hope of Lambert for the school in 1907 became plausible in the mid-1920s.

The new Egyptian deans and professors were nationalists and anti-imperialists who also admired French law and culture. They held doctorates from France and had studied with luminaries of the period such as Édouard Lambert, Albert Wahl, Henri Lévy-Ullmann, and Marc Desserteaux. Their doctoral theses had treated matters of European, Egyptian, Islamic, international, and comparative law. Of 23 Egyptian teachers at the Cairo Faculty in 1929–30, at least sixteen held doctorates in law from France. Among them were ʿAbd al-Ḥamīd Badawī (Grenoble, 1912), ʿAbd al-Ḥamīd Abū Hayf (Toulouse, 1912), Muḥammad Kāmil Mursī (Dijon, 1914), ʿAbd al-Salām Dhuhnī (Lyon, double doctorate, 1914, 1921), Muḥammad Ṣāliḥ (Grenoble, 1922), ʿAbd al-Fattāh al-Sayyid (Dijon, 1922), Muḥammad Ṣādiq Fahmī (Paris, 1923), Kāmil Amīn Malash (Paris, 1924), Muḥammad ʿAbd Allāh al-ʿArabī (Lyon, 1924), ʿAlī Muḥammad Badawī (ca. 1924),[15] ʿAbd al-Razzāq al-Sanhūrī (Lyon, double doctorate, 1925, 1926), Muḥammad ʿAbd al-Jawād (Lyon, 1926), (see Fig. 9.1), Maḥmūd Iḥsān Zuhdī (Paris, 1927), Muḥammad Muṣṭafá Qulalī (Paris, 1927), Muḥammad Ḥilmī Baḥjat (Paris, 1929), and ʿAbd al-Ḥakīm Rifāʿī (Paris, 1929).

The five professors holding doctorates from Lyon were students of Édouard Lambert. Dhuhnī, Fahmī, al-ʿArabī, al-Sanhūrī, and al-Jawād published their theses as part of his *Séminaire Oriental* series.[16] Although al-Sanhūrī has become the most, if not the only, famous figure among the new Franco-Egyptian jurists, he was not their leader. As can be seen from the dating of dissertations, books, and first faculty appointments, seven other scholars preceded al-Sanhūrī on the path from a doctoral program in France to the Cairo Faculty. If only the Lyon group is counted, al-Sanḥūrī was preceded by three others: Dhuhnī, Fahmī, and

[12] See pp. 119–20. [13] See Chapter 7.

[14] Léon Duguit, *Leçons de droit public général faites à la Faculté de Droit de l'Université Égyptienne pendant les mois de janvier, février et mars 1926* (Paris: E. de Boccard, 1926), 7–21.

[15] His doctoral institution is unknown.

[16] See Lambert, *L'Institut orientale*. See also Bibliography for the theses.

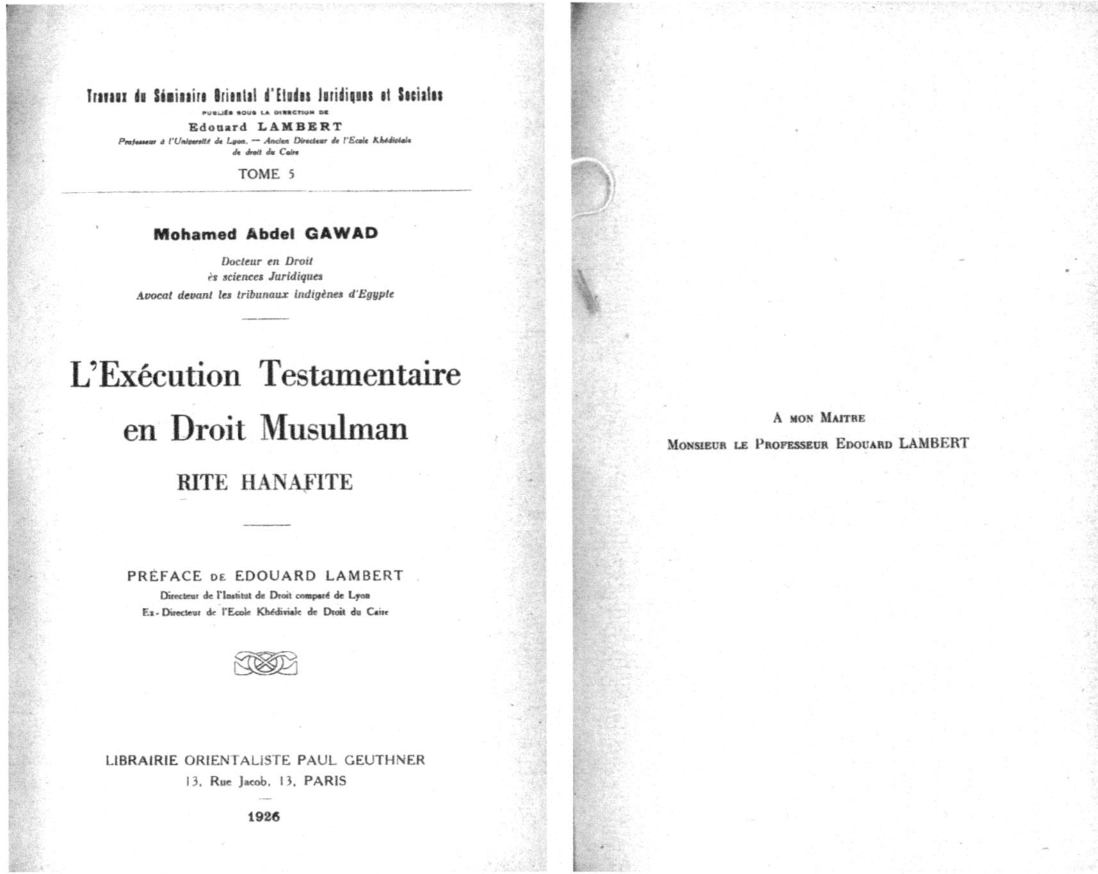
Travaux du Séminaire Oriental d'Etudes Juridiques et Sociales
PUBLIÉS SOUS LA DIRECTION DE
Edouard LAMBERT
Professeur à l'Université de Lyon. — Ancien Directeur de l'Ecole Khédiviale de droit du Caire
TOME 5

Mohamed Abdel GAWAD

Docteur en Droit
ès sciences Juridiques
Avocat devant les tribunaux indigènes d'Egypte

L'Exécution Testamentaire en Droit Musulman

RITE HANAFITE

PRÉFACE DE EDOUARD LAMBERT
Directeur de l'Institut de Droit comparé de Lyon
Ex-Directeur de l'Ecole Khédiviale de Droit du Caire

LIBRAIRIE ORIENTALISTE PAUL GEUTHNER
13, Rue Jacob, 13, PARIS

1926

A MON MAITRE
MONSIEUR LE PROFESSEUR EDOUARD LAMBERT

Fig. 9.1 Title page and first dedication page of Muḥammad ʿAbd al-Jawād's *L'Exécution testamentaire en droit musulman* (1926). Muḥammad ʿAbd al-Jawād dedicated his 1926 dissertation to his mentor, Édouard Lambert.

al-ʿArabī.[17] In Lambert's preface to al-ʿArabī's 1924 dissertation, Lambert named his previous Egyptian doctoral students and remarked that Dhuhnī and Fahmī were his "favorite students."[18] He mentioned that they had recently embarked on a program to transform the Cairo Faculty, and he complimented Cairo as the "brain [and] the scientific center of the Islamic world." As of that moment, Lambert had nothing to say of the now-renowned al-Sanhūrī.

As students of French-style comparativism and enthusiasts of the above-outlined universalist tenets, this generation of professors viewed the French language as essential to cultivating advanced and comparative studies. It was the lingua franca of international comparative law. Thus, even as they were publishing and teaching in Arabic and realizing the Arabization of instruction and published scholarship, they were recultivating French as a second language of instruction.

In 1929, Dean Muḥammad Kāmil Mursī expressed disappointment with the level of French among students.[19] "The student of Egyptian law," he observed, "cannot do without foreign references of law and in particular the works of French *doctrine*. Right now many Egyptian students cannot read French well enough. A source of the problem is that they do not receive teaching in French language. This needs to be improved especially so we can strengthen the connection between the *licence* section and the doctoral section."[20] He created a one-year program at the Faculty of the Arts to educate students in the humanities, arts, and basic sciences, and he instituted twelve hours per week of French instruction. This program was for students who showed promise but were unprepared for the rigors of the law school. The Cairo Faculty then established new French-language classes at the *licence* level in Franco-Egyptian criminal law, commercial law, and parts of civil law.[21] This policy was later extended to public law. These classes had been taught in Arabic since 1923—criminal law was taught by Jean Grandmoulin, commercial by G. L'Abbatté, and aspects of civil law by Albert Chéron.[22] The policy led to the creation of four posts for junior lecturers, chosen from the best students who had studied in French and intended to enroll in the graduate courses. The Egyptian deans were trying to ensure that Egyptian law students who received Egyptian doctorates in law would one day teach courses at the school in French.

[17] He was preceded by four if one includes Maḥmūd Fatḥī (Mahmoud Fathy), who did not teach at the Cairo Faculty, but whose thesis on the theory of the abuse of rights in Islamic law was the first publication in Lambert's *Séminaire Oriental* series.

[18] El-Araby, *Conscription des neutres*, xvii–xxi.

[19] This policy is confirmed in the exam registers. The annual faculty prospectuses of the 1920s and 1930s (*taqwīmāt*, *annuaires*) printed exams from the previous year. On Mursī, see Nantes/Cairo 171, "Le Réorganisation de la Faculté de Droit: Un Intéressant rapport du doyen de la Faculté Dr. Mohamed Kamel Moursy Bey," untitled newspaper clipping, ca. 1929.

[20] Ibid. See also Nantes/Cairo 171, "Développement des connaissances de langue française," an unsigned, undated memo in a dossier on Muḥammad Kāmil Mursī's reforms, and "Un Projet de réforme: Le Doyen de la Faculté de Droit, Kamel Moursi Bey, demande le développement de l'enseignement du français," unsigned newspaper clipping, ca. Sep. 16, 1930. See also "Règlement intérieur de la Faculté de Droit," *Journal officiel du gouvernement égyptien* 60,66 (July 20, 1933): 1–3.

[21] Nantes/Cairo 171, "Réforme à la Faculté de Droit," *Journal officiel du gouvernement égyptien* 99 (Nov. 3, 1930).

[22] Nantes/Cairo 171, "Le Réorganisation de la Faculté de Droit."

The revival of French language, law, and cultural prestige did not mean precisely a full-scale return of personnel from France. Among the Frenchmen serving on the faculty in the 1920s and 1930s were Albert Chéron, Lucien Chéron, Grandmoulin, Léon Mazeaud, J. A. Boyé, and Léon Duguit. However, the combined number of Italians, Belgians, and British personnel teaching in French usually was greater than the number of French personnel. The French revival was French not in the mere sense of things properly and uniquely French—it was also a revival of things more broadly Francophone, European-continental, and civil law related, all as distinct from British and common law related.

In the 1920s only a few courses were taught and examined, in whole or in part, in French. In the 1940s, fewer *licence* classes were taught in French. In the two years before the 1952 revolution, there were no classes remaining in French at the *licence* level. The graduate program, however, followed a different path. When graduate classes appeared in the late 1920s, almost all classes were taught in French. This situation continued through the 1940s. The key exception was graduate classes listed under "comparative civil law," which were taught in Arabic.

Before discussing the "comparative civil law" classes further, it is important to underline that advanced instruction and research in comparative Islamic-European law was taking place during the early 1930s, in Arabic, and alongside advanced studies in comparative civil law. These were classes taught by ʿAbd al-Razzāq al-Sanhūrī and Muḥammad Ṣādiq Fahmī, among other Franco-Egyptian professors. Under this rubric, they lectured on sophisticated topics in civil law and introduced students to fundamentals of legal theory and comparative law as they had encountered those subjects in France. Notably, "comparative civil law" also comprised advanced Sharia study. The teachers for these lessons were Aḥmad Ibrāhīm, ʿAbd al-Wahhāb Khallāf, and Muḥammad Abū Zahrah.

A look at the composition of grading panels for the 1938–39 graduate exams reveals that several of the panels were composed of one European and one Egyptian (see Table 9.1). A tutelage system was in place in which European faculty members were ostensibly mentoring Egyptian faculty members in the work of training graduate students. Whether the Egyptian professors really embraced this system or not, as they publicly claimed, cannot be known. One advantage of having Europeans on grading juries is that it boosted the prestige of the doctoral program in the eyes of French legal academicians.

The Cairo Faculty's favorable view of French law and influence still had limits, however, for the Egyptian professors were nationalists. They ensured that French law, personnel, and language came second in priority to Egyptian law, personnel, and Arabic. The school was trying to produce younger Egyptian scholars who would one day assume the law-teaching jobs held by Europeans, and so the number of Frenchmen appointed to law-teaching posts remained limited.

In a related move, the Cairo Faculty adopted an aggressive posture toward the French Faculty and its graduates who obtained a French *licence*. In 1930, the Cairo Faculty abolished the equivalency exam that allowed holders of the non-Egyptian *licence* degree to enter the Egyptian Bar. This policy adversely affected graduates of the French Faculty who held such degrees as well as any other graduate who

Table 9.1. Examination boards for exams in the graduate diploma courses.

Diploma	Language	Subject	Examiners
Private Law	Arabic	Droit civil (*qānūn madanī*)	ʿA. R. al-Sanhūrī Wadīʿ Faraj ʿA. M. Khayyāl
Private Law	French / Arabic	Droit civil comparé et approfondi	G. Stephani Muḥ. Ṣādiq Fahmī
Private Law	Arabic	Sharia	Aḥ. Ibrāhīm ʿAbd al-Wahāb Najjār
Private Law Elective	French	Droit commercial	Gaston Caby ʿA. M. Khayyāl
Private Law Elective	French	Droit roman	V. Arangio-Ruiz M. ʿA. al-Munʿim Badr
Private Law Elective	French	Droit international privé	M. Siotto-Pintor Ḥāmid Zakī
Public Law	French	Droit international public	M. Siotto-Pintor Maḥ. Sāmī Junaynah
Public Law	French	Droit public	P. Dubois-Richard Waḥīd Raʾfat
Public Law	French	Droit criminal	Albert Chéron ʿAlī Muḥ. Badawī
Public Law Elective	French	Histoire du droit public	V. Arangio-Ruiz Jouget
Public Law Elective	French	Finances et législation financière	Umberto Ricci Aḥ. ʿAbd al-Wahhāb
Political Economy	French	Économie politique approfondie	C. Bresciani-Turroni ʿA. Ḥ. al-Rifāʿī
Political Economy	French	Hist. des doctrines, faits économiques	T. H. Frazer C. Bresciani-Turroni
Political Economy	French	Finances et législation financière	Umberto Ricci Aḥ. ʿAbd al-Wahhāb
Political Economy Elective	French	Economie et législation sociales comparés	T. H. Frazer C. Bresciani-Turroni

Compiled from Jāmiʿat Fuʾād al-Awwal, *Taqwīm Kulliyyat al-Ḥuqūq 1938–1939* (1938), appendix, "Asʾilāt al-ikhtibārāt al-taḥrīriyyah fī l-sanah al-dirāsiyyah 1937–1938." For each exam, the examiners are ordered top-to-bottom as in the source.

had recently obtained a European *licence* elsewhere. In addition, any individual holding a French law degree was required to obtain exceptional permission from the Cairo Faculty dean in order to pursue a doctorate at the Cairo Faculty. These policies were somewhat ironic since French universities and the French Bar accepted holders of the *licence en droit égyptien* without any restrictions. The exam was eventually reinstated, but only after considerable struggle by the French Faculty and France's embassy in Cairo.[23]

[23] Beginning in 1899 the Cairo Faculty offered the equivalency exam every year. Graduates of the French Faculty had been among the principal beneficiaries. The Cairo Faculty's threat to cancel the exam for the first time in many years was almost natural given the anti-French inclinations of some British personnel at the Ministry of Education and the Cairo Faculty in the early 1900s. This longstanding problem is documented in Nantes/Cairo 171 (and 159), "Aide-mémoire au sujet de l'équivalence des licences en droit français et égyptien."

FRANCO-EGYPTIAN SCHOLARSHIP

Egyptian jurists who returned to the Cairo Faculty after completing doctorates in France wrote books to usher in a new era of Arabic legal scholarship.[24] These books had novel characteristics. First, the books transformed Franco-Egyptian legal scholarship from English and French into Arabic. This involved stabilizing the Arabic lexicon of translations for French legal terms and concepts, a project begun but left unfinished in the nineteenth century.[25] Second, the books introduced to Arabic-Egyptian scholarship the gamut of legal theories, methodological sensibilities, and ancillary topics known in French legal academia (international general jurisprudence). New Arabic books appeared explaining Roman law, the Egyptian civil codes, Egyptian criminal law, Western legal history, and the various schools of European and international critical legal theory—the schools of historical, conceptual, and social jurisprudence, as well as others. Notable were books by ʿAbd al-Salām Dhuhnī, Muḥammad Kāmil Mursī, Muḥammad Ṣādiq Fahmī, Muḥammad Ṣāliḥ, Aḥmad Ṣafwat, and ʿAbd al-Razzāq al-Sanhūrī.

The most senior of Lambert's doctoral students was ʿAbd al-Salām Dhuhnī, who penned long treatises in the 1910s and 1920s. The first book he produced for Egyptian students after returning from Lyon was an Arabic, six-hundred-page memorandum on Roman law, which explained Roman legal concepts in Arabic and ventured to provide definitive Arabic translations for Latin terms.[26] In 1924, Dhuhnī published *Fī l-iltizāmāt: al-Naẓariyyah al-ʿāmmah* (Obligations: The General Theory). In 1926, he published *al-Amwāl* (Property) on European and Franco-Egyptian property law. Both books focused on creating definitive Arabic translations for French and Roman terms and concepts in law. They also aimed to evaluate Egyptian law through reference to theoretical frameworks that were predominant in European legal academia.

Other books supported this effort to build Arabic-language, Franco-Egyptian law scholarship. In 1926, Muḥammad Ṣādiq Fahmī produced a commentary on the Egyptian Civil Code that situated the code in a context of European legal history and legal theory.[27] In 1930, he followed with a book for Egyptian students that explained the European theory of contract law, in Arabic, but presenting this theory with special reference to Franco-Egyptian law.[28] In 1931, Muḥammad Ṣāliḥ published *Uṣūl al-taʿahhudāt* (Theory of Obligations), which sought to create a definitive Arabic lexicon for the general theory of contract in civil law, and which commented on Franco-Egyptian law through references to theoretical frameworks from Europe.

ʿAbd al-Razzāq al-Sanhūrī made his mark in this new stream of publications when he returned from France to join the Civil Law department in 1926. Al-Sanhūrī's first books brought to bear on his study of Franco-Egyptian civil law

[24] See Appendix. [25] See pp. 155–6 and 238–9.
[26] ʿAbd al-Salām Dhuhnī, *al-Qānūn al-rūmānī* (n.p, n.d.).
[27] Muḥammad Ṣādiq Fahmī, *Sharḥ al-qānūn al-madanī* (Miṣr: Maṭbaʿat al-Iʿtimād, 1926).
[28] This book first appeared as a memorandum. Muḥammad Ṣādiq Fahmī, *Mudhakkirāt fī naẓariyyat al-iltizāmāt* (Miṣr: Maṭbaʿat al-ʿŪluww, 1930).

the full force of "social" critique that was popular in Europe. His first manuscript following graduate school, *ʿAqd al-ījar* (Lease Contracts), originally appeared as a widely circulated draft in 1929.[29] The book critiqued individualism in the Franco-Egyptian rent laws and incorporated the critical evaluations of Bufnoir, Gény, Lévy-Ulmann, and Saleilles. The first chapter was entitled "Hiring Contracts from Social, Economic, and Legal Standpoints." Al-Sanhūrī spent the next years preparing the groundwork for his monumental *Naẓariyyat al-ʿaqd* (Theory of Contract) (1934), an explanation of the Native Civil Code and the theory of obligations. The book furnished a thorough critique of the Native Civil Code from the social-critical standpoint.

This brief review of the new Franco-Egyptian legal literature would be incomplete without mentioning the books on "sources of law" (or "theory of law") that appeared after 1923.[30] Chapter 8 discussed Muḥammad Raʾfat's book on the theory of positive law. This genre was further pursued in the 1920s by Muḥammad Kāmil Mursī, who in 1923 produced *Uṣūl al-qawānīn* (Sources of Laws) based almost entirely on French sources, and Aḥmad Ṣafwat, who in 1924 published *Muqaddimat al-qānūn* (Introduction to Law).[31] Ṣafwat drew ideas from French theorists but also from English theorists such as John Austin, Henry Maine, and Albert Venn Dicey. Al-Sanhūrī contributed to this genre in 1938 with *Uṣūl al-qānūn* (Sources of Law).[32] Al-Sanhūrī situated the current legal systems within their given legal histories—Roman, continental *ius commune*, Arab customary, Islamic, and so forth. These books attempted to acclimatize the Egyptian student to living with two legal systems, the Franco-Egyptian and the Islamic, that each had its own history and theories. But, these books also appear to have aimed to assuage popular concerns about the apparent differences between these systems.

A characteristic of the newer works in the sources of law was that they were less critical of the Franco-Egyptian law than had been the work of Muḥammad Raʾfat.[33] These books adopted universalist premises that guided their elaboration, and implicit defense, of an Egyptian legal system that mixed laws derived from Islamic primary sources and laws derived from other sources, such as modern customs and conceptions of equity, and codes of a foreign genealogy. Aḥmad Ṣafwat, for example, posited that "law" (*qānūn*) in modern Egypt had, and should have, six sources: custom (*ʿādah*), religion (*dīn*), state-made legislation (*tashrīʿ*), opinions of jurists and commentators (*arāʾ al-fuqahāʾ wa-l-shurrāḥ*), court precedents (*aḥkām al-maḥākim*), and principles of justice and equity (*qawāʿid al-ʿadl wa-l-inṣāf*).[34]

The Franco-Egyptian doctrinal works could be argued to have supported "secularizing" trends in Egyptian legal thought, at least insofar as the term is understood by Talal Asad and like-minded theorists. The concept of "secularism," if understood as a simple separation between religion and state, has minimal currency among historians of this era of Egyptian history because Egypt did not officially

[29] See n. 41. [30] See pp. 126–7 and 188.

[31] Ṣafwat, *Muqaddimat al-qānūn*.

[32] In 1936, al-Sanhūrī taught "Introduction to the Study of Law" to first-year *licence* students. See al-Sanhūrī and Abū Sitīt, *Uṣūl al-qānūn*.

[33] Esmeir, *Juridical Humanity*, 48–53. [34] Ṣafwat, *Muqaddimat al-qānūn*, 95.

pursue this objective. In place of this understanding, Asad and Hussein Ali Agrama have articulated a more helpful and now widely recognized understanding of secularism for Egypt.[35] They suggest that for the purpose of studying Egypt and certain other places, secularism refers not to a situation where the state and religion are wholly separated, but to a situation where the state, as opposed to a class of politically independent jurists, controls the articulation of Sharia, partly by relegating Sharia to more limited jurisdictions than were known in the past, and also by subsuming Sharia into the field of state-made and state-controlled law and thereby subjecting Sharia to substantive manipulation. Thus Asad, in an often-cited discussion of the emergence of "secular modernity" in Egypt, characterized Ṣafwat's writing as an effort to "adapt Islamic ethics and law to Western jurisprudential thinking."[36] A similar perspective might be offered about al-Sanhūrī. For al-Sanhūrī writing in the 1920s, Islam was a "religion and a state." However, he added to this aphorism his view that where the state's law serves the ends of Islam, the state's law is therefore compliant with and part of the Sharia order.[37]

Ṣafwat and al-Sanhūrī, like other Muslim Franco-Egyptian jurists, appear to have been consciously trying to avoid association with the aspiration of separating religion and state. These jurists knew that secularism was a concept widely considered antagonistic to Islam. They considered themselves pious Muslims. The Muslim Franco-Egyptians were not necessarily opponents of Islamic legal revivalism, but rather lived with it and to some extent within it. They tried to shape its course from within, where possible.

Ṣafwat's book does not advocate explicitly for a separation of religion and state, but it does make ample references to European doctrinalists tied in one way or another to the Lambertian style of thought. What can this mean for present-day analysis? It means that there may be no problem with investigating, between the lines, aspects of "secular modernity" and "secularizing" trends in writings by Egyptian jurists, through methods and concepts developed by Asad and Agrama. But it also suggests, on the other hand, that a more proximate influence on Franco-Egyptian thinking was Lambertian-style universalism and associated ideas.[38] Ṣafwat was giving expression to a type of Islamic belief, and a type of Islamic legal thought, that held that a genuinely Islamic society could accept manifold sources of law. One notes this bearing in mind, as the Franco-Egyptians did, that Islamic *fiqh* had its own deeply-rooted traditions to this effect.[39]

Generally speaking, Ṣafwat's immediate colleagues were seeking pious innovations within Islamic law, and not necessarily ways around Islam wholesale; they were seeking authentic Islamic reform, not necessarily a qualified or cautious adaptation of Islamic belief to Western legal theory. Ṣafwat, like Lambert—and

[35] See Asad, *Formations of the Secular*, 205–27; Hussein Ali Agrama, *Questioning Secularism: Islam, Sovereignty, and the Rule of Law in Modern Egypt* (Chicago: University of Chicago Press, 2012), 23–36.

[36] Asad, *Formations of the Secular*, 240.

[37] See al-Sanhuri, "al-Dīn wa-l-dawlah fī l-islām."

[38] This style of thought was also articulated in certain ways by Muḥammad ʿAbduh and certain of his devotees.

[39] See Frank E. Vogel, "Siyāsa Sharʿiyya," *Encyclopaedia of Islam*, 2nd ed.; Wood, "Legislation as an Instrument of Islamic Law."

slightly less than al-Sanhūrī in his *Uṣūl al-qānūn*—was most likely trying to avoid the very kind of "secular vs. Islamic" conflict in Egyptian society that present-day scholars, writing about the emergence of secularism in legal thought, risk imposing on this period and Islamic thought in general. On a cultural plane, the Franco-Egyptians likely saw such a battle as a losing one. In this regard, certain present-day scholars, Asad and Agrama among them, share premises with harder-line Islamic thinkers who rejected, and still reject, Franco-Egyptian approaches to the conception of Islam and the Sharia-compliant legal order.

For the time being, the point is to put this genre of books on the map of Egyptian legal and intellectual history. More could be said about these books—they merit further attention for how they advanced Egyptian legal scholarship and illustrate the interactions between European and Egyptian legal thought. If one seeks to assess the precise nature of the reception of European legal theory within Egyptian scholarship, these are central texts.

The reception of European law in Egypt during the nineteenth and early twentieth centuries did not, therefore, begin and end with the installation of new codes and the activation of new courts that applied the codes. The reception of European law and legal thought also occurred in the world of academic thought and *doctrine*.[40] Most of that new thought and *doctrine* came from the law schools, particularly the Cairo Faculty.

The highest stage of Egyptian engagement with European legal ideas occurred in the 1920s, 1930s, and 1940s with the creation of this Franco-Egyptian *doctrine*. This was the period when Egyptians moved to a new stage of interpreting, critiquing, and elaborating upon their codes, fully equipped with the latest methods and theories from European legal thought. The interwar period was also the first time in which Egyptian scholars realized the extent to which their Franco-Egyptian codes had been written according to individualist and capitalistic premises of eighteenth- and nineteenth-century legal, political, and economic thought. This recognition provided the basis for a new era of social critique of Egyptian laws, a process that culminated in al-Sanhūrī's writing of a new Egyptian Civil Code between 1934 and 1948. This engagement with European theories and ideas in Arabic would also affect the ways that jurists in the Sharia department of the Cairo Faculty approached the study of Sharia.

VISIONARY SCHOLARS, ADVANCED STUDIES, AND THE GRADUATE PROGRAM

After Egyptianization, Arabization, and the revival of French proficiency, the priorities of the new deans and professors were to improve education at the *licence* level, to develop a graduate program that would be competitive with programs in

[40] On the meaning of *doctrine*, see Chapter 6.

France, and to use a graduate program as the starting point for promoting advanced scholarship. The professors envisioned a movement of comparative law studies flourishing in the graduate program. They pursued these aims simultaneously.

Founded in the mid-1920s, the graduate program only started to meet the expectations of its founders in the early 1930s. Among the first to publicly envision the pursuit of advanced studies was Muḥammad Ṣādiq Fahmī, the new assistant professor of civil law. Although al-Sanhūrī has received the most credit for establishing advanced studies at the Faculty, his colleagues such as Fahmī also made contributions.[41]

Muḥammad Ṣādiq Fahmī wrote a French article for *L'Égypte contemporaine* in 1924 on comparative law in Egypt.[42] *L'Égypte contemporaine* was the most prestigious social science journal in Egypt at the time, having interests in law, political economy, and legal and economic statistics. The article explained the author's vision of the future of comparative law; he extolled it as a new field and urged colleagues to take action in advancing its study. Mastering comparative law, Fahmī claimed, was essential if Egyptians were to participate in the project of international modernity and development. He viewed the civilized world as moving in the direction of legal cooperation and unification.

Fahmī urged Egyptian students to seek out mentorship of French or Italian teachers.[43] This viewpoint goes some distance in explaining why European professors were able to remain in a tolerant environment during the 1920s and 1930s. It was a view shared by his colleague and future dean, Muḥammad Kāmil Mursī. Throughout the 1920s, European comparativists and doctrinalists visited the Cairo Faculty to lecture. Among them were purportedly Henri Capitant, René Demogue, Henri Lévy-Ullmann, Salvatore Messina, and Édouard Lambert.

In 1926, the Cairo Faculty agreed on the principle of establishing a graduate program leading to a doctorate in laws. There were several impetuses. A graduate program would facilitate comparative studies and assert Egypt's prestige and independence. Egyptians would be empowered to teach Egyptians about Egypt's law and legal heritage. The professors believed that "Egyptian law" had become sufficiently different from French law to merit the creation of a doctoral program wherein (Franco-) Egyptian law was the main interest. In the program's first decade, all doctoral theses examined Egyptian or Islamic law, at least in part.

Although envisioned during Duguit's deanship, the graduate program started classes in 1927–28, the first year of Muḥammad Kāmil Mursī's deanship, which

[41] See Hill, "Islamic Law as a Source."

[42] Mohamed Sadek-Fahmy, "Le Droit comparé: Son utilité particulière en Égypte," *L'Égypte contemporaine* 15 (1923): 397–411. See also Henri Lévy-Ullmann, "De l'Utilité des études comparatives," *Revue de droit* (Québec) 1 (1923): 385–98.

[43] Italians were always on the faculty. Among the European faculty members of this era were Jean Grandmoulin (criminal), Léon Mazeaud (civil), Albert Chéron (civil and criminal), Lucien Chéron (criminal), M. Ritchie (public), Gaston Caby (commercial), Paul Dubois-Richard (public), M. Mouskheli (public), Manfredi Siotto-Pintor (international), Vincente Arangio-Ruiz (history of law), Costantino Bresciani-Turroni (economy), T. H. Frazer (economy), and R. D. Melville (Roman). Among the more obscure faculty were Montbrand (criminal), R. Leballe (civil), G. Stephani (civil), Bésson (civil), and Carfian (public).

lasted from 1928 to 1936. Slightly older than Fahmī, Mursī had obtained his *licence* from the Cairo Faculty in 1910 and a doctorate in law from Dijon in 1914. He was steeped in the French tradition of legal study.

Mursī publicly expressed concern for the "quality" and "intellectual level" of students and teachers involved with the graduate program.[44] When he assumed the deanship, no dissertations had yet passed. Examiners had been asked to employ the standards applied in France, and one European professor sat on any given committee. In the Spring term of 1929, the Cairo Faculty failed all eight dissertations submitted. In a report, Mursī cited the displeasure of French examiners who claimed that students had not mastered their French sources.[45]

One of Mursī's first policies to remedy weakness at the graduate level was to improve the quality of instruction at both the *licence* and graduate levels. Already mentioned earlier was his decision to enhance French instruction in the *licence* curriculum. His idea was that stronger education in French at the *licence* level would lead to stronger research at the doctoral level. Further, claiming that many of his best professors had left for more lucrative positions in government, he launched a campaign to hire better instructors. He hired lawyers out of government offices, among them Najīb al-Hilālī, a royal adviser, Muḥammad ʿAshmāwī Bey, the General Secretary of the Ministry of Education, and Sayyid Muṣṭafá, Chief of the Parquet. He lured Muḥammad Ṣāliḥ from the university's Faculty of Commerce. He also insisted on the necessity of keeping European professors on staff. Their purpose, he said, would be to "nurture this new department so that it can be established on firm ground."[46]

In response to the failed dissertations, the Cairo Faculty prepared a statement explaining how students should craft their scholarship. The technical requirements they established sought to initiate changes in academic publishing practices.[47] The subject could not have been explored previously; dissertations were to pursue original research only. To ensure that requirement, each dissertation topic now needed the dean's approval. Dissertations were required to have a meticulous footnoting apparatus. Students were to footnote all sources and ideas taken from other writers. Students were to use quotation marks for all borrowed language. A point-by-point lesson was given in how to incorporate European punctuation into Arabic prose.[48] A rigid format for quoting, citing, and footnoting books, journals, and legal documents was provided.

The insistence on these standards was a step forward for an institution that wanted to put its graduate program on a par with those of French universities. The Cairo Faculty saw itself as building on old knowledge, developing new knowledge, and protecting the intellectual property of individual scholars. The professors mandated originality and set criteria for judging it. They wanted

[44] Nantes/Cairo 171, "Développement des connaissances de la langue française."

[45] Ibid. [46] Ibid. [47] Al-Jāmiʿah al-Miṣriyyah, *Taqwīm, 1929–1930*, 31.

[48] Students were to use inverted commas for quotations. They were not to change an author's original language within the quotations. Split paragraphs were to be notated with the ellipsis. The dissertation author's commentary or emendation within a quote was to be notated with square brackets. Ibid.

empirical, comparative, and theoretical rigor. A young scholar's reputation would be pinned to the originality and rigor of his dissertation.

It then became possible to speak of a new wave of Arabic-Egyptian legal scholarship and research. The Franco-Egyptian professors saw themselves as implementing the standards of scientific learning and authorship that they had encountered in Europe. Reflecting on his move to the Egyptian University in 1926 after having spent his career in the Sharia College, Aḥmad Amīn's memoir commented on the importance that the Cairo Faculty attached to originality:

> I learnt from this milieu that the difference between the university and the school (*madrasah*) lay in research. The school teaches what is in the books while the university reads books in order to extract something new from them. The school teaches the latest advancements in learning while the university tries to discover the unknown, criticizes the achievements of learning, introduces amendments, replaces the old by the new, destroys one viewpoint and builds up another instead, and so on. This is the university's first and last function: if it does not fulfill it, it is then a school not a university. This was what I understood in the first year I taught at the university; I understood it from what I heard from foreign professors who had undertaken various new researches in their individual fields; I understood it from my association with some orientalists at the university as I came to know what they were doing; and I understood it from a few Egyptian professors who had adopted their plans and used their methods. For this reason I began to try my hat at research in this year, and I chose to offer a course in which my research dealt with dictionaries. . . .[49]

The stage was thereby set for new developments in the Sharia department. Fahmī had reorganized the Faculty into six departments: Private Law, Public Law, Economic Sciences, International Law, Penal Law, and History of Law. The Private Law department housed two sections: Civil and Comparative Law, and Sharia. This arrangement would facilitate cooperation between the professors of Franco-Egyptian civil law and Sharia in teaching programs.

Here, al-Sanhūrī enters the picture. So far, this discussion of the foundations of comparative law in Cairo has scarcely mentioned the Cairo Faculty's most famous comparativist. This is because the foundation of advanced studies was a collective project undertaken by a plurality of professors. Yet with that in mind, the importance of al-Sanhūrī to the graduate program must be recognized.

Al-Sanhūrī's ambition to bring comparative law to Egypt can be traced to 1922, when he was Lambert's doctoral student in Lyon. In memoirs written from that time, he laid out four objectives for the reform of the Cairo Faculty, his alma mater.[50] He intended to establish a doctoral program in comparative law, to improve the study of comparative law, to improve the study of European languages, and to revive Sharia law studies as a facet of comparative law study. Thereafter, decisive moments in the institutionalization of comparative law occurred in

[49] He also mentions that he attended the Congress of Orientalists in Leiden in 1932 and met the orientalist David Margoliouth. Amin, *My Life*, 78–80, 185.

[50] ʿAbd al-Razzāq al-Sanhūrī, *al-Sanhūrī min khilāl awrāqihi*, 56–7.

the years 1926 to 1931, when al-Sanhūrī was an assistant professor, in 1931–33, when he was a full professor, and in 1936–37, when he was dean.

Al-Sanhūrī was absent from the school's faculty for much of the 1930s. He was connected to the Saʿdist political party, and in 1934 a personal fallout with the Wafd Party led to his being ousted from the school. He left for two years.[51] In 1936, the Saʿdist party returned to power in parliament and reinstated al-Sanhūrī as dean. He then left his post permanently after 1937. In the years when he was not present, his Franco-Egyptian colleagues filled his shoes.

ISLAMIC LEGAL REVIVALISM IN THE NEW CURRICULUM

In the Sharia department, a new generation of professors took an interest in the new spirit of Islamic-European comparativism and became proponents of advanced research and new approaches to teaching Islamic law. They collaborated with their Franco-Egyptian colleagues. They were involved in the graduate program. They published books on all aspects of Islamic law, applied and non-applied. They tried to develop *fiqh* in the areas of law where Sharia was not applied in Egypt but where, hypothetically, it could one day be applied. The first and best proof of their efforts is their publications.[52]

As young jurists of Franco-Egyptian law were rising at the Cairo Faculty in the 1920s, older professors of Sharia were still in place but gradually retiring. It took ten years for a new generation of Sharia professors to arrive, partly because of a retirement system that had professors retire twice. The first retirement led to an emeritus term of five years, during which the professor would continue to teach. Thus, although Muḥammad Salāmah retired in 1919, he taught until 1923. Aḥmad Abū al-Fatḥ retired in 1926 but taught until 1931. Muḥammad Zayd retired in 1930 but taught until 1936.

The new generation of Sharia professors came from the Sharia College. In 1924, Shaykh Aḥmad Ibrāhīm—a graduate of Dār al-ʿUlūm who had been teaching at the Sharia College since 1907—assumed the chair of the Sharia section at the Cairo Faculty and took over classes formerly taught by Muḥammad Salāmah

[51] In 1934–36, he assumed the deanship at the newly founded Baghdad Law School, where he developed the *licence* curriculum and created a fourth-year course comparing civil law to the Ottoman *Mecelle*. "Drs. Abdul Razaq Sanhury and Zuhair Jarana; R.I. reg. appt. as Dean of the Law College and teacher of Public Rights respectively," in *Iraq Government Gazette*, no. 4 (Baghdad, January 26, 1936): No. of Notification: 34, Office of Origin: C.M., p. 50. See also "Regulation for the Law College – No. 8 of 1936," in *Iraq Government Gazette*, no. 18 (Baghdad, May 3, 1936): No. of Notification: 239, Office of Origin: C.M., 236.

[52] As a starting point, see Shubayr, *al-Shaykh ʿAlī al-Khafīf*; Shubayr, *Muḥammad Abū Zahrah*; Dasūqī, *Muḥammad Yūsuf Mūsá*. The Cairo Faculty's library holds memoranda that the professors wrote for students. See their articles in *Majallat al-qānūn wa-l-iqtiṣād* (1932–) and contributions of Aḥmad Ibrāhīm in the rare source *Majallat Kulliyyat al-Ḥuqūq li-l-mabāḥith al-qānūniyyah wa-l-iqtiṣādiyyah* 1–2 (1927). This journal of the Cairo Faculty preceded *Majallat al-qānūn wa-l-iqtiṣād*. Just as Aḥmad Ibrāhīm had been a frequent contributor to *Majallat al-qaḍāʾ al-sharʿī* when he was teaching at the Sharia College, he was the most frequent contributor to this lesser-known journal of the Cairo Faculty, in which, see, for example, "al-Zawāj al-madanī wa-l-zawāj al-dīnī," 2,27: 6–9; "Takhṣīṣ al-qaḍāʾ wa-baḥth fīh," 2,2: 3–11.

and Aḥmad Abū al-Fatḥ. He began teaching advanced research seminars in comparative law, offering tenure track positions to his best Sharia College students. Muḥammad Abū Zahrah and ʿAbd al-Wahhāb Khallāf, classmates at the Sharia College from its first year in 1907, joined the faculty as assistant professors in 1934. ʿAlī al-Khafīf joined the faculty as an assistant professor in 1939. In 1941, Muḥammad Yūsuf Mūsá was hired as an assistant professor. He was an Azharite but also held a doctorate in philosophy from the Sorbonne. He was the only professor among the four in this generation who read French fluently and had obtained a degree outside of the high Islamic institutions.

In 1969, Muṣṭafá Muḥammad Qulalī, a professor of Franco-Egyptian criminal law and one-time dean, reflected on the work of these second-generation Sharia jurists at the Cairo Faculty. Writing of them generally and of ʿAlī al-Khafīf specifically, he articulated his admiration for their advanced studies as well as his esteem for Islamic legal revivalism, despite his own status as a professor of Franco-Egyptian law:

> The interaction between the Sharia professors and the *qānūn* professors and their work together in one professional environment was a productive, mutual exchange. Naturally, this resulted in comparisons between opinions and theories (*naẓariyyāt*) on different topics. They also took into consideration what previous Muslim jurists had said about different legal matters in question. They took account of previous scholars' well-established views and their fatwas. This reflected their profound thinking and brilliant minds....
>
> In the midst of those times Western civilization had imposed itself upon us in such a way that it almost made us forget ourselves and what was ours; it almost made us give up all of what was ours. We were following at that time the lead of Western legislation, which had become the basis of our current laws. This prevented us from studying our own great cultural wealth in Islamic *fiqh*. We had lost touch with much of its technical vocabulary.
>
> But there were those among our greatest teachers—and in the vanguard of them our great professor [Shaykh ʿAlī al-Khafīf]—who deserve the most credit for pointing us back in the direction of that astounding cultural wealth, which had until then been buried in the depths of [old] books.
>
> That is what led me in those days to begin researching whether the classical Islamic jurists had written opinions on the topic of legal defenses (*difāʿ sharʿī*)....[53] Among other difficult legal questions that appeared in my research on legal defense was the question of the use of mechanical devices in the defense of property.... These topics had been a point of strenuous debates and differences among commentators and the courts, especially in France. So I was amazed when I found that such questions did not escape the classical Sharia jurists.... The classical Islamic jurists had dealt with these procedural questions with judiciousness, precision, and profound consideration....

[53] The comparative movement also progressed in the criminal field. See, for example, ʿAlī Ṣādiq Abū Hayf, "al-Diyah fī l-sharīʿah al-islāmiyyah" (doct. diss., Law Faculty of the Egyptian University, 1933); Muḥammad Muṣṭafá al-Qulalī, *Fī l-masʾūliyyah al-jināʾiyyah* (Cairo: Maṭbaʿat Jāmiʿat Fuʾād al-Awwal, 1948); al-Qulalī, *Uṣūl qānūn taḥqīq al-jināyāt* (Cairo: Maṭbaʿat Fatḥ Allāh Ilyās Nūrī, 1941).

Shaykh ʿAlī al-Khafīf considered this kind of work to be among the best kind of work that he had helped to develop.[54]

Evident from Qulalī's reflections is the creative milieu in which the Sharia department pursued new advanced studies and thought in Islamic law. The graduate program compelled students and faculty to pursue new research. The fruits of exploratory and comparative considerations in the classroom inspired original dissertations, memoranda, and books.

The graduate program required students to follow coursework and write a dissertation. For coursework, students needed to take two diplomas in graduate studies in two separate fields. Each diploma required one academic year of coursework. The three diplomas offered were originally Private Law, Public Law, and Political Economy. New diplomas were added later. Following the completion of two diplomas, the student would write, submit, and defend a dissertation. The completion of the dissertation would lead to the conferring of a doctorate.[55] The first graduate diplomas were awarded in May 1927; the first dissertation passed in 1931.[56]

The diploma courses were interested in what the professors called "advanced study" (*al-dirāsah bi-l-taʿammuq, études approfondies*) and "comparative study" (*al-dirāsah al-muqāranah, études comparatives*). Many of the classes were exploratory, with the professors pursuing new topics that they planned to write about in articles and books. There was often a correspondence between what a professor taught one year and what he published the next year.[57] It will be useful to consider examples of how this curriculum worked for the diploma in Private Law, which generated some of the most important, new ideas in comparative Islamic-European law.

On the Franco-Egyptian side, the professors were usually Muḥammad Kāmil Mursī, Muḥammad Ṣādiq Fahmī, ʿAbd al-Razzāq al-Sanhūrī, and Albert Chéron. On the Islamic law side, the professors were, at first, Aḥmad Ibrāhīm and Muḥammad Zayd al-Abyānī. Soon to follow were members of the second generation of Sharia professors—Aḥmad Ibrāhīm, ʿAlī al-Khafīf, Muḥammad Abū Zahrah, ʿAbd al-Wahhāb Khallāf, and Muḥammad Yūsuf Mūsá. They taught a diploma course called Sharia but also taught lessons in comparative civil law.

[54] Muḥammad Muṣṭafá al-Qulalī, "Kalimat al-duktūr Muḥammad Muṣṭafá al-Qulalī fī ḥafl istiqbāl al-shaykh ʿAlī al-Khafīf fī l-Majmaʿ," *Majallat Majmaʿ al-Lughah al-ʿArabiyyah (bi-l-Qāhirah)* 25 (1969): 209–11, as quoted in Shubayr, *al-Shaykh ʿAlī al-Khafīf*, 33–4.

[55] In France, the holder of a doctorate in law was required to take the *agrégation* in order to teach in a university. This was not required for teaching law in Egypt.

[56] Ḥusayn Fahmī, "Baḥth fī l-ḥālah al-iqtiṣādiyyah li-sikak ḥadīd al-ḥukūmah," (doct. diss., Law Faculty of the Egyptian University, 1931).

[57] In 1929–1930, al-Sanhūrī lectured to graduate students on hiring and leasing. He published a memorandum on the topic in 1929. The first version of the book appeared in the early 1930s under the title *ʿAqd ījar al-ashyāʾ*, according to al-Jāmiʿah al-Miṣriyyah, *Taqwīm, 1929–1930*. See ʿAbd al-Razzāq Aḥmad al-Sanhūrī, *ʿAqd al-ījār: Sharḥ al-qānūn al-madanī fī l-ʿuqūd* (Beirut: Dār al-Fikr, ca. 1980). Aḥmad Ibrāhīm delivered lectures offering a new approach to Islamic contract law, which led to a corresponding book: Aḥmad Ibrāhīm, *Kitāb al-Muʿāmalāt al-sharʿiyyah al-māliyyah* (Cairo: al-Maṭbaʿah al-Salafiyyah, 1936). On "advanced study," see Lambert, *Fonction*, 45–6.

To obtain the graduate diploma in Private Law in the first half of the 1930s, the student followed four courses across one academic year. The fall courses of (1) "Review of Civil Law" and (2) "Advanced Civil Law" were required. The first was a review of material covered at the *licence* level and the second focused on one or more sophisticated topics in civil law. In the spring, the student chose two electives from five options: (3) Sharia, (4) Roman Law and the History of Private Law, (5) Commercial Law, (6) Civil, Commercial, and Criminal Investigation Procedures, and (7) International Private Law.

The first teacher for "Advanced Civil Law" was al-Sanhūrī. The course title was only a rubric. Under this rubric, the professor taught one or two courses that had separate names. In 1929–30, al-Sanhūrī taught under this rubric "Islamic Law as a Source of Egyptian Positive Law" and "The Social-Economic Question in Hiring Contracts." In the second semester, Muḥammad Zayd al-Abyānī taught the Sharia elective. His course on "Pleadings and Evidence" was a standard study of the law of procedure in force in the Sharia Courts.[58] There was a direct connection between what the professors wrote in their books, what they taught in the classrooms, and what, if anything, they were contributing to the world of actual legal practice.[59]

In 1933–34, Aḥmad Ibrāhīm taught the Sharia elective and broke new ground in pedagogy and the conceptualization of private law in *fiqh*. He created a course in "Islamic Contract Law." Its content was new for a few reasons. First, the course posited a "general law of contract" in Sharia. Historically, Sharia courses had taught Islamic contracts by teaching the so-called nominate contracts of sale, lease, mortgage, gift, and so forth. In this new course format, the professor posited a series of general rules that applied to all contracts. It was French *doctrine* that had a "general theory of contract" and a "general law of contract."

In Aḥmad Ibrāhīm's class, graduate students learned an approach to Islamic contract law that was modeled on the French approach for conceptualizing and organizing rules in contracts. This new approach resulted from the fact that the Franco-Egyptian professors taught a general theory of contract for European and Franco-Egyptian law. Another novelty of the class is that it was teaching substantive contract law beyond what was applied in the Sharia Courts at the time. The class was effectively envisioning a general theory of contract for Islamic law—one that existed independently of sure precedent in Hanafi, Shafiʿi, and Maliki *fiqh* tradition, and one that existed independently of the applied law of the Sharia Courts.

The course catalogue provided a detailed description of the course's novel approach.[60] The new method was tested in exams.[61] Aḥmad Ibrāhīm explained that the "subjects are studied in a comparative manner, comparing the different

[58] Compare with al-Abyānī, *Mabāḥith al-murāfaʿāt*; al-Abyānī, *Mukhtaṣar al-murāfaʿāt al-sharʿiyyah* ([Cairo], ca. 1925).

[59] See below on al-Sanhūrī and the 1948 Egyptian Civil Code.

[60] Al-Jāmiʿah al-Miṣriyyah, *Taqwīm, 1933–1934*, 100.

[61] One question came in three parts: (1) Discuss the capacity of the contracting party in all of the contracts, then indicate the characteristics that do not affect capacity but affect the effect of the contract (*ḥukm al-ʿaqd*) in special terms. (2) What is the séance of the contract (*majlis al-ʿaqd*) and what is its connection to effects? (3) Define "effect of the contract" (*ḥukm al-ʿaqd*) and "rights of the contract" (*ḥuqūq al-ʿaqd*). Ibid., appendix "Asʾilāt al-ikhtibārāt al-taḥrīriyyah . . .," 5.

schools of Islamic law and with exhaustive treatment."[62] This course was "comparative" in the sense that it presented rules of Sharia in such a way that they would be easily comparable to rules in the French general theory of contract. However, the class was comparative additionally in that Aḥmad Ibrāhīm was transcending the typical focus on Hanafi *fiqh*.

Egyptian legal thinkers since the beginning of the century had been calling for cross-*madhhab* approaches to studying Islamic law. However, the Sharia courses and textbooks at the Cairo Faculty had continued to prefer Hanafi law through the 1920s. The second generation of Sharia professors was thoroughly concerned with the other three schools, particularly the Maliki and Hanbali schools.

It was not Rashīd Riḍā, Muḥammad ʿAbduh, or any of the other most famous clerics who brought cross-*madhhab* legal reasoning to the Cairo Faculty—it was the professors of the Cairo Faculty themselves.[63] The innovation was to impact the way they and their successors wrote about modern Islamic law in the 1930s and 1940s, and for the rest of the century. This impact is explored in the next chapter.

New approaches for teaching Sharia at the doctoral level also reached *licence* students. In 1933–34, the first-year class in Sharia was also taught the "General Law of Contracts."[64] In 1936–37, the first-year Sharia class was revised to teach "General Principles of Property and Contract."[65] The focus on "general principles" in Islamic law became popular in the mid-1930s. In 1938–39, the first-year course in Islamic contract law was renamed "General Rules of Contracts" (*al-qawāʿid al-ʿāmmah li-l-ʿuqūd*).[66] The teacher for this course was ʿAbd al-Wahhāb Khallāf. This interest in general principles of contract law was generated by interests in the idea of codifying Islamic law and comparing the classical Islamic contract laws to the European contract laws in force in Egypt. These changes had certain pre-1923 precursors;[67] however, the 1930s marked the first moment when these changes were applied, applied thoroughly, and retained as a permanent feature in Sharia instruction.

THE NEXUS OF ISLAMIC LEGAL REVIVALISM AND INTERNATIONALIST SOPHISTICATION: DIVERSITY, COMPETITION, INTERNATIONAL OUTLOOKS, AND COMPARATIVE LAW AT THE CAIRO FACULTY

The interwar years were a time of intellectual growth, innovation, and increasing academic sophistication at the Cairo Faculty. In addition to the changing approaches

[62] Al-Jāmiʿah al-Miṣriyyah, *Taqwīm, 1934–1935*, 102.

[63] See Ibrāhīm, "Wujūb waḍʿ qānūn sharʿī," 1–5.

[64] *Journal officiel du gouvernement égyptien* 66 (June 20, 1933), 1–2. Jāmiʿat Fuʾād al-Awwal, *Taqwīm 1934–1935*, 52.

[65] Université Égyptienne, *Annuaire, 1936–1937*, 51.

[66] Jāmiʿat Fuʾād al-Awwal, *Taqwīm 1938–1939*.

[67] Aḥmad Abū al-Fatḥ taught a course like this in 1917. However, the approach was not a constant in the curriculum. For several years, there was no first-year class on property and contracts in Sharia. *Recueil des documents officiels du gouvernement égyptien* (1917), 24.

in the teaching, research, and writing of Franco-Egyptian and Islamic private law, the school also grew in other areas and ways.

The new studies in private law already mentioned took place within a broader context of innovation and ambition. Developments occurred in the advanced and comparative study of public, criminal, procedural, and administrative law and political economy. Four institutes of advanced study were created for criminal law, administrative law, economic and finance law, and diplomatic and consular affairs. The institutes offered diplomas for professionals and public servants. The Faculty's course offerings sought to keep pace with global developments in legal, social, and medical science. Special courses and programs were developed, for example, on banking law, stocks, public utilities, and forensics. The number of faculty members, students, and courses continuously expanded into the 1940s, excepting some contractions during the Second World War. The Faculty passed sixty-nine dissertations in all fields between 1931 and 1952.[68] The Faculty's law review, *Majallat al-qānūn wa-l-iqtiṣād*, founded in 1932, is the best monument to this golden age of Egyptian legal studies and its diversity.

The intellectual culture of interwar Egypt hosted proponents of every ideological orientation and school of thought in Europe and the Muslim world; at the Cairo Faculty, professors came together from a wide variety of political, ideological, and religious orientations. The Egyptian professors had different schooling experiences, some having been formed in Francophone schools, others in Anglophone schools, others in Egypt's secular-oriented state schools, and others in Islamic institutions. Some were multilingual and had lived abroad; others spoke only Arabic and had not lived abroad. Some were Muslim and took an interest in Islamic legal revival; some were Muslim and did not take such an interest; some were not Muslim and looked for ways to dampen, to shape, or to politely ignore Islamic legal revivalism.[69]

The intellectual, spiritual, political, and sentimental leanings of the faculty and graduate students were reflected in their publications. To find evidence of such leanings, a reader must read closely and often between the lines. An appreciation of the context in which these professors worked is essential to that task.

As mentioned, professors expressed their intellectual and cultural orientations through their choice of dress and their use of language—the European suit and tarboush vs. the cloak and turban; French vs. Arabic. The clothes were meant to have meaning. Aḥmad Amīn recalled in his memoir that when he migrated from the Sharia College to the Cairo Faculty in 1926, ʿAbd al-Razzāq al-Sanhūrī inquired as to why he still wore his turban, suggesting it was out of fashion and reflected the orientation of the Islamic institutions.[70] Aḥmad Amīn began wearing a suit, but the second-generation Sharia professors kept their traditional dress. As for language, the Franco-Egyptians were distinguished from other colleagues by

[68] See *al-ʿĪd al-miʾawī*, 493–503. The list in that source may be incomplete. See the catalogues of dissertations in the individual departments at the Cairo University Law Faculty Library.

[69] See, for example, discussion of the work of Sulaymān Murqus, an Egyptian law professor, in Bechor, *God in the Courtoom*, 4–8, 165–80, 220–74.

[70] Amin, *My Life*, 148.

their ability to speak fluent French. One wonders how and to what extent the Sharia professors communicated with the European teaching personnel who did not know Arabic. The link between the two groups was the group of Franco-Egyptians, who made French knowledge comprehensible in Arabic and vice versa.

At the Cairo Faculty, the 1920s and 1930s witnessed a level of interest and investment in the revival of Islamic law studies that was not evident beforehand. This is not to say that interest in Sharia overtook scholarly effort in the non-Islamic aspects of Egyptian law. Franco-Egyptian law remained the overwhelming interest, if measured by course offerings, publications, dissertations, diplomas, and faculty appointments. However, Sharia received more attention and a share in the movement of advanced studies. Franco-Egyptian law professors acknowledged this heightened interest.[71] The Sharia professors heralded the new work in their books, and they were celebrated by others for their work.[72]

The Sharia professors eventually gave some credit for their own reformist efforts to collaborations with the Franco-Egyptians. In 1952, Muḥammad Yūsuf Mūsá reflected on the interwar years: "It was God's work that the study of Islamic *fiqh* came to be studied in detail at the University's Law Faculty and that it reached men of the positive law (*rijāl al-qānūn*), so that each party could benefit from the other. As a result of that, mutual influence between positive law and *fiqh* was manifested in the way that rules are presented and explained."[73]

Both groups of scholars published dozens of books and articles on Sharia, whereas this had not been a common topic at the Cairo Faculty in previous years. While the professors of the Cairo Faculty who wrote on Sharia usually published in Arabic, some also published their ideas in foreign languages.[74] The volumes of *Majallat al-qānūn wa-l-iqtiṣād* included articles by faculty members on Sharia, both applied and theoretical.[75] The same authors had previously published in the law journals of the Sharia College and the Sharia Bar Association. The opening article of the Faculty's first student-run journal featured a reformist argument by Aḥmad Ibrāhīm on cross-*madhhab* legal reasoning.[76] When the new diploma in

[71] ʿAbd al-Salām Dhuhnī, "al-Tawaththub li-l-nuhūḍ al-fiqhī wa-ʿuddatuh," *Majallat al-Azhar* 8,1 (1937): 28–35; al-Qulalī, "Kalimat."

[72] See, for example, Abū Bakr ʿAbd al-Rāzī, *Abū Zahrah fī rāʾy ʿulamāʾ al-ʿaṣr* ([Cairo]: Dār al-Iʿtiṣām, ca. 1980); al-Qulalī, "Kalimat."

[73] Muḥammad Yūsuf Mūsá, *al-Amwāl wa-naẓariyyat al-ʿaqd fī l-fiqh al-islāmī* (Cairo: Dār al-Kitāb al-ʿArabī, 1952), 250.

[74] See later on the Hague congresses. Abdel Razzaq al-Sanhuri (ʿAbd al-Razzāq al-Sanhūrī), "Le Standard juridique," in *Recueil d'études sur les sources du droit en l'honneur de Francois Gény* (Paris: Librarie du Recueil Sirey, 1935), 144–56; Albert Chéron and Mohamed Sadek Fahmy Bey (Muḥammad Ṣādiq Fahmī), "Le Transport de dette dans les législations européennes et en droit musulman," *L'Égypte contemporaine* 22 (1931): 35–66, 137–90; Chafik Chehata, "Le Project de nouveau Code civil," *Journal de tribunaux mixtes* 25/26 Feb. (no. 3579) and 22/23 Dec. 1948 (no. 4015). Others appeared in *L'Égypte contemporaine, Revue de droit et économie politique* (*Majallat al-qānūn wa-l-iqtiṣād*), and *Revue internationale de droit comparé*.

[75] See, for example, Aḥmad Ibrāhīm Ibrāhīm, "al-ʿUqūd wa-l-shurūṭ wa-l-khiyārāt" 1 (1934): 641–722; ʿAbd al-Wahhāb Khallāf, "al-Sulṭāt al-thalāth fī l-islām" (1935, 1936, and 1937); Ibrāhīm Zakī al-Dīn Badawī, "Naẓariyyat al-ribā al-maḥram" (1939); ʿAbd al-Wāhhāb Khallāf, "al-Sharīʿah al-islāmiyyah: Maṣdar ṣāliḥ li-l-tashrīʿ" (1940); ʿAlī al-Khafīf, "Taʾthīr al-mawt fī ḥuqūq al-insān wa-iltizāmātih" (1940); Abdel Razzak A. Sanhoury Bey (al-Sanhūrī), "La Responsabilité civile et pénale en droit musulman" (1945).

[76] Ibrāhīm, "Wujūb waḍʿ qānūn sharʿī."

Sharia was offered in 1945, it attracted the highest enrollment in the history of the graduate diploma program.[77] Of the forty-eight dissertations written between 1931 and 1946, twelve were primarily concerned with a question of Islamic legal doctrine (not including those that touched on Islamic law in a comparative framework). At least five of these authors became professors at the Cairo Faculty.[78]

The interest of the professors in comparative law paralleled international trends. The International Academy of Comparative Law was founded in The Hague in 1924. The Locarno Treaties were signed in 1925. Throughout Europe there was interest in codifying private international law.[79] In 1927, France and Italy produced the Franco-Italian Draft Code of Obligations. Although the code was not applied in France or Italy, the document became a source of academic authority to Egyptian code writers.[80] In 1930, Dean Roscoe Pound of Harvard Law School heralded a revival of comparative law.[81]

The International Academy of Comparative Law hosted two International Congresses of Comparative Law in 1932 and 1937 in which Édouard Lambert participated alongside Egyptian colleagues—some his students, and others graduates of the high Islamic institutions. For his own part, he pushed his comparative law agenda as forcefully in those years as he had in the first decade of the century.[82] In 1932, he spoke on the imminent revival of Islamic law in Egypt.[83] At least six Egyptian professors from the Cairo Faculty presented papers at the congresses: ʿAbd al-Ḥamīd Badawī, ʿAbd al-Munʿim Riyāḍ, al-Sanhūrī, Muḥammad ʿAbd al-Jawād, Muḥammad Abū Zahrah, and Aḥmad Ibrāhīm.[84] Their contributions argued for giving Islamic law a place in the world of comparative law and legislation. The signing of the Montreux Conventions in 1937 further inspired Egyptian initiative in advanced legal study and comparative law and legislation.[85]

The comparative study of European and Islamic law played a role in the practical arena of Egyptian lawmaking. In the mid-1930s, al-Sanhūrī lectured in Cairo

[77] See "Décret créant un diplôme d'études supérieures en droit musulman à la Faculté de Droit de l'Université Fouad I," *Journal officiel du gouvernement égyptien* 125/149 (1944).

[78] See theses of ʿAlī Ṣādiq Abū Hayf (1932), Muṣṭafá al-Saʿīd (1932), Chafik Chehata, (1936), Ḥasan Aḥmad Baghdādī (1937), and Ṣāliḥ Ḥasan Manṣūr (1939).

[79] Pierre Arminjon and Société de législation comparée, *La Codification du droit international privé* (Paris: LGDJ, 1932); Hug, "History of Comparative Law."

[80] See generally S. G. Vesey-FitzGerald, "The Franco-Italian Draft Code of Obligations, 1927" *Journal of Comparative Legislation and International Law* 14,1 (1932): 1–19. Regarding the interest of Egyptians in this draft, see its frequent mention in the Egyptian Civil Code's preparatory works. See n. 89.

[81] Roscoe Pound, "The Revival of Comparative Law," *Tulane Law Review* 5 (1930–31): 1–16.

[82] See, for example, Lambert, "Comparative Law"; Lambert, "Le Droit comparé et la formation d'une conscience juridique internationale," *Revue de l'Université de Lyon* 5 (1929): 441–63.

[83] E. Lambert, "Comments on the Egyptian Law System and Islamic Law's Potential for Development and Expansion," presentation given at the Congrès international de droit comparé, The Hague, 1932.

[84] Édouard Lambert, "Les Rapports du droit et de la religion dans le monde musulman moderne," in *Le Congrès International de droit comparé de 1932* (Paris: A. Rey, Librairie du Recueil Sirey, 1934), 90–100; ʿAbd al-Razzāq Aḥmad al-Sanhūrī, "L'Université Égyptienne au Congrès international de droit comparé de La Haye," in *Maqālāt wa-abḥāth al-ustādh al-duktūr ʿAbd al-Razzāq al-Sanhūrī* (special issue of *Majallat al-qānūn wa-l-iqtiṣād*), 2 vols. (Cairo: Maṭbaʿat Jāmiʿat al-Azhar, 1990), 1: 525–31; al-Sanhūrī, "Droit musulman comme élément de refonte"; Hill, "Al-Sanhuri and Islamic Law."

[85] ʿAbd al-Razzāq Aḥmad al-Sanhūrī, "Wājibunā baʿd al-muʿāhadah," *al-Ahrām* (Jan. 1, 1937).

and The Hague about his project to rewrite the Egyptian Civil Code accounting for principles and substance of Islamic law.[86] Assisting him was Édouard Lambert, who advised on the drafting of parts of the code. Ultimately, the code was shaped heavily by the substance of European codes and the priorities of European legal theory.[87] However, Islamic considerations were a factor in the code's original conception and in the parliamentary debates that preceded its adoption.[88] Al-Sanhūrī's meticulous comparative studies are preserved in ten volumes of preparatory works published in the 1940s.[89]

At the same time as al-Sanhūrī was rewriting the Egyptian Civil Code, ostensibly with the interest of incorporating Islamic law, multiple professors and students of the Cairo Faculty penned books on Islamic contract and property law. Each scholar appears to have intended to shape the modern conceptualization of Islamic contract doctrine.[90] Graduate students, for example, produced exploratory theses. Chafik Chehata's 1936 dissertation on the "theory of obligations" in Hanafi law proved to be transformational in the realm of contract and obligations doctrine.[91] Ḥasan ʿAlī al-Dhannūn wrote a dissertation on the Islamic theory of contract annulment.[92] The Sharia professors Aḥmad Ibrāhīm, Muḥammad Abū Zahrah, ʿAlī al-Khafīf, and Muḥammad Yūsuf Mūsá all wrote reform-minded treatises, textbooks, and memoranda on Islamic obligations, contract, and property doctrine.[93] Contributing to this discourse were their colleagues in Damascus and Beirut, Shaykhs Muṣṭafá Aḥmad Zarqāʾ and Ṣubḥī Rajab Maḥmaṣānī.[94] All of these scholars wrote their texts conscious of al-Sanhūrī's codification project. They were aware of the Egyptian delegations to The Hague. They were working to make Islamic law intelligible, practical, and relevant in the eyes of Egyptian colleagues, students, and an international community of scholars.

Although al-Sanhūrī vacated his chair at the Cairo Faculty in 1937, and although his Civil Code drafts provoked disappointment among many proponents of

[86] Al-Sanhūrī, "Droit musulman comme élément de refonte"; "Wujūb tanqīḥ"; "ʿAlá ayy asās"; "Muḥāḍarat al-duktūr ʿAbd al-Razzāq al-Sanhūrī Bey allatī alqāhā bi-l-Jamʿiyyah al-Jughrāfiyyah al-Malakiyyah fī 24 abrīl sanat 1942 ʿan mashrūʿ tanqīḥ al-qānūn al-madanī," *al-Muḥāmāh* 22,4 and 6 (1942): 419–31.

[87] Guy Bechor, *The Sanhuri Code* (Leiden: Brill, 2007); Amr Shalakany, "Between Identity and Redistribution: Sanhuri, Genealogy and the Will to Islamise," *Islamic Law and Society* 8,2 (2001): 201–44.

[88] See Bechor and Shalakany, cited in n. 86, for more precise readings of the code's level of commitment to Islamic law.

[89] Ministry of Justice, *Mashrūʿ tanqīḥ al-qānūn al-madanī: Mudhakkirah īḍāḥiyyah*, 4 vols. (Cairo: Maṭbaʿat al-Iʿtimād, 1948); *al-Qānūn al-madanī: Majmūʿat al-aʿmāl al-taḥḍīriyyah*, 6 vols. (Cairo: Maṭbaʿat Dār al-Kitāb al-ʿArabī, 1950). The post-1948 commentary on the code, in twelve volumes, also provides insight into the preparatory research. See ʿAbd al-Razzāq Aḥmad al-Sanhūrī, *al-Wasīṭ fī sharḥ al qānūn al-madanī* (Cairo: Dār al-Nashr li-l-Jāmiʿah al-Miṣriyyah, 1952–69).

[90] Ibrāhīm, "al-ʿUqūd wa-l-shurūṭ"; Dhuhnī, "al-Tawaththub"; Chafik Chehata, *Essai d'une théorie générale de l'obligation en droit musulman* (Cairo: F. E. Noury et Fils, 1936); Ibrāhīm, *al-Muʿāmalāt al-sharʿiyyah al-māliyyah*; Muḥammad Abū Zahrah, *al-Milkiyyah wa-naẓariyyat al-ʿaqd fī l-sharīʿah al-islāmiyyah* (Cairo: Dār al-Fikr al-ʿArabī, 1939). See Chapter 10.

[91] See Chapter 10.

[92] "Al-Naẓariyyah al-ʿāmmah li-l-faskh: al-Fiqh al-islāmī wa-l-qānūn al-madanī" (doct. diss., Cairo University Law Faculty, 1946).

[93] See next chapter. Also, by two professors of Franco-Egyptian civil law, Soliman Morcos and Chafik Chehata, *Introduction à l'étude du droit civil* (Cairo: F. E. Noury et Fils, 1938).

[94] See Chapter 10.

Islamic legal revival, including Muḥammad Ṣādiq Fahmī,[95] he remained in contact with his colleagues at the Cairo Faculty and especially in the Sharia department with whom he disagreed on many issues. His personal library, housed at the Cairo Faculty, reveals that nearly every important professor of the era gave books to him from the 1930s until his death in 1971. Such gifts do not prove friendship, but they indicate collegiality.

While serving as Minister of Education in 1948, al-Sanhūrī founded the Arab League Institute for High Arab Studies.[96] His ambition was to create a research center for pioneering Egyptian jurists. He chaired the institute and placed on its governing board Muḥammad Abū Zahrah, ʿAlī al-Khafīf, and Muḥammad Yūsuf Mūsá. The center became a hub for publishing on Islamic law, especially private law, during the 1950s and 1960s. Professors of Sharia published with the institute as well as jurists of Franco-Egyptian and other national laws. Contributors included Chafik Chehata, Sulaymān Murqus, and ʿAbd al-Munʿim Faraj Ṣaddah.

New works on Islamic property and contract law were comparative in nature, sometimes rigorously so. New works in comparative Islamic-European scholarship were considerably more sophisticated than those that had appeared in recent years. The comparative works of the Cairo Faculty professors outdid the pieces of scholarship that had appeared in the Sharia Law Journal and the Sharia Bar Association journal. Some scholars pursued comparative studies in the style of Lambert and the French comparativists; others tried to craft a different approach. Taken collectively, these books reflect the various approaches of professors who sought to bridge or otherwise reinforce differences between European and Islamic legal doctrine. Many of the writers created new conceptions about Islamic property and contract law, effectively reforming Islamic doctrine as a direct result of their consultations in European and Franco-Egyptian *doctrine*.

[95] Bechor, *Sanhuri Code*, 87.

[96] ʿImārah, *al-Duktūr ʿAbd al-Razzāq al-Sanhūrī*, 62–5.

Section IV

New Forms of Islamic Legal Thought

10

The Origins of "General Theory" in Islamic Legal Thought

As has been seen, the reception of European law and legal thought was one factor that drove the transformation of Egyptian-Islamic legal scholarship between the mid-nineteenth and mid-twentieth centuries. Although historians of modern Islamic and Arab law have typically focused on the European-style law code as the major impetus and inspiration of European extraction behind the modernization of Islamic legal thought during the colonial era, the emergence in the 1930s and 1940s of a genre of Arabic legal literature called "general theory" played an equal and in some regards greater role than codes in this regard.

The emergence of the general theory genre, which articulated rules in specific areas of *fiqh*, was academically and legally significant; the genre became a popular method for expounding on Islamic legal doctrine and a standard for Islamic legal writing in Egypt and the Arab world, and, as an innovative and efficient structure for writing about law, it was a conduit for the transmission of European ideas and laws. Reformist jurists used it to reshape premises and laws advocated by Egyptian-Islamic legal doctrine, and it was employed either to bridge gaps between European and Islamic law or to showcase what jurists considered to be points of tension or irreconcilable differences between the two traditions. The primary site of intellectual production in this area was the Cairo Faculty.

The inspiration behind the formation of general theory writing in Egypt and how the innovation led Egyptian jurists to articulate a new "theory of obligation," "theory of contract," and "theory of freedom of contract" for Egyptian-Islamic legal doctrine require elaboration.[1] The new general theory writing was evidently an academic event in that it involved changes in methodology and substantive legal thought; it was also a political event in that Egypt's reception of European law and legal thought was controversial in the early and mid-twentieth century—as it is today. Although Egyptian law scholars agreed on its utility, they differed in their enthusiasm for European influence, and they disagreed about

[1] The modern origins of the general theory genre and its significance for the history of modern Islamic legal thought have not been the object of much study. But see Ḥalīmah Bū Karūshah, *Maʿālim tajdīd al-manhaj al-fiqhī: Unmūdhaj al-Shawkānī* (Doha: Wizārat al-Awqāf wa-l-Shuʾūn al-Islāmiyyah, 2002), 90–1; ʿAbd al-Wahhāb Abū Sulaymān, "al-Naẓariyyah wa-l-qawāʿid fī l-fiqh al-islāmī," *Majallat Jāmiʿat al-Mālik ʿAbd al-ʿAzīz* 2 (1978): 53.

Islamic Legal Revival: Reception of European Law and Transformations in Islamic Legal Thought in Egypt, 1875–1952. First Edition. Leonard Wood.

the degree to which the general theory method should be an engine for driving substantive changes in Islamic law.

FRANCO-EGYPTIAN LAW AND NEW SCHOLARSHIP

Central to the formation of the genre of general theory was the deployment of the Arabic terms *naẓariyyah* and *naẓariyyah ʿāmmah*, which were taken to be equivalent in meaning to *théorie* and *théorie générale*, respectively, in French legal discourse. The term *naẓariyyah* represented a mode of legal exposition, a method for conceptualizing distinct fields of law and for organizing law into a hierarchical structure of categories, principles, and rules. The *naẓariyyah* method was modeled on one within French *doctrine juridique*, which had flourished during the nineteenth century[2] and which from the 1890s into the 1920s had been encountered by the Egyptian doctoral students studying in France who later became leading law scholars at the Cairo Faculty.

This exposure to general theory eventually led Egyptian law scholars to recast areas of Islamic legal thought, and the *naẓariyyah* method was used to treat "obligations" and "contract" law, which were thus newly conceived as "fields" of Islamic *fiqh*.[3] The term *naẓariyyah* ("theory")—a neologism that was applied to law for the first time in the twentieth century—became increasingly more common in the titles and content of Egyptian Arabic books on Franco-Egyptian law. In the 1930s, 1940s, and 1950s, at least ten books were written in Egypt and neighboring Arab countries to explicate the "general theory of obligation" and the "general theory of contract" "in Islamic law." This approach to exposition in Islamic legal thought, which has no exact parallel in classical Islamic legal writing, was gradually replicated in all other subjects, beyond obligations and contracts, during the twentieth century.

Today, students of Islamic law in Egyptian and Arab universities find innumerable academic books on Islamic law with titles written in the form *al-Naẓariyyah al-ʿāmmah fī...fī l-fiqh al-islāmī* (The General Theory of...in Islamic Legal Thought). Almost every topic in Islamic law now has a book of general theory.[4] Books on Islamic contract doctrine will elaborate a general theory of contract, whether or not the term "general theory" is used.[5]

From its inception, the general theory genre, as applied to Islamic legal thought, has contributed to the production of reformist Islamic legal discourse that seeks

[2] On the origin of general theory in Europe, see generally Jestaz and Jamin, *La Doctrine*.

[3] Books and ideas about the "theory of obligations" and the "theory of contract" are from continental Europe's civil law tradition and do not have parallels of equal prestige or weight in the Anglo-American common law tradition.

[4] See, for example, Muḥammad Muḥammad Farḥāt, *al-Naẓariyyāt al-ʿāmmah fī l-fiqh al-islāmī* (Cairo: al-Risālah al-Dawliyyah li-l-Ṭibāʿah, 2002); Rushdī Shiḥātah Abū Zayd, *al-Madkhal li-dirāsat al-fiqh al-islāmī, al-Juzʾ al-thānī: al-Naẓariyyāt al-ʿāmmah* (Cairo: Dār al-Naṣr, 2001); Aḥmad Farrāj Ḥusayn and ʿAbd al-Wadūd al-Sarītī, *al-Naẓariyyāt al-ʿāmmah fī l-fiqh al-islāmī wa-tārīkhih* (Beirut: Dār al-Nahḍah al-ʿArabiyyah, 1992).

[5] See, for example, "ʿAqd," in *al-Mawsūʿah al-fiqhiyyah* (Kuwayt: Wizārat al-Awqāf, 1983).

to revive, reform, and ultimately reapply Islamic law in the Egyptian and other Arab legal systems. The genre helped to advance conceptions of a unified Islamic law that transcends differences among and within the four Sunni law schools. It also informed practical endeavors to reform and reapply Islamic law through legislative projects.

The general theory genre facilitated the production of comparative Islamic-European legal scholarship. As a mechanism for comparing European and Islamic doctrines, the genre became a vehicle to introduce European influences into Islamic legal thought. Sometimes, legal borrowing was obvious and direct; at other times, and alternatively, the new genre merely helped to inspire changes—that is, a European rule found in European *doctrine* became a desired end for an Egyptian author writing about Islamic rules, but the juridical method and the textual primary source the author used to produce the parallel Islamic rule came from the traditional repertoire of Islamic legal methodology and sacred sources.

The application of general theory writing to Islamic law was consequential to the future of Islamic legal doctrine for one reason above others. By reorganizing the categorical and conceptual premises of a field of Islamic legal doctrine, the *naẓariyyah* model made it easier for comparative scholars to place Islamic and European laws side by side and to compare their premises and rules. In this way the model exerted and facilitated downward pressure for change on the middle-level rules of traditional Islamic legal doctrine, as the jurists' attention became focused on those aspects of substantive Islamic law that could be seen as needing reform in a modern era. This downward pressure happened especially in topics where Islamic doctrine conflicted with conveniences or advantages of modern European law (e.g., comparatively relaxed rules on interest). With specific reference to Islamic contract law, this mechanism of "general theory" led Egyptian scholars to continually revise substantive legal doctrine from the top down, that is, by proceeding from higher-order principles, to middle-level generalities, and finally to substantive minutiae of legal rules.

ORIGINS OF GENERAL THEORY WRITING IN EGYPTIAN *FIQH*

In 1936, Chafik Chehata, a doctoral student at the Cairo Faculty, produced a paradigm-shifting dissertation, which he wrote in Arabic and French versions.[6] The French version was published by an academic publisher and sold in different countries of the world. This was the first Arabic treatise on Islamic law that used the term *naẓariyyah* in the title. The Arabic version was entitled "Al-Naẓariyyah al-ʿāmmah li-l-iltizāmāt fī l-sharīʿah al-islāmiyyah," while the French version was

[6] Shafīq Shiḥātah, "Al-Naẓariyyah al-ʿāmmah li-l-iltizāmāt fi-l-sharīʿah al-islāmiyyah, al-juzʾ al-awwal: Ṭarfā al-iltizām" (doct. diss., Law Faculty of the Egyptian University, 1936); Chafik Chehata, *Essai d'une théorie générale de l'obligation en droit musulman, tome premier: Les Sujets de l'obligation, avec une bibliographie, une méthodologie et un tableau général de la théorie de l'obligation en droit hanéfite* (Cairo: F. E. Noury et Fils, 1936).

entitled "Essai d'une théorie générale de l'obligation en droit musulman" (Essay on the General Theory of Obligation in Muslim Law). Directly influenced by French *doctrine*, the dissertation made "obligations" a master category for organizing rules of contract and civil delict[7] in Islamic law. Classical *fiqh*, by contrast, explicated the rules of obligation by treating obligation as the effect of nominate contracts.[8] Classical *fiqh* had neither an explicit general theory of obligation nor an explicit general theory of contract. The building blocks of such a theory existed, but the consolidated and explicit theory had never been formed.[9]

Chehata's promotion of "obligation" to a master category of rules constituted a step in the direction of making "contract" a master category of general rules above the subjacent rules of specific nominate contracts—all within *Islamic* legal discourse. The maneuver was not, in fact, entirely novel to modern Egyptian-Islamic legal writing. The 1893 French version of Muḥammad Qadrī Pasha's *Murshid al-ḥayrān* had posited obligation as a master category for contract and delict law in Islamic law.[10] However, Qadrī Pasha's elaboration of Islamic obligations was brief and incomplete. Despite their interest in his work, succeeding jurists in Egypt made a neglible effort to improve on it. One partial exception was Aḥmad Abū al-Fatḥ at the Cairo Faculty, who wrote a book in 1913 that treated the rules of "contracts in general" (*al-ʿuqūd ʿalá al-ʿumūm*).[11] He developed fundamentals of a theory of contract, putting them into a narrative form. On the other hand, he theorized only slightly on the concept of an Islamic "law of obligation" that was superior to and would subsume a general law of contract.

Chehata did not invent the concepts of obligation (*iltizām*), contract (*ʿaqd*), right (*ḥaqq*), liability (*ḍamān*), and related concepts for the discourse of Sharia and *fiqh*. These already pervaded the classical Islamic *fiqh* literature. In classic *fiqh*, as in any legal system, there was a conception that a person or entity can obligate and be obligated; there was a conception of a person's or entity's "capacity" to be obligated; there was a conception of a person's or entity's "right" vis-à-vis a thing, person, or another entity.

In Chehata's view, the classical jurists had certainly articulated a conception of obligation and related concepts, but they had not consolidated a theory, standardized it, perfected it, made obligation the master category for organizing

[7] I.e., torts. English translations are to the terms of civil law, since this was the point of reference for Chehata and his colleagues where comparisons to European law were concerned.

[8] A civil law term, "nominate" is an English, Latinate translation of the French *contrat nommé* ("named contract"). The French *Code civil* provides rules for twelve such contracts: Sale, Exchange, Hire, Partnership, Loan, Deposit, Insurance, Agency, Surety, Pledge, Options, and Hypothecs. Nineteenth-century French law provided specific rules for these nominate contracts. Modern Islamic jurists are familiar with this term and concept because of the presence of nominate contracts in Islamic *fiqh* and because continental European civil law has been practiced in Muslim countries, especially the Arab countries, since the nineteenth century. The connection of Arab countries to civil law is the reason that Arabic books on Arab civil law and Islamic law speak of "named contracts" (*al-ʿuqūd al-musammá*).

[9] See Frank Vogel, "Contract Law of Islam and the Arab Middle East," in *International Encyclopedia of Comparative Law* (Tübingen: Mohr Siebeck, 2006), 7: 1–77; M. E. Hamid, "Islamic Law of Contract or Contracts?," *Journal of Islamic and Comparative Law* (Nigeria) 3 (1969): 1–10.

[10] The 1893 French edition introduced the chapter on obligation; earlier Arabic versions of 1890 and 1891 did not include such a chapter. This chapter was integrated into Arabic editions in 1911 and thereafter.

[11] Abū al-Fatḥ, *Kitāb al-Muʿāmalāt.*

and explaining a substantial part of private law, or committed the conception to writing.

Chehata's 1936 dissertation surpassed all precursors in fleshing out an Islamic theory of obligation. It was based on a greater degree of research in classical sources to establish its argument. It made a case for the authenticity and legitimacy of positing general theories within Islamic *fiqh* discourse. It also represented the greatest achievement in Egypt, to date, of the application of French-style comparative law—particularly the brand advanced by Édouard Lambert—to the study of classical Islamic *fiqh*. By advancing a new structural and categorical conception of Islamic private law, Chehata advanced a mechanism that facilitated subsequent changes in the substance of Islamic doctrine on contract, delict, property, and other legal subjects.

Chehata convinced his mentors and colleagues in the Cairo Faculty's Sharia department of the utility of focusing on the concept of obligation, standardizing its meaning, and using it as a first principle for organizing the better part of private laws in interpersonal transactions (*muʿāmalāt*). As such, he advanced Egyptian-Islamic *fiqh* discourse in one direction, the direction of theorizing on obligation and contract. At the same time his dissertation sharpened a divide at the Cairo Faculty between proponents of French-style methodology in the field of *fiqh* and proponents of more traditional Islamic methodology, those who held degrees from Egypt's high Islamic institutions.

CHEHATA AND EUROPEAN-ISLAMIC COMPARATIVE LAW AT THE CAIRO FACULTY

Aspects of Chehata's personal history illuminate the politics of the reception of European law and legal thought in Egypt. Chehata was an Egyptian citizen, born in Egypt in the early years of the twentieth century. His family may have originated from Lebanon or Syria. He may have graduated from a French *lycée* in Cairo. He entered the graduate diploma program at the Cairo Faculty in 1929 and obtained graduate diplomas in private and public law in 1930 and 1931. His dissertation was written between 1930 and 1936. After completing his doctorate, he taught civil law and legal history at the Cairo Faculty and later at the law faculty of ʿAyn Shams University. In the 1950s, he assumed a chair at the College de France in Paris where he taught Islamic and Arab law. He published many books and articles on Islamic law, Egyptian law, and legal history throughout his career.

Chehata was a Christian. Although senior Egyptian law professors who remember Chehata regard this point as inconsequential, it seems to have been a relevant factor in his life and in the history of his 1936 dissertation. In concert with other factors, Chehata's Christian identity helps explain why his study received a mixed reception from Sharia scholars—influencing them on the one hand, and apparently displeasing them on the other.

The graduate courses in private law offered by the Cairo Faculty in the early 1930s afforded students new opportunities to conduct advanced research in

Sharia, particularly in "comparative" research. Al-Sanhūrī and Shaykh Aḥmad Ibrāhīm were among the faculty teaching these courses when Chehata was a graduate student. Chehata was one of the earliest beneficiaries of the focus on training students in Franco-Egyptian law, Western legal theory (including Western philosophy), and French approaches to comparative law. As pointed out earlier, all three areas of legal thought were packed with premises and biases, many of which were inimical to traditional viewpoints on Islamic law and legal method. Of the many premises, ambitions, and methods that were applied to Islamic law and legal reform in French-style comparativism, three were of special importance in shaping Chehata's dissertation.

The first was the presumption that the methods, theories, and ambitions of the European fields of "Legal History," "Conceptual Jurisprudence," and "Social Jurisprudence" could be brought to bear on the reform of modern Islamic law, even if these schools of legal thought and theory—at that time already beyond their prime and fading from fashion in Europe itself—were opposed to one another in their historical origins and ambitions.[12]

The second was the critical attitude toward traditional conceptions in Islamic *uṣūl al-fiqh*, and the view that a reformed conception of Islamic legal theory and methodology was necessary to revive, reform, and (re)apply modern Islamic law. The French-style comparativist who studied Islamic law and aimed for its reform was aware of the importance that traditional theories, sources of law, and methods played in Muslims' understanding of Sharia and *fiqh*, but he looked for ways to formulate reformed methods that would make *fiqh* more workable in modern society. Like Lambert and al-Sanhūrī before him, Chehata took action in his 1936 dissertation on Islamic private law.

Finally, the third was the perception of Islamic law through the lens of universalist conceptions. In this worldview, Islamic law was one subset of human law, a part among equals, but neither Sharia nor *fiqh* was a source of normative authority that superseded the rest of the world's legal traditions in importance and rightness.

Knowing the history of developments in comparative law and in the Cairo Faculty's curriculum, which was primarily devoted to promoting comparative studies in private as opposed to public law, it is not surprising that Chehata's study appeared in 1936. This observation is not to slight Chehata's originality, genius, or industry, but rather only to point out that many preparatory steps had already been taken. Zealous in their enthusiasm for comparative law and for the revived study of Islamic law, his professors of Franco-Egyptian law had been writing their own general theory works on a range of topics in European and Franco-Egyptian law and legal history. They encouraged comparative studies with Islamic law and collaboration with the Sharia professors of the Faculty. Al-Sanhūrī was not Chehata's official dissertation adviser, but Chehata evidently considered al-Sanhūrī his greatest influence, and he told him so in a handwritten dedication to a gift copy he gave al-Sanhūrī in 1936.[13]

[12] Additionally, a special esteem was harbored for codes and the role of academic jurists in shaping legislation for modern society.

[13] Appendix.

For a concerted movement of French-styled, European-Islamic comparative law to take hold in Egypt, a comparative work on European and Islamic obligation theory and contract theory needed to be written. For enthusiasts of European comparativism around the world, and for any jurist trained in the legal thought of nineteenth-century Europe, the general theory of obligation and the general theory of contract were the starting points for comparing and reforming all areas of private law, and possibly public law as well. To satisfy the expectations of the Egyptian comparativists holding chairs in the Franco-Egyptian law departments of the Cairo Faculty, a general theory of contracts and obligations for Islamic law needed to be written by an author using concepts, categories, methods, and methodological premises from European comparativism,[14] that is, the premises and objectives established by the schools of Historical, Conceptual, and Sociological Jurisprudence. Islamic substantive law would be, perhaps, the raw material poured into the French-style comparativist mold. The study needed to be written by someone who would deploy European-inspired revisionist Islamic legal history as a tool of modern legal reform.[15] It needed to be written by someone who was knowledgeable about prevailing policy and theoretical concerns of European legal thought. It needed to be written by someone fluent in Arabic and French. And, the study needed to be written in Egypt, not in France, so that the author could have the fullest possible access to classical *fiqh* works in manuscripts and edited form.

Chehata's project was a Lambertian approach to comparative law—although it was also more than this. His dissertation was an academic study in "comparative legal history" written according to "scientific method" (as understood at the time), with an interest in developing interlocking, hierarchical concepts, all to prepare the way for the practical work of "comparative legislation." This was a roadmap that Lambert had designed at the beginning of the century for studying, improving, and ultimately uniting different legal systems of the world.[16]

CHEHATA'S STATUS AT THE CAIRO FACULTY

To the Egyptian professors of Franco-Egyptian law who admired European-style comparativism, Chehata was a suitable candidate for the project he undertook. He spoke French and Arabic, he held a *licence* in French law, and as a Christian he was unlikely to have a deep loyalty to orthodox Sunni legal theory, methods, or legal substance.

It is reasonable to consider that Chehata's advisers may have perceived another possible effect of tasking him with refashioning a major subject of Islamic *fiqh*: Chehata might use his dissertation to reshape Islamic doctrine to benefit Egypt's non-Muslim communities. During the 1930s, many Egyptian academics were concerned

[14] See generally Zimmermann and Reimann, eds., *Oxford Handbook of Comparative Law.*

[15] See Chapter 6 on Lambert's *La Fonction de droit comparé.*

[16] Société de législation comparée, *Congrès international de droit comparé.* See also Lambert, *Fonction*, introduction.

with the legal future of Egyptian Christians, given the state's Muslim majority and the fact that reviving Sharia was a popular cause.[17]

To accept the ways of European comparativism, and to bring the power of European legal theory to bear on classical *fiqh*, a student needed to be induced by the lure of notions of universalism and the universality of scientific inquiry. Through the universalist prism, Islam and Islamic law could be seen as a manifestation of universal science and normativity rather than as the unique and supreme source of normativity. This worldview made it easier to submit the study of Sharia to the methods and premises of a foreign legal science. The appeal to universalism was the inducement that affected al-Sanhūrī, a young, pious, religiously conservative, Muslim Egyptian student, when he was in Lyon in the 1920s and that helped him commit to European styles of comparative legal study,[18] and it was likely the same inducement for Chehata. However, a possible difference between the two figures is that Chehata needed less in the way of such inducements. Adopting premises of European scientific thought did not force him to question tenets of his own religious tradition, or face a crisis of faith by attaching himself to ideas and tools of a European discipline.

As a doctoral candidate aspiring to a professorship at the Cairo Faculty, Chehata did not have to worry about his credibility in the high Islamic institutions like al-Azhar. The clerics he needed to please were his adviser, Shaykh Muḥammad Abū Zahrah, and examiner, Shaykh Aḥmad Ibrāhīm, who taught at the Cairo Faculty in the Sharia department. Both Aḥmad Ibrāhīm and Muḥammad Abū Zahrah had been affiliated, as students and teachers, with the high Islamic institutions. In retrospect, it seems they approved of Chehata's project insofar as it was a provocative experiment in a new way of thinking, and insofar as it met standards for conferring a doctorate at the Cairo Faculty. Although it was a project that they and most Sharia jurists at the Cairo Faculty could not undertake themselves, given their limited ability to read French or to independently access the most sophisticated European legal thought, this was the type of research project that all of their Franco-Egyptian colleagues were interested in during the 1930s.

It is impossible to know for certain what Chehata's Sharia professors thought about his dissertation. The books they wrote about the theory of obligations and contract after 1936[19] show that they were inspired by Chehata's work. The titles, objectives, and categorical structures Abū Zahrah and Aḥmad Ibrāhīm employed in their respective books about Islamic contract law in 1939 and 1944 were similar. They took some of his most important arguments and advanced them—for example, Abū Zahrah took Chehata's tentative musings about the possibility of achieving a doctrine of freedom of contract in Islamic law and then declared that

[17] Leonard Wood, "Sharīʿah Revivalist Thought in the First Years of the *Sharīʿah Lawyers Bar Association Journal*," in *Maghreb Review* 32,2–3 (2007): 196–217.

[18] See his memoirs and his entries from his time in Lyon in the 1920s, in al-Sanhūrī and al-Shāwī, eds., *Al-Sanhūrī min khilāl awrāqih*. For further insight into al-Sanhūrī's universalistic attitude in the 1920s, see the front matter in his second dissertation, *Le Califat* (Paris: P. Geuthner, 1926).

[19] Aḥmad Ibrāhīm, *Mudhakkirah mubtadaʾah fī bayān al-iltizāmāt wa-mā yataʿallaq bihā min al-aḥkām fī l-sharʿ al-islāmī* (Miṣr: Maktabat ʿAbd Allāh Wahbah, 1944–45); Abū Zahrah, *al-Milkiyyah wa-naẓariyyat al-ʿaqd*.

Islamic law did in fact have a doctrine of freedom of contract.[20] However, neither Abū Zahrah nor Aḥmad Ibrāhīm paid tribute to Chehata in their respective books, despite the fact that they had supervised his thesis and had since become faculty colleagues with him, in an era in which Egyptian law professors assiduously cited one another's work.

Chehata's non-Muslim background was not necessarily the chief problem—although it is impossible to know for certain. More ascertainable is that his being a Christian was a reflection of a more important, inescapable truth, namely, that he had not been "raised since childhood on Islamic *fiqh*."[21] He had not attended a *madrasah*, never memorized the Quran, and spent no significant time in al-Azhar, Dār al-ʿUlūm, or the Sharia College. He would never wear the turban or be called *shaykh*. Some Muslim jurists may have suspected that his agenda for Egypt's legal future was different from their own. This is an interpretation of events that rules out prejudice or a simple preference for Muslims on the part of the Sharia professors.

For Muḥammad ʿAbd al-Jawād, the biographer of the graduates of Dār al-ʿUlūm, Chehata was an example of how Abū Zahrah—a bona fide expert of the Sharia—stretched himself to accommodate the interests of the new French-style comparativists at the Cairo Faculty who were the professors and students of Franco-Egyptian law.[22] In the parlance of the times, the comparativists were the *madaniyyūn* (civilists), *ḥuqūqiyyūn* (positive law lawyers), *qānūniyyūn* (positive law lawyers), and *mutafarnijūn* ("self-Frenchified"). They were *fuqahāʾ madaniyyūn* (civil jurists), but they were not *fuqahāʾ* (jurists of Sharia law). They could be Muslim, they could dabble in *fiqh*, and they could learn a few things quite well. But they would never master *fiqh* or have the final, authoritative word on a question in Islamic jurisprudence. Aḥmad Ibrāhīm said as much in a textbook on *uṣūl al-fiqh* written, not coincidentally, in 1938.[23]

From the outset, it seems that Chehata was operating in an environment that on the one hand encouraged his project, but on the other hand allowed him access only to certain professional opportunities and echelons of prestige. Professors in the Sharia department at the Cairo Faculty encouraged new research, but they were advising students of Franco-Egyptian law who, as such, could never personally replace them as Sharia professors. Chehata would be able to teach civil law and legal history, but he would forever be a member of the Franco-Egyptian side of legal academia. More importantly, his thesis would always be seen by Sharia professors as a work written from a Franco-Egyptian perspective that had crept over into Sharia studies as a kind of intellectual adventure. Like Chehata himself, Chehata's thesis sat on the "positive law" side of Egyptian legal academia, expressed in Arabic in various terms: *waḍʿī* (positive), *qānūnī* (positive-legal), *ūrūbi* (European), *madanī* (civil), *ḥuqūqī* (modern law), *miṣrī* (Egyptian), and *faransī* (French).

[20] Abū Zahrah, *al-Milkiyyah wa-naẓariyyat al-ʿaqd*, 223.

[21] See Muḥammad ʿAbd al-Jawād, "Abū Zahrah wa-ārāʾ al-ʿulamāʾ fīh," in *Abū Zahrah fī raʾy ʿulamāʾ al-ʿaṣr*, ed. al-Rāzī, cited in Shubayr, *Muḥammad Abū Zahrah*, 53.

[22] See n. 21.

[23] "One who has not attained the rank of *ijtihād* from among the students of the Sharia is required to take his rules from the *faqīh*." Aḥmad Ibrāhīm, *Mudhakkirah mūjizah fī ʿilm uṣūl al-fiqh* ([Miṣr]: Maṭbaʿat al-ʿUlūm, 1938–39), 1–10.

Nevertheless, the dissertation had a lasting impact on Egyptian scholars, including those same Sharia professors who apparently regarded the work and its author with some reservation.

NAẒARIYYAH AND *NAẒARIYYAH ʿĀMMAH*

As said earlier, the Arabic term *naẓariyyah* is a neologism. It is a noun, derived from the Arabic root *n-ẓ-r* ("scientific investigation"),[24] itself possibly a calque of the Greek *theoria*, and from its relative adjective *naẓarī*, meaning "theoretical" (as opposed to *ʿamalī* "practical"). More could be said about classical uses of this root, but it is enough to say that *naẓariyyah* was not a classical Arabic term.

Egyptian authors only gradually settled on the Arabic terms for *théorie* and *théorie générale*. In 1924, Aḥmad Najīb al-Hilālī and Ḥāmid Zākī, civil law professors at the Cairo Faculty, published *Sharḥ al-qānūn al-madanī fī l-ʿl-ʿuqūd*, a commentary on the civil law of contract.[25] The book was about continental European legal theory and Franco-Egyptian law. It applied the notion of general theory and its organizing principles, but it did not include the term *naẓariyyah* in the title or table of contents. In 1931, Muḥammad Ṣāliḥ used the general theory model but not the term *naẓariyyah* in a book entitled *Uṣūl al-taʿahhudāt* (Principles of Obligations). A professor of political economy and commercial law at the Cairo Faculty, Ṣāliḥ was an examiner of Chehata's thesis. Although in his title and text he used *uṣūl* instead of *naẓariyyah* to express "general theory," the same concept and its ramifications were applied to the organization and exposition of legal rules of Franco-Egyptian civil law. The term *uṣūl*, literally "roots," conveys the idea of "sources," "theory," and "principles," and was an acceptable way to articulate the concept in 1931.

The terms *naẓariyyah* and *naẓariyyah ʿāmmah* themselves appear infrequently in Arabic law books and articles in the 1910s and then more frequently in the 1920s. The upswing in the 1920s may be seen as a reflection of the increased popularity of the term *théorie* in titles of French legal books in the 1910s and 1920s.

One of the earliest deployments of the term *naẓariyyah* within an Egyptian law book is found in ʿAbd al-Ḥamīd Abū Hayf's 1915 treatise on Franco-Egyptian civil procedure, *al-Murāfaʿāt al-madaniyyah*.[26] ʿAbd al-Fattāḥ Sayyid and Aḥmad Qamḥah replicated the usage in their 1923 treatise on Sharia court procedure.[27] It is not surprising that the term *naẓariyyah* would have been innovated and then replicated in this way, at this time. ʿAbd al-Ḥamīd Abū Hayf obtained his doctorate in Toulouse in 1912 and returned to Egypt where he began writing new Arabic textbooks about Franco-Egyptian law. ʿAbd al-Fattāḥ Sayyid obtained his doctorate from Dijon in 1922. This generation was committed to stabilizing modern Arabic

[24] *Naẓar*'s meaning as "scientific investigation" was probably as late as the ninth century; Th. de Boer and H. Daiber, s.v., *Encyclopaedia of Islam*, 2nd ed.

[25] It was an edition of an earlier book by Aḥmad Najīb al-Hilālī.

[26] 2nd ed. (Miṣr: Maṭbaʿat al-Maʿārif, ca. 1921), 26.

[27] Qamḥah and al-Sayyid, *Sharḥ lāʾiḥat al-ijrāʾāt*.

legal vocabulary, a project that had been ongoing since Rifāʿah Rāfʿi al-Ṭahṭawī's first translations of the Napoleonic codes in the mid-nineteenth century. They were likely candidates to borrow a popular French term and concept and to support the innovation of an Arabic word that best represented the French concept.

The first Egyptian writer to use the term *naẓariyyah* in an Arabic title with reference to law—continental European civil law with references to Franco-Egyptian civil law—was ʿAbd al-Salām Dhuhnī, the most prolific among the Franco-Egyptian jurists before the rise of al-Sanhūrī.[28] The event that stabilized it as a term, concept, and approach to law was the 1934 publication of ʿAbd al-Razzāq al-Sanhūrī's masterwork *Naẓariyyat al-ʿaqd* (Theory of Contract), a work concerned with Franco-Egyptian law.[29] Yet, as of 1936, there still was no Arabic book on Islamic *fiqh* deploying the term and using the concept to reconceptualize an area of Islamic private law. All that existed for *fiqh* in the way of general theory literature was a handful of references in scattered French works.[30]

CHEHATA'S INNOVATIONS

The first innovation of Chehata's dissertation was the title, "al-Naẓariyyah al-ʿāmmah li-l-iltizāmāt fī l-sharīʿah al-islāmiyyah"; in French, "Essai d'une théorie générale de l'obligation en droit musulman." Every term was significant from terminological, conceptual, and historical standpoints. The title reflected the reduction of Islamic *fiqh* to a field called *droit musulman*—one result of colonial intervention on the territory of Islamic legal thought.[31] It reflected the ongoing Egyptian preoccupation with Hanafi law, a preoccupation with nineteenth-century roots that was finally subsiding in the 1930s. It also reflected the ongoing Egyptian movement to speak of a uniform Islamic *fiqh* as opposed to a *fiqh* divided by *madhhabs*, and it contributed to the beginning of the now-ubiquitous phrase "in Islamic *fiqh*" (*fī l-fiqh al-islāmī*) in the titles of Arabic books on Islamic law. Finally, it thrust the term *naẓariyyah* into published discourse on Islamic law.

Chehata assumed the existence of a first-order distinction in the field of private law between property law on one hand and obligations law on the other hand. From there, he treated obligation as a master category of rules (beneath the category of "private law") from which emanated two, ostensibly distinct, second-order categories of law, one concerned with contract, and the other concerned with delict. This conceptual and categorical approach, taken straight from the fundamentals of French *doctrine* literature, prevailed for the rest of the century in many writings

[28] Dhuhnī, *Fī l-iltizāmāt*. For more on Dhuhnī, see pp. 188 and 192.

[29] Volume one of al-Sanhūrī, *Sharḥ al-qānūn al-madanī: al-Naẓariyyah al-ʿāmmah li-l-iltizāmāt* (Cairo: Maṭbaʿat Dār al-Kutub al-Miṣriyyah, 1934). The course catalogues at Cairo Faculty reveal that al-Sanhūrī was lecturing on the *naẓariyyah* of Franco-Egyptian contract law before the publication of his book.

[30] See Ch. Cardahi, "Théorie générale des actions en droit musulman," *Bulletin de la société de législation comparée* (1929): 379–99; Sim Tolédo, *Analyse de la théorie des contrats et obligations en droit civil ottoman* (Montpellier: Imprimerie Générale du Midi, 1915); Van den Berg, *Beginselen* (Fr. trans. *Principes*); Gatteschi et al., *Manuale di diritto*, 421. It is possible that Van den Berg relied on the writings of the French-Algerian jurist Ernest Zeys.

[31] See pp. 4–5 and 49–50.

about Islamic private law. (It is incidentally relevant to note that speaking of Islamic "private law," as Chehata did, is to invoke a category from Roman and French law.) The conceptual origin of these divisions can be achieved if one's approach to the law begins with, among other things, a conceptual distinction between rights *in personam* (rights vis-à-vis a person) and rights *in rem* (rights vis-à-vis a thing), a distinction that Egyptian jurists struggled to equate to the distinction in Islamic *fiqh* between *ḥaqq shakhṣī* (personal right) and *ḥaqq ʿaynī* (material right). They debated the issue into the 1950s.[32]

At the outset, Chehata made a variety of maneuvers in articulation and conceptualization that were not traditional to Islamic *fiqh*. He began his exposition on Islamic *fiqh* with a statement about organizing principles in Roman, French, and German law and legal-academic doctrine. He cited Roman, French, and German jurists. This was a completely different beginning than was standard in Islamic books of law. If there was an introduction at all in classical *fiqh* books on the topic of interpersonal transactions (*muʿāmalāt*), it discussed the standard Islamic categorical distinction between *muʿāmalāt* and rules of worship (*ʿibādāt*). Works were often prefaced with a reference to the "rights of God" (*ḥuqūq Allāh*) versus the "rights of God's servants" (*ḥuqūq al-ʿibād*).

Classical works in Hanafi *fiqh* did not begin their discussions of *muʿāmalāt* by distinguishing between property, obligations, and contracts, and making obligations a master category for the conception of general rules of contract. Chehata states in his introduction that the classical Muslim jurists had not elaborated on a theory of obligation: they did not separate the discussion of obligations from discussions within chapters on contract; they did not articulate a general theory of contract; they did not propose that a general "law of contract" existed under a general "law of obligation." Nevertheless, Chehata maintained that such conceptualizations were implicit in the classical *fiqh* texts and could be extracted from those texts to construct—that is, to reconstruct—an authentic organizing theory. In fact, Chehata followed the lead of the German historical school in proposing that his base texts were "cases" (*les cas*) found in classical *furūʿ* and *fatāwá* works, and that it is from such texts that a modern jurist extrapolates "general principles" that inhere in and govern the Islamic contract "system."[33]

Chehata built on previously existing "theories" of French and Franco-Egyptian law, and he may also have built on writings by European orientalists and colonial agents.[34] (See Chehata with Louis Milliot in Fig. 10.1.) Chehata also developed a far more elaborate scheme than Aḥmad Abū al-Fatḥ's effort of 1913.[35] Chehata worked to bring the Islamic theory of obligations to a European standard of completeness by taking a major European work in obligations theory as his model. The categorical scheme of his work seems to have followed Raymond Saleilles's *Essai d'une théorie générale de l'obligation d'après le projet de Code civil allemand* (1890). (See Table 10.1 and Fig. 10.2.)

[32] See, for example, ʿAbd al-Razzāq Aḥmad al-Sanhūrī, *Maṣādir al-ḥaqq fī l-fiqh al-islāmī* (Cairo: Jāmiʿat al-Duwal al-ʿArabiyyah, 1954–59), 1: 13–15.

[33] Chehata, *Essai*, 42–3. [34] See n. 30. [35] Abū al-Fatḥ, *Kitāb al-Muʿāmalāt*.

Fig. 10.1. Chafik Chehata and Louis Milliot, Paris, 1951.
Source: Louis Milliot and Université de Paris, *Travaux de la semaine internationale de droit musulman, Paris, 2–7 juillet 1951* (Paris: Recueil Sirey, 1953).

Although Chehata tried to prove every point about substantive law by reference to methods or arguments acceptable to traditional Islamic methodologies and sensibilities, he did not work hard to justify his application of European categories, methods, and theories to restructure a field of Islamic legal thought. He did not appear too pressed to justify his innovative employment of the concept of a "general theory of obligation" as a means to reconceptualize classical *fiqh*. Instead, he stated that the concepts he was invoking were prominent in European legal thought and that these concepts could be a guide for reforming and reviving Islamic law. He argues that the same conceptual structure had been underlying classical works of Hanafi *fiqh*, even if the classical jurists did not know it. The explanation for his approach might be attributed to his accepting Lambertian premises for his study of legal history, as well as premises advanced earlier by the German schools of Legal History and Conceptual Jurisprudence. He was writing, additionally, with universalist premises:

> The notion of obligation is the foundation of law. In private law, the notion appears as a fundamental category juxtaposed to property law. The rules that govern the diverse cases of obligation were abstracted in the Roman juridical system and its tributary systems. These rules formed the general theory of obligation, which all regard as the masterpiece of the juridical genius of Rome. This theory groups together the general

> principles that govern the infinite variety of situations created by free will as well as all of the obligatory relationships to which a diversity of acts can give birth.[36] This theory delineates the effect of the obligating bond, elaborates its modes of formation, and establishes its sources and its modes of extinction.[37]

He continues:

> These general principles have never been derived in Muslim law. In this system, the jurists were always focused on the casuistry without preoccupying themselves with general rules. Nevertheless, Muslim law comprises an inexhaustible trove of juridical norms. *Justifying the interest that would lie in a work of synthesis in this domain is therefore unnecessary.* It aims at nothing less than to create a science of Muslim law, given that science is defined as the knowledge of phenomena by their primary principles.... This formidable undertaking should not be left uncompleted. [In the history of legal scholarship], synthesis always succeeded the analysis of cases. It is time to pick up once again this thread of centuries' old juridical activity, which has been interrupted. Only a scientific study undertaken with a method and rigor will yield an exact and systematic understanding of Muslim law. With this, a renaissance of studies in Muslim law will set in motion a new "reception" of this law in the countries that saw its birth—and where it is necessary to act upon the highest aspirations of the juridical conscience, a pure product of the national genius.[38]

Chehata's statement of purpose and his proposed methodology are imbued with premises, ideas, and methods from nineteenth-century German legal scholars, among whom Savigny, Puchta, and Jhering. Particularly noticeable among those ideas is the proposition of a scientific-historical method that will yield undiscovered truths about the nature of Islamic law.

In a society that was not accustomed to such innovations in Islamic legal writing, that was living in the midst of anti-colonial political struggle, and that saw as controversial any non-Muslim intervention in an Islamic science, Chehata was cautious about how he presented this European-inspired intellectual endeavor to his examiners. Although the Arabic and French texts are generally identical, the rhetoric differed subtly in important parts of the introduction.[39] For the Franco-Egyptian scholars who were his French readers, he emphasized his devotion to the European disciplines; for his Arabic readers, he emphasized his esteem for Islam and the Egyptian-Islamic intellectual tradition.

[36] Compare with Friedrich Karl von Savigny, *System of the Modern Roman Law* (Madras: J. Higginbotham, 1867), bk. 2, chap. 1, sec. 1.3.

[37] Chehata, *Essai*, 41.

[38] Ibid., 41–2 (emphasis added). He references either the "reception" of Roman law in continental Europe in the twelfth century, or the "reception" of Roman law in German legal scholarship in the sixteenth century. Both events intensified the study of Roman law, conceived at the time by Chehata as part of Egypt's legal heritage.

[39] The French introduction invoked a Muslim "national genius" (*Volksgeist*—an allusion to Puchta and Savigny); the Arabic text did not. The French text invoked *science*, suggesting European methods for researching law and legal history; the Arabic version claimed that Chehata's methodology was in keeping with tradition in Islamic sciences. The French version claimed that the book would serve a renaissance of Muslim law "studies"; the Arabic version implied that the thesis would serve a revival of Islamic "legislation." The cover of the French version offered a quote from Charles Maurras; the cover of the Arabic version offered a quote from prophetic hadith (see Appendix).

Throughout the work, Chehata appears to be informed by two different traditions of legal thought, theory, method, and inquiry. Ample sections of the work are concerned with traditional Islamic methodological sensibilities—perhaps most especially in the second half where Chehata writes an elaborate treatment of "subjects of obligation." In the first half, where he explains his methodological influences and sketches a structure for the Islamic theory of obligation, he shows allegiance to European schools of thought and invokes Lambert's notion of a first stage of comparative law study, which is to say the rewriting of "legal history." That is, Chehata claims that he is writing an authentic revisionist history of Islamic law and doctrine by writing a revisionist history, and he believed this revisionist history could be used by other scholars as a basis for "comparative study" and "comparative legislation." He admitted that his own attempt at legal history was pre-informed by concepts, premises, and categories from European comparative law. "With my method thus established," he wrote, "I intend to delve into the Muslim law and harness its innermost realities. . . . [E]ven if I don't speak openly of comparative law, it goes without saying that the various questions here are studied in light of the *droit commun législatif* of which Lambert spoke.[40] A latent work of *comparison* is read between the lines."[41]

Chehata follows with a justification for his use of Roman legal categories, explaining that these categories help to bring out the authentic Islamic law:

> It would be dangerous to impose on the Muslim system notions and categories that are foreign to it. Every system can have, in effect, its own technique; and that technique may admit the existence of certain notions for the sole reasons of its own needs. Nevertheless, I will provisionally use the categories of Roman law, even if it means discarding some that do not correspond exactly with the notions under consideration. These categories have, in reality, already proven themselves. They consist, in some part, of "the alphabet of the law" as put by Jhering. Even Jhering did not reject the application of Roman categories to Germanic law when such categories were conducive to making a science of German law. "By the Roman Law, it might be said, but above and beyond the Roman law."[42]

Ultimately, Chehata justified his recourse to Roman law and its categories by invoking the authority of Rudolph von Jhering. Jhering's words had also appeared in French legal scholarship through the writings of Gény, the leading contemporary of Lambert and Saleilles. Gény famously adapted Jhering's words when criticizing the French school of exegesis,[43] arguing at the end of the nineteenth century that modern jurists could reform the civil law without dismantling the *Code civil*—that is, "by the *Code civil*, but beyond the *Code civil*."

[40] See Société de Législation Comparée, *Congrès International de droit comparé*, 26–60.

[41] Chehata, *Essai*, 59 (emphasis added). See also pp. 132–3, 141, and 147.

[42] Chehata, *Essai*, 59, 45–6.

[43] On the critique of the school of exegesis and its effects in Egyptian legal thought, see Shalakany, "Between Identity and Redistribution"; Shalakany, "Sanhuri."

FRENCH-STYLE COMPARATIVISM APPLIED

Chehata adopted a twofold methodology comprised of "historical" and "objective" methods, taken from Lambert's writings and Saleilles's 1890 work on obligations theory.[44] The objective method of studying law entails comparing its rules and institutions without reference to historical context. The historical method of studying law involves understanding rules, institutions, sources, and methods within the context of their historical evolution and function.

Chehata was more interested in the historical method, which, as designed by his predecessors, helped him explain, through prefabricated arguments (i.e., theoretical constructs), why the classical Muslim jurists did not form general rules of obligations. Premises of the Historical School also legitimized Chehata's effort to mine the classical Islamic "casuistry" for underlying general rules of obligation. By adopting Lambert's ideas about the history of human law in general and the history of Islamic law in particular, Chehata presumed that an authentic Islamic obligations theory was out there to be discovered, underlying the case law of classical *fiqh*.

As seen in Chapter 6, Édouard Lambert had earlier constructed a theory about the global history of law that informed Chehata's work—in essence, that all law begins with custom and is gradually elaborated by jurists and the state. Since Lambert's understanding of history stripped Islamic *fiqh* of much of its prestige, the understanding rendered *fiqh* amenable to extensive reform by modern jurists. Lambert had also earlier attacked fundamental conceptions of Islamic legal history, such as the valorization of the four *madhhab*s, the reigning theory of consensus (*ijmāʿ*), and the authority of Muslim jurists after the tenth century. Most of these arguments had been adopted from select orientalists as a tool for suggesting pathways for the reform of modern Islamic legal method and substance.

In a similar way, Chehata used European revisionist narratives of Islamic legal history as a tool for promoting modern legal reform. The use of revisionist arguments about Islamic legal history allowed him to make revisionist claims about "authentic" Islamic legal practice, and to contrast ostensibly authentic practice with the divergent doctrine of contemporary Muslim scholars. He compared what he considered "authentic" Islamic law to European law, suggesting cautiously how rapprochement between the two systems could be achieved.

More specifically, Lambertian historical premises appeared in Chehata's work in at least seven ways.

(1) Chehata tried to strip Islamic contract *fiqh* of much of its religious quality. In keeping with Lambert's theories and in common with arguments marshaled by French jurists in Algeria, Chehata made the case that Islamic

[44] Raymond Saleilles, *Essai d'une théorie générale de l'obligation d'après le projet de code civil allemand* (Paris: F. Pichon, 1890). See also Raymond Saleilles, "Le Code civil et la méthode historique," in *Le Code civil, 1804–1904*, ed. Société d'études législatives (Paris: A. Rousseau, 1904), 97–129; Saleilles, "École historique et droit naturel"; Saleilles, "Quelques mots sur le rôle de la méthode historique dans l'enseignement du droit."

contract *fiqh* is a human creation, the extrapolation of jurists, and thus amenable to modern reform.

(2) Chehata cast doubt on the authority of classical jurists collectively. Since they were only human, he argued, their views could be challenged.

(3) Chehata rejected widespread interpretations of Islamic legal history that prevailed among Muslims. By way of this, he cast doubt on the authority of orthodox legal methods of the *madhhabs*. In turn, he opened the way for proposing a new scheme for arranging Islamic private law.

(4) Chehata championed the function of the modern jurist in reforming *fiqh*. Jhering and Lambert had held that the modern jurist of a civilized society needed to serve as a middle man between law and legal doctrine as a static and conservative phenomenon, on the one hand, and human society, on the other hand, which is ever-changing and ever in need of flexible and forward-looking laws. Jhering and Lambert had assailed nineteenth-century French and German jurists for their alleged formalism and ignorance of social realities. They urged European jurists to take greater account of modern needs and to adopt a flexible approach to law, as a means to reform law and make it more useful to society. Chehata took this line of critique and applied it to the *fiqh* discourse, downgrading the authority of classical doctrine and jurists, upgrading the reforming potential of modern doctrine and jurists.

(5) Chehata followed Lambert's theory of global historical legal development, which held that all human legal systems necessarily needed to progress through particular stages. As far as Chehata was concerned, the next stage of development for *fiqh* was the elaboration of general principles. According to the theory, the *fiqh* had begun with custom, then was transformed into formalized casuistry during the medieval centuries. Now, in the modern era, jurists needed to elaborate *fiqh*'s general principles.

(6) Chehata's revisionist claims about Islamic legal history were part of a wide-ranging effort to undermine the authority of orthodox *uṣūl al-fiqh* and to refashion modern Islamic legal methodology. Lambert had adopted from Snouck Hurgronje the attitude that *uṣūl al-fiqh* makes Islamic law resistant to modernization and change; unlike Snouck Hurgronje, Lambert was dedicated to reforming understandings of Islamic legal theory and Islamic history so that Islamic legal theory could be a catalyst, and not an impediment, to the development of new law in the modern era. Chehata followed in this path, although he did so with caution. He critiqued traditional theories regulating the use of primary sources of Islamic legal doctrine and legislation (Quran, sunnah, *ijmāʿ*, and *qiyās*) and proposed alternative theories. Whereas traditional legal methodology held that the foundation of Islamic law is the textual guidance of the Quran and prophetic tradition, Chehata claimed that the starting point for his method was "the cases," or the academic extrapolations of classical jurists.[45]

[45] Chehata, *Essai*, 43.

Chehata also strove to transcend the classical tolerance of juristic difference (*ikhtilāf*). Whereas it was a tenet of *uṣūl al-fiqh* that jurists within and from different Sunni schools of thought could legitimately hold different rulings on the same legal question, Chehata wanted to erect a uniform system of rules for obligations. He therefore proposed a method for how jurists could move beyond *ikhtilāf*. One sees here reverberations of the drive for unity in the legal system, a key preoccupation of nineteenth-century German and French legal theory.[46]

(7) There was a European-inspired policy driver behind Chehata's interest in the reconceptualization and reform of Islamic private law through the means of general theory. Lambert had been intensely concerned with injecting a greater measure of social justice into French civil law. In Lambert's view, French civil law's valorization of the autonomy of the will created conditions in which stronger parties routinely exploited weaker parties through contracts, thereby entrenching problematic social and economic inequalities. Chehata showed some inclination in bringing this line of social critique to bear on considerations about the reform of modern Islamic contract law.[47]

With such challenges to the authority of orthodox Islamic legal thought thus set forth, Chehata empowered himself to reconceptualize the system of Islamic private law according to different lead categories. He did not go as far in the construction of his theory as he might have; however, he went further than any Egyptian jurists before him, and further than many who succeeded him.

THE GENERAL THEORY OF OBLIGATION AND THE GENERAL THEORY OF CONTRACT

Chehata's general theory pushed Islamic *fiqh* in new conceptual and substantive directions. His general theory was a new kind of attempt at standardizing and unifying Islamic contract law—despite his research scope being limited to Hanafi *fiqh*. He paved the way for an elaboration of a general theory of contract in Islamic law, and began along the paths, although leaving them incomplete, of constructing an Islamic doctrine that explicitly enforced innominate contracts and supported the principle of freedom of contract. He suggested paths for relaxing traditional Hanafi constraints on contractual freedoms, specifically on interest, contracts with a "future object," and adjoining conditions (*al-shurūṭ al-muqtārinah bi-al-ʿaqd*).

As displayed in Table 10.1, the categorical paradigm bore a close resemblance to that found in a book written by Lambert's mentor, Saleilles. (See also Fig. 10.2.)

[46] As of 1936, Chehata's observations on *uṣūl al-fiqh* literature were radical for an Egyptian author in Egypt, writing from within an Egyptian educational institution. Arguably, his statement would not be well received in present-day Egypt given the climate of religious conservatism and the power of *uṣūl al-fiqh* orthodoxy in the universities.

[47] Chehata, *Essai*, 58.

Table 10.1. The General Theory Books of Saleilles and Chehata compared.

Raymond Saleilles, *Essai d'une théorie générale de l'obligation d'après le projet de code civil allemand* (1890)	Chafik Chehata, *Essai d'une théorie générale de l'obligation en droit musulman* (1936)
Sec. 1. Obligation in Itself	**Sec. 1. Obligation in Itself**
	1. Elements
	Subject
1. Object	Object
	Cause
2. Effects	**2. Effects**
Liability of Debtor	Obligation to Give
Vicarious Liability	Obligation to Do
Execution and Refusal	Breach of Contract
Lien Rights	Fault
Acts of God	Force Majeure and Acts of God
Fault	Excuse
Notice to Debtor	Calculation of Sums
Notice to Creditor	Obligation for Money Sums
	3. Clauses
	Term
	Condition
3. Extinguishment	**4. Extinguishment**
Payment	Payment
Deposit	Accord and Satisfaction
Offsetting	Offsetting
Discharge	Merger of Debt
Merger of Debt	Discharge
	Lapse
	Other Modes
4. Transfer	**5. Transfer**
5. Plurality of Creditors or Debtors	
Sec. 2: Sources of Obligation	**Sec. 2: Sources of Obligation**
I. Acts	**I. Acts**
Contract	1. General Notions
Simple Promise	2. Declared Will
	3. Real Will
2. Object of Contracts	
.... Nullities....	4. Nullities
3. General Effects of Contracts	5. General Effects of Contracts
4. Special Effects of Certain Contracts	
5. Secondary Effects of Contracts	
	Dissolution of Contracts
II. Delict	**II. Delict**
1. General Notions	
Quasi-Delict	
2. Elements and Conditions	**1. Acts**
Illicit Act	Illicit Act
Fault	Fault
Privilege	Risk
3. Liability	**2. Liability**
	Causality
	Damage
	Reparation
III. Unjust Enrichment	**III. Unjust Enrichment**

ESSAI

D'UNE

THEORIE GENERALE DE L'OBLIGATION

EN

DROIT MUSULMAN

TOME PREMIER

LES SUJETS DE L'OBLIGATION

AVEC UNE BIBLIOGRAPHIE, UNE MÉTHODOLOGIE
ET UN TABLEAU GÉNÉRAL DE LA THÉORIE DE L'OBLIGATION
EN DROIT HANÉFITE

« ...ayant adopté ma carrière et choisi pour objet la figure abstraite du vrai... »
Ch. MAURRAS

LE CAIRE
IMP. F. E. NOURY & FILS
1936

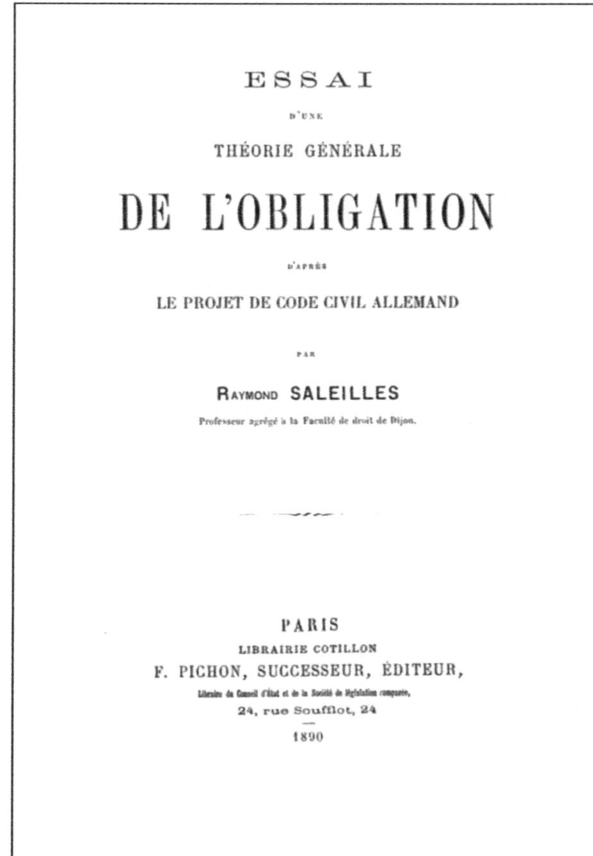

ESSAI

D'UNE

THÉORIE GÉNÉRALE

DE L'OBLIGATION

D'APRÈS

LE PROJET DE CODE CIVIL ALLEMAND

PAR

RAYMOND SALEILLES

Professeur agrégé à la Faculté de droit de Dijon.

PARIS
LIBRAIRIE COTILLON
F. PICHON, SUCCESSEUR, ÉDITEUR,
Libraire du Conseil d'État et de la Société de législation comparée,
24, rue Soufflot, 24
1890

Fig. 10.2. Title pages of Saleilles's and Chehata's books on the theory of obligations.

UNIFYING CONTRACT LAW AND ESTABLISHING NEW MASTER CATEGORIES

Chehata posited the "general laws of contract" as subsidiary to the "general laws of obligation," although he would leave it for other jurists to flesh out an Islamic theory of contract. He lists two principal sources of obligations: the "juridical act" (contracts and unilateral will) and the "juridical event" (delict and unjust enrichment). He identifies delict as a cause of obligations but notes that Islamic juridical texts historically did not theorize on delict. He admits that classicial *fiqh* was concerned with civil liability (*ḍamān*), but suggests that the classical *fiqh* did not provide general theories of civil liability, much less as a subset of the theory of obligation. He underlines the distinction between contractual and delictual liability. He proceeds to advance a theory of delict as a source of obligation and its relationship to damages. Finally, he studies "unjust enrichment" as a source of obligation.

The section on obligation comprises five main parts: elements (subjects and object), effects (doing, conveying, etc.), clauses (term and condition), extinguishment (payment, conveyance, offset, etc.), and transfer (active and passive). Chehata then comes to the section on sources of obligation, of which contract is his first part. He lists six main categories in the law of contract: declared will (offer and acceptance), the session, real will (which he contrasts with its vitiating factors: coercion, misrepresentation, unequal compensation, lesion, error, and incapacity), nullities (non-existence, vitiated, etc.), effects, and dissolution. He therefore provides a map of the theory, modeled on French doctrine.

It would be for later writers of this genre—Muḥammad Abū Zahrah, ʿAlī al-Khafīf, Aḥmad Zarqāʾ, al-Sanhūrī, and others—to posit a unified Islamic law of contract that was trans-*madhhab* and purported to represent the complete view on obligations and contract law of the Sharia. Chehata probably deserves some credit for the fact that those jurists, after 1936, endeavored to pen comprehensive, trans-*madhhab* Islamic general theories on topics such as obligations, rights, capacity, and liability.

FREEDOM OF CONTRACT AND THE LIMITS OF CHEHATA'S INTERVENTION

Chehata was concerned with the variety of constraints on contracting in Hanafi *fiqh*. Constraints were posed, for example, on interest, contracts with future objects, and certain types of contract conditions. Like other jurists concerned with the question of Islamic law's relevance and revival in the contemporary nation and economy, Chehata saw these constraints as possible areas for reform.[48]

[48] Since the end of the nineteenth century, European jurists and several of Chehata's colleagues had determined that it was good for a legal system to impose constraints on contracting, for the benefit of social and individual welfare in the modern industrial economy. See Kennedy, "Three Globalizations." American law came around to this view years later, most notably with the U.S. Supreme Court decision of *West Coast Hotel v. Parrish* (1937). Nonetheless, Chehata was concerned about whether the specific

Yet, for all of Chehata's innovative engagements with classical *fiqh* at the level of organizing categories, he did not innovate a rule of freedom of contract for Hanafi *fiqh*—even though such a rule featured prominently in French and Franco-Egyptian *doctrine* (albeit, this concept had been under sustained attack by European social jurists for three decades). He was willing to challenge orthodox conceptions when working at the top of the system, that is, with fundamental questions of juridical methodology or with high-level substantive law categories like obligations, contract, and liability. He was less comfortable with manipulating well-known rules in the middle-level substance of Hanafi *fiqh*. In the latter area, Chehata acted mostly as a historian of the Hanafi *fiqh* as he understood it. He avoided taking up the mantle of a reformist *mujtahid,* a claim he could never have made for reasons discussed earlier.

The main obstacles to a Hanafi rule of freedom of contract, Chehata claimed, were classical jurists' restrictions against *ribā*, contracts with a future object, and "adjoining conditions," and jurists' ambivalence concerning innominate contracts. Chehata allowed those inhibiting factors to stand, as had Egyptian jurists writing about Hanafi law in prior decades. However, unlike his predecessors, Chehata identified those restrictions as obstacles to a rule of freedom of contract.

It was a significant innovation for Chehata merely to have asked whether Hanafi *fiqh* comprised a doctrine of "freedom of contract" (*ḥurriyyat al-taʿāqud*). No Arabic book on Islamic law from before 1936 had posed this question or used this Arabic term. In a section entitled "Freedom of Contracting," a rubric possibly borrowed from Saleilles, Chehata argued that Hanafis acknowledge, at some level, the principle of freedom of contract. At the root of Hanafi discussions on contracts, he claims, is the principle of *ibāḥah* ("that which is [not forbidden is] licit"). However, he concludes that by European standards, there is no comparable freedom of contract in Hanafi *fiqh*: the number and weight of restrictions placed on the contracting parties is too great.

For a few paragraphs, it appears as though Chehata drives toward an argument for freedom of contract in Hanafi *fiqh*.[49] Momentarily, he makes a case for how Hanafi law might enforce innominate contracts. Following on an argument once made by Lambert,[50] Chehata points out that the traditional Islamic legal sources of custom (*ʿurf*) and consensus (*ijmāʿ*) could lend weight to such a rule. Momentarily, he challenges the prevailing notion that Hanafi *fiqh* is absolutely risk averse and therefore absolutely inimical to contracts with a future object where risk is involved. He gives examples of two Islamic nominate contracts that betray tolerance for risk: the hire/rent contract (*ijārah*) and the service contract[51] (*istiṣnāʿ*). And momentarily, he challenges dominant interpretations of the Hanafi restrictions on adjoining conditions to nominate contracts.

constraints posed by Hanafi *fiqh*, and the extent of those constraints, were workable in contemporary Egypt. The observations in this paragraph are based on my reading between the lines of Chehata's work. He does not state these concerns explicitly, but a reading of his text in historical context justifies the claims made. Chehata invited his readers to "read between the lines" to discern the underlying theoretical, policy, and comparative law concerns at stake in his work. Chehata, *Essai*, 59.

49 Ibid., 105–6.

50 Lambert, *Fonction*, 325–6, 334–48.

51 Chehata uses the civil law term, *locatio operis*.

These ideas amounted only to prodding in the direction of a rule of freedom of contract, inspired by a style of legal critique and theorization popularized in Europe. Nonetheless, Chehata's text suggested room for further development of the *fiqh*. As mentioned, the Egyptian jurists who followed him in writing on this topic did, in fact, enter through some of the doors that he opened. It is possible to portray Chehata as a non-Muslim civil lawyer meddling in the substance of sacred law on this topic, but it becomes harder to dismiss him in this way when one considers that Shaykh Muḥammad Abū Zahrah, Chehata's own adviser and a famous Muslim jurist, endorsed the freedom of contract rule for Islamic law three years later, in 1939.

NEXUSES OF INFLUENCE BETWEEN EUROPEAN LAW AND ISLAMIC *FIQH*

With Chehata's work taken as a case study, it appears that European law was influencing Islamic *fiqh* discourse during the 1930s on at least six levels: expository; conceptual and categorical; substantive; methodological, theoretical, social-scientific, and policy; source-wise; and philosophical/religious.

Expository. Chehata's study was modeled, in its most outward manifestations, on one of the most famous books in the French and German *doctrine* genre—Saleilles's *Essai d'une théorie générale de l'obligation*. His study also shows Islamic *fiqh* being written, in Arabic, in new rhetorical form. The Arabic version employed a modern style of Arabic that had become popular in other intellectual circles, for example, in the writings of Ṭāhā Ḥusayn and Qāsim Amīn. In the 1930s, a Europeanized rhetorical style signaled that an author was advertising his European intellectual pedigree. More pertinent to the content of the text, Chehata took European terms and inserted them into *fiqh* discourse, even when this meant deploying new Arabic coinages to accommodate French meanings. One example given is *ḥurriyyat al-taʿāqud* (freedom of contracting). Notably, the experimental positing of such a term was the beginning of the concept's eventual adoption among jurists as a point of substantive legal doctrine.

Concepts and Categories. Chehata took a conceptual and categorical model from a foreign system of law and imposed it on Islamic *fiqh*. He argued that he was, merely, and in fact, uncovering the true nature of the *fiqh* and the Sharia. Nevertheless, it is clear that he was following the lead of European jurists. This categorical model would take hold for future writers for the rest of the century, even if most Egyptian and Arab jurists lost track of the model's historical origins and Chehata's place in its history.

Substance. Chehata was cautious in handling the middle-level rules of the system. However, by taking European categories for a model, he provided a new foundation on which to debate and reform traditional rules from Islamic *fiqh*.

Method, Theory, Social Science, and Policy. Chehata was influenced by European trends in juridical methodology, theory, social science, and policy. Ideas from orientalists and European comparativists found their way into his work. In methods, Chehata adopted some premises of orientalists regarding Islamic legal history; he followed the lead of Roman legal categories in restructuring Islamic legal rules; he followed the lead of French law in seeking out lacunae and problems in classical Islamic legal rules; he adopted Lambert's belief in the power of history, as a science, to reveal truths about the legal past. On the level of policy concerns, Chehata was influenced by the social critique of law that was popular in Europe.

Sources and Authority. Chehata differed from Egyptian writers on Islamic contracts before him by engaging a range of scholarly sources that previous Muslim jurists had not used. The drafters of the *Mecelle*, for example, relied on classical Hanafi works of *fiqh*, and occasionally looked to major classical works from other schools. Muḥammad Qadrī Pasha referred to the classical Hanafi works and, particularly, to more recent works such as those by Ibn ʿĀbidīn. Chafik Chehata availed himself not only of these classical *fiqh* sources but also of the full range of writings by European orientalists, comparativists, and theoretical texts that would have been available to Lambert and the Egyptian jurists of Franco-Egyptian law.

Philosophy and Religion. In the long term, during the remainder of the twentieth century Arabic-Islamic general theory books would be interested in the question of *why* contracts are binding. Chehata was not concerned with the deontological bases of Islamic obligations law. He may have made this choice because of his worldview or because he considered himself an exponent of the secular-oriented "*science*" of legal history, like Lambert or Snouck Hurgronje.[52] In 1936, European obligations theory was largely devoid of religious underpinnings.[53] At any rate, his decision not to comment on the religious underpinnings of obligations seems to have been interpreted by later Muslim jurists as the result of undue European influence and a purposeful decision to avoid addressing Islamic beliefs about the place of God in the normative order.

Later writers in this field, especially Sharia professors at the Cairo Faculty, brought the religious dimension back into the fold of the theory of contract, insisting on the existence of a divine underpinning of human obligations. One can say then that Chehata brought European influence into the Islamic general theory discourse by what he did *not* say, and by giving Sharia jurists an idea for how the Islamic theory of obligation could distinguish itself from European theories.

CHEHATA'S LEGACY

Chehata's basic ambition would take hold among jurists in Egypt and the Arab world. In the fourteen years following 1936, his colleagues in Cairo, Beirut, and

[52] The European discipline of legal history may have been secularly inclined, but not all European proponents of advanced legal studies and theory were secular in outlook or ambivalent about their own religion. See also p. 138 n. 16.

[53] See generally James Gordley, *The Philosophical Origins of Modern Contract Doctrine* (Oxford: Oxford University Press, 1991).

Damascus published at least ten books that addressed the same topic as his 1936 dissertation.[54] These colleagues, most of them senior to him, included Shaykhs Aḥmad Ibrāhīm, ʿAlī al-Khafīf, Muḥammad Abū Zahrah, Muḥammad Yūsuf Mūsá, Ṣubḥī Maḥmaṣānī, Muṣṭafá Aḥmad Zarqāʾ, and ʿAbd al-Razzāq al-Sanhūrī. Their books followed the general theory paradigm, pursued many of the same questions, and carried titles that bore a similarity to that of Chehata's dissertation.

These jurists and their works were divided into two strains. One group, represented by Aḥmad Ibrāhīm, ʿAlī al-Khafīf, Muḥammad Abū Zahrah, and Muḥammad Yūsuf Mūsá—all Sharia professors of the Cairo Faculty—attempted to strengthen the general theories of obligation and contract while seeking to rid the discourse of other European-inspired premises and methods. In opposition to Chehata's challenges to classical Islamic legal theory and method, they made their theory books platforms for championing classically oriented Islamic legal theory and method. The other group, represented by al-Sanhūrī and Chehata in his later years, favored synthesis of European and Islamic premises and methods.

That story—one could say, that clash—falls beyond the scope of this work. It will suffice to underline that in 1939, Shaykh Muḥammad Abū Zahrah threw his weight behind the conception of an Islamic theory of contract and an Islamic doctrine of freedom of contract.[55] Aḥmad Ibrāhīm, Muḥammad Yūsuf Mūsá, al-Sanhūrī, and the others followed in step. Al-Sanhūrī went so far as to chip away at traditional Islamic prohibitions on *ribā*, working within a general theory paradigm.[56] The Muslim jurists thereby gave ultimate legitimacy to ideas and certain methods that Chehata had proposed. Throughout the Arab world, many of the subsequent changes to Islamic contract doctrine, as well as changes in other legal subjects, happened on the playing field of the general theory genre.

[54] See Ibrāhīm, *al-Muʿāmalāt al-sharʿiyyah al-māliyyah*; Abū Zahrah, *al-Milkiyyah wa-naẓariyyat al-ʿaqd*; ʿAlī al-Khafīf, *al-Ḥaqq wa-l-dhimmah* (Cairo: Maktabat al-Wahbah, 1940); ʿAlī al-Khafīf, *Aḥkām al-muʿāmalāt al-sharʿiyyah* (Cairo: Maṭbaʿat Lajnat al-Taʾlīf wa-l-Tarjamah wa-l-Nashr, 1942); Aḥmad Ibrāhīm, *al-Iltizāmāt fī l-sharʿ al-islāmī* (Cairo: Dār al-Anṣār, 1980); Muṣṭafá Aḥmad Zarqāʾ, *al-Madkhal ilá naẓariyyat al-iltizām al-ʿāmmah fī l-fiqh al-islāmī* (Damascus: Dār al-Qalam, 1946); Ṣubḥī Rajab Maḥmaṣānī, *al-Naẓariyyah al-ʿāmmah li-l-mūjibāt wa-l-ʿuqūd fī l-sharīʿah al-islāmiyyah* (Beirut: Maktabat al-Kashshāf, 1948); ʿAlī al-Khafīf, *Mukhtaṣar Aḥkām al-muʿāmalāt al-sharʿiyyah* (Cairo: Maṭbaʿat al-Sunnah al-Muḥammadiyyah, 1949); Mūsá, *Amwāl wa-naẓariyyāt al-ʿaqd*; al-Sanhūrī, *Maṣādir al-ḥaqq*.

[55] Muḥammad Abū Zahrah, *Al-milkiyyah wa-naẓariyyat al-ʿaqd fī-al-sharīʿah al-islāmiyyah* (Cairo: Dār al-Fikr al-ʿArabī, 1939).

[56] Emad Khalil, "The Modern Debate over Riba and Its Resolution in the Codes of Sanhuri" (S.J.D. diss., Harvard Law School, 1990); Chibli Mallat, "The Debate on Riba and Interest in Twentieth Century Jurisprudence," in *Islamic Law and Finance*, ed. C. Mallat (London: Graham and Trotman, 1988), 69–88.

Epilogue: The Waxing of Conservative Revivalists and the Waning of Franco-Egyptians

The ideological and academic dimensions of Islamic legal revivalism persisted through the 1940s and 1950s. Enthusiasm for the application of Sharia increased in the public consciousness and in the rhetoric of opposition movements, especially in social quarters removed from the comparatively rarified environs of the Cairo Faculty. The exhortations of Ḥasan al-Bannā, Sayyid Quṭb, and the Muslim Brotherhood in favor of the application of Sharia are widely known. More attention should be afforded to the academic work that buttressed these ambitions. The Sharia professors of the Cairo Faculty, conservative-minded reformists, incorporated into their textbooks and scholarly articles assertions about the superiority of Islamic law. Aḥmad Ibrāhīm, for example, opened a 1944 treatise with an exhortation against "positive law," intended as a reference to man-made law:

> Islamic law surpasses positive laws in the way of redeeming the soul and purifying it, in preserving the intellect of mankind, and in defending the intellect from all that does not enrich it. By contrast, the positive laws (man-made law) regulate only the material aspects of life. Positive law leaves each person completely free in his private affairs so long as he does not harm others, with a few exceptions. By contrast, Islamic law provides for man by way of its virtuous spirit, and through the highest human ethics, divine grace, and God's supervision over human beings in all of their words and deeds, "those which are overt, and those which are concealed."[1]

The revivalist statements of Sharia professors at the Cairo Faculty became more explicit in the later 1940s and 1950s. One of the most outspoken was the Azhar- and Sorbonne-educated Muḥammad Yūsuf Mūsá, who had ties to the Muslim Brotherhood. He published academic articles in the al-Azhar journal, *Majallat al-Azhar*, during the early 1950s, including during the first years of the Egyptian revolution of 1952.

An impressive aspect of Islamic legal revivalism in the late 1940s and 1950s is that more elaborate and comparative approaches were deployed beyond the

[1] Ibrāhīm, *Mudhakkirah mubtada'ah*, 4. The quote is Quran *al-A'rāf* (7):33; see also *al-An'ām* (6):151.

Islamic Legal Revival: Reception of European Law and Transformations in Islamic Legal Thought in Egypt, 1875–1952. First Edition. Leonard Wood.

Cairo Faculty and its classrooms, books, and journals. Comparative inquiry ceased to be the work of only, or predominantly, those professors. Zakī al-Dīn Shaʿbān published articles of revivalist interest for *Majallat al-Azhar* while teaching as an assistant professor at the new ʿAyn Shams Law Faculty. Other efforts appeared by writers directly affiliated with al-Azhar, the Sharia Courts, and the Muslim Brotherhood, for instance Sayyid ʿAbd Allāh Ḥusayn's four-volume comparison of Maliki *fiqh* and French law.[2] He accomplished this project while working in government service and for the Sharia Courts.

Sayyid ʿAbd Allāh Ḥusayn was one among a relatively small number of al-Azhar graduates who had studied law in France. After obtaining the *ʿalamiyyah* degree in 1917, he spent 1921 to 1925 studying for the *licence* in Lyon. Unlike the doctoral students discussed in previous chapters, the scholars of Franco-Egyptian law, he did not assume a position at the Cairo Faculty and did not become a professor of Franco-Egyptian law. Instead, he remained connected to his roots in the Islamic institutions. His treatise comparatively evaluated theories of law and substantive rules on the family, inheritance, succession, contracts, delicts, and criminal punishment. The book was written to furnish the Sharia revivalist ambition with academic weight. The rhetorical tone was sharp. In addition to championing Islamic legislation, he argued that French law, in its best aspects, had been based on Islamic law. That particular historical argument, one that contradicted the theory of Lambert and some of his orientalist colleagues and predecessors, had roots in Egyptian-Islamic historical discourse—controversial discourse—from earlier decades. He claimed in his four-volume, comparative law masterwork:

> It is unusual in law and history for a body of legislation to be created from scratch, without it drawing on law that was already in place, and still appealing to men as a law that is sensible and easy to follow. For 1360 years, this has been the difference between Islamic law and the Roman law that appeared in 50 B.C. As for French law, it was born after the Islamic conquests, and after the consequent spread of science and learning, and after the conquests' appeal to justice. The French jurists knew the differences between Islamic and Roman law, and they chose to adopt whatever was most sensible and easy to work with, and whatever was most helpful to mankind.... But the writer of today's positive law is too proud. He declines to admit the truth. And so he intentionally declines to mention his debt to Islamic law.... Yet none of them can truly hide their debt to the grace of Islam, however they may try, or fail to acknowledge the grace Islam bestows on its people. Every aspect of Islamic law provides guidance to secure the peaceable interactions among men. Islam legislated for humankind fundamentals and rules that provide peace of mind and serenity to parties in dispute. Islam renders disputing parties mutually desirous of Islam's trial and judgment. For Islam is trial by logic and reason. Mankind asks for nothing more than the security of justice and the prevention of injustice.... Roman law was the first to come into existence, and

2 ʿAbd Allāh Ḥusayn, *al-Muqāranāt al-tashrīʿiyyah*, ed. M. A. Sirāj and ʿA. J. Muḥammad, 4 vols. (Cairo: Dār al-Salām, 2001 [1947–49]). Biographical remarks are based on the editors' introduction to the 2001 edition. See also al-Minyāwī, *Muqāranāt*. Compare with ʿAbd Allāh Ḥusayn, "al-Qaḍāʾ al-sharʿī wa-l-muḥāmūn al-sharʿiyyūn," *al-Muḥāmāh al-sharʿiyyah* 1,1 (1929): 15–17.

then Islamic law appeared. And Islam's law was no great secret. On the contrary, people applied it and followed its rules even in France, Spain, Germany, and Africa. After this, French law came, which its authors claimed was different from Roman law. As for Islamic law, my esteemed friends, it is pure logic and justice, and a source of French law. And how could you deny that, when you see before you palpable evidence....

"Their intention is to extinguish God's light by blowing with their mouths;
But God will complete the revelation of His light, even though the unbelievers detest it."[3]

ʿAbd al-Qādir ʿAwdah, a civil court judge and a member of the Muslim Brotherhood, was among the outspoken advocates of the view that all law in Egypt should be based on Sharia. His provocative ideological manifesto, *al-Islām wa-awḍāʿunā al-qānūniyyah* (Islam and Our Legal Practices, 1951), called for reorienting the Egyptian constitution around principles of Sharia.[4] He is also remembered as a proponent of the revival of Islamic criminal law. However, less appreciated are the structure and intellectual origins of his four-volume treatise on that subject, *al-Tashrīʿ al-jināʾī al-islāmī muqāranan bi-l-qānūn al-waḍʿī* (Islamic Criminal Law Compared to Positive Law, 1949). This book was more than an ideological manifesto—its approach was academic; it offered research to support its claims; it provided an elaborate, if contestable, structure of categories, claims, and evidence; and it endeavored to make a comparative study between two legal traditions.

For all of its controversial ideas, ʿAwdah's criminal law book employed a comparative approach that resembled approaches pioneered in the 1930s and 1940s. Although ʿAwdah did not apply a Lyonaise or Lambertian method, his approach would have been recognizable to the Sharia jurists at the Cairo Faculty. They had been interested in making lengthy comparisons between European and Islamic law, but they were not as interested in certain premises, requirements, and rigors of French-style comparativism. Lyon-style universalism, for example, was not as appealing to them as the theory of Islam's uniqueness, originality, and supremacy.

ʿAwdah's confidence in the value of his case for Islamic criminal legislation derived, in part, from confidence in his comparative method. He wrote in his introduction:

This book is a comparative study of the Islamic criminal law with particular reference to Egyptian law. It essentially consists of an inquiry into the respective principles and theories underlying the Islamic laws and other laws, and it aims at identifying the points of difference and similarity between them. May God grant me the strength and guidance to accomplish this noble task. After the completion of the work in hand, I propose to undertake a comparative study of the civil laws....

My contention may astonish some people, since truth has become unfamiliar in the world today. However, those whom God has endowed with reason and understanding can certainly distinguish between good and evil.

[3] Quran *al-Ṣaff* (61):8, translation based on Yusuf Ali. Ḥusayn, *Muqāranāt*, 2: 652.

[4] ʿAbd al-Qādir ʿAwdah, *al-Islām wa-awḍāʿunā al-qānūniyyah* (Cairo: Dār al-Kitāb al-ʿArabī, 1951); Nathan J. Brown, *Constitutions in a Nonconstitutional World* (Albany: State University of New York Press, 2002), 165–9.

> No doubt the new is better than the old, but this holds true only when the new and the old are both man-made. Nothing can stand in comparison with anything old made by God Almighty....
>
> This study is not confined to any one school of Islamic jurisprudence....I have deliberately avoided in this book the use of traditional jargon of our jurists....
>
> I have begun this comparative study with the criminal law since it is this part of the Islamic Sharia that has suffered the greatest injustice and has been abandoned as impracticable....
>
> Indications of the superiority of the Sharia are found in Muḥammad Qadrī Pasha's book *Murshid al-ḥayrān*, which has made it easier to compare and contrast the Islamic Sharia with the modern law.... The readers will notice that in arranging the text of this book, I have followed the same method as is generally adopted in the modern law books....
>
> On the basis of my comprehensive study of the Islamic law, I maintain that declaring this law incompatible with the demands of the modern age is untenable; it is not the result of research or logical reasoning. In fact, academic research and logical arguments lead to the conclusion that Islamic law is unique among all human laws and is applicable to the conditions of every age.[5]

A believer, a judge, a comparativist, and then a revolutionary, ʿAwdah was eventually charged with involvement in a plot to assassinate President Gamal Abd al-Nasser, and was executed in 1958.

AUTHORITARIANISM AND FRANCO-EGYPTIANS

The Egyptian Revolution and the rise of Gamal Abd al-Nasser brought a decline of standards in legal academia and also a suppression of Islamic reformist initiatives.[6] As suggested, Islamic legal revivalism still persisted as a discourse in the 1950s and 1960s. Some who engaged in this discourse went to prison, and some died there. Others, however, managed to support Islamic legal revivalist principles without facing prison. Professors with chairs in law schools were usually safe from the harshest varieties of government attention. The Cairo Faculty professors provide a good example, as do the professors at the Universities of al-Azhar, Alexandria, and ʿAyn Shams. Many contented themselves to write about topics that did not provoke the government. New treatises positing a modern Islamic theory of contract—to give one example—were novel and interesting to professors, but such expositions did not provoke much interest among the colonels.

[5] ʿAbd al-Qādir ʿAwdah, *al-Tashrīʿ al-jināʾī al-islāmī muqāranan bi-l-qānūn al-waḍʿī* (Cairo: Dār Nashr al-Thaqāfah, 1949), Eng. trans., A. Q. ʿO Shaheed and S. Z. Aijaz, *Criminal Law of Islam*, 4 vols. (New Delhi: Adam Publishers and Distributors, 2005), 1: 3–11. The translation above is based on that of Shaheed and Aijaz, with modifications.

[6] See generally Tamir Moustafa, "The Islamist Trend in Egyptian Law," *Politics and Religion* 3,3 (2010): 610–30, at 613–18. See also works in Bibliography of Donald M. Reid, Byron Cannon, and Nathan Brown.

The revolutionary government intervened in the management of law faculties.[7] This was an established practice, of course. Historically, consonant with political practice in France, the Ministries of Education and Justice had always overseen the Cairo Faculty in its hiring and firing, governance, and instruction. However, Nasser's revolutionary government managed the law schools in its characteristically revolutionary ways. It manipulated curricula and saturated classrooms with overflowing enrollments—arguably to weaken the prestige and power of lawyers; it suppressed rights of expression; it slashed faculties' budgets. Under Egyptian nationalist and anti-European policies, and under the squeeze of an increasingly poor public sector that paid meager salaries to professors, Egyptian law scholars travelled less and more rarely became truly fluent in foreign languages. The government also transferred teaching personnel around the schools as a method for building loyalty networks, spreading intimidation, and controlling messages. Nasserist policies also led to a decline in the quality of Egyptian social science departments, and this decline dragged on the quality of Egyptian legal scholarship.

A separate but telling event involved al-Sanhūrī, who by the 1950s was known by the honorific al-Sanhūrī Pasha. In 1954, he was President of Egypt's Supreme Administrative Court. He was also a three-time Education Minister, a former Deputy Minister of Justice, a former President of the Arab League's Cultural Commission, a senior statesman who had represented Egypt in international congresses, and author of Egypt's new Civil Code. In 1952–53, he supported the Free Officers in their ascent to power. He had been on cordial terms with Colonel Muḥammad Najīb (Naguib) (see Fig. 11.1). In 1954, in his capacity as President of the Supreme Administrative Court, al-Sanhūrī opted to challenge the Free Officers' constitutional machinations. The Revolutionary Command Council dispatched a mob that attacked him in his chambers and beat him severely (see Fig. 11.2). Although al-Sanhūrī would survive and continue to write and speak publicly until his death in 1971, he suffered a lifetime ban from government service.

Al-Sanhūrī's political fate symbolized changes that would occur in the law and legal education during subsequent decades. Authoritarianism, corruption, emergency law, censorship, cultural consequences of anti-European nationalism, failures of statist economic policies, and weakened academic standards were factors that took a toll on the well-being of the Franco-Egyptian approach to legal thought, as well as on the ideological and administrative power of its adherents. In the meantime, Islamic legal revivalist thought persisted for the rest of the century in the secular-oriented universities, Islamic universities, intellectual culture, and radical Islamist milieus. It flourished without having to contend with pre-1952 levels of ideological tempering, legal-theoretical influence, and internationalist influence which Franco-Egyptian scholars had once supplied with greater force.

Scholars of Franco-Egyptian law had historically countered both conservative and radical tendencies of certain quarters of Islamic legal revivalism through the

[7] Moustafa, "The Islamist Trend in Egyptian Law," 613–18.

Fig. 11.1. Al-Sanhūrī Pasha with Colonel Muḥammad Najīb (Naguib), ca. 1953.

Fig. 11.2. Al-Sanhūrī Pasha following the attack on him at the Supreme Administrative Court, March 29, 1954.

weight of Franco-Egyptian juridical rigor and prestige. Having diminished the abilities and prestige of next-generation Franco-Egyptian jurists, the post-1952 Egyptian state principally countered the ideas of Islamic legal revivalism, in the urban parts of Egypt, with ideas of nationalism and socialism, and with force—all poor and fleeting counterweights to an Islamist conviction that focuses on the primacy of Sharia. If anything, nationalism, statist economic policy, and, above all, authoritarianism exercised by the post-1952 military state made Islamic legal revivalist conviction stronger, more methodologically and morally conservative, more radical in some of its quarters, and harder to argue against.

Conclusion

An understanding of present-day Islamic law—theoretical and applied, and for all countries—requires an appreciation of Egyptian legal thought and education between 1875 and 1952. That appreciation, in turn, requires knowledge of the reception of continental European law in Egypt, the origins of Egyptian efforts to revive Islamic law, and foundations of transformations in twentieth-century Egyptian-Islamic legal thought.

The late nineteenth and early twentieth centuries witnessed the evolution of a movement to reform, revive, and apply Islamic law in the face of European law reception. This book has called the movement Islamic legal revivalism. On the one hand, Islamic legal revivalism was ideology: it constituted tenets and a platform for political activism. Proponents wanted Islamic *fiqh* to be competitive with European law in terms of prestige, comprehensiveness, ease of use, and relevance. Many proponents took the additional step of asserting that Islamic law was qualitatively, morally, and overall spiritually superior to European law. On the other hand, Islamic legal revival was a field of technical scholarship dedicated to accomplishing Islamic legal revivalism, whose lead players were more than ideologues—they were academic jurists, lawyers, and judges, and their primary contributions came in the form of intellectual exploration and rigor.

Characteristics that the early Islamic legal revivalists yearned to attribute to their modern, reformed Islamic *fiqh* were those that they first attributed to European law. Early revivalists praised codification and famous European reference works.[1] They were attracted to the Napoleonic ideal, and fiction, of a unified legal system offering uniform and definitive answers to every question. They seized on a popular assumption that European law was more comprehensive and fitting to the changing world and economy than Islamic law *qua fiqh*; responding to this notion, they claimed that Islamic law, *qua* Sharia, was itself, instead, the singularly comprehensive and best law to handle all matters old and new.

Islamic legal revivalists also advocated the development of fields in Islamic *fiqh* such as "Islamic constitutional law" and women's rights, human rights, and judicial independence "in Islamic law." Revivalists often encountered concepts in European law, searched out parallels in classical Islam, and claimed that the parallels

[1] See al-Jazīrī, *Fiqh ʿalá al-madhāhib al-arbaʿah.*

Islamic Legal Revival: Reception of European Law and Transformations in Islamic Legal Thought in Egypt, 1875–1952. First Edition. Leonard Wood.

were as good or better. Often they additionally claimed that the classical Islamic version of a concept—for example, "women's rights"—was, in fact, the source of the European concept. They embraced parliaments and processes by which political legislators give force to the opinions of jurists. Many took for granted institutions and premises of contemporary Egyptian statecraft that had been created under conditions of colonial occupation and were grounded, on paper, in the machinery of European public law.

Before the mid-1930s, Islamic legal revivalists accomplished minimal gains in technical scholarship. They articulated general ideas about methods for reviving Islamic law; they suggested ways to develop substantive law in famously controversial areas, such as Islamic criminal punishment, the Islamic prohibition of adultery, and the Islamic prohibition of usury; they critiqued traditionalism in the *madhhabs* by recourse to general arguments well known since at least Muḥammad ʿAbduh; they demonstrated a light grasp of the Franco-Egyptian and European laws they opposed; and they made rudimentary comparisons between European, Franco-Egyptian, and Islamic law.[2]

After the mid-1930s, the rigor of revivalist legal thought improved, but its flourishing was not solely in the hands of Egyptians or forged entirely within Egypt. Europeans played a direct role in shaping the course and content of the technical dimension of Islamic legal revivalism. This kind of claim is unpopular in present-day academia, where historians typically strive to afford as much agency as possible to colonized people when narrating their past.[3] Yet, the claim is true. During the nineteenth and early twentieth centuries, scholars in Europe and other European colonies created fields of knowledge and academic practices that would come to inform Egyptian approaches to studying, conceptualizing, and re-conceptualizing Islamic law. Among those fields were orientalism, the legal expertise of colonial administrators in other colonies, comparative law, and Western legal theory.

European academics and agents of colonial authority worldwide had made experiments in Islamic legal thought before the ascent of Egyptian-Islamic legal revivalism in the 1930s. They had translated classical Arabic texts that they thought approximated the form of modern codes; situated Islamic legal rules in the organizational and conceptual paradigms of European codes; and recommended changes to Islamic substantive law (sometimes tampering with the substance of Islamic doctrine, changing it from what they knew it to be to what they wanted it to be). Agents of colonial authority and orientalists took an interest in *madhhabs* beyond the dominant *madhhab* in their local colonial environment. They produced textbooks critiquing traditional elements of *uṣūl al-fiqh*, produced revisionist conceptions of Islamic legal history, and wrote doctrinal treatises about Islamic law that resembled, in form, the doctrinal treatises of nineteenth-century European jurists.

2 It would be useful to know more about the standards that emerged at al-Azhar's Sharia Faculty, constituted between 1928 and 1930.

3 See relevant perspectives in Esmeir, *Juridical Humanity*, 41–2.

European orientalists and agents of colonial authority developed the view that Europeans and non-Muslims could change Islamic legal thought not just by exercising physical power over colonial environments, but by entering the authentic domain of Islamic legal discourse as savants fortified by the power of "European" "science." It was characteristic of such Europeans to presume that their powers of scientific analysis were superior to powers of analysis possessed by Muslims. A corollary to such presumptions was the presumption of European superiority in mores and civilizational standards. Although not all orientalists and colonial scholars displayed these pretensions to this degree, several did.

Merely showing that some Egyptians produced ideas and forms of legal literature similar to those of orientalists and colonial agents does not prove that Egyptians relied upon, partly copied, adapted, or were aware of efforts by orientalists and colonial scholars. But, evidence points to such connections. Muḥammad Qadrī Pasha's famous personal status code—always treated in historical literature as a product of pure Egyptian ingenuity—resembled an earlier work by French scholars from Algiers. Continental European law scholars who had taught in Algeria, among whom Louis Milliot, Eugène Clavel, L. W. C. van den Berg, and Édouard Lambert, worked with Egyptians in France and Egypt. Egyptian authors cited these scholars, other orientalists, and colonial agents by name. Chafik Chehata cited orientalists and Algerian and Indian colonial law manuals. When al-Sanhūrī publicly spoke about revising Egypt's Civil Code, he quoted orientalists as authorities on Islamic legal history.[4] Muḥammad Yūsuf Mūsá, an Azharite and Cairo Faculty professor of Sharia, engaged with the ideas of orientalists in his books. Aḥmad Amīn attended orientalist congresses in Leiden. The Sharia Lawyers Journal, published by the Sharia Bar Association itself, engaged with ideas of orientalists, revealing that although Egyptian specialists in Islamic law could not always read European foreign-language texts, they could still be familiar with distilled and translated versions of European texts and ideas.

The Cairo Faculty was a principal site of reception of European legal thought in Egyptian and Egyptian-Islamic legal thought. Reception involved acceptance, contestation, change, and rejection. Europeans imported and imposed knowledge; Egyptians, for their part, variously sought that knowledge, accepted it, resisted it, adapted it, changed it, created it, advanced it, and rebelled against it.

The most intellectually and culturally diverse of Egypt's law schools, the Cairo Faculty was a site of serious education and research in European, Franco-Egyptian, and Islamic law. It taught in both Arabic and foreign languages. The professors included Egyptians and Europeans. Leading Egyptian professors obtained doctorates in France, many having written on topics relevant to comparative law or Islam. Under their leadership, Franco-Egyptian legal academia came into its own as an Arabic-language arena, autonomous from its parent arenas of French-, English-, and Italian-language scholarship. Their projects in comparative Islamic-European scholarship and pedagogy provide the best evidence for how Egyptians were masters as well as objects in the reception of European law.

[4] Al-Sanhūrī, "ʿAlá ayy asās."

As advanced research and comparative law found a home at the Cairo Faculty, technical changes took place in approaches to studying Islamic law that became permanent in Egyptian legal academia. In the curriculum of the mid-1930s, students and scholars were taught to do more than criticize the secular-oriented legal order and the European foundations of legislation. They thought in rigorous ways about how Islam and Islamic law would supplement or supplant a European-inspired order that had been in place for over fifty years and had become sophisticated and rooted.

Communication between Franco-Egyptian and Sharia jurists facilitated new directions in Islamic legal thought. They collaborated in the teaching and supervision of graduate students. Al-Sanhūrī maintained collegial relations with the Sharia professors at the Cairo Faculty, even though they had significant differences. As a doctoral student, Chafik Chehata managed to merge Islamic and European legal studies and faced Albert Chéron and Shaykh Aḥmad Ibrāhīm on the same examination committee. His mentor on the civil side was al-Sanhūrī, and his adviser on the Sharia side was Shaykh Muḥammad Abū Zahrah.

Professors concerned with Islamic law at the Cairo Faculty did not all share the same methods, premises, and inclinations when it came to making comparative inquiries and shaping the future of Islamic legal doctrine. The principal ideological, theoretical, and methodological divide fell between those who were academically oriented toward European and Franco-Egyptian law, legal thought, and philosophy, and those who were academically oriented toward traditional approaches in Islamic theology, legal theory, and law. Many of the faculty members—Muslim faculty in particular—positioned themselves between these two orientations, influenced by European ideas while also loyal to Muslim traditions and norms.

In the decade before the Egyptian revolution of 2011, scholars in North America and Europe had grown tired of the conservative/reformist analytical binary in studies of Egypt's intellectual history. They had also grown tired of the analytical binary between Islamic-oriented (Islamist) Egyptians and secular-oriented (secular) Egyptians. Hostility to these dyads was strong enough that invoking them too forcefully in a book of history, or perhaps in a doctoral dissertation, would have put the work in jeopardy of backlash by colleagues. The prevailing view among scholars was that the binaries were stale and insufficiently mindful of the nuances of social, economic, and colonial history, and that to whatever extent these binaries were based in truth, they did not map accurately enough relevant divides among Egyptians. All of this was before the tumult of 2011–2013, when much of the Egyptian population divided itself roughly along the lines of these two binaries, at least for certain purposes and at certain political moments.

This book rarely invokes the once taboo binaries—articulated by figures no less than Rashīd Riḍā, Chafik Chehata, and Muḥammad Abū Zahrah—even though they might have been useful at times. Egyptian jurists conceived of themselves as falling on spectrums between the poles of those binaries, and that makes the binaries worth bearing in mind and exploring. This book instead posited and relied upon a somewhat different conception of alignments. It introduced the concept of Franco-Egyptian jurists, identified al-Azhar as a bastion of conservatism (while acknowledging the presence of reformists), and singled out the Sharia jurists of the Cairo Faculty as a separate group—a conservative-minded but reform-inclined offshoot with roots in the high Islamic institutions.

The Sharia jurists of the Cairo Faculty were distinct from their Franco-Egyptian colleagues. The best proof would have to be presented through extended discussion of their books on law and legal theory. This book has, for its part, pointed to differences between the first and second generation of Sharia professors at the Cairo Faculty, or the generation preceding 1930 and the one following 1930. The second-generation Sharia jurists collaborated with the Franco-Egyptians in teaching and research. They contributed to the "theory of obligations" discourse. Their textbooks advanced new rules in Islamic substantive law and theory, but held the line in some areas, as in the prohibition on illicit gain (*ribā*). Franco-Egyptian jurists, by contrast, remained under the influence of Lambertian comparativism and related fields of knowledge, theory, and science from Europe. Chafik Chehata's dissertation still provides one monument to the distinctiveness of Franco-Egyptian methods in Egyptian comparative law, although it does not represent the entire gamut of such methods.

LEGAL HISTORY AND CONTEMPORARY TRENDS

The history of Egyptian legal thought provides keys to appreciating the origins and content of present-day Islamic legal thought worldwide, and this book has attempted to facilitate the positing of connections between past and present. To find connections, one can look to contemporary practices that would have appeared novel to a jurist in 1875. Many attitudes of today were either hard to conceive or inconceivable then. In what follows, I summarize novel practices and attitudes from present-day Egypt that can also be, in most cases, observed worldwide.[5] Each of these practices and attitudes has precursors from the years between 1875 and 1952.

Jurists today take for granted the desirability of presenting the rules of Sharia and *fiqh* in the form of positive law (*qānūn waḍʿī*). Although they frequently assail positive law in polemical terms, they are not assailing positive law per se. They are instead assailing "man-made" positive law. The goal of Islamic legal positivization is to produce a positive law that is "God-made" as opposed to "man-made." This concept was part of the Muslim Brotherhood's ideology during the 2011 Egyptian revolution.

The world of published Islamic legal doctrine constitutes, in certain respects, a world of hypothetical law. Islamic legal doctrine stands at the ready to refine, supplement, or supplant portions of the legal order as it is. Revivalists, after all, have over a thousand years of legal opinions at their disposal. Published Islamic

[5] Each characteristic that I list has a wealth of relevant citations. Rather than listing these, I refer the reader to sources cited in the introduction.

legal doctrine is a world of academic scholarship about an imagined modern legal order; that world of knowledge shadows the world of legal scholarship that addresses the legal system as it actually is. A trip to Egypt's law bookstores today shows that one group sells books about the actual legal system, and another group sells books about the hypothetical and theoretical Islamic system. Nowhere has this been more apparent than in the scores of bookstores in the center of Cairo.

Jurists today commonly downplay, ignore, or regard as historical trivia the heavily evidenced proposition that Muslim societies, for centuries, found ways to accept man-made law as Sharia-compliant and as part of the legitimate legal order of a Muslim society.[6] In turn, one popular conception of Islamic history envisions historical legal orders that were unsullied or unbothered by the encroachment of man-made law. An alternative, common trope in widespread, Arabic and Egyptian, boilerplate legal-historical narrative holds that the cause of all injustices in Islam after the death of the Prophet Muhammad stemmed from legal consequences of foreign intervention in Muslim lands—Persians, Greeks, Crusaders, Mongols, Turks, Circassians, all before the French, British, and Americans. These views persist in Egypt today as core tenets of Islamic legal revivalist ideology.

Jurists today commonly accept Sharia-based positive law, applied or hoped for, as a legitimate instrument of political and social governance; and they commonly accept the idea of Sharia-based positive law as an instrument that can be legitimately promulgated, managed, and enforced by a centralized national government. While not necessarily accepting the legitimacy of the people presently ruling their country, jurists do commonly accept that new rulers working in similar governmental institutions could provide and manage a better kind of law.

There is a common expectation that a singular "Islamic law of" any topic can and should be explicated in academic doctrine. For examples, one looks to the proliferation of texts and media events explicating the "Islamic law of" intellectual property, the "Islamic law of" corporations, the "Islamic law of" bankruptcy, and so forth. The widespread popularity of books styled in this manner is a quintessential facet and result of Islamic legal revivalism.

The tolerance in classical Islam for the simultaneous existence of multiple rulings to singular questions (*ikhtilāf*) is not out of fashion in the theory of jurists; but the theoretical acceptability of such legal difference is often overshadowed by efforts to determine, with finality, single and uniform rules for single questions.

There is a common expectation that uniform, comprehensive, and largely self-contained Islamic law codes can and should be written for vast fields of law such as contract, commercial, and criminal law. Legislators and academic committees have attempted to draft such codes, but have less commonly taken guidance from hard lessons learned in code law jurisdictions about the need for creative judges and lawyers, seasoned in practical experience, who breathe vitality into codes. A feature of European-law reception in Islamic legal revivalist thought is that revivalism absorbed early European trends of formalism but many—certainly not

[6] See Shalakany, "Islamic Legal Histories"; Wood, "Legislation as an Instrument of Islamic Law."

all—revivalists later ignored or were unaware of subsequent trends in European and North American legal realism, let alone the successes, and practicality, of Anglo-American approaches to codes, legislation, and common law adjudication. For all of his devotion to continental civil law, Édouard Lambert admired American realist approaches to and theories of legislation and adjudication. The decline of Franco-Egyptian prestige and power provides one explanation for these inconsistencies in legal and legal-theoretical reception.

Western legal categories are continually imposed on the material of classical *fiqh* and the conception of Sharia—thus, one finds abundant treatises and draft codes concerning Islamic "civil rights," "human rights," "economic rights," and women's rights. This point is made not to say that the wealth of classical Islamic legal thought and the wealth of the primary sources and pre-modern cases do not provide guidance for law in these fields, but rather to suggest that jurists today adopt foreign categories; furthermore, it is to suggest, more tentatively, that the adoption of these categories has transformative implications for the substantive elaborations of jurists who seek to develop law within the categories.

A common view holds that Sharia can and should be distilled into "principles" for the use of constitutional jurisprudence. Although ideas about "Islamic" constitutional jurisprudence gained the greatest momentum in Egypt after 1952, the pre-1952 Egyptian legal scene, deeply influenced by civil code theory and interpretive methods from the European continent, was focused on inducing higher-level legal "principles," for all areas of law, from which smaller rules could be deduced. Thus, the Supreme Constitutional Court of Egypt today exercises the power to uphold or reverse legislation and government action on the claim that one or the other complies with or violates the "principles" of Sharia.[7] In the process, the Court has formulated particular methods of reasoning celebrated in the early twentieth century—yet also rooted in nineteenth-century French formalism—and it has assumed a power unknown to the state courts of Egypt before 1875.

It is common for people who were not rigorously trained in Islamic law—or in Islamic schools and degree programs—to assume positions wherein they make authoritative pronouncements about it. This is the case for Egyptian judges, many of whom hand down judgments on matters of Islamic law in appellate courts and the Supreme Constitutional Court. This situation also extends to private individuals who write legal-academic *doctrine*. Many of those referred to earlier in this Conclusion as "jurists" are not Muslim jurists in the conventional and historically accurate sense. They are rather individuals who studied other topics for much of

[7] This trajectory parallels the American experience, which is noteworthy because the U.S. Supreme Court provided Egyptians of the second half of the twentieth century with their model for constitutional review of legislation and government action. Although ordinary American state and federal courts operate in many areas of law according to traditional practices of common law (i.e., generating holdings through the reasoned application of judge-made precedent), American constitutional jurisprudence, established in the early nineteenth century, was built on methods more commonly associated with continental European, civil law adjudication. The U.S. Supreme Court treats the U.S. Constitution much like French judges (theoretically) treat the *Code civil*—as a self-sufficient document that is not gapless, but which provides all the rules, and implies all the "principles," that would ever be needed to guide the filling of gaps in constitutional law when new questions arise. Salient exceptions in American constitutional history have not negated this tendency and preference of the American Supreme Court justices.

their lives and then dabbled in *fiqh*, or trained themselves in it, or sought instruction outside of a high Islamic institution, or performed some combination thereof. Historians of Egypt have generally attributed this development—the rise of the less-than-formally trained Islamic jurist—to the influences of Ḥasan al-Bannā and Sayyid Quṭb. Those figures, however, were products, as well as exponents, of this trend within the broader trend of Islamic revivalism.

There is enthusiasm among jurists for aspects of public law that have roots in European law: constitutions, parliaments, bills of rights, separation of powers, checks and balances, administrative law, and international public law. Islamic legal revivalism of the early twentieth century was intensely concerned with developing Islamic public law, since public law was one area that had been wholly occupied in the courts by European law.

Jurists today display interest in Islamic doctrines that accommodate policy, equity, and flexibility in statutory interpretation. This interest has been related to the vast, ongoing proliferation of writings on "aims of the law" (*maqāṣid al-sharīʿah*), public and individual welfare (*maṣlaḥah*), juristic preference (*istiḥsān*), custom (*ʿurf*), necessity (*ḍarūra*), reason (*ʿaql*), "Sharia-compliant policy" (*siyāsah sharʿiyyah*), and what one could call the doctrine of ease and sufficiency (*yusr al-Islām*). These discussions operate mostly in a theoretical realm in lieu of a system of Islamic courts that are routinely applying Islamic legal rules. The discourse is driven by academic theorists. Islamic legal revivalists have been concerned with this line of research.

Although the scholar of Islamic law need not look far into the history of *fiqh* to find doctrines for flexibility and policy-accommodation in law, the great interest of Egyptians in such doctrines in the nineteenth and twentieth centuries was prompted, in part, by interactions with Western jurists. No sooner did the Europeans bring new codes and legal formalism to Egypt than they also began to import concepts of "social" jurisprudence, comparative law, and proto-legal realism as a means to moderate legal formalism in Franco-Egyptian legal thought. There is a link in legal literature of Egypt's interwar period between the Franco-Egyptian jurists who were expounding on social jurisprudence and their Islamic legal revivalist colleagues who were dusting off and elaborating doctrines such as *maṣlaḥah* and *siyāsah sharʿiyyah*. The common notion that Muḥammad ʿAbduh was the major force behind Egyptian interests in these subjects has been, to date, overstated by historians.

Among contemporary jurists in Egypt, there is a popular interest in Hanbali and Maliki *fiqh* and especially in the doctrines of Ibn Taymiyyah and Ibn Qayyim al-Jawziyyah. Leaving aside those who take an interest in Ibn Taymiyyah's writings on jihad, mainstream Muslim jurists commonly refer to Ibn Taymiyyah's and Ibn Qayyim's theories of *siyāsah sharʿiyyah* and their distinctive, creative approaches to contract law as a means to modernize Islamic contract and commercial law. The early twentieth-century revivalists are the people who brought Ibn Taymiyyah and Ibn Qayyim to the fore for the purposes of developing Islamic legal thought to address contemporary economic needs.

Comparative law is a contentious discursive space in contemporary Egyptian academia. The common expectation is that, on balance, "Islamic" rules will trump "non-Islamic" rules. In general, whatever seems good and pious, regardless of its most apparent and proximate historical origins, is ultimately stamped as "Islamic." This makes sense, given the worldview undergirding much of Islamic legal revivalist literature: if another system has a rule that is better than the rule known in *fiqh*, this means that the other system contained a rule from the Sharia and that previous Muslim jurists holding a different rule were mistaken in their interpretation of the Sharia. This sensibility is widespread in Islamist circles worldwide.

Universalism, in the sense advocated by Lambert and the Franco-Egyptians, is irrelevant in many quarters, that is, unless universalism is taken to mean that all world religions and cultures are in a process of catching up with Islam or meeting its standards. In the universalism of today's Islamic legal revivalists, everyone in the world is invited to and called to participate and submit to Islam, but the guiding values come from within Islam; the guiding values cannot be accreted to Islam by customs and notions that originated outside of Islam. In essence, the normative supremacy of Islamic primary sources, theology, and law are taken for granted and as the starting point of doctrinal exposition and comparative inquiry. The mid-century Islamic legal revivalists, such as Muḥammad Abū Zahrah and Aḥmad Ibrāhīm, steered Egypt's approach to universalism in this direction. It was a victory over the old guard of Franco-Egyptian jurists and helped to steer much of mainstream Egyptian-Islamic legal thought in particularistic, formalist, and sometimes chauvinist directions.

Today, conservatism prevails in many Sunni Islamic educational institutions, and even in secular-oriented institutions like Cairo University, regarding methods and substantive norms in Islamic legal thought. It is mainly outside of those institutions—for example, in European and American universities—that one can test radical methods for interpreting Islamic law and posit alternative ideas about what the substantive Islamic legal order should be. Some of this conservatism may have resulted from the defensive posture that Sharia jurists adopted earlier in the twentieth century, including at the Cairo Faculty, when they perceived their values, beliefs, and institutions to be under attack by foreign theories and theorists. As discussed in the Epilogue, Egypt's brand of authoritarian rule has provided an additional impetus to conservativism and defensiveness in Islamic legal revivalist thought.

Looking beyond 1952, Franco-Egyptian jurists achieved less than a triumph in their competition with Sharia jurists for control of theories, methods, and substance in Islamic legal thought. One cannot, however, speak of winning and losing in absolute terms. The Egyptian revolution of 1952, Nasserism, reform at al-Azhar, the evolution of the Muslim Brotherhood, the closure of the Sharia Courts in 1956, socialism, and Saudi intellectual influence in Egypt during the 1970s and 1980s were among many factors to have affected the equation in the competition between Franco-Egyptians and Islamic legal revivalists. To say that the Franco-Egyptians at the Cairo Faculty did not win the competition for control of Islamic legal science is not to say that they lost and that the Sharia jurists across the hall won.

After 1952, however, the ascent of the Muslim Brotherhood and its writers, the ongoing conservativism of al-Azhar, and the fact that Azharites and Dār ʿĀmīs always outnumbered Franco-Egyptians in Islamic-legal intellectual quarters point to the Franco-Egyptian sensibilities and approach to Islamic legal thought falling short in terms of power. Additionally, although Sharia jurists of the Cairo Faculty reformed Islamic legal thought in important ways, they held the conservative line on other fundamental questions of theory, method, and substance. At the Cairo Faculty, Muḥammad Abū Zahrah, ʿAlī al-Khafīf, ʿAbd al-Wahhāb Khallāf, Muḥammad Yūsuf Mūsá, and their students maintained into the 1970s a kind of monopoly on final authority in questions pertaining to Islamic law.

With regard to the present day, the Islamic legal revivalism movement is still multi-factional and displays various different tendencies, but it is also still coherent enough to be treated for certain analytical purposes as a single phenomenon. Rooted in profound conviction, the movement is unlikely to die out in the face of intimidation. It has survived imperialism, autocracy, repression, and multiple revolutionary upheavals. It feeds on the perennial failings of statist economic policies and the moral problems that inevitably come to be associated with despotism. At the time of writing, it has been seen that three of the harshest military dictatorships in the Arab world—in Iraq, Syria, and Libya—were the birthplace of some of the most radical, extra-governmental Islamist movements of the Arab world. Egypt has also witnessed the evolution of its own radical currents within the broader scope of the Islamic movement. One could therefore conjecture that Islamic legal revivalism, like Islamic movements more generally, will only be vindicated, or else exhausted, when its exponents have had a real and complete opportunity to succeed or fail.

Such a conjecture, however, and put in such terms, reflects a problem in contemporary thought about, and within, Islamic politics as much as it provides one pathway to settlement. The prevalent aspiration for a perfect legal system that can succeed entirely—one that has all the right answers, and is all things to all people, even if only for all Muslims—is a utopian conception, and as such, may be an obstacle to peace, functionality, prosperity, and moral and spiritual fortitude.

The present-day utopian aspiration of total Islamic legal triumph may have proximate roots in the reception of European legal formalism, where and to the extent that such reception was not tempered, for many revivalists, by a later stage of European legal realism. As this book has helped to prove, ideas of a Western origin are a source of certain impractical ends sought by Islamic legal radicalism or extremism—or whichever slippery, but still useful, terms one chooses to use. It could behoove more Islamic legal revivalists to consider this point, and to consider the possibility that certain performances of juridical rigidity and aspirations for total perfection in law may be more performances of imitation and foreignness than performances of revolution, authenticity, Islam, and autochthonous agency. On the other hand, certain ideas, theories, and practices in law well known to certain Western countries may still hold out the best hope for solutions. One could reject this suggestion out of hand as a deplorable instantiation of neo-colonialist sentiment, were it not the case that many of the most powerful ideas and practices of European and American law and legal realism have sure corollaries, and many antecedents, in Islamic history and legal theory. Nobody ever examined this fact more forcefully and amply than Egypt's early- and mid-twentieth-century jurists.

It may be important for people interested in law and legal reform on a system-wide level to think creatively and critically about what success should mean for a legal system implemented and operated by fallible humans as distinct from an infallible prophet. Legal systems of the world that have delivered to their citizens high degrees of peace, functionality, prosperity, and moral fortitude have keyed the concept of success not only to maintaining consistency with certain sources of law—be it legislation, a constitution, or a divine mandate—and what some people think are the correctly formulated fundamental principles of the legal system, but also to prioritizing the welfare of people on an urgent basis, and especially the health of their economy. This is a form of assessment and aspiration-building that does not derive from a single-minded focus on juridical methodology—specifically, the methods of deriving laws from other principles and laws—but from looking at the legal system as it is, looking at the society as it is, and asking what works, and how law can help people. It is no innovation in Islamic thought to entertain the notion that Sharia demands that people make law both to serve God and to help themselves, and that believers may view both objectives as mutually consistent. These considerations are well known within Islamic legal revivalism—for example, through the doctrines of *maṣlaḥah, maqāṣid al-sharīʿah*, and *siyāsah sharʿiyyah*—but more often as methodological tools to assist casuistic adjudication; these same considerations have not as commonly been elevated within Islamic legal revivalist thought of recent years to the level of affecting and tempering revivalists' aspirations for reform and revolution of the macro legal system.

The chief dilemmas for the opponents of Islamic legal revivalism, or at least for those who wish to counter the inclinations of some groups toward extremism, are twofold: Islam cannot fail in the eyes of its adherents, and many Islamic legal revivalists, lacking real experience in day-to-day law practice in a sophisticated economy and social structure, have impractical, if not also religiously problematic, conceptions of success. One antidote to radicalism, extremism, and legal utopianism—if one considers these facets of the movement a problem—might be found through popularizing the notion that there can never be a perfect legal system—one that knows all the right answers to every issue and is all things to all people. An antidote might also be found in re-popularizing the notion that a legal system should strive to be consistent with its foundational moral and legalistic imperatives, but that this adherence to and pursuit of foundational imperatives must also be influenced and tempered by the imperative to help people to prosper economically and to live in peace. This means aspiring to a legal system not guided by bookish juridical methodologies and operations of logical reasoning alone, but to a system that accepts complexity, is informed and enhanced by world-class social science, prioritizes the function of practice and fluid case law development over theory and dogma, remains systematically responsive to the needs of its subjects, learns from the experiences of other nations as well as its own, and accepts that it will always have to face, and to continuously handle, constant and inevitable failures that surface in the system. These were powerful ideas in interwar Egypt, propagated and substantiated by the Franco-Egyptian legal academy, as well as by the early Islamic legal revivalists, at their pre-1952 zenith.

APPENDIX

Images

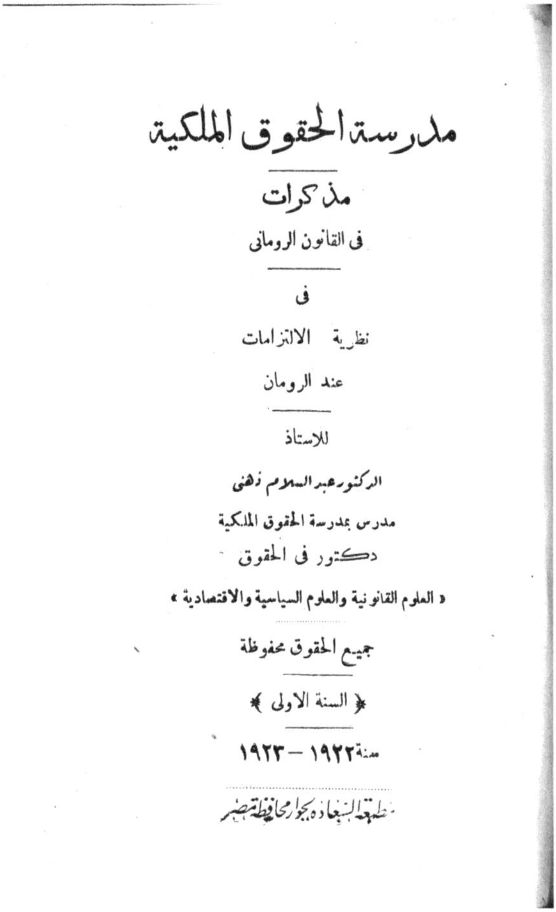
مدرسة الحقوق الملكية

مذكرات

فى القانون الرومانى

فى

نظرية الالتزامات

عند الرومان

للاستاذ

الدكتور عبد السلام ذهنى

مدرس بمدرسة الحقوق الملكية

دكتور فى الحقوق

« العلوم القانونية والعلوم السياسية والاقتصادية »

جميع الحقوق محفوظة

السنة الاولى

سنة ١٩٢٢ – ١٩٢٣

مطبعة السعادة بجوار محافظة مصر

Royal Law School

Memoranda on Roman Law

The Roman Theory of Obligations

Doctor ʿAbd al-Salām Dhuhnī
Teacher in the Royal Law School

Doctor in Laws

First Year

1922–1923

Title Page of ʿAbd al-Salām Dhuhnī, *Mudhakkirāt fī l-qānūn al-rūmānī fī naẓariyyat al-iltizāmāt ʿind al-rūman* (Memoranda on Roman Law: The Roman Theory of Obligations) (1922–1923)

Pp. 4–5 on obligations, from ʿAbd al-Salām Dhuhnī, *Mudhakkirāt fī al-qānūn al-rūmānī fī naẓariyyat al-iltizāmāt ʿind al-rūman* (Memoranda on Roman Law: The Roman Theory of Obligations) (1922–1923)

This page shows Dhuhnī's discussion of fundamental concepts in the Roman law of obligations as conceived in Justinian's *Institutes.* Prior to 1923, students used French and English texts to study these topics.

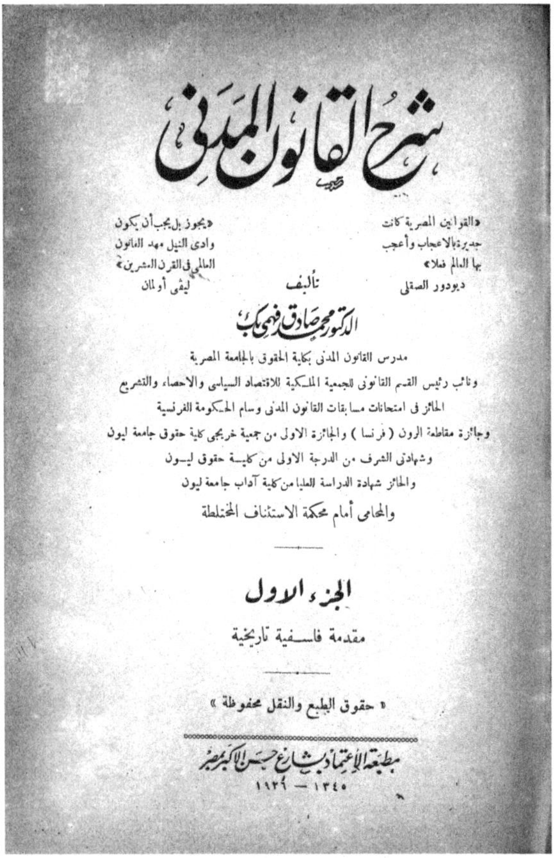

شرح القانون المدنى

«القوانين المصرية كانت جديرة بالاعجاب وأعجب بها العالم فعلا»
ديودور الصقلى

«يجوز بل يجب أن يكون وادى النيل مهد القانون العالمى فى القرن العشرين»
ليفى أولمان

تأليف

الدكتور محمد صادق فهمى بك

مدرس القانون المدنى بكلية الحقوق بالجامعة المصرية
ونائب رئيس القسم القانونى للجمعية الملكية للاقتصاد السياسى والاحصاء والتشريع
الحائز فى امتحانات مسابقات القانون المدنى وسام الحكومة الفرنسية
وجائزة مقاطعة الرون (فرنسا) والجائزة الاولى من جمعية خريجى كلية حقوق جامعة ليون
وشهادتى الشرف من الدرجة الاولى من كليـة حقوق ليـون
والحائز شهادة الدراسة العليا من كلية آداب جامعة ليون
والمحامى أمام محكمة الاستئناف المختلطة

الجزء الاول

مقدمة فلسفية تاريخية

« حقوق الطبع والنقل محفوظة »

مطبعة الإعتماد بشارع حسن الاكبر بمصر
١٣٤٥ — ١٩٢٦

Title Page of Muḥammad Ṣādiq Fahmī, *Sharḥ al-qānūn al-madanī* (Commentary on the Civil Code) (1926)

Commentary on Civil Law

"The Egyptian laws once inspired awe. They were truly the most wondrous of the world." Diodorus of Sicily

"It is conceivable, nay, a requirement, that the Nile Valley become the cradle of world law in the twentieth century." Lévy-Ullman

Doctor Muḥammad

Ṣādiq Fahmī Bey

Professor of Civil Law in the Law Faculty of the Egyptian University. Vice President of the Legal Division of the Royal Society for Economics, Politics, Statistics, and Legislation. Holder of the Order of the French Government for Competitive Examinations in Civil Law. Prize of the Department of Rhône (France). First Prize from the Alumni Association of the Law Faculty of Lyon University. Two diplomas of honor, first class, from the Law Faculty of Lyon. Holder of the Graduate Diploma in Humanities from the University of Lyon. Lawyer at the Mixed Court of Appeals.

Part One: Philosophical and Historical Introduction

1926/1345

١٦ (القانون والحق)

§ ٢ — من هو واضع القانون ؟

مجمل المذاهب في وضع القانون

٤ — قلنا في بند ٢ « القانون مجموع الاحكام التي وضعت . . » وبقينا الفعل للمجهول نظراً لاختلاف العلماء والفلاسفة في معرفة واضع القواعد القانونية وحقيقة منشئها وكيفية تكوينها

فذهب فريق الى أن واضع القواعد القانونية هو الحاكم ذو السلطان بما له من الولاية والقوة

وذهب فريق آخر الى أن وضع القواعد القانونية يرجع الى الفكر الانساني وادراكه لقواعد العدل التي قررتها الطبيعة ويسمى هذا المذهب بمذهب القانون الطبيعي L'école du droit naturel ويقرب من هذا المذهب من يقول ان الاصل في وضع القوانين المحافظة على حرية الفرد وتحديد تلك الحرية لتنظيم علائقه بغيره ويسمى هذا المذهب الفردي La doctrine individualiste

وقال فريق رابع ان القوانين تتكون من تقسها في كل بيئة معينة بتأثير العوامل الاجتماعية والدينية والاقتصادية والسياسية وطبيعة البلاد فهي كالثمرة تتكون من الزهرة ويسمى هذا المذهب بالمذهب التاريخي L'école historique

وفريق خامس يعتقد ان العامل في وضع القوانين هو الارتباط الاجتماعي بين الناس وان المجتمع الذي يندمج فيه الفرد هو الموجد للقواعد التي تضبط أعمال الناس ويسمى هذا المذهب بالمذهب الاجتماعي L'école sociologique

تلك هي المذاهب بالاجمال وسنبين أن كل واحد منها قد ألم بطرف من الحقيقة والواقع أن وضع القوانين يرجع الى كثير من هذه العوامل مجتمعة غير أن درجة تأثير كل عامل تختلف باختلاف الاحوال وهناك عامل جديد هو مقارنة الشرائع وهذا العامل هو المهيمن اليوم على الحركة التشريعية في العالم المتمدين وسيؤدي الى توحيد بعض القوانين لا سيما الخاص منها بالمعاملات وربما كان ذلك داعياً للتفاهم بين الامم فيسود السلام والاخاء (١)

[٤] (١) كتابنا الاثبات في القانون المدني المقارن جزء ١ ص ١٠ و ٣٥٩ وما بعدها

١٧ (من هو واضع القانون ؟)

١ : الحاكم ذو السلطة

٥ — ممن قال ان واضع القانون هو الحاكم ذو السلطة توماس هوبز الانجليزي(١) Thomas Hobbes وتبعه في رأيه مواطنه جون أوستن Austin (٢) فأحكم مذهبه وفصله وقد أفاض الاستاذ الفرنسي الفريد فوييه Alfred Fouillée في بيان تشيع عدد عظيم من علماء الالمان ورجال سياستهم بهذا المبدأ لا سيما في القرن التاسع عشر ومن بينهم هيجل Hegel وشوبنهاور Schopenhauer والبرنس بسمارك de Bismarck (٣) وعلى الاخص العالم الكبير اهرنج Jhering ومن أقواله المأثورة : «l'État est la seule source du Droit .... le Droit est conditionné par l'État. » (٤)

ولهذه النظرية أنصار في فرنسا فان العلامة رينيه دموج R. Demogue (الاستاذ بجامعة باريس الآن) يرى أن وضع القاعدة القانونية يرجع الى السلطة المنظمة التي تؤيدها القوة والتي لا ينقض قرارها(٥) — وهو رأي أغلب شراح القانون الفرنسي في أول عهده وهم الملقبون بمفسري « نصوص » القانون

[٥] (١) ولد سنة ١٥٨٨ وتوفي سنة ١٦٣٩ وهو من أشهر فلاسفة قومه في عصره في العلوم السياسية وأشهر مؤلفاته « de cive » و « Leviathan » طبعا بأمستردام الاول سنة ١٦٤٧ والثاني سنة ١٦٦٨ ، وقد أراد أن يثبت أن أصل سلطة الحاكم هو اتفاق الرعية على تعيين شخص يرضخون اليه فيما يصدره من الاحكام ، وقد ذهب الى أن حكم الفرد المطلق هو خير للامة — بواستل A. Boistel بند ٥٩ — مقدمة لدراسة القانون لجودبي F. M. Goadby ص ٣٤ — ويجاري هوبز في نظرية العقد الاجتماعي روسو J. J. Rousseau الفرنسي الشهير، ولكنهما يختلفان في تصوير ذلك العقد الاجتماعي وفي نتائجه : راجع التفصيل في كتاب مبادئ القانون الدستوري المصري والمقارن للاستاذ مصطفى الصادق ص ٢٩ وما بعدها — راجع بند ٧ حاشية ٥ هنا
(٢) كان مدرساً لفلسفة القانون بجامعة لندن ولد سنة ١٧٩٠ وتوفي سنة ١٨٥٩ وقد طبعت مذكراته العلمية بعد وفاته بالعنوان الآتي Lectures on jurisprudence or the philosophy of the positive law. الطبعة الثانية بلندره سنة ١٩٠٧
(٣) راجع الفرد فوييه L'idée moderne du droit ص ٢٩ وما بعدها وعلى الاخص ص ٤٦ حاشية ١ فقد حلل بعض مبادئ البرنس بسمارك — قارن بونكاس بند ١٥
(٤) عن بونكاس Bonnecase بند ١٦ ص ٦٩
(٥) راجع مؤلفه Les notions fondamentales du droit privé. p 4.

(٣ — مدني)

Pp. 16–17 on legal theory, from Muḥammad Ṣādiq Fahmī, *Sharḥ al-qānūn al-madanī* (Commentary on the Civil Code) (1926)

مذكرات

فى

نظرية الالتزامات

الباب الخامس فى مصادر الالتزامات

بقلم

الدكتور محمد صادق فهمى بك

أستاذ القانون المدنى بكلية الحقوق

بالجامعة المصرية

١٩٣٠ — ١٣٤٨

مطبعة العلوم بشارع الخليج بجنينة لاظ

Memoranda on the Theory of Obligations

Part Five: The Sources of Obligations

Doctor Muḥammad Ṣādiq Fahmī

Professor of Civil Law in the Law Faculty of the Egyptian University

1930/1348

Title page of Muḥammad Ṣādiq Fahmī, *Mudhakkirat fī naẓarriyat al-iltizāmāt* (Memoranda on the Theory of Obligations) (1930)

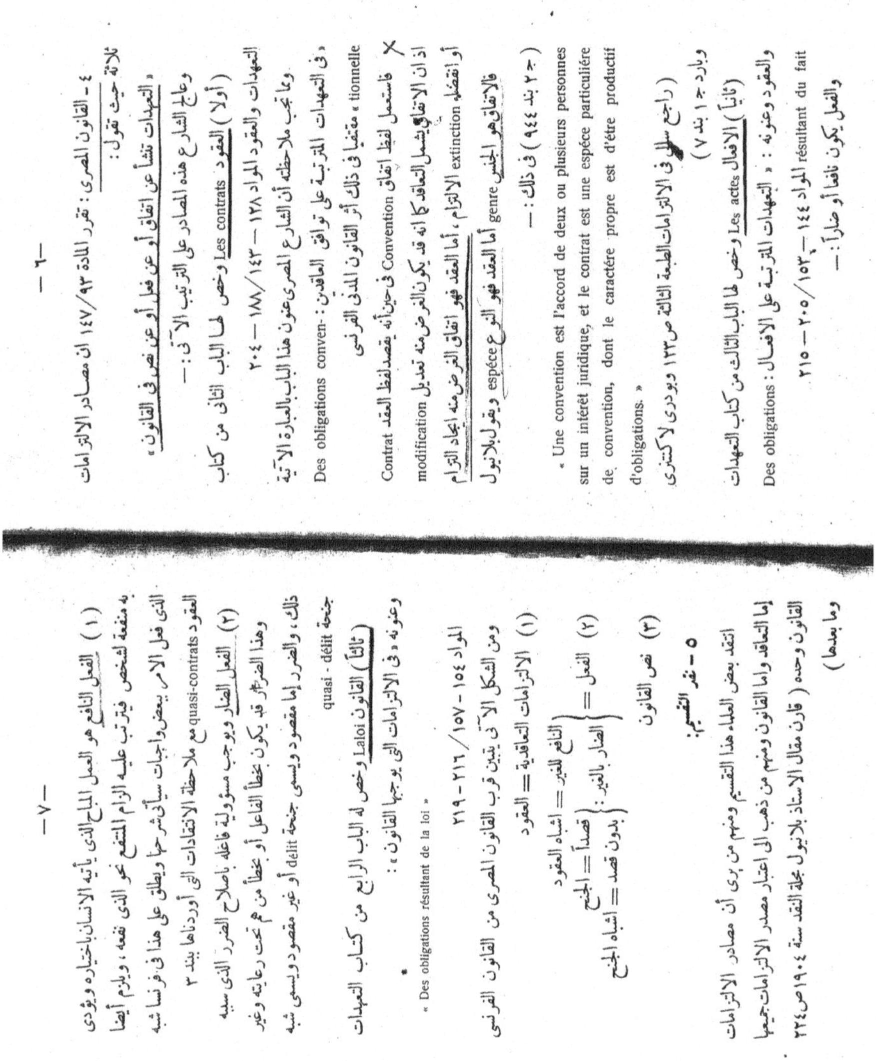

— ٦ —

٤ ـ القانون المصرى : تقرر المادة ٩٣/١٤٧ ان مصادر الالتزامات ثلاثة حيث تقول :

« التعهدات تنشأ عن اتفاق أو عن فعل أو عن نص فى القانون »

وعالج الشارع هذه المصادر على الترتيب الآتى : —

(أولا) العقود Les contrats وخص لها الباب الثانى من كتاب التعهدات والعقود المواد ١٢٨ — ١٤٣/١٨٨ — ٢٠٤

ومما تجب ملاحظته أن الشارع المصرى عنون هذا الباب بالعبارة الآتية « فى التعهدات المترتبة على توافق العاقدين : Des obligations conventionnelle » مقتفيا فى ذلك أثر القانون المدنى الفرنسى

فاستعمل لفظ اتفاق Convention فى حين أنه يقصد لفظ العقد Contrat اذ ان الاتفاق يشمل التعاقد كما انه قد يكون الغرض منه تعديل modification أو انقضاء extinction الالتزام ، أما العقد فهو اتفاق الغرض منه ايجاد التزام فالاتفاق هو الجنس genre أما العقد فهو النوع espéce ويقول بلانيول (جـ ٢ بند ٩٤٤) فى ذلك : —

« Une convention est l'accord de deux ou plusieurs personnes sur un intérêt juridique, et le contrat est une espéce particuliére de convention, dont le caractére propre est d'étre productif d'obligations. »

(راجع سلى فى الالتزامات الطبعة الثالثة ص ١٢٣ وبودرى لاكنتنرى وبارد جـ ١ بند ٧)

(ثانياً) الافعال Les actes وخص لها الباب الثالث من كتاب التعهدات والعقود وعنونه : « التعهدات المترتبة على الافعال : Des obligations résultant du fait المواد ١٤٤ — ١٥٣/٢٠٥ — ٢١٥

والفعل يكون نافعا أو ضاراً : —

— ٧ —

(١) الفعل النافع هو العمل المباح الذى يأتيه الانسان باختياره ويؤدى به منفعة لشخص فيترتب عليه الزام المنتفع نحو الذى نفعه ، ويلزم أيضا الذى فعل الامر ببعض واجبات سيأتى شرحها ويطلق على هذا فى فرنسا شبه العقود quasi-contrats مع ملاحظة الانتقادات التى أوردناها ببند ٣

(٢) الفعل الضار ويوجب مسؤولية فاعله باصلاح الضرر الذى سببه وهذا الضرر قد يكون بخطأ الفاعل أو بخطأ من هم تحت رعايته وغير ذلك ، والضرر إما مقصود ويسمى جنحة délit أو غير مقصود ويسمى شبه جنحة quasi - délit

(ثالثاً) القانون Laloi وخص له الباب الرابع من كتاب التعهدات وعنونه « فى الالتزامات التى يوجبها القانون » :

« Des obligations résultant de la loi »

المواد ١٥٤ - ١٥٧ / ٢١٦ - ٢١٩

ومن الشكل الآتى يتبين قرب القانون المصرى من القانون الفرنسى

(١) الالتزامات التعاقدية = العقود

(٢) الفعل = { النافع للغير = اشباه العقود
الضار بالغير : { قصداً = الجنح
بدون قصد = اشباه الجنح } }

(٣) نص القانون

٥ — نقد التقسيم:

انتقد بعض العلماء هذا التقسيم ومنهم من يرى أن مصادر الالتزامات إما التعاقد واما القانون ومنهم من ذهب الى اعتبار مصدر الالتزامات جميعها القانون وحده (قارن مقال الاستاذ بلانيول بمجلة النقد سنة ١٩٠٤ ص ٢٢٤ وما بعدها)

Pp. 6–7 on contracts, from Muḥammad Ṣādiq Fahmī, *Mudhakkirāt fī naẓariyyat al-iltizāmāt* (Memoranda on the Theory of Obligations) (1930)

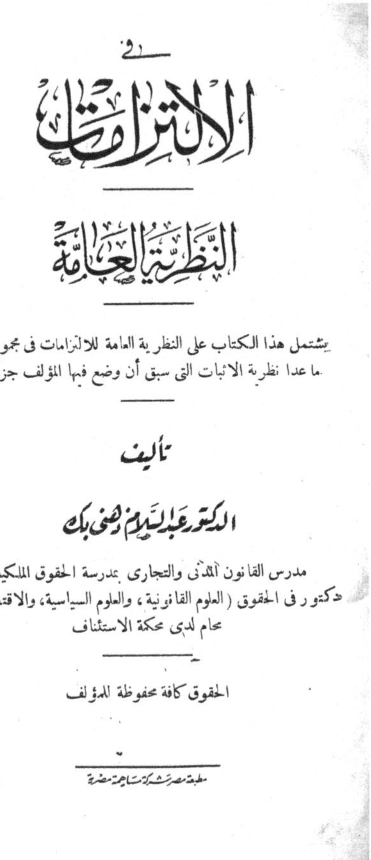

في

الالتزامات

النظرية العامة

يشتمل هذا الكتاب على النظرية العامة للالتزامات فى مجموعها ،
ما عدا نظرية الاثبات التى سبق أن وضع فيها المؤلف جزأين.

تأليف

الدكتور عبد السلام ذهنى بك

مدرس القانون المدنى والتجارى بمدرسة الحقوق الملكية
دكتور فى الحقوق (العلوم القانونية ، والعلوم السياسية، والاقتصادية)
محام لدى محكمة الاستئناف

الحقوق كافة محفوظة للمؤلف

مطبعة مصر شركة مساهمة مصرية

Obligations:
The General Theory

Doctor ʿAbd al-Salām Dhuhnī Bey

Professor of Civil and Commercial Law in the Royal Law School.
Doctor in Laws (Legal Science and Political and Economic Science)

Title page of ʿAbd al-Salām Dhuhnī, *Fī l-iltizāmāt: al-Naẓariyyah al-ʿāmmah* (Obligations: The General Theory) (1924)

تمهيد عام

لنظرية العقود

الالتزام من حيث هو

٥٧ ـ الالتزامات (١) أو حقوق الدائنية (٢) أو كما يسميها البعض الحقوق الشخصية (٣) هي ثانى الحقوق المالية (٤) بعد الحقوق العينية (٥)

والالتزام هو ضرورة قانونية (٦) يترتب عليها أن شخصاً يلتزم أمام شخص آخر بعمل شيء (٧) ايجابي أو سلبي أي عمل مادى (٨) أو الامتناع عن عمل (٩) أو هو كما قررت المادة ١٤٤/٩٠ مدنى : « التعهد هو ارتباط قانونى (١٠) الغرض منه حصول منفعة لشخص بالزام المتعهد بعمل شيء معين أو بامتناعه عنه » (راجع المادة ١١٠١ مدنى فرنسى)

ومادة الالتزامات واسعة الأطراف تتمشى على جميع الأعمال القانونية الخاصة بالافراد . وأكبر مظهر لها العقود (١١) وهى الاداة التى يرجع اليها فى اكتساب الحقوق العينية (المادة ١٤٥/٩١ مدنى و ١١٣٨ فرنسى)

(١) وقال عنها تارد (١٢) « بأن لنظرية الالتزامات فى مجال القضاء نفس الدور الذى تمثله نظرية القيمة والقدر (١٣) فى مجال علم الاقتصاد السياسى » أى ان كلا منها يعتبر مركزاً عاماً تتلاقى فيه أمهات الأصول الرئيسية العامة »

وقد غلا بعض المفسرين وأراد الحاق الحقوق العينية بالالتزامات وإدماجها فيها (١٤) وقالوا فى ذلك بأن الحق العينى لم يخرج عن كونه التزاماً يقوم به جميع الافراد نحو صاحبه فى ترك هذا الأخير يتمتع وينتفع بحقه . ولكن هذا غير صحيح ، لأن هناك فروقاً هامة بين الحق العينى (١٥) وحق الدائنية (١٦) ، ذلك لأن حقوق الدائنية حقوق

(١) obligations (٢) droits de créance (٣) droits personnels (٤) droits patrimoniaux (٥) droits réels (٦) nécessité juridique (٧) prestation (٨) fait (٩) abstention (١٠) lien de droit (١١) contrats (١٢) (انظر كتاب تارد فى تطور الحق ص ١٢٥ Tarde, Transformation du droit (١٣) valeur (١٤) دموج فى الالتزامات ج١ ن ٥ ص٨ وما بعدها (١٥) droit réel (١٦) droit de créance

نسبية (١) تربط شخصين معينين ويرى أحدهما أن حريته مقيدة قبل الآخر وأن لهذا الآخر سلطانا عليه، والحق العينى غير ذلك، فانه حق مطلق (٢)، وهو حق لا ينحصر فى ربط شخصين معينين، بل هو امتياز لدى صاحبه، كحق الملكية ، ينصب على شيء معين يستغله وينتفع به بقدر ما أعد له هذا الشيء . والحق العينى خالد دائم (٣) وهو يدوم بدوام الشيء الذى ينصب عليه الحق ، وينتقل من شخص الى آخر دون أن يزول من عالم الوجود . واما حق الدائنية فهو بأصله وطبيعته حق مؤقت (٤) بين شخصين وهو قابل للزوال بسبب من الاسباب القانونية كالوفاء (٥) وفوق ما تقدم فان الالتزام اذا انصرف الى غير المعنى المعد له من قبل فان ذلك يفسد عليه معناه القانونى الصحيح لان الالتزام فى ذاته مظهر غير عادى (٦) بين الافراد باعتبار أن الاصل فيهم استقلال بعضهم قبل البعض الآخر فالالتزام وارد عليهم أى هو حالة استثنائية للحالة العامة لهم ، أى هو استثناء للقانون العام (٧) وأما الحق العينى وهو احترام الافراد لصاحبه وعدم العمل على ما يعطل لديه مزية الانتفاع بحقه، فهو هذا المظهر العادى للحق العام، وهو الاساس الذى تستند اليه حياة الافراد . هذا والالتزامات على نوعين : نوع عام ونوع خاص . ونريد بالعام منها المبادىء القانونية العامة التى لا تتغير مطلقاً من عهد الرومان للآن . وهذه المبادىء لا تسرى فقط على الأحوال التى نص عليها القانون بل تسرى أيضاً على كل ما يتولد عن الحياة الاجتماعية وما تتطور فيه من الأدوار المختلفة من مختلف العقود والمعاملات .

واما النوع الخاص فانه يتعلق بالاحاطة بالمبادىء الخاصة ببعض الاعمال القانونية وهى تلك الاعمال التى يكون من شأنها ربط الافراد بروابط قانونية خاصة (ن ٥٨). وهذا القسم فى حالة تطور مستمر . والسبب فى عدم استقراره على حال واحدة هو أنه نظراً للتغييرات الاقتصادية والسياسية يبطل العمل ببعض العقود ، مثل عقود ترتيب المعاش طول الحياة، وعلى العكس من ذلك يكثر العمل بعقود اخرى نظراً لاهميتها فى عالم الحياة العملية، مثل عقد الشغل (٨) وعقد الاشتراك (٩) وعقد النقل (١٠) وقد تظهر

(١) droits relatifs (٢) droit absolu (٣) perpétuel (٤) temporaire (٥) paiement (٦) anormal (٧) droit commun (٨) contrat de travail (٩) contrat d'association (١٠) contrat de transport

Pp. 58–9 on contracts, from ʿAbd al-Salām Dhuhnī, *Fī l-iltizāmāt: al-Naẓariyyah al-ʿāmmah* (Obligations: The General Theory) (1924)

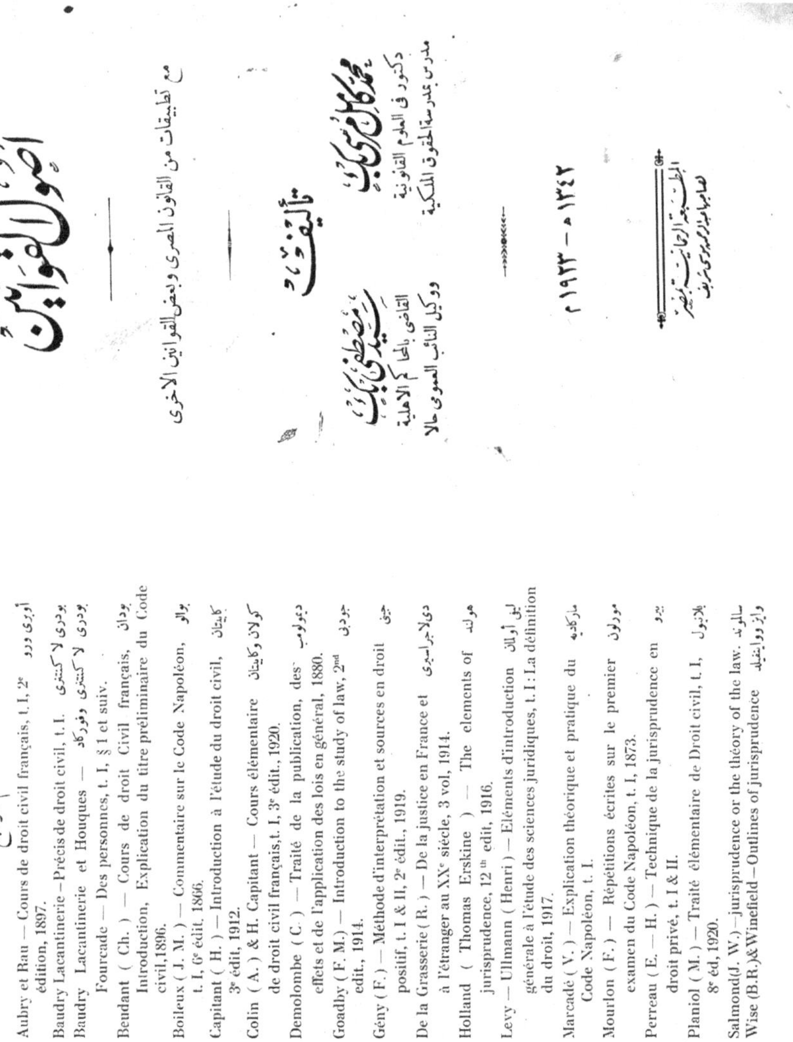

أصول القوانين

مع تطبيقات من القانون المصرى وبعض القوانين الاخرى

تأليف

محمد كامل مرسى بك
دكتور فى العلوم القانونية
مدرس بمدرسة الحقوق الملكية

سيد مصطفى بك
القاضى بالمحاكم الاهلية
ووكيل النائب العمومى حالا

١٣٤٢ هـ - ١٩٢٣ م

المطبعة الرحمانية بمصر
لصاحبها عبد الرحمن موسى شريف

— ٣ —

أهم المراجع

Aubry et Rau — Cours de droit civil français, t. I, 2e édition, 1897. أوبرى ورو

Baudry Lacantinerie – Précis de droit civil, t. I. بودرى لا كنتنرى

Baudry Lacantinerie et Houques — Fourcade — Des personnes, t. I, § 1 et suiv. بودرى لا كنتنرى وفوركاد

Beudant (Ch.) — Cours de droit Civil français, Introduction, Explication du titre préliminaire du Code civil, 1896. بودان

Boileux (J. M.) — Commentaire sur le Code Napoléon, t. I, 6e édit. 1866. بوالو

Capitant (H.) — Introduction à l'étude du droit civil, 3e édit, 1912. كابيتان

Colin (A.) & H. Capitant — Cours élémentaire de droit civil français, t. I, 3e édit., 1920. كولان وكابيتان

Demolombe (C.) — Traité de la publication, des effets et de l'application des lois en général, 1880. ديمولومب

Goadby (F. M.) — Introduction to the study of law, 2nd edit., 1914. جودبى

Gény (F.) — Méthode d'interprétation et sources en droit positif, t. I & II, 2e édit., 1919. جينى

De la Grasserie (R.) — De la justice en France et à l'étranger au XXe siécle, 3 vol, 1914. دى لاجراسيرى

Holland (Thomas Erskine) — The elements of jurisprudence, 12th edit, 1916. هولند

Levy — Ullmann (Henri) — Eléments d'introduction générale à l'étude des sciences juridiques, t. I : La définition du droit, 1917. ليفى أولمان

Marcadé (V.) — Explication théorique et pratique du Code Napoléon, t. I. ماركاديه

Mourlon (F.) — Répétitions écrites sur le premier examen du Code Napoléon, t. I, 1873. مورلون

Perreau (E. — H.) — Technique de la jurisprudence en droit privé, t. I & II. بيرو

Planiol (M.) — Traité élémentaire de Droit civil, t. I, 8e éd, 1920. بلانيول

Salmond (J. W.) — jurisprudence or the théory of the law. سالموند

Wise (B.R.) & Winefield — Outlines of jurisprudence وايز ووانيفيلد

Title page and reference list of Muḥammad Kāmil Mursī and Sayyid Muṣṭafá Bey, *Uṣūl al-qawānīn* (Sources of Laws) (1923)

— ٨ —

بهذا المعنى قد يسمى بالقانون الوضعى Jus positivum = Positive Law
وينقسم علم القانون المدنى civil Jurisprudence الى :
١) منهاجى systematic ، ٢) تاريخى Historical ، ٣) وانتقادى Critical
فالأول يبحث عن القانون كما هو بحالته الحاضرة ، والثانى يبحث عن الماضى وتطورات القانون وتدرجه ، والثالث يبحث عن وجوه النقص فى القانون وما يجب أن يكون عليه فى المستقبل ، ويسمى بالتشريع (١)

رابعا — قد يقصد بها ، لا كل القانون المدنى ، بل جزء معين منه ، وهو الجزء النظرى Theoretical Jurisprudence ، لا العملى

وهـذا هو المعنى الذى يقابل علم أصول القوانين السابق شرحه فى هـذا الكتاب (٢) ولذلك يمكن تعريفها بأنها عـلم المبادىء الأولية للقانون المـدنى ، وموضوعها النظريات العامة للقانون (٣)

٤ معنى كلمة Jurisprudence — فى فرنسا — تستعمل هذه الكلمة فى القانون الفرنسى فى جملة معان ، فيقصد بها :

أولا — معرفة القوانين ، أى مجموع الأحكام التى تحتملها النصوص وتكون النظرية العامة للقانون ، وبهذا المعنى تكون مرادفة لكلمة Droit ، أى القانون بمعناه الأعم (٤) ولكن هذا المعنى تلاشى شيئا فشيئا

ثانيا — التفسير القضائى للقانون ، أى الطريقة التى تؤول بها المحاكم النصوص القانونية وتطبقها (٥)

ثالثا — النتيجة التى وصلت اليها المحاكم واعتادت على اتباعها فى تفسير القانون ، أى مجموع الأحكام المتماثلة (٦)

(١) سالموند نبذة ٢
(٢) هذا الكتاب نبذة ٢
(٣) سالموند نبذة ٣
(٤) ديمولومب نبذة ١٣ بودان نبذة ٥ — كولان وكابيتان ص ٢
(٥) فيقال La jurisprudence de la cour esf prononcée en tel sens
بودان نبذة ٥ ديمولومب نبذة ١٣
(٦) ديمولومب نبذة ١٣

— ٩ —

٥ — أصول القوانين علم لا فن — ودرس أصول القانون علم ، وان كان تطبيقه فنا ، كعمل القضاة والمحامين والموثقين ، ولكن هذا الفن لم يكن الا تطبيق علم اكتسب قبله ، ومن ذلك يظهر أن درس القانون قد يكون فنا وقد يكون علما ، فيكون فنا اذا كان المقصود منه تحقيق الأغراض العملية والنتائج القانونية ، اذ الفن مجموع الطرق التى ترمى الى الوصول الى نتيجة مفيدة حسنة ، أما ما يتعلق بدرس أصول القوانين فعلم ، لأن العلوم هى درس القوانين الطبيعية بطريقة منظمة ، وكل علم عبارة عن معرفة جزء معين من قواعد الطبيعة بصفة منظمة فيما يختص بنوع خاص من الكائنات (١) ، وقد قال بعضهم عن العلم بأنه ما يبحث فى المسائل المرتبطة بعضها ببعض بعلاقات ضرورية استكشفت وتسمى بالقواعد الثابتة (٢) ، والعلم لغة هو ادراك الشىء بحقيقته ، ويطلق العلم مجازا على مجموع مسائل فى موضوع واحد ، أما فى الاصطلاح المصرى فيطلق على مجموع المعارف الطبيعية المحضة الخالية من شوائب الظنون والاوهام (٣)

٦ — علاقة أصول القوانين بالعلوم الاخرى — علم أصول القوانين من العـلوم الاجتماعية ، مثل علم الآداب والسياسة والتاريخ والاقتصاد الخ ، فانها كلها تبحث فى الانسان بصفته عضوا فى الهيئة الاجتماعية (٤) التى لا يمكن أن يعيش فى غيرها

وعلوم الاجتماع تحلل العلاقات المختلفة بين الناس بصفتهم المتقدمة ، وتبحثها بحثا دقيقا ، فما كان منها خاصا بالاجتماع فى حد ذاته ، كالدين والعادات ، اختص به علم الاجتماع ، وما كان خاصا بالعلاقات المادية من جهة الثروة اختص به علم الاقتصاد ، وما كان متعلقا منها بالسياسة اختص به علم النظام السياسى ، وما

(١) بودرى لاكنترى وفوركاد نبذة ١٣ — كولان وكابيتان جزء ١ ص ٦
(٢) او القوانين بالمعنى المجازى . راجع شارل جيد الاقتصاد السياسي الكتاب الاول نبذة ٢
(٣) كنز العلوم واللغة لمحمد فريد وجدى ص ٦٨٠
(٤) بودرى لاكنترى وفوركاد نبذة ١٣ — كولان وكابيتان ١ ص ٦

(٢)

Pp. 8–9 on legal theory, from Muḥammad Kāmil Mursī and Sayyid Muṣṭafá Bey, *Uṣūl al-qawānīn* (Sources of Laws) (1923)

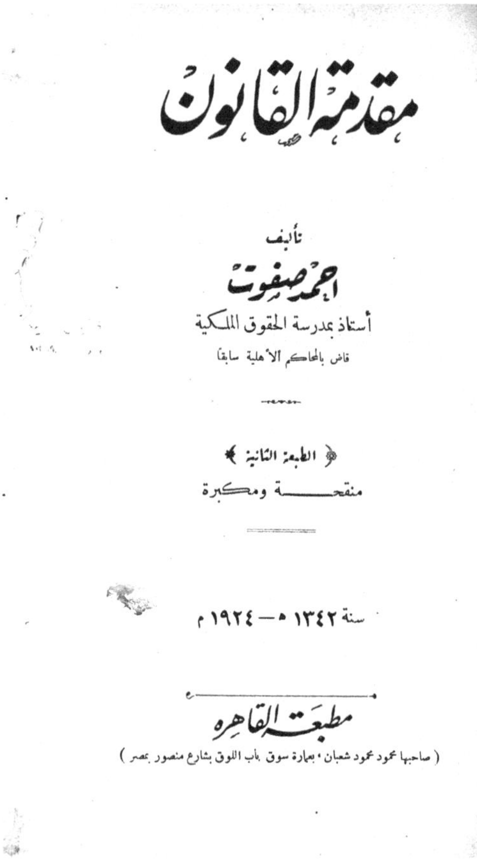

مقدمة القانون

تأليف

احمد صفوت

أستاذ بمدرسة الحقوق الملكية

قاض بالمحاكم الأهلية سابقاً

﴿ الطبعة الثانية ﴾

منقحة ومكبرة

سنة ١٣٤٢ هـ — ١٩٢٤ م

مطبعة القاهرة

(صاحبها محمود محمود شعبان ، بعمارة سوق باب اللوق بشارع منصور بمصر)

Introduction to Law (Qānūn)

Aḥmad Ṣafwat

Professor in the Royal Law School

Former Judge of the Native Courts

Title page of Aḥmad Ṣafwat, *Muqaddimat al-qānūn* (Introduction to Law) (1924)

— ٣٠ —

وهي عبارة عن ظواهر طبيعية مطردة النظام كأنها تسير على قانون ، لـكن فى الواقع لا يوجد قانون ، ومثل ذلك حالة أن الجائع يأكل ، فالناموس أى النظام الواقع فعلا هو أن الجائع يأكل ، فلا يقال ان هناك قانوناً بان الجائع يأكل ، بل هى حالة ثابتة تعرف بالمشاهدة وبالتجارب .

وانما أطلق لفظ القانون على النواميس الطبيعية مجازاً تشبيهاً لها بالقوانين الوضعية بجامع النظام المطرد فى كل منهما . وأوجه التناقض بينهما أن القوانين الوضعية تتبع اختياراً فمن شاء أخل بها ، أما القوانين الطبيعية فتتبع اضطراراً بحكم الطبيعة ، فالـكواكب لا يمكن ان تخرج عن دائرة فلكها . وان نتيجة مخالفة القوانين الطبيعية تقع من نفسها وجوباً بلا واسطة(١) . فمن خالف قوانين الطبيعة المتعلقة بالصحة يمرض ومن ألقى نفسه من علو يسقط ويصاب ، فى حين أن الجزاء على مخالفة القوانين الوضعية يقع بواسطة الحاكم .

﴿ القوانين الوضعية والفروض الدينية ﴾

الفروض الدينية أو العبادات هي الواجبات المفروضة على الانسان بحكم دينه نحو خالقه مثل الصلاة والصيام والامتناع عن المحرمات ، وتميز عن الواجبات أو الالتزامات القانونية بأنها (أولا) لا تعتبر علاقات بين الناس بل واجبات مفروضة على الانسان نحو خالقه ، و (ثانياً) ان الجزاء عليها دينى محض يقع فى الحياة الأخرى .

لـكن إذا قام السلطان بمراقبة إجراء هذه الفروض واجبار الناس

«1» Automatiquemnt

— ٣١ —

على القيام بها ومعاقبة من يهملها صارت واجبات قانونية بين السلطان والأفراد ، لأن السلطان يتطلب من الأفراد القيام بها أو يعاقبهم على إهمالها ، فتأخذ حكم القوانين الوضعية وتعتبر جزءاً من القانون العام الذى يحدد علاقة الفرد بالحكومة ، مثل قانون العقوبات ، وذلك علاوة على صفتها الدينية ، كما كان الحال فى عصر الخلفاء الراشدين .

﴿ القانون والعدل (١) ﴾

يختلط معنى القانون أحياناً بمعنى العدل بسبب أن تطبيق القانون على جميع الحالات التى يشملها يوصف بأنه عدل فى تطبيق القانون ، حتى لو كانت نصوص القانون من الأصل لم تسوّ فى الحكم بين الحالات التى تشملها ويحسن أن نفهم أولا معنى العدل فى ذاته .

العدل فى ذاته — العدل فى ذاته هو المساواة فى تطبيق قاعدة بين الناس (٢) . وعرفه جستنيان أنه « الرغبة الدائمة فى إعطاء كل انسان حقه » (٣) وعرفه أفلاطون أنه « قول الصدق وإعطاء كل ذى حق حقه » (٤) .

لـكن على أى قاعدة يعطى الانسان حقه ؟ فالعدل كتصور معنوى لا يفهم الا بنسبته الى قاعدة ، ويكون اتباع هذه القاعدة هو العدل فى تطبيقها .

(1) La justice [2] Jhering; Evolution du Droit , p.244

[3] Levy-Ullmann ; Eléments d'Introduction Générale ; p. 10.

[4] Republic of Plato ; Book IV, no. 331.

Pp. 30–1 on legal theory in man-made and religious law, from Aḥmad Ṣafwat, *Muqaddimat al-qānūn* (Introduction to Law) (1924)

الجامعة المصرية – كلية الحقوق

النظرية العامة للالتزامات
فى
الشريعة الإسلامية

الجزء الأول

طرفا الالتزام

وبه بيان المراجع ومقـــدمة فى طريقة البحث
وعرض عام لنظرية الالتزامات
فى الفقه الحنفى

« وانه ليستغفر لطالب العلم
من فى السموات ومن فى الأرض
حتى حيتان البحر وهوام البر »
حديث شريف

رسالة للحصول على درجة الدكتوراه فى القانون

تأليف

شفيق شحاتة

مقدمة للمناقشة العلنية فى يوم الأحد ٢٤ مايو ١٩٣٦

لجنة المحكمين
الأستاذ أحمد ابراهيم بك . رئيس
الأستاذ البير شيرون
الأستاذ محمد صالح

مطبعة الاعتماد بشارع حسن الأكبر بمصر

Arabic version of Chafik Chehata, *Essai d'une théorie générale* (1936)

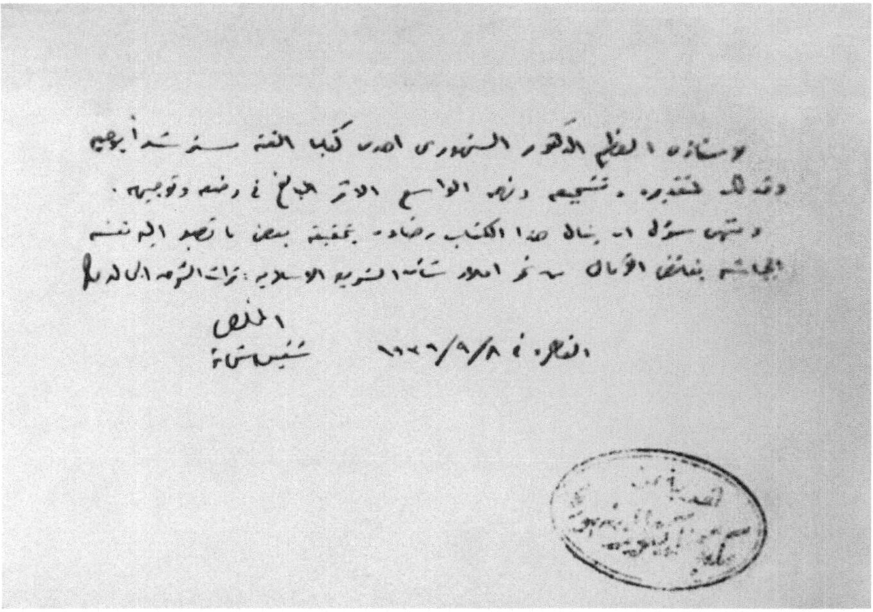

Handwritten dedication of Chafik Chehata to ʿAbd al-Razzāq al-Sanhūrī, inside al-Sanhūrī's personal copy of *Essai d'une théorie générale de l'obligation en droit musulman* (1936).
(From the library of ʿAbd al-Razzaq al-Sanhūrī, Cairo University Law Faculty)

"To my Esteemed Professor, Doctor al-Sanhūrī, I present this book which has been guided by his inspiration, and whose esteem, discernment, and vast intellect have been the greatest influences in its writing and direction. My utmost hope is that this book will obtain his approval by making some achievement toward serving his abundant hopes for the advancement of Islamic Sharia and the Heritage of the East eternal.

Cairo
September 8, 1936
Yours sincerely
Chafik Chehata"

References

Interviews

Professor Fu'ad Arini, Alexandria, June 13, 2009.
Professor Borham Atallah, Alexandria, June 13, 2009; Cairo, June 16, 2009.
Professor Muhammad Serag, Cairo, June 14, 2009.
Professor Muhammad Kamal al-Din al-Imam, Alexandria, June 15, 2009.

Newspapers and Periodicals

Al-Aḥkām al-sharʿiyyah (Cairo, 1902–).
Al-Ḥuqūq (Cairo, 1886–).
Al-Manār (Cairo, 1898–1935).
Al-Muḥāmāh al-sharʿiyyah (Cairo, 1929–56).
Al-Muqtaṭaf (Beirut, 1885–1914).
Al-Waqāʾiʿ al-miṣriyyah (Cairo, 1828–).
Journal officiel du gouvernement égyptien (Cairo, 1886–).
Le Bosphore égyptien (1890s).
Bulletin de l'Institut Égyptien (Cairo, 1859–1918).
Bulletin des lois et décrets et de documents officiels du gouvernement égyptien (Cairo, ca. [1880]-1902).
The Egyptian Gazette (Alexandria, 1880–1938).
Majallat al-aḥkām al-sharʿiyyah (Cairo, 1902–10).
Majallat al-Azhar (Cairo, 1939–).
Majallat Kulliyyat al-Ḥuqūq li-l-mabāḥith al-qānūniyyah wa-l-iqtiṣādiyyah (Cairo, 1927).
Majallat al-qaḍāʾ al-sharʿī: Sharʿiyyah, ʿilmiyyah, adabiyyah (Cairo, 1922–31).
Majallat al-qānūn wa-l-iqtiṣād (Cairo, 1932–).
Official Bulletin of the Native Courts (Cairo, 1900–).
Le Phare d'Alexandrie (Alexandria, 1878).
Revue internationale de droit comparé (Paris, 1949–).
Revue internationale de l'enseignement (Paris, 1881–).
Revue internationale de législation et de jurisprudence musulmanes (Cairo, 1895–96).

Official Documents, Printed, and Reference Works

ʿAbd al-Jawād, Muḥammad. *Taqwīm Dār al-ʿUlūm: al-ʿAdad al-māsī yuṣdar li-murūr 75 ʿāman ʿalá al-madrasah 1872–1947*. Miṣr: Dār al-Maʿārif, 1952.

Britain, and Lord Cromer. *P.P., Despatches from Sir E. Baring Respecting the Employment of Europeans in the Egyptian Public Service, Egypt. No. 6 (1887), C. 4997 XCII 1888*. London, 1887.

Britain, and Lord Cromer. *(P.P.) Reports by His Majesty's Agent and Consul-General on the Finances, Administration, and Condition of Egypt and the Soudan, in 1905. Egypt. No. 1 (1906)*. London, 1906.

Britain, and Lord Cromer. *(P.P.) Reports on the Finances, Administration, and Condition of Egypt, and the Progress of Reforms. May 1898. Egypt. No. 1 (1898)*. London, 1898.

The Code of the Civil and Commerical Procedure of the Egyptian Native Tribunals, Translation. Oxford: Horace Hart, 1903.

The Egyptian Codes, Preceded by the Statute of Judicial Organization. London: W. Clowes and Sons Ltd., 1892.

Egyptian Ministry of Education. *Projet de règlement organique de l'École Khédiviale de Droit.* Cairo: Imprimerie Nationale, 1904.

Egyptian Ministry of Education. *Rapport sur l'enseignement public en Égypte.* Cairo: Imprimerie Nationale, 1885–89.

Egyptian Ministry of Justice. *Mashrūʿ tanqīḥ al-qānūn al-madanī: Mudhakkirah īḍāḥiyyah.* 4 vols. Cairo: Maṭbaʿat al-Iʿtimād, 1948.

Egyptian Ministry of Justice. *Projet de code civil révisé.* 3 vols. Cairo, 1941.

Egyptian Ministry of Justice. *Reports for the Years 1903, 1907–1915, 1916.* Cairo, 1904–.

Egyptian Native Civil Code. Oxford: Hart, 1901.

Encyclopaedia of Islam, 2nd ed. Ed. P. J. Bearman et al. Leiden: Brill, 1960–2004.

al-Jāmiʿah al-Miṣriyyah. *Taqwīm Kulliyyat al-Ḥuqūq.* Cairo: al-Maṭbaʿah al-Amīriyyah, 1929–1940 (annual volumes).

al-Jāmiʿah al-Miṣriyyah, and Kulliyyat al-Ḥuqūq. *Asmāʾ man ḥaṣalū ʿalá līsans fī l-ḥuqūq min sanat 1874 li-sanat 1931 wa ʿalá diblūmāt al-dirāsah al-ʿulyā min sanat 1928–1931.* Cairo: al-Maṭbaʿah al-Amīriyyah, 1933.

Jāmiʿat al-Qāhirah. *Al-ʿĪd al-miʾawī li-Kulliyyat al-Ḥuqūq.* Cairo: Jāmiʿat al-Qāhirah, Kulliyyat al-Ḥuqūq, 1980.

Jāmiʿat al-Qāhirah. *Taqwīm Jāmiʿat al-Qāhirah.* Cairo: Jāmiʿat al-Qāhirah, 1956–1958 (annual volumes).

Les juridictions mixtes d'Égypte 1876–1926: Livre d'or édité sous le patronage du Conseil de l'ordre des avocats à l'occasion du cinquantenaire des tribunaux de la réforme. Alexandria: Journal des tribunaux mixtes, 1926.

Madrasat al-Ḥuqūq al-Khidīwiyyah. *al-Qawānīn wa-l-brūgrām.* Cairo: al-Maṭbaʿah al-Amīriyyah bi-Miṣr, 1910.

Madrasat al-Qadāʾ al-Sharʿī. (1) *al-Amr al-ʿālī al-ṣādir 12 muḥarram sanat 1325 (25 fabrāyir 1907) bi-inshāʾ al-madrasah*, (2) *al-Lāʾiḥah al-dākhiliyyah li-l-madrasah*, (3) *Brugrām mawādd al-dirāsah.* Miṣr: al-Maṭbaʿah al-Amīriyyah, 1907.

Madrasat al-Qaḍāʾ al-Sharʿī. *Mudhakkirāt ʿan al-muʿāmalāt fī fiqh al-imām Abī Ḥanīfah raḥimahu Allāh.* Cairo: Maṭbaʿat al-Wāʿiẓ, 1327/1909.

Madrasat al-Qaḍāʾ al-Sharʿī, and Wizārat al-Maʿārif al-ʿUmūmiyyah. *Manhaj al-dirāsah al-muʾaqqat.* Cairo: al-Maṭbaʿah al-Amīriyyah, 1929.

al-Qānūn al-madanī: Majmūʿat al-aʿmāl al-taḥḍīriyyah. 6 vols. Cairo: Maṭbaʿat Dār al-Kitāb al-ʿArabī, 1950.

Recueil des documents officiels du gouvernement égyptien. Cairo: Imprimerie Nationale, 1881–1917.

ʿUmar, Aḥmad, and ʿAlī ʿAbd al-ʿAzīz. *Majmūʿat al-imtiḥānāt al-nihāʾiyyah li-madrasat al-ḥuqūq al-malakiyyah min sanat 1906 li-ghāyat imtiḥān māris sanat 1925.* Miṣr: Maṭbaʿat al-Iʿtimād, 1925.

Université Égyptienne. *Annuaire 1908–1910.* Cairo: Imprimerie de l'Institut Français d'Archéologie Orientale, 1911.

Université Égyptienne. *Annuaire de la Faculté de Droit, année 1936–1937.* Cairo, ca. 1936.

Université Fouad Ier. Université Fouad Ier [Annuaire]. Cairo: Université Fouad Ier, 1950.

Wathelet, J. A., et al. *Codes égyptiens et lois usuelles en vigueur en Égypte.* Cairo: Imprimerie Noury, 1939.

Unpublished Documents

Amos-Bunting-Moncrieff-Legg-Hawthorn Family Papers, London. Private collection maintained by Mrs. Ruth Hawthorn and Sir Thomas Legg of London. Includes the papers of Andrew Amos, Sheldon Amos, Maurice Sheldon Amos, and Colin Scott-Moncrieff.

Archives rapatriées de l'Ambassade de France au Caire 1870–1956, Centre des archives diplomatiques de Nantes, Ministère des affaires étrangères, Nantes.

Dissertations (*Qāʿat al-rasāʾil*), Cairo University Law Faculty, Cairo.

Foreign Office 78, 141, 143, 371, 407, 566, 605, 608, 624, 738, 804, 847, National Archives, Kew, London.

Four notebooks of George Nassif, written in classes at the Khedivial School of Law, circa 1908. College de la Sainte Famille, Cairo.

Papers of Lord Cromer (Evelyn Baring), Bodleian Library, Oxford.

Papers of William Brunyate, Bodleian Library and Rhodes House, Oxford.

Papers of Lord Dufferin, Rhodes House and St. Antony's College Middle East Centre Archive, Oxford.

Papers of Benson Maxwell, Rhodes House, Oxford.

Papers of John Scott, Bodleian Library and Rhodes House, Oxford; British Library, London.

Secondary Works

ʿAbd al-Bārī, Muḥammad, and ʿAbd al-Razzāq Aḥmad al-Sanhūrī. *Al-Imtiyāzāt al-ajnabiyyah.* Miṣr: Lajnat al-Taʾlīf wa-l-Tarjamah wa-l-Nashr, 1930.

ʿAbd al-Rāzī, Abū Bakr. *Abū Zahrah fī raʾy ʿulamāʾ al-ʿaṣr.* [Cairo]: Dār al-Iʿtiṣām, ca. 1980.

ʿAbd al-Rāziq, ʿAlī. *Al-Islām wa-uṣūl al-ḥukm: Baḥth fī l-khilāfah wa-l-ḥukūmah fī l-islām.* Cairo: Maṭbaʿat Miṣr, 1925.

ʿAbduh, Muḥammad. "Al-Azhar al-sharīf wa-l-gharaḍ min iṣlāḥ ṭuruq al-taʿlīm fīh." In *al-Aʿmāl al-kāmilah li-l-imām Muḥammad ʿAbduh*, ed. M. ʿImārah, 3: 203–9. Cairo: Dār al-Shurūq, 2001.

ʿAbduh, Muḥammad. "Ikhtilāf al-qawānīn bi-ikhtilāf al-umam." *Al-Waqāʾiʿ al-miṣriyyah* (June 19, 1881). Repr. in Muḥammad ʿAbduh, *al-Aʿmāl al-kāmilah li-l-imām Muḥammad ʿAbduh*, 5 vols, ed. M. ʿImārah, 1: 337–42. Cairo: Dār al-Shurūq, 2001.

ʿAbduh, Muḥammad. "Iṣlāḥ al-Azhar." In Muḥammad ʿAbduh, *al-Aʿmāl al-kāmilah li-l-imām Muḥammad ʿAbduh*, ed. M. ʿImārah, 3: 191–215. Cairo: Dār al-Shurūq, 2001.

ʿAbduh, Muḥammad. "Al-Quwwah wa-l-qānūn." *Al-Manār* 1 (1899): 917–23; 2 (1899): 174.

ʿAbduh, Muḥammad. *Risālat al-tawḥīd.* Bulaq: al-Maṭbaʿah al-Kubrá al-Amīriyyah, 1898.

ʿAbduh, Muḥammad. "Shaykh al-Azhar yukhālif qānūnah." In Muḥammad ʿAbduh, *al-Aʿmāl al-kāmilah li-l-imām Muḥammad ʿAbduh*, ed. M. ʿImārah, 5 vols., 3: 197–201. Cairo: Dār al-Shurūq, 2001.

Abécassis, Frédéric. "De la Protection par l'école: La Sédimentation des traditions d'enseignement du français en Égypte au XIXe siècle." In *France-Levant: De la fin du XVIIe siècle à la première guerre mondiale*, ed. B. Delpal et al., 117–44. Paris: Geuthner, 2005.

Abū al-Fatḥ, Aḥmad. *Kitāb al-Muʿāmalāt fī l-sharīʿah al-islāmiyyah wa-l-qawānīn al-miṣriyyah.* 2 vols. Miṣr: Maṭbaʿat al-Busfūr, 1913.

Abū al-Fatḥ, Aḥmad. *Kitāb al-Mukhtārāt al-fatḥiyyah fī tārīkh al-tashrīʿ wa-uṣūl al-fiqh.* 4th ed. Miṣr: Maṭbaʿat al-Nahḍah, 1924.

Abū Hayf, ʿAbd al-Ḥamīd. *Al-Murāfaʿāt al-madaniyyah wa-l-tijāriyyah wa-l-niẓām al-qaḍāʾī fī Miṣr*. 2nd ed. Cairo: Maṭbaʿat al-Maʿārif, 1915, 1921.
Abū Hayf, ʿAlī Ṣādiq. "Al-Diyah fī l-sharīʿah al-islāmiyyah." Doct. diss., Law Faculty of the Egyptian University, 1933.
Abu-Odeh, Lama. "Politics of (Mis)Recognition: Islamic Law Pedagogy in American Academia." *American Journal of Comparative Law* 52 (2004): 789–824.
Abū Sulaymān, ʿAbd al-Wahhāb. "Al-Naẓariyyah wa-l-qawāʿid fī l-fiqh al-islāmī." *Majallat Jāmiʿat al-Mālik ʿAbd al-ʿAzīz* 2 (1978): 53.
Abū Zahrah, Muḥammad. *Al-Milkiyyah wa-naẓariyyat al-ʿaqd fī l-sharīʿah al-islāmiyyah*. Cairo: Dār al-Fikr al-ʿArabī, 1939.
Abū Zayd, Rushdī Shiḥātah. *Al-Madkhal li-dirāsat al-fiqh al-islāmī*. Vol. 2, *Al-Naẓariyyāt al-ʿāmmah*. Cairo: Dār al-Naṣr, 2001.
al-Abyānī, Muḥammad Zayd. *Kitāb Mabāḥith al-murāfaʿāt wa-ṣuwar al-tawthīqāt wa-l-daʿāwá al-sharʿiyyah*. Miṣr: ʿAbd Allāh Wahbah al-Katbī, 1924.
al-Abyānī, Muḥammad Zayd. *Mukhtaṣar al-murāfaʿāt al-sharʿiyyah*. [Cairo], ca. 1925.
al-Abyānī, Muḥammad Zayd. *Mukhtaṣar Sharḥ al-aḥkām al-sharʿiyyah fī l-aḥwāl al-shakhṣiyyah*. Miṣr: Maṭbaʿat al-Waʿiẓ, 1326.
al-Abyānī, Muḥammad Zayd. *Sharḥ al-Aḥkām al-sharʿiyyah fī l-aḥwāl al-shakhṣiyyah*. Miṣr: Maṭbaʿat ʿAlī Sukkar Aḥmad, 1903.
al-Abyānī, Muḥammad Zayd, and Muḥammad Salāmah al-Sanjalfī. *Sharḥ Murshid al-ḥayrān ilá maʿrifat aḥwāl al-insān fī l-muʿāmalāt al-sharʿiyyah ʿalá madhhab al-imām al-aʿẓam Abī Ḥanīfah al-Nuʿmān mulāʾiman li-ʿurf al-diyār al-miṣriyyah wa-sāʾir al-aqṭār al-islāmiyyah*. Miṣr: Maṭbaʿat al-Wāʿiẓ, 1908.
Adams, Charles C. *Islam and Modernism in Egypt: A Study of the Modern Reform Movement Inaugurated by Muhammad Abduh*. London: Oxford University Press, 1933.
Ahmad Atif Ahmad, "Lawyers: Islamic Law." *Oxford Encyclopedia of Legal History*, 4: 47–8. Oxford: Oxford University Press, 20.
Ali Agrama, Hussein. *Questioning Secularism: Islam, Sovereignty, and the Rule of Law in Modern Egypt*. Chicago: University of Chicago Press, 2012.
ʿĀlamgīr, Muḥammad Awrangzeb, and al-Ḥasan ibn Manṣūr al-Ūzjandī al-Farghānī Qāḍīkhān. *Al-Fatāwá al-hindiyyah wa-tuʿarraf bi-l-fatāwá al-ʿālamgīriyyah fī madhhab al-imām Abī Ḥanīfah al-Nuʿmān*. 6 vols. Repr. of Bulaq ed. 1310/1891. Beirut: Dār al-Maʿrifah li-l-Ṭibāʿah wa-l-Nashr, 1973.
ʿAlī, ʿAbd al-Raʾūf Ibrāhīm. "al-Ijtihād wa-l-taqlīd." *al-Muḥāmāh al-sharʿiyyah* 2,1 (1930): 16–18.
ʿAlī, ʿAbd al-Raʾūf Ibrāhīm. "Kutub al-fiqh al-islāmī." *Al-Muḥāmāh al-sharʿiyyah* 1,6 (1929): 482–4.
Allen, Roger. *A Study of Hadīth ʿĪsā ibn Hishām: Muhammad al-Muwaylihī's View of Egyptian Society during the British Occupation*. Albany: State University of New York Press, 1974.
Allen, Roger. *A Period of Time*. Part 1: *A Study of Muhammad al-Muwaylihi's* Hadith ʿIsa Ibn Hisham. Reading, UK: Ithaca Press, 1992.
Amīn, Aḥmad. "Khaṭarāt." *Majallat al-qaḍāʾ al-sharʿī* 1,3 (1922): 139–41.
Amīn, Aḥmad. *My Life: The Autobiography of an Egyptian Scholar, Writer and Cultural Leader*. Trans. I. J. Boullata. Leiden: E. J. Brill, 1978.
Amīn, Aḥmad. "Al-Qānūn al-rūmānī wa-l-fiqh al-islāmī (1)." *Al-Muḥāmāh al-sharʿiyyah* 1,1 (1929): 20.
Amos, Maurice Sheldon, and Pierre Arminjon. *Collection of Problems and Exercises in the Civil and Commercial Law of Egypt*. Cairo, 1904.

Ancel, M. "La Tendance universaliste dans la doctrine comparative française au début du XXème siecle." In *Festschrift für Ernst Rabel*, ed. H. Dölle et al., 2 vols., 1: 17–38. Tübingen: Mohr, 1954.

Anderson, J. N. D. "Law Reform in Egypt: 1850–1950." In *Political and Social Change in Modern Egypt: Historical Studies from the Ottoman Conquest to the United Arab Republic*, ed. P. M. Holt, 209–30. London: Oxford University Press, 1968.

"ʿAqd." In *al-Mawsūʿah al-fiqhiyyah*. Kuwayt: Wizārat al-Awqāf, 1983.

Arabi, Oussama. *Studies in Modern Islamic Law and Jurisprudence*. The Hague: Kluwer Law International, 2001.

Aragoneses, Alfons. *Recht im* Fin de Siècle*: Briefe von Raymond Saleilles an Eugen Huber (1895–1911)*. Frankfurt am Main: V. Klostermann, 2007.

Aristarches, Gregorius. *Législation ottomane, ou recueil des lois, réglements, ordonnances, traités, capitulations et autres documents officiels de l'empire ottoman*. Constantinople: Freres Nicolaïdes, 1873–88.

Arminjon, Pierre. "Charles Testoud: Ses années d'Égypte." *Annales (Université de Grenoble)* (1907): 19–25.

Arminjon, Pierre. "Le Droit international privé interne." *Journal Clunet* (1912, 1913): 79–172.

Arminjon, Pierre. "Égypte: Notice sur les lois promulguées pendant l'année 1907." In *Annuaire de législation étrangère*, 924–6. Paris: Libraire Générale de Droit et de Jurisprudence, 1908.

Arminjon, Pierre. *L'Enseignement, la doctrine et la vie dans les universités musulmanes d'Égypte*. Paris: Felix Alcan, 1907.

Arminjon, Pierre, and Société de législation comparée. *La Codification du droit international privé*. Paris: LGDJ, 1932.

Asad, Talal. *Formations of the Secular: Christianity, Islam, Modernity*. Stanford: Stanford University Press, 2003.

al-ʿAshmāwī, Muḥammad Saʿīd. *Al-Sharīʿah al-islāmiyyah wa-l-qānūn al-miṣrī*. Cairo: Maktabat Madbūlī al-Ṣaghīr, 1996.

ʿAṭṭār, ʿAbd al-Nāṣir Tawfīq. *Taṭbīq al-sharīʿah al-islāmiyyah fī l-ʿālam al-islāmī*. Cairo: Dār al-Faḍīlah, 1993.

ʿAwdah, ʿAbd al-Qādir. *Al-Islām wa-awḍāʿunā al-qānūniyyah*. Cairo: Dār al-Kitāb al-ʿArabī, 1951.

ʿAwdah, ʿAbd al-Qādir. *Al-Tashrīʿ al-jināʾī al-islāmī muqāranan bi-l-qānūn al-waḍʿī*. Cairo: Dār Nashr al-Thaqāfah, 1949. Eng. trans. in A. Q. ʿO Shaheed and S. Z. Aijaz, *Criminal Law of Islam*, 4 vols. New Delhi: Adam Publishers and Distributors, 2005.

Ayubi, Nazih N. M. *Over-Stating the Arab State*. London: I. B. Tauris, 1995.

al-Azhar, Lajnat Iṣlāḥ. *Mashrūʿ iṣlāḥ al-Azhar*. Cairo, 1919.

Aziz, Joseph. *Concordance des codes égyptiens mixtes et indigènes avec le code Napoléon, suivie d'un appendice relatant la jurisprudence de la Cour d'Appel Mixte d'Alexandrie*. Alexandria, 1886.

al-ʿAẓm, Rafīq Bey. "Al-Iṣlāḥ al-islāmī bi-ʿadl al-qiwām aw al-takāful al-ʿāmm." *Al-Manār* 2 (1899): 71–8.

al-Azmeh, Aziz. *Islams and Modernities*. London: Verso, 1993.

ʿAzzām, ʿAbd al-Wahhāb. "Al-Nahḍah." *Majallat al-qaḍāʾ al-sharʿī* 1,2 (1922): 81–6.

Badawī, ʿAbd al-Ḥamīd. "Athar al-imtiyāzāt fī l-qaḍāʾ wa-l-tashrīʿ fī Miṣr." In *al-Kitāb al-dhahabī li-l-maḥākim al-ahliyyah 1883–1933*, 2 vols., 1: 1–61. Bulaq: al-Maṭbaʿah al-Amīriyyah, 1937.

Badawī, ʿAbd al-Ḥamīd (Badawi, Abd El-Hamid Bey). "Du Principe qu'en droit musulman la succession n'est ouverte qu'après aquittement des dettes." *L'Égypte contemporaine* 5 (1914): 14–51.

Badawī, Ibrāhīm Zakī al-Dīn. "Naẓariyyat al-ribā al-muḥarram." *Majallat al-qānūn wa-l-iqtiṣād* (1939): 387–446.

Baer, Gabriel. "The Development of Private Ownership of Land." In Baer, *Studies in the Social History of Modern Egypt*, 62–78. Chicago: University of Chicago Press, 1969.

Baer, Gabriel. "Social Change in Egypt: 1800–1914." In *Political and Social Change in Modern Egypt*, ed. P. M. Holt, 135–61. London: Oxford University Press, 1968.

Baer, Gabriel. "Tanzimat in Egypt: The Penal Code." *Bulletin of the School of Oriental and African Studies* 26 (1963): 29–49.

Balboni, L. A. *Gl'italiani nella civiltà egiziana del secolo XIX°: Storia, biografie, monografie*. 2 vols. Alexandria: V. Penasson, 1906.

al-Bannā, Jamāl. *Al-Ḥukm bi-l-qurʾān wa-qaḍiyyat taṭbīq al-sharīʿah*. Cairo: Dār al-Fikr al-Islāmī, 1986.

Barclay, Thomas. "The Teaching of Law in France." *Journal of the Society of Comparative Legislation* 2,1 (1900): 131–6.

Basdevant-Bastid, Suzanne. "L'Institut de Droit Comparé de Lyon." In *Introduction à l'étude du droit comparé: Recueil d'études en l'honneur d'Édouard Lambert*, 11–15. Paris: LGDJ, 1935.

Baudry-Lacantinerie, G. *Précis de droit civil*. Paris: Larose et Forcel, 1882.

Bayitch, S. "Codification in Modern Times." In *Civil Law in the Modern World*, ed. A. N. Yiannopoulus, 161–91. Baton Rouge: Louisiana State University Press, 1965.

Bechor, Guy. *God in the Courtroom: The Transformation of Courtroom Oath and Perjury between Islamic and Franco-Egyptian Law*. Leiden: Brill, 2011.

Bechor, Guy. *The Sanhūrī Code, and the Emergence of Modern Arab Civil Law (1932–1949)*. Leiden: Brill, 2007.

Bedir, Murteza. "*Fıkıh* to Law: Secularization through Curriculum." *Islamic Law and Society* 11,3 (2004): 378–401.

Beinin, Joel. "Egypt: Society and Economy, 1923–1952." In *The Cambridge History of Egypt*, vol. 2, *Modern Egypt from 1517 to the End of the Twentieth Century*, ed. M. W. Daly, 309–33. Cambridge: Cambridge University Press, 1998.

Belleau, Marie-Claude. "The ʿJuristes Inquiets': Legal Classicism and Criticism in Early Twentieth-Century France." *Utah Law Review* 2 (1997): 379–424.

Bellomo, Manlio. *The Common Legal Past of Europe, 1000–1800*. Washington, DC: Catholic University of America Press, 1995.

Bemmelen, Pieter van. *L'Égypte et l'Europe*. Leiden: E. J. Brill, 1882.

Bencheneb, M. "Khalīl b. Isḥāḳ." *Encyclopaedia of Islam*, 2nd ed., 4: 964.

Benda, Harry J. "Christiaan Snouck Hurgronje and the Foundations of Dutch Islamic Policy in Indonesia." *The Journal of Modern History* 30,4 (1958): 338–47.

Berg, L. W. C. van den. *De beginselen van het mohammedaansche recht volgens de imâm's Aboe Hanîfat en Sjâfe'î*. Batavia: Bruining, 1874. Russ. trans. V. F. Girgas, St. Petersburg, 1882; Fr. trans. R. de France de Tersant, Algiers, 1896.

Berg, L. W. C. van den, trans. *Minhādj aṭ-ṭālibīn: Le Guide des zélés croyants. Manuel de jurisprudence musulmane selon le rite de Chāfi'ī*. Batavia: Imprimerie du Gouvernement, 1882.

Bernand, M. "Muʿāmalāt." *Encyclopaedia of Islam*, 2nd ed., 7: 255–7.

Bernhöft, Franz. "Über Zweck und Mittel der vergleichenden Rechtswissenschaft." *Zeitschrift für vergleichende Rechtswissenschaft* 1,1 (1878).

Berque, Jacques. *Egypt: Imperialism and Revolution*. Trans. J. Stewart. London: Faber and Faber, 1972.

al-Bishrī, Ṭāriq. *Al-Ḥiwār al-islāmī al-ʿalmānī*. Cairo: Dār al-Shurūq, 1996.

al-Bishrī, Ṭāriq. *Al-Muslimūn wa-l-aqbāṭ fī iṭār al-jamāʿah al-waṭaniyyah*. Cairo: al-Hayʾah al-Miṣriyyah al-ʿĀmmah li-l-Kitāb, 1980.

al-Bishrī, Ṭāriq. *Al-Waḍʿ al-qānūnī al-muʿāṣir bayna l-sharīʿah al-islāmiyyah wa-l-qānūn al-waḍʿī*. Cairo: Dār al-Shurūq, 1996.

Blaustein, Albert P. et al. *Independence Documents of the World*. Vol. 1. Dobbs Ferry, NY: Oceana Publications, 1977.

Blevis, Laure. "Une Université française en terre coloniale: Naissance et reconversion de la Faculté de Droit d'Alger (1879–1962)." *Politix* 4,76 (2006): 53–73.

Bobrovnikov, Vladimir O. *Musul'mane severnogo Kavkaza: Obychai, pravo, nasilie*. Moscow: Vostochnaia Literatura, 2002.

Boer, Tj. de, and H. Daiber. "Naẓar." *Encyclopaedia of Islam*, 2nd ed., 7: 1050–2.

Bonnecase, Julien. *L'École de l'exégèse en droit civil*. Paris, 1919.

Borelli, Octave. *La Législation égyptienne annotée*. Brussels: P. Weissenbruch, 1892.

Botiveau, Bernard. *Loi islamique et droit dans les sociétés arabes: Mutations des systèmes juridiques du Moyen-Orient*. Paris: Karthala, 1993.

Botman, Selma. "The Liberal Age, 1923–1952." In *The Cambridge History of Egypt*, vol. 2, *Modern Egypt from 1517 to the End of the Twentieth Century*, ed. M. W. Daly, 285–308. Cambridge: Cambridge University Press, 1998.

Bouckaert, Baudouin. "Sources du droit." In *Dictionnaire encyclopédique de théorie et de sociologie du droit*, ed. A. J. Arnaud and J. G. Belley, 45–53. Paris: Libraire générale de droit et de jurisprudence, 1993.

Bousquet, G. H. *Abrégé de la loi musulmane selon la rite de l'imâm Mâlek*. 4 vols. Algiers-Paris, 1956–62.

Bousquet, G. H. "L'École de Droit (1880–1909)." Available at http://alger-roi.fr/Alger/documents_algeriens/culturel/pages/30_droit.htm. Accessed April 21, 2015.

Brett, Michael. "Legislating for Inequality in Algeria: The Senatus-Consulte of 14 July 1865." *Bulletin of the School of Oriental and African Studies* 51,3 (1988): 440–61.

Brinton, Jasper Yeates. *The Mixed Courts of Egypt*. Rev. ed. New Haven: Yale University Press, 1930.

Brinton, Hasper Yeates. "The Closing of the Mixed Courts of Egypt." *American Journal of International Law* 44,2 (1950): 303–12.

Broadley, Alexander M. *How We Defended Arabi and His Friends*. London: Chapman and Hall Ltd., 1884.

Bron, Jean. *Histoire du mouvement ouvrier français*. 3 vols. Paris: Editions Ouvrières, 1968–82.

Brower, Daniel R., and Edward J. Lazzerini, eds. *Russia's Orient: Imperial Borderlands and Peoples, 1700–1917*. Bloomington: Indiana University Press, 1997.

Brown, Nathan J. "Brigands and State Building: The Invention of Banditry in Modern Egypt." *Comparative Studies in Society and History* 32,2 (1990): 258–81.

Brown, Nathan J. *Constitutions in a Nonconstitutional World*. Albany: State University of New York Press, 2002.

Brown, Nathan J. "Law and Imperialism: Egypt in Comparative Perspective." *Law and Society Review* 29,1 (1995): 103–26.

Brown, Nathan J. "The Precarious Life and Slow Death of the Mixed Courts of Egypt." *International Journal of the Middle East* 25,1 (1993): 33–52.

Brown, Nathan J. *The Rule of Law in the Arab World: Courts in Egypt and the Gulf.* Cambridge: Cambridge University Press, 1997.
Brown, Nathan J. "Shariʿa and State in the Modern Muslim Middle East." *International Journal of Middle East Studies* 29,3 (1997): 367–8.
Brugman, Jan. "Snouck Hurgronje's Study of Islamic Law." In *Leiden Oriental Connections 1850–1940*, ed. W. Otterspeer, 82–93. Leiden: E. J. Brill, 1989.
Brun-Durand, Justin. "Edouard Sautayra." In *Dictionnaire biographique et biblio-iconographique de la Drôme*, 2: 334–5. Grenoble: Librairie Dauphinoise, 1901.
Brunyate, William. "The Private Reading of a Law Student." *L'Égypte contemporaine* 8 (1918): 195–214.
Bū Karūshah, Ḥalīmah. *Maʿālim tajdīd al-manhaj al-fiqhī: Numūdhaj al-Shawkānī.* Doha: Wizārat al-Awqāf wa-l-Shuʾūn al-Islāmiyyah, 2002.
Bullard, Sir Reader. *The Middle East: A Political and Economic Survey. American Political Science Review* 53,4 (1959): 1133–5.
Cairns, John W. "Development of Comparative Law in Great Britain." In *The Oxford Handbook of Comparative Law*, ed. R. Zimmermann and M. Reimann, 131–74. Oxford: Oxford University Press, 2006.
Cannon, Byron. *Politics of Law and the Courts in Nineteenth-Century Egypt.* Salt Lake City: University of Utah Press, 1988.
Cannon, Byron. "Social Tensions and the Teaching of European Law in Egypt before 1900." *History of Education Quarterly* 15,3 (1975): 299–315.
Capitant, Henri. *Introduction à l'étude du droit civil.* Paris: A. Pedone, 1898.
Cardahi, Ch. "Théorie générale des actions en droit musulman." *Bulletin de la société de législation comparée* (1929): 379–99.
Chaouiche, Abd el Aziz (ʿAbd al-ʿAzīz Jāwīsh). "Nécessité d'avoir égard aux circonstances de temps et de lieu dans l'application des préceptes de la chériat." In *Recueil des travaux du premier congrès égyptien réuni à Héliopolis du samedi 30 rabi-ul-sani 1329 (29 avril 1911) au mercredi 5 gamadi-ul-awl 1329.* Alexandrie: Imprimerie d'Alexandrie, 1911.
Chehata, Chafik (Shafīq Shiḥātah). *Essai d'une théorie générale de l'obligation en droit musulman.* Cairo: F. E. Noury et Fils, 1936.
Chehata, Chafik (Shafīq Shiḥātah). "Le Project de nouveau Code civil." *Journal de tribunaux mixtes* 25/26 Feb. (no. 3579)–22/23 Dec. 1948 (no. 4015).
Chéron, Albert, and Mohamed Sadek Fahmy (Muḥammad Ṣādiq Fahmī). "Le Transport de dette dans les législations européennes et en droit musulman." *L'Égypte contemporaine* 22 (1931): 35–66, 137–90.
Cheta, Omar Youssef. "Rule of Merchants: The Practice of Commerce and Law in Late Ottoman Egypt, 1841–1876." Ph.D. diss., New York University, 2014.
Christelow, Alan. *Muslim Law Courts and the French Colonial State in Algeria.* Princeton: Princeton University Press, 1985.
Clément, Anne Marie. "*Fallāḥīn* on Trial in Colonial Egypt: Apprehending the Peasantry through Orality, Writing, and Performance (1884–1914)." Ph.D. diss., University of Toronto, 2012.
Crecelius, Daniel. "The Emergence of the Shaykh of al-Azhar as the Preeminent Religious Leader in Egypt." In *Colloque international sur l'histoire du Caire, 27 mars–5 avril 1969*, ed. Ministry of Culture of the Arab Republic of Egypt, 109–203. [Cairo]: General Egyptian Book Organization, 1972.
Crecelius, Daniel. "Nonideological Responses of the Egyptian Ulama to Modernization." In *Scholars, Saints, and Sufis: Muslim Religious Institutions in the Middle East since 1500*, ed. N. R. Keddie, 167–209. Berkeley and Los Angeles: University of California Press, 1972.

Crews, Robert D. *For Prophet and Tsar*. Cambridge, MA: Harvard University Press, 2006.

Cromer, Evelyn Baring. *Modern Egypt*. 2 vols. London: Macmillan, 1908.

Crone, Patricia. *Roman, Provincial, and Islamic Law: The Origins of the Islamic Patronate*. Cambridge: Cambridge University Press, 1987.

Daguin, Fernand. Book review of Amos and Arminjon, *Espèces, problèmes juridiques et questions pratiques de droit civil, de droit commercial et de droit international privé*. *Bulletin de la société de législation comparée* 34 (1905): 110–11.

Daly, M. W., ed. *The Cambridge History of Egypt*. Vol. 2, *Modern Egypt from 1517 to the End of the Twentieth Century*. Cambridge: Cambridge University Press, 1998.

Dasūqī, Muḥammad al-Sayyid. *Muḥammad Yūsuf Mūsá, 1317–1383h/1899–1963m: al-Faqīh al-faylasūf wa-l-muṣliḥ al-mujaddid*. Damascus: Dār al-Qalam, 2003.

David, René. *Le Droit comparé*. Paris: Economica, 1982.

"Décret créant un diplôme d'études supérieures en droit musulman à la Faculté de Droit de l'Université Fouad I." *Journal officiel du gouvernement égyptien* 125/149 (1944).

Delpal, Bernard, Bernard Hours, and Claude Prudhomme. *France-Levant: De la fin du XVIIe siècle à la première guerre mondiale. Colloque internationale, Lyon, 13, 14, 15 juin 2002*. Paris: Geuthner, 2005.

Demolombe, Ch. *Cours de code civil*. Paris: Durand, 1845.

al-Dhannūn, Ḥasan ʿAlī. "Al-Naẓariyyah al-ʿāmmah li-l-faskh: al-Fiqh al-islāmī wa-l-qānūn al-madanī." Doct. diss., Cairo University Law Faculty, 1946.

Dhuhnī, ʿAbd al-Salām. *al-Qānūn al-rūmānī*. n.p, n.d.

Dhuhnī, ʿAbd al-Salām. *Fī l-iltizāmāt: al-Naẓariyyah al-ʿāmmah* (Obligations: The General Theory). N.p., 1924.

Dhuhnī, ʿAbd al-Salām. *Mudhakkirāt fī l-qānūn al-rūmānī fī naẓariyyat al-iltizāmāt ʿind al-rūman* (Memoranda on Roman Law: The Roman Theory of Obligations). N.p., 1922–1923.

Dhuhnī, ʿAbd al-Salām. "Al-Tawaththub li-l-nuhūḍ al-fiqhī wa-ʿuddatuh." *Majallat al-Azhar* 8,1 (1937): 28–35.

DiCaprio, Lisa. *The Origins of the Welfare State*. Urbana: University of Illinois Press, 2007.

Di-Capua, Yoav. "The Professional Worldview of the *Effendi* Historian." *History Compass* 7,1 (2009): 306–28.

Dölle, H., M. Rheinstein, and K. Zweigert. *Festschrift für Ernst Rabel*. 2 vols. Tübingen: Mohr, 1954.

Donahue, Charles. "Comparative Legal History in America: A Report." *Tijdschrift voor rechtsgeschiedenis* 65,1–2 (1997): 1–17.

Donahue, Charles. "Roman Law Influence on the Civil Law." *Michigan Law Review* 81,4 (1983): 972–6.

Dozy, Reinhart. *Essai sur l'histoire de l'islamisme*. Trans. V. Chauvin. Leiden: E. J. Brill, 1879.

Duguit, Léon. *Leçons de droit public général faites à la Faculté de Droit de l'Université Égyptienne pendant les mois de janvier, février et mars 1926*. Paris: E. de Boccard, 1926.

"École de Droit: Élèves boursiers." *Bulletin des lois et décrets, année 1887*, 996–7.

El-Araby, Mohamed Abdullah. *La Conscription des neutres dans les luttes de la concurrence économique: Les Coalitions du journalisme et la liberté de la presse. Sorrell v. Smith*. Paris: Marcel Giard, 1924.

Ellul, Jacques. *Histoire des institutions*. Vol. 2. Paris: Presses Universitaires de France, 1958.

Esmeir, Samera. *Juridical Humanity: A Colonial History*. Stanford: Stanford University Press, 2012.

Fahmī, Ḥusayn. "Baḥth fī l-ḥālah al-iqtiṣādiyyah li-sikak ḥadīd al-ḥukūmah." Doct. diss., Law Faculty of the Egyptian University, 1931.

Fahmī, Muḥammad Ṣādiq (Mohamed Sadek-Fahmy). "Le Droit comparé: Son utilité particulière en Égypte." *L'Égypte contemporaine* 15 (1923): 397–411.
Fahmī, Muḥammad Ṣādiq. *Mudhakkirāt fī naẓariyyat al-iltizāmāt.* Miṣr: Maṭbaʿat al-ʿŪluww, 1930.
Fahmī, Muḥammad Ṣādiq. *Sharḥ al-qānūn al-madanī.* Miṣr: Maṭbaʿat al-Iʿtimād, 1926.
Fahmy, Khaled. "Justice, Law and Pain in Khedival Egypt." In *Standing Trial: Law and the Person in the Modern Middle East,* ed. B. Dupret, 85–115. London: I. B. Tauris, 2004.
Fahmy, Khaled. "The Police and the People in Nineteenth-Century Egypt." *Die Welt des Islams* 39,3 (1999): 340–77.
Fahmy, Khaled. "The Sound of Silence: Criminal Law, Forensic Medicine and Subaltern Agency in Khedival Egypt." Unpubl. art., 2005.
Fahmy, Ninette S. *The Politics of Egypt: State-Society Relationship.* London: RoutledgeCurzon, 2002.
Fakhrī, Ḥusayn. "Mudhakkirāt Ḥusayn Fakhrī bāshā nāẓir al-ḥaqqāniyyah li-majlis al-nuẓẓār?" In *al-Kitāb al-dhahabī li-l-maḥākim al-ahliyyah 1883–1933,* 2 vols., 1: 107–16. Bulaq: al-Maṭbaʿah al-Amīriyyah, 1937.
Farḥāt, Muḥammad Muḥammad. *Al-Naẓariyyāt al-ʿāmmah fī l-fiqh al-islāmī.* Cairo: al-Risālah al-Dawliyyah li-l-Ṭibāʿah, 2002.
Fathy, Mahmoud. *La Doctrine musulmane de l'abus des droits. (Étude d'histoire juridique et de droit comparé).* Lyon: H. Georg, 1913.
Faure, Fernand. "L'École française de Droit du Caire en 1914 (1)." *Revue internationale de l'enseignement* 69 (1915): 307–12.
Fauvarque-Cosson, Bénédicte. "Development of Comparative Law in France." In *The Oxford Handbook of Comparative Law,* ed. R. Zimmermann and M. Reimann, 35–67. Oxford: Oxford University Press, 2006.
Feldman, Noah. *The Fall and Rise of the Islamic State.* Princeton: Princeton University Press, 2008.
Flory, Maurice, and Jean-Robert Henry. *L'Enseignement du droit musulman.* Paris: Editions du CNRS, 1989.
Gans, Eduard. *Das Erbrecht in Weltgeschichtlicher Entwicklung.* [Berlin: Maurer, 1824].
Gatteschi, Domenico et al. *Manuale di diritto pubblico e privato ottomano.* Alexandria: V. Minasi, 1865.
Gaudemet, E. "Raymond Saleilles (1855–1912)." *Revue bourguignonne de l'Université de Dijon* 22,4 (1912): 161–263.
Gavillot, A. "Notice sur Vidal Pacha." *Bulletin de l'Institut Égyptien, année 1891.* 3rd ser., no. 2: 122–34.
Gavillot, J. C. Aristide. *Essai sur les droits des européens en Turquie et en Égypte: Les Capitulations et la réforme judiciaire.* Paris: E. Dentu, 1875.
Genton, Stanislas. *De la juridiction française dans les échelles du Levant.* Lyon: Imprimerie du Salut Public, 1873.
Gerber, Haim. "Rigidity Versus Openness in Late Classical Islamic Law: The Case of the Seventeenth-Century Palestinian Muftī Khayr al-Dīn al-Ramlī." *Islamic Law and Society* 5,2 (1998): 165–95.
Gerber, Haim. *State, Society, and Law in Islam: Ottoman Law in Comparative Perspective.* New York: SUNY Press, 1994.
Gershoni, I., and James P. Jankowski. *Redefining the Egyptian Nation, 1930–1945.* New York: Cambridge University Press, 1995.
al-Ghāzī, Murād. "Al-Qānūn al-rūmānī wa-l-fiqh al-islāmī (Part 3)." *Al-Muḥāmāh al-sharʿiyyah* 1,3 (1929): 167–70.

Gillotte, Ch., et al. *Traité de droit musulman précédé du décret du 31 décembre, 1859*. 2nd ed. Constantine: Alessi and Arnolet, 1860.
Giraud, Arthur. *Principes de colonisation et de législation coloniale*. 4th ed. Paris: L. Tenin, 1921–23.
Goadby, Frederic Maurice. *Commentary on Egyptian Criminal Law*. Cairo: Government Press, 1914.
Göçek, Fatma Müge. *Rise of the Bourgeoisie, Demise of Empire: Ottoman Westernization and Social Change*. New York: Oxford University Press, 1996.
Goldschmidt, Arthur. *Biographical Dictionary of Modern Egypt*. Boulder, CO: Lynne Rienner, 2000.
Goldziher, Ignác. *Introduction to Islamic Theology and Law*. Princeton: Princeton University Press, 1981.
Goldziher, Ignác. *Muslim Studies: On the Development of Hadith*. Chicago: Aldine Pub. Co., 1968.
Gordley, James. *The Philosophical Origins of Modern Contract Doctrine*. Oxford: Oxford University Press, 1991.
Gottlieb, Stephen E. *Jurisprudence: Cases and Materials. An Introduction to the Philosophy of Law and Its Applications*. 2nd ed. Newark, NJ: LexisNexis, 2006.
Grande, Elisabetta. "Development of Comparative Law in Italy." In *The Oxford Handbook of Comparative Law*, ed. R. Zimmermann and M. Reimann, 107–30. Oxford: Oxford University Press, 2006.
Grasserie, Raoul de la. "Analyses: E. Lambert, *Études de droit commun législatif ou de droit civil comparé*." *Revue de l'histoire des religions* 49 (1904): 195–200.
al-Ḥakīm, Tawfīq. *The Maze of Justice: Diary of a Country Prosecutor*. London: Saqi Books, 1989.
Hallaq, Wael B. *An Introduction to Islamic Law*. Cambridge: Cambridge University Press, 2009.
Hallaq, Wael B. "A Prelude to Ottoman Reform: Ibn ʿĀbidīn on Custom and Legal Change." In *Histories of the Modern Middle East: New Directions*, ed. I. Gershoni et al., 37–61. Boulder, CO: Lynne Rienner, 2002.
Hallaq, Wael B. *Sharīʿa: Theory, Practice, Transformations*. Cambridge: Cambridge University Press, 2009.
Hallaq, Wael B. "Was the Gate of Ijtihad Closed?" *International Journal of Middle East Studies* 16,1 (1984): 3–41.
Hamid, M. E. "Islamic Law of Contract or Contracts?" *Journal of Islamic and Comparative Law* (Nigeria) 3 (1969): 1–10.
Hamilton, Charles, trans. *The Hedaya, or Guide: A Commentary on the Mussulman Laws*. London: T. Bensley, 1791.
Hanley, Will. "Foreignness and Localness in Alexandria, 1880–1940." Ph.D. diss., Princeton University, 2007.
Hartmann, Martin. *The Arabic Press of Egypt*. London: Luzac & Co., 1899.
Hayman, Robert L. Jr., et al., eds. *Jurisprudence: Classical and Contemporary*. Vol. 2. St. Paul: West Group, 2002.
Hayward, J. E. S. "Solidarist Syndicalism: Durkheim and Duguit." *Sociological Review* 8 (1960): 17–36.
Heidborn, Adolf. "A Muslim University." *Imperial and Asiatic Quarterly Review* 16,31–32 (1903): 310–13.
Herget, James E. *Contemporary German Legal Philosophy*. Philadelphia: University of Pennsylvania Press, 1996.

Hilbāwī, Ibrāhīm. *Mudhakkirāt Ibrāhīm al-Hilbāwī: Tārīkh ḥayāt Ibrāhīm al-Hilbāwī Bik, 1858–1940*. Ed. ʿI. Ḍiyāʾ al-Dīn Sayyid. Cairo: al-Hayʾah al-Miṣriyyah al-ʿĀmmah li-l-Kitāb, 1995.

Hill, Enid. "Al-Sanhuri and Islamic Law: The Place and Significance of Islamic Law in the Life and Work of ʿAbd Al-Razzaq Ahmad al-Sanhuri, Egyptian Jurist and Scholar, 1895–1971." *Arab Law Quarterly* 3,1–2 (1988): 33–64, 182–218.

Hill, Enid. "Islamic Law as a Source for the Development of a Comparative Jurisprudence: Theory and Practice in the Life and Work of Sanhuri." In *Islamic Law: Social and Historical Contexts*, ed. A. al-Azmeh, 146–97. London: Routledge, 1988.

Hindī, ʿAbd al-ʿAzīz. *Al-Azhar wa-taqnīn al-sharīʿah al-islāmiyyah*. Cairo: Majmaʿ al-Buḥūth al-Islāmiyyah, 1982.

Hourani, Albert. *Arabic Thought in the Liberal Age, 1798–1939*. London: Oxford University Press, 1962.

Hoyle, Mark S. W. *Mixed Courts of Egypt*. London: Graham and Trotman, 1991.

Hoyle, Mark S. W. "The Mixed Courts of Egypt: An Anniversary Assessment." *Arab Law Quarterly* 1,1 (1985): 60–8.

Hoyle, Mark S. W. "The Structure and Laws of the Mixed Courts of Egypt." *Arab Law Quarterly* 1,3 (1986): 327–45.

Hug, W. "The History of Comparative Law." *Harvard Law Review* 45,6 (1932): 1027–70.

Ḥusayn, ʿAbd Allāh. *Al-Muqāranāt al-tashrīʿiyyah bayna l-qawānīn al-waḍʿiyyah al-madaniyyah wa-al-tashrīʿ al-islamī: Muqāranah bayna fiqh al-qānūn al-faransī wa-madhhab al-imām Mālik ibn Anās*. 4 vols. Ed. M. A. Sirāj and ʿA. J. Muḥammad. Cairo: Dār al-Salām, 2001 (2nd ed.) [1947–49 (1st ed.)].

Ḥusayn, ʿAbd Allāh. "Al-Qaḍāʾ al-sharʿī wa-l-muḥāmūn al-sharʿiyyūn." *Al-Muḥāmāh al-sharʿiyyah* 1,1 (1929): 15–17.

Ḥusayn, ʿAbd Allāh. "Taghyīr lāʾiḥat al-maḥākim al-sharʿiyyah sanat 1899." *Al-Muḥāmāh al-sharʿiyyah* 2,4 (1931): 306–39.

Ḥusayn, Aḥmad Farrāj, and ʿAbd al-Wadūd al-Sarītī. *Al-Naẓariyyāt al-ʿāmmah fī l-fiqh al-islāmī wa-tārīkhih*. Beirut: Dār al-Nahḍah al-ʿArabiyyah, 1992.

Ḥusayn, Muḥammad al-Khiḍr. "Al-Sharīʿah al-islāmiyyah ṣāliḥah li-kull zamān wa-makān." *Al-Muḥāmāh al-sharʿiyyah* 2,2 (1930): 119.

Husayn, Taha. *The Future of Culture in Egypt*. Washington, DC: American Council of Learned Societies, 1954.

Huxley, Andrew. *Religion, Law and Tradition: Comparative Studies in Religious Law*. London: Routledge Curzon, 2002.

Hyland, R. "Comparative Law." In *A Companion to Philosophy of Law and Legal Theory*, ed. D. Patterson, 184–99. Cambridge, MA: Blackwell, 1996.

Ibn ʿArnūs, Maḥmūd ibn Muḥammad. *Kitāb Tārīkh al-qaḍāʾ fī l-islām*. Cairo: al-Maṭbaʿah al-Miṣriyyah al-Ahliyyah al-Ḥadīthah, 1934.

Ibn ʿArnūs, Maḥmūd ibn Muḥammad. "Tārīkh al-qaḍāʾ wa-l-quḍāh fī l-islām: Ṣaḥīfah maṭwiyyah min tārīkh al-qaḍāʾ bi-Miṣr (Part 3)." *Al-Muḥāmāh al-sharʿiyyah* 1,10 (1930): 869–71.

Ibn ʿĀṣim, Muḥammad ibn Muḥammad. *Traité de droit musulman: La Tohfat d'Ebn Acem*. Trans. O. Houdas and F. Martel. Algiers: Gavault Saint-Lager, 1882.

Ibrāhīm, Aḥmad. *Al-Iltizāmāt fī l-sharʿ al-islāmī*. Cairo: Dār al-Anṣār, 1980.

Ibrāhīm, Aḥmad. *Kitāb al-Muʿāmalāt al-sharʿiyyah al-māliyyah*. Cairo: al-Maṭbaʿah al-Salafiyyah, 1936.

Ibrāhīm, Aḥmad. *Mudhakkirah mubtadaʾah fī bayān al-iltizāmāt wa-mā yataʿallaq bihā min al-aḥkām fī l-sharʿ al-islāmī*. Miṣr: Maktabat ʿAbd Allāh Wahbah, 1944–45.

Ibrāhīm, Aḥmad. *Mudhakkirah mūjazah fī ʿilm uṣūl al-fiqh*. [Miṣr]: Maṭbaʿat al-ʿUlūm, 1938–39.

Ibrāhīm, Aḥmad. "Takhṣīṣ al-qaḍā' wa-baḥth fīh." *Majallat Kulliyyat al-Ḥuqūq li-l-mabāḥith al-qānūniyyah wa-l-iqtiṣādiyyah* 2,2 (1928): 3–11.

Ibrāhīm, Aḥmad. "al-ʿUqūd wa-l-shurūṭ wa-l-khiyārāt." *Majallat al-qānūn wa-l-iqtiṣād* 1 (1934): 641–722.

Ibrāhīm, Aḥmad. "Wujūb waḍʿ qānūn sharʿī ghayr muqayyad bi-madhhab muʿayyan." *Majallat Kulliyyat al-Ḥuqūq li-l-mabāḥith al-qānūniyyah wa-l-iqtiṣādiyyah* 1,1 (1927): 2–5.

Ibrāhīm, Aḥmad. "Al-Zawāj al-madanī wa-l-zawāj al-dīnī." *Majallat Kulliyyat al-Ḥuqūq li-l-mabāḥith al-qānūniyyah wa-l-iqtiṣādiyyah* 2,[27] (1928): 6–9.

Ibrahim, Yasir S. "The Spirit of Islamic Law and Modern Religious Reform: Maqasid al-Shariʿa in Muhammad ʿAbduh and Rashid Rida's Legal Thought." Ph.D. diss., Princeton University, 2004.

ʿImārah, Muḥammad. *Al-Duktūr ʿAbd al-Razzāq al-Sanhūrī: Islāmiyyat al-dawlah wa-l-madaniyyah wa-l-qānūn*. Cairo: Dār al-Rashād, 1999.

ʿImārah, Muḥammad, ed. *Al-Aʿmāl al-kāmilah li-l-imām Muḥammad ʿAbduh*. 5 vols. Cairo: Dār al-Shurūq, 2001.

ʿImārah, Muḥammad. *al-Shaykh al-Marāghī wa-l-iṣlāḥ al-dīnī fī l-qarn al-ʿishrīn*. Cairo: Majallat al-Azhar, 1428/2007.

ʿInān, Muhammad ʿAbd Allāh. *Tārīkh al-jāmiʿ al-Azhar*. Vol. 2. Cairo: Mu'assasat al-Khānjī, 1958.

ʿĪsá, Muḥammad Ḥilmī. *Sharḥ al-bayʿ fī l-qawānīn al-miṣriyyah wa-l-faransiyyah wa-fī l-sharīʿah al-islāmiyyah*. [Cairo]: Maṭbaʿat al-Maʿārif, 1916.

Issawi, Charles P., ed. *The Economic History of the Middle East, 1800–1914: A Book of Readings*. Chicago: University of Chicago Press, 1966.

Issawi, Charles P. "Egypt since 1800: A Study in Lopsided Development." *Journal of Economic History* 21,1 (1961): 1–25.

Jamin, Christophe. "Le Vieux rêve de Saleilles et Lambert revisité: À Propos du centenaire du congrès international de droit comparé de Paris." *Revue internationale de droit comparé* 52,4 (2000): 733–51.

Jankowski, James P., and Israel Gershoni. *Rethinking Nationalism in the Arab Middle East*. New York: Columbia University Press, 1997.

Jawādī, Muḥammad Muḥammad. *Fī riḥāb al-ʿadālah: Mudhakkirāt ʿAbd al-Fattāḥ Ḥasan, Fatḥī Raḍwān, Yūsuf Naḥḥās, Maḥmūd Kāmil*. Cairo: al-Hay'ah al-Miṣriyyah al-ʿĀmmah li-l-Kitāb, 2007.

al-Jazīrī, ʿAbd al-Raḥmān. *Kitāb al-Fiqh ʿalá al-madhāhib al-arbaʿah*. Cairo: Dār al-Kitāb al-ʿArabī, 1938.

Jersild, Austin. *Orientalism and Empire: North Caucasus Mountain Peoples and the Georgian Frontier, 1845–1917*. Montreal: McGill-Queen's University Press, 2002.

Jestaz, Philippe. *Doctrine et jurisprudence: Une Liaison de 25 siècles*. Montreal: Thémis, 2001.

Jestaz, Philippe, and Christophe Jamin. *La Doctrine*. Paris: Dalloz, 2004.

Jindī, ʿAbd al-Ḥalīm. *Ibrāhīm al-Hilbāwī: al-Muḥāmūn wa-siyādat al-qānūn*. Egypt: Majallat al-Muḥāmāh Niqābat al-Muḥāmīn, 1982.

Jindī, ʿAbd al-Ḥalīm. *Nujūm al-muḥāmāh fī Miṣr wa-Ūrubbā: al-Hilbāwī, al-Sanhūrī, Muṣṭafá Marʿī, Marshāl Hawl, Ḥanrī Rawbayr*. Cairo: Dār al-Maʿārif, 1991.

Johansen, Baber. "Casuistry: Between Legal Concept and Social Praxis." *Islamic Law and Society* 2,2 (1995): 135–56.

Johansen, Baber. *Contingency in a Sacred Law: Legal and Ethical Norms in the Muslim* Fiqh. Leiden: Brill, 1999.

Johansen, Baber. "Legal Literature and the Problem of Change: The Case of Land Rent." In Johansen, *Contingency in a Sacred Law: Legal and Ethical Norms in the Muslim* Fiqh, 446–64. Leiden: Brill, 1999.

Jones, William, trans. *Al Sirájiyyah, or, the Mohammedan Law of Inheritance, with a Commentary*. Calcutta: Printed by Joseph Cooper, 1792.

Jori, Mario. "Formalisme." In *Dictionnaire encyclopédique de théorie et de sociologie du droit*, ed. A. J. Arnaud and J. G. Belley. Paris: Libraire générale de droit et de jurisprudence, 1993.

Jumayʿī, ʿAbd al-Munʿim Ibrāhīm al-Dusūqī. *Madrasat al-Qaḍāʾ al-Sharʿī: Dirāsah tārīkhiyyah li-muʾassasah taʿlīmiyyah, 1907–1930*. Cairo: Maktabat al-Khānjī bi-Miṣr, 1986.

Juynboll, A. W. T., trans. *Jus Shafiiticum: At-Tanbîh*. Leiden: E. J. Brill, 1879.

Juynboll, A. W. T. *Handleiding tot de kennis van de mohammedaansche wet volgens de leer der Sjâfi'itische school*. Leiden: E. J. Brill, 1903.

Juynboll, Th. W. *De hoofdregelen der Sjafi'itische leer van het pandrecht, met een onderzoek naar haar ontstaan en naar haren invloed in Ned.-Indië*. Leiden: E. J. Brill, 1893.

Kalenský, Pavel. *Trends of Private International Law*. Prague: Academia, 1971.

Kalmbach, Hilary. "From Turban to Tarboush: Dār al-ʿUlūm and Social, Linguistic, and Religious Change in Interwar Egypt." D.Phil. diss., University of Oxford, 2011.

Kāmil, Maḥmūd. *Yawmiyyāt muḥāmin miṣrī: al-Jānib al-insānī min ḥayāt al-maḥākim fī ʿishrīn ʿāman*. Cairo: al-Dār al-Qawmiyyah li-l-Ṭibāʿah wa-l-Nashr, 1963; Eng. trans., *Diary of an Egyptian Lawyer: The Human Side of a Court of Law*. [Cairo]: General Egyptian Book Organization, 1980.

Kedourie, Elie. "The Genesis of the Egyptian Constitution of 1923." In *Political and Social Change in Modern Egypt*, ed. P. M. Holt, 347–61. London: Oxford University Press, 1968.

Keijzer, Salomon. *Handboek voor het mohammedaansch regt*. The Hague: Belinfante, 1853.

Keijzer, Salomon, trans. *Précis de jurisprudence musulmane selon le rite châfeite*. Leiden: E. J. Brill, 1859.

Kennedy, Duncan. *The Rise and Fall of Classical Legal Thought*. Washington, DC: Beard Books, 2006.

Kennedy, Duncan. "Three Globalizations of Law and Legal Thought: 1850–2000." In *The New Law and Economic Development: A Critical Appraisal*, ed. D. Trubek and A. Santos, 19–73. Cambridge: Cambridge University Press, 2006.

Kerr, Malcolm H. *Islamic Reform: The Political and Legal Theories of Muḥammad ʿAbduh and Rashīd Riḍā*. Berkeley and Los Angeles: University of California Press, 1966.

al-Khafīf, ʿAlī. *Aḥkām al-muʿāmalāt al-sharʿiyyah*. Cairo: Maṭbaʿat Lajnat al-Taʾlīf wa-l-Tarjamah wa-l-Nashr, 1942.

al-Khafīf, ʿAlī. *Al-Ḥaqq wa-l-dhimmah*. Cairo: Maktabat al-Wahbah, 1940.

al-Khafīf, ʿAlī. *Mukhtaṣar Aḥkām al-muʿāmalāt al-sharʿiyyah*. Cairo: Maṭbaʿat al-Sunnah al-Muḥammadiyyah, 1949.

al-Khafīf, ʿAlī. "Taʾthīr al-mawt fī ḥuqūq al-insān wa-iltizāmātih." *Majallat al-qānūn wa-l-iqtiṣād* 10,5–6 (1940): 3–92.

Khalil, Emad. "The Modern Debate over Riba and Its Resolution in the Codes of Sanhuri." S.J.D. diss., Harvard Law School, 1990.

Khallāf, ʿAbd al-Wahhāb. "Al-Sharīʿah al-islāmiyyah: Maṣdar ṣāliḥ li-l-tashrīʿ." *Majallat al-qānūn wa-l-iqtiṣād* 10,3–4 (1940): 3–34.

Khallāf, ʿAbd al-Wahhāb. "Al-Siyāsah al-sharʿiyyah aw niẓām al-dawlah al-islāmiyyah." *Al-Muḥāmāh al-sharʿiyyah* 2,2 (1930): 100–6; 2,3 (1930): 196–206.

Khallāf, ʿAbd al-Wahhāb. "al-Suluṭāt al-thalāth fī l-islām." *Majallat al-qānūn wa-l-iqtiṣād* (Jun. 1935, Mar. 1936, and Apr. 1937).

Khallāf, ʿAbd al-Wahhāb. "Al-ʿUqūbāt al-sharʿiyyah: Li-man ḥaqq al-ʿiqāb?" *Majallat al-qaḍāʾ al-sharʿī* 1,1 (1922): 12–17; 1,2 (1922): 59–61.

Khankī, ʿAzīz. "Al-Tashrīʿ wa-l-qaḍāʾ qabla inshāʾ al-maḥākim al-ahliyyah." In *al-Kitāb al-dhahabī li-l-maḥākim al-ahliyyah 1883–1933*, 62–96. Bulaq: al-Maṭbaʿah al-Amīriyyah, 1937.

Khānkī, ʿAzīz. *Majmūʿat Mudhakkirāt.* Miṣr: Maṭbaʿat al-Akhbār, 1912.

Khānkī, ʿAzīz, and Jamīl Khānkī. *al-Muḥāmāh qadīman wa-ḥadīthan.* Cairo: s.n., 1940.

al-Khaṭīb, Muḥibb al-Dīn. "Al-Fiqh al-islāmī wa-l-tashrīʿ." *Al-Muḥāmāh al-sharʿiyyah* 1,1 (1929): 5–7.

Kholoussy, Hanan. *For Better or Worse: The Marriage Crisis That Made Modern Egypt.* Stanford: Stanford University Press, 2010.

Khuḍarī, Muḥammad. *Kitāb Uṣūl al-fiqh.* Miṣr: Maṭbaʿat al-Jamāliyyah Muḥammad Amīn Khānjī, 1911.

Khūrī, Fāʾiz. *Muqābalah bayna l-ḥuqūq al-rūmāniyyah wa-l-ḥuqūq al-islāmiyyah wa-l-faransiyyah wa-l-inglīziyyah.* Damascus: al-Maṭbaʿah al-Ḥadīthah, 1924.

Knight, Nathaniel. "Grigor'ev in Orenburg, 1851–1862: Russian Orientalism in the Service of Empire?" *Slavic Review* 59,1 (2000): 74–100.

Kosugi, Yasushi. *Fihris majallat al-Manār, 1898–1935.* Beirut: Turāth, 1998.

Lajnat Iṣlāḥ al-Azhar. *Mashrūʿ iṣlāḥ al-Azhar.* Cairo, 1919.

Lambert, Édouard. "Comments Found on the Egyptian Law System and Islamic Law's Potential for Development and Expansion." Presentation given at the Congrès international de droit comparé. The Hague, 1932.

Lambert, Édouard. "Comparative Law." In *Encyclopaedia of the Social Sciences*, ed. E. R. A. Seligman, 127. New York: Macmillan, 1931.

Lambert, Édouard. "Le Droit comparé et la formation d'une conscience juridique internationale." *Revue de l'Université de Lyon* 5 (1929): 441–63.

Lambert, Édouard. *Études de droit commun législatif ou de droit civil comparé. Première série. Le régime successoral. Introduction: La fonction du droit civil comparé. Tome I.* Paris: V. Giard et E. Brière, 1903.

Lambert, Édouard. *L'Institut oriental d'études juridiques et sociales de Lyon: Séminaire libre ouvert aux étudiants de l'orient musulman.* Lyon: Imprimerie du Moniteur Judiciaire, 1910.

Lambert, Édouard. "La Lettre de M. Lambert: Dunlop et sa politique anti-française et anti-égytpienne. Comment on étouffe une nation." *Le Temps*, 1907.

Lambert, Édouard. "Muḥāḍarāt al-ustādh Lāmbīr bi-Kulliyyat al-Ḥuqūq." *Majallat al-qānūn wa-l-iqtiṣād* 7,3 (1937): 439–54.

Lambert, Édouard. "Les Rapports du droit et de la religion dans le monde musulman moderne." In *Le Congrès International de droit comparé de 1932*, 90–100. Paris: A. Rey, Librairie du Recueil Sirey, 1934.

Lambert, Édouard. "Une Réforme nécessaire des études de droit civil." *Revue international d'enseignement* 40 (1900): 216–43.

Layish, Aharon. "The Contribution of the Modernists to the Secularization of Islamic Law." *Middle Eastern Studies* 14,3 (1978): 263–77.

Layish, Aharon. "Notes on Joseph Schacht's Contribution to the Study of Islamic Law." *BRISMES Bulletin* 9,2 (1985): 132–3.

Layish, Aharon. "The Transformation of the Shariʿa from Jurists' Law to Statutory Law in the Contemporary Muslim World." *Die Welt des Islams* 44,1 (2004): 85–112.

Levasseur, Émile. *Questions ouvrières et industrielles en France sous la troisième république.* Paris: A. Rousseau, 1907.

Lévy-Ullmann, Henri. "De l'Utilité des études comparatives." *Revue de droit* (Québec) 1 (1923): 385–98.
Lévy-Ullmann, Henri. "Vers le droit mondial du XXème siècle." In P. Lepaulle, *De la Condition des sociétés étrangères aux États Unis d'Amérique*, preface. Paris: Rousseau et cie., 1923.
Lewis, Bernard. "The Question of Orientalism." *New York Review of Books* 19,11 (1982).
Libson, Gideon. "On the Development of Custom as a Source of Law." *Islamic Law and Society* 4,2 (1997): 131–55.
Libson, Gideon, and F. H. Stewart. "ʿUrf." *Encyclopaedia of Islam*, 2nd ed., 10: 887–92.
Liebesny, Herbert J. *The Law of the Near and Middle East: Readings, Cases, and Materials.* Albany: State University of New York Press, 1975.
Linant de Bellefonds, Y. *Traité de droit musulman comparé.* Paris: Mouton, 1965.
Linant de Bellefonds, Y., et al. "Ḳānūn." *Encyclopaedia of Islam*, 2nd ed., 4: 556–62.
López Medina, Diego Eduardo. "Comparative Jurisprudence: Reception and Misreading of Transnational Legal Theory in Latin America." S. J. D. diss., Harvard Law School, 2001.
Loutfy, Omar Bey (ʿUmar Luṭfī). *De l'Action pénale en droit musulman: Rite hanefite.* Paris: Marchal et Billard, 1897.
Lusena, Ugo. *Eléments de procédure civile et commerciale d'après le code indigène comparé au code mixte.* 3rd ed. 2 vols. Cairo: Imprimerie Nationale, 1903, 1906.
Macnaghten, William. *Principles and Precedents of Moohummudan Law.* Calcutta: Church Mission Press, 1825.
al-Maghribī, ʿAbd al-Qādir. "Najtahid fī ījād al-mujtahid." *al-Muḥāmāh al-sharʿiyyah* 1,10 (1930): 873–8.
Maḥmaṣānī, Ṣubḥī Rajab. *al-Naẓariyyah al-ʿāmmah li-l-mūjibāt wa-l-ʿuqūd fī l-sharīʿah al-islāmiyyah.* Beirut: Maktabat al-Kashshāf, 1948.
Majlis al-shūrá li-qawānīn. *Majmūʿat maḥādir jalsāt sanat 1884, 1885, 1886 (24 nūvambir sanat 1883 - 22 dīsambir sanat 1886).* Miṣr, 1895.
Makad, Adib. *Notions générales sur les jurisdictions mixtes d'Égypte.* Alexandria: Imprimerie de l'École Professionelle des Frères, 1922.
Makhlūf, Muḥammad. "Al-Zawāj fī l-islām." *Majallat al-qaḍāʾ al-sharʿī* 1,4 (1922): 149–58.
Mallat, Chibli. "The Debate on Riba and Interest in Twentieth Century Jurisprudence." In *Islamic Law and Finance*, ed. C. Mallat, 69–88. London: Graham and Trotman, 1988.
Mallat, Chibli. *Introduction to Middle Eastern Law.* Oxford: Oxford University Press, 2007.
Malortie, Karl von. *Egypt: Native Rulers and Foreign Interference.* 2nd ed. London: W. Ridgway, 1883.
Malosse, Louis. *Impressions d'Égypte.* Paris: Librairie Armond Colin, 1896.
Manṣūr, ʿAlī ʿAlī. *Niẓām al-tajrīm wa-l-ʿiqāb fī l-islām: Muqāranan bi-l-qawānīn al-waḍʿiyyah.* Medina: Muʾassasat al-Zahrāʾ li-l-Īmān wa-l-Khayr, 1976.
Marṣafāwī, Fatḥī. *Dirāsat taṭbīq al-sharīʿah al-islāmiyyah fī Miṣr.* [Cairo]: Dār al-Fikr al-ʿArabī, 1981.
Marshall, Alex. *The Russian General Staff and Asia, 1800–1917.* London: Routledge, 2006.
Marsot, A. Lutfi al-Sayyid. "The Ulama of Cairo in the Eighteenth and Nineteenth Centuries." In *Scholars, Saints, and Sufis: Muslim Religious Institutions in the Middle East since 1500*, ed. N. R. Keddie, 149–65. Berkeley and Los Angeles: University of California Press, 1972.
Mattila, Heikki E. S. *Comparative Legal Linguistics.* Aldershot: Ashgate, 2006.
al-Mawlá Bey, Muḥammad Aḥmad Jād. "Al-Qurʾān al-karīm." *Al-Muḥāmāh al-sharʿiyyah* 1,10 (1930): 838–50.
Meysonasse, V. *Code civil musulman suivant le cadre du code civil français: Rite malekite.* Paris: A. Chevalier-Marescq et cie., 1898.

Milliot, Louis. "Le Mouvement des études juridiques musulmanes en France." *Revue algerienne, tunisienne et marocaine de legislation et de jurisprudence* (1922–23): 103–10.

Milliot, Louis, and Université de Paris. *Travaux de la semaine internationale de droit musulman, Paris, 2–7 juillet 1951*. Paris: Recueil Sirey, 1953.

Miltitz, Alexandre de. *Manuel des consuls*. Londen and Berlin: A. Asher, 1837.

Minda, Gary. *Postmodern Legal Movements: Law and Jurisprudence at Century's End*. New York: New York University Press, 1995.

al-Minyāwī, Makhlūf ibn Muḥammad al-Badawī. *Al-Muqāranāt al-tashrīʿiyyah: Taṭbīq al-qānūn al-madanī wa-l-jināʾī ʿalá madhhab al-imām Mālik*. 2 vols. Ed. M. A. Sirāj and ʿA. J. Muḥammad. Cairo: Dār al-Salām, 1999.

Moaddel, Mansoor, and Kamran Talattof. *Contemporary Debates in Islam*. Basingstoke: Macmillan, 2000.

Mogahed, Dalia. "Islam and Democracy," Special Report: Muslim World. The Gallup Organization, Princeton, NJ (2006).

Morand, Marcel. *De l'Abus du droit dans la législation musulmane*. Algiers: Typographie A. Jourdan, 1906.

Morcos, Soliman (Sulaymān Murqus), and Chafik Chehata. *Introduction à l'étude du droit civil*. Cairo: F. E. Noury et Fils, 1938.

Moustafa, Tamir. "The Islamist Trend in Egyptian Law." *Politics and Religion* 3,3 (2010): 610–30.

Muḥammad, ʿAlī Jumʿah. *Al-Madkhal ilá dirāsat al-madhāhib al-fiqhiyyah*. Cairo: Dār al-Salām, 2004.

Muḥammad, Fāʾiz Muḥammad Ḥusayn. *Al-Manhaj al-fiqhī li-l-imām Muḥammad ʿAbduh*. Cairo: Dār al-Nahḍah al-Miṣriyyah, 2000.

Muḥammad, Makhlūf. "Bāb al-muwāzanāt wa-l-muqāranāt bayna l-sharīʿah al-islāmiyyah al-gharrāʾ wa-bayna l-qawānīn al-waḍʿiyyah." *al-Muḥāmāh al-sharʿiyyah* 2,2 (1930): 135–7.

Mursī, Muḥammad Kāmil, and Sayyid Muṣṭafá. *Uṣūl al-qawānīn*. Miṣr: al-Maṭbaʿah al-Raḥmāniyyah, 1923.

Mūsá, Muḥammad Yūsuf. *Al-Amwāl wa-naẓariyyat al-ʿaqd fī l-fiqh al-islāmī*. Cairo: Dār al-Kitāb al-ʿArabī, 1952.

Nadolski, Dora Glidewell. "Ottoman and Secular Civil Law." *International Journal of Middle East Studies* 8,4 (1977): 517–43.

al-Najjār, ʿAbd Allāh Mabrūk. *Fatāwá l-imām Muḥammad ʿAbduh: Dirāsah fiqhiyyah taʾṣīliyyah*. Cairo: Dār al-Nahḍah al-ʿArabiyyah, 1995.

al-Nakadī, ʿĀrif Bey. "Al-Qānūn al-rūmānī wa-l-fiqh al-islāmī (Part 2)." *Al-Muḥāmāh al-sharʿiyyah* 1,2 (1929): 72–3.

Nanji, Azim, ed. *Mapping Islamic Studies: Genealogy, Continuity, and Change*. Berlin: Mouton de Gruyter, 1997.

Naṣr, ʿAbd al-ʿAzīz, ed. *Marjiʿ al-qaḍāʾ*. 4 vols. Miṣr: Maṭbaʿat al-Iʿtimād, 1923.

Nauphal, I. de. *Cours de droit musulman présenté à l'Institut des langues orientales du Ministère des Affaires Étrangères en l'année 1884/85*, fasc. 1: *La Propriété*. St. Petersburg: Trenké et Fusnot, 1886.

Nauphal, I. de. *Législation musulmane: Filiation et divorce*. St. Petersburg: Trenké et Fusnot, 1893.

Nauphal, I. de. *Système législatif musulman: Mariage*. St. Petersburg: Trenké et Fusnot, 1890.

D'Ohsson, Ignatius Mouradgea. *Tableau général de l'empire ottoman, divisé en deux parties, dont l'une comprend la législation mahométane, l'autre, l'histoire de l'empire ottoman*. 7 vols. Istanbul: Isis, 2001.

Otterspeer, W., ed. *Leiden Oriental Connections, 1850–1940*. Leiden: E. J. Brill, 1989.

Owen, Roger. *Lord Cromer: Victorial Imperialist, Edwardian Proconsul*. Oxford: Oxford University Press, 2004.
Owen, Roger. *The Middle East in the World Economy, 1800–1914*. Rev. ed. London: I. B. Tauris, 1993.
Owen, Roger, and Sevket Pamuk. *History of Middle East Economies in the Twentieth Century*. London: I. B. Tauris, 1998.
Perron, N. *Précis de jurisprudence musulmane ou principes de législation musulmane civile et religieuse selon le droit malékite*. Paris: Imprimerie Nationale, 1848–54.
Peters, Rudolph. "The Codification of Criminal Law in Nineteenth Century Egypt: Tradition or Modernization?" In *Law, Society, and National Identity in Africa*, ed. J. M. Abun-Nasr et al., 211–25. Hamburg: H. Buske, 1990.
Peters, Rudolph. *Crime and Punishment in Islamic Law: Theory and Practice from the Sixteenth to the Twenty-First Century*. Cambridge: Cambridge University Press, 2005.
Peters, Rudolph. "Egypt in the Age of the Triumphant Prison: Legal Punishment in Nineteenth Century Egypt." *Annales Islamologiques* 36 (2002): 253–85.
Peters, Rudolph. "From Jurists' Law to Statute Law or What Happens When the Sharia Is Codified." In *Shaping the Current Islamic Reformation*, ed. B. A. Roberson, 82–95. London: Frank Cass, 2003.
Peters, Rudolph. "Ijtihad and Taqlid in 18th and 19th Century Islam." *Die Welt des Islams* 20,3–4 (1980): 131–45.
Peters, Rudolph. "Islamic and Secular Criminal Law in Nineteenth Century Egypt." *Islamic Law and Society* 4,1 (1997): 70–90.
Peters, Rudolph. "State, Law and Society in Nineteenth Century Egypt." *Die Welt des Islams* 39 (1999): 267–72.
Pound, Roscoe. "The Revival of Comparative Law." *Tulane Law Review* 5 (1930–31): 1–16.
Powers, David S. "Orientalism, Colonialism, and Legal History: The Attack on Muslim Family Endowments in Algeria and India." *Comparative Studies in Society and History* 31,3 (1989): 535–71.
Qadrī, Muḥammad. *Droit musulman: Du statut personnel et des successions d'après le rite hanafite*. Alexandria: Imprimerie Française A. Mourès, 1875; Eng. trans., Nasib Abcarius and Wasey Sterry, *Code of Mohammedan Personal Law According to the Hanafite School*. London: Spottiswoode and Co., 1914.
Qadrī, Muḥammad. *Kitāb Murshid al-ḥayrān ilá maʿrifat aḥwāl al-insān fī l-muʿāmalāt al-sharʿiyyah ʿalá madhhab al-imām al-aʿẓam Abī Ḥanīfah al-Nuʿmān mulāʾiman li-ʿurf al-diyār al-miṣriyyah wa-sāʾir al-aqṭār al-islāmiyyah*. Bulaq: al-Maṭbaʿah al-Kubrá al-Amīriyyah, 1890.
Qadrī, Muḥammad, and Muḥammad Zayd al-Abyānī. *al-Aḥkam al-sharʿiyyah fī l-aḥwāl al-shakhṣiyyah (wa-sharḥ li-Muḥammad Zayd al-Abyānī)*. 4 vols. Ed. M. A. Sirāj and ʿA. J. Muḥammad. Cairo: Dār al-Salām, 2006.
Qamḥah, Aḥmad, and ʿAbd al-Fattāḥ al-Sayyid. *Niẓām al-qaḍāʾ wa-l-idārah*. Cairo: Maṭbaʿat al-Nahḍah, 1923.
Qamḥah, Aḥmad, and ʿAbd al-Fattāḥ al-Sayyid. *Sharḥ lāʾiḥat al-ijrāʾāt al-sharʿiyyah wa-l-qawānīn wa-lawāʾiḥ al-murtabiṭah bihā*. Miṣr: Maṭbaʿat al-Nahḍah, 1923.
Qaṭṭān, M. K. *Muʿawwiqāt taṭbīq al-sharīʿah al-islāmiyyah*. Cairo: Maktabat Wahbah, 1991.
al-Qulalī, Muḥammad Muṣṭafá. *Fī l-masʾūliyyah al-jināʾiyyah*. Cairo: Maṭbaʿat Jāmiʿat Fuʾād al-Awwal, 1948.

al-Qulalī, Muḥammad Muṣṭafá. "Kalimat al-duktūr Muḥammad Muṣṭafá al-Qulalī fī ḥafl istiqbāl al-shaykh ʿAlī al-Khafīf fī l-Majmaʿ." *Majallat Majmaʿ al-Lughah al-ʿArabiyyah (bi-l-Qāhirah)* 25 (1969): 209–11.
al-Qulalī, Muḥammad Muṣṭafá. *Uṣūl qānūn taḥqīq al-jināyāt*. Cairo: Maṭbaʿat Fatḥ Allāh Ilyās Nūrī, 1941.
Qurrāʿah, Saniyyah. *Tārīkh al-Azhar fī alf ʿām*. Cairo: Maktabat al-Ṣaḥāfah al-Dawliyyah, 1968.
Quṭb, Muḥammad. *Ḥawla taṭbīq al-sharīʿah*. Cairo: Maktabat al-Sunnah, 1991.
Raʾfat, Muḥammad. *Kitāb Uṣūl al-qawānīn*. Cairo: n.p., 1898.
Rahman, Fazlur. *Islam and Modernity*. Chicago: University of Chicago Press, 1982.
Rahnema, Ali, ed. *Pioneers of Islamic Revival*. Atlantic Highlands, NJ: Zed Books, 1994.
Rausas, G. Pélissié du. *Le Régime des capitulations dans l'empire ottoman*. Paris: A. Rousseau, 1902.
Reid, Donald Malcom. *Cairo University and the Making of Modern Egypt*. Cambridge: Cambridge University Press, 1990.
Reid, Donald Malcom. *Lawyers and Politics in the Arab World, 1880–1960*. Minneapolis: Bibliotheca Islamica, 1981.
Reid, Donald Malcom. "The National Bar Association and Egyptian Politics, 1912–1954." *International Journal of African Historical Studies* 7,4 (1974): 608–46.
Reid, Donald Malcom. "The Rise of Professions and Professional Organizations in Modern Egypt." *Comparative Studies in Society and History* 16,1 (1974).
Reid, Donald Malcom. "The ʿUrabi Revolution and the British Conquest, 1879–1882." In *The Cambridge History of Egypt*, vol. 2, *Modern Egypt from 1517 to the End of the Twentieth Century*, ed. M. W. Daly, 217–38. Cambridge: Cambridge University Press, 1998.
Reimann, Mathias. "Nineteenth Century German Legal Science." *Boston College Law Review* 31 (1990): 837–900.
Riḍā, Muḥammad Rashīd. "Al-Dīn wa-l-dawlah aw al-khilāfah wa-l-salṭānah." *Al-Manār* 2 (1899): 353–60.
Riḍā, Muḥammad Rashīd. "Al-Ḥukm bi-l-sharīʿah fī l-Sūdān." *Al-Manār* 1 (1899): 759–60.
Riḍā, Muḥammad Rashīd. "Iqtirāḥ al-qayṣar." *Al-Manār* 1 (1898): 484–95.
Riḍā, Muḥammad Rashīd. "Al-Iṣlāḥ al-dīnī: al-Muqtaraḥ ʿalá maqām al-khilāfah al-islāmiyyah." *Al-Manār* 1 (1898): 764–71.
Riḍā, Muḥammad Rashīd. "Khiṭāb waʿẓī li-l-insān." *Al-Manār* 2 (1899): 1–2.
Riḍā, Muḥammad Rashīd. "Madrasat al-Qaḍāʾ bayna l-Azhar wa-l-Maʿārif." *Al-Manār* 10 (1907): 77–8.
Riḍā, Muḥammad Rashīd. *Al-Manār wa-l-Azhar*. Miṣr: Maṭbaʿat al-Manār, 1353/1934.
Riḍā, Muḥammad Rashīd. "Musāwāt al-marʾah bi-l-rajul: al-Ḥukm fī l-bilād al-islāmiyyah, ʿalāqat al-maḥākim al-sharʿiyyah wa-l-ahliyyah bi-l-sharīʿah al-islāmiyyah." *Al-Muḥāmāh al-sharʿiyyah* 1,7 (1929): 574–8.
Riḍā, Muḥammad Rashīd. "Muwāfaqah wa-intiqād." *Al-Manār* 1 (1899): 841–3.
Riḍā, Muḥammad Rashīd. "Rabbanā innā aṭaʿnā sādatanā wa-kubarāʾanā fa-aḍallūnā al-sabīlā." *al-Manār* 1 (1898): 606.
Riḍā, Muḥammad Rashīd. *Tafsīr al-Manār*. 12 vols. in 5. Cairo: Dār al-Manār, 1948–56.
Riḍā, Muḥammad Rashīd. "Taḥrīf al-kalim ʿan mawāḍiʿih." *Al-Manār* 2 (1899): 385–91.
Riḍā, Muḥammad Rashīd. "Al-Taʿlīm al-qaḍāʾī." *Al-Manār* 2 (1899): 117–21.
Riḍā, Muḥammad Rashīd. *Tārīkh al-ustādh al-imām al-shaykh Muḥammad ʿAbduh: Wa-fīh tafṣīl siratih wa-khulāṣat sīrat mūqiẓ al-sharq ḥakīm al-islām Jamāl al-Dīn al-Afghānī*. 3 vols. Miṣr: Maṭbaʿat al-Manār, 1906–31.

Roberson, Barbara A. "The Emergence of the Modern Judiciary in the Middle East." In *Islam and Public Law: Classical and Contemporary Studies*, ed. C. Mallat, 107–39. London: Graham and Trotman, 1993.

Rosen, Lawrence. "Beyond Compare." In *Comparative Legal Studies: Traditions and Transitions*, ed. P. Legrand and R. J. C. Munday, 439–510. Cambridge: Cambridge University Press, 2003.

Rousseau, S. *A Dictionary of Mohammedan Law, Bengal Revenue Terms, Shanscrit, Hindoo, and Other Words, Used in the East Indies*. London: Printed for J. Sewell, 1802.

Roux, Amédée. "Manuel de droit public et privé ottoman, par le docteur Domenico Gatteschi." *Revue historique de droit français et étranger* 11 (1865): 646–50.

Rubin, Avi. *Ottoman Nizamiyye Courts: Law and Modernity*. New York: Palgrave Macmillan, 2011.

Russell, Mona. "Competing, Overlapping, and Contradictory Agendas: Egyptian Education under British Occupation, 1882–1922." *Comparative Studies of South Asia, Africa and the Middle East* 21,1–2 (2001): 50–60.

Ruxton, F. H., trans. *Mâliki Law: Being a Summary from French Translations of the Mukhtasar of Sîdî Khalîl*. London: Luzac and Co., 1916.

Ryzova, Lucie. "Egyptianizing Modernity through the New Effendiya." In *Re-Envisioning Egypt, 1919–1952*, ed. A. Goldschmidt et al., 124–63. Cairo: American University in Cairo Press, 2005.

Ryzova, Lucie. *The Age of the Efendiyya: Passages to Modernity in National-Colonial Egypt*. Oxford University Press, 2014.

Ṣabrī, Muḥammad Ḥāfiẓ. *Al-Muqāranāt wa-l-muqābalāt bayn aḥkām al-murāfaʿāt wa-l-muʿāmalāt wa-l-ḥudūd fī sharʿ al-yahūd wa-naẓāʾirihā min al-sharīʿah al-islāmiyyah al-gharrāʾ wa-min al-qānūn al-miṣrī wa-l-qawānīn al-waḍʿiyyah al-ukhrá*. Miṣr: Maṭbaʿah Hindiyyah, 1902.

Sachau, Eduard. *Muhammedanisches Recht nach schafiitischer Lehre*. Stuttgart: W. Spemann, 1897.

Ṣafwat, Aḥmad. *Muqaddimat al-qānūn*. 2nd ed. Cairo: Maṭbaʿat al-Qāhirah, 1924.

Said, Edward W. *Orientalism*. 2nd ed. New York: Vintage Books, 1994.

Ṣaʿīdī, ʿAbd al-Mutaʿāl. *Tārīkh al-iṣlāḥ fī l-Azhar wa-ṣafaḥāt min al-jihād fī l-iṣlāḥ*. Miṣr: Maṭbaʿat al-Iʿtimād, 1943.

Saleilles, Raymond. "Le Code civil et la méthode historique." In *Le Code civil, 1804–1904*, ed. Société d'études législatives, 97–129. Paris: A. Rousseau, 1904.

Saleilles, Raymond. "Droit civil et droit comparé." *Revue international de l'enseignement* 61 (1911): 5–32.

Saleilles, Raymond. "École historique et droit naturel." *Revue trimestrielle de droit civil* 1 (1902): 80–112.

Saleilles, Raymond. *Essai d'une théorie générale de l'obligation d'après le projet de code civil allemand*. Paris: F. Pichon, 1890.

Saleilles, Raymond. "Préface." In Francois Gény, *Méthode d'interpretation et sources en droit privé positif*. Paris: A. Chevalier-Marescq et cie., 1899.

Saleilles, Raymond. "Quelques mots sur le role de la méthode historique dans l'enseignement du droit." *Revue internationale de l'enseignement* 19 (1890): 482–505.

Sālim, Laṭīfah Muḥammad. *Al-Niẓām al-qaḍāʾī al-miṣrī al-ḥadīth 1875–1914*. 2 vols. Cairo: al-Hayʾah al-Miṣriyyah al-ʿĀmmah li-l-Kitāb, 2000.

al-Sanhūrī, ʿAbd al-Razzāq Aḥmad (ʿAbdel Razzak al-Sanhoury). "ʿAlá ayy asās yakūn tanqīḥ al-qānūn al-madanī al-miṣrī." In *al-Kitāb al-dhahabī li-l-maḥākim al-ahliyyah 1883–1933*, 2 vols., 2: 76–94. Bulaq: al-Maṭbaʿah al-Amīriyyah, 1937.

al-Sanhūrī, ʿAbd al-Razzāq Aḥmad. *ʿAqd al-ījār: Sharḥ al-qānūn al-madanī fī l-ʿuqūd*. Beirut: Dār al-Fikr, ca. 1980.

al-Sanhūrī, ʿAbd al-Razzāq Aḥmad. *Le Califat*. Paris: P. Geuthner, 1926.

al-Sanhūrī, ʿAbd al-Razzāq Aḥmad. "Al-Dīn wa-l-dawlah fī l-islām." *Al-Muḥāmāh al-sharʿiyyah* 1,1 (1929): 8–14.

al-Sanhūrī, ʿAbd al-Razzāq Aḥmad. "Le Droit musulman comme élément de refonte du code civil égyptien." In *Introduction à l'étude du droit comparé: Recueil d'études en l'honneur d'Édouard Lambert*, 621–42. Paris: LGDJ, 1935.

al-Sanhūrī, ʿAbd al-Razzāq Aḥmad. *Maṣādir al-ḥaqq fī l-fiqh al-islāmī*. 6 vols. Cairo: Jāmiʿat al-Duwal al-ʿArabiyyah, 1954–9.

al-Sanhūrī, ʿAbd al-Razzāq Aḥmad. "Muḥāḍarat al-duktūr ʿAbd al-Razzāq al-Sanhūrī Bey allatī alqāhā bi-l-Jamʿiyyah al-Jughrāfiyyah al-Malakiyyah fī 24 abrīl sanat 1942 ʿan mashrūʿ tanqīḥ al-qānūn al-madanī." *Al-Muḥāmāh* 22,4 and 6 (1942): 419–31.

al-Sanhūrī, ʿAbd al-Razzāq Aḥmad. "La Responsabilité civile et pénale en droit musulman." *Majallat al-qānūn wa-l-iqtiṣād* 1,2–3 (1945): 1–26.

al-Sanhūrī, ʿAbd al-Razzāq Aḥmad. *Al-Sanhūrī min khilāl awrāqihi l-shakhṣiyyah*. Ed. N. al-Sanhūrī and T. al-Shāwī. Cairo: Dār al-Shurūq, 2005.

al-Sanhūrī, ʿAbd al-Razzāq Aḥmad. *Sharḥ al-qānūn al-madanī: al-Naẓariyyah al-ʿāmmah li-l-iltizāmāt*. Cairo: Maṭbaʿat Dār al-Kutub al-Miṣriyyah, 1934.

al-Sanhūrī, ʿAbd al-Razzāq Aḥmad (ʿAbdel Razzak al-Sanhoury). "Le Standard juridique." In *Recueil d'études sur les sources du droit en l'honneur de Francois Gény*, 144–56. Paris: Librarie du Recueil Sirey, 1935.

al-Sanhūrī, ʿAbd al-Razzāq Aḥmad. "L'Université Égyptienne au Congrès international de droit comparé de La Haye." In *Maqālāt wa-abḥāth al-ustādh al-duktūr ʿAbd al-Razzāq al-Sanhūrī*, 1: 525–31. Cairo: Maṭbaʿat Jāmiʿat al-Azhar, 1990.

al-Sanhūrī, ʿAbd al-Razzāq Aḥmad. "Wājibunā baʿd al-muʿāhadah." *Al-Ahrām* (Jan. 1, 1937).

al-Sanhūrī, ʿAbd al-Razzāq Aḥmad. *Al-Wasīṭ fī sharḥ al qānūn al-madanī*. Cairo: Dār al-Nashr li-l-Jāmiʿah al-Miṣriyyah, 1952–69.

al-Sanhūrī, ʿAbd al-Razzāq Aḥmad. "Wujūb tanqīḥ al-qānūn al-madanī al-miṣrī." *Majallat al-qānūn wa-l-iqtiṣād* 6,1 (1936): 3–144.

al-Sanhūrī, ʿAbd al-Razzāq Aḥmad, and Aḥmad Ḥishmat Abū Sitīt. *Uṣūl al-qānūn*. Cairo: Maṭbaʿat Lajnat al-Taʾlīf wa-l-Tarjamah wa-l-Nashr, 1941.

Ṣaqqāl, Fatḥ Allāh. *Min dhikrayātī fī l-muḥāmāh fī Miṣr wa-Sūriyā*. Aleppo: Maṭbaʿat al-Ḍād, 1958.

Saroufim, Ebeid. "England and the Criminal Legislation of Egypt from 1882." D.Phil. diss., University of Oxford, 1950.

Saʿūdī, Jumaʿah ʿAbd al-Ḥamīd ʿAlī. "Al-Qānūn fī Miṣr bayna l-sharīʿah al-islāmiyyah wa-l-tashrīʿāt al-waḍʿiyyah." Doct. diss., Cairo University Faculty of Law, 1995.

Sautayra E., and E. Cherbonneau. *Droit musulman du statut personnel et des successions*. Paris: Maisonneuve et cie., 1873–74.

Savigny, Friedrich Karl von. *Geschichte des römischen Rechts im Mittelalter*. 6 vols. Heidelberg: Mohr und Zimmer, 1815. Fr. trans. Charles Guenoux, *Histoire du droit romain au moyen age*, 4 vols. Paris: Alexandre Mesnier, 1830.

Savigny, Friedrich Karl von. *Histoire du droit romain au moyen age*. Trans. C. Guenoux. 4 vols. Paris: Alexandre Mesnier, 1830.

Savigny, Friedrich Karl von. *System of the Modern Roman Law*. Madras: J. Higginbotham, 1867.

Savigny, Friedrich Karl von. *Vom Beruf unserer Zeit für Gesetzgebung und Rechtswissenschaft*. Heidelberg: Mohr und Zimmer, 1814.

Savvas Pacha, J. *Le Droit musulman expliqué: Réponse à un article de M. Ignace Goldziher paru dans le Byzantinische Zeitschrift, II, 2, p. 317–325, 1893*. Paris: Marchal et Billard, 1896.

Savvas Pacha, J. *Étude sur la théorie du droit musulman, 2ème partie*. 2 vols. Paris: Marchal et Billard, 1898.

Savvas Pacha, J. "Société d'économie politique: Réunion du 5 février 1892." *Journal des économistes*, 5e sér., 9 (1892): 284–300.

Ṣāwī, Ṣalāḥ. *Qaḍiyyat taṭbīq al-sharīʿah*. Shubrah al-Khaymah, Egypt: Bayt al-Ḥikmah, 1990.

Sayour, Homère. *Répertoire de la jurisprudence des appels sommaires des tribunaux mixtes d'Égypte*. Alexandria: Société des Publications Égyptiennes, 1916.

al-Sayyid, ʿAbd al-Fattāḥ, and Muḥammad Kāmil Mursī. *Majmūʿat qawānīn al-maḥākim al-ahliyyah wa-l-sharʿiyyah*. Misr: Maṭbaʿat al-Raghāʾib, 1921.

Schacht, Joseph. "L'Évolution moderne du droit musulman en Égypte." *Melanges Maspero* 3 (1940): 323–34.

Schacht, Joseph. "Ikhtilāf." *Encyclopaedia of Islam*, 2nd ed. 3: 1088.

Schacht, Joseph. "Islamic Law in Contemporary States." *American Journal of Comparative Law* 8,2 (1959): 133–47.

Schrage, Eltjo, and Viola Heutger. "Legal History and Comparative Law." In *Elgar Encyclopedia of Comparative Law*, ed. J. Smits, 393–406. Cheltenham: Edward Elgar, 2006.

Scott, John. "Rapport sur les Tribuneaux indigènes 1890–1894." *Recueil des documents officiels du gouvernement égyptien 1894* [1894], 81–100.

Seikaly, Samir. "Coptic Communal Reform: 1860–1914." *Middle Eastern Studies* 6,3 (1970): 247–75.

Shadid, Anthony. "Egypt's Islamists Show Their Might and Numbers, Demanding Religious Law." *New York Times* (July 30, 2011), 1.

Shaham, Ron. *Family and the Courts in Modern Egypt: A Study Based on Decisions by the Sharīʿa Courts, 1900–1955*. Leiden: Brill, 1997.

Shāhid, Ṣalāḥ. *Dhikrayātī fī ʿahdayn*. Miṣr: Dār al-Maʿārif, 1976.

Shalakany, Amr A. "Between Identity and Redistribution: Sanhuri, Genealogy and the Will to Islamise." *Islamic Law and Society* 8,2 (2001): 201–44.

Shalakany, Amr A. "Islamic Legal Histories." *Berkeley Journal of Middle Eastern and Islamic Law* 1 (2010): 1–82.

Shalakany, Amr A. "Sanhuri and the Historical Origins of Comparative Law in the Arab World (or How Sometimes Losing Your Asalah Can Be Good for You)." In *Rethinking the Masters of Comparative Law*, ed. A. Riles, 152–88. Oxford: Hart, 2001.

Shalaqānī, ʿAmr (Amr Shalakany). "'I Heard it All Before': Egyptian Tales of Law and Development." *Third World Quarterly* 5,27 (2006): 833–53.

Shalaqānī, ʿAmr (Amr Shalakany). *Izdihār wa-inhiyār al-nukhbah al-qānūniyyah al-Miṣriyyah, 1805–2005*. Cairo: Dār al-Shurūq, 2013.

al-Shaʿrānī, ʿAbd al-Wahhāb ibn Aḥmad. *Balance de la loi musulmane, ou, ésprit de la législation islamique et divergences de ses quatre rites jurisprudentiels*. Trans. N. Perron and J. D. Luciani. Algiers: Imprimerie orientale, P. Fontana, 1898.

Shiḥātah, ʿAbd Allāh Maḥmūd. *Manhaj al-imām Muḥammad ʿAbduh fī tafsīr al-qurʾān al-karīm*. [Cairo]: al-Majlis al-Aʿlá li-Riʿāyat al-Funūn wa-l-Ādāb wa-l-ʿUlūm al-Ijtimāʿiyyah, 1963.

Shiḥātah, Shafīq (Chafik Chehata). "Al-Naẓariyyah al-ʿāmmah li-l-iltizāmāt fi-l-sharīʿah al-islāmiyyah, al-juzʾ al-awwal: Ṭarfā al-iltizām." Doct. diss., Law Faculty of the Egyptian University, 1936.

Shiḥātah, Shafīq (Chafik Chehata). *Tārīkh ḥarakat al-tajdīd fī l-nuẓum al-qānūniyyah fī Miṣr mundh ʿahd Muḥammad ʿAlī*. Cairo: al-Jamʿiyyah al-Miṣriyyah li-l-Dirāsāt al-Tārīkhiyyah, 1961.

Shubayr, Muḥammad ʿUthmān. *ʿAbd al-Wahhāb Khallāf: al-Faqīh al-uṣūlī al-mujaddid*. Dimashq: Dār al-Qalam, 2010.

Shubayr, Muḥammad ʿUthmān. *Muḥammad Abū Zahrah: Imām al-fuqahāʾ al-muʿāṣirīn wa-l-mudāfiʿ al-jarīʾ ʿan ḥaqāʾiq al-dīn*. Damascus: Dār al-Qalam, 2006.

Shubayr, Muḥammad ʿUthmān. *Al-Shaykh ʿAlī al-Khafīf 1309–1398h/1891–1978m: al-Faqīh al-mujaddid*. Damascus: Dār al-Qalam, 2002.

Ṣiyām, ʿAbd Allāh. "Al-Siyāsah al-sharʿiyyah wa-qawāʿid al-ʿadl wa-l-inṣāf." *Al-Muḥāmāh al-sharʿiyyah* 1,7 (1929): 579–81.

Smith, Charles D. *Islam and the Search for Social Order in Modern Egypt*. Albany: State University of New York Press, 1983.

Snouck Hurgronje, Christiaan. "Le Droit musulman (Review of Savvas Pacha, *Le Droit musulman expliqué*: Réponse à un article de M. Ignace Goldziher (1893)." *Revue de l'histoire des religions* 37 (1896): 1–22, 174–203.

Snouck Hurgronje, Christiaan. *Verspreide geschriften*. Bonn and Leipzig: K. Schroeder, 1924.

Société de l'Enseignement Supérieur. "Étudiants et examens." *Revue internationale de l'enseignement* 30 (1895): 163.

Société de législation comparée. *Congrès international de droit comparé tenu á Paris du 31 juillet au 4 août 1900*. Paris: Librairie générale de droit et de jurisprudence, 1905.

Soliman, Mohamed (Muḥammad Sulaymān). "Mise en harmonie de la nouvelle législation égyptienne avec le concept de la loi musulmane." *L'Égypte contemporaine* 26 (1935): 367–84.

Sonbol, Amira El Azhary. *The Last Khedive of Egypt: Memoirs of Abbas Hilmi II*. Cairo: American University in Cairo Press, 2006.

Sprenger, Aloys. *Das Leben und die Lehre des Mohammad*. Berlin: Nicolai'sche Verlagsbuchandlung, 1861.

Sulaymān, Muḥammad (Mohammed Soliman). "Bi-ayy sharʿ nuḥkam?" *L'Égypte contemporaine* 26 (1935): 289–365.

Sulaymān, Muḥammad (Mohammed Soliman). "Ḥaqq al-ruʾyah (Part 2)." *Majallat al-qaḍāʾ al-sharʿī* 1,3 (1922): 144.

Sunderland, Willard. "The Caucasian Tangle." *Kritika: Explorations in Russian and Eurasian History* 7,1 (2006): 111–22.

Tādrus, Tādrus Mikhāʾīl. *Dhikrayāt min ʿālam al-muḥāmāh wa-l-qaḍāʾ*. Cairo: al-Dār al-Qawmiyyah li-l-Ṭibāʿah wa-l-Nashr, 1966.

Tartari, Charles. *Charles Testoud, professeur à la Faculté de Droit de Grenoble*. Grenoble: Imprimerie Allier Frères, 1903.

al-Ṭawīl, Amānī. *al-Muḥāmūn bayna l-nahḍah wa-l-siyāsah*. Cairo: Dār al-Shurūq, 2007.

Theolin, Sture. *The Torch of the Empire*. Istanbul: Yapi Kredi Kültür, 2002.

Timmermans, G. *La Réforme judiciaire en Égypte et les capitulations*. Ghent: Librairie Générale de Ad. Hoste, 1875.

Toledano, Ehud R. "Social and Economic Change in the 'Long Nineteenth Century'." In *Cambridge History of Egypt*, ed. M. W. Daly, 2: 252–84.

Tolédo, Sim. *Analyse de la théorie des contrats et obligations en droit civil ottoman*. Montpellier: Imprimerie Générale du Midi, 1915.

Tornau, Baron Nikoli Egorovich. *Le Droit musulman, exposé d'après les sources*. Trans. Louis Prosper Auguste Eschbach. Paris: Cotillon, 1860.

Tornau, Baron Nikoli Egorovich. *Izlozhenïe nachal musul'manskago zakonoviedienïia*. St. Petersburg: 1850.

Unger, Roberto. "The CLS Movement." *Harvard Law Review* 96 (1983): 561–73, 665–75.

Van Dyck, Edward A., trans. *Real Property, Mortgage and Wakf According to Ottoman Law*. London: Wyman and Sons, 1884.

Varisco, Daniel M. *Reading Orientalism: Said and the Unsaid*. Seattle: University of Washington Press, 2007.

Vatikiotis, P. J. *The History of Egypt*. Vol. 2. Baltimore: Johns Hopkins University Press, 1980.

Vesey-FitzGerald, S. G. "The Franco-Italian Draft Code of Obligations, 1927." *Journal of Comparative Legislation and International Law* 14,1 (1932): 1–19.

Vidal, Victor. "Notice sur les travaux de l'Institut Égyptien depuis sa fondation." In *Verhandlungen des VII. internationalen Orientalisten-Congresses, gehalten in Wien im Jahre 1886*, 1: 89–108. Wien: Alfred Holder, 1886–89.

Vikør, Knut S. *Between God and the Sultan*. Oxford: Oxford University Press, 2005.

Vincent, M. B. *Études sur la loi musulmane: Legislation criminelle*. Paris: Joubert, 1842.

Vizetelly, Edward. *From Cyprus to Zanzibar*. London: C. A. Pearson Ltd., 1901.

Vogel, Frank. "Contract Law of Islam and the Arab Middle East." *International Encyclopedia of Comparative Law*, 7: 1–77. Tübingen: Mohr Siebeck, 2006.

Vogel, Frank. "Siyasa Sharʿiyya." *Encyclopaedia of Islam*, 2nd ed., 9: 694–6.

Waardenburg, J. D. J. *L'Islam dans le miroir de l'occident*. Paris: Mouton, 1963.

Waardenburg, J. D. J. "Mustashriḳūn." In *Encyclopaedia of Islam*, 2nd ed., 7: 735–53.

Walton, Frederick Parker. "Egyptian Law, Sources and Judicial Organisation." In *Pars Orientalis (Aegyptus—Palaestina—Sina—Japonia)*, ed. E. Balogh, 11–38. Berlin: Sack et Montanus, 1929.

Warburg, Gabriel. *Islam, Sectarianism, and Politics in Sudan since the Mahdiyya*. London: Hurst & Co., 2003.

Warburg, Gabriel. *The Sudan under Wingate: Administration in the Anglo-Egyptian Sudan, 1899–1916*. London: Cass, 1971.

Watson, Alan. *The Making of the Civil Law*. Cambridge, MA: Harvard University Press, 1981.

Weiss, Bernard G. *The Spirit of Islamic Law*. Athens, GA: University of Georgia Press, 1998.

West, Raymond. "Modern Developments of Mohammedan Law: Its Origin and Growth." *Journal of the Society of Comparative Legislation* 2,2 (1900): 27–44.

Whitman, James Q. *The Legacy of Roman Law in the German Romantic Era: Historical Vision and Legal Change*. Princeton: Princeton University Press, 1990.

Wieacker, Franz. *A History of Private Law in Europe*. Oxford: Oxford University Press, 1995.

Wilson, Roland Knyvet. *A Digest of Anglo-Muhammadan Law, Setting Forth in the Form of a Code, with Full References to Modern and Ancient Authorities, the Special Rules Now Applicable to Muhammadans as Such by the Civil Courts of British India*. London: W. Thacker, 1895.

Wilson, Roland Knyvet. *An Introduction to the Study of Anglo-Muhammadan Law*. London: W. Thacker, 1894.

Wilson, Roland Knyvet. *Tables Shewing the Differences between English and Indian Law, under the Several Heads of I. Substantive Criminal Law. II. Law of Evidence. III. Contract Law*. Cambridge: University Press, 1890.

Wood, Leonard. "Legislation as an Instrument of Islamic Law." In *The Oxford Handbook of Islamic Law*, ed. Anver Emon and Rumee Ahmed. Oxford Handbooks Online. May 2016. Available online at http://www.oxfordhandbooks.com.

Wood, Leonard. "Reception of European Law, Origins of Islamic Legal Revivalism, and Foundations of Transformations in Islamic Legal Thought in Egypt, 1875–1960." Ph.D. diss., Harvard University, 2011.

Wood, Leonard. "Sanhuri, ʿAbd al-Razzaq Ahmad al-." In *Dictionary of African Biography*, ed. Emmanuel K. Akyeampong and Henry Louis Gates Jr., 5: 266–8. New York: Oxford University Press, 2012.

Wood, Leonard. "Shariʿah Revivalist Thought in the First Years of the *Shariʿah Lawyers Bar Association Journal*." *Maghreb Review* 32,2–3 (2007): 196–217.

Worsfold, W. Basil. *The Redemption of Egypt*. London: G. Allen, 1899.

Young, George. *Corps de droit ottoman*. 7 vols. Oxford: Clarendon, 1906.

Zaghlūl, Aḥmad Fatḥī. *Al-Muḥāmāh*. Miṣr: Maṭbaʿat al-Maʿārif, 1900.

Zaghlūl, Aḥmad Fatḥī. *Sharḥ al-qānūn al-madanī*. Cairo: al-Maṭbaʿah al-Amīriyyah bi-Miṣr, 1913.

Zaghlūl, Saʿd. "Al-Akhbār wa-l-ārāʾ: Madrasat al-qaḍāʾ bayna l-Azhar wa-l-maʿārif." *Al-Manār* 10,1 (1907): 77–8.

Zarqāʾ, Muṣṭafá Aḥmad. *Al-Madkhal ilá naẓariyyat al-iltizām al-ʿāmmah fī l-fiqh al-islāmī*. Damascus: Dār al-Qalam, 1946.

al-Ẓawāhirī, Muḥammad ibn Ibrāhīm al-Aḥmadī. *Al-ʿIlm wa-l-ʿulamāʾ wa-niẓām al-taʿlīm*. Tanta: al-Maṭbaʿah al-ʿUmūmiyyah, 1904.

Ze'evi, Dror. "The Use of Ottoman Sharīʿa Court Records as a Source for Middle Eastern Social History." *Islamic Law and Society* 5,1 (1998): 35–56.

Zenkovsky, Serge A. "Kulturkampf in Pre-Revolutionary Central Asia." *American Slavic and East European Review* 14,1 (1955): 15–41.

Zeys, Ernest. *Essai d'un traité méthodique de droit musulman (école malékite)*. Algiers: A. Jourdan, 1884.

Zeys, Ernest. *Traité élémentaire de droit musulman algérien (école malékite)*. 2 vols. in 1. Algiers: A. Jourdan, 1885.

Ziadeh, Farhat. *Lawyers, the Rule of Law and Liberalism in Modern Egypt*. Stanford: Hoover Institution, 1968.

Zimmermann, Reinhard. "Comparative Law and the Europeanization of Private Law." In *The Oxford Handbook of Comparative Law*, ed. R. Zimmermann and M. Reimann, 539–78. Oxford: Oxford University Press, 2006.

Zimmermann, Reinhard. "Roman Law and European Legal Unity." In A. S. Hartkamp and Christian von Bar, *Towards a European Civil Code*, 2: 21–43. Nijmegen: Ars Aequi Libri, 1998.

Zimmermann, Reinhard, and Mathias Reimann, eds. *The Oxford Handbook of Comparative Law*. Oxford: Oxford University Press, 2006.

Zubaida, Sami. *Law and Power in the Islamic World*. London: I. B. Tauris, 2003.

Index

Page numbers followed by an '*f*' denote reference to illustrations.

The manufacturer's authorised representative in the EU for product
safety is Oxford University Press España S.A. of El Parque Empresarial
San Fernando de Henares, Avenida de Castilla, 2 - 28830 Madrid
(www.oup.es/en or product.safety@oup.com). OUP España S.A. also acts
as importer into Spain of products made by the manufacturer.
Printed and bound by CPI Group (UK) Ltd, Croydon, CR0 4YY
14/09/2026
02216306-0009